TOWARD BELIEF

TOWARD BELIEF

Essays in the Human Sciences, Social Ethics, and Philosophical Theology

W. Widick Schroeder

Exploration Press
Chicago, Illinois

Printed in the United States of America.

Exploration Press
Chicago Theological Seminary
5757 University Avenue
Chicago, Illinois 60637

ISBN: 0-913552-59-3

Library of Congress Catalog Card Number: 95-83405

To my mother, Irene Schroeder,
whose generation was the first to consider
the mode of constructive thought employed here,

and to my grandchildren,
Erin and Matthew Schroeder
and
Amy, Julie and Mark Seidel,
whose generation will be the next
to explore the issues addressed in this volume.

Table of Contents

Part Three
On Religious Institutions: Constructive and Analytical Studies

Part Four
Alternative Primal Interpretations: Analyses and Critiques

Preface

Throughout my academic career I have been interested in actual and conceivable relations between the human sciences, social ethics, and theology. Persuaded that the fact-value disjunction rooted in the neo-Kantian tradition and exemplified *par excellance* by Max Weber is spurious, I have held that one must not only analyze human life but one must also try to discern fitting modes of human conduct and to promote fitting forms of human social organization. At the same time, I have been wary of the ideological biases embodied in neo-Marxist analysis and have appreciated Weber's protest against Marxist modes of social analysis. Weber's existentialist interpretation of human experience emphasized the role of human beings and their cultural creations in human life. To my mind, these emphases are most commendable.

I am committed to the Christian movement, and I have spent most of my academic life on the faculty of the Chicago Theological Seminary, an institution closely related to the United Church of Christ. This denomination was formed in the 1950s through the merger of the Congregational-Christian Churches and the Evangelical and Reformed Church. My own roots are in the Congregational tradition, which was more influenced by modern modes of thought than was the Evangelical and Reformed tradition.

In the last decade of the nineteenth century and the first half of the twentieth century, many faculty and students of the Chicago Theological Seminary, which had been founded in 1855 by a group of Congregational lay people, were influenced by the Social Gospel. Participants in this movement of thought, which will be addressed at some length in one of the chapters in this volume, sought to utilize the emerging human sciences to enhance the quality of human life and to promote social justice. Although the movement had waned by the time I joined the faculty, many persons in the institution continued to have interest in the relations between the human sciences, social ethics, and theology.

During my career, I have been involved in several empirical studies in the sociology of religion and have worked at the metatheoretical level, seeking to develop a framework of interpretation that affirmed the authenticity of religious experiences as human responses to the Divine

Presence in their lives. In undertaking this effort, I have been led to explore a variety of theoretical perspectives. Some of this work is embodied in the essays included in this volume.

I have found the seminal work of Alfred North Whitehead most suggestive. His work, particularly *Process and Reality,* has been an invaluable resource for me. I am in the debt of Charles Hartshorne, Bernard Loomer, Alvin Pitcher, and Daniel Day Williams for helping me to see the significance of Whitehead for my work during my graduate study at the University of Chicago during the 1950s. The contribution of Whitehead's thought to my work is manifest in every essay in this volume, but that contribution is more directly apparent in some of them than in others.

I want to express my appreciation to the participants in numerous seminars of the Center for the Scientific Study of Religion in the 1960s and 1970s and to my colleagues and graduate students in the Center for Theology, Ethics, and the Human Sciences of the Chicago Theological Seminary in the 1970s, 1980s and 1990s for sustaining an ethos which encouraged interdisciplinary work. I am especially grateful to Dorothy Bass, Robert Benne, Thomas C. Campbell, John B. Cobb, Jr., Franklin I. Gamwell, Philip Hefner, Perry LeFevre, Robert L. Moore, Victor Obenhaus, W. Alvin Pitcher, and Gibson Winter for their roles in stimulating my interest in the topics addressed in this volume.

I am in the debt of Eva Salmons and Max Havlick for their highly competent editorial work and manuscript preparation. Finally, I want to thank my wife, Gayle, for her encouragement and support of my work in countless ways.

W. Widick Schroeder

Acknowledgments

The following essays have been reproduced with minor stylistic changes from the journals and books cited here. The copyright holders generously gave me permission to reprint these essays in this volume.

W. W. S.

1. "Evolution, Human Values and Religious Experience: A Process Perspective." *Zygon: Journal of Religion and Science*, 17:3 (September, 1982). Copyright © 1982 by the Joint Publication Board of *Zygon*. Used by permission.
2. "Toward Belief: A Process Perspective on the Social Sciences and on Social Ethics." From *Belief and Ethics: Essays in Ethics, the Human Sciences, and Ministry in Honor of W. Alvin Pitcher*. Edited by W. Widick Schroeder and Gibson Winter. Chicago, IL: Center for the Scientific Study of Religion, 1978. Copyright © 1978, Center for the Scientific Study of Religion. Used by permission.
3. "Structure and Context in Process Political Theory: A Constructive Formulation." From *Process Philosophy and Social Thought*. Edited by John B. Cobb, Jr. and W. Widick Schroeder. Chicago, IL: Center for the Scientific Study of Religion, 1981. Copyright © 1981, Center for the Scientific Study of Religion. Used by permission.
4. "Unity and Diversity among Humans: A Framework for Interpretation." *Zygon: Journal of Religion and Science*, 13:1 (March, 1978). Copyright © 1978 by the University of Chicago. Used by permission.
5. "Political Economy: A Process Interpretation." From *Economic LIfe: Process Interpretations and Critical Responses*. Edited by W. Widick Schroeder and Franklin I. Gamwell. Chicago, IL: Center for the Scientific Study of Religion, 1988. Copyright © 1988 by the Center for the Scientific Study of Religion. Used by permission.
6. "American Democratic Capitalism: A Sympathetic Appraisal." From *Liberation and Ethics: Essays in Religious Social Ethics in Honor of Gibson Winter*. Edited by Charles Amjad-Ali and W. Alvin Pitcher. Chicago, IL: Center for the Scientific Study of Religion, 1985. Copyright © 1985 by the Center for the Scientific Study of Religion. Used by permission.

7. "The Socialist/Communitarian Vision: New Dream or Old Nightmare?" From *Christianity and Capitalism: Perspectives on Religion, Liberalism, and the Economy.* Edited by Bruce Grelle and David A. Krueger. Chicago, IL: Center for the Scientific Study of Religion, 1986. Copyright © 1986 by the Center for the Scientific Study of Religion. Used by permission.
8. "Religious Institutions and Human Society: A Normative Inquiry into the Appropriate Contribution of Religious Institutions to Human Life and to the Divine Life." From *Belonging and Alienation: Religious Foundations for the Human Future.* Edited by Philip Hefner and W. Widick Schroeder. Chicago, IL: Center for the Scientific Study of Religion, 1976. Copyright © 1976 by the Center for the Scientific Study of Religion. Used by permission.
9. "The Idea of a Liberal Christian Theological Seminary." From *Theology and the Human Spirit: Essays in Honor of Perry LeFevre.* Edited by Theodore W. Jennings and Susan Brooks Thistlethwaite. Chicago, IL: Exploration Press, 1994. Copyright © 1994 by Exploration Press of the Chicago Theological Seminary. Used by permission.
10. "Measuring the Muse: Reflections on the Use of Survey Methods in the Study of Religious Phenomena." *Review of Religious Research,* 18:2 (Winter, 1977). Copyright © 1977 by the Religious Research Association, Inc. Used by permission.
11. "The Emergence of the Voluntary Church." From *The American Religious Experience: Piety and Practicality.* Edited by Clyde L. Manschreck and Barbara Brown Zikmund. Chicago, IL: Exploration PRess, 1976. Copyright © 1976 by Exploration Press of the Chicago Theological Seminary. Used by permission.
12. "The Variety of American Religious Expression: A Framework for Interpretation." *The Chicago Theological Seminary Register,* 68:29 (Spring, 1978). Copyright © 1978 by the Chicago Theological Seminary. Used by permission.
13. "The United Church of Christ: The Quest for Denominational Identity and the Limits of Pluralism." From *The United Church of Christ: Studies in Identity and Polity.* Edited by Dorothy C. Bass and Kenneth B. Smith. Chicago, IL: 1987. Copyright © 1987 by Exploration Press of the Chicago Theological Seminary. Used by permission.
14. "The Development of Religious Research in the United States: Retrospect and Prospect." *Review of Religious Research,* 13:1 (Fall, 1971). Copyright © 1971 by the Religious Research Association, Inc. Used by permission.

15. "Liberation Theology: A Critique from a Process Perspective." From *Process Philosophy and Social Thought.* Edited by John B. Cobb, Jr. and W. Widick Schroeder. Chicago, IL: Center for the Scientific Study of Religion, 1981. Copyright © 1981 by the Center for the Scientific Study of Religion. Used by permission.
16. *"The Human Prospect and the 'Lord of History'*: A Process Critique." *Zygon: Journal of Religion and Science,* 12:1 (March, 1977). Copyright © 1977 by The University of Chicago. Used by permission.

****

The extended quotations in Chapter 17 are drawn from Paul Tillich, *Systematic Theology,* Volume I, Chicago: University of Chicago Press, 1951, copyright © 1951 by the University of Chicago Press, Paul Tillich, *Systematic Theology,* Volume II, Chicago: University of Chicago Press, 1957, copyright © 1957 by the University of Chicago Press, and Paul Tillich, *Systematic Theology,* Volume III, Chicago: University of Chicago Press, copyright © 1963 by the University of Chicago Press. Used by permission.

The extended quotations in Chapter 18 are drawn from Jürgen Moltmann, *The Crucified God: The Cross of Christ as the Foundation and Criticism of Christian Theology,* New York: Harper and Row, Publishers, Inc., copyright © 1974 by SCM Press, Ltd. Used by permission.

TOWARD BELIEF

Introduction

This volume brings together a number of studies which have appeared in various books and journals during the past quarter of a century. It also includes three previously unpublished essays. All are informed at the metatheoretical level by the basic categories of process philosophy, a mode of thought initiated by Alfred North Whitehead in the 1920s and 1930s. In a trilogy of major works, *Science and the Modern World, Process and Reality,* and *Adventures of Ideas,* Whitehead laid the foundations of a postmodern philosophic perspective rooted in his appropriation and transformation of Platonism.[1] Inverting Platonic thought, Whitehead insisted on the ultimacy of becoming rather than of being. For him, the "really real" were not the Platonic forms or ideas; rather, the "really real" were concrete particular actual entities or occasions. God and a puff of existence in the farthermost reaches of space were both actual entities, differing greatly in richness and complexity of vision and feeling, but both "really real."

In an epoch in which theistic interpretations of experience are not fashionable in either the natural or the human sciences, it is scarcely surprising that workers in these fields have rarely employed the metatheoretical framework of process philosophy. Nonetheless, the paucity of theistic interpretations of experience in general and of process theism particularly in the contemporary academic community is an historical accident, not a metaphysical necessity. One may hope that alternative modes of thinking may become more widespread in the twenty-first century.

In any event, each scholar working in the natural or the human sciences has to appropriate, either implicitly or explicitly, some basic mode of thought in which to set the more specialized propositions related to his/her particular subject matter. In my case, I have sought to do studies in social ethics and the human sciences self-consciously informed by Whitehead's metaphysics. As a result, I have had to cast my research so that the more specialized formulations and interpretations cohere with the basic categories of process thought and to focus on those facets of process thought most central to the human sciences and to social ethics.

Four key notions, central to Whitehead, inform the constructive portions of these essays: the ontological principle, the principle of relativity, the ultimacy of the category of creativity, and a faith in rationalism. According to the ontological principle, the reasons for things are to be found in actual entities — in particular entities in the world and in God. Based on this philosophical realism, I have emphasized both the particularity of actual occasions and also the reality of the Divine Life.

The principle of relativity, which in its most general form states that every being constitutes a potential for every becoming, is the basis for the necessary social character of existence and for the reciprocity and mutual influence of God and the world. The logic of sociality and the character and properties of various types of societies in their interrelationships are central concerns in these essays.

Taken conjointly, the principle of relativity and the ontological principle give rise to what Whitehead calls the reformed subjectivist principle. According to this principle, one's own subjective experience is the primary datum for interpreting experience. This existentialist view differs very significantly from most contemporary existentialism, for in Whitehead's version the actual occasions embodied in an emerging subject's causal past are objectified in that subject. As a result, one's subjective experience necessarily includes aspects of the world outside the emerging subject.

The fact-value disjunction is spurious, for our experience begins with our valuation of other entities. Existence is inextricably social, and the basic rhythm of the cosmos is participation-individuation-participation-individuation-participation, and so on. The many become one, and the one adds to the many. This basic relational matrix clarifies many complex issues about the relation of the individual and the community in social theory and in social ethics.

The ultimacy of the category of creativity is the third fundamental notion informing process metaphysics. The dynamic creative urge for the many constituting the universe disjunctively to become the one constituting the universe conjunctively lies behind all forms and is not explicable by forms.

In elaborating the dynamic ontology this view entails, Whitehead develops a rich doctrine of emergent evolution. Emerging creatures, appropriating but surpassing the past in their becoming, seek aesthetic satisfaction and intensity of feeling. Beauty is a central category of interpretation in a Whiteheadian perspective, and emergent novelty is a key idea.

Faith in rationalism is the fourth fundamental notion shaping Whitehead's philosophy. Whitehead had faith that there was a relational matrix inherent in the nature of things which reason could penetrate. This faith was transrational. It was a hope seeking satisfaction, not something that could be demonstrated. This faith in intrinsic reasonableness was balanced by a distrust in the ability of language to express the truth.

(Whitehead's confidence in reason has led some process thinkers to develop arguments for the existence of God.)

Whitehead himself sought to move through the obscurity of existing thought and language toward a more adequate but never final system of thought. Whitehead's own work focused on more penetrating descriptions of the given rather than on formal argument. He never attempted to develop proofs for the existence of God.

These emphases have led other process thinkers to emphasize the ambiguous relation between linguistic symbols and forms, on the one hand, and the depths of experience, on the other. These thinkers are somewhat skeptical about formal arguments for the existence of God. I myself am closer to Whitehead on this issue than to the most rationalistically inclined process thinkers.

Whitehead affirmed the actuality of a Divine Entity that served as the locus of potentiality, the evoker of the becoming of the actual occasions, the mediator of experience from one occasion to another, and the ultimate receptor of all that has become. By incorporating the principle of relativity in the center of his thinking, he became the first major philosopher to generalize notions central to contemporary postmodern physics.

Whitehead's understanding of the complexity of actual occasions and of the significance of the higher phases of experience in human life provide one with a rich context from which to explore the interplay between the influence of the causal past and the novelty of human responses to the past in the emerging present. Events in the causal past influence but do not determine the nature of an emerging occasion. High grade organisms such as human beings have substantial capacities for novel responses to the influence of the causal past. Human freedom and human responsibility are central elements in a process social ethic.

In addition to Whitehead, Henry Nelson Wieman and Charles Hartshorne were intimately associated with the emergence of process philosophy. Wieman did not have as much confidence in speculative reason as did Whitehead, and he developed a view which sought to discern the creative good in concrete structures and processes. For him, God is immanent and unconscious. Wieman refused to engage in what he felt were unwarranted claims for the reality of forms of definiteness and their envisagement by God.[2] Hartshorne had relatively greater confidence in speculative reason that Whitehead did, and he devoted much attention to the exploration of logically exhaustive formulations of God's nature and to proofs for the existence of God.[3]

This "family quarrel" has resulted in some differences in emphasis and interpretation among those who trace their intellectual roots to process philosophy. In my own constructive work, I stand closer to Whitehead than to Wieman or Hartshorne.[4] I want to highlight a distinction between metaphysics and the other sciences, for people frequently engage in complex controversies in which both metaphysical and specialized propositions are involved. Metaphysics seek to develop generic propositions applicable to all actual entities. A particular science seeks to develop more specialized notions applicable to its particular subject matter. Because specialized notions are always intertwined with more general propositions, no specialized discipline can avoid some metaphysical propositions.

Scientists may verbally disavow metaphysics, but they cannot avoid the use of some metaphysical propositions in their own work. In the human sciences this issue becomes critical, because all human interpretations impact human life directly. The shape of one's analysis and the shape of one's character are affected by one's view of the nature of things.

In an earlier volume, I explored a variety of issues in theology and sociology from the perspective of process thought.[5] My subsequent efforts have expanded on the work reflected in that volume. Although I have continued to address sociological issues, in the last two decades I have broadened my work to address more directly normative issues in the economic and political spheres of the human social order and in social ethics.

In our historical epoch, the human sciences are dominated by nontheistic phenomenological or reductionist interpretations of human life. Consequently, it is inevitable that interpretations developed in this work will stand in some contrast and in some conflict with the dominant modes of thought in our epoch. Although their primary interpretations differ, Karl Marx, Sigmund Freud, Emile Durkheim, John Stuart Mill, and Max Weber, as well as most of their successors, do not employ theistic modes of interpretation in their work.

An anecdote illustrates this phenomenon. A featured session at an annual meeting of the Society for the Scientific Study of Religion in the late 1980s dealt with new theoretical approaches to the sociology of religion. I was curious to see if any of the participants would suggest that theistic interpretations of religious phenomena might be among the "new" theoretical approaches to the study of religion. None did.

In the discussion period following the formal presentations, I asked the members of the panel whether any of them thought that an exploration of some of the modes of thought extant prior to the emergence of the human sciences in the nineteenth century might provide some resources for the development of new theoretical perspectives in the sociology of religion. Wanting to get behind the nineteenth century founders of the modern human sciences, whose assumptive worlds were non-theistic, I asked the members of the panel if any of them thought that Hegel, Kant, Aquinas, Augustine, Aristotle, or Plato (all of whom incorporate the notion of a *sui generis* divine reality in their interpretations) might be helpful in facilitating the development of new theoretical perspectives. One of the two past S.S.S.R. presidents on the panel responded that he hadn't the slightest idea. The other past president launched a positivist attack against the value of studying the history of ideas, asserting that a science that did not forget its founders was not going to progress.

The essays in this volume are informed by the notion of a Divine Reality that is, in some senses, *sui generis.* In contrast to interpretations that locate the genesis of religion in charismatic leaders (as Max Weber does) or in more basic underlying structures or processes (as Karl Marx, Emile Durkheim, and Sigmund Freud do), the interpretations developed in the essays in this volume ground religion in human responses to the Divine Presence in their experiences.

The reader informed by contemporary variations of existentialist or reductionist modes of interpretation will necessarily take issue with the interpretation offered in this volume.

The reader informed by contemporary versions of the dominant interpretations of the Christian movement will also necessarily take issue with the interpretation elaborated here. Two issues are salient: the place of natural theology and the uniqueness and elevated status of Christianity among the world religions.

Theologians and social ethicists rooted in the Christian movement who reject the idea of a natural theology must take issue with the mode of thought informing the constructive portions of this volume. Because Aquinas appropriated Aristotelian thought in his work, many Roman Catholics are sympathetic to the idea of a natural theology in principle. In Aquinas' view, divine revelation supplemented but was complimentary with the understanding of God developed through human efforts. For Aquinas a "one-way" God-world relation existed between God and the world. God influences the world but the world does not influence God.

Most Protestant theologians and social ethicists have also entertained one-way God world relations; in addition, they have rejected the idea of a natural theology, in which unaided human reason can illumine at least some facets of the Divine Reality. In their view, divine relation to humankind through Jesus Christ is unique and unanticipatable.

In contrast to both Roman Catholic and the dominant classical Protestant views, the view advanced in this volume envisages a "two-way" God-world relation, in which God influences the world and the world influences God. In addition, the particularism and elevated status of the Christian movement among world religions advanced by most Protestant and Catholic theologians and social ethicists are challenged and markedly reinterpreted. Finally, the ability of human reason to illumine the nature of the Divine Reality is more forcefully affirmed that is the case in Roman Catholicism, for the Catholic view of the supplementation of unaided human reason by Divine revelation is challenged. Persons informed by classical Protestant views will surely challenge my faith in rationalism, even though, as noted, it is more qualified than in some versions of process thought.

Thus, for different reasons than the ones advanced by many human scientists, one may expect many thinkers rooted in the Christian movement to be critical of the constructive views informing these essays.

Nonetheless, persuaded that religious experience is grounded in the authenticity of human experience of the Divine Presence, I offer these essays informed by a metatheory consistent with and informing this conviction. I hope they will be suggestive to people who are uneasy with the points of view dominant in the human sciences and in some religious bodies today and who are seeking to develop alternative interpretations of the human situation which they can maintain with emotional and intellectual integrity.

This work is divided into four parts. Part One includes three essays dealing with the basic categories of process thought and with my use of these categories and of contingent empirical data to elaborate basic notions in social theory and social ethics. These foundational essays illumine the concepts that are used in the other essays in the book.

Part Two includes five essays dealing primarily with the economic and political spheres of human society. They focus on post-traditional societies generally and on the United States in particular. Chapters 4 and 5 address the nature of political science and the state. Chapters 6, 7, and 8 focus on political economy. Democratic capitalism is defended as a desirable form of political economy. Chapter 6 develops the viewpoints most fully. Chapters 7 and 8 address Christian religious social ethicists, many of whom are persuaded that democratic socialism is the preferred form of political economy.

Part Three includes eight essays dealing with religious institutions and the study of religious phenomena. It is divided into two sections. Section A includes four chapters that are predominately constructive. Although they incorporate analytical dimensions, these essays develop a point of view about the topics being considered. Section B includes four chapters that are predominately analytical. Explicit constructive concerns are muted.

Part Four includes critical studies of three contemporary thinkers who have contributed much to the ongoing discussion of the relation between religion and science. Paul Tillich and Jürgen Moltmann formulate Protestant interpretations, and Ralph Wendell Burhoe formulates a view informed by facets of contemporary science, especially biology and anthropology. The introduction to Part Four and the critical discussions of these three thinkers illustrate the contrasts between my perspective and those of representative thinkers with their intellectual roots in the Christian and in the scientific communities.

Each part of this volume opens with a general introduction designed to provide an overview of the topics in that part. Within each part, more specialized introductions precede particular essays or clusters of essays. They contextualize the essays and illumine the socio-cultural factors leading to the development of the essay. An understanding of the context out of which a particular work comes is a useful but not a sufficient basis for considering the work. It is not sufficient because some propositions transcend the specificity of the context of which they come and are embodied in other contexts as well.

As noted earlier, many of the essays included in this volume appeared originally in other publications; all were written to be read independently. Except for a few stylistic changes, the essays stand as they were originally written. As a consequence, the same basic notions are repeated in several of the essays. I ask the reader's indulgence for these repetitions. Because they are integral to the discussion in a given essay, their deletion would have seriously distorted the structure of a given essay and the sequence of the discussion.

Notes and References

1. *Science and the Modern World* (New York: Macmillan, 1925); *Religion in the Making* (New York: Macmillan, 1926); *Process and Reality: An Essay in Cosmology,* corrected edition, ed. David Ray Griffin and Donald W. Sherburne (New York: Free Press, 1978) [Gifford Lectures, 1927-28, pub. 1929]; Alfred North Whitehead, *Adventures of Ideas* (New York: Macmillan, 1933); *Symbolism: Its Meaning and Effect* (1927; Reprint ed., New York: G.P. Putnam's Sons, Capricorn Books, 1959); *Modes of Thought* (1938; Reprint ed., New York: G.P. Putnam's Sons, 1958).

2. See Henry Nelson Wieman, *The Source of Human Good* (Chicago: University of Chicago Press, 1946) for a statement of his views.

3. Charles Hartshorne's writings are very extensive. He is a major exponent of what he calls "neo-classical" theism. Beginning with his early book *Man's Vision of God* (Chicago: Willett, Clark & Co., 1941), he has devoted his life to exploring the theistic question. *Philosophers Speak of God,* ed. Charles Hartshorne and William L. Reese (Chicago: University of Chicago Press, 1953), is an excellent reader in which various philosophical views of the Divine are ordered according to a typology informed by Hartshorne's views. They offer commentaries and critiquies of contrasting interpretations. Charles Hartshorne, *Creative Synthesis and Philosophic Method* (LaSalle, IL: Open Court, 1970), and *A Natural Theology for Our Time* (LaSalle, IL: Open Court, 1967) continue his work on the theistic question. For a critical discussion of his work see *Existence and Actuality: Conversations with Charles Hartshorne,* edited by John B. Cobb and Franklin I. Gamwell (Chicago: University of Chicago Press, 1984).

4. Numerous philosophical theologians within the Christian movement who have appropriated process modes of thought in their constructive work. Bernard Loomer, Bernard Meland, and Perry LeFevre develop interpretations informed by Wieman's constructive views. Daniel Day Williams, John B. Cobb, David Ray Griffin, Marjorie Suchocki, Delwin Brown, and Lewis Ford develop views whose understanding of speculative reason is more closely aligned with Whitehead. Franklin I. Gamwell, Schubert Ogden, and David Tracy espouse the most rationalistic views more closely associated with Charles Hartshorne.

5. See my *Cognitive Structures and Religious Research: Essays in Theology and Sociology* (East Lansing: Michigan State University Press, 1970).

PART ONE

Foundational Notions

Introduction to Part One

The three essays included in Part One discuss the foundational issues one must consider in the development of a process perspective on the human sciences, religious social ethics, and theology. They elaborate the basic notions employed throughout this volume: actual occasions as the "really real," the ultimacy of creativity in the nature of things, the hierarchy of nature, the universality of the principle of relativity, the basic factors involved in the becoming of actual occasions, the bases for the spheres of the human social order, the interrelation of fact and value, the principles of justice, and the exploration of normative forms of human social organization.

Chapter 1 elaborates most fully the basic factors involved in the becoming of an actual occasion and explores the nature of human values and human religious experience. Chapter 2 draws on the basic concepts of process philosophy and the defining characteristics of various subject matters as interpreted by process philosophy to suggest an ordering of the sciences and to develop guidelines for the seasonal relevance of subhuman sciences in the study of human beings.

Chapter 3 addresses the issues of human rights and peace. This chapter constitutes the fullest and most comprehensive discussion of the facts which must be addressed in the development of a process social ethic. The more specialized essays the rest of the volume draw selectively on the concepts developed here and in the other chapters in Part One.

Introduction to Chapter 1

This chapter is an expanded version of a paper presented during the 1980 annual meeting of the American Association for the Advancement of Science at a symposium honoring Ralph Burhoe, who had been awarded the Templeton Prize for advancing the relation between science and religion. Because it engages the range of issues addressed in this volume and delineates the basic mode of interpretation employed in my appropriation of process thought, it is placed at the beginning of this volume. One who is unfamiliar with process thought may find it helpful to begin with this chapter.

Beauty is a key notion, and emergent evolution is a central theme. The following topics are addressed: the emergence of modern evolutionary thinking and alternative responses to it; the nature of human nature in a process perspective; the place of humans in nature; the immanence of laws; emergent evolution on this planet; some implications of the hierarchy of nature for the interpretation of human life, human morality, and human values; and human religious experience.

CHAPTER 1

Evolution, Human Values and Religious Experience: A Process Perspective

The place of humans in nature has long been problematic, and the foundational issues pertaining to humankind's relation to nature emerged in the West long before the development of modern science. Nonetheless, the impact of science upon the world and popular culture in the past three or four centuries has dramatically affected the loci of discussions and has led to the accentuation of themes and foundational modes of interpretation which were minor motifs during the medieval and early modern epochs. Today western scholars and scientists emphasize inordinately efficient causes and minimize final causes; just the opposite situation prevailed in the Middle Ages.

The problem of interpretation is complicated by the intertwining of propositions and theories informed by particular researches in specialized fields of scientific investigation with propositions embodying more general notions not being considered directly in the more specialized studies. For example, many studies in the biological and human sciences refer to the "passage of time." This conception, informed by a Newtonian understanding of time, usually is not discussed in detail in more specialized monographs. The different notion that time is measured by motion, embodying an alternative cosmology associated with Plato's *Timaeus* and advanced by the twentieth-century philosopher and cosmologist Alfred North Whitehead, is rarely discussed in specialized monographs in biology, sociology, psychology, economics, or political science.

When one seeks to discern the place of humans in nature, broad general presuppositions giving shape to one's interpretation of scientific data are unavoidably intertwined with more specialized notions pertaining to data in a particular field of investigation. One may seek to generalize the findings and the interpretative framework drawn from the study of one subject matter to other subject matters, but two dangers are inherent in such analogical efforts. First, the characteristics of the primary subject matter and the secondary subject matter may be significantly different, so that findings informing the first subject matter may be unfitting for the second. Second, the implicit, generic notions inherent in the interpretative framework informing one area of investigation may be applied in an unexamined manner to another area. When this happens, an implicit interpretation of experience rooted in a particular philosophic tradition may be imposed uncritically on the secondary subject matter. Some propositions may seem to be relatively adequate for the purpose of studying a particular subject matter but may be unfitting for other subject matters without substantial qualifications and revisions.

The principle that our understanding of nature may enhance our understanding of human beings is a sound one, but the principle is double-edged. What we know of human beings may also enhance our understanding of nature. If theories developed primarily in the context of the physical and biological sciences are used to interpret human nature and human action, serious distortions and misinterpretations of the human situation may result. The widespread use of a Freudian world view in the interpretation of human nature is a case in point, for both the gratification-deprivation interpretation of human motivation and also the rewards-punishment scheme of human social control stemming from that tradition are inordinately mechanistic and reductionistic.

This chapter elaborates an interpretation of the evolutionary process informed by process philosophy. Process philosophy was initiated by Whitehead through a series of writings in the 1920s and 1930s during the time he was professor of philosophy at Harvard.[1] Deeply informed by the broad contours of modern science, Whitehead appropriated the Platonic heritage to develop a cosmology incorporating a complex and rich doctrine of emergent evolution.

Before addressing this constructive task, it is fitting to describe briefly the context from which the "evolutionary epoch" emerged and to note some theological responses to it.

The Evolutionary Epoch

The Emergence of Modern Evolutionary Thinking. The epoch-making work of Charles Darwin initiated a movement in theory and research that has brought the topic of evolution to a central place in both scientific and popular culture in the contemporary world. Darwin himself emphasized both the conflictful and also the adaptive dimensions of nature through his ideas about the struggle for survival and the survival of the fittest.

Social theorists in the late nineteenth and early twentieth centuries sought to apply evolutionary ideas to the changes being manifest in human society. Lloyd Morgan, Herbert Spencer, and Emile Durkheim are illustrative of those who sought to develop interpretations focused on the evolution of human forms of social organization. Most social theorists informed by evolutionary notions undertook either phenomenological or reductionistic interpretations of experience. They saw no reason to appeal to a Divine reality that was at least in some senses *sui generis* to interpret the evolutionary process. In addition to the intellectual issues involved in their interpretations of the evolutionary process, two socio-cultural factors affected their approaches. First, the general climate of opinion prevailing in European scientific circles disparaged "metaphysics" and ontic interpretations of experience. Second, in the early modern period most independent thinkers and scientists in Europe had to struggle with university establishments which had been dominated for centuries by the church and the clergy. The scars of these struggles have run deep, and they undoubtedly affected the intellectual interests and the emotional tone of persons working in both the natural and the human sciences.[2]

Some biblical scholars became interested in evolutionary theories in the latter part of the nineteenth century and applied evolutionary notions to the analysis of biblical documents and to the interpretation of ethical and theological ideas. Also, in addition to the detailed studies undertaken by biologists, historians, psychologists, and sociologists, persons concerned with cosmological and ontological matters began to incorporate evolutionary thinking in their work. Henri Bergson, Charles Sanders Peirce, Nikolai Berdyaev, and Samuel Alexander all elaborated dynamic ontologies embodying evolutionary understandings.

Today evolutionary thinking is overwhelmingly predominant in the scientific community. To be sure, differences exist among scientists regarding both the details of the evolutionary processes and also the most fitting interpretations of the processes, but very, very few challenge the basic vision of the emergence of increasingly complex creatures on this planet.[3] In this sense, the present epoch may be termed "the evolutionary epoch."

Theological Responses. The primal vision embodied in evolutionary thinking did clash with cosmological interpretations advanced by classical Christian thinkers, and evolutionary theories have evoked varied theological responses.

St. Augustine (354-430) most fully formulated the cosmology which became dominant in the Christian movement for the next fourteen-hundred years. Although he insisted that knowledge of the theories and details of the workings of nature were not critical to matters of faith and theological belief, he himself did develop a theory of the origin of things that stands at variance with evolutionary perspectives. Augustine posited a world with a beginning, a middle, and an end. In his view God created *ex nihilo* a perfectly harmonious world—a literal Garden of Eden and a literal Adam and Eve, created with their wills in perfect accord with the Divine will. Consequently, their minds were in perfect harmony with their wills, and their bodies were also in perfect harmony with their minds and wills. When they turned away from the Divine will and centered themselves around their own wills, thereby committing the sin of pride, they disrupted the perfect harmony of their bodies, minds, and wills. Their actions along with the actions of fallen angels, who were creatures with minds and spirits but no bodies, introduced disharmony in nature and death to humans.[4] God, knowing that they would sin inevitably but not necessarily, had initiated efforts to redeem some of the fallen people and to condemn others to eternal separation from It. Redemption was carried out through the life, death, and resurrection of Jesus Christ and through the salvational mediation of the church.

It is obvious that evolutionary theory, rejecting the idea of a perfectly created world which was subsequently distorted and suggesting the increasing complexification of life forms on this planet, constituted a major challenge to this style of thinking.[5]

Biblical fundamentalists, insisting on the literal interpretation of the Adam and Eve account in Genesis incorporated in the thinking of

Augustine, have persistently and consistently challenged evolutionary thinking. The current "creationist" controversies in North America are a contemporary manifestation of this conflict.

Christian theologians wanting both to sustain facets of the theological tradition and also to respond sympathetically to evolutionary thinking made two types of responses. Some made very sharp distinctions between the inner experiential warrants for theological formulations and external scientific and cosmological formulations; others incorporated the broad contours of evolutionary thinking in their theological formulations. In different ways Paul Tillich and Karl Barth, two of the most distinguished Protestant theologians of the twentieth century, took the former route; Pierre Teilhard de Chardin and process theologians took the latter route.

Arguing that the movement from essence to existence was irrational, Tillich insisted that the impingement of the Divine Spirit into the human spirit is a consequence of the Divine initiative.[6] With one exception, theologians *qua* theologians have no business dealing with the issues embodied in the specialized sciences. These sciences have developed fitting methodologies and accepted methods of investigation about which the theologian has nothing to say *qua* theologian. The one exception is the sciences dealing with human beings. If scientists studying human beings deny that humans are deliberating free subjects, their objectification and thingification of human beings has to be challenged. (Tillich's personal experiences with the Nazis and their treatment of Jews accentuated his views on this matter, but the general notion was, of course, not dependent on this particular occurrence.) Any research or experimentation on human beings violating their freedom and subjectivity must be challenged.

Because Tillich thought theology could provide the answers to the questions philosophy raised about human existence, he was willing to use the cultural forms of the modern epoch to raise the questions to which he felt theology could provide answers. In this manner, he was able to relate to evolutionary thinking in his work.

Barth insists even more vigorously than Tillich that the Divine reality is utterly transcendent and only through Its self-revelation to humankind could humans become aware of It. He insists on the ultimacy of God's revelation in Jesus Christ and in the primacy of biblical forms to convey God's revelation to humankind. Although Barth was a most learned person thoroughly conversant with the major thought forms shaping the modern world, in his theological work he refused to engage in speculation about evolutionary theory. He viewed his task as a theologian to seek illumine the meaning of God's revelation in Jesus Christ to which witness was borne through Scripture primarily and in the tradition secondarily in relation to one's personal experience. The radical contrast between human works and God's grace led him to insist that human thinking about God apart from human awareness of God's revelation to humankind would either be idolatrous or secular. For Barth, Scripture is the form through which God's revelation is manifest.[7]

Due to a rather static ontology and the qualified appropriation of the Augustinian view of creation, nineteenth-century Catholic theologians were very wary of evolutionary theories, but in more recent times some have sought to relate to evolutionary thinking, for example, Karl Rahner and Bernard Lonergan.

In contrast to thinkers like Barth and Tillich who sharply distinguished theology and science, some theologians responded to evolutionary theories by incorporating evolutionary theory in their theological work. Teilhard de Chardin is the most widely recognized Roman Catholic to do this. His presentation of the emergence of the *nous sphere* in the evolutionary process accentuates the emergent side of evolution, but his view of the culmination of history in an Omega point accentuates the notion of a single mode in perfection to be attained at the end of history, a motif which is predominant in the Christian movement.[8] Catholic theologians Bernard Lee and David Tracy have utilized the process perspective informing the constructive portions of this essay in their work.[9]

The contemporary line of theistic thinking most fully appropriating evolutionary views is the movement of thought broadly characterized as process philosophy and its corollary, process theology. As noted earlier, the distinguished mathematician and philosopher Alfred North Whitehead initiated this line of thinking in the 1920s. Numerous Protestant theologians and a few Catholic theologians have appropriated this approach.[10]

The body of this essay is devoted to the formulation of a perspective informed by process philosophy. It seeks to discern the place of humans in nature, to affirm one type of evolutionary theory, to describe the processes by which an emerging creature becomes and is objectified for other creatures in its casual future and in the Divine life, and to delineate the nature of human nature, the nature of religious experience, and the status of human values.

Even though the framework of interpretation developed here is informed by evolutionary theory, it contains two elements absent from most contemporary scientific accounts. First, forms of definiteness termed eternal objects are an integral part of this interpretation; analogous to the Platonic forms, they constitute the potential which may be actualized by emerging creatures. An indefinite number of creatures may participate in the same eternal object. Second, a Divine reality that is in some senses *sui generis* is an integral part of this interpretative framework. God functions in the universe as the locus of potentiality, the mediator of experience from one creature to another, the lure for feeling, and the ultimate receptor of all that has become.

These two components and the interpretative framework in which they are set are not fashionable today among most workers in either the natural or social sciences. Some form of metaphysical skepticism, involving a rejection of a faith in rationalism beyond the confines of one's specialized discipline, some form of reductionism, involving an explanation of the higher aspects of experience on the basis of more fundamental or elemental components, and/or some form of causal determinism, involving an explanation of current occasions on the basis of events in the causal past of an emerging creature, are currently more widespread.[11]

The Nature of Human Nature in a Process Perspective

The Human Organizing Center. A detailed consideration of the human organism, the biological and biochemical processes transpiring in the human body, and the mechanisms of sense reception and perception lie in the special provinces of the biologist, the biochemist, and the physiological psychologist. These analyzes are beyond the scope of this essay and are not directly pertinent to the salient aspects of human activity considered here, for the peculiarly human aspects of human life are embodied in the human organizing center.

This organizing center is a sequence of occasions arranged in serial order and embodied in a form so protean it can only be characterized by the occasions which it receives. This organizing center is here termed a "soul," and each event constituting its life is termed a "regnant ultimate percipient occasion."[12] This regnant ultimate percipient occasion receives data from the body, from the Divine life, and from preceding ultimate percipient occasions. (The way in which these entities contribute to the emerging regnant ultimate percipient occasion will be discussed subsequently.)

In process thinking the reasons for things are always to be found in actual occasions. One's primary data for developing an interpretation of experience are one's conscious experiences; there is no place else to begin. Our own foundational experience illumines the centrality of deliberations and decisions in human life. Human beings are meaning-seeking, meaning-posting creatures with substantial capacities for deliberation and self-determination. These factors shape the entire tone of human life; they are too central and too widespread among humankind to be set aside as mere illusion.

These aspect of human nature are central for *human* social theory. They are integral to interpretations of *human* history and *human* group life, for with the emergence of humans life has taken on new dimensions of novelty and intensity. Because all creatures possess some capacities to respond to the data they appropriate in the process of their becoming, the differences between human and subhuman entities on this planet are a matter of degree; but the differences in degree are so substantial they are almost differences in kind.

In spite of this emphasis upon the importance of the human organizing center in human life, the regnant ultimate percipient occasions constituting our conscious "selves" are intimately related to our bodies. Conscious human experience begins with a flood of feelings coming from the occasions constituting our bodies. In this initial physical phase of the becoming of a regnant ultimate percipient occasion, feeling is primary. The body functions as a giant amplifier, sensing and transforming data having their origins both within and beyond the body. In the supplemental or mental phase of the occasion's becoming, the emerging occasion supplements and synthesizes the feelings and forms received from the physical phase of the occasion's becoming.

A dynamic and reciprocal relation exists between the body and the regnant ultimate percipient occasion. Sometimes the regnant ultimate percipient occasion is preoccupied with the body, as in cases of great pain, intense hunger, or sexual excitement. Sometimes it exercises substantial directive influence on the body, as in the cases of intense intellectual activity, appropriation of a rich aesthetic experience, or participation in facets of the Divine life.

The Structure of the Becoming of Actual Occasions (Creatures). The description of the emergence and becoming of actual occasions is central to a process perspective on emergent evolution. In process modes of thought, actual occasions are the basic units constituting the components of the cosmos. They differ in complexity and importance, but they all exhibit the same basic structure.

All creatures are dipolar. Except for God, they begin their process of becoming by appropriating data embodied in the creatures of the emerging occasion's causal past.[13] This physical appropriation is termed the "physical pole." It is "followed" by a conceptual appropriation of forms of definiteness embodied in the primordial facet of the Divine life. This appropriation is termed the "conceptual" pole, and the forms of definiteness are termed "eternal objects." Eternal objects are not necessarily embodied in the occasions in the causal past of an emerging creature, but they are necessarily embodied in the primordial facet of the Divine nature. Novelty and the emergence of new forms and novel propositions in the evolutionary process are due to the "abrupt" appropriation by an emerging creature of forms of definiteness either not previously embodied in the world or else not previously embodied in the same patterning in the world.

The verb "followed" in the preceding paragraph is placed in quotes, for the process of the coming together of the several forms and feelings comprising an emerging actual occasion cannot be divided into temporally earlier and later phases. The temporal thickness of an emerging experience is termed a duration. Physical time itself is measured by the sequence of events which become, and change is the "movement" of eternal objects form one creature to another.

In process thinking, the potentiality represented by eternal objects must be located somewhere. That somewhere is the primordial facet of the Divine nature. Not only does God provide a locus for potentiality; It also orders the forms of definiteness. Through Its ordering God assures that an emerging creature can integrate the data it appropriates into a novel unity. Without God's functioning any situation would be riddled with ambiguity. God's envisagement of all potentiality provides a locus for potentiality and the lure for feeling. It permits a rational explanation for the emergence of novel entities in the evolution of the cosmos.

In the supplemental phase of the becoming of an actual occasion, the emerging creature effects syntheses and contrasts between the data appropriated from occasions in the emerging creature's casual past and the eternal objects appropriated from the primordial facet of the Divine nature. In higher-grade organisms the supplemental phase is enhanced and prolonged, so the contrasts between the initial data and the supplemental data are richer and more complex. In lower-grade organisms the past is appropriated in the present with a modicum of novelty; the laws of nature hold sway, for zest, novelty, and innovation are at a minimum.

In its becoming a creature seeks aesthetic satisfaction and intensity of feeling. As is synthesizes and integrates the data it has received, it is guided by its subjective aim. This aim is informed by God's subjective aim, for God's overarching rationality, Its harmonization of all forms of definiteness, and Its grading of seasonal relevance of the forms of definiteness for emerging occasions give shape to the subjective aims of emerging creatures. God is immanent in the creatures of the world whether or not they are aware of it. The process of the becoming of an actual entity just described is illustrated in Figure 1.

Individual creatures may share complex eternal objects with other creatures and may derive satisfaction from their common participation in the same defining characteristics. Creatures sharing the same defining characteristics may constitute a society. In the case of creatures in the physical and biological spheres, these defining characteristics contribute to the apparent substantiability of what is in fact a myriad sequence of emerging actual entities.

Human beings participate in some of the forms of definiteness embodied in entities in both the physical and biological spheres, but they also share many complex conceptual forms and feelings grounded in the rich and complex supplemental phase of the regnant ultimate percipient occasion.[14] Humans may participate in multiple social worlds, each with varying defining characteristics. The realm of human culture is a complex realm of propositions and precipitates of meaning and feeling created by humans and shared by persons in specified societies of human beings.

As noted earlier, the prolongation and enhancement of the supplemental phase of the serial sequence of regnant ultimate percipient occasions constituting the human organizing center provides the basis for the richer elaboration and the greater complexification of human life than is the case for other living organisms on this planet. Human societies are much more variegated and innovative than subhuman societies. This prolongation also greatly increases a creature's capacity for depth and breadth of aesthetic satisfaction, providing the bases for human values and human religious experiences. These human-defining characteristics give human history a qualitatively different character than subhuman history.

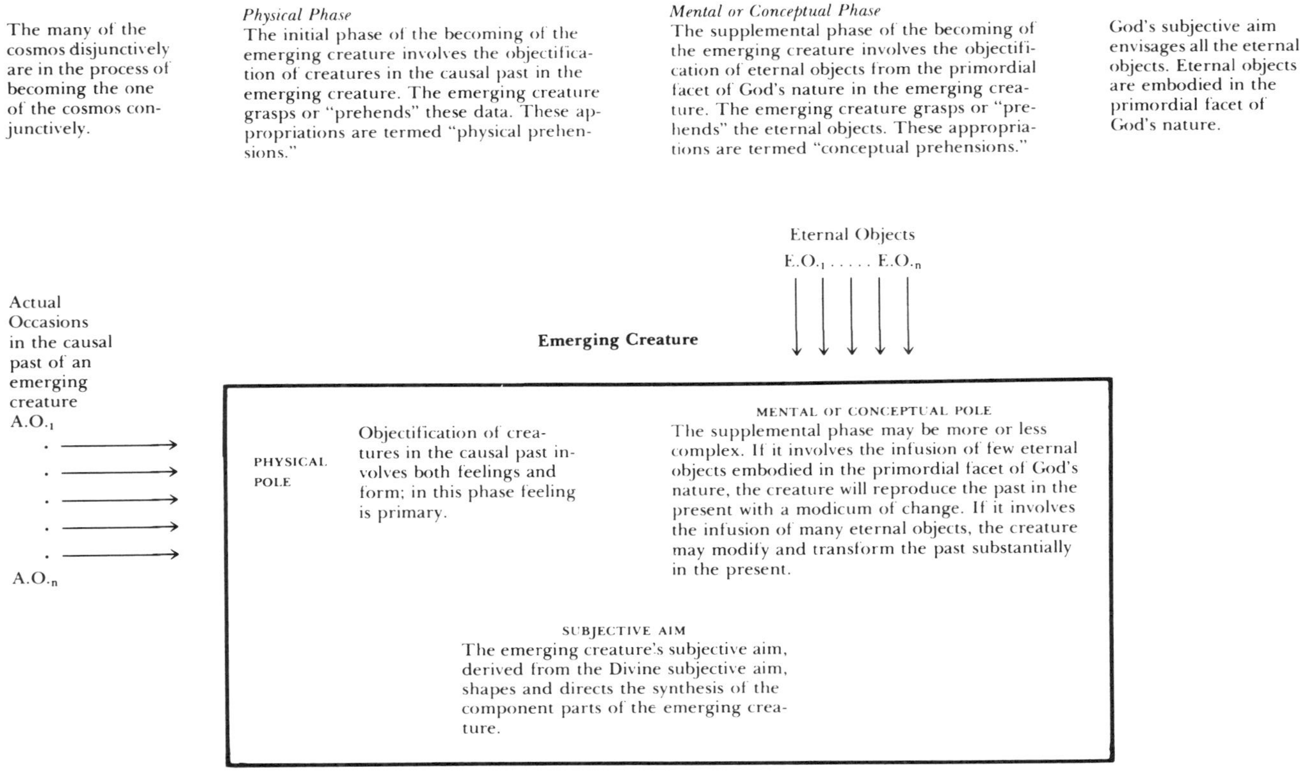

Fig. 1.—The becoming of an Actual Entity

History, Facts, and Values. The dynamic and emergent character of human societies is rooted in the nature of human nature indicated above by the human-defining characteristics. Human *history* involves heightened intentionality and directionality. Purposiveness and meanings embodied in human social groups loom large in human life. In addition, theoretical understanding developed in one human generation and/or society can be transmitted to another, increasing the human cultural storehouse.

The infusion of feelings and forms constituting perception in the mode of causal efficacy is primary in human experience. This physical phase of becoming is more primitive than the complex conceptual development constituting the supplemental phase.[15] The objectification of creatures in an emerging occasion's causal past integrates fact and value, for *what* something is and *how* that thing functions are interrelated. The "facts," that is, entities in their causal pasts which humans appropriate in their emerging presents, are laden with meanings and feelings.

Science is concerned with percepta rather than the humans' feelings about the percepta—at least not human feelings in their immediacy. Religion is concerned with human responses to the data it receives—both from creatures in the world and from the Divine entity. Philosophy seeks to discern the relation between science and religion and to develop a framework of interpretation which incorporates both spheres of human experience in an integral whole. Humans seek intellectual justifications for both science and religion. This issue will be considered subsequently in the discussion of human religious experience. But before this is done, humans must more clearly be set in the context of nature by examining the organization of the human organism and its place in the order of nature.

The Place of Humans in Nature

The Organization of the Human Organism. The human organism is an exceedingly complex society including a vast number of subordinate societies and myriad living occasions. It incorporates in serial order a sequence of regnant ultimate percipient occasions of very high grade in what earlier was termed the organizing center or the soul. As noted earlier, an emerging regnant ultimate percipient occasion receives a complex array of data from the subsocieties and occasions constituting the body and from preceding regnant ultimate percipient occasions. It synthesizes them with conceptual forms and with subjective feelings in its process of becoming. As observed previously, these regnant ultimate percipient occasions are embodied in the organizing center or soul, a "formless" form so protean it can "contain" the occasions which occur in serial order "within" it.

The living occasions constituting the human being's organizing center are bound together by hybrid prehensions, which in this instance are the "physical" prehensions of earlier regnant occasions. Hybrid prehensions, by which an emerging occasion may feel the conceptual feelings of other occasions physically and *vice versa*, are required to explain memory. Through memory the living occasions lying in the causal past of the emerging occasion are objectified in that occasion.[16]

Humans are organized hierarchically, for the human organizing center coordinates and directs the human organism. Lower grade organisms such as rose bushes and oak trees are more democratically organized; they do not have a dominant organizing center.

In spite of the importance of the human organizing center, many parts of the human organism exist quite independent of it. Overall, the organizing center and the rest of the human organism maintain symbiotic and mutually reciprocal relations.[17] Due to this intimate relation between the "soul" and the body, the body has a substantial impact on human behavior. Some psychic disorders have their roots in bodily disorders. Research in biochemistry has discovered the physiological bases for some psychic disorders and will undoubtedly discover physiological bases for other psychic maladies.

Nonetheless, the exceedingly complex and reciprocal relations between the soul and the body, the abruptness of the becoming of a regnant ultimate percipient occasion, the capacity of present occasions to surpass past occasions, and the significance of human relations in human life suggest the multifaceted sources of human pathological behavior. Human psychic pathology cannot be reduced unequivocally to physiological phenomena.

No advances in biochemistry or in related areas can eliminate all disharmony in human experience, for finitude, ignorance, sloth, lethargy, and inordinate self-interest are persistent bases of disharmony. Furthermore, the emergence of new, novel, and more creative human relations, grounded in the Divine evocation for harmony and intensity of feeling and in the capacity of emerging occasions to respond novelly to their pasts, is always a potential source of disharmony; for the quest for richer and more complex harmonies always involves the risk of greater disharmony and attenuation of feeling.

The Hierarchy of Nature. Humans are at the apex of a hierarchy of nature on this planet, but they are integrally involved in the order of nature. This order needs to be sketched to illumine the direction of emergent evolution on this planet. The most general defining characteristics, shared by all creatures in our cosmic epoch and also by creatures in other cosmic epochs, are the properties of extensive connection. Creatures are bound together by their common participation in an extensive continuum. The properties of the extensive continuum include extensive connection, whole-part relations, and various geometrical elements derivable from these properties.[18]

Those more general geometric properties do not include measurement, for measurement presupposes the embodiment of more specialized geometric forms permitting straight lines to be defined. Consequently, more specialized defining characteristics are also embodied in the creatures in our cosmic epoch. These more specialized defining characteristics make measurement possible.

A multiplicity of competing families of straight lines is possible, giving rise to different systems of measurement. In our cosmic epoch, this ambiguity is resolved in favor of one family of straight lines and a system of metric measurement.

In our cosmic epoch more specialized societies with additional defining characteristics have evolved. These societies include numerous subatomic entities, atoms, molecules, societies of molecules organized as inorganic bodies, living cells closely related to inorganic molecules and societies, and societies of living cells. On this planet vegetable and animal bodies illustrate complex societies composed of both inorganic societies and living cells.

The human organism is set in the context of this broad order of nature. The human organism itself consists of a hierarchy of societies more or less integrated into a complex whole. However, as noted earlier, humans possess a soul, a serial sequence of regnant ultimate percipient occasions, constituting the conscious self.

The Immanence of Laws

According to this view of the character of geometric forms and other defining characteristics and their relations to the "facts" of emergent evolution, the laws of nature are immanental. They pass into existence with the emergence of creatures possessing particular defining characteristics, and they pass out of existence with the emergence of new creatures embodying different defining characteristics. Plato made this point poetically in the *Timaeus* when he observed that nature could only tell a likely tale.

The view of law as immanental must be qualified, for according to process thought the divine reality is seeking to evoke creatures capable of experiencing more intense feelings and richer harmonies. Both the forms of definiteness embodied in the order of nature, from which a creature begins to become, and the Divine evocation for harmony and intensity of feeling contribute to the shape and feeling of an emerging new creature. In its becoming, a creature not only appropriates but also surpasses the "laws" embodied in the creatures constituting its causal past.

The aim of existence is aesthetic satisfaction and intensity of feeling. The Divine persuasion seeks to evoke creatures capable of greater aesthetic satisfaction. In this evocation, one can discern the teleology of the universe. This point of view provides a framework to interpret the process of emergent evolution on this planet.

Emergent Evolution on this Planet

In evolution on earth, two salient trends are discernible. First, some societies and some societies of societies have become increasingly complex. Second, the mental or conceptual pole of some occasions has been enhanced. Life, constituting a bid for freedom from the bonds of the causal past, has emerged.

In ways that permit some of their members to attain greater breadth and depth of experience, complex structured societies have evolved. The creatures of these societies participate in common forms, and these societies are able to survive in the midst of a shifting and changing environment. The enhancement of an occasion's mental pole facilitates the emergence of these structured societies, which are enduring objects with substantial survival capabilities.

The enhancement of the mental pole may occur in one of two ways. In the first instance, the enrichment of the conceptual pole permits an emerging creature to consider the many members of a society as one. The unity of the society is accentuated in the experience of each emerging members, and the individuality of the many actual occasions comprising the society is minimized. The fitting uniformity of structure pervading the society is enhanced, and the diversity of its individual members is minimized.

This mode of conceptual enhancement is typical of the occasions of societies termed physical bodies, for both organic and inorganic physical bodies are closely associated with presented loci definable by straight lines. The creatures sharing these forms are prone to reproduce them, for the commonly shared forms are imposed upon them. These societies are stable and endure many changes in their surrounding environment.

This type of mentality is rather low grade, a step above the level of the mere reproduction of the past in the present. There is evidence of conceptual integration, but minimal evidence of conceptual originality. This mentality is characteristic of societies termed "inorganic."

In the second instance, the emerging occasion's mental pole is further enriched to produce conceptual originality. In this way a creature may both appropriate more elements of the environment into its own becoming and entertain novel eternal objects that may not have been embodied in the occasions in the emerging entity's causal past. The complexity of this conceptual originality varies from the merest aesthetic adjustment lured by an ideal of harmony in the case of low-grade living organisms to thought about a range of experiences and the exercise of negative judgments in the case of high-grade living occasions.

In both of these instances, an impulse original to the emerging occasion qualifies the data received by the physical pole of the occasion. The emerging occasion initiates a response aimed to preserve and enrich the society of which the emerging creature is a member.

The transition from nonliving to living societies is not clear cut, so the members of a society may be more or less living. For example, "viruses" represent transitional societies that are neither organic nor inorganic. Further, as noted earlier, on this planet living societies are intimately associated with inorganic ones. In complex living organisms, living and nonliving occasions interact with and relate to each other.

The abruptness of the embodiment of eternal objects, or new forms of definiteness, in the conceptual phase of the becoming of a creature and the discreteness of some geometrical forms provide the basis for a rational interpretation of the emergence of new forms of life on this planet. New life evolves as an emerging creature appropriates forms of definiteness that are not identical with the forms embodied in its causal past but that may be integrated with them to produce a novel proposition. What begins as a novel conceptual form may then be embodied in an emerging creature and subsequently become a physical datum for the entities which succeed it. In this manner a mutation may take place. The fecundity of nature is vast; some of the mutations may enhance the capacity of subsequent occasions to survive and live better, and others may not. Thus, one may speak of the survival of the fittest, but this notion should not be emphasized inordinately for nature manifests cooperative as well as the conflictful aspects.

The discreteness of geometric forms enables one to interpret the rather clear-cut species in nature, for there is not a continuum of organic life grouped around an amorphous central type. Instead, species of organic life are reasonably distinct. The same situation holds in the realm of inorganic entities. In these instances, creatures of the same species seem to share common geometric forms.

Although the abruptness of the embodiment of eternal objects in the conceptual phase of the becoming of a creature need not necessarily result in the rapid emergence of a new species, it certainly would lead one to suspect such phenomena have occurred. The current biological discussions about the possible rapid development of human beings cohere with one of the likely possibilities suggested by this theory. Human beings, for example, may have emerged as a result of an abrupt mutation. If so, the quest for intermediate species between humans and other primates may well be a futile one. In one sense, these abrupt mutations, if they in fact occurred, could be interpreted as a form of "new creation."

In the case of humans, the most significant factor in their mentality is the prolongation of the supplemental phase of the regnant ultimate percipient occasions constituting the human organizing center.

The peak of consciousness is the negative judgment. In a negative judgment one can imagine the absence of that which is present or the presence of that which is absent. These experiences involve a new level of contrasts in the conscious entity. This capacity appears to differentiate humans rather sharply from other earthly creatures, but some analogous judgments seem to be manifest in some subhuman animals.

Because the evolutionary process is unending, it is conceivable that new and novel creatures with capacities for contrasts and intensities of feelings surpassing those of humans will emerge on this planet. Considering the vastness of the cosmos, alternative life forms superior to human forms may well have evolved in some environments or will do so in the future.

However, possessing enhanced capacities for thought, aesthetic satisfaction, and depth of feeling, humans can qualify, modify, and shape that which they receive in ways which greatly exceed the capabilities of other creatures on this planet. Both intentionally and unintentionally humans impinge on the processes of natural evolution in ways that greatly exceed the abilities of subhuman entities.

Human moral values, cultural works, and religious experiences also are grounded in these enhanced capacities for aesthetic satisfaction and creative formulation. These aspects of human experience will be considered in the concluding sections of this essay. Before turning to them, however, the implications of the hierarchy of nature for human social theory and social ethics need to be further considered.

Some Implications of the Hierarchy of Nature for the Interpretation of Human Life

The enhanced conceptual phase of the becoming of the regnant ultimate percipient occasion of a human being has important consequences for the interpretation of human life. The recognition of this reality permits one to delineate the relative importance of the physical and biological spheres in human social theory and social ethics and to illumine the nature of consciousness and the self.

The Relative Importance of the Physical, Biological and Human Spheres in Human Social Theory and Social Ethics. The increasing complexification of some societies on this planet and the increasing capacities of some organisms to respond novelly to the data they appropriate permits one to assess the relative importance of facts and theories in the physical and biological sciences for human life.

For purposes of human social theory and social ethics, many of the persistent patterns manifest in the physical world are relatively insignificant. The "laws" shaping the behavior of many nonliving creatures which are of special interest to mathematicians and physical scientists are not directly pertinent to the human scientist and social ethicist.[19]

Due to the intimate relation between the soul and the body noted earlier, findings in the biological sciences are more directly relevant for human studies than findings in the physical sciences. However, due to the innovative character of the regnant ultimate percipient occasions constituting the human soul, biological components are modified, qualified, and transformed in human life. Human behavior is *not* reducible to its biological dimension, for, as noted earlier, purposiveness, meaning, and intentionality loom too large in human life to be put aside as epiphenomenal.

The actions of human beings and the feelings and meanings informing these actions are at the center of human life, for the conscious experience of a regnant ultimate percipient occasion is the primary datum for all human reflections and interpretations. In assessing the validity of any formulation, the ultimate court of appeal is the individual thinker's experience. An individual's feelings, meanings and interpretations are primary in understanding *human* behavior.

This existentialist bias of process thought is qualified by a principle of relativity and a principle of rationality. According to the principle of relativity, every being is a potential for every becoming. Consequently there is a *necessary* relation between an emerging creature and other creatures, for all other creatures in the universe lying in the causal past of an emerging creature contribute positively to the emerging creature. Conscious creatures are able to understand some aspects of the order of nature because patterned forms of definiteness embodied in other creatures are also embodied in the emergent conscious subject.

Although the structures emerge in individual experiences, they have a public character. Rational analysis can illumine aspects of these structures. This interplay between the public and private aspects of experience can be illustrated in human social relations. The principles of justice and the forms of human social organization contributing to the conduct of human life are inherent in every human experience. Even though all humans participate in these structures, not all humans are self-conscious about them. Some humans, being more selfconsciously aware of these principles of justice and alternative forms of social organization, may illumine them through rational analysis. In this manner, those persons raise the consciousness of their fellows. This enhanced consciousness may lead to more general understandings to guide human life and to enhace its quality.

In this way, the primacy of individual preferences and tastes in human experience is acknowledged, but a critique of particular human tastes, preferences, and actions based on the development of a more public mode of interpretation is possible. Tastes, preferences, and particular social institutions are not equal in excellence; by using more public principles of evaluation, a critique of individual values and modes of conduct is possible.[20]

The Nature of Consciousness and the Self. Earlier in this essay the dipolar character of occasions was noted. In the discussion of emergent evolution, the prolongation and complexification of the supplemental phase of the becoming of a creature were outlined to interpret the foundational bases for the movement toward organisms with enhanced capacities for manifesting novelty and intensity of feeling in their becoming. This movement reaches its apex on this planet with the emergences of organisms with human-defining characteristics. As noted earlier, humans embody a series of sometimes conscious regnant actual occasions of a very high grade.

Humans apparently share consciousness with some other animals on this planet, but only a very small proportion of actual occasions on this planet are conscious. So far as we can discern, this low proportion of conscious creatures extends throughout the cosmos.

Mentality is more general than consciousness; the two cannot be equated. Mentality at a very low level is manifest in every entity due to the dipolar nature of becoming. In low-grade occasions the supplemental mental phase is minimal, and the past is reproduced in the present with minimal contrasts and changes. Low-grade occasions must entertain some contrasts between the eternal objects objectified in the physical phase of their becoming and those ingressing in the conceptual phase, but in most occasions this contrast is merely a senseless aesthetic one. Most occasions do not appear to exhibit even an embryonic consciousness.

Consciousness is the identifying mark of high-grade occasions. In conscious occasions the supplemental phase of their becoming is prolonged and enhanced. In conscious occasions contrasts develop between the objectified creatures in the occasion's causal past that are embodied in the emerging creature through its physical pole and the complex eternal objects derived from the primordial facet of the Divine nature that are embodied in the emerging creature through its mental pole. This contrast may be incorporated with additional eternal objects to produce another contrast. This second contrast may be incorporated with still additional eternal objects to produce yet another contrast, and so on. This enrichment gives rise to a hierarchy of contrasts, having a relation but not a correspondence with the objectified entities lying in the emerging subject's causal past.

The peak of consciousness is the negative judgement. In the negative judgment, the judging subject imaginatively contrasts that which is with that which might be but is not. For example, more creatures can experience blackness than can contrast their experience of blackness with their experience of not-blackness. In the latter instance, the individual experient must imagine the proposition "B is not black" and contrast it with the proposition "A is black." This contrast heightens one's consciousness of blackness and deepens the feeling of blackness in the emerging creature.

Life is a claim for freedom from the bonds of the past. In its simpler forms there seems to be little evidence to suggest that living occasions transmit their experience from one living occasion to another. But higher forms of living occasions are bound together in serial order; life has been canalized and turned in on itself. In this way both memory and novelty of response to circumstances can be combined to enhance the experience of the conscious regnant actual occasion. In these instances antecedent living occasions are felt physically in the initial phase of the becoming of a subsequent living occasion. The subsequent occasions can sustain complex values and discern formal principles which may inform their behavior and shape their social institutions. These occasions are salient in human life and give rise to morality, values, and religious experience.

Human Morality and Human Values

According to the point of view being developed here, the aim of existence is beauty. Human moral principles and human values that enhance harmony and intensity of feeling are "good"; those that diminish them are "evil."

The primacy of creativity means that morality is ultimately contextual. As contexts change, fitting creaturely responses also change. Moral values fitting for one historical epoch or culture may be inappropriate for a different epoch or a different culture.

At the same time forms are embodied in every emerging creature, and some pervasive forms may generally increase harmony and intensity of feeling for creatures with particular defining characteristics. In this manner, the formal side of morality may assume importance.

Thus, both contexts and forms need to be considered in a social ethic. Some persons may accentuate the contextual side leading to a dynamic and emergent morality. Others may accentuate the formalistic side leading to a more formalistic and conservative morality. Some process thinkers look for general principles of justice and seek normative forms of human social organization to inform human morality; others emphasize more forcefully the relational, dynamic emergent facets of experience and do not focus on principles of justice and normative forms of social organization.[21]

From the point of view shaping this essay, both formal and contextual facets of morality need to be considered in a process social ethic. Equality appropriate to form, self-determination informed by excellence, and order constitute the formal principles of justice which must be embodied in the judicial rules and regulations of a particular living community in a given historical epoch. Normative forms of social organization include monogamy, a fitting ethnic and racial pluralism, a fitting separation of economic and political institutions, a federated form of democracy, and fitting cultural religious pluralism.[22]

The inevitable contrasts between liberty, equality, and order and the multiple situations to which they have to relate underscore the contextual side of morality. Similarly, the wide variety of forms of social organization manifest on this planet and the lack of seasonal relevance of normative forms in many human societies also accentuate the contextual side of morality.

The significance of the contextual side of morality should not lead one to denigrate the formal side of morality. Principles of justice and a vision of desirable forms of social organization can help people seek the relative "better" rather than the relative "worse" in the familial, social, ethnic, economic, political, cultural and religious spheres.

Human Religious Experience

Human religious experience is intimately related to rather exceptional experiences of the conscious regnant occasions constituting the human organizing center. Only creatures with enhanced capacities for harmony, contrasts, and intensity of feeling can be religious. On this planet some lower animals may have some aesthetic experiences which may be termed "religious," but adequate data are lacking. In any event, both historical and contemporary human beings have participated in religious rituals, developed religious beliefs, and elaborated rational theologies.[23]

As noted earlier, an important distinction should be made between the loci of scientific inquiry and religious experience: science is concerned with the objects an experiencing subject perceives while religion is concerned with the sensitive response of the experiencing subject to the percepta it is receiving. Because the two dimensions of experience are intertwined, one will likely experience aesthetic disharmony and tedium unless one effects a supreme fusion between these two dimensions of experience.

Religious experience involves an intuition of an ultimate harmony of harmonies, a consummate peace of peaces. Religious experience may be evoked by and may evoke a sense of moral fitness, a sense of the rightness of specialized truths, and a feeling of aesthetic satisfaction. However, because the aesthetic dimension of experience embodied in an emerging creature's subjective aim surpasses the formal aspects of experience embodied in propositions and eternal objects, the feeling of aesthetic satisfaction is more foundational than moral fitness or the rightness of specialized truths. Without aesthetic satisfaction and religious experience, morality deteriorates into moralisms and truth into narrow dogmatisms. Because truth and goodness may contribute to beauty, they are important. In addition, as truth, beauty, and goodness are three-in-relation, an experience centered on any one may evoke the others and shade off into religious experience.

Two implications of these relations should be noted, for they invert the priorities espoused by those who place preeminence on the quest for truth and/or those who equate religion and morality. First, an intuition into the rightness of things and a faith that there is a relational essence to things which reason may penetrate—at least in part—is transnational. Second, rational proofs for the existence of God are of secondary importance and will be unconvincing to one who with intentionality wills to exercise negative judgments about any human efforts to delineate the Divine nature.

Nonetheless formulations characterizing the Divine nature can be developed. Theological propositions *about* the Divine nature may increase human religious experience *of* the Divine nature, but they cannot unequivocally evoke human religious experience. Religious experience entails an especially intense awareness of the Divine subjective aim—an aim which harmonizes all the eternal objects and evokes harmony and intensity of feeling in the creatures of the world. In human experience, these occasions are rather infrequent and may be misinterpreted or explained away.

The phases of becoming provide a basis for interpreting the various dimensions of religious expressions discerned among humans. The rhythms embodied in the physical side of experience give rise to the ritual and emotional dimensions of religious expression. Rituals are the external data appropriated by emerging subjects to evoke feelings and emotions eliciting religious experience. Because of the significance of the supplemental phases in the becoming of regnant ultimate percipient occasions constituting the human organizing center, feelings demand interpretations. Consequently religious beliefs emerge among humankind to explain the religious practices in which humans engage. At the folk level religious beliefs are often inchoate and contain inconsistent and incongruous propositions.

Humans also quest for some coherence and logicality in their beliefs, and they want them to fit the facts. Consequently, even though theological developments are uneven and are more fully elaborated in some cultures than in others, rational theologies have emerged to provide a more coherent and logical account of religious beliefs and practices. Characterizations of a Divine reality that is at least in some senses *sui generis* are an integral part of rational theologies.

According to the interpretation advanced here, religious experiences, beliefs, and interpretations are evoked by the Divine presence in human life. Because the persons initiating the evolutionary epoch were informed by phenomenological or reductionistic interpretations of human values and religious experiences, they frequently interpreted them by appealing either to what they held were underlying or more fundamental phenomena or by resorting to descriptive or subjective interpretations.[24] Process thinking can both honor the "facts" about evolution and also interpret them in a manner which may enhance human religious experience. It also permits one to understand one's deepest aesthetic and religious intuitions in ways which enable one to affirm the *sui generis* and authentic character of these experiences. It remains to be seen how and to what extent this mode of thinking is incorporated in the future work of scientists and theologians and is appropriated in human life.

Notes and References

1. Alfred North Whitehead's major writings in this period include *Science and the Modern World* (1925; reprint ed., New York: New American Library, Mentor Books, 1964); *Religion in the Making* (1926; reprint ed., Cleveland, Ohio: World Publishing, Meridian Books, 1965); *Symbolism: Its Meaning and Effect* (1927; reprint ed., New York: G.P. Putnam's Sons, Capricorn Books, 1959); *The Function of Reason* (1929; reprint ed., Boston, Mass.: Beacon Press, 1958); *Process and Reality,* corrected ed., ed. David Ray Griffin and Donald W. Sherburne (1929; corr. ed., New York: Free Press, 1978); *Adventures of Ideas* (1933; reprint ed., New York: New American Library, Mentor Books, 1967); and *Modes of Thought* (1938; reprint ed., New York: G.P. Putnam's Sons, Capricorn books, 1958).

2. In the context of the American experience the conflicts have taken a different shape. Scientists working in most universities did not have to deal with a clergy establishment, for most of the major universities were public in the nineteenth century. The major private universities made the transition from substantial church relatedness to negligible or nonexistent church relatedness with relative felicity. Indeed, in the context of the American experience many church groups themselves appropriated many of the interpretations and findings of modern science.

Political bodies, secondary schools, and some church related colleges bore the brunt of the controversy. The Scopes trial was the high water mark of the political impingement upon science in America, but some "creationist" advocates in the current epoch seem intent to raise similar issues. Some scientists and some church people entertain, in different ways, rather unbending viewpoints on creationist issues.

3. See, for example, Ernst Mayr and William B. Provine, eds., *The Evolutionary Synthesis: Perspectives on the Unification of Biology* (Cambridge, Mass.; Harvard University Press, 1980). For a most interesting analysis of the evolutionary process emphasizing periods of rapid change associated with major evolutional transitions, see Steven M. Stanley, *Macroevolution: Pattern and Process* (San Francisco: W. H. Freeman, 1979). Although Stanley does not use the categories of process philosophy to interpret his data, the abruptness of the emergence of eternal objects in the conceptual phase of an actual occasion's becoming provides a basic explanation for the mutations and rapid emergence of novel creatures sometimes observed in nature. This issue is discussed subsequently in the section entitled "Emergent Evolution on this Planet."

Many biologists and social anthropologists reject the notion that nature has a purpose. See, for example, G. G. Simpson, *The Meaning of Evolution,* rev. ed. (New York: Bantam Books, 1971). In his *Chance and Necessity* (New York: Vintage Books, 1972) Jacques Monod holds that chance alone accounts for every creation in the biosphere. For him, chance is absolutely free but it is blind.

On the other hand, Ralph W. Burhoe in his "The Human Prospect and the 'Lord of History,'" (*Zygon* 10 {September 1975}: 299-375) discerns a deterministic pattern in the evolutionary process.

For a most interesting interpretation of the evolutionary process having much in common with the constructive facets of this paper, see John F. Haught, *Nature and Purpose* (Lanham, Md.: University Press of America, 1980). He develops the notion that nature exhibits a "loose teleology," somewhere between the randomness of Monod and the determinism of Burhoe.

4. It is beyond the scope of this essay to elaborate the richness and complexity of the Augustinian formulations. The person reading this summary statement who has not read the Augustinian texts should be alerted to the breadth and the scope of his thought. It would be interesting to see what Augustine would have written if he had been living in an evolutionary epoch, for he ranks among the major intellects produced on this planet.

5. One cannot fault the logicality and coherence of Augustine's formulations. His thinking cannot be challenged on the rational side. It must be challenged on the empirical side, for it does not seem to fit the facts. The evidence for the emergence of creatures on this planet with increasingly complex structures and with increasingly enhanced capacities for intensity of feeling and thinking and for greater capacities to respond to circumstances seems very persuasive indeed.

6. Tillich affirms confessionally the revelatory power of Jesus as the Christ. It is beyond the scope of this essay to pursue this matter, but it is a central aspect of his theological system. Tillich's view than philosophy can raise questions about the Divine but cannot answer them is Augustianian, for Augustine held that humans did not lose the craving for happiness in the Fall. Barth entertains a more radical view of the Fall than either Augustine or Tillich.

7. For this reason an uninitiated person might think Barth was a biblical fundamentalist. There is a tantalizing relation between Barth and biblical fundamentalists, but he is definitely not a fundamentalist.

8. See Pierre Teilhard de Chardin, *The Phenomenon of Man* (New York: Harper & Row, 1959).

9. See, for example, Bernard Lee, *The Becoming of the Church* (New York: Paulist Press, 1974) and David Tracy, *Blessed Rage for Order* (New York: Seabury Press, 1975).

10. See, for example, John B. Cobb, Jr. and David Ray Griffin, *Process Theology: An Introductory Exposition* (Philadelphia: Westminster Press, 1976). This volume contains an excellent annotated bibliography of works by persons informed by process thought. Those wanting bibliographical references for work done prior to 1976 are referred to this text. (For an exhaustive bibliography of writings relating to Whitehead prior to 1976, see Barry Woodbridge, *Alfred North Whitehead: A Primary-Secondary Bibliography* [Bowling Green, Ohio: Philosophy Documentation Center, Bowling Green State University, 1977].)

Cobb and Griffin also edited *Mind in Nature: Essays on the Interface of Science and Philosophy* (Lanham, Md.: University Press of America, 1977). This volume contains several essays of direct relevance to the topic of emergent evolution.

For a rich and complex critique of process views of God, see Robert Neville, *God and Creativity* (New York: Seabury Press, 1980).

For a collection of essays dealing with the implications of process thought for the human sciences, social ethics, and liberation theology, see John B. Cobb, Jr. and W. Widick Schroeder, *Process Philosophy and Social Thought* (Chicago: Center for the Scientific Study of Religion, 1981).

Lewis Ford has incorporated evolutionary thinking in his work, *The Lure of God* (Philadelphia: Fortress Press, 1978).

11. As noted in the opening paragraphs of this essay, the specialized scientist will inevitably incorporate some presuppositions in his or her analysis not directly derived from work in his or her specialized field of endeavor. These more general notions will effect the shape and tone of his or her interpretation. If the scientist is informed by reductionist views, he or she is apt to seek to "explain" the activity of the human organism on the basis of some underlying elements internal and/or external to the organism. Some evolutionary theory is of this type. E. O. Wilson's *Sociobiology* (Cambridge, Mass.: Harvard University Press, 1975) is informed by such views.

In this essay, the informing evolutionary theory is "emergent evolution." In this view the causal past conditions the present, but it does not determine the present. The more complex and high grade the organism, the greater its capacity for novelty in response to circumstances. Life is fittingly interpreted as a claim for freedom from the bonds of the causal past.

12. The unity of the self constitutes a major problem in process modes of thought. Process philosophy entertains an atomic view of reality, for the ultimately real are drops of experience. Varying in richness and complexity, the occasions constituting the world are, nonetheless, all on the same level of actuality.

This view does justice to the experience of diversity, but it does not adequately deal with the *unity* of human experience. The notion of a formless form is advanced here to account for the *unity* of the human person. God contributes to the experience of the soul, due to the significance of the mental phase in occasions constituting the soul and the richness of the human subjective aim.

13. In the case of the Divine entity, the mental pole of Its becoming is prior to Its physical pole. This exception has far-reaching consequences for an interpretation of the Divine life. The implications of this exception are not explored systematically in this essay, but some of the consequences are considered in the latter part of the essay.

14. Some subhuman animal societies have some transphysical feelings and meanings. Dolphins and primates probably have the richest subhuman cultures. In the future humans may devise better ways to communicate with such creatures and may be able to empathize more sensitively with their symbolic worlds.

15. The order of nature manifest in our cosmic epoch is partially objectified in the regnant ultimate percipient occasion through sense reception in the mode of casual efficacy. This version of philosophic realism is central to process modes of thought.

16. Telepathy and other psychic phenomena—insofar as they are authentic—also involve the hybrid prehension of the mental pole of another creature or creatures.

17. The interrelatedness of nature and the intimate relations existing between the organizing center and the rest of the body underscore the importance of a congenial sustaining environment to support human life. The ecological concerns emerging in our time are grounded on this interrelatedness. For a discussion of ecology by a process theologian see John B. Cobb, Jr., *Is It Too Late? A Theology of Ecology* (Beverly Hills, Cal.: Bruce, 1972).

18. For a rich discussion and elaboration of the order of nature and the properties of the extensive continuum, see Whitehead, *Process and Reality*, corrected ed. (n. 1 above), pp. 66-129, 283-333. An extended discussion of the extensive continuum and the geometrical implications of it are beyond the scope of this essay. The discussion here is designed to set the human organism within its broader environment and to illumine the form of emergent evolution which is envisaged in the framework of process philosophy.

For helpful discussions of these issues, see Elizabeth Krause, *The Metaphysics of Experience* (New York: Fordham University Press, 1979) and Robert M. Palter, *Whitehead's Philosophy of Science* (Chicago: University of Chicago Press, 1960).

19. Of course, the *human* consequences of developments in scientific theory and application are important for human life. High technology has helped transform many human societies, and the scientific mind set has greatly influenced modern culture. Because such work is inevitably informed by some implicit or explicit metaphysical assumptions, the human impact of such work may be substantial.

These factors need to be considered in the human sciences, but it is not necessary to understand the most recent specialized work in the natural or biological sciences to elaborate a human social theory or social ethic. Because so many scientists formally eschew metaphysics, the communication problems between scientists and others are increased.

20. In this way a double understanding of human freedom emerges. In one sense, freedom is doing what one wants to do. In a second sense, authentic human freedom consists in doing what one ought to do.

The "is/ought" contrast deeply embedded in human experience is ultimately grounded in the intense human awareness of the Divine subjective aim. Its once-and-for-all envisagement and harmonization of the forms of definiteness provide the basis for the "ought" aspect of human experience. Finitude, ignorance, sloth, lethargy and inordinate self-interest provide the basis for the "is" aspect of human experience.

21. For an illustration of alternative approaches to a process social ethic, see Cobb and Schroeder (n. 10 above).

22. It is beyond the scope of this essay to elaborate these notions in detail in this chapter. The other chapters in Parts One and Two and Section A of Part Three address these issues in greater detail.

23. It is beyond the scope of this essay to examine alternative interpretations of religious phenomena. For a typological discussion of alternative perspectives, see W. Widick Schroeder, *Cognitive Structures and Religious Research* (East Lansing: Michigan State University Press, 1970), pp. 145-80.

24. Because so few contemporary workers in the sciences—natural or human—are informed by views rooted in the Platonic or Aristotelian traditions, most scientists entertain either skeptical, phenomenological, or reductionistic views of a Divine reality. Because most Western theologians entertain "one-way" God-world relations, their views of the Divine reality contrast substantially with process views. Process theists suggest that a "two-way" God-world relation exists. God is immanent in and transcends the world, and the world is immanent in and transcends God.

From the point of view of most contemporary scientists, many process thinkers are willing to say more about a Divine reality that is, in some senses, *sui generis* than they are. From the point of view of most Western theologians, process thinkers limit the Divine in ways they do not.

Introduction to Chapter 2

In order to see one's work in context, one must set one's subject matter in its systematic relation to other subject matters. To delineate the context of one's studies, one must elaborate and order the various sciences to clarify the relations between them and to set boundaries for one's own work. In some fashion, one must address the so-called inorganic, the organic, the psychological, the spiritual, and the historical dimensions of existence. People disagree about the relative interdependence of the spheres, the relative autonomy of the spheres, the bases for distinguishing between the spheres, and the status of descriptive/analytical and prescriptive analysis.

My interest in both analytical and descriptive work in the human realm led me to address the question of the ordering of the sciences early in my own work. My special interest in religious institutions and in religious social ethics forced me to think through the relations between the several human sciences and between the human sciences and social ethics. It also forced me to clarify my understanding of the bases for religious institutions.

This chapter is the product of these efforts. It seeks to discern the grounding of the several human sciences in the defining characteristics of human experience and in foundational human experience. It is informed by the basic categories of process philosophy outlined in Chapter 1. The principles of justice and normative forms of social organization formulated in this chapter are elaborated at greater length in Chapter 3 and in Part Two.

The consequentialist social ethic posited here is a contextual one. However, principles have an important but not definitive role in this process social ethic. This issue is also addressed at greater length in Chapter 3 and in Part Two.

The intrinsic interrelation of truth, beauty, and goodness, and of fact and value evokes a muddle-headedness, for one cannot delineate unequivocally clear and sharp distinctions between subject matters or between analytical and prescriptive work. In my view, the distinctions between the theoretic, the practical, and the aesthetic disciplines advanced by Aristotle and embodied in the neo-Thomist tradition, the reductionist unity of the sciences proposed by Democritus and embodied in the Marxist and Freudian traditions, and the fact-value disjunction promoted by Weberians and other neo-Kantians are spurious.

In this essay I sketch my view of normative forms of social organization, but I do not elaborate them. I subsequently became more fully persuaded of the desirability of democratic capitalism as a form of political economy in human societies. These views are elaborated in later essays. Chapters 6, 7, and 8 illumine most fully this development of my thinking.

CHAPTER 2

Toward Belief: A Process Perspective on the Social Sciences and on Social Ethics

Introduction

Process thought, involving a transposition of the Platonic tradition, has had slight impact on the social sciences to date. The theoretic foundations of the modern social sciences emerged primarily in Europe in the nineteenth and early twentieth centuries. Karl Marx, John Stuart Mill, Herbert Spencer, August Comte, Emile Durkheim, Sigmund Freud, and Max Weber are among the seminal thinkers contributing to their emergence in that epoch. In spite of the internal diversity between these cited figures, they shared one characteristic; none of them thought it was necessary to appeal to a God who was in some sense *sui generis* to interpret human life. All were interested in religion and sought to interpret it, but their approaches to the study of religious phenomena were phenomenological, residualistic, or reductionistic.

These early emphases continue, for today only a few social scientists are informed by the Platonic, Aristotelian, or Christian traditions. Broadly viewed, contemporary social scientists have more intellectual kinship with Democritus or the Sophists than with Plato, Aristotle or classical Christian thinkers.[1]

The voluntaristic facet of contemporary social science, rooted in the tradition of Max Weber primarily, and John Stuart Mill and other nineteenth-century English liberals and some evolutionists secondarily, has more in common with a process view of the social sciences than the more causally oriented views rooted in the traditions of Karl Marx, Sigmund Freud, and Emile Durkheim. At the same time, the staunch phenomenological and interactionist views of contemporary voluntarists differentiate them from process perspectives; for process thinkers have to appeal to a Divine Reality to discern a locus for potentiality, to explain the human experiences of the lure for harmony and intensity of feeling, to interpret the mediation of data from one creature to another, and to delineate the ultimate receptor of all that has become.

This essay explores some of the implications of process thought for the social sciences and social ethics. It deals primarily with the ordering of the social sciences in the mode of process thought, the understanding of human nature and human experience from this perspective, and the bases for a process social ethic. This focus on generic notions will permit readers to contrast this perspective with their own understandings and with the views of the social theorists whom they happen to know.[2]

A Resume of the Ordering of the Sciences in the Perspective of Process Thought

The complexity of actual entities and groupings of actual entities in societies has given rise to the hierarchical ordering of nature discernible in this cosmic epoch. It is the basis for the ordering of the sciences.

Metaphysical propositions apply to all creatures. They constitute the matrix in which more specialized propositions applying to particular entities and societies are set. Theological propositions apply to the Supreme Subject-Object, for from the perspective of process thought God exemplifies the metaphysical propositions supremely. Thus, a reciprocal relation exists between theology and metaphysics — a fully adequate theology awaits a fully adequate metaphysics. Since limitations of insight and language preclude the full realization of the latter, the former is likewise precluded.

Mathematics deals with geometric relations and derivative notions. Insofar as mathematics is exploring potentiality, it is "pure." In its "applied" form, mathematics seeks to discern the forms of definiteness associated with particular creatures in this cosmic epoch.

The physical sciences are saliently concerned with geometric forms and with measurements involving intervals and ratios. The biological sciences retain these interests, but organismic purpose becomes increasingly important. In the human sciences, such interest becomes central.

This pattern of increasing complexification is grounded in the natures of the creatures and societies of creatures constituting the subject matters of the several sciences. All creatures are dipolar. Excepting God, they begin their experience with their appropriation of data from the world. This physical phase is supplemented by a mental phase in which creatures appropriate forms of definiteness embodied in God's primordial nature. Guided by its subjective aim, the emerging creature synthesizes these two phases into an integrated unity.

The hierarchy of nature is twofold. First, there are substantial differences in the importance of the supplemental phase in the lives of various creatures. Some creatures and some societies of creatures merely reproduce their pasts in their presents with a modicum of novelty. They convey the impression of stability, endurance, and relative changelessness. So-called "inorganic" societies are composed of such creatures. Other creatures respond with greater novelty to the context in which they find themselves. Some creatures in so-called "organic" societies are illustrative. They are "alive." As the presence of viruses and other transitional societies indicates, the dividing line between organic and inorganic societies is not clear cut.

Second, there are substantial differences in the complexity and structuring of groups of creatures. Some societies, such as gases are less structured than others, such as solids. Living organisms involve the integration of groups of societies and sub-societies and are sometimes co-ordinated to support an entirely living nexus.

Human beings are the most complex creatures of which we have any direct knowledge at present. The human is comprised of a large number of living and nonliving sub-societies, co-ordinated in such a way that there are reciprocal relations between the regnant center and the rest of the organism. This regnant center, a "formless form" so protean that it can "contain" the sequence of ultimate percipient occasions constituting it, is of very high grade. The supplemental phase is greatly enhanced in the creatures constituting it, so humans are able to respond to and to shape their initial data with a very substantial measure of novelty. Subjective species of eternal objects and a welter of subjective forms are enhanced in high grade organisms, so feelings and meanings loom large in human life. Purposiveness and intentionality are also salient in human experience. Any rendering of the human sciences that loses sight of these foundational experiences is suspect, for their recognition is too widespread in the life of civilized humankind to be put aside as mere error.[3]

The Relation Between Internal and External Factors in Human Experience

When social scientists consider emotions, meanings, and actions, they are considering other people's emotions, meanings, and actions. Their *own* emotions, meanings, and actions are provisionally excluded from consideration. Such exclusion is fitting and proper, for it is possible to analyze values and social structures, discern the intensity of other people's feelings, and examine other people's actions provisionally without evaluating them.

This provisional distinction, however, is ultimately only heuristic, for the internal and external dimensions of experience are inextricably intertwined. According to the principle of relativity, fundamental to process modes of thought, every being is a potential for every becoming. Consequently, what a creature *is* cannot be separated from *how* a creature functions. Creatures begin their process of becoming with the *valuation* of the data they appropriate.

It is arbitrary to distinguish absolutely between the analytical and descriptive and the synthetic and evaluate sides of social scientific theory, for social scientists also participate in the pervasive attraction towards beauty, truth, and goodness which is at the base of things. If they ignore or deny these experiences in their study of human life, they are going to distort their interpretation of the human situation. Social scientists confront the question of the adequacy of their foundational perspective more forcefully than natural scientists (though natural scientists also confront the issue), for in a more direct way than is the case for studies of subhuman subject-objects, both the findings of specific social scientific studies and also the general conceptual schemata employed by social scientists affect their subject-objects.[4]

Human cultural phenomena have both objective and subjective dimensions. As objects for study, they are part of the subject matter of the social sciences. As sources and expressions of meaning, cultural objects — artistic products, musical compositions, and thought forms — are necessarily related to human internal experiences. Both dimensions need to be explored in the elaboration of a more adequate human science.

In the context of the social sciences, the inner side of experiences gives rise to morality and the science of morals — for human behavior is concerned with the good.

Since the good (action pertaining to the seasonally relevant future) is intimately related to the beautiful (the actualization of harmony and intensity of feeling) and to the true (the elaboration of propositions fitting to various subject-objects), experiences in one dimension may elicit or reinforce experiences in the other dimensions. Religious experience involves the sensitive response to and/or awareness of these dimensions of experience. It both surpasses and also shades off into experiences heightening human awareness of the beautiful, the true, and the good.

This chapter does not consider the ordering of the aesthetic disciplines or the ordering of the natural sciences; it is focused on the implications of process modes of thought for the social sciences. For the reasons noted in the preceding paragraph, these omissions are somewhat arbitrary. They have been dictated by the author's specialized interest in the implications of process thought for the social sciences and by space limitations.

The Spheres of the Social Order: The Subject Matter of the Social Sciences

Introduction

As noted previously, the external and internal factors of experiences are interrelated. The drop of experience constituting our conscious self begins to become by appropriating facets of other creatures in its causal past. In the supplemental phase of its becoming it appropriates forms of definiteness embodied in the primordial facet of God's nature and not necessarily actualized in other creatures. The emerging creature is aiming at satisfaction, a focus lured forth by God's subjective aim.

The organizing regnant center of an individual human being constitutes the subject matter of psychology. Social institutions, meanings, values, and norms in the several spheres of the social order abstracted from the individuals comprising them constitute the subject matter of the other human sciences.

The meanings, values, and norms giving shape to social institutions in the several spheres of the social order cannot be definitively separated from the humans shaping them and participating in them, for function and meaning are interrelated; both are rooted in human decisions. As noted earlier, this interrelation makes an evaluative consideration of societal norms, art objects, and scientific and philosophic thought forms — the fruits of inner human experiences of the good, the beautiful, and the true — integral to an adequate social science.

The good is especially related to norms and institutions in the familial sphere, primary and quasi-primary group spheres, the economic sphere, and the political sphere. In the cultural sphere, the beautiful is related especially to art objects; and the true is related especially to scientific and philosophic thought forms.

In the religious sphere, the beautiful is especially related to constitutive acts of worship giving rise to religious institutions. The reality of God needs to be considered in an adequate interpretation of religious institutions, for they are grounded in human experiences of a Divine Reality who is, in some senses, *sui generis.*

The intrinsic interrelatedness of the beautiful, the true, and the good means these distinctions are equivocal, but the priority of factors in the various spheres of the social order legitimates the distinctions and sustains the differentiations of the spheres.

The interdependency and interrelation of the spheres are reflected in the evolution of various "hybrid" disciplines such as demography, geography, social psychology, and urban and regional studies. They are also reflected in the tendency for each of the social sciences to incorporate facets of other disciplines in their own work.

The remainder of this section sketches the bases for the ordering of the "major" social scientific disciplines. They are grounded in the biological, social, intellectual, aesthetic, and religious characteristics of humankind. These characteristics give rise to the several spheres of the social order and provide the subject matters for the various social sciences.

The Organizing Center of Human Beings: The Subject Matter of Psychology

The subject matter of psychology is the regnant center of the human being. Psychology is the most concrete social science, for feelings, attitudes, values, beliefs, norms, and decisions are ultimately referable to the human beings in which they are rooted. The hierarchy of nature noted earlier gives some guidance about the degree of precision to be anticipated in various sub-disciplines of psychology. Sub-disciplines dealing with the impact of the body on the regnant center are apt to develop more precise "laws" than sub-disciplines focusing primarily on the regnant center itself. The latter sub-disciplines deal with attitudes, values, beliefs, and actions involving intentionality, purpose, and decision.

Consequently, physiological psychologists may expect to develop theories possessing more predictive power than social psychologists. Theories predicting the impact of certain drugs on sense perception, for example, are more precise and less culture-bound than theories predicting the impact of social attitudes on electoral behavior.

The Abstractive Net of Human Relations: The Subject Matter of the Other Social Sciences

The subject matter of other social sciences is the entire net of human relations in the social order abstracted from the concrete relations of human beings comprising the net. Individuals are inextricably interrelated with social institutions in the several spheres of the social order, for the defining characteristics of social institutions are immanent in the human beings comprising them. As individuals surpass the structures reflected in the several spheres of the social order, studies of social institutions in one sphere cannot be isolated from studies of social institutions in all the spheres or from the actions of individual humans. The social sciences must deal with human meaning, intentionality, and social structures in their interrelatedness.

Sociology is an inclusive abstractive social science, for it is concerned with forms of social organization in all the spheres of the social order. Various other social scientific disciplines may be distinguished by the special attention they give to one or more spheres of the social order. Economics, political science, and anthropology are often related to the economic, the political, and the cultural spheres, respectively.

The Family Sphere, the Quasi-Primary Sphere, the Ethnic Sphere, and the Social Sphere: A Special Domain of Sociology

It is arbitrary to limit the actual interests of sociologists to groups in the spheres of the social order composed of familial and of the quasi-primary groups, ethnic groups, and status groups, for in fact sociologists study forms of social organization in all the spheres. This sequence of discussion is shaped by the desire for systematic clarity and is not intended to be an accurate empirical description of the subject matters sociologists actually study.

The *family* is rooted in biological necessity and in human trans-rational social needs for intimate, diffuse, primary relations. Human sexual and social needs account for the multiplicity of forms of family organization, shaped by values, beliefs, and norms. Other small primary groups, grounded in human trans-rational social needs for intimacy, emerge in all societies.

Biological and socio-historical factors working in concert with human capacity for feeling and thinking contribute to the development of persons who feel they belong to particular *ethnic* or *racial* groups. Racial groups are defined by real or imagined common biological characteristics, and ethnic groups are defined by commonly shared historical experiences.

Human beings have the capacity to shape sentiments and values in relation to particular socio-historical groupings. As a result, people developed varied and distinctive life styles to which honor or prestige is differentially accorded. Persons in the same *status* group manifest comparable styles of life. Though status groups are frequently reinforced by values associated more directly with one of the other spheres of the social order, members of the same status groups may be drawn from different groups in the other spheres of the social order.

Sociologists have made innumerable studies of familial and other primary groups, ethnic and racial groups, and status groupings. As noted earlier, they also study economic, political, and religious groups as well. Two of these spheres — the economic and the political — have been the special subject matter of other social scientists.

The Economic Sphere: The Subject Matter of Economics

Human creativity, reason, capacity for novelty of response, and biological necessity combine to create and to sustain institutions in the economic sphere of the social order. Human economic behavior and institutions in this sphere constitute the subject matter of the science of economics.

Rational calculation in a means-end pattern is salient in this sphere. "Technical" reason is predominant in the economic sphere.[5]

The data on which economics is based ultimately refer back to the human beings from which they have been abstracted. For this reason, the predictive capacity of economic science — even in those societies in which calculating reason is forcefully accentuated — is less than in the sub-human sciences.

Humans, embodying both technical and ontic reason, reproduce some values for extended periods, so economic analysis is possible and often useful. Nonetheless, humans surpass technical rationalism, and contemporary human decisions surpass the past, so the tales told by laws in economics and the other human sciences are less certain than the tales told by laws in the sub-human sciences.

The Political Sphere: The Subject Matter of Political Science

Human creativity, human reason, human capacity for novelty of response, and social necessity combine to create and to sustain institutions in the political sphere, the subject matter of political science.

The rational side of the political sphere includes the objectification of the values sustaining particular forms of political organization, the principles of justice, and the rules and regulations of justice. Groups rooted in any of the other spheres of the social order may and do become political groups, for they may seek to attain group objectives through political processes. In these processes, they both compete with and also cooperate with other groups.[6]

The subject matter of political science differs in specificity from the subject matter of economics. Economics, especially in industrial societies, focuses on highly rationalized relations, so its subject matter is relatively specific. This specificity, coupled with the widespread tendency of most people in some societies to follow reasonably well the rules of a rational economic game, enhances the predictive power of economics in such societies.

Political science studies trans-rational decisions and "power" relations directly, so its subject matter is more diffuse. The unique character of crucial decisions and actions of political leaders more sharply limits the predictive capacity of political science than is the case for some of the other social sciences.

The Cultural Sphere: The Subject Matter of the "Science of Culture"

The cultural creations of human beings constitute the subject matter of the "science of culture." Human reason and the human capacities for novelty of response interplay with inner experiences and the conditions of human existence to produce human culture, for fundamental beliefs, values, and norms give shape to the forms of social organization in every sphere of the social order.

Disembodied cultural objects, which some define as the subject matter of anthropology, are human products. Social scientists reifying these concepts or dealing with the objects independent of the creatures in whom they are embodied deal inadequately with the science of culture. From the perspective of process thought social scientists separating the *function* of moral, aesthetic, and intellectual objects from their *meaning* to the creatures embodying and creating them are acting arbitrarily. The especially human character of culture accentuates the need for a broader conceptual scheme with which to interpret intellectual, aesthetic, and moral objects than is currently fashionable in the social sciences.[7]

The disciplines are embryonic or non-existent within the social sciences, but a "science of belief," a "science of aesthetics," and a "science of morals" to study the cognitive and ideational side of the science of culture can be envisaged. Each of these disciplines would have an external side, analyzing the extant objects, and an internal side, considering the inner grounds for human creation of both analytic and descriptive dimensions and also normative and evaluative dimensions.

Because of its pertinence here, the evaluative and normative dimensions of a "science of morals" are elaborated briefly in the following section of this essay. This "science" is related to all of the social sciences, for it would seek to evolve normative forms of social organization in all the spheres of the social order to permit an evaluation of existing forms of social organization and to lure forth more adequate forms.

The Religious Sphere: The Subject Matter of the "Science of Religion"

Religious rituals, symbols, beliefs, and institutions constitute the subject matter of the "science of religion." These subject matters are often studied in the sociology of religion.

As noted earlier, religious experience arises as a human fuses its physical and conceptual experiences into an emerging unity. This foundational experience constitutes the basic subject matter of the psychology of religion. Rituals, emotions, symbols, beliefs, and institutions emerge out of and contribute to human religious experience. Because of these reciprocal relations it is arbitrary to separate sharply the sociology of religion from the psychology of religion.

The science of religion should study both the conceptual, moral, and aesthetic objects arising from religious experience and also the forms of religious organization evolved in relation to human religious experience.

If function and meaning are intertwined, as has been affirmed frequently here, social scientists ought to study the inner meaning of and grounds for religious experience. These analyses will lead ultimately to analysis of the nature of religious experience and its relation to human experiences of the beautiful, the true, and the good and to a consideration of the relation of these experiences to the Divine Life. Facets of this exploration are developed in the final portion of this essay.

The Integrated Whole: The Subject Matter of Historical Studies

Conceived in its broadest sense, history is the discipline studying the factors giving rise to the cosmos at a given state of its becoming. Insofar as the factors giving rise to the present state of the cosmos can be rationalized by explaining how successors are determined by causal antecedents, historians may attain some success in their efforts. Since there is no reason intrinsic to the historical process for the necessary actualization of a given flux of forms, historians cannot fully and adequately rationalize history; they simply must accept it as "given."

Human history may be conceived more narrowly as the discipline tracing the interplay between human decisions and social-institutional configurations. Causal analysis in human history incorporates human decisions as part of the causal factors. For this reason historical study is necessarily *post facto*, integrative, and wholistic.

Historians should seek to interpret the values, decisions, and actions of particular people in their relation to particular social institutions in particular societies in particular historical epochs. In this disciplined artistic synthesis, historians draw on data provided by the other social sciences. Since a whole is more than the sum of its parts, history is the social science most able to delineate the character of the various epochs constituting the history of civilized humankind. Historians perform both a most difficult and also an indispensable role in the interpretation of human life.[8]

The *resume* of the status of history concludes this outline of the ordering of the subject matters of the social sciences dealing with the external side of human community-in-individuality. As previously noted, the question of *how* an entity functions cannot be divorced from the question of *why* an entity becomes. Efficient cause and final cause are inter-related; an analysis of function cannot be separated from an analysis of meaning.

Morality is intimately related with the internal side of human meanings. These meanings shape forms of social organization and norms of human conduct. The concluding section of this essay elaborates the shape of a process social ethic.

Morality in a Process Perspective: The Bases for a Social Ethnic

Introduction

The lure to accentuate harmony and intensity of feeling in the future is at the base of morality. Although one may be a bit oblivious to morals at certain times and in certain places, the lure for aesthetic satisfaction, truthful formulations, and good actions constitutes a basic trinity inherent in the nature of things. Prescription and interpretation are as intrinsic to an adequate social science as are description and analysis.

Morality incorporates both formal and volitional dimensions. The delineation of principles of justice, the elaboration of the relations between form (justice), dynamics (power), and unification (love) in various interpersonal and intergroup relations, and the description of the forms of familial, social, economic, political, cultural, and religious organizations normatively desirable for human beings constitute the formal dimension. The social sciences provide empirical data to help humans discern the probability of actualizing the normative forms in a particular context and the probable consequences of alternative actions and policy.

Human moral decisions, guided by but surpassing factors included in the formal dimension, constitute the volitional dimension. This contrast between volitional and formal dimensions is one facet of an "isness-oughtness" contrast, a part of the experience of all humans.

The more fundamental contrast is rooted in human intuition of the primordial facet of the Divine nature, one ground for the human experience of the lure for the beautiful, the true, and the good. Humans are persuaded by the lure for harmony embedded in this dimension of experience and in some facets of their causal pasts to enhance the beautiful, to seek the true, and to try to do the good. They are also coerced by finitude and ignorance, i.e., the limitations of existence, so harmonious and disharmonious experiences are both part of human experience. Persuasion is a more desirable kind of power than coercion, but the two kinds are intermingled in human experience. Insofar as is possible in a given context, persuasion rather than coercion should be exercised.

Finitude, ignorance, sloth, and lethargy combine with inordinate self-interest to preclude the possibility of a perfect harmony of life with life under the conditions of existence. The only "perfect" harmony is the ordering of the forms of definiteness by God's subjective aim, and this harmony is deficient in actuality.

Evil involves experiences of disharmony and of loss. Loss is the more fundamental evil, for discord may signal the dawn of an emerging order that is richer and more complex than its predecessors. As the ultimate receptor and synthesizer of all that has become, God retains everlastingly and without loss all the creatures of the world. In this fashion, that which appears to be lost or evil from the human perspective is transformed and retained in Divine Life.

The Formal Side of Morality

Forms are an integral part of every experience. Humans may surpass particular forms as they become, but they must appropriate some forms in their becoming. The primacy of the category of creativity in process thought gives it a dynamic bias, but this primacy is balanced by the necessity of the presence of some forms of definiteness in all creatures.[9]

In this introduction of this section the three dimensions of the formal side of morality were cited: the principles of justice, the relations between form (justice), dynamics (power), and unification (love) in various interpersonal and intergroup relations, and the normative forms of social organization. These dimensions are considered in this sub-section.

The Principles of Justice[10] — There are three formal principles of justice. These principles are based on the universality of the experience of the unification of a formal dimension in the dynamic process of the becoming of creatures. These principles are: *self-determination* informed by excellence, *equality* appropriate to form, and the *order, love* and *peace* harmonizing the other two principles.

At the metaphysical level, the dynamic process is rooted in the creativity which is at the base of things; the formal dimension is grounded in the forms of definiteness envisaged by God and embodied in creatures; and the unification dimension is grounded in God's subjective aim and is manifest in the emerging creatures' aims for harmony and intensity of feeling, in their unification of forms and feelings in their becomings, and in their everlasting objectifications in the Divine Life.

These general principles are embodied in the rules and regulations of justice of a living community through its decision-making processes. Humans then have to apply these rules and regulations of justice to particular contexts.

Because of this movement from the more general to the more specific, the general principles of justice are less ambiguous than the rules and regulations of justice. For the same reason, the rules and regulations of justice are less ambiguous than the application of the rules and regulations in a given context. The "power" component of the form-dynamic couplet is salient in the actualization of the principles of justice in concrete situations.

Relative Priority of Form (Justice), Dynamics (Power), and *Unification (Love) in the Spheres of Human Life* — Form, dynamics, and unification are three-in-relation, so these factors are each present in every sphere of human life. Even so, the saliency of the factors differs, permitting an assessment of the potential contribution of social institutions in the several spheres to interpersonal and intergroup life. There are six possible priorities of relations between these factors: dynamics, unification, and form; form, unification, and dynamics; form, dynamics, and unification; dynamics, form, and unification; unification, dynamics, and form; and unification, form and dynamics.

In human life, dynamics refers to power or self-determination informed by excellence; form refers to defining characteristics and principles of justice; and unification refers to the harmony or love uniting dynamics and form.

The sequence of priority "dynamics, unification, and form" points to the emergence of the novel creature *per se.* Any emergent creature (dynamics) with its subjective aim fostered by God (unification) seeks to actualize itself by harmonizing forms in its experience.

The sequence of priority "form, unification, and dynamics" points to the priority of factors in interpersonal relations. The priority of the principle of equality appropriate to form is dominant, so a person can be treated more fully as a person in small primary and quasi-primary groups than in any other contexts. Among these groups, the family is paramount. Love, involving sensitive and empathetic response to the needs of the other, is second in emphasis. Self-determination, involving the actualization of one's own aims, is third in emphasis; for, at least in principle, one's own aims are intimately related to the aims of the other members of the primary group which may be taken more fully into account.

The sequences of priorities "form, dynamics, and unification" and "dynamics, form, and unification" relate to social institutions and groups abstracted from the concrete network of relations in which human beings are enmeshed. This abstraction precludes fuller human relations in the racial, ethnic, status, economic, political, and cultural spheres. Groups in these spheres may become vehicles for more inclusive interpersonal relations, but in themselves they do not permit the fuller and richer human interplay characterizing interpersonal relations in small groups.

In every sphere except the political sphere, the sequence of priority of "form, dynamics, and unification," for groups in the other spheres are dominantly shaped by defining characteristics (forms). These defining characteristics are sometimes enhanced by actions rooted in the political sphere. People will to belong to these groups (dynamic), and they have a sense of shared values and/or common participation (unification).

In the political sphere, the sequence of priority of factors is "dynamics, form, and unification." Power considerations (dynamics) are leading; but the state, which is the organizing center of a society, gives shape to the structures (form) defining relations between groups in a given geographical territory. To facilitate this effort, the state develops rules and regulations of justice (form). Citizens of a state participate (unification) in common values and at least tacitly approve of political leadership. Leders trying to impose their wills (power) without regard to justice (form) or to the expectations of the citizens (unification) may succeed for a while, but eventually such leadership will be deposed.

The state seeks both domestic and international order and harmony. Harmony in the international sphere is especially difficult, for there is little consensus about justice (form) and minimal sense of the common destiny of humankind (unification).

The sequences of priorities "unification, dynamics, and form" and "unification, form, and dynamics" refer to God-world relations. From the Divine point of view, the former sequence applies; from the human point of view, the latter sequence applies. Love, power, and form delineate the sequence of sensitivity of response, lure for feeling, provision of seasonally relevant forms, and objectification of the world characterizing the Divine functioning in the world. Love, form, and power delineate the sequence of sensitivity of response, development of subjective aim, appropriation of forms, and self-actualization characterizing the realization of creatures in the world.

Institutions in the religious sphere are grounded in human religious experience and in interpretations of that experience. The priority of the sequence "unification, form, and dynamics" from the human perspective on God-world relations provides criteria to guide the relation of religious institutions to other social institutions and groups. The Divine Reality functions by suasion, and institutions lured forth by that reality should do likewise. Religious institutions should not use force or violence, and they should become involved directly in the political sphere most infrequently. The priority of form over dynamics implies that reason contributes positively to human experience of the Divine Presence, but the salience of unification or love implies that religious experience is more fundamental and elemental than any analysis of it or of the Supreme Subject-Object of religious devotion. Consequently, faith precedes reason in human religious experience, but reason may help elicit or may reinforce faith.

Due to the relative priority of factors in the spheres of the social order and in the networks of human relations, the fulfillment of human life is most realizable in interpersonal relations and in the everlasting objectification of creatures in the Divine Life. Desirable forms of familial, social, economic, political, cultural, and religious organizations may foster richer human life, but social institutions and groups cannot be the end or fulfillment of human life.

In some ways, the more the spheres are differentiated, the more intense the sense of disharmony becomes between interpersonal and intergroup relations. In most modern societies in which high technology is predominant, the differentiations are very substantial. A qualified critique of inordinate social differentiation may be appropriate, but it is a mistake to criticize inordinately forms of familial, social, economic, political, cultural, or religious life on the grounds they prevent full humanness. Some forms of social organization are more adequate than others and should be fostered, but the most any form of social organization can ever do is to provide a more congenial environment for the development of richer, fuller, and more harmonious human life. Temporal fulfillment of human life surpasses institutional forms and historical groups and is embodied in individual human beings through concrete relations with other human and non-human beings; eternal fulfillment of human life surpasses the perishing of the temporal and is manifest in the everlasting objectification of creatures in the Divine Life.

Normative Forms of Social Organization— Even though human life surpasses social institutions, desirable forms of social organization may contribute positively to human life. The delineation of normative forms of familial, social, economic, political, cultural, and religious organizations developed in this sub-section is based on a consideration conjointly of the principles of justice, the relative priority and form, dynamics, and unification in the spheres of the social order, and the conditions of human existence.

The dominantly bi-sexual character of human beings and the necessity for sociability among them give rise to the family, the fundamental and elemental unit in the social structure. The biological basis of the family is the diadic character of human sexual relations. The social basis is the necessity for continuity and intensity of social interaction to elicit intensity and contrast of feeling among people and to provide a stable sustaining environment for the development of children. Monogamy is the form of family organization best able to harmonize biological and social necessity.

Diverse racial, ethnic, and status groups are a part of the life of any complex society. Racial, ethnic, and status pluralism is desirable, for it provides a context for a more diverse and potentially richer societal unity. The diversity is limited by the self-understanding of the diverse groups and by the possibilities for integration into a reasonably harmonious whole.

It is not possible to state the limits of diversity formally, for the limits depend on the nature of the society. Some societies are able to sustain greater complexity harmoniously than others. Too much complexity fosters disintegration of a given society; too little diversity results in a dull and monotonous whole. Racial, ethnic, and status groups rejecting a pluralistic harmony are least desirable and cause the most difficulty for a society.

No normative form of economic organization can be delineated, but some guidelines can be indicated. Greater direction can be provided negatively than positively. The decisions of the persons in the system should provide some direction for the allocation of resources, so any non-primitive economic system should contain supply-demand pricing mechanisms insuring a relatively efficient allocation of resources. The system should also permit some measure of individual and group self-initiation in the production of economic goods and services. Finally, the system should not abuse unduly the nature of the human beings who participate in it.

Representative democracy is the form of political organization best able to harmonize self-determination informed by excellence and equality appropriate to form. Because these principles of justice are partially contradictory, neither an egalitarian society nor a rigidly stratified one is desirable. Some social differentiation is essential, but it must be balanced by a measure of equality. As the state integrates and harmonizes community-in-individuality, it necessarily develops rules and regulations pertinent to institutions in the other spheres. The state must retain a monopoly on the legitimate use of force in a society, but its use of force must be subject to careful review by a multiplicity of agencies.

As there is no single mode of perfection in the cosmos, a qualified cultural pluralism is desirable in a society. The "best" society is the one which can harmonize the greatest cultural diversity, but there are limits to the degree of diversity sustainable in a society without personal and corporate disintegration. No narrowly conceived notions of artistic, educational, or literary uniformity can be supported, but no sharp judgment about the desirable diversity of creations can be made independent of the context.

In a good society, most of its citizens will share some common unifying beliefs and values transcending the diverse ones of sub-groups. A relatively "better" society is one in which the large majority of its participants share the normative forms of social organization outlined here.

This necessity for unifying integrative values limits the range of social and cultural pluralism a society can tolerate. No society can escape some limitations on pluralism without anarchical disintegration into conflicting groups. In efforts to impose order, governments may become tyrannical. Humans should try to chart a course of unity and diversity in values, avoiding the polar opposites of tyranny and anarchy.

Because the Subject-Object to which religious institutions bear witness is supreme, the religious sphere should be separated from the other spheres. Worship, education, and the fostering of close interpersonal relations are direct responsibilities of religious institutions. The religious institution should uphold principles of justice and cultivate an *ethos* which fosters rich human life, but it should not impinge directly in particular issues in the political sphere except in the most extraordinary circumstances. Religious institutions should seek to give direction to a society, but they should refrain from giving directives to a society.

The religious professional possesses no unique sacerdotal role, but through his or her training and special skills he or she may contribute positively to the life of a worshipping community. Voluntarism is especially prized in the religious sphere, for people cannot be coerced to worship. Some structures beyond local religious institutions are necessary to provide them with a broader breadth of vision and a higher level of excellence. As in the political sphere, some type of representative democratic structure is desirable.

No human society reflecting perfectly those normative forms of familial, social, economic, political, cultural, and religious organization has existed or will exist. Clearly delineated normative forms are not even possible in the social, economic, and cultural spheres.

The normative forms of social organization developed here presuppose creatures possessing human characteristics. Some of these defining characteristics will shift in due course, and new normative forms of social organization will then emerge. If sexual relations were triadic or quadratic, for example, new normative forms of family organization would evolve.

Some of these normative forms have been more adequately institutionalized in Western democracies than in any other part of the world. Persons in those societies in which monogamy, social pluralism, a modified enterprise economic system, representative democracy, cultural pluralism, and religious pluralism and voluntarism are institutionalized tolerably well should seek to preserve and to improve such patterns.

Some of these normative forms are obviously not seasonally relevant in many countries at the present time. Persons who live in such countries must balance the vision of normative forms with their social context as they decide what forms of social organization are most appropriate in their situation. In every instance they may be guided by a concern for the proper balance between self-interest and the common good.

People have to make judgments about the forms of social organization they seek or support in a given society; they also have to make innumerable moral decisions about interpersonal and inter-group relations in their existing social order. This reality leads to a consideration of the volitional side of morality.

The Volitional Side of Morality

As people seek to decide what to do to enhance harmony and intensity of life with life in a given context, they cannot attain unqualified guidance by intellectual analysis and interpretation. Contexts change, and there is no single mode of perfection in the universe. Informed by their understanding of the principles of justice, the relative priority of form, dynamics, and unification in various spheres of the social order, and their view on seasonally relevant forms of social organization, they must make judgments about the most appropriate mode of action in their situation.

Progress is possible in morality, for forms are a necessary part of moral decisions. Perfection is impossible in morality; for no form fits a context perfectly, and finitude, ignorance, sloth, lethargy, and inordinate self-interest preclude the possibility of the perfect harmony of life with life.

Human moral experience — the sense of a "rightness" of fit between form and context elicited by God's evocation of harmony — shades off into religious and aesthetic experiences. People are sustained in their awareness of the impossibility of an unqualifiedly proper moral decision by their awareness of the presence of the One Who is able to make the best of whatever is offered to It and Who is able to retain everlastingly all the world offers It. In this fashion, one may interpret disharmonious elements in human experience as contrasts in a broader, richer, and more complex unity. At the same time, since each person contributes his or her bit to the Divine Life, one is sustained in his or her quest for love and justice in the life of civilized humankind.

Without such a Supreme Referee, all is ultimately sound and fury, signifying nothing.

Notes and References

1. For extended discussions of these issues see, for example, Gregory Baum, *Religion and Alienation* (New York: Paulist Press, 1975), Robert W. Friedrichs, *A Sociology of Sociology* (New York: The Free Press, 1970), W. Widick Schroeder, *Cognitive Structures and Religious Research* (East Lansing: Michigan State University Press, 1970), and Gibson Winter, *Elements for a Social Ethic* (New York: Macmillan, 1966).

2. As this essay is primarily a constructive one, no references are made to other theorists in the body of the text, and space limitations prevent discussion in the "Notes and References" section. The following texts have been most suggestive in raising and/or illumining the problems addressed here:

Ernest Barker, *Reflections on Government* (New York: Oxford University Press, 1958).

Emil Brunner, *The Divine Imperative* (Philadelphia: The Westminster Press, 1974).

T.S. Eliot, *The Idea of a Christian Society* (New York: Harcourt, Brace and Company, 1940).

The Federalist Papers

Milton Friedman, *Capitalism and Freedom* (Chicago: University of Chicago Press, 1962).

Hans Morgenthau, *Politics Among Nations* (New York: A. Knopf, 1948).

Reinhold Niebuhr, *The Children of Light and the Children of Darkness* (New York: Charles Scribner's Sons, 1944).

Reinhold Niebuhr, *The Nature and Destiny of Man* (New York: Charles Scribner's Sons, 1949).

Reinhold Niebuhr, *The Structure of Nations and Empires* (New York: Charles Scribner's Sons, 1960).

Talcott Parsons, *The Social System* (Glencoe: The Free Press, 1951).

Plato, *The Republic.*

Paul Tillich, *Love, Power and Justice* (New York: Oxford University Press, 1954).

Paul Tillich, *Systematic Theology* (Chicago: University of Chicago Press, 1951, 1955, 1963).

Max Weber, "Politics as a Vocation" and "Science as a Vocation" in C. Wright Mills and Hans Geuth, editors *From Max Weber: Essays in Sociology* (New York: Oxford University Press, 1946).

Max Weber, *Theory of Social and Economic Organization,* translated by A. R. Henderson and Talcott Parsons (New York: Oxford University Press, 1947).

Alfred North Whitehead, *Adventures of Ideas* (New York: Macmillan, 1933).

Alfred North Whitehead, *Process and Reality* (New York: Macmillan, 1929).

Alfred North Whitehead, *Science and the Modern World* (New York: Macmillan, 1925).

Whitehead's *Process and Reality* is the primary text for an appropriation of the basic categories of process thought. Valuable interpretations of Whitehead's thought include William Christian, *An Interpretation of Whitehead's Metaphysics* (New Haven: Yale University Press, 1959); John Cobb, Jr. and David Ray Griffin, *Process Theology: An Introductory Exposition* (Philadelphia: Westminster, 1976); and Donald W. Sherburne, *A Key to Whitehead's Process and Reality* (New York: Macmillan, 1966).

3. For this reason the voluntaristic facet of social science theory rooted in the tradition of Max Weber and manifest in various phenomenologies has more in common with process views than the causal facet rooted in the traditions of Durkheim, Pareto, Freud, Marx, and other strongly causally oriented theorists.

4. The fact-value disjunction, manifest in the neo-Kantian understanding of social scientific theory associated with Max Weber and his followers, is spurious. The inner and exterior factors in human experience are necessarily related.

5. In its broader meaning, "reason" refers to human participation in forms of definiteness embodied in God's primordial nature. This "ontic" reason, coupled with human capacity to think by a method of difference and by the exercise of negative judgments, enables humans to analyze and to interpret human experience.

Technical reason is grounded in ontic reason, and in appropriate contexts the two meanings of reason should be explored. Such explorations are currently not fashionable among economists or, for that matter, among social scientists generally.

6. In a society in which technical reason is highly valued, the legal order may be richly elaborated. Lawyers and the "law" become very important in such societies.

7. This interdependence is the basis of a process critique of structural-functional analysis.

8. Needless to say, their formulations also must be set in the context of a more inclusive interpretative scheme. The notion of the historian writing history as it really was is a figment of the imagination.

9. The relatively "conserving" nature of the version of a process social ethic elaborated here is grounded on a relatively greater emphasis on the formal side of experience than is the case for most process thinkers addressing this problem.

10. Space limitations dictated the propositional character of the delineations advanced here and preluded an extended elaboration and clarification of these propositions in this essay. These discussions are expanded and elaborated in Chapter 3, in Part Two, and in Section A of Part Three.

Introduction to Chapter 3

This chapter is based on a paper prepared for a conference on issues of peace and human rights held in Kyoto, Japan in the spring of 1987. It draws on ideas dealing with principles of justice, the spheres of the social order and the priority of love, power and justice in the various spheres developed in the preceding chapters. The issues related to these ideas are elaborated at much greater length in this chapter than in the two preceding chapters. Because of the state's centrality in the quest for human rights and peace, it is given special attention in the discussion. The relation of the state and the economic sphere are addressed briefly in this chapter. These relations are discussed in much more detail in Part Two, especially in Chapter 6. The role religious institutions *ought* to play in the quest for peace and social justice is also addressed briefly. Their role is considered at much greater length in Chapter 9.

CHAPTER 3

Human Rights: A Process Interpretation

Introduction

People have quested for peace for as long as human reflection on experience has been recorded. Undoubtedly, human desires for peace were intuited and transmitted through oral traditions prior to the first written records. Humans have sought an inner peace in the human soul, a harmony of the soul and the body, and an external harmony of human life with human life, of social group with social group, and of humans with nature. Humans have experienced cooperation, tenderness, affection, kindness, and love. They have also experienced competition, harshness, disaffection, indifference, and hatred.

Physical compulsion, human volition, and the divine persuasion combine to evoke the admixture of harmony and discord which humans experience in their lives. Because the complex hierarchy of societies comprising the human organism is not perfectly coordinated, the human soul, which is the recipient of much data from the body with which it is intimately associated, cannot avoid some discordant experiences. Such experiences are sometimes exacerbated by the impact of events beyond the body, for the actions of other human beings and nonhuman creatures also evoke discordant experiences.

Finitude, ignorance, sloth, lethargy, and inordinate self-interest all contribute to the discord which is ubiquitous in human experience. Humans may be able to modify and/or transform some of the bases for human discord, but other contributing factors are relatively intractable. One of the functions of human reason is to facilitate the discernment of factors which human efforts may modify and to explore appropriate measures which humans may undertake to effect these transformations. A second function is to facilitate the accommodation of factors which are intractable.

Humans also intuitively claim certain rights as human beings and sense some responsibility for securing such rights for themselves and others. The particular shape of the claim varies from society to society and from historical epoch to historical epoch, but the variety of manifestations should not obscure the universality of the claim.

This essay is concerned primarily with the quest for human rights, but this issue is intimately associated with the quest for peace. Because persons associated with the organizing center of a human society must be concerned with developing and maintaining an earthly peace, the human rights question always involves politics and the public order.

This essay is informed by the mode of thought that has come to be called process philosophy. Rooted in the work of Alfred North Whitehead, Charles Hartshorne, and Henry Nelson Wieman, process philosophy and its correlate, process theology, have attracted the interest of religious social ethicists in the last couple of decades.

Process metaphysics has been both used and abused in religious social ethics. It has been used to provide generic notions in which to set more specialized propositions; it has sometimes been abused to legitimate views on public policy issues that are based on more specialized data than metaphysics can provide.

Process religious social ethicists differ on many public policy matters. Because one cannot move directly from metaphysical propositions, which — if the propositions are, in fact, metaphysical — apply to all actual entities, to contingent propositions applying to specific actual entities with particular defining characteristics, disagreements are inevitable.

One cannot discern the particular from an understanding of the general. One can derive a genus from species, but one cannot derive species from a genus. Even if we were able to develop a fully adequate metaphysics—which most process people hold is impossible—this achievement would not insure a consensus among process thinkers on issues in religious social ethics.

For example, one of the basic metaphysical propositions in process thought is the principle of relativity. This principle holds that every being is a potential for every becoming. This doctrine of internal relations is universal, applying to all actual occasions. The proposition does not and cannot illumine how much influence one actual entity has on its successors. All the principle states is that the actual entity has some *influence,* which may vary from the most negligible to the most salient. The contribution may range from little more than the sharing of the geometric properties of the extensive continuum to the most profound reciprocal influences between a particular parent and a particular child, or between a particular husband and a particular wife.

In addition to the need to discern more particular patterns, structures and facts to describe and to assess the influence of specific contingent phenomena on one another, one also needs to formulate criteria to guide one's assessment of the normative desirability of a particular pattern, structure, or course of action. Because process religious social ethicists may differ in their assessment of both descriptive and evaluative factors, they may differ both in their analysis of a particular human situation and also in their evaluation of what ought to be done in that situation. For example, most process thinkers understand that the becoming of an actual occasion involves the appropriation of physical and conceptual data in a novel synthesis in the emerging present. However, they may draw different implications from the relation of the past, the present, and the future in an emerging creature and from the contrast between potentiality and actuality.

One distinguished process thinker seeks to legitimate abortion on the basis of the relative depth and intensity of feeling in the experience of the mother in contrast to that of the embryo. By emphasizing the ultimacy of present actuality and minimizing the potentiality inherent in the fetus, he argues that the mother may abort a very undifferentiated and relatively unfeeling embryo because it has minimal capacities for integration and depth of feeling. Using the same informing metaphysical framework but emphasizing more forcefully our knowledge of the relation between the present and the future and between potentiality and actuality, one could argue either that the fetus should not be deprived of the opportunity to evolve in the direction inherent in its character, or that such deprivation should be strictly limited.

Process religious social ethicists may also make contrasting prudential judgments, based on alternative assessments of the consequences of present actions for future events. The issue of the development and/or use of nuclear weapons will serve to illustrate this point, for the vast majority of process thinkers are opposed to nuclear war. The widespread use of nuclear weapons would wreak massive destruction on human beings, those creatures having the greatest capacity for harmony and intensity of feeling on this planet. It would also have profound impact on many other life forms, making the continuation of life as we know it on this planet very problematic.

In spite of this broad consensus, process religious social ethicists may disagree on the most appropriate means to prevent and/or to limit the use of nuclear weapons. Some may propose unilateral nuclear disarmament of their nation as the most appropriate means to minimize the likelihood of widespread use of nuclear weapons. Others may urge both the continuation of arms reduction negations and also the retention of current nuclear weapons. Still others may propose both continued arms reduction negotiations and also continued development of nuclear weapons. Because the future is real but not actual in the present, no one knows that the future will hold in full detail.

This essay is divided into seven sections. The first section explores the bases of human rights from a process perspective. The second section discusses the fundamental factors embodied in human experience and uses the analogical method to formulate the principles of justice. The third section explores the bases of the three principles of justice in more detail and relates them to the evolution of human societies. The fourth section explores the bases for disharmony in the human social order. The fifth section explores the bases for the forms of human social organization and notes some historical developments. The sixth section advances some normative assessments about what the state should do to promote and to defend human rights. The final section notes the forms of political action that may be available to persons seeking to promote their particular vision of the fitting pattern of human rights in their particular historical context.

I
The Bases of Human Rights: A Perspective of the Nature of Human Nature

Human beings are complex structured societies consisting of many integrated and coordinated subsocieties and millions of living occasions. Members of some of the subsocieties can and do exist naturally outside the organism, albeit in slightly different patterns; members of other subsocieties depend on the entire organism to provide an appropriate sustaining environment for their reproduction. Their survival outside the organism—if it is possible at all—depends upon the construction of an artificial sustaining environment.

At the apex of the human organism is a serially-ordered sequence of high grade occasions which are the ultimate recipients of a wide variety of data coming from other parts of the organism. This sequence of ultimate percipient occasions constitutes the regnant center of the human being. It is the "soul" of the organism, a formless form so protean it can encompass the multiple occasions that constitute it.

Human beings possess very substantial capacities for novelty of response to the circumstances in which they find themselves. They are the only organisms of which we have any direct knowledge who have the capacity to formulate general principles to order and to interpret particular patterns of behavior and experience. Other animals seem to be aware of forces and factors at work on the planet, but they do not seem to possess the capacity to generalize from this awareness. A cat may intuitively assess the attraction between objects in its deftly executed leaps from the ground to a fence or a tree limb, but a human and not a cat formulated the laws of gravity.

This human capacity is a consequence of the prolongation of the supplemental conceptual phase in the becoming of the ultimate percipient occasions constituting the human soul. This prolongation permits humans to contrast what is with what might be and to entertain negative judgements. In a negative judgment the human being imagines the absence of something that is present or the presence of something that is absent. In this way, humans can play with consistency and inconsistency, developing interpretations of both natural and human phenomena.

The expanded capacities of humans, compared to other living creatures on this planet, to think and to respond volitionally to their environment, highlight human freedom from the bonds of the causal past in the emerging present. The human senses of responsibility, of morality, of individual initiative, of approbation and condemnation, of qualification and redirection of data derived from the causal past, and of individual attainments are all derived from the foundational experience of human self-determination.

The evolutionary process of this planet has been shaped by the evocation of creatures with enhanced capacities for harmony and intensity of feeling. In this process the various types of organisms cohabitating the planet have evolved complex interdependent relations. Because of these interdependencies, an appropriate sustaining environment is necessary to support complex life forms. Until the emergence of humans, the evolutionary process was largely unconscious and/or intuitive. Humans have intervened in the evolutionary process both intentionally and as an unintended consequence of other activities. Since the early modern period (circa 1500), humans have modified natural processes much more rapidly than was the case earlier. Humans are rightly concerned about the impact of many new and novel materials in the ecosystem, for no one knows the full impact of such rapid transformations. At this organic level, human rights are dependent on a congenial sustaining environment. If humans violate the limits nature imposes on them, the rights of human and subhuman species are violated. The intrinsic right to sustain the forms that enable humans to survive is the most elemental and fundamental human right.

Because of their plasticity, living organisms can respond and adjust to their changing environment within limits. One is advised to err on the side of caution in the introduction of human made products into the environment, for no one knows the long-run impact of synthetic products, waste materials, and altered biological organisms into the delicately balanced web of life on this planet.

Because of the intimate relation between the soul, which embodies both capacities for freedom and for rationalism, and the body, any discussion of human rights must consider the well-being of the human body, the vessel which partly sustains the soul. At the most elemental level, humans claim the right to sustain their bodies from the ravages of hunger and the elements. A minimum of food, fiber, and shelter is a basic human right.

The nature of the body also helps define the shape of other human rights. Human sexuality, mental and physical handicaps, and age-grading are salient biological factors which must be considered in a discussion of human rights.

Humans are individuals-in-community. The most intimate community an individual experiences is his/her body and the ultimate percipient occasions in the individual's causal past. Beyond the body and one's memory, the closest human communities are found in the family and/or clan. These primary groups sustain inclusive, holistic relations. In addition to these primary relations, people in societies of more than a few people establish numerous secondary relations, involving persons with more role-specific associations with a given individual.

These differing levels of human intimacy and frequency of human interaction are rooted in human finitude and in the fact that objectification entails loss from the human point of view. One cannot sustain close and intimate relations with more than a small finite number of people. In secondary relations, the many are frequently counted as one. (This situation is exacerbated in societies in which technical rationalism is a prized value, for the resultant bureaucratization makes a virtue of segmented roles and limited relations between people.) Without such simplification, the human organism would be unable to harmonize the many into a unified experience.

The idea of the love of humankind as such is a noble idea, derived as a generalization from the experience of the love of particular human beings and an interpretation of Divine love. It is a concept which contributes to a doctrine of human rights, for the notion evokes a general concern about the well-being of all humankind. This vision must always be embodied in a particular society in a particular historical epoch. The particular environment imposes limits on the forms this embodiment may take.

The human soul's relations with its body, with nature, and with other humans provide the basic data for the discussion of human rights. The following two sections develop some more specialized notions which must be considered in the formulation of a process perspective on human rights.

II
The Fundamental Factors Embodied in Human Experience

Human experience entails the dynamic unification of formal components by an emerging feeling subject. Some of these formal components are derived from subject-objects lying in the causal past of the emerging subject. Other formal components are forms of definiteness embodied in the primordial facet of the Divine Nature. The emerging subject clothes both types of forms with feelings. These feelings are partly derived in the objectification of formal components lying in the causal past of the emerging subject, are partly derived from the divine subjective aim which informs the emerging creature's subjective aim, and are partly a *sui generis* creation of the emerging subject under the urge of creativity. The emerging subject's aim at unification is guided but not determined by the divine evocation for harmony and intensity of feeling. The emerging entity synthesizes the components of its experience into a completed whole that constitutes the creature as subject. It then becomes an object for the entities that succeed it. Thus every creature is a subject-object. In its becoming it is an emerging subject. After it has become, it is an object contributing data to the creatures that succeed it.

The basic rhythm inherent in the nature of things is the movement from the community of the many to the individuation of the one which then becomes one of the many constituting the community from which a new entity emerges. The emerging entity begins its becoming by appropriating data from the many entities in the world, supplements these data with forms of definiteness embodied in the primordial facet of the Divine Nature, and unifies these contrasting data in the privacy of its becoming.

In human beings the canalized sequence of serially ordered ultimate percipient occasions constitutes the human personality or soul. As noted earlier, this community is the one with which emerging ultimate percipient occasions have the closest relations, except for their relations with the Divine Reality. One's body, some other humans, some other living beings, and some other parts of nature are also closely related to one's organizing center.

The basic social nature of life is grounded in these relations. Both the freedom of the individual from the community and the obligation of the individual to the community are inherent in these relations. Indeed, one of the perennial problems in social ethics is the relation of the individual to the community. Human freedom cannot be bound by one's relation to one's community, but neither individuals nor representatives of the community can ignore their relations to and responsibilities to the living community of human beings of which they are a part. As will be elaborated later, representatives of one's community frequently claim more than they have a right to claim for the community and for their stake in those claims. The magistrates' own self-interests complicate and exacerbate the relation of the individual good and the good of the living community.

The relations between the individual and the community ought to be guided by just relations. At a basic level, *intrinsic justice* entails a respect for the form defining the characteristics of human beings. The respect involves the acknowledgement that human beings are free, deliberating responsive creatures and should be respected as such. At the level of guiding relations between humans in living communities, *distributive justice*, emphasizing the application of fitting rules and regulation of justice to particular situations, is dominant. At the highest level, *creative justice* entails the transformation of old rules and regulations of justice in a novel, concrete setting. This uniting form surpasses distributive justice for the sake of justice.

There are three principles of distributive justice. They represent the most formal and abstract components involved in the quest for the justice and the attainment of human rights. The principles are grounded in the dynamic, formal, and unifying facets of the becoming of a creature. This basic triad may be used analogically to formulate these general principles of justice and may be used analytically to examine their embodiment in the life of a living community. Because the dynamic-form-unification triad is three-in-relation, the principles of justice are interrelated.

Freedom informed by excellence is the constitutive principle of justice, rooted in the dynamic facet of experiences. It is based on the ultimacy of creativity and the primacy of process in the nature of things. In human life, the human capacity for self-determination, which is too salient in human experience to be interpreted epiphenomenally, is the basis for this principle.

Equality appropriate to form is based on the form facet of experience, and order, peace, and harmony is based on the unifying facet of experience. These principles are regulative principles of justice. As such, they qualify the constitutive principle of justice.

These principles will be discussed in more detail in the following section of this essay. However, it is fitting to consider the relation of these principles of justice to human life in a living community in this section. The basic form-dynamic-unification triad delineated at the beginning of this section may be used analytically to examine the way in which the principles of justice become embodied in the life of a living community.

In a given living community, persons representing its organizing center have a monopoly on the legitimate use of coercion. The living community occupies a given geographical area within which this force may be used. Unless most of the members of this living community share certain common core values and are persuaded rather than coerced to recognize the legitimacy of the rule of the constituted authorities and of the rules and regulations of justice shaping the life of that community, disorder and conflict will loom large in its life. In the extreme case, anarchy may prevail, and civil war will exist.

As just noted, the principles of justice—freedom informed by excellence, equality appropriate to form, and order/peace/harmony—represent the most formal and abstract aspect of justice and are grounded in the dynamic, formal, and unifying facets of the becoming of a creature. At the next level of embodiment a living community codifies these principles in the rules and regulations of justice in its legal order. As the members of a particular society codify the principles, they are conditioned by the level of technological development and the unique historical background of that society. These factors influence the way in which its members interpret the scope of human freedom and the limits which forms impose on equality. In addition, the dominant climate of opinion and the particular forms of social organization extant in a given society will affect the process by which the rules and regulations of justice are promulgated and enforced.

The final level of embodiment involves the application of the rules and regulations of justice in a particular situation. As is the case with the formulation of rules and regulations of justice, the general cultural conditions and the judicial structure of a particular society will effect the way the rules and regulations of justice are applied.

Because the formal, dynamic, and unifying facets of experience are intrinsically interrelated, justice cannot simply be identified with the formal aspect of experience. On the contrary, because of the ultimacy of the category of creativity, the highest form of justice is creative or transformative justice. In this form of justice, old forms are transformed for the sake of justice in a new and novel situation.

The sequence from principles of justice to rules and regulations of justice to the application of the rules and regulations of justice in a specific context embodies the form-dynamics-unification triad in increasingly specific ways. The generality of the principles of justice is translated into more specific rules and regulations which are then applied to a concrete situation. In the application, creative justice is required, for no rules and regulations fit any actual situation perfectly.

The bases for the principles of justice have been stated in this section, but the topic requires a more extended discussion. The following section considers the bases for the principles of justice in more detail and selectively illustrates the way they have been incorporated in various human societies.

III
The Principles of Justice: Bases and Historical Manifestations

Freedom Informed by Excellence as the Constitutive Principle of Justice

As noted earlier, in fundamental human experience the emerging subject unifies an inrush of feelings and forms. Humans are aware that they undertake shifts of emphasis, weigh alternatives, and make decisions affecting both the inner life of the emerging subject and of the emerging subjects which succeed the subject once it has actualized itself. This experience of becoming illumines the ultimate dynamic bias of the universe.

This experience of individual decision making is too salient in human experience to be illusory. In spite of the undeniable influence of the causal past in the emerging present, there is a *sui generis* dimension to human becoming. The reality of human freedom governs the whole tone of human life. Life is a bid for freedom from the bonds of the causal past, and human beings have a greater capacity for novelty of response to circumstances than any other living organisms of which we have any direct knowledge.

In the course of human history, there has been a broad drift toward the extension of human freedom in human communities. This extension entails a reduction in the ways in which some human beings can claim the right to abridge the liberty of other human beings. As Whitehead and many others have noted, in the ancient world slavery was presupposed as necessary for the sustenance of many human social orders. In the modern world, freedom is presupposed in most societies, and slavery as practiced in the ancient world is virtually absent. Even in those societies with caste systems—in which relations between people and various subgroups in the society are circumscribed by law—the view that one human being is the property of another human being is absent.

Individuals appeal to their experiences of a basic inner freedom and the idea of equality to claim this human right for other people. Unless one qualifies the understanding of freedom, one is affirming a sophistic view at this level—freedom is simply being able to do what one wants to do.

Both the persuasive lure for harmony and intensity of feeling at the base of things and also the social nature of existence make this view of freedom inadequate. If self-determination is unqualified, it leads to inordinate self-centeredness and self-indulgence. The more excellent way of love requires the qualification of freedom by the phrase "informed by excellence." Consequently freedom informed by excellence is one of the principles of social justice. Because of the dynamic bias inherent in the nature of things due to the ultimacy of the category of creativity, freedom informed by excellence is the constitutive principle of justice.

Equality Appropriate to Form and Order/Peace/Harmony as the Regulative Principles of Justice

In addition to the primal dynamic and volitional facet of experience giving rise to freedom informed by excellence as the constitutive principle of justice, two other factors are embodied in our experience: formal components and the unification of forms and feelings in the emerging subject. The former gives rise to equality appropriate to form as a regulative principle of justice. The latter gives rise to order/peace/harmony as a regulative principle of justice.

Equality Appropriate to Form — As humans encounter other human beings in human communities and seek to accommodate their claims in the community, they often evoke the principle of equality to help guide the formulation of the rules and regulations of justice. Persons with an egalitarian bias emphasize this principle very forcefully in their promotion of public policy proposals and in their visions of desirable forms of human social organization.

This view must be challenged, for equality is one of the regulative principles of justice, but it is not a constitutive principle. Even when equality is appropriately qualified, it is in some tension with the constitutive principle of freedom.

Equality is a mathematical ideal, for no two actual entities are exactly equal. On the contrary, the actualization of an entity requires some contrast with the contribution that entities in the causal past make to that emerging entity. In the case of the rhythmic contrasts in simple entities, the difference between two entities may be minimal; but, even in the case of low grade occasions, no two occasions are identical. In the case of human beings, who are very complex high-grade organisms, the differences between them may be very substantial.

In some religious circles, people evoke the notion that God loves everyone equally to legitimate the primacy of the principle of equality in social ethics. This notion of the Divine equality of love is a curious one, for it is not clear what equal love means. If it is used to mean that God responds fully to all that a creature has to offer it, then God's love must be unequal; for creatures are unequal and must be responded to unequally. In any event, such a view, even if in some sense it is true, cannot be applied directly to the human social order; for relations between humans always entail relations between creatures that are not fully equal.

Even though the principle of equality cannot be fully actualized in existence, it can be used to formulate relations among creatures that do possess many common defining characteristics. In other words, the principle may be applied to creatures who are roughly equal. Consequently, the phrase "appropriate to form," which is used to distinguish between various types of organisms based on selected common forms must be used to qualify the regulative principle of equality.

Some of the forms that historically have qualified equality in human life are age, sex, social status, race, ethnicity, economic class, political position, and religion. Because many of the rules and regulations of justice informed by these qualifications have limited substantially the freedom of persons in some of these categories, these qualifications have become less salient over the past two or three millennia of human history. For those who affirm strongly the constitutive principle of freedom, the most objectionable qualifications are those associated with some of the social characteristics. The qualifications that will probably persist in human life center on the biologically grounded age and sex characteristics and some of the sociologically grounded differences in social function.

The increasing inclusiveness in the application of equality as a regulative principle of justice has generally been associated with the transition from traditional to post-traditional societies. This trend has been associated with the rise in technical rationalism as a criterion for evaluating human activity and with the increasing differentiation of the spheres of the human social order.

Technical rationalism seeks the most efficient means to attain a given end. It has evoked the growth of bureaucracies, the division of labor, the widespread interest in growth and efficiency in the economic sphere, the growth of voluntary associations in all the spheres of the social order, and the evaluation of human beings on the basis of achieved rather than ascribed social characteristics.

In this way individual competencies come to be more highly valued, and sociological characteristics associated with sex, age, race, ethnicity, and religion become less highly valued. In some spheres of the human social order, the forms which limit the application of the principle of equality are reduced, but the organic character of community life is loosened. Rational-legal authority becomes relatively more important, and customs become relatively less important. Arbitrators and lawyers become very important in societies in which technical rationalism is a salient value. As "organic" traditional ways of resolving differences recede, legal means become more important.

The drift toward freedom is uneven, and the quasi-feudal character of many bureaucracies sharply circumscribes the freedom of individuals. An individual in principle may be free to withdraw from a given position in a bureaucratic hierarchy, but in fact he/she may be bound to it by economic necessity.

Historically the extension of freedom has been more evident in the West than in other parts of the planet and in the more industrialized countries than in the more agrarian countries. Part of the contemporary differences in the understanding of human rights in various societies is a result of the contrasting limits on equality as a principle of justice which have emerged in various societies.

The biological forms of age and sex impose some necessary limits on the reduction in the limitations of forms qualifying equality. Because human nature is quite plastic, one cannot formulate precisely the ways in which sex and age must qualify equality, but there are limits beyond which one cannot go in the extension of equality. The precise age at which children are treated as adults is subject to discussion and to change, but the changes are ultimately limited by age grading. No one would argue that a two-year-old should have the law applied to him/her in the same way it would be applied to a thirty-year-old, but the precise age at which one is considered an adult for legal purposes is somewhat arbitrary. The limit that nature imposes is somewhere between the onset of puberty and the early-to-mid twenties. The precise limit will be determined in the give-and-take within the life of a living community.

In all human societies for much of human history and in most human societies today, sex is one of the forms substantially qualifying the principle of equality. Men and women have traditionally been subject to both some common and to some different rules and regulation of justice. Generally, the liberty of men has been more broadly defined than the liberty of the woman. The drift toward the extension of liberty as the constitutive principle of justice and the increasing importance of technical rationalism have combined to facilitate the dimunition of qualifications that sexual differences have made on equality as a principle of justice in many living communities in this historical epoch.

The plasticity of nature with respect to sex is of a different character than with age, for the limits have little or nothing to do with the developing capacity for foresight in relation to self-determination. Instead, biological functions are at the base of whatever qualifications on equality sexual forms evoke. The current debates in many societies—significantly most frequently in post-traditional societies and among middle and upper status social groups—represent efforts to discern the limits sexual differences should impose on equality. The discussions are multi-faceted and take a different shape in the different spheres of the social order, but supporters of women's rights generally seek more equal rights in most of the spheres of the social order.

The position of people in the social structure is the final basis for limitations which forms impose on the principle of equality. Differences in social function and differences in social status have always evoked limitations on the principle of equality. Kings, princes, lords, and divines have historically been granted special privileges in most societies. Lawyers, judges, journalists, and government officials have also been afforded special privileges in many societies.

In feudal time, the principle of equality was limited by one's station in a hierarchically ordered society. The rights and obligations of persons within and between different strata in the social order were based on these differentiations. Equality of persons within a given strata was balanced by inequality of persons in different strata.

As with other forms limiting the regulative principle of equality, the enhancement of the constitutive principle of freedom has sharply reduced inequality due to social function. In spite of these reductions, the nature of human social life suggests that the limitations which social functions impose on the principle of equality cannot be eliminated in human life. The ways in which social functions limit equality are also subject to debate and to reinterpretation in the lives of living communities.

Earlier it was noted that freedom informed by excellence and equality appropriate to form are not perfectly harmonizable. Human self-determination, shaped by biological and social factors, leads to inequality. Some limits on inequality for the sake of justice are fitting, but too stringent a quest for equality leads to excessive restraint on self-determination, including the right to make mistakes and to bear the consequences for errors in judgment.

The inevitable tension between freedom and equality is resolved in the ongoing life of a living community. The resolutions are always tentative, but people's decisions ought to be guided by an understanding of certain basic human rights.

Order/Peace/Harmony — This issue leads to a discussion of order/peace/harmony, the other regulative principle of justice. The principle of order/peace/harmony is focused directly on the community, for it is grounded in the necessity for representatives of the organizing center of the community to coordinate and to harmonize its constituent components. Both suasive and coercive power are involved in this necessity for the representatives of a living community to attain a measure of order among its constituents, as well as internal and external peace.

As noted earlier, freedom and equality cannot be perfectly harmonized, and both biological and sociological factors limit these two principles. In some societies, individual freedoms and some legitimate claims for equality are often suppressed for the sake of order. Through the enforcement of both codified and informal rules and regulations of justice, representatives of the organizing center of society shape the way in which the principles of liberty and equality are embodied in the life of a particular living community. As shifts in the general climate of opinion and in the technological status of a given living community occur, the community will redefine liberty and equality and the relations between them. In this complex and ongoing interplay, older configurations pass away, and new ones emerge. In some societies, these transformations are gradual and evolutionary. In societies in which innovations are suppressed by coercion, the culminating transformations may be radical and revolutionary. Because such radical changes are rarely if ever attained without bloodshed, the evolutionary pattern is preferable to the revolutionary one.

These principles of justice are never adequately embodied in the life of any living community. As noted in the Introduction, finitude, ignorance, sloth, lethargy, and inordinate self-interest are perennial sources of disharmony and imperfection. These factors are elaborated in some detail in the next section.

IV
The Bases of Disharmony in the Human Social Order

Introduction

Religious social ethicists informed by process modes of thought differ in the relative importance they attach to finitude, ignorance, sloth, lethargy, and inordinate self-interest, the fundamental bases for conflict and disharmony among humans. These differences effect their views on desirable forms of social organization, public policy proposals, and the degree of harmony of life with life they think is possible under the conditions of existence. In this section, the author grounds his views on these bases for human conflicts and disharmonies.

Finitude

Finitude is the most fundamental ground for conflict and disharmony. The primordial facet of the Divine Nature has envisaged all of the eternal objects; its gaze, as it were, orders and harmonizes all potentiality. However, this potentiality lacks the concreteness and particularity of actuality. Because the fully actual is more ultimate than the merely potential, this abstractness is a deficiency.

All actualization is finite actualization. It is limiting and exclusive. The realization of *this* potentiality requires the exclusion of *that* potentiality. A given actual occasion harmonizes more or less well with other actual occasions in its immediate sustaining environment. The more fitting its relations to its environment, the greater the harmony it evokes in its successors.

However, because some discord is an inevitable concomitant of actualization, the lure for new and novel occasions in a changing environment will evoke some disharmony with the prevailing ethos. All perfections are finite, and as seasons change, those things contributing to a relative perfection of one epoch may become an evil in another epoch. The mere repetition of old forms and old patterns becomes tedious. Although the transition to new forms and new patterns may result in new and richer contrasts, it will evoke some discord in the occasions facilitating the transition.

In addition, more than mere harmony is sought in experience. The lure for aesthetic satisfaction requires both harmony and intensity of feeling. The growth in intensity of feeling requires a proper balance between breadth and depth of experience. A proper vagueness and a proper triviality are necessary to evoke higher contrasts which enhance intensity of feeling. In this process, the experience of intense disharmony may be a concomitant of the development of creatures with enhanced capacity for intensity of feeling. For this reason, it is "better" to be an unhappy human than a contented cow.

Finitude evokes disharmony in a second way. Objectification involves loss. Achievements of the present fade into memories of the past. The vivid immediacy of the present passes away. High-grade organisms who are self-conscious about these losses experience a sense of melancholy and of tragedy in their self-awareness of the transitory character of great achievements. Of course, the anesthesia which occurs is welcome in the case of heinous and/or very discordant experiences.

Ignorance

Ignorance also contributes to the disharmony which is an inevitable facet of human experience. The independence of action which contemporary occasions enjoy is the basis for elbow-room in the universe. No actual occasion knows precisely what its contemporaries are going to do. This ignorance means that even well intentioned persons are going to make decisions which evoke disharmony in the future. It also means that in some instances humans may be a bit oblivious to morality, for not all human decisions focus heavily upon the consequences of present actions for the future.

The lack of full knowledge of the decisions of contemporaries is not the only way in which ignorance contributes to the human experience of conflict, discord, and disharmony. Humans often do not possess an adequate theory to know what course of action will minimize discord in the future. The practice of medicine is full of illustrations of this fact. Bloodletting is a dramatic illustration of the way in which ignorance contributed to practices which are now seen to be harmful or at best ineffectual. Undoubtedly our successors will look back at our epoch and cite many practices which were of a similar type. In many instances, good practice awaits good theory, and good theory requires a growth in understanding resulting from the interplay between conceptual formulations and rational experimentation. In some spheres, good human practice may be more sharply limited by an intrinsic inability to project the consequences of one's actions with great clarity because of human capacities to respond in new ways to changing conditions.

Sloth and Lethargy

Sloth and lethargy in human experience are pervasive in human life, for the drag of the causal past on the emerging present is most substantial. Laziness, indifference, and a general disinclination to action or labor are persistent phenomena among human beings. Humans are often disinclined to make the effort to undertake activities which might enhance the quality of human life. Public policies must take account of the pervasiveness of sloth and lethargy in human affairs.

Inordinate Self-Interest

Inordinate self-interest is the final source of disharmony in human life. Because of the structural necessity to become *something*, self-interest cannot be eliminated from the world. Indeed, the quest for an appropriate relation between the individual and the community is perennial in human life. A proper balance between the rights and obligations of individuals and the communities to which they belong is a central human rights question. The attainment of the proper balance would produce a fitting self-interest, in which the individual would have space both for the pursuit of individual interests and the promotion of the good of the community.

In the Christian movement, the persistence of inordinate self-interest has been addressed in a more specialized way. It has been set in the context of the doctrine of original sin and of contrasting doctrines of personal and social transformation and sanctification. Transformation focuses on the means by which inordinate self-interest may be ameliorated, and sanctification focuses on the possibility of the diminution or elimination of inordinate self-interest under the conditions of existence.

From processes perspectives, all occasions both give to and receive from others. The exemption of the Divine Reality from this reciprocity in classical theism led to the notion that a completely giving and selfless person constitutes an ethical ideal. This view is in error, for it entails a denial of the reciprocal character of giving and receiving. It reduces the dignity of the recipient of the giving, for in principle it denies the contribution which the recipient can make to the giver. In fact, one who gives cannot avoid receiving some form of gift from the recipient. A proper view of these relations helps alleviate the sanctimony which one-sided interrelations of giving and receiving often induce.

Morality and Progress

Those persons who hold there can be no progress in morality accentuate the ultimacy of human freedom above the formal elements of experience and envisage the inevitability of inordinate self-interest in the human moral act. In the Christian movement, persons informed by the views of Martin Luther have frequently advanced such views. Because humans are constantly falling in and out of grace, being grasped by the loving forgiveness of the Divine Love and failing to respond adequately to it, the moral life of the person is most ambiguous. Human sinfulness constantly thwarts growth in grace and moral stature.

Although this view of sanctification is too pessimistic, one cannot ignore the reality reflected in this interpretation of human morality. Humans do pursue their own self-interest at the expense of others all too frequently. The "saint" is inordinately self-centered some of the time, and most of humankind is inordinately self-centered much of the time.

In spite of this reality, there can be some progress in morality, for forms are an integral part of every becoming. Both the embodiment of more fitting forms and the more sensitive awareness of the claims which others make for their basic rights contribute to the enhance harmony of life with life. The promotion of forms of social organization which enhance peace and promote human rights and the formulation of justice enhance human morality. These "trapped universals," embodied in the feeling and thinking of human beings, may promote better conduct and more social justice.

The divine lure for harmony and intensity of feeling, the plasticity of human nature, the persuasive capacity of ideals, the evocation of "better" forms of social organization, the more adéquate embodiment of the principles of justice in rules and regulations of justice, and the growth of feelings of kindness and tenderness among humankind provide a hope for progress in human morality. The conflict and discord evoked by finitude, ignorance, sloth, lethargy, and inordinate self-interest limit progress in human morality and may lead to a regression in human morality.

In formulating public policy proposals and in delineating desirable forms of social organization, these dual propensities of humankind must be taken into account. Neither too pessimistic nor too optimistic an assessment of human possibilities will contribute to the quest for peace and human rights. A realistic assessment will seek to consider both the limits the causal past imposes on the present and the foreseeable future and also the opportunities new and novel ideas and situations provide for social transformation. This assessment will take account of human propensities for altruistic behavior and for self-centered behavior. One should prefer persuasion and nonviolent coercion to coercion and physical force whenever feasible, but one must acknowledge the necessity for coercion and physical force in some contexts.

These observations provide the guidelines informing the discussion of desirable forms of social organization in the several spheres of the human social order. The next two sections of this essay address this topic.

V
The Spheres of the Human Social Order: Bases and Historical Developments

Introduction

The spheres of the human social order are rooted in the characteristics and the experiences of human beings. The way in which the spheres are organized and related to each other depends upon the prevailing ethos in a given society. This ethos itself is a product of the interplay between natural necessity, human rational shaping capacities, and human self-determination. Human rational shaping capacities are objectified in the cultural sphere. Dominant ideas give rise to a formal and/or informal legal order. This legal order supports particular forms of social organization and defines the relations between social institutions in the several spheres of the social order.

The spheres include the familial sphere, the social sphere, the ethnic sphere, the economic sphere, the political sphere, the cultural sphere, and the religious sphere. The spheres are abstractions derived from the complex network of specific human relations in which people are enmeshed.

The forms of human social organization in the various spheres of the human social order have varied widely among human societies. For instance in the familial sphere, which is grounded in biological necessity, in human needs for intimacy and affection, and in human rational shaping capacities, monogamy, polygamy, polyandry, and polygyny have all existed among humans. Similarly, in the political sphere, which is rooted in social necessity and human rational shaping capacities, monarchy, aristocracy, and democracy (and their perversions, tyranny, oligarchy, and anarchy) have all existed, and complex modifications and qualification of all three forms of political organization have existed in various human societies.

The degree of differentiation between familial, social, ethnic, economic, political, cultural, and religious groups has also varied widely between groups in various historical epochs and within groups in the same historical epoch. For example, relations between economic and political institutions range from the dominance of institutions in one sphere or the other to a very substantial independence of the two spheres.

The degree of differentiation between the spheres of the social order in a given society depends on the general cultural conditions dominant in that society in the given historical epoch. Individual human rights are generally less sharply defined in societies in which the distinctions between the various spheres are not very clearly delineated. These societies are traditional in character; custom and oral traditions dominate. Because the primacy of the community is accentuated, individual liberty is minimized.

A complex differentiated social order requires a high degree of rationalization and the presence of substantial numbers of persons and groups self-consciously seeking to shape and to coordinate various components of the complex social order. The codified legal order is very important in such societies, for the degree of rationalization required to evoke and to sustain such societies requires an elaborate development of rules and regulations of justice. (The self-conscious formulation of human rights themselves depends upon these general cultural conditions.) Lawyers proliferate and play a significant role in such post-traditional societies.

In this section, the bases for the spheres of the human social order are explored, and some salient historical developments are highlighted. Through the rules and regulations of justice it establishes, the state promotes or represses human rights in the several spheres of the human social order. In section VI a normative discussion of what forms of social organization and values the state *qua* state *ought* to sustain is undertaken.

The Familial Sphere

The familial sphere is rooted in biological and social necessity. The predominantly bisexual nature of human nature, the dyadic requisites for human procreation, and the relatively long period of gestation and maturation of human beings are the biological bases for the family. Human needs for intimacy, tenderness, affection, inclusive shared experience, common memories, and relatively uncritical supportive relations are the psychological and spiritual bases for the family.

Enhanced human freedom for both men and women and the concomitant extension of the principle of equality have modified substantially traditional forms of family organization in parts of the planet. Historically, in most of the planet, patriarchy has been the predominant form of family organization. With the extension of the principles of freedom and equality and with the increasing emphasis on technical rationalism, the patriarchal family has been challenged, and its organic character has been modified. More equalitarian and more contractual values have emerged in families in post-traditional societies. The increase in divorce rates in societies, the emergence of serial monogamy as an increasingly popular form of family organization, and the press for enhanced rights for homosexuals and bisexuals are all related to these shifts in the value orientations affecting forms of family organization.

Humankind is never certain what it is seeking and what the consequence of transformative patterns will be. The extension of human sexual rights and the extension of more equality and freedom to women and to homosexuals and to bisexuals have much merit, but the contributions such extensions have made to the harmony of the family and to the enhancement of the quality of human life are ambiguous. Both biological and social factors suggest strongly that a monogamous form of family organization is normatively desirable for human life. If this is so, the current epoch is to be seen as one in which the quest for a more fitting form of family organization is evoking substantial disharmony and discord among many men, women, and children. A proper harmony between freedom and equality in this area is being explored. and the limits which nature imposes upon human sexual relations are being reexamined.

The Social Sphere

The social sphere of the human social order is characterized by style of life. Social status is largely determined by contrasting life-styles and concomitant factors such as linguistic usage and education. Some degree of social differentiation is present in all human societies, but it is accentuated in post-traditional societies. The embodiment of the principle of freedom and the extension of the principle of equality have accentuated social mobility in post-traditional societies. Because the organic facets of life are diminished by these extensions, persons are freer to adopt alternative life-styles than in other epochs.

As is the case in the familial and ethnic spheres, an increase in pluralism and a broader tolerance for alternative life-styles are concomitants of the enhanced freedom of the individual. Again, the limits are being pressed, and the obligations humans have for the broader community are being reassessed.

The Ethnic Sphere

The ethnic sphere of the human social order is closely related to the social sphere. In both spheres people share specialized histories set within the context of history of a broader society, contributing to the sense of identity among persons identifying with a particular status or ethnic group. Social honor and style of life are central characteristics of both spheres. However, in the ethnic sphere, real or imagined difference in physical characteristics usually augment distinctions based on social characteristics, such as life-style and shared common memories.

In numerous instances social distinctions based on status and/or ethnicity have been incorporated within the legal order of a society. In these instances, social relations between members of subgroups within the broader society are legally prescribed. In such instances, a caste system has been institutionalized. The most salient modern form of such a system has been the recently abolished apartheid system in the Republic of South Africa, but in modified forms caste systems are extant in several societies in the modern world.

In all such instances, the human rights of the persons in the designated groups are being restricted by the existing government which enforces the laws established in that state. If liberty and equality are to be extended, such limitations on human freedom and such a narrow understanding of equality must be challenged. In instances in which such patterns have been institutionalized for a long period of time, the adjustments which must be made to minimize or to eliminate these legal restrictions may well induce very substantial discord and disharmony in the society. Even though one may reject pleas from some for the maintenance of an existing peace and harmony, there is no question that, if effected, the radical social transformation sought by some protagonists would entail much discord and disharmony.

Because order/peace/harmony is one of the three principles of justice, the please for order and stability which some make are never without at least a modicum of merit. The task falling on the magistrates, which sometimes is beyond their ability, is the task of promoting innovation in the context of conservation. It is one thing to offer this proposal for a wholesome social order; it is another thing to embody it in the life of a living community.

The Economic Sphere

The economic sphere is grounded in biological necessity and in human rational shaping capacity. Human needs for food, clothing and shelter are universal, and every human society organizes itself to provide these basic necessities for its members. Because humans are able to make generalizations, to develop theories, to conduct experiments, to engage in toolmaking, and to anticipate the consequences of various alternatives to a greater degree than any other creatures on this planet, they have developed far more elaborate and complex ways to attain their basic economic needs than have members of any subhuman societies.

Because of their rational shaping capacities and their dexterity, humans have created arts and artifacts far exceeding those needed for bare existence. They seek well-being beyond mere being. Some moralists challenge some of the forms which this quest has taken, and market hedonism is a phenomenon of concern in all advanced industrialized societies.

The precise shape of the economic order depends on particular historical circumstances. The most important historical factors impacting on economic institutions are the general cultural conditions which both contribute to the state of technology and also shape the relations between economic and political institutions.

In post-traditional societies in which substantial differentiation of the spheres of the social order has occurred, the division of labor, the specialization of economic functions, and a complex, money-based exchange system have evolved.

The Political Sphere

The political sphere is rooted in social necessity and human rational shaping capacity. The large number of human beings inhabiting the planet and the accompanying need for coordination and conflict reduction within and between human social groups have fostered the emergence of organizing centers within human social groups. Political leaders representing the organizing centers may be selected by traditional hereditary succession, by charismatic leadership qualities, by some rationally prescribed selection process, or by some combination of these ways.

The state, the name given to the organizational center of a society, is paramountly important in the promotion of human rights, for people in this sphere enact, administer, and enforce the rules and regulations of justice which defined relations of humans within and between the spheres of the human social order. The general cultural conditions set the broad climate of opinion which guides the formulations of the rules and regulations of justice in a given society.

Power—both coercive and persuasive—is central in the political sphere, for persons related to institutions in this sphere must *make, administer,* and *enforce* laws, maintain domestic tranquility, and defend the state from external threats.

As noted earlier, the state must maintain a monopoly on the legitimate use of physical force in its geographical territory. Because of the dominance of the dynamic dimension of experience and the necessity to use coercion from time to time, analogies drawn from experiences rooted in the other spheres of the social order and applied to the political sphere are circumscribed and often inappropriate.

Formal components of experience and the persuasive power associated with love are important in the political sphere, but they are more salient in the other spheres of the social order.

The Cultural Sphere

The cultural sphere is rooted in the interplay between the particularity of human experience and the free play of human imagination. The supplemental phase of the ultimate percipient occasions constituting the human soul evokes art, science, philosophy, and the multiplicity of ideas-feelings which give shape to human actions and interpretations. These ideas-feelings both legitimate existing forms of human social organization and also promote the emergence of new patterns of human actions and interpretations and new forms of human social organization.

Educational, scientific, and artistic institutions are especially responsible for promoting cultural activities, and museums have developed to house historical artifacts. The cultural sphere includes both general notions and specialized ideas exceptional human beings create and the more diffuse ideas and feelings which produce the general climate of opinion dominant in a given society in a given cultural epoch.

The Religious Sphere

The religious sphere is rooted in exceptional human experiences and in human rational shaping capacity. In this context the term *exceptional* means "out of the ordinary," and not an unequivocally unique experience confined to one person or to one historical context. The intuition of an intense harmony, persuasion, peace, and ultimacy embodied in religious experience requires interpretation, but the experience itself is more fundamental and elemental than any interpretation which is proposed to understand it. This condition exists because the aesthetic experience of the Divine Reality is more fundamental than a rational analysis of the Divine Nature. Because of the interrelated character of beauty and truth, some interpretations of religious experience enhance the character of the experience itself and other interpretations diminish the character of the experience.

The uneven extension of human freedom and the broader interpretation of equality noted earlier have led to greater freedom of expression and freedom of religion in some part as the planet over the past several centuries. As a consequence, both cultural and religious pluralism are widespread in the modern epoch. In many states, the peace and harmony of the state are not explicitly associated with a particular body of religious beliefs or with particular cultural or artistic forms. Of course, underlying such shifts are the adoption of other more fundamental notions such as pluralism, liberty and tolerance, ideas which were widely associated with the Enlightenment.

As these observations suggest, the issue of human rights is ultimately centered in the political sphere of the human social order, for persons associated with the organizing center shape, administer and enforce the rules and regulations of justice which limit and guarantee human rights in a particular state. The following section of the essay focuses upon the political sphere and the role of th state in promoting and sustaining human rights in the various spheres of the human social order. The relations between states in the promotion of human rights is briefly considered in this context.

VI
The Political Sphere and Human Rights: Some Normative Considerations

Introduction

Actions by people in the political sphere are critical in the promotion of human rights, for people in the political sphere promulgate the rules and regulations of justice and enforce these rules and regulations.

In the modern world, the state is the central institution in the political sphere. Political leaders, who initiate and promote proposed rules and regulations of justice, are the central actors in this sphere. They are dependent for their authority on the implicit or explicit consent of the persons in the geographical territory in which the acknowledged political leaders possess, at the minimum, a legitimate monopoly on the use of physical coercion to enforce the claims of the state on its members.

The Dynamics-Form-Unification Triad

As noted earlier, power is the leading component in the political sphere, justice is the secondary component, and love is the tertiary component. Because these three factors are three in relation, derived from the dynamics-form-unification triad inherent in the becoming of an actual occasion and employed analogically to discern their embodiment in institutions in the several spheres of the human social order, all are present in each sphere of the social order. However, the priority of the components of the spheres varies. On the basis of empirical observations, priority may be established in each sphere.

In interpersonal relations, the form of the persons who are interacting may be taken most fully into account as persons. Love, entailing sensitive and empathetic responses to the needs of others, is secondary. Self-determination, involving an intimate relation between one's own aims and the aims of others in the primary group, is tertiary, and reciprocal power may be maximized in interpersonal relations. (Of course, for the same reasons that offer the promise of the richest and most wholesome human relations, in fact intimate primary group relations may be the source of the most gross and inhumane treatment.) In the status, ethnic, economic, and cultural spheres, the sequence is justice, power, and love, for defining characteristics are salient in identifying these groups. People participate in these groups and share the values inherent in the forms. From the human point of view, in the religious sphere the sequence is love, justice, and power. God's receptivity of that which the world offers it and God's evocation of the aim for harmony and intensity of feeling, the appropriation of forms and feelings, and their harmonization in the emerging subject constitute this sequence.

As noted earlier, because of the priority of power in the political sphere, analogies drawn from experience in the other spheres of the social order have only qualified value in the political sphere.

Self-Determination and the Quest for Human Rights

The quest for human rights entails the extension of self-determination consonant with the regulative principles of equality and order. It entails a reduction of tradition or custom as the basis for social organization and an increase in self-determination as a basis for social organization.

In order for these patterns to evolve, a society must incorporate some common cultural values. Substantial pluralism, tolerance, and freedom in forms of family organization, social and ethnic styles of life, and artistic and religious expression are natural concomitants of enhanced freedom of self-determination. Democracy is an inevitable concomitant of enhanced self-determination in the political sphere, but the particular form of democracy depends on a variety of circumstances. In large heterogeneous nation states, some form of representative democracy is most appropriate.[1] An economic system based on production and consumption patterns informed by supply-demand pricing mechanisms, and grounded in consumer preference is an inevitable concomitant in the economic sphere.

Because freedom is abused, equality appropriate to form and order in the life of a living community are regulative principles of justice, and custom and tradition limit all human actions, freedom is invariably qualified in one way or another. The uneven and unbalanced enhancement of human rights in the various nation-states now dominant in the world is a consequence of these varied developments.

Abuses of Freedom and the Limits on Self-Determination

Unfortunately, not all freedom is informed by excellence. The abuse of freedom, related to ignorance, sloth, lethargy, and inordinate self-interest, requires the state to limit some forms of self-determination. It is beyond the scope of this essay to explore the implications of this abuse in all the spheres of the social order, but the implications for the relations between institutions in the political sphere and the other spheres of the social order must be considered. Because humans both quest for the harmony of the community and also thwart the quest for both good and dubious reasons, the efforts to attain community are perennial and are never fully successful. In fact, sometimes utopianists seeking a harmonious community may help more cynical political realists thwart the quest for human rights.

The enhancement of human self-determination has evoked a plethora of voluntary associations in some human societies. They are a most important part of community life in the United States of America, in parts of Western Europe, and in parts of the world influenced by Great Britain. Various international professional societies constitute specialized forms of the voluntary associations. These groups are important, for they promote multiple centers of initiative in complex post-traditional societies. They contribute new and novel ideas and prevent the inordinate concentration of power in the hands of the politicians. Persons related to specialized voluntary associations have often been promoters of human rights. By their political efforts, they have often helped to embody human rights in rules and regulations of justice and to implement them in the life of a society and in the community of nation-states.

In very recent times, the increased globalization of the economic sphere and the dramatic improvements in communication are impacting the life of nation-states in profound ways. The long-term impact of these changes is difficult to discern. As the increase of ethnic self-conscious in recent decades indicates, these unifying forces are being countervailed by differentiating ones. The nature of the whole (relation of nation-state to nation-state) and the nature of the parts (ethnic groups within one or several nation-states) in the modern epoch is the most recent illustration of the perennial problem of the integration of parts into a viable whole.

Every nation-state risks balkanization, and responsible leaders must adopt public policies which minimize the risk.

Checks and Balances in the Social Order

The desirability of multiple centers of initiative in a living community and the need to prevent inordinate concentrations of power in the hands of representatives of the state both suggest the merit of a separation of institutions in the several spheres of the social order, a system of checks and balances, and a multiplicity of factions. The state must provide a framework for coordinating and promoting institutions in the several spheres of the social order, but it should not usurp the functions belonging to institutions in the other spheres of the social order. Indeed, the "common good" is best promoted if substantial self-determination is sustained in the familial, social, ethnic, economic, cultural, and religious spheres of the social order.

Although nineteenth-century English liberalism may have overstated the rights of the individual in relation to the community, those who stress inordinately the priority of the common good in social ethics understate the rights of the individual and overestimate the goodness of politicians. Considering the power of the community over the individual and the propensity of politicians to pursue their own self-interests inordinately, those who stress the freedom of the individual in relation to the community may be waging a losing battle. Nonetheless, in the quest for a fitting balance between the rights and duties of the individual in relation to the community, their contributions are very important.

The Role of the State in the Familial, Social, and Ethnic Spheres

The state should seek to promote a stable and harmonious family life consonant with the principle of self-determination. It is beyond the scope of this essay to discuss in detail the nature of the family. In the present context, only a very brief sketch can be advanced. In the main, the state should prefer to let men and women make their own decisions in this area, but the impact of these decisions on others requires the state to provide a stable framework in which humans make decisions. The cumulative wisdom of the race and the characteristics of human beings combine to suggest the normative desirability of monogamy, and the state should seek to support that form of family organization through the legal order.

However, the state *qua* state should be very wary of the extent of the limits it imposes on humans, granted its bias in favor of monogamy. Homosexuals and bisexuals should be free to experiment with alternative forms of family organization, but the state should be very wary about granting legal recognition to such relations.

Human freedom legitimates state support of substantial pluralism in the social and ethnic spheres. In practice, this support entails equality of legal treatment for person in various ethnic and status groups. At the same time, there are limits as to what the state can or should do to shelter people from the consequences of the status and/or ethnic values they hold. These limits in practice will be worked out in the life of a living community.

The problem becomes most acute in connection with persons associated with social and ethnic groups who reject the basic notions of liberty, tolerance, and pluralism. These notions, grounded in the Enlightenment and in nineteenth-century liberalism, are central to the constructive views being developed here. Persons associated with social and ethnic groups rejecting these basic notions cannot sustain a society supporting broad extensions of liberty and equality. One who supports the ideas developed here may be forced to support measures to restrain some activities of such persons. This situation illustrates the limits which a "liberal" state must impose on some people.

The Role of the State in the Economic Sphere

Because social necessity is at a higher level than biological necessity, in principle the state has the right to intervene in the economic sphere. In its interventions, the state must consider both the principle of equality and the impact of public policies on the growth and efficiency of the economic system. Some income redistribution within a human living community is almost always necessary to provide the youth, the handicapped, the old, and the inordinately poor with a minimal standard of living, at least according to existing community standards. In so doing, public policy should work with rather than against market forces whenever possible. Because of the importance of market incentives for the growth and efficiency of the economic system, substantial variation in wealth and income within a living community is warranted. What constitutes "substantial" will invariably become a matter of political disagreement. Used properly, the principle of equality can promote both the extension of liberty and the enhancement of opportunity. One must not forget, however, the tension at many levels between freedom and equality. In some instances the extension of freedom for some limits the freedom of others.

Capitalism as a form of economic organization has been severely criticized by some religious social ethicists informed by process modes of thought. Social market or democratic capitalism deserves more support than such persons give it, for democratic capitalism sustains both liberty and economic growth and efficiency.

Although the state may intervene in the economic sphere for the sake of equality, its intervention should be circumspect. However, distinctions between economic and political institutions should be maintained. Economic growth and efficiency are thereby promoted, and multiple centers of initiatives are thereby sustained. Private ownership of the modes of production limits the power of the state, and state regulation and taxation limit the power of private ownership. These issues are addressed in much greater length in Part Two of this volume.

The Role of the State in the Cultural and Religious Spheres

Human freedom is at a maximum in the cultural and religious spheres, for the free play of imagination is most salient in the cultural sphere and the persuasive aspects of experience are at the apex of religious experience. Consequently, freedom of expression and freedom of religion are precious human rights.

Because human expression is often uninformed by the quest for excellence and religious practices and beliefs are often much less than sublime, no community has or will grant its members unlimited freedom of expression or freedom of religion. As in the other spheres of the social order, the public policy bias should be in the direction of the greatest possible freedom of expression and freedom of religion. The limits will depend both on the general cultural conditions extant in a given society and also on the impact of certain modes of expression and particular religious beliefs and practices upon the members of that society.

Equality, the other regulative principle of justice, helps facilitate judgments about the limits which representatives of the organizing center of a state should impose on freedom of expression and freedom of religion. Because the denial of freedom of expression and freedom of religion is itself a limitation on the constitutive principle of justice, those persons who would deny substantial freedom of expression and freedom of religion are most suspect.

Even when it is quite clear to most people that limitations on freedom of expression and freedom of religion must be imposed on a minority because of the highly negative impact of these expressions or religious beliefs and/or practices on other human rights of their followers and/or members of the larger community, these restrictions are a most unfortunate necessity.

The Relations between States

The numerous nation-states now extant and the most limited shared symbols and histories between them preclude the possibility of greatly enhanced harmony of life with life between nation-states in the foreseeable future. The lure of the love of humankind as such, an analogical notion derived from human experiences of the Divine eros, may sustain humans in their quest for freedom, equality, and community among the peoples of the planet, but finitude, ignorance, sloth, lethargy, and inordinate individual and group self-interest will continue to thwart their visions. Rational egoistic theories of international relations are inadequate; they must be supplemented by visions of the enhanced harmony of life with life under the conditions of existence and of the value of the whole. Although humans may fail, the quest for such enhancement is evoked again and again by the Divine lure for harmony and intensity of feeling which is at the base of all creaturely experience.

The Religious Sphere and Human Rights

As discussed in Chapter 1, God is the locus of all potentiality, the lure for feeling, the mediator of experience from one creature to another, and the ultimate receptor of all that has become. In evoking creatures to become, God functions by persuasion. It seeks to promote harmony and intensity within and between the creatures of the world, and It receives them into Its life. It manifests a tender loving care in which the attainments of the creatures who have become are retained everlastingly in the Divine Life. (Whether the limits for harmony in the present imposed by the causal past constitute a coercive facet in the Divine Nature need not be addressed here.) Worship is the fitting human response to awareness of Divine Immanence in experience. It is the constitutive basis for religious institutions, which exist to facilitate human awareness of the Divine and to enhance peace and human rights in the world.

Because of the priority of love in the love-justice-power triad in the religious sphere, religious institutions should primarily bear witness and offer testimony to God's love for the world. God's love is persuasive and not coercive; God is supremely sensitive to the needs of emerging creatures and is supremely sensitive to that which they offer Its life. Religious institutions should encourage their participants to promote the human quest for peace and human rights through their participation in groups in other spheres of the social order. Because of the centrality of the political sphere for these concerns, much activity will focus on groups in this sphere.

In the blend of coercive and persuasive power embodied in human experience, religious institutions ought to be especially sensitive to persuasive power. Because of their symbolic role, leaders of religious institutions should be extremely wary about engaging in and promoting religious institutional involvement in direct military action, where coercion is dominant. They should also be wary of indirect involvement.

Power is the leading component in the political sphere, as noted earlier. Though the exercise of persuasive power is the preferable mode of power in this sphere, sometimes political leaders must initiate coercive power for the sake of both justice and love. This topic is addressed more fully in Chapter 9 and in passing in the chapters of Part Two.

VII
Primal Visions and Political Action for Human Rights

This essay has grounded human rights in a process framework, but the discussion has emphasized aspects of human experience that put this interpretation at odds with some process interpretations of religious social ethics. Assuming the metaphysical differences constitute a modest family quarrel, the primary reasons for the contrasts relate to differing emphases given to the components of human experience directly relevant to religious social ethics. Thus the lack of consensus on public policy issues results form contrasting judgments on a variety of other issues: the plasticity of human nature, the consequences of present actions for future occasions, the priority among the principles of justice, normative forms of human social organization, the persistence of inordinate self-interest among humankind, the limits of freedom and pluralism in the various spheres of the human social order, the bases of and limits to analogies drawn from basic human experience in the analysis of the various spheres of the human social order, the importance of growth and efficiency in economic institutions, the best means to attain economic growth and efficiency, the appropriate degree of social and economic differentiation in human societies, and/or the relative importance of forms to give guidance to moral decisions.

Some basic guidelines can be drawn. Because of the basic relational character of existence, both the individual and the community must be addressed in any process social ethic. Neither the individual nor the community can be given unqualified priority. Similarly, all three principles of justice must be considered in evaluating forms of social organization and particular public policy proposals. In countries in which democracy is functioning in a tolerably adequately manner and elemental human rights are respected, one may expect persons seeking social changes to work within the political framework. (As observed earlier, in some cases one may feel obligated to promote revolutionary groups seeking a radical change in the form of political organization extent in a given territory. Because of the danger of bloody conflicts in such situations, one must be very strongly convinced that efforts at peaceful change are out of the question before promoting revolution.) Persons whose basic metaphysical viewpoints are very similar may well come to different prudential judgments in such situations.

In those parts of the world in which participation in the existing political processes is a preferred option, people must relate to those groups they judge are most adequately pursuing politics designed to promote peace and human rights. They must apply some pragmatic tests for their political involvement and their associational relations, for there are several viable ways to pursue peace and human rights.

As a result of its historical destiny, voluntary associations have proliferated in the United States. Influenced by ideas rooted in the Enlightenment and the left wing of the Calvinist facet of the Protestant Reformation, and articulated persuasively in *The Federalist Papers*, voluntary associations are more pervasive than in any other part of the world. In this context, persons informed by process social ethics may participate with integrity in a plethora of such organizations. As noted, it is most unlikely that such people would associate with groups promoting unequivocally either the rights of the individual or the rights of the community. If one accentuates the community in relation to the individual, emphasizes the principles of equality, does not focus strongly on issues of growth and efficiency in the economic sphere, and is relatively sanguine about the concentration of power in the government, one will probably associate with relatively more "left-wing" groups. If one seeks a balance between the freedom of the individual and the authority of the community, emphasizes the principle of self-determination, desires to promote a proliferation of centers of power and initiative in the social order, and is concerned with growth and efficiency in the economic sphere, one will probably associate with relatively centrist or moderately "right-wing" groups. In some instances on certain issues, persons of both broad perspectives may participate in the same special interest groups.

In these involvements, one need not press for an explicit consensus among participants on the bases for one's views on the various principles and priorities informing one's own participation; a common effort to develop public policy broadly cohering with one's basic perspective is sufficient ground for one's involvement. The same pragmatic approach ought to apply to one's involvement in international bodies seeking to promote human rights.

Given the pluralism of special interest groups, one may well participate in several groups with somewhat contrasting emphases, for one cannot expect a perfect fit of one's own public policy concerns with those of any particular special interest group. The contingencies of life cannot be captured in predetermined forms.

The full harmonization of these contrasting emphases is beyond the capacity of mortals. Hopefully the persuasive aspects of human life may become more dominant in the future and human rights will be extended, but it seems most unlikely that all coercion can ever be eliminated, or that all human rights will be sustained. The ultimate harmonizer of the conflicts evoked by physical realization is the Divine Reality, Who transforms our conflicts into contrasts within a broader unity. God continually seeks richer and more harmonious experience for the creatures of the world and receives into Itself all which the world has to offer. These facts sustain the quest for human rights, earthly peace, and the harmony of the parts within a larger whole.

Notes and References

1. Today in the United States and in much of the rest of the world, Christian churches are staunch supporters of political democracy. It has not always been so. Historically, the relation between democracy and Christianity has been complex, sometimes conflictive, and often ambiguous. Church social teachings on political economy have both contributed to and been influenced by ideas prevalent in a given historical epoch. Broadly viewed, until the sixteenth and seventeenth centuries, Christianity supported monarchy or aristocracy. Slavery was presupposed in the ancient world, and Christians accepted slavery with minimal problems. Indeed, the slow drift from slavery to freedom took well over a millennium. Over three centuries before Christ, Plato advanced the view that the divine eros at the base of things evoked human freedom. However, it took almost 1,500 years for this idea to become embodied in the political structures of some living communities in the West. Even today, democratic ideals are very unevenly distributed throughout the planet.

The claims of the Catholic Church to wield not only spiritual but also absolute temporal power reached its apex in the bull *Unum Sanctum* of Pope Boniface VIII in 1302. It asserted kings and knights should wield the temporal sword "at the will and sufferance of the priest." Obviously, kings, knights, and others did not share this view. Since that epoch, the political power of the Papacy and the Catholic Church has generally been in decline.

Catholic social teachings held that slavery was morally acceptable from the time of St. Paul until well into the nineteenth century. While it was obligatory to treat slaves humanely and to permit them to marry, it was commendable but not obligatory to give them their freedom. Finally, in 1890 Pope Leo XIII condemned slavery. It was not until the Christmas message of 1944 that Pope Pius XII gave a full endorsement to liberal democracy, stating that such a form of government has the dignity of the person as "its subject, its foundation, and its end."

During the Reformation, the Protestant churches displayed similar patterns. Luther supported princely control of the quasifeudal political structure of his time. While abstractly expressing a preference for democracy, Calvin supported the monarchical form of political organization in the western European countries of his time. Only in the left wing of the Calvinist influenced Reformation did some people express democratic sentiments. While some groups, notably the Quakers, spoke out against slavery in the eighteenth century, the Protestant churches as a whole had a checkered record on the matter until well into the nineteenth century.

In addition to the Reformation, two other movements of thought and feeling shaped the development of the early modern period—the Renaissance (1300s-1600s) and the Enlightenment (1700s). Although the Renaissance focused people's attention on humans themselves and on the natural world and promoted art, music, and science, it did not contribute directly to the movement toward popular democracy. The Enlightenment ideas about human rights, individualism, the free use of reason, and historical progress motivated the leaders of both the French and American revolutions. (The American values of religious liberty, religious tolerance, religious pluralism, and church-state separation are grounded in Enlightenment ideas, complemented by some Quaker and Baptist contributions.)

In the American context, Enlightenment democratic ideas were fused with the Christian idea of human sinfulness to develop a constitution shaping a representative form of democracy replete with many checks and balances. The congregational form of church organization (self-governance by local congregations) associated with groups such as the Baptists, the Quakers, and the Congregationalists indirectly promoted the idea of self-government in the political sphere and fostered the proliferation of voluntary associations contributing to democratic processes.

Once democratic values became widespread in the American culture, almost all the churches espoused them. By the latter part of the nineteenth century, values supporting democracy and church-state separation were overwhelmingly dominant in the United States. Lest one think these ideas became dominant overnight, one should note that the last state to disestablish a church was Massachusetts. In 1833 the Congregational churches (which some wrongly think were early champions of religious liberty) were disestablished, and the American religious experiment was fully launched. The struggle to enter completely into this experiment persists to this day.

PART TWO

On Political Economy

Introduction to Part Two

The five chapters in Part Two all address issues in what was classically called political economy, dealing with the interrelation of political and economic institutions. In the modern epoch political science departments have maintained more explicit interest in philosophical matters than have economic departments. The emergence of so-called higher economics, emphasizing mathematical model building, has led many economists to disparage explicit attention to philosophical or theological issues. In fact, economists frequently use the term "theological" to indicate great disgust at what they think are dogmatic viewpoints. Because political philosophy was historically embodied in the great universities of the Middle Ages and the early modern period, political philosophers have persistently been members of political science faculties. In fact, substantial tension frequently exists between those in these departments who have explicit philosophical interests and those who focus on "empirical" studies.

These chapters explore the shape of a process-informed political science, consider the problems that unity and diversity pose for life on this planet, and address the issue of a desirable form of political economy. I hold that democratic capitalism is the most desirable form of political economy in our historical epoch and in the foreseeable future. Although this view is clearly the dominant one in much of the world at the present time, there was much more controversy about this matter in the 1970s and 1980s when these essays were developed. My own social location within the Christian movement helped shape some of the issues addressed in these essays, for many Christian social ethicists still express a preference for democratic socialism. Many of them prefer much greater and more direct government involvement in the economic sphere than I am prepared to support. In addition, the appeal of neo-Marxist modes of social analysis and socialism in that school of thought that has come to be called "Liberation Theology" was and is widespread in some theological circles.

The polemical passages in Chapters 6, 7, and 8 were evoked by my rejection of these modes of thought and of social analysis and my development of an alternative interpretation. I became increasingly persuaded of the desirability of that form of political economy which Michael Novak and others have called democratic capitalism. The bases for this conviction are elaborated most fully in Chapter 6 and are set in opposition to alternatives in Chapters 7 and 8. (Chapter 18 centers on my critique of one form of liberation theology. The interested reader may want to examine that chapter in relation to some of the issues raised in the essays in Part Two.)

These chapters were written in the aftermath of the Vietnam War and the 1960s civil rights movement. While critical of the Vietnam War and sympathetic to the Civil Rights Movement, I did not share the radical critique of American society popular among many of my colleagues in religious social ethics. Consequently, the themes of both conservation and innovation appear in all these essays.

Chapter 4, "Structure and Context in Process Political Theory: A Constructive Formulation," expands the discussions of the political sphere which were developed in Chapters 2 and 3. It incorporates metaphysical propositions with propositions pertaining to human beings to elaborate the shape of my political theory. Chapter 5, "Unity and Diversity among Humans: A Framework for Interpretation," explores this problem and suggests that the resolution of the disharmony excessive diversity poses—insofar as it can be resolved—centers on actions that politicians must initiate.

Chapter 6, "Political Economy: A Process Interpretation," elaborates the bases for my preference for democratic capitalism in this historical epoch and in the foreseeable future. It draws especially on ideas developed in Chapter 3 to argue that democratic capitalism represents the form of political economy most able to promote basic human rights and peace. Chapter 7, "American Democratic Capitalism: A Sympathetic Appraisal," a more compact formulation of this viewpoint, sets my defense of democratic capitalism in the context of discussions within the Christian movement. Chapter 8, "The Socialist/Communitarian Vision: New Dream or Old Nightmare?" is a critical and polemical response to an essay promoting a socialist/communitarian vision.

Introduction to Chapter 4

This chapter is based on a paper presented at the 1975 annual meeting of the American Academy of Religion. It was part of a session on the theme "Process Philosophy and the Social Sciences," the first session held on the topic at a learned society meeting.

The chapter draws on notions developed in Chapters 2 and 3 to elaborate a political theory shaped by process theory and the facts of political life, discusses the sources of the experience of an "isness-oughtness" contrast and the implications of this contrast for the political sphere, highlights the relation of dynamic, formal, and unifying components in the political sphere developed in Part One, utilizes the principles of justice as criteria to guide public policy formation, and affirms the normative value of a democratic form of political organization. It concludes with a brief discussion of the level of human fulfillment to be expected in and through politics. This issue is explored more fully in Chapter 9.

CHAPTER 4

Structure and Context in Process Political Theory: A Constructive Formulation

Introduction

The development of human social theory in a process mode of thought requires a blending of metaphysical propositions and propositions applying to particular actual occasions or societies of actual occasions, i.e., human beings in human societies.

Metaphysical propositions apply to all actual occasions. Consequently, the matrix of propositions making up a process social theory should be consistent with the matrix of propositions believed to be metaphysical (or, at least applicable to a very wide range of actual occasions) and should also be applicable to the more limited range of actual occasions constituting human beings and to societies of human beings. An adequate social theory should both describe and analyze and also prescribe, for fact and value are intertwined in process thought.[1]

Just as the development of metaphysical propositions has a rational side and an empirical side, so the development of propositions comprising human social theory has a rational side and an empirical side. Metaphysical propositions and propositions relating to human societies differ in the emphases given to the two sides. Because of the contingent character of the subject matter of human social theory, empirical observations are more salient in its formulation, for the social theorist is seeking to delineate those special characteristics of human beings which must be considered in the development of an adequate and applicable social theory.

The questions "How much?", "What is distinctive?" and "In what degree?" are of critical importance in distinguishing issues in human social theory from issues in metaphysics. For instance, the proposition that "The concrescence of each individual actual entity is internally determined and is externally free" is purportedly a metaphysical proposition, applying to all actual entities.[2] The question of the degree of novelty, purposiveness, and intentionality embodied in a particular individual actual entity is an empirical question, requiring some attention to the characteristics of individual actual entities.

Fortunately, our own experience can provide an empirical basis for a consideration of the defining characteristics of human beings and our relations to other humans. These characteristics must by taken into account in the formulation of a process human social theory.

This essay focuses on a consideration of the political sphere of human life, which is the subject matter of political science. It seeks to characterize the nature of the political sphere, to explore the implications of the "isness-oughtness" contrast for the political sphere, to delineate the relation of dynamic, formal, and unifying components in the political sphere, to elaborate principles of justice which can provide guidance to leaders formulating public policy, and to suggest a normative form of political organization. In this discussion the bases for conflict and the grounding of morality are considered.

THE POLITICAL SPHERE IN HUMAN SOCIETIES

According to the principal of relativity, one of the basic notions of process thought, every being is a potential for every becoming. In other words, every creature that has become, i.e., has completed its process of becoming, is a datum for every creature that is yet to emerge.[3]

In the initial phase of its emergence, a creature appropriates data from its settled past. In the supplemental phase of its becoming, an emerging subject synthesizes the data appropriated from its causal past and from the primordial facet of God's nature. After it has completed its becoming, this subject becomes an object for the creatures which succeed it. Thus, the becoming of creatures begins with a public side, emerges in private, and then again becomes public. In this way, every creature is both a subject and an object.

In this basic rhythm, life is both social and private, involving participation and individuation. The principle of relativity expresses the inextricably social character of existence.

The degree of importance of other creatures for an emerging creature may range from a very high degree to a very low degree. In human life, the Divine, the creatures in one's body, and persons in primary relationships—the family and intimate friends—contribute very greatly to the life of emerging human subjects. A graded relevance of persons in other spheres of the social order and of non-human entities is apparent.

A human being incorporates an extraordinarily large number of societies, organized and co-ordinated to provide a wide range of data to a regnant center, one's conscious self. The sequence of ultimate percipient occasions constituting this regnant center is partly dependent on the body, partly directive for the body, and partly independent of the body. The regnant center possesses substantial rational capacity and is able to exercise negative judgments, imaginatively envisaging the absence of that which is present or the presence of that which is absent. The negative judgment, which is the peak of consciousness, is more fully developed in humans than in any other creatures of which we currently have direct knowledge.

Although the causal past, constituting the destiny dimension of human experience, always influences the present, humans possess substantial capacities to surpass the causal past in the present and to interject novel elements into the world. Purposiveness and intentionality loom too large in human experience to be interpreted epiphenomenally.[4]

The form dimension of human experience is grounded in the objectification in an emerging creature of forms of definiteness embodied in creatures in the causal past and in the primordial facet of God's nature. The dynamic dimension of human experience is grounded in the emerging synthesis of feelings and forms in the developing subject. The unifying dimension of human experience is grounded in the harmonious togetherness of forms and feelings in the centered creature who becomes.

Human beings find themselves enmeshed in complex networks of relations with other humans. These networks include relations in familial, social, ethnic, economic, political, cultural, and religious spheres.[5] In some societies, the degree of differentiation of the several spheres is minimal. In others, the degree of differentiation of the several spheres is moderate, and in others very substantial.[6]

The more complex the society, the greater the degree of differentiation of the spheres. A good human society is one in which the parts are unified in a harmonious whole, a whole which retains some regard for the uniqueness and novelty of its component parts and embodies the principles of justice to be characterized later in this essay in fitting rules and regulations of justice.

The members of a society require an organizing center to co-ordinate and to harmonize the component parts. Social necessity—the fact that a substantial number of human beings find themselves occupying a particular geographical area and sharing a common history of shared feeling and meaning—and human rational capacities—the ability to devise structures of governance and to discern principles and rules and regulations of justice—combine to produce a political sphere characterized by political leaders and a structure of government acting for and on behalf of the members of the group.[7]

The classical one-some-all triad may be used to delineate rule by one, some, or all. The further classical distinction between a good ruler, concerned with the common good, and a bad ruler, concerned with the ruler's own good, may be used to develop the familiar six-fold characterization of forms of governments. The good forms are monarchy, aristocracy, and democracy; the bad forms are tyranny, oligarchy, and anarchy. The complexity of political life and the persistence of inordinate self-interest among humans suggest all leaders act from complex motives, leading to a "mixed" category.

The complexity of many contemporary large nation-states limits the usefulness of this classificatory typology, but it does point toward some authentic differences between types of governments and between the general orientations of political leaders.

THE IMPLICATIONS OF THE ISNESS-OUGHTNESS CONTRAST IN HUMAN EXPERIENCE FOR THE POLITICAL SPHERE

The contrast between the human experience of an ultimate harmony of harmonies, an ultimate peace of peaces, and an ultimate perfection, and the human experience of great disharmony, great disorder, and substantial imperfection is reflected in common human experience and in the literature of the race. The Christian doctrine of original sin, the Stoic doctrine of a Golden Age before a fall, the Platonic doctrine of the Good, and the Marxist vision of the enhanced harmony of life with life following the reorganization of the economic sphere bear witness to the pervasiveness of the human experience of an "isness-oughtness" contrast.

From my process perspective, the experience of a perfect harmony is engendered by a particularly intense awareness of God's subjective aim, its envisagement and ordering of the forms of definiteness. Because this facet of the Divine Life encompasses potentiality, it is an error to think that a "perfect harmony" can be actualized, for actualization inevitably requires some limitations and a sense of an "isness" involving some disharmony and some sense of contrast with an "oughtness" which cannot be. Thus, finitude, imposing a limitation of all which might be in favor of something which is, is one ground for the "isness-oughtness" contrast, for humans participate in both the boundlessness of potentiality and the particularity of actuality. In addition, actualization embodied in the past may limit the possibilities of the present and the foreseeable future.

The limitations which finitude imposes on creatures are not the only grounds for the "isness-oughtness" contrast. Ignorance, sloth, lethargy and inordinate self-interest also contribute to this contrast.

An emerging creature appropriating entities in its causal past does not fully objectify them. As our own experience indicates, objectification entails loss. We appropriate portions of the past, but we are not fully aware of what our predecessors have become and might contribute to their successors. Consequently, the decisions we make in the present are done without the full knowledge of the implications of the past for ourselves and our contemporaries. This ignorance makes impossible a response to a context which can most fully enhance the harmony of that situation. Approximations are possible, but the haunting feeling that a more adequate response might have been made contributes to awareness of an "isness-oughtness" contrast.

Ignorance contributes to this contrast in another way. An emerging creature is not fully aware of the way in which its contemporaries are going to shape and to integrate the data they receive from their causal pasts. The freedom of contemporaries to respond novelly to the data they appropriate may contribute to a lack of harmony in the future. Disharmony in the present is often the price that must be paid for novelty and for the possibilities of richer and/or more complex harmonies in the future.

Sloth, lethargy, and inordinate self-interest accentuate human frailties contributing to the "isness-oughtness" contrast. Laziness and indolence are persistent phenomena among human beings. While the hyper-activism of the profesional do-gooder may well cause more disharmony than harmony in the life of a society, the unresponsive reproduction of the causal past in the emerging present is not likely to accentuate the harmonious intensity of experience in the present.

The persistence of the doctrine of original sin in Christian theology cannot be readily dismissed. The process perspective being advanced here does not accept the cosmology and the view of God-world relations informing various classical views of the doctrine. However, evidence that humans and collectivities of humans pursue their own self interest inordinately is very pervasive in human affairs. This propensity, coupled with the universality of the experience of the "isness-oughtness" contrast, is the basis on which this process perspective interprets the attraction and persistence of this classical Christian doctrine.

If political theory is to relate adequately to the realities of political life, it must take persistent self-interest into account. Power, understood as the ability to actualize one's own will, individual or collective, in conflict with other wills, is not the whole story in political life, but it is an important part of the story.[8] The interplay between self-interest and the common good is a manifestation of the "isness-oughtness" contrast in the body politic and of the contrast between individuation and participation.

THE IMPLICATIONS OF THE PRIORITY OF POWER IN THE POWER-JUSTICE-LOVE TRIAD IN THE POLITICAL SPHERE

In the emergence of a new creature, feelings and forms are unified in a dynamic process of becoming. A creature begins to become by appropriating forms of definiteness embodied in creatures in its causal past. As the creature synthesizes these forms and its feelings of them into a novel unity, it appropriates forms of definiteness from the primordial facet of the Divine nature. This process is guided by the creature's subjective aim, initially derived from but not determined by the Divine subjective aim.

Dynamic, unifying, and formal dimensions are thus enmeshed in the emergence of creatures. These dimensions are three-in-relation, so they cannot be isolated from each other. Nonetheless, it is possible to discern by empirical observation which of these components is salient in the several spheres of the social order. In this way, the predominant character of the several spheres may be characterized.

The form dimension of experience may be translated to justice in human life, the dynamic dimension to power, and the unifying dimension to love, Justice, power and love become a basic trinity embedded in the nature of human experience. Power is the leading component in the power-justice-love triad in the political sphere; justice is the secondary component; and love is the tertiary component.

Politicians live in a house of power. Through the exercise of power, they have to formulate the rules and regulations that guide and shape the lives of the members of a particular society and to define the relations prevailing in other spheres of the social order. In this manner, they seek to attain a degree of peace and harmony.

The interrelatedness of power, justice and love, the hierarchical ordering of human society, the reciprocal nature of relationships, and the shape of Divine-world relations serve to illumine the nature of power.

Power needs a fitting form to enhance harmony and intensity of feeling in human life. Naked power, the use of unmitigated coercion to enforce the will of the ruler, may sustain the ruler on the short run, but unless it is informed by the form of justice and by the persuasive aspect of love, the wielders of naked power cannot sustain their leadership on the longer run. Without the form of justice and the lure of love, political leaders will lose their power. If the state is to remain viable, the members of a state must share and affirm its common history.

In this way, authentic power is reciprocal power. The politicians exercising power respond to the needs and interests of the citizens in shaping the rules and regulations of justice, and the citizens exercising power respond to the values and interests embodied in the political leaders.

There are limits to reciprocal power, and these limits are embodied in nature, which has hierarchical tendencies. The human organism itself is organized hierarchically and has an organizing regnant center which is a deliberative responsive conscious entity capable of exercising negative judgments. If it is treated like an unresponsive "thing," its fundamental character is violated.

Hence, although one may analogically refer to the organizing center of a social group, the analogy between the relation of the parts of the human body to its organizing center and the individual to the state must be qualified. An individual is not a member of the state in the way the hand is a member of the body. A human is a member of multiple communities including the state, but a human is not merely a member of a state. The individual has a right to pursue a variety of interests and relationships, some of which are independent of the state; for one possesses an organizing center not fully included in any of its relations, including the state. Indeed, something akin to this relation exists between the sequence of events constituting the human organizing center and the myriad of events and sub-societies encompassed in the human body.

At the same time the hierarchical patterning of societies precludes egalitarianism and equal participation by all in the affairs of the state. Every state must have a relatively small group of leaders who often act on behalf of its members.

This centeredness is especially evident in periods of crisis. In recent American history, the Cuban missile crisis and the infamous Gulf of Tonkin "crisis" illustrate the way in which a small group of leaders act on behalf of a country in time of emergency.

The saliency of self-interest and of "one-way" power relations is especially evident in international affairs, for humans share relatively few common universal loci of feeling and meaning. In the foreseeable future, this situation will likely continue to prevail. Mutual self-interest and balance of power patterns are the guiding components contributing to international tranquility. A magistrate ignoring this reality will not remain in office for long, but such a magistrate would be most unlikely to be selected in the first place.[9]

Social necessity and human rational shaping capacities interplay in the civil community. This interplay is illustrated by the use of technical reason and the elaboration of bureaucracies to govern human societies, by the development rules and regulations of justice to coordinate relations between members and social institutions in the state, and by the emergence of forms of meaning and feeling in which members of a particular society participate.

Order, peace, and harmony consonant with liberty and equality are the aims of the civil community. Through the use of persuasive and coercive power and through the use of reason, leaders of the state seek to coordinate, harmonize and unify its component parts.

All civil communities confront two dangers. The first is the excessive differentiation and self-determination of the parts, leading to anarchy. The second is excessive centering and suppression of the parts, leading to tyranny. Both extremes need to be avoided, and an adequate political theory needs to consider forms of political organization which will minimize both of these undesirable polar opposites.

In the process perspective, as persons interact, they mutually affect one another. In the political sphere, this reciprocity of power is manifest in the interactions between political leaders and the citizens.

Power is not "one-way" or linear in any state, but the reciprocity that exists in intergroup relations in the state is not an equal reciprocity. No direct analogy between interpersonal and intergroup relations can be drawn, for the sequence of priority of power, justice, and love is different in intergroup than in interpersonal relations. The form of the person may be taken more fully into account in interpersonal than in intergroup relations, and the sequence of priority in interpersonal relations in justice, power, and love.

Because of the hierarchical ordering of nature and of human life just noted, rulers necessarily have more power and greater influence than individual citizens. Further, a state must maintain a monopoly on the legitimate use of physical power, i.e., police and military power, for a state to remain viable. In this circumstance, organizations of citizens and a variety of checks and balances to constrain the coercive power of the state are needed. At the same time, persons not seeking an overthrow of an existing government must acknowledge the legitimacy of its monopoly on the use of force.

Persuasion and coercion interplay in any human community.[10] In a good society, the majority of the citizens will be lured into coordinating their activities to harmonize the whole. However, coercion cannot be eliminated. The relatively infrequent use of police power to enforce laws can mask the deterrent power of the threat of coercion. The inevitability of finitude and ignorance, the persistence of sloth, lethargy and inordinate self-interest among human beings, and the capacity of humans to surpass substantially their causal pasts preclude the existence of a human society without some coercion.

The primordial facet of the Divine Agency functions in the world by persuasion. God's supreme rationality, manifest in Its once-for-all envisagement of all the forms of definiteness, seeks to evoke harmony and intensity of feeling within and among the creatures of the world that are becoming.

God's persuasive agency is, however, limited by the conditions of existence. The persistence of particular forms of definiteness, embodied in creatures in the causal past, and the clash of diverse interests in the present impose limits on the possible and exert coercive power upon the present. Because these creatures and the forms they embody are objectified in the consequent facet of God's nature, God also has coercive as well as suasive dimensions.

These limitations may range from the actualization of particular families of straight lines in this cosmic epoch limiting inexorably the physical side of creatures participating in them to the actualization of particular forms of social, economic or political organization in a particular society limiting the range of possibilities available in the present and in the near to intermediate future.[11]

Because of the freedom of creatures, which includes the capacity to act in ways violating others, and the limits the past imposes on the present, human agents must exercise some coercive power. In some instances, humans must use force to protect human persons and human societies from predators, both human and sub-human. Universal pacificism is not possible in the present cosmic epoch, but persuasion is always to be preferred over coercion in resolving interpersonal and intergroup conflicts.

PRINCIPLES OF JUSTICE AND THE POLITICAL SPHERE

As noted in the preceding section, leaders in the political sphere must promulgate rules and regulations of justice to guide and to shape life in the civil community. If these rules and regulations are to enhance human life, the principles of justice must inform them.

There are three principles of justice discoverable in experience. These principles, analogs of principles advanced in classical natural law theory, are equality appropriate to form, self-determination informed by excellence, and order, peace or harmony.[12]

These three principles are derived from the form-dynamics-unification triad inherent in the nature of things. Equality is grounded in an implicit recognition of an "oddness-evenness" contrast and the intuition of the principle of congruence.[13]

Equality without qualification cannot serve as a principle of justice, for the principle can be applied only to creatures possessing similar defining characteristics. For this reason, the phrase "appropriate to form" is added to the term "equality".

Among humans, the forms qualifying equality have included ascribed characteristics, such as age, sex, and ethnicity, and achieved characteristics, such as social status, education and occupation. Because the extent to which these forms should qualify the principle of equality is not unequivocally clear, there is a continued debate about the limits particular forms should place on humans.[14]

Self-determination (or freedom) informed by excellence is grounded in the experience of purposiveness and intentionality associated with the becoming of the ultimate percipient occasions constituting our conscious selves.[15] The human capacity for novelty of response to shifting contexts underscores the significance of self-determination.

As human beings become, the Divine subjective aim seeks to evoke in them a harmonious and intense unification of feelings and forms. For this reason, the phrase "informed by excellence" is added to the term "self-determination" in the formulation of this principle of justice.[16]

Equality appropriate to form and self-determination informed by excellence are not perfectly harmonizable. The equivocalness of appropriate forms, the widespread manifestations of self-determination lacking excellence, and the multiple and contextual character of "perfection"—understood as the maximization of harmony and intensity of feeling in a particular situation—preclude the perfect ordering of equality and self-determination in a particular context.

Order, peace, or harmony is grounded in the experience of the unification of the dynamic and formal facets of experience and in the human experience of the Divine subjective aim. It is the third principle of justice, for equality and self-determination must be co-ordinated. In some situations, order may be as important a principle of justice as equality or self-determination.

The difficulties involved in co-ordinating these three principles of justice, all of which are necessary but not perfectly harmonizable, are great. Different historical epochs and different societies in the same historical epoch have blended the principles in different ways.

In most complex traditional societies, a hierarchical ordering in which the forms qualifying equality are salient has been predominant. Only in segments of the Occident in relatively recent times have both comparatively more egalitarian and more self-determining societies emerged.

Individuation has been accentuated in these liberal Western societies and the community's influence on its citizens has been restricted.[17] The zenith of this movement has probably been reached, and the citizenry of these nations will most likely be subject to increased restriction of their activities in the coming decades.

The principles of justice must be embodied in the rules and regulations of justice applicable in a given society in a given historical epoch. In turn, the rules and regulations must be formulated and applied in a given situation. The implementation of the rules and regulations of justice requires legislative, executive, and judiciary functions. In practice, these functions may be differentiated, or they may be undertaken by the same person or persons.

The form-dynamics-unification triad is exhibited in the progressive levels of concreteness leading to the application of particular rules and regulations of justice in a particular context. First, the principles of justice (form) must be translated (dynamics) into rules and regulations of justice (unification). The rules and regulations of justice (form) must in turn be applied (dynamics) to a particular situation (unification). The equivocalness inherent in the principles of justice are accentuated both at the level of the formulation of the rules and regulations of justice and also at the level of the application of the rules and regulations of justice to a particular situation.

Because of this equivocalness, the age old complaint that laws are not adequate to the situation is a partial truth. Without creative reformulations and surpassments of old laws, the law becomes an oppressive element in society. Because of the ontological priority of creativity, laws are always becoming outmoded; because of the necessity for the inclusion of forms in every occasion, laws contribute in an ambivalently positive way to human life. A society without some laws would be chaotic, but there is no such society. Creative and transforming justice surpasses old laws for the sake of justice.

The necessary embodiment of forms in emerging creatures gives rise to a principal facet of morality. The dynamic bias inherent in the nature of things gives rise to a contextual facet of morality. A large part of morality concerns the implications of present actions for the future. The discernment of these implications requires some understanding of cause and effect relations and some assessment of the probable consequences of present action for the future.[18]

Morality has both formal and volitional dimensions. The formal dimension provides guidance for but does not determine the volitional dimension. Progress is possible in morality; for the development of more adequate forms of social organization, enhancing the harmony of our lives together and consonant with the defining characteristics of human beings and with the principles of justice, can accentuate the harmony of our lives together. Perfection in morality is impossible, for finitude, ignorance sloth, lethargy and the persistence of inordinate self-interest preclude a fully adequate human response to any situation.

The following section delineates the normative form of political organization for human beings. This form most adequately takes account of the factors associated with human experience and human nature discussed in this and the preceding sections.[19]

A FEDERATED FORM OF DEMOCRACY: THE NORMATIVE FORM OF POLITICAL ORGANIZATION

The human quest for harmony and intensity of feeling is enhanced by fitting forms and attenuated by inappropriate forms. In human life, those forms of social organization most consonant with the defining characteristics of human beings and most able to promote the actualization of the principles of justice should be elaborated.

Although these forms may not be seasonally relevant in many parts of the planet, they offer a lure which may encourage their actualization in the future. In those portions of the globe in which they are partially actualized, desirable forms of social organization should be supported and improved.

Because forms are an integral element of moral behavior, a vision of normative forms of social organization to guide and to enhance moral action is needed. A given context may preclude their near-term actualization, and less desirable forms of social organization may be the best that can be actualized. In this manner, the contextual side of morality must be considered in any human action; for, as noted earlier, morality involves contexts as well as general forms and general principles.

In the development of the normative form of political organization, the principles of justice, the power-justice-love sequence of priority in intergroup relations, the hierarchical ordering of nature, the bases for the persistence of disharmony in human life (finitude, ignorance, sloth, lethargy and inordinate self-interest) and the isness-oughtness contrast must be taken into account conjointly.

As observed earlier, the first two principles of justice, equality appropriate to form and self-determination informed by excellence, are not perfectly harmonizable. No consensus about the forms which legitimately qualify equality exists. Self-determination leads to inequalities, and equality limits self-determination. This situation creates disorder and disharmony, contrasting with order and harmony, the third principle of justice.

In human societies, representatives of the organizing center of a society must seek to order or harmonize these partially contradictory principles in fitting rules and regulations of justice. As noted earlier, both suasive and coercive power are involved in this process. Persuasion is more desirable than coercion, for persuasive power involves greater reciprocity and more mutual participation than coercive power. Therefore, structures of government that promote relatively free discussions of issues, encourage the participation of their members in decision making processes, and seek to develop a consensus on foundational issues and to sustain an acknowledgment of the legitimacy of the rules and regulations of justice on most other issues are desirable.

Some form of democracy is most likely to foster this process of participation and consensus formation, for democracy maximizes the number of citizens involved in the governmental process. Competing and sometimes conflictual individuals and groups seek to advance their views on issues of public policy and seek to establish particular rules and regulations of justice. Political leaders, representing the apparatus of government, seek to harmonize and to coordinate the multiplicity of interests represented by the various component parts of the society.

As observed in the discussion of the sequence of priority in the power-justice-love triad in the political sphere, power is salient in this process. Various individuals and groups seek to attain their wills in partial conflict with other wills. In a healthy democratic society various groups internalize unifying components of meaning and feeling embodied in the society with sufficient intensity to surpass their particular interests. They are willing to make some individual or interest group sacrifices for the common good.[20]

The ambivalence of the term "the common good" reflects the perennial contrasts between the individual and the community. Self-interest may be qualified and modified by one's identification of one's self interest with the common good, but self-interest cannot be eliminated. At the metaphysical level, the necessity to become *some* thing requires some self-interest. The priority of feeling in the becoming of a creature requires the emerging creature to pay some attention to its causal past and its immediate sustaining environment as it becomes. The enhanced capacity of human beings to surpass the causal past and to envisage a larger whole may permit them to minimize self-interest in some contexts, but self-interest is always a factor in human social relations.

These capacities increase the possibilities for broader extensions of community among humans. Conversely, they also increase the possibilities for inordinate concern with one's self-interest. This commingling of self-interest and concern for larger wholes poses both vexing problems and promising opportunities for political leaders. Because the state can be oppressive and because novelty is often suppressed, the individual also needs some protection from the "common good."[21]

The separation of executive, legislative, and judicial powers in the organizing center of the society, the development of a multiplicity of initiating centers, and the necessity for public officials to be accountable to an electorate who may remove them all deter inordinate self-interest, provide some enhancement of the vision of the welfare of the broader community, and offer to the individual some protection from the community.[22]

The persistence of the factors contributing to the disharmony of human life and the emergence of the new and the novel in human life suggest the desirability of democracy, for this form of political organization is most capable of dealing with both factors. Even in a well-functioning democracy, the state must have the resources to restrain those illegitimately challenging its authority, including a monopoly on the legitimate use of physical force. At the same time, multiple review bodies to minimize abuses of the state's awesome power are desirable.

The "isness-oughtness" contrast discussed earlier contributes to the emergence of zealots of the left and of the right who envisage the possibility of a greatly enhanced if not perfect harmony of life with life under the conditions of existence through some changes in cultural and/or religious values and/or in forms of social organization. Grasped by an experience of the intense harmony embodied in the primordial facet of God's nature, confusing potentiality with actuality, and often envisaging a single mode of perfection, such zealots frequently challenge the principle of order institutionalized in an established government and existing forms of social organization in the name of greater equality, greater self-determination or both.[23]

Sometimes an authentic revolution, involving the radical transformation of established values and institutions and the violent overthrow of an existing government, may be necessary for the attainment of greater justice and a richer and more harmonious society in the longer run.

However, there has never been an authentic revolution without widespread bloodshed and many casualties, and the likelihood of a bloodless one in the foreseeable future seems remote. Because of the dangers involved in radical transformation, innovation in the context of conservation is generally preferable to an authentic revolution.

The pure conservative is fighting the universe and cannot win. The radical revolutionary seeks to run roughshod over history, customs, and established social institutions, and he or she will not attain the "perfection" he or she desires. The radical revolutionary often does not adequately appreciate the fragile character of "order" and its ambivalently positive contribution to the body politic.

Democracy provides the best political framework to sustain both conservation and innovation in the body politic. The "form of democracy" should be conserved and enhanced; but, as circumstances change, the proximate solutions to social, ethnic, economic, political, cultural, and religious problems forged in the decision-making process should always be open to possible revision.

In formulating the most fitting form of democracy, the hierarchical ordering of nature and the necessity for some centering of authority in human decision making discussed earlier must be taken into account. At the same time, the need for checks and balances to blunt the darker side of human nature occasioned by sloth, lethargy and inordinate self-interest must also be considered.

The separation of powers between law-giving, law-enforcing, and judiciary bodies noted earlier provides checks and balances between various components of government. Although the system cannot prevent governmental office holders from sometimes acting from inordinate self-interest and from a centering of authority in times of crisis, it is better than the alternative, i.e., the concentration of law-giving, law-enforcing, and judiciary functions in the hands of one or a few persons.

Not all persons have the intellectual gifts, the personal inclinations, or the necessary information to consider complex public policy issues and to enact legislation to deal with them. Smaller bodies should be delegated responsibility for detailed legislative activities.[24]

While the citizenry should have a voice in the direction of public policy through the election of officials whose views are matters of general knowledge, the more specific directives involved in the implementation of public policy should be left to more elite bodies. Within the legislative branch itself, a more popular body and a more elitist body may be desirable, for their interaction may facilitate the proper harmonization of conservation and innovation.

In sum, a federated form of democracy, in which the electorate, the legislators, the judges, and the executives have appropriate functions to perform, is a more desirable form of democracy than pure democracy, for this form takes the nature of human nature more adequately into account.

Democracy is not a political possibility at the present time in many parts of the planet. The sentiments and feelings sustaining democracy have historical roots, and these ideals have not been embodied in all civilizations. Democracy requires a relatively well-educated citizenry to function effectively; such citizenries are not present in many contemporary societies.

One must exercise judgments to discern whether democracy is possible in a particular society. If the rule is by the one or by the some, leaders should seek the common good rather than their own good. In any case, those who are persuaded that democracy is the best possible form of political organization in human societies should seek to promote it in fitting ways in those portions of the planet where it is absent and to foster it in those portions of the planet where it is embodied.

The presence of democratic nation states does not guarantee international tranquility. As noted earlier, power is the leading component in the power, justice, love triad in the political area. Because there are so few meaning-embodying forms informing humankind in the political sphere, coercive power and self-interest loom especially large in international affairs.

These components seem likely to be salient in the foreseeable future. Mutual self-interest and balance of power strategies are likely to continue to dominate international relations.

HUMAN FULFILLMENT BEYOND THE POLITICAL SPHERE

The inevitability of conflict and disharmony in the political sphere leads to the question of the locus of potentially greater harmony in human life. Such human fulfillment will be found in those spheres of the social order in which justice or love is the leading component, i.e., in interpersonal relations in the family and small primary groups and in the religious sphere.

In interpersonal relations, the form of the person may be taken into greater account than in intergroup relations. In the religious sphere, humans may become aware of the Divine Presence in human life and may be lured to sense the way in which the conflict and turmoil of the world is received and transformed in the consequent facet of the Divine Nature.

The recognition of the possibilities and the limits of the contribution of institutions in the political sphere to human life can prevent one from expecting too much or too little from political institutions. Political activity can contribute to the enhancement of human life, and it is important. Humans should seek to cultivate political structures to improve the quality of human life.

At the same time, political activity cannot fulfill human life, and it is not all important. Humans should look to involvements in the other spheres of the social order to attain richer human satisfaction and to the Divine Life to attain ultimate fulfillment.

Notes and References

1. This fact-value interrelation means that theory and practice are intertwined. Good theory can lead to good practice, and good practice can suggest good theory.

   Both Plato and Aristotle maintained an interrelation between theory and practice. Plato refused to distinguish in principle between the various sciences, but Aristotle did separate the theoretical, practical, and aesthetic disciplines. For Aristotle, politics and ethics, which were reflexively related to each other, constitute the subject matters of the practical disciplines.

   For Plato, the distinction between subject matters was a matter of degree, depending on the salient characteristics being manifest in given creatures. The process perspective is more Platonic than Aristotelian, but the priority of becoming over being in process thought inverts the Platonic vision.

   As will be observed in later notes, this existentialist emphasis of process thought relates it to the voluntaristic strand of contemporary social scientific thinking, but its insistence on the inter-connectedness of fact and value and its view of a Divine Reality that is in some senses *sui generis* distinguishes it from the voluntaristic tradition. Max Weber was the most distinguished classical exemplar of this voluntaristic tradition in the human sciences. (See, for example, his "Politics as a Vocation" in *From Max Weber; Essays in Sociology* edited by Hans Gerth and C. Wright Mills (New York: Oxford University Press, 1946).

Hans Morgenthau's interpretive theory of international politics as outlined in his *Politics among Nations* (New York: Alfred A. Knopf, 1953) stands in this voluntaristic tradition.

Both Weber and Morgenthau emphasize the saliency of self-interest in political life. Both sustain a fact-value disjunction, contrasting scientific analysis and moral prescription.

2. Alfred North Whitehead, *Process and Reality*. Corrected edition edited by David Ray Griffin and Donald W. Sherburne (New York: The Free Press, 1978), p. 27.
3. *Ibid.*, p. 22.
4. This understanding coheres with the voluntaristic strand of social scientific theory noted earlier. It contrasts with the view of human social theory elaborated by Talcott Parsons in *The Social System* (Glencoe: The Free Press, 1953), by David Easton in *The Political System: An Inquiry into the State of Political Science* (New York: Alfred A. Knopf, 1966), and in B. F. Skinner, *Beyond Freedom and Dignity* (New York: Bantam paperback, 1972). Because of the principle of relativity and the functioning of the Divine Reality in the world, process thought does not cohere fully with voluntaristic views. Whitehead's "reformed subjectivist principle" qualifies the radical existentialism of some voluntaristic theories and much nineteenth century "liberal" thought.
5. It is beyond the scope of this essay to elaborate the bases for all the spheres in the social order. For more extended discussions, see Chapter 2 and Chapter 9 of this volume.
6. In contemporary America the differentiation of the spheres is very substantial. Parcularly, the familial and the religious spheres have become privatized; and they are not directly pertinent to the activities of the other spheres, especially activities in the economic and the political spheres.
7. These formulations are similar to those developed by Paul Tillich in Chapter VI of *Love, Power and Justice*, (New York: Oxford University Press, 1953) and Reinhold Niebuhr in Chapter IX of volume two of *The Nature and Destiney of Man: Vol. I Human Nature; Vol. II Human Destiny*, (New York: Charles Scribner's Sons, 1949).
8. This type of power is akin to what Bernard M. Loomer has termed "linear" power, in which a "one-way" influence from one agent to another is dominant.

"Relational power," the term Loomer uses to characterize reciprocal interplay between creatures, is a more desirable form of power. Empirically, one can seek to determine the relative significance of the two forms of power, granted the impossibility of unequivocal "linear power" in the cosmos.

The emphasis given in this version of a process social theory to the persistence of inordinate self-interest in human affairs is one of the reasons for its more "conservative" character compared to other versions of a process political theory. A second reason for this "conservatism" is the relatively greater emphasis on freedom understood as self-determination and the relatively lesser emphasis on equality and community. A third reason is the relatively greater emphasis on the formal side of experience compared to other versions.

Consequently, the doctrine of sanctification inherent in these formulations has a less perfectionistic character. These contrasts are analogous to differences in classical Christian thought between the perfectionistic tendencies of Pietists and some Methodists and the vivid sense of the persistence of sinfulness among the redeemed manifest in Lutheran and Calvinist theologians.

9. Over the longer run, inordinate self-interest may be mitigated, and creative transformation of some patterns of international relations may occur. However, in the shorter run, international relations will probably continue to be shaped by balance-of-power and enlightened self-interest. In this regard, the point of view developed here is close to that of Reinhold Niebuhr in *The Nature and Destiny of Man (op. cit.)* and *The Structure of Nations and Empires: A Study of the Recurring Patterns and Problems of the*

Political Order in Relation to the Unique Problems of the Nuclear Age (New York: Scribner, 1959).

10. Whitehead's discussion of the contributions of brute force (the harnessing of steam and industrialization) and of new ideals (democratic notions emerging in western civilization) illustrates this interplay. (See A. N. Whitehead, *Adventures of Ideas* (New York: Macmillan, 1933), Part I.
11. All laws are immanental, passing into existence as the forms to which the laws relate are embodied in societies of creatures and passing out of existence as the forms are no longer actualized in later emerging creatures. The relatively more rapid transformation of forms in human creatures than in non-human creatures is manifest in the great variety of human social organizations and in the relatively more rapid changes in them than in sub-human societies. The "laws" of physics, referring to non-human subject matter, are, for example, more precise and persistent than the "laws" of sociology. Nonetheless, in both sub-human and human sciences, nature provides only a plausible story.

    My process viewpoint differs from others who seek to discern only suasion in the Divine and who reinterpret the conditioning effects of the causal past.
12. The Stoic principles of liberty and equality are typical. Some harmonization of these principles implies the principle of order. Because of the dynamic bias inherent in process thought, the shape of natural law in this perspective is more fuzzy than in classical Roman Catholic social ethics or in classical Calvinism.

    It is more akin to the formulations put forth by the contemporary Protestant theologian, Reinhold Niebuhr. In *The Nature and Destiny of Man (op. cit.)* Niebuhr posited liberty and equality as universal principles of justice. In a later essay, "The Problem of a Protestant Social Ethic" (*Union Seminary Quarterly Review*, November, 1959, pp. 1-11), he added order to the other two principles. If the pre-trinitarian formulation, form-dynamics-unification, is valid, one would expect the emergence of three principles time and again. Niebuhr did not qualify the principles of liberty and equality as fully as is done here, but he made similar observations about their relations.
13. The questions of whether there are other bases for the recognition of "evenness" and "oddness" and for the establishment of the principle of congruence are left open here.
14. At the present time, the political conflict about the proposed Equal Rights Amendment to the Constitution of the United States is illustrative. The extent to which sex should qualify the principle of equality is the focus of the debate.

    Broadly speaking, in post-traditional societies the ascribed characteristics of sex and ethnicity and most achieved characteristics have not qualified the principle of equality as markedly as in traditional societies. Nonetheless, both achieved and ascribed characteristics continue to modify the principle. Because there is legitimacy in some qualification of the principle, the debates will undoubtedly persist.

    Age is the one ascribed characteristic which universally qualifies this principle. The same rules and regulations cannot be applied to children as to adults. In spite of this reality, the line of demarcation is not clear-cut, so debates about the way in which age should qualify equality are also interminable.
15. The ultimacy of the category of creativity in process modes of thought results in a dynamic ontology. The causal past limits but does not determine the present. God-world relations are a structural necessity, and some forms are a necessary constituent of every experience. Even though process thought shares the modern preference for a dynamic ontology, for these reasons it is not as dynamic of the ontologies of thinkers such as Karl Barth, Martin Heidegger or Paul Tillich.
16. The failure to attain excellence, a consequence of some combination of finitude, ignorance, sloth, lethargy, and inordinate self-interest, is widespread in human affairs. The understanding of freedom as the ability to do what one wants to do, first elaborated by the Sophists and advanced in a qualified way in nineteenth century liberalism, emerges from an inordinate emphasis on self-determination unqualified by excellence and by a minimization of the principle of equality. Our constructive sympathies with aspects of the nineteenth century liberal tradition are based in part on both the positive and negative aspects of self-interest in human life.
17. The major exception has been the vast expansion in the scale of warfare. It is ironic that nations in those portions of the planet in which civil liberties are most respected have

conscripted extraordinarily large numbers of citizens into their armed forces. Large numbers of them have given their lives for the nation state.

My somewhat greater emphasis on self-determination and individuation place my process interpretation between the views of Samuel H. Beer in *The City of Reason* (Cambridge: Harvard University Press, 1949) and the views of some other process informed thinkers, such as John B. Cobb, Jr., Franklin I. Gamwell and Douglas Sturm. At the same time, the formal side of experience is emphasized more forcefully here.

18. The basic aim of existence is aesthetic satisfaction. Because the true and the good enhance the beautiful, beauty, truth, and goodness are three-in-relation. Because the present is all one has, an excessive concern about the future, real but not actual in the present, may attenuate experience. Puritans, old and new, who are inordinately preoccupied with the future undercut the appreciation of the present. At some times and in some contexts, one may be a bit oblivious to morality.
19. It is beyond the scope of this essay to elaborate the normative forms of familial, ethnic, status, economic, cultural, and religious organizations. A comprehensive process social theory should also consider these spheres of the social order. See Chapter 2 and Chapter 9 for more extended consideration of these spheres.
20. In the United States, the multiplication-of-factions doctrine and the principle of checks and balances, as elaborated in *The Federalist Papers*, were designed to blunt inordinate self-interest.

    In the American experience, special interest groups have become extraordinarily important in the political process. The danger in such a situation is a movement toward anarchy. Indeed, as Plato long ago observed, the special dangers of democracy are mediocrity and anarchy.
21. For this reason, the author is uneasy about democratic socialism. In his judgment, the need for individuation and the opportunities for self-direction require some separation between economic and political institutions. Because social necessity has priority over physical necessity, the state in principle has the right to intervene in the economic sphere. However, it should not usurp the institutions in this sphere.

    In his volume, *Capitalism and Freedom*, (Chicago: University of Chicago Press, 1962), Milton Friedman explores these relations. He suggests that political democracy and economic capitalism are interdependent. The argument has much merit.

    At the same time the inordinate competitiveness and widespread adversary relations which may be enhanced in societies dominated by enterprise systems are major problems; they need to be blunted and co-operation needs to be fostered.

    The remaining chapters in Part Two explore these issues.
22. This separation need not take the form that has evolved in the United States. The English system represents an alternative form.
23. In the Christian tradition, one's views of the possibility of the harmony of life with life under the conditions of existence effect one's view on the merits of social reorganization. Christian "perfectionists" and Marxists may converge on their vision of the human future.
24. This theme is elaborated in Ernst Barker's *Reflections on Government*, (New York: Oxford University Press, 1952).

Introduction to Chapter 5

This chapter is a revised version of a presentation to the participants at a 1976 summer conference of the Institute on Religion in an Age of Science. The first third of the chapter rehearses the basic notions elaborated in Chapter 1 in order both to interpret the bases for the unity and diversity manifest in human experience and also to characterize the order and hierarchy of nature leading to unity and diversity. The other two-thirds of the chapter integrate these generic notions with more specialized propositions applying to human life. This portion of the chapter focuses primarily on politicians and the political sphere of the human social order, for I hold that on the shorter run political leadership and political action are central to the survival of the human race. The cultural sphere is critical on the longer run, for ideas shape human forms of social organization and the values guiding many aspects of human action. The lack of shared values and memories on the world level underscores the significance of the leaders of the nation-states dominating the current world political structure. This theme was accentuated in this essay, for the vast majority of the people attending this conference were academics in the natural sciences, psychology, sociology, anthropology, or theology. Political scientists, economists, business people, and politicians were conspicuous by their absence.

I did not anticipate the demise of the Soviet Union at this time this essay was written. While this development greatly reduces the danger of a nuclear holocaust, it does not eliminate either the centrality of political leadership in the quest for an earthly peace or the importance of the development of a broad climate of opinion to support their actions. In fact, the resurgence of ethnic and regional conflicts following the end of the cold war in the late 1980s illustrates both the way in which military force and coercion helped sustain an earthly peace and also the persistence at ethnic anomisities among humankind.

CHAPTER 5

Unity and Diversity among Humans: A Framework for Interpretation

Both biological and sociocultural factors contribute to human unity and diversity. Differences in sex, racial characteristics, physical vigor, and some aspects of intellectual prowess are rooted primarily in the biological dimension of human experience. Differences in basic values and forms of social organization are rooted primarily in the sociocultural dimension.[1] The two dimensions together contribute to the emergence of creatures who, relative to other creatures on this planet, possess very substantial capacities for self-initiation and for novelty of response to circumstances.[2]

Three aspects of the unity-diversity problem are addressed here. The first section sketches a broad framework to interpret our common human experience of the complex unification of diversity in the unity of an emerging creature. The second section delineates the hierarchy of creatures and the order of nature discernible on this planet. The third section, the longest of the three due to its primacy for this topic, focuses on the characteristics of human beings and their social institutions.

Human freedom greatly complicates strategies designed to foster a fitting synthesis of human unity and diversity, for it prevents the success of any simple strategy. Human actions and decisions in the political sphere are especially significant for the formulation of strategies for human survival, for politics is central for coordinating and harmonizing activities in human societies. In the foreseeable future politicians in nation-states will bear primary responsibility for initiating and implementing appropriate strategies for human survival. Wise political leaders should seek counsel and data from experts in the various fields of human endeavor, but politicians must bear primary responsibility for the major decisions shaping our lives together on this planet.[3]

Interpretative Perspective on the Human Experience of Unity and Diversity

Foundational human experience involves the synthesis of contrasting and commonly shared data into a complex unity. As humans become, they aim at aesthetic satisfaction and intensity of feeling. In order to attain rich and complex experiences humans require a proper blending of breadth of experience with depth of experience.[4]

A commonly shared background provides the foundation upon which a superstructure of contrasts and of contrasts of contrasts giving rise to rich aesthetic experiences is built. For humans these uniform components range from geometric forms shared by all the creatures in our cosmic epoch to cultural values shared by most of the human beings in a particular society in a particular historical epoch.

The contrasts eliciting depth of feeling are grounded in the selective appropriation of forms embodied in creatures in the causal past of an emerging creature and of forms embodied in the primordial facet of God's nature, that facet of the Divine Nature which is the locus of potentiality. Without such a locus, emergent novelty would not be possible, for unactualized forms must be located somewhere.

Sometimes there is too much diversity in a sustaining environment, for different creatures may be trying to attain mutually incompatible objectives. Disharmonies result, and creatures with lesser capacities for encompassing a rich diversity in a complex unity of experience are apt to emerge in the future. Consequently there is likely to be a decline in qualitative excellence in an environment in which there is too much diversity.

Sometimes there is too little diversity in a sustaining environment, for most creatures may be reproducing their pasts in their presents with minimal novelty. Relatively simple creatures predominate in such an environment, and the intensity of experience is truncated.

The terms "too much diversity" and "too little diversity" are not very precise, for "too much" and "too little" refer to specific creatures in specific environments. The bewildering complexities of creatures and societies of creatures observed in nature highlight its fecundity. They also limit the formulation of an optimum range of unity and diversity in a given environment, for the emerging future may suffer by human efforts to suppress inordinately excessive diversity in the present.

Nonetheless, too much uniformity in a sustaining environment may evoke simple creatures lacking in zest, vigor, and intensity of feeling. Conversely too much diversity in a sustaining environment may evoke simpler creatures lacking the capacities for integrating complex diversities into rich unities.

Nature confronts the task of evoking societies of creatures with substantial survival ability. One way to enhance survival capacity is to develop societies of creatures able to endure through many environmental changes. Such societies must reproduce their pasts in their presents with minimal change. To do so creatures in these societies massively simplify the data they receive from their pasts; so many count as one. Such creatures can continue to reproduce themselves with minimal innovation in spite of major changes in the surrounding environment. Inorganic societies, such as rocks, are societies possessing great endurance capacities, but they have minimal capacities for novel responses to their changing environment.

The other way to enhance survival capacity is to develop societies of creatures able to respond novelly to changing circumstances. Creatures in these societies must have enhanced conceptual capacities. These creatures are alive, and in their becoming they appropriate novel forms and feelings.

Life is a claim for freedom from the bonds of the causal past. So far as we can observe clearly, creatures possessing "life" are intimately associated with societies of inorganic creatures, with which they often have reciprocal relations. The inorganic societies serve as a life support system, permitting the emergence of living occasions within the organism. In this manner survival capacity is combined with capacities for novelty and intensity of feeling.[5]

The evolution of societies and hierarchies of societies is aimed at the evocation of creatures with enhanced capacities for novelty and intensity of feeling. This aesthetic aim at the harmonic intensification of feeling is at the base of things. A harmony/lack of harmony contrast inheres in the nature of things and provides the basic category for interpreting human experience.

The increased complexity of creatures, based on the enhancement of the conceptual side of experience and on a hierarchy of societies coordinated to sustain the proper balance of unity and diversity in an environment, permits a delineation of the order of nature and of the hierarchy of creatures discernible on this planet. The following section elaborates this hierarchy.

Order of Nature and Hierarchy of Societies of Creatures

The lure for aesthetic satisfaction and intensity of feeling inherent in the nature of things has brought forth entities and societies of entities differing substantially in complexity. The evolution of some conscious, relatively high-grade organisms on this planet is the outcome of this process of evocation spanning many millennia.

Our own self-conscious organizing centers, which are the ultimate percipient occasions receiving and integrating data transmitted from our bodies, from past ultimate percipient occasions, and from forms of definiteness embodied in the Divine Life, constitute the apex of this evolutionary process on this planet. The human organism consists of many inorganic and organic societies. There are literally millions of living occasions in the human organism but—except in pathological cases—only one organizing or regnant center, a serial sequence of ultimate percipient occasions. This center is partly dependent on the body, partly determinative of the activities of the body, and partly independent of the body. All interpretations of experience are grounded in this organizing center's perceptions.

By imaginatively sorting out the components embodied in our conscious experience and by using a method of analogy, which presupposes some elements of commonality among all occasions, it is possible to elaborate certain propositions applying to all—or at least a very great number of creatures—and to delineate a hierarchy of nature exhibited in our particular cosmic epoch.

Our own self-conscious drops of experience are the result of a synthesis of diverse forms and feelings into a complex unity. In the initial phase of its experience the emerging ultimate percipient occasion appropriates forms of definiteness embodied in creatures lying in its causal past. A mental or conceptual phase supplements this physical phase of its experience. This phase may be minimal. If it is, the past is reproduced in the present with a modicum of change.

In such instances so-called physical laws hold sway, and the predictive capacities of theories utilizing mathematical forms may be very substantial. In so-called inorganic entities the supplemental or conceptual pole is relatively shallow. Even among such creatures the past is not reproduced in the present without some novelty, so "laws" are statistical.

Laws are also immanental. They come into existence with the emergence of creatures embodying them, and they pass out of existence with the demise of the creatures embodying them. In this sense nature provides only a plausible tale, for the creature's selection of some forms of definiteness rather than others is somewhat arbitrary.

In the case of so-called organic entities the emerging creature's conceptual phase is prolonged. In this supplemental phase, forms of definiteness not embodied in the immediate causal past and perhaps not embodied by any creatures in the past may emerge into saliency. The contrasts and contrasts of contrasts evoked in this phase of the experience of complex entities heighten both their capacity for novelty and their aesthetic sensitivity. An emerging creature's subjective aim is derived from but not completely determined by the divine subjective aim, an all-inclusive rationality which primordially has envisaged all the forms of definiteness. The creature's subjective aim guides the satisfaction toward which the creature is aiming.

In sum, an emerging creature begins to become as its physical pole appropriates data from its causal past. In its supplement phase the emerging entity's conceptual pole introduces novel feelings and forms of definiteness. The creature contrasts these forms of definiteness and feelings with those appropriated from its causal past. Guided by its own subjective aim, the creature unifies these two sets of data into an emergent whole. After it has become, this creature becomes an object which other emerging creatures appropriate as they become. Hence every creature is both a subject and an object, for after the emerging subject "closes up" it is an object for every subsequent emerging subject.

In some instances many creatures mutually participate in common defining characteristics, producing a society. If these shared defining characteristics are reproduced by many creatures commonly participating in them, the many creatures may appear to be one stable, solid object to the human observer.

In nature many societies are organized hierarchically. Some very general defining characteristics are shared by creatures in our entire cosmic epoch; more specialized defining characteristics are shared by a limited number of creatures in a small segment of our cosmic epoch. The general pattern seems to be thus: selected geometric forms defining the most general relations of a whole to its parts, contiguity, and overlap; particular families of straight lines defining the relations among creatures in our own cosmic epoch and giving rise to metric measurement; electromagnetic occasions whose defining characteristics physicists are exploring; various inorganic societies such as gases, liquids, and solids; and various organic societies such as plants and animals. As the presence of entities such as viruses indicates, the dividing lines among these various societies of entities are somewhat vague. At the same time the differentiation among species is rather clear-cut, suggesting that differing entities appropriate forms of definiteness with different properties.

As noted earlier, the hierarchy of nature is twofold. First, the importance of the supplemental phase of an emerging creature varies greatly. Second, there is a wide variety in the complexity and the structuring of groups of creatures.

Human beings are the most complex societies of which we have any direct knowledge at present. Humans are comprised of living and non-living societies, coordinated to produce reciprocal relations between the regnant center and the rest of the organism.

The regnant center is a protean "formless form" capable of "containing" the sequence of ultimate percipient occasions constituting it. In this regnant center the supplemental or conceptual phase is enhanced greatly. Consequently humans are able to respond novelly to the initial data received from their past.

Consciousness is rooted in the human capacity to entertain contrasts and contrasts of contrasts. The peak of consciousness is the negative judgment. In a negative judgment a person is able to imagine the absence of something which is present or to imagine the presence of something which is absent.

As a result of the regnant center's rich capacities for feeling and thinking, feelings and meanings are central in human life. Purposiveness and intentionality are too salient in human experience to be interpreted epiphenomenally.

The development of creatures with these capacities has interjected a new note into the processes of emergent evolution. The processes on this planet were relatively spontaneous and unreflective prior to the emergence of humankind. Both conflict and harmony are manifest in nature, but prior to the emergence of humans the various creatures had relatively modest capacities for altering the process intentionally or for effecting the short-term relations among them. The symbiotic relationships emerging between and among creatures were the outcome of unplanned interaction between them. To be sure, some creatures destroyed others and were destroyed by them, but they did not drastically alter the structure of the simpler societies to which the lives of high-grade organisms on this planet are related intimately.

Sometimes between the sixth century B.C. and the first century A.D. systematic or quasi-systematic thought and new levels of human sensitivity emerged in several portions of the planet. In the West the emergence of Greek philosophy and the Judeo-Christian religion reflects this movement of thinking and feeling.[6]

It was not until the time of the Renaissance that modern science—with all its ambivalences—dawned, for in the Renaissance epoch humans fused rational speculation, particularly related to mathematical forms, with the carefully conducted experiment. As the history of the past five or six centuries reveals, the development of the science has vastly increased human capacity to alter the evolutionary process in both conscious and unconscious ways. The modern sciences have introduced a dramatically new and novel dimension to the evolutionary processes on this planet.[7] The decisions people make to use and to abuse science are primarily political ones. This situation leads to the final section of this paper, for the political process is central to the development of a fitting synthesis of unity and diversity in human life.

Human Beings and Their Social Institutions

As previously observed, human beings are the most complex creatures of which we have any direct knowledge. As self-conscious bearers of feeling and meaning, they are meaning-seeking, meaning-positing creatures. The elements of foresight, intentionality, and purposiveness loom large in their lives compared with those of other creatures on the planet. Compared with those of subhuman groups, their creative capacities have accentuated greatly the range of diversity in human societies. They make and bear history in a unique manner, and they often display substantial adjustive capacities to changing circumstances. They can create universes of meaning and can probe the structure of things in ways far surpassing the capabilities of other creatures on this planet. In short, relative to other creatures, the human organizing center is extraordinarily rich and complex.

As a result of these characteristics, human beings have accelerated and modified the evolutionary process markedly. Humans display much greater variations in values and styles of life than non-human creatures. This diversity raises forcefully the central theme of this essay, for the issue of the proper balance between uniformity and diversity becomes especially critical in human life. Not only can human beings reflect self-consciously about the problem; they also possess some capacities to qualify and to modify intentionally the balance between uniformity and diversity in nature and in human life. Nature and historical destiny limit these capacities, and the political problems involved in seeking to attain a relatively harmonious unity of our diversity are monumental.

If humans cannot attain a proper balance between unity and diversity with subhuman entities and societies, nature will impose it. The disturbance of the ecosphere and the disruptions of the balance of nature are stark testimony to nature's limits. Even though limits are imposed by nature, the precise boundaries are unclear. This murkiness is partly because all creatures relate to and respond to one another. It is also partly because in the evolving ecosystem it is "natural" for some life forms to pass away and for others to emerge.

In spite of this intrinsic vagueness regarding precise limits to the changes humans can impose on nature, human actions—particularly in the areas of applied science and of technology—may so alter the ecosystem as to make life or at least human life as we know it impossible.

Since human beings are related intimately to nature and many human needs are grounded in the biological side of human experience, humans are concerned rightly about the range of organic and inorganic diversity desirable on this planet and about human impingement upon the "natural" process evoking unity and diversity. Prudence suggests one exercise great caution in applying biological techniques or using chemical compounds which may alter subhuman forms of life markedly.[8]

The notion that humans are called to subdue, master, and change nature, a secularized Calvinistic notion deeply ingrained among many people in the West in general and in the United States in particular, needs to be balanced by the notion that humans are called to appropriate, appreciate and receive nature. This secularized Lutheran notion, emphasizing receptivity and aesthetic appreciation of nature, is necessary to attain a proper balance between the dual relation of humans and nature. Among those seeking to discern a strategy for human survival this issue undoubtedly will continue to be debated.[9]

As in the case of human-human encounters to be discussed next, the task of modifying the untoward impact of the dramatic human intervention on the evolutionary process falls primarily on political leaders. Experts in other fields serving as consultants and as participants in the public dialogue leading to political decisions may contribute significantly to the political process, but politicians will consummate the decisions. In the long run humans will have to be persuaded of the merits of restraint and conservation to sustain political decisions. Many natural scientists can share in this consensus-formation process, but the resolutions are primarily political.

This emphasis on the importance of the political process in shaping facets of the human future underscores the emergent character of the future. In spite of human efforts to discern the future's shape and pattern, the future is unknown and unknowable in many of its most important details. Alternative models can be projected; but the projections rest on assumptions about human behavior and patterns of nature, the validity of which is always questionable.

As creators and bearers of meaning and feeling, humans are distinguished from other creatures on this planet by the variety of historical forms they have evolved. The enhancement of human freedom led to a surpassing of the rather simple rhythms of primitive life and has resulted in an increase in the degree of diversity of human social organization.

Even though humans have greater capacities to surpass and to transform the past than other creatures on this planet, they are limited by the past.

Freedom and Destiny in Human Life.

In areas of the world in which technical reason is salient, as it is in the United States, the destiny dimension in human life is not sufficiently emphasized. Seeking the most efficient means to attain given ends, people in these areas often strongly insist that humans can subdue nature and shape their own future. They seek to enhance the novel, to surpass traditional modes of life, to ignore history, and to minimize the limits the past imposes on the present. They frequently envisage the rapid transformation of the rest of the planet—much of Asia, Africa, and Latin America—into the Western mold, unattentive to the fact that the emergence of technical reason to a position of preeminence in parts of Europe, the United States, Canada, and a few other areas is itself the product of a very complex historical movement evolving from the Renaissance and the Reformation.[10]

Many Western efforts to effect social and cultural transformation in the so-called Third World have failed and have met with indifferent results. These consequences highlight the difficulty of direct intervention in the life of one culture by people from another. The impact certainly has had some effects—witness the dramatic decline in the death rate, particularly among infants, in many cultures appropriating Western medicine. At the same time, as the dramatic increase in the population in Southeast Asia, much of Africa, and much of Latin America indicates, the appropriation of one cultural complex developed outside a given culture without the substantial modification of customs and values of the recipient culture can induce as many or more problems than it reduces.[11]

The prospects for preventing widespread famine in much of Asia, Africa, and Latin America in the next generation seem dim. Scientific, social and political solutions of population, production, and consumption problems seems almost impossible, and nature probably will impose limits on population growth in these areas through famine, disease, and war—the restraints Malthus elaborated almost two centuries ago.[12]

Unity and Diversity in Human Social Organization.

The great diversity of familial, social, economic, political, cultural, and religious institutions on the planet makes very improbable the emergence of sufficient unity to effect the social, economic, and political transformations necessary to arrest the widespread hardship likely to emerge in the next generation or two in many parts of the earth.

The unifying symbols which might serve as a focus for global brotherhood are almost nonexistent. Mutual self-interest may serve to mitigate disaster, but it seems unlikely that self-interest can serve to overcome the famine and suffering already present in some areas and likely to emerge in others in the next generation. Indeed relatively wealthy countries will likely isolate themselves to protect themselves and to prevent inordinate domestic discord.[13]

The great world religions cannot provide unifying symbols within this time span, for each of them is enmeshed in the particularity of one or several of the great world civilizations. Within the Christian movement the persistence of high christologies, in which the categorical uniqueness of Jesus as the Christ is affirmed and reaffirmed, accentuates the ultimate superiority of one faith community over others. It is very, very difficult to see how such views—however subtle, rich, and sophisticated they might be—can serve to unify all of humankind under the conditions of existence.

At one time it appeared that the United Nations might serve as a symbol of human unity. However, its intimate relations to the principalities and powers in the political sphere have precluded this development. Even though the United Nations continues to sustain some significant economic, political, scientific, and cultural activities, it now primarily mirrors the economic and political interests and policies of its member states and cannot serve as a symbol unifying humankind.[14]

The excessive diversity of the familial, social, ethnic, economic, political, cultural, and religious spheres in the several societies of the world is mitigated by developments in some spheres of the social order and exacerbated by developments in others. Viewed broadly, the emergency of technical rationalism to a salient position in segments of the world has fostered developments reducing diversity in certain spheres of the social order, and the proliferation of nation-states has fostered developments increasing diversity in other spheres. The sciences, particularly mathematics, the natural sciences, and applied technology, have contributed substantially to human uniformity, for certain methods of scientific procedure and modes of production are accepted throughout the world.

Technical rationalism challenges traditional views of life, and the impact of its widespread appropriation on the familial, social, ethnic, political, cultural, and religious spheres of life has been complex and multifaceted. Technical rationalism fosters the segmentalization of the spheres of the social order, accentuates social stratification by achievement rather than by ascription, puts substantial strains on traditional family structures, fosters the proliferation of secondary social relationships, and contributes to the elaboration of bureaucratic structures in all the spheres of the social order. The bureaucratic structures are most evident in the economic and political spheres.

Technical rationalism affects religious institutions markedly. It encourages people to qualify inherited religious beliefs and practices by challenging traditional views and by confining the significance of religious beliefs to the non-public spheres. Religious liberty and/or the privatization of religion is most common in the highly industrialized countries, for technical reason both sustains industrialization and minimizes the direct effect of traditional religious values on the economic sphere.[15]

On the productive side of the economic sphere technical reason reduces the diversity of human society, for it encourages the development of efficient forms of economic organization, the elaboration of specialized competencies, and the evolution of standardized and regularized work procedures and productive activities. It also tends to atomize and objectify the individual person, for he or she is evaluated primarily on the basis of his or her competence to perform specific and specialized tasks. Critics of large-scale economic enterprises and high technology often cite this objectification as one basis for their critiques.[16]

On the consumption side of the economic sphere technical reason increases the diversity of human society, for it fosters the continuous outflow of new inventions and an endless proliferation of consumer products. Humans often cannot integrate this substantial novelty into a harmonious whole. The rapidity of social and economic change then attenuates rather than intensifies the harmony of human experience.[17]

The global tendencies toward uniformity resulting from the extension of technical rationalism are counterbalanced by the diversity resulting form the proliferation of nation-states in the post-World War II era. Technical rationalism knows nothing of honor and history, but these factors loom large in the political life of nation-states. Increasing political diversity, the result of decolonization, has accentuated the already formidable problems of coordination among states. The attainment of a political unity of the world's nation-states in the foreseeable future seems utterly out of the question, and the attainment of a tolerable harmony incorporating a measure of equality seems problematic.

Centrality of Political Leadership.

As noted earlier, political leaders are directly responsible for the cultivation of a tolerable balance of uniformity and diversity between humans and nature and among humans. This subsection elaborates the grounds for this judgment and considers the implications for strategies for human survival.

There are three factors embodied in every experience. The first is a formal component appropriated from creatures in the causal past and from forms of definiteness embodied in the primordial facet of God's nature. The second is a dynamic component, embodied in the very process of becoming. The third is a unifying component, involving the ordering of the formal and dynamic components into an emerging unity. Because of the ultimacy of creativity in the nature of things, there is a dynamic bias in the universe. The pure conservative is defying the cosmos and cannot win. Nonetheless, the process of unification of formal components in any particular context requires some order.

Governments live in a house of power. Persuasion is preferable to coercion, but governments have used, are using, and will continue to use force as one of the means of maintaining order. The saliency of power in the political sphere does not preclude the presence of formal or unifying elements in this sphere of human society, but it does relegate them to secondary and tertiary positions.[18]

In the political sphere the imposition of too much order to suppress dynamic components results in tyranny; the parts are inordinately suppressed for the sake of unity. Conversely too much freedom results in anarchy; the parts are accentuated inordinately for the sake of diversity. The state, as the organizing center of a society, seeks to foster the proper balancing of uniformity and diversity, both of which are necessary for the harmony of the whole.[19]

There are limits to the degree of familial, social, ethnic, economic, cultural, and religious diversity a given society can tolerate without lapsing into inordinate disharmony. Due to a complex historical evolution, post-traditional societies generally are more able than traditional societies to sustain greater diversity, particularly in the familial, social, ethnic, cultural, and religious spheres.

In any viable state most people must be lured to obey the state's laws by suasion. Nonetheless, states always must reserve the right to enforce obedience by coercion, for humans are motivated to action both by the lure for harmony and by the threat of disharmony.

Excepting times of the threat or reality of civil war, the element of coercion or threat of coercion is generally greater between states than within states, for, as observed earlier, universal unifying symbols and a sense of universal unifying history are almost absent among humankind. Thus coercive elements loom large in interstate relations.[20]

The establishment of rules and regulations defining economic relations within and between states is a political act. Political decisions produce the forms shaping the context for economic activities. As a consequence the dynamic component in the form-dynamics-unification triad is the leading component in the political sphere, and the formal component is the leading component in the economic sphere. In the political sphere the formal component is the secondary component, and the unifying component is the tertiary one. In the economic sphere the dynamic component is the secondary one, and the unifying component is the tertiary one.

The tertiary character of the unifying component in both political and economical spheres is the fundamental and inexorable basis for the frustration and alienation people so frequently express toward economic and political institutions. People's deeply felt needs for wholistic, integrating, loving relations cannot be met fully by any political or economic system, for power and forms predominate in the political and economic spheres. This reality should serve to chasten advocates of radical economic and/or political transformation, for no rearrangement or reorganization of economic or political institutions can lead to human fulfillment. At the same time modifications of these institutions may enhance human life, and such modifications ought to be fostered. More suasion and more humane forms of social organization can contribute positively to human life.

At the legal level the formal dimension is manifest in the rules and regulations of justice—formal and informal, written and unwritten—which evolve in the life of a living community. Generally speaking, the more highly rationalized the society, the greater the importance of formal, written legal codes, lawyers, and courts. The unifying dimension is manifest in the actions of officials who apply the rules and regulations of justice to specific situations.

At the cultural level the formal dimension is manifest in the meaning-giving symbols and in voluntary observance of the rules and regulations of justice, producing the persuasive aspect of community life noted earlier.

Implications for Strategies for Human Survival.

The predominance of dynamics in the political sphere and the persistence of self-interest among humans highlight the importance of power in the relations between states. Ecological imbalances precipitated in part by human innovation, persistent ethnic strife within and between nation-states, inordinate economic inequality, political instability, and inordinate cultural and religious diversity contribute to the disharmony manifest on this planet.

So far as temporal life is concerned, it falls primarily upon the political leaders of the several states to try to coordinate this diversity into a tolerable if not an enriching unity. Because power, understood as the ability to attain one's will in conflict with other wills, is so salient in this sphere, the leaders of the superpowers—the USSR, the United States, and, to a lesser extent, present-day China—bear a special responsibility in these matters.

Various suasive efforts through international agreements to minimize ecological imbalances, economic injustices, and political controversies point to the possibilities of cooperation among the human family. The continued manifestations of self-interest in all the spheres of the social order, the persistent antagonisms between nations, the inability of people in some nations to limit population growth, and the ambivalences of technical rationalism point to the persistence of coercion and disharmony among the human family.

The development of technology and of a reasonably productive economy requires substantial capital accumulation. Such capital accumulations are limited in many countries in the so-called Third World, and often the government is the only agency large enough to accumulate sufficient capital to enhance economic productivity.[21]

In many of these nations the concentration of political leadership in the hands of elites, the need for development capital, and the rapid transition from traditional to post-traditional modes of life foster the emergence of the rule of the one or the few. Because of a need for order, dictators or oligarchs often emerge in these nations.[22] Such governments are likely to continue in the foreseeable future, for the confluence of factors giving rise to Western-type democracies was unique in human history. As the Vietnam and Korean experiences vividly revealed to Americans, democracy is not easily exportable to peoples with markedly different lived histories.

Multinational corporations and economic diplomacy have received much criticism in some circles in recent years. Some of it undoubtedly is deserved, but force is subordinate to persuasion in economic relations.[23] Granted the inevitability of some coercion in human affairs, economic coercion may be preferable to political or military coercion. If so, one of the factors offering some hope for the future of humankind is the growth of reciprocally beneficial world trade.

It is naive to expect the element of coercion to be absent in economic interchange. It is similarly naive to think governments will refrain from imposing their self-interest on economic matters. Cartels, tariffs, government subsidies, and the intermeshing of government economic and political policies attest to this reality. Nonetheless, the growth of trade does represent a move from coercion toward persuasion in the relations between states.

Whether ameliorative efforts will prove adequate to the ecological, social, economic, and political problems confronting humankind is a moot question. The radical critics and doomsayers say no; more moderate prognosticators say yes or maybe. Since none of us is graced with the wisdom to know that which is yet to be, the best one can do is to make judgments informed by past and present experience and by visions of better paths to follow. Unforeseeable historical events, technological innovations, and novel emergent entities inevitably will obscure the future, but some of the foreseeable consequences of human action can inform current and future public policy.

A Concluding Note

Concerned humans with a vision of the whole, a sense of proportion, and a sense of responsibility are among those most likely to foster the proper balance between uniformity and diversity in human life. Both by participating in the political process and by offering appropriate counsel to the magistrates, they may seek to contribute to our lives together.

In spite of the best of human efforts, humans are likely to continue to experience substantial disharmony in the next century or so. Scarcities of food and natural resources, the proliferation of nuclear weapons, the continued technologization of the human spirit, slower rates of economic growth, and an increase in tension between the more industrialized and the less industrialized nations seem likely. Statesmen and politicians will have to be exceedingly gifted and fortunate to assure human survival.

It is beyond the power of any of us to know whether this level of statesmanship can be attained and sustained. Some modifications of current patterns and values, involving some dimunition of diversity and some enhanced concern for the whole, seem necessary for human survival. Through a blending of suasion and coercion an increased concern for the whole of humankind may emerge. Some problems, such as inordinate population growth and continued conflicts between states, seem intractable, and they will have to be endured.

In order to sustain itself the human spirit must have the capacity to receive and to appreciate that which is given to it in the present. To enhance aesthetic satisfaction in the specious present, humans need to maintain a proper balance among their concerns for the past, for the present, and for the future. If the reality of the future is ignored or is inordinately preoccupying, the present also is enfeebled.

The greater part of morality lies in the assessment of the impact of the present on the future; but if one is to accentuate the aesthetic satisfaction of the specious present, at times one must be a bit oblivious of morals. Those Puritans, old and new, who are preoccupied excessively about the future risk the loss of all they actually possess—the present.

To sustain themselves in the coming century, humans will need some sense of fulfillment beyond the strife and conflict embodied in the temporal world. Whether many humans will or can attain this sense of peace is a moot question.

The theological notion of ultimate fulfillment in the Kingdom of God is related to the sense of peace. For a variety of reasons, traditional theological formulations are currently not attractive to many contemporary people. Nonetheless, some reformulation and/or reappropriation of the idea of a kingdom not of this world which people can maintain with emotional, intellectual, and spiritual integrity is much needed. If the quest for a harmonious unification of human diversity is even modestly successful in the coming century, the realization of this reformulation and of a nontemporal fulfillment may be essential.[24]

Notes and References

1. The debate on the relative importance of the biological and sociocultural factors in human life emerged early in the history of Western thought, and it has continued to the present day. In *The Republic* Plato opted for the predominant importance of heredity, and he proposed an elaborate eugenics plan. In *Politics* and *Nicomachean Ethics* Aristotle emphasized the importance of the environment and proposed to focus on the sustaining environment to cultivate good habits leading to virtue. In various forms the debate is still carried on today. Some will emphasize one factor but may not eliminate the other, blunting the sharpness of the debate. If it is held that both factors are inextricably and interrelatedly involved in human experience, as it is held here, the debate will be interpreted as an endless one.

2. This volitional emphasis relates this point of view to the strand of social scientific theory rooted in the tradition of Max Weber and some nineteenth-century English liberals (see, e.g., Max Weber, *Theory of Social and Economic Organization,* trans. A.R. Henderson, and Talcott Parsons [New York: Oxford University Press, 1947], and John Stuart Mill, *On Liberty* [Chicago: Henry Regnery Co., n.d.]). It contrasts with the causal strand of social scientific theory rooted in the traditions of Karl Marx, Sigmund Freud, and Emily Durkheim (see, e.g., Karl Marx and Friedrich Engels, *Basic Writings on Politics and Philosophy,* ed. Lewis S. Feuer [Garden City, N.Y.: Doubleday & Co., 1959]; A. A. Brill, ed., *The Basic Writings of Sigmund Freud* [New York: Random House, 1938]; and Emily Durkheim, *The Rules of Sociological Method* [Glencoe, Ill.: Free Press, 1938]).

3. In some portions of the world, political leaders must engage in a substantial consensus-formation process to modify existing life patterns; in other portions, elitists—at least in the short run—formulate policy with much less concern about a public consensus. In the short run political leaders in democracies must try to cultivate substantial domestic support for their foreign policy. Leaders in nondemocratic countries are not under such direct, short-run pressures.

4. The informing perspective shaping the discussion in secs. 1 and 2 is rooted in process philosophy. See esp. Alfred North Whitehead's *Adventures of Ideas* (New York: Macmillan Co., 1933) and *Process and Reality* (New York: Macmillan Co., 1929). See also Charles Hartshorne, *Creative Synthesis and Philosophic Method* (LaSalle, Ill.: Open Court Publishing Co., 1970), and William Christian, *An Interpretation of Whitehead's Metaphysics* (New Haven, Conn.: Yale University Press, 1959).

5. Whether a sequence of entirely living occasions can exist without an inorganic support system is a moot question. Certainly there is no metaphysical necessity for an underlying support system. It is beyond the scope of this paper to explore this issue. Problems of telepathy and the persistence of the sequence of events constituting the "soul" after the demise of the "body" are of special interest (see, e.g., William A. Beardslee, *A House for Hope* [Philadelphia: Westminster Press, 1972]).

6. See, e.g., Karl Jaspers, *The Origin and Goal of History* (New Haven, Conn.: Yale University Press, 1953), and Arnold Toynbee, *A Study of History* (London: Oxford University Press, 1939).

7. See, e.g., William Cecil Dampier, *A History of Science* (New York: Macmillan Co., 1944); E.A. Burtt, *The Metaphysical Foundations of Modern Science* (Garden City, N.Y.: Doubleday & Co., 1954); and Max Weber, *The Protestant Ethic and the Spirit of Capitalism* (London: George Allen & Unwin, 1930).

8. Rachel Carson's *Silent Spring* (New York: Hougton Mifflin Co., 1962) and Barry Commoner's *The Closing Circle* (New York: Alfred A. Knopf, Inc., 1972) reflect these concerns. Some may hold that the arguments in these volumes are exaggerated and polemical, but they do not point toward legitimate and authentic concerns.

9. Max Weber's *Protestant Ethic* is the classic study exploring the relationship between Calvinism and capitalism. For a neo-Lutheran critique of the mind-set overemphasizing mastery, see Paul Tillich's intellectual autobiography in Charles W. Kegley and Robert W. Bretall, eds., *The Theology of Paul Tillich* (New York: Macmillan Co., 1952) and Paul Tillich, *The Protestant Era* (Chicago: University of Chicago Press, 1948). For a discussion of the saliency of technical reason and the vision of the human mastery of nature in contemporary American society, see Robin Williams, *American Society: A Sociological Interpretation* (New York: Alfred A. Knopf, Inc., 1970). For an analysis and critique of technocracy, see Theodore Roszak, *The Making of a Counter Culture* (Garden City, N.Y.: Doubleday & Co., 1969).

10. See, e.g., Robert N. Bellah, *Beyond Belief* (New York: Harper & Row, 1970), pt. 2: "Religion in the Modernization Process," and Wilbert E. Moore, *Social Change* (Englewood Cliffs, N.J.: Prentice-Hall, Inc., 1963).

11. For a trenchant critique of Western efforts to facilitate the "development" of countries in Asia, Africa, and Latin America, see Gustavo Gutierrez, *A Theology of Liberation* (Maryknoll, N.Y.: Orbis Books, 1973).

12. See, e.g., S.J. Behrman et al., eds., *Fertility and Family Planning: A World View* (Ann Arbor: University of Michigan Press, 1970); Daniel Callahan, ed., *The American Population Debate* (New York: Anchor Books, 1971); Paul Ehrlich, *The Population Bomb*, rev. ed. (New York: Ballantine Books, 1971); George R. Lucas, Jr., and Thomas W. Ogletree, eds., *Lifeboat Ethics* (New York: Harper & Row, 1976).

13. For four contrasting views of the emerging future, see Daniel Bell, *The Coming of Post-industrial Society* (New York: Basic Books, 1973), and *The Cultural Contradiction of Capitalism* (New York: Basic Books, 1976); Victor Ferkiss, *The Future of Technological Civilization* (New York: George Braziller, Inc., 1974); Robert L. Heilbroner, *An Inquiry into the Human Prospect* (New York: W. W. Norton & Co., 1974); and Donnella H. Meadows et al., *The Limits to Growth* (New York: Universe Books, 1972). For two suggestive discussions and summaries of this literature, see Robert Benne's "Values, Technology and the American Future" and J. Ronald Engel's "The 'New Primitivism'" in *Belonging and Alienation*, ed. Philip Hefner and W. Widick Schroeder (Chicago: Center for the Scientific Study of Religion, 1976).

14. For two suggestive discussions of symbolism, see Paul Tillich's *Love, Power, and Justice* (New York: Oxford University Press, 1954) and Alfred North Whitehead's *Symbolism: Its Meaning and Effect* (New York: Macmillan Co., 1927).

15. For a discussion of this situation, see W. Widick Schroeder et al., *Suburban Religion: Churches and Synagogues in the American Experience* (Chicago: Center for the Scientific Study of Religion, 1974).

16. See, e.g., Herbert Marcuse's *One-Dimensional Man* (Boston: Beacon Press, 1964) and Gibson Winter's "Symbol and Society" in Hefner and Schroeder, pp. 219-48.

17. Alvin Toffler elaborates this theme in *Future Shock* (New York: Random House, 1970).

18. For two differing but complementary interpretations of this situation, see Chapter 9 and Tillich's *Love, Power and Justice.*

19. For two analysis of this problem from different but complementary perspectives, see Ernst Barker's *Reflections on Government* (New York: Oxford University Press, 1958) and Reinhold Niebuhr's *The Children of Light and the Children of Darkness* (New York: Charles Scribner's Sons, 1944).

20. See e.g., Hans Morgenthau, *Politics among Nations* (New York: Alfred A. Knopf, Inc., 1948); Reinhold Niebuhr, *The Structure of Nations and Empires* (New York: Charles Scribner's Sons, 1959); Frederick L. Schuman, *International Politics* (New York: McGraw-Hill Book Co. 1969).

21. Broadly viewed, no social institution should be larger than is necessary to enable it to fulfill its functions effectively (see e.g., Pope John XXIII's "Mater et Magistra," in *Seven Great Encyclicals* [Glen Rock, N.J.: Paulist Press, 1963] and E.F. Schumacher's *Small is Beautiful* [New York: Harper & Row, 1973]).

22. See, e.g., Moore and Bellah (n. 10 above).

23. For a volume offering a balanced assessment of the impact of corporations and governments of industrialized powers on economic affairs in other areas, see Kenneth E. Boulding and Tapan Mukerjee, eds., *Economic Imperialism* (Ann Arbor: University of Michigan Press, 1972).

24. The most significant movement in contemporary theology seeking to reformulate classical views is process theology, rooted in the seminal work of Alfred North Whitehead. The following representative texts illustrate various dimensions of this mode of thought: Beardslee, *A House for Hope* (n. 5 above); Delwin Brown, Ralph E. James Jr. and Gene Reeves, eds., *Process Philosophy and Christian Thought* (Indianapolis: Bobbs-Merrill Co. 1971); John B. Cobb, Jr., and David Ray Griffin, *Process Theology: An Introduction* (Philadelphia: Westminster Press, 1976); Ewert Cousins, ed., *Process Theology* (New York: Newman Press, 1971); Charles Hartshorne, *The Divine Relativity* (New Haven, Conn.: Yale University Press, 1948); Schubert M. Ogden, *The Reality of God and Other Essays* (New York: Harper & Row, 1966); Daniel D. Williams, *The Spirit and the Forms of Love* (New York: Harper & Row, 1968).

Introduction to Chapter 6

During the 1970s and 1980s, many academics in the humanities and in the human sciences (with the notable exception of economists) were very critical of a private enterprise market economy. Informed by neo-Marxist modes of thought, many liberation theologians have joined in this critique. Other Christian social ethicists, informed by desires for community and equality and by a relatively optimistic view of human nature, also shared in the general critique. Theological students, most of whom have had very little work in economics, frequently joined their mentors in critiquing the market-oriented economy. Official Catholic teachings supported private property, but they also promoted elaborate income redistribution schemes, emphasizing equality rather than growth and efficiency. Some process-informed religious social ethicists participated in the critiques.

As this chapter and the subsequent two chapters reveal, I have not shared the views of many religious social ethicists. In fact, I uphold the legitimacy of private property, affirm self-determination more forcefully than equality or community, and both want to maintain multiple centers of economic initiative and also to pay substantial attention to growth and efficiency in the economic sphere.

Chapter 6 utilizes empirical data and notions elaborated in Chapters 2 and 3 to promote democratic capitalism as the most desirable form of political economy in this historical epoch and in the foreseeable future. After reviewing the various spheres of the human social order and the relation of love, power, and justice in the several spheres of the human social order, it treats the sources of disharmony in human life. It then suggests that capitalism and a democratic polity are a fitting mode of political economy, given the nature of the social order, the quest for freedom, equality, and peace, and the persistence among humans of both altruism and inordinate self-interest.

CHAPTER 6

Political Economy: A Process Interpretation

I
Introduction

The normatively desirable forms of economic and political institutions and the proper relations between them are the central topics of this essay. The mode of thought which has come to be called process philosophy is used to address this topic. Rooted in the seminal work of Alfred North Whitehead and Charles Hartshorne and deeply in the debt of the Platonic tradition, process philosophy and its correlate, process theology, have become significant philosophical and theological movements in the six decades since Whitehead initiated this style of thinking in several major volumes in the 1920s and 1930s.[1]

In spite of the common debt to Whitehead and to Hartshorne, religious social ethicists informed by the process perspective have not attained a consensus on appropriate modes of economic and political organization and other topics in social ethics.

In their development of process religious social ethics, ethicists have both used and abused process metaphysics. Insofar as ethicists have appealed to process thought to develop generic notions and to formulate propositions applicable to all actual creatures, they have used process metaphysics. Insofar as ethicists have sought to legitimate more specialized propositions by citing more general ones, they have abused process metaphysics, for one cannot derive more specialized propositions from more general ones. One must base specialized propositions on the defining characteristics of particular concrete actual entities or societies of actual entities. One may legitimately set these more specialized propositions in the context of more general propositions, but one must verify them by observing creatures with particular defining characteristics and by using the analogical method.

At this less inclusive level, religious social ethicists informed by process metaphysics disagree about the nature of the pertinent facts, the sequence of priority of formal, dynamic and unifying factors in the several spheres of the human social order, the constitutive and regulative principles of justice, the best conditions and structures to evoke maximal harmony for human beings under the conditions of existence, the plasticity of human nature, the relative importance of form and context in social ethics, the possibility and extent of human sanctification under the conditions of existence, and the probable consequences of alternative public policy proposals.

This essay characterizes the nature of the human social order using categories of interpretation consonant with process metaphysics, formulates principles of justice which are applicable to human beings in this historical epoch, and addresses the bases for persistent disharmony in human life. In the light of these considerations, the essay proposes the most fitting form of human economic and political organizations. In developing these themes, process metaphysics provides the generic notions in relation to which the more specialized propositions pertaining to the topics addressed here are set.

Democratic capitalism is defended as a fitting form of economic/political organization. Both socialism, involving state ownership of the modes of production, and laissez-faire capitalism, involving private ownership unrestrained by the state, are rejected. (Of course, these bald alternatives are ideal types. Under the conditions of existence neither type exists, and many proponents of these types will qualify them in some ways.)

In arguing democratic capitalism is most consonant with the principles of justice and with the nature of human nature, the author takes issue with many religious social ethicists, including both those informed by process modes of thought and also those informed by alternative philosophical or theological perspectives, who promote democratic socialism as the preferred political economy.[2]

The following section of this essay is devoted to a delineation of the spheres of the human social order. This quasi-descriptive analysis is a precondition for the succeeding constructive formulations.

II
The Spheres of the Human Social Order

Human beings are enmeshed in a network of social relations shaped by their locations in the spheres of the human social order. The sequence of events constituting the organizing center of the human being is more fundamental and elemental than abstractions that are derived from it. Consequently, humans transcend and are not unequivocally bound by their location in the human social order, but their lives are shaped by the pattern of relations in which they are set.

The defining characteristics of human beings and the environment in which they find themselves provide the basis for the delineation of the spheres of the human social order. This delineation is necessary in order to set the economic sphere in the context of the other spheres of the social order. By viewing the characteristics of each sphere and by discerning their relations to each other, one can illumine the limits human life places on economic institutions.

The human organism consists of complex societies and sub-societies which are organized hierarchically. Some of the societies and sub-societies can exist outside the human organism. Others apparently depend upon the sustaining environment within the human organism for their survival. The organizing center of the human organism is a sequence of very high-grade occasions, some of which are conscious. They are unified by memory, by their objectification in the Divine Life, and by a formless form so protean it can contain within it all the occasions it encompasses.

The ultimate percipient occasions constituting the human organizing center are partially dependent on the body, partly independent of the body, and partly determinative of bodily activities. Although all occasions have some capacities for novelty of response to circumstances, human freedom is focused in the organizing center. Human rational shaping capacities are also embodied in the organizing center. The peak of consciousness is the negative judgment. In a negative judgment one imagines the absence of something which is present, thus intensifying experience and permitting the development of theory. Compared to other living creatures of which we have any direct knowledge, humans possess the greatest capacity for novelty of response to circumstances. This capacity enhances the ability of humans to live and to live well.

The aim of existence is the evocation of harmony and intensity of feeling. Human freedom should be evaluated by the extent to which human actions maximize harmony and intensity of feeling of the whole.[3] It is easier to formulate this proposition than it is to actualize it. In seeking to maximize the harmony and intensity of feeling of the whole, one must make complex judgments about the consequences of present actions for future events. Because of finitude, ignorance, and the freedom of other creatures, one is never certain of the future consequences of one's actions. One must exercise prudential judgments and humans do not necessarily agree on these judgments. Therefore, one's decisions about actions designed to maximize harmony and intensity of feeling are ambiguous. The best means to attain the objective are never unequivocally clear.

In the delineation of the spheres of the human social order, one must consider human biological, social, rational, and decision-making factors. In addition one must assess the relative importance of formal, dynamic, and unifying facets of human experience in the several spheres of the human social order. The spheres of the social order include the familial, the social, the ethnic, the economic, the political, the cultural, and the religious.

The Familial Sphere

The family and other small primary groups are rooted in biological necessity and human needs for intimacy and inclusive personal relations. Humans can be accepted more fully in the totality of their being in these small groups than in groups identified with institutions in most of the other spheres of the human social order. The form of the person and the sensitivity and fullness of responses which characterize love can best be manifest in the familial sphere and in the religious sphere. (The possibility does not ensure the reality, as heinous activities among people in both spheres starkly reveal.) Power, both linear and reciprocal, is tertiary in family relations.[4] Because the form of the person may be taken more fully into account in interpersonal relations in small groups, reciprocal power and love may be enhanced in primary groups.

The Social and Ethnic Spheres

The social and ethnic spheres of the human social order are rooted in biological necessity, social destiny, and human rational shaping capacities. Persons affirming comparable life styles share a common social status, and persons with a common historical destiny in a subculture may constitute an ethnic group. People in ethnic groups may share common real or imputed racial characteristics. Except insofar as status and ethnic characteristics may condition the formation of primary groups and economic/political interest groups, status and ethnic groups are not directly pertinent to the central topic of this essay. Formal factors are dominant in these spheres; dynamic and unifying factors are set in relation to formal components.

The Economic Sphere

The economic sphere is grounded in biological necessity and human rational shaping capacities. Human needs for food, fiber, and shelter are the basic and elemental factors evoking an economic sphere. Because humans want not only to live but to live well, they have evolved a plethora of economic activities. Indeed, because no human activity can be carried on without some physical base, economic factors are intimately associated with activity in all human social institutions. Nonetheless, economic activity focuses primarily on the production, exchange, and consumption of goods and services.

In earlier historical epochs and in some relatively undifferentiated social systems in the current historical epoch, the spheres of the social order were not as sharply separated and rationally organized as they are in modern post-traditional societies. People often produced the goods they consumed. In such instances, they had relatively simple exchange relations, and they often bartered with one another.

An economy based on a monetary system and the rationalization of production, consumption and exchange relations requires an extensive rationalization of the spheres of the social order, one of the characteristics of post-traditional societies. Cost/benefit calculations and the promotion of the most efficient means to attain given economic ends become much more important in post-traditional societies. People prize technical rationalism in these societies, and they promote its widespread use.[5] Because economic power is shaped by rules and regulations of justice, the legal order is very important in shaping economic life.

Formal rational values dominate economic considerations in the economic sphere in all societies, but they become more salient in post-traditional societies. Because of the primary importance placed on these factors in the economic sphere, a person must be evaluated primarily on the basis of his/her competence in a particular job, not on the basis of his/her general character.

The primacy of evaluation based on rationally delimited competencies precludes the fulfillment of human life in economic relations, for the whole person in his/her rich particularity cannot be central in the economic sphere. Forms are primary in the economic sphere, power is secondary, and the inclusivisity of love is tertiary.

The Political Sphere

Social necessity and human rational shaping capacity produce the political sphere in human life. Humans find themselves in social groups. Because of the number of people in the groups and the legitimate and illegitimate desires of people to pursue their own activities, coordination is necessary to enhance the harmony of group life and to defend the group from others. Humans respond to this social necessity by evolving governments to develop rules and regulations of justice to shape and to coordinate human life.

The power given people in the political sphere to make and to enforce the rules and regulations of justice illustrates the primary position of power and the secondary position of forms in the political sphere. Informed in part by the lure of the harmony of life with life and will with will, people in the political sphere are aware of the love which unifies a community and sustains reciprocal power between its members. Love is tertiary in the political sphere, but it works to enhance the degree of reciprocal power and to evoke fitting rules and regulations of justice.

Reciprocal power is "two-way" or relational power. In reciprocal power, agents mutually influence and are affected by each other. This mode of power is central in process thought. According to the principle of relativity, a primary notion in process thought, every being is a potential for every becoming.

The *degree* of reciprocal influence varies widely from creature to creature and may be more fully manifest in some of the spheres of the human social order than in others. Because political leaders cannot ignore public opinion and the responses of people to their actions, power in the political sphere, as in all the spheres of the social order, is reciprocal. However, reciprocity is *not* equal. Political leaders influence the people to a greater degree than the people influence the political leaders. Representative democracy may enhance the reciprocity between the people and their political leaders, but even representativeness cannot eliminate the inequality of relations.

Politicians live in a house of power. Unfortunately, under the conditions of existence, reciprocal power is frequently diminished and the conflict of will with will and life with life often takes place. An approximation of linear or "one-way" power emerges. However, even in the most blatant physical conflicts, the seeds of redemption are present, for humans have at least some vague intuition of the divine evocation of the harmony of life with life and the enhancement of intensity of feeling within and between human beings.

Relations between economic and political institutions have always been problematic.[6] Social necessity, the "natural" ground for political organization, is grounded in the higher phases of experience. In contrast, biological necessity, the "natural" ground for economic organization, is grounded in the lower phases of experience.[7]

Because social necessity is superior to biological necessity, the state, which is rooted in social necessity, in principle has the right to intervene in the economic sphere, which is rooted in biological necessity. In fact, state intervention varies widely, depending opon the dominant values in a given society, the political conditions in a particular given society, and the status of technology and science in the given society.

The enforcement of the rules and regulations of justice entails the apprehension of those persons who have been alleged to violate the law, to try them, and to punish those who have been found to violate the laws of a given state. Without embodying the form of justice and the lure of love in its life, a state cannot long endure. People will withdraw their loyalty to the political leadership and a pre-revolutionary or revolutionary condition will exist.

The Cultural Sphere

Human rational shaping capacities and the free play of imagination combine to produce a cultural sphere. Art, music, drama, sports, literature, poetry, science, and philosophy are all productions of the free play of imagination with the conditions of existence. Institutions in this sphere include those which evoke, sustain, transmit, and store these human cultural creations, such as schools, research institutes, libraries, and museums.

The most generally held cultural values give shape to the forms of social organizations extant in a given society. These general cultural conditions become embodied in a legal order which both legitimates and sustains various social institutions. The legal order also defines the relations which *ought* to exist between social institutions within and between the various spheres of the human social order.

The free play of imagination evokes various forms of definiteness, some of which participate in the harmonization of life. In this manner, justice, power, and love are embodied in cultural forms.

The Religious Sphere

The religious sphere is the final sphere of the human social order. Human awareness of the divine presence evokes religious institutions. Love, entailing an intuition of an ultimate harmony of harmonies and involving reciprocity and sensitivity of response, is the leading component in God-world relations.

It is beyond the scope of this essay to explore this sphere in detail, but the place of religious institutions in the human social order must be noted. Religious institutions' constitutive acts are worship, and these activities are the hallmarks of religious institutions.

Because power and justice are salient in the social, ethnic, economic, political, and cultural spheres of the human social order, human fulfillment can be most adequately expressed in interpersonal relations in the religious and familial spheres where love is primary or secondary.

Economic and political institutions, in which love is the tertiary component, cannot sustain inclusive human fulfillment, but better forms of economic and political organization may enhance it. The contribution of economic and political institutions to the harmony of life with life will be discussed in the fifth section of this essay. Before this discussion can be developed, it is necessary to address the levels and the principles of justice in relation to the spheres of the human social order and to delineate the bases for disharmony in human life.

III
Justice and the Spheres of the Human Social Order

Power, Justice and Love in the Spheres of the Human Social Order

Justice is the great regulator sustaining interpersonal and intergroup relations. Because dynamic, formal, and unifying components are embodied in every instance of becoming, these universal components of experience are three-in-relation.

These components are found in every instance of our self-conscious experience. Using the analogical method, one can posit their presence in the becoming of all creatures. Certainly the components are present in all entities of which we have any direct knowledge.

In human social life, power refers to the dynamic facets of human life, justice refers to the formal facets of human life, and love refers to the empathizing and unifying facets of human life. In order to indicate the limits nature imposes on the possibilities for human fulfillment in the spheres of the human social order, the sequence of priority of power, justice, and love in each of the spheres must be elaborated. These priorities were sketched in the discussion in the preceding section, but they need to be set in the context of the discussion of the principles of justice, the focus of this section.

In interpersonal relations, justice is the leading component, love is the secondary component, and power is the tertiary component. The form of the person may be more fully taken into account in interpersonal relations than in any other relations. Reciprocal power, in which each agent directly effects and is directly affected by the other, is potentially and sometimes actually most fully realized in interpersonal relations. In these instances love, which is the secondary component in interpersonal relations, is saliently manifest. Power is tertiary in interpersonal relations, and linear power relations may be minimized in interpersonal relations.

Because the form of the person may be most fully taken into account in interpersonal relations, reciprocity in power relations may be maximized in interpersonal relations. Primary groups potentially and sometimes actually offer the greatest possibilities for human fulfillment, for the particularity of persons can be most richly taken into account in small groups. Such rich fulfillment is not possible in human relations shaped by economic or political structures. Because of the scale of relations in these spheres, the many frequently have to be counted as one, so the particularity of a person is not fully acknowledged. In addition, human relations shaped by institutions in these spheres tend to be circumscribed and less inclusive than relations in groups in the familial, social, and religious spheres.

In the economic sphere, formal components are primary, dynamic factors are secondary, and unifying factors are tertiary, so justice, power, and love constitute the sequence of the triad in this sphere. In societies prizing technical rationalism, the primacy of the formal facet of experience is manifest in the application of cost/benefit analysis techniques to enhance efficiency and to maximize profits, in bureaucratic organization, and in the use of money to assess the value and to facilitate the exchange of the goods and services produced by people in institutions in this sphere.

Power is the secondary component in the economic sphere. Because of the priority of formal components in the economic sphere, peaceful "persuasion" characterizes economic transactions. A stable social order and general agreement about exchange practices are essential to the efficiency of economic institutions. In economic activity, voluntary actions and reciprocal power predominate. Acquisition by plunder is the way of war through political action, not the way of economic interchange.

Power is the leading component in the political sphere, justice is the secondary component, and love is the tertiary component. Through political action the state determines the rules and regulations of justice which define relations between institutions in all the spheres of the human social order. Informed by the general climate of opinion and the political configurations in a given society, the people in the political sphere promulgate, administer, and enforce the rules and regulations of justice in that society.

Without the form of justice and the lure of love, people in a society will not support their political leadership over an extended period of time. *Realpolitik* may be a short-term expedient, but it cannot serve as a long-term policy. Reciprocal power is incompatible with *realpolitik*.

One of the perennial appeals of a democratic polity is its promotion of persuasive and reciprocal power. In democracies politicians must try to persuade the public, and, in turn, they are persuaded by the public.

Nonetheless, reciprocal power is frequently less salient in this sphere than in the other spheres of the social order. In fact, persons representing institutions in the other spheres of the human social order frequently appeal to persons representing political institutions to enforce the rules and regulations of justice by coercing recalcitrant individuals.

The basic reason for the diminution of reciprocal power in the state is its monopoly on the legitimate exercise of physical force within a given geographical territory. (In revolutionary situations, some groups challenge this right, and civil war erupts.) Agencies of the state must ultimately maintain order, peace and harmony within and between the multiple subcommunities in the state. If political leaders fail to persuade recalcitrant individuals and/or groups to obey the law and they consider changes in the rules and regulations of justice to be impossible and/or undesirable, the state must use its coercive power—ultimately physical force—to sustain domestic tranquility. In addition, it must sometimes utilize force or the threat of force to defend its people from external threats.

In the cultural sphere, novel forms and novel propositions are evoked by the free play of human imagination responding to forms embodied in actual occasions in the world. Persuasive power is dominant, for humans are moved toward propositions that are true, actions that are good, and objects that are beautiful by persuasion and not by coercion.

Informed by the general climate of opinion evoked by values embodied in cultural objects and in the feeling tones and intellects of most people in a given society, politicians shape the rules and regulations of justice in a given society.

The slow drift toward greater freedom for more humans in more societies that has characterized the past three millenia is a function of novel ideas and novel technologies. Freedom and destiny have interplayed in this long process.

In the religious sphere, love is the leading component from both the human and divine perspectives. From the divine point of view the sequence is "love, power, and justice"; from the human point of view the sequence is "love, justice, and power." Because reciprocal power is so closely related to love, the intrinsic interrelatedness of the components is maximized in the religious sphere.

Given this qualification, one may say that God first manifests Its love by responding to the contribution the creatures of the world make to Its life and then by seeking to evoke the becoming of new creatures by supplying them with an initial aim. This initial aim ensures that the forms of definiteness appropriated by a new emerging creature can be unified by that creature. In the process, God seeks to evoke harmony and intensity of feeling. After this creature unifies itself, it is then objectified in the Divine Life, and the process is repeated.

From the human point of view, God's subjective aim evokes the human's initial aim. The human rightly or "justly" appropriates forms of definiteness from creatures in its causal past and from the primordial facet of God's nature.

The creature actualizes itself through a dynamic process of unification of data from its physical and conceptual poles. In this process it is guided by its subjective aim. After it is actualized, the emerging creature in its role as an object is a "power" which affects all subsequent creatures.

Religious institutions ought to be shaped by persuasive love. If this is the case, human associations shaped by religious institutions provide rich opportunities for inclusivity and relationality. Along with the family and small friendship groups, they potentially offer the greatest opportunities for rich and inclusive human relations.[8]

This discussion of the sequence of priority in the various spheres of the human social order sets the stage for the discussion of the levels and the principles of justice. These notions provide guidance for the discussion of the normatively desirable relations between the economic and political spheres.

The Levels of Justice

There are three dimensions or levels of justice, intrinsic, legal, and transformative. Intrinsic justice refers to the defining characteristics of a particular actual entity, subsociety, or society. For example, rocks, trees, animals, and humans possess different defining characteristics and hence differ in claims for intrinsic justice. Human capacities for deliberation, reflection, and sensitivity of response to changing circumstances exceed those of any other creatures of whom we have any direct knowledge. Humans have an intrinsic claim to be treated as centered, deliberating, sensitive creatures. Intrinsic justice acknowledges the legitimacy of this claim.

In the human realm, there are two other dimensions of justice. The first is a formal or legal dimension analogous to the classical idea of distributive justice. The second is a dynamic dimension analogous to the classical notion of unifying, creative or transformative justice. In this dimension formal justice is surpassed for the sake of justice.

Creative or transformative justice is essential to human life, for no formal rule or regulation of justice is fully applicable to a given circumstance. In addition, circumstances change, and laws applicable to one historical epoch may be inappropriate to succeeding ones.

Creative justice is grounded in the primacy of the dynamic side of experience and in the unifying facet of experience. In process thought, this dynamic primacy is reflected in the ultimacy of the category of creativity. Creativity stands beyond the forms and is inexplicable by the forms. It is always manifest through the dynamic realization of actual entities, but it is never exhausted by the realization of actual entities. It is the universal of universals. Because of its ultimacy, it cannot be demonstrated by appeal to a penultimate principle. The sole appeal is to intuitive insight. One may employ linguistic symbols to focus one's attention on creativity, but one cannot demonstrate its ultimacy by appeal to linguistic symbols.

The unification of the dynamic and formal aspects of experience is a result of creative synthesis or creative transformation. By analogy, this elemental unification is seen in the surpassment of particular rules and regulations of justice for the sake of justice. A process social ethic is ultimately a contextual or situational social ethic.

Because of the dynamic bias in emergent evolution, life would be unbearable without creative justice. At the same time, without legal or distributive justice, life would be chaotic and arbitrary. In human life, transformative justice evokes changes in legal justice to help legal justice more closely fit new and novel situations.

The state is necessarily concerned primarily with legal justice. However, the widespread prevalence of the pardon of human actions or commutation of juridical sentences among human communities points to the ubiquity or at least implicit awareness of the ultimacy of creative justice.

Principles of Justice

Every society evolves rules and regulations of justice. These rules and regulations are more formally rationalized in some societies than in others. General cultural conditions determine the extent to which the rules and regulations of justice are elaborated and formalized. In the Occident, the rules and regulations have been richly elaborated, and lawyers and judges have become key agents in this extensive rationalization of the legal order.

Three general principles of justice stand behind and are embodied in the specific rules and regulations of justice shaping social life in a given society in a given historical epoch. The three principles are self-determination informed by excellence, equality appropriate to form, and order/peace/harmony. These principles are rooted in the dynamic, formal, and unifying aspects of our experience.

As noted earlier, creativity is the ultimate category, inexplicable by any other notion. In human life, it is manifest in the dynamic aspects of our experience, including our capacity to deliberate and to make decisions. This capacity for freedom and self-determination is too widespread and too foundational to be put aside as a misconstruction. Purposiveness, valuation, and responsibility inform the entire tone of human life.

Freedom is the constitutive principle of justice. However, freedom understood merely as the ability to do what one wants to do or has the power to do is a sophistic view of freedom. Freedom needs to be informed by excellence. The person who is authentically free seeks to act so as to enhance the harmony and intensity of feeling of the whole.[9] It is much easier to state this maxim than it is to actualize it. Because humans are finite, ignorant of some things, and make excessive claims for themselves, it is impossible to actualize fully the principle. The implications of this observation for political economy will be considered subsequently.

The quest for excellence is rooted in the divine lure for harmony and intensity of feeling. The initial aims of the ultimate percipient occasions constituting the human soul are derived from the divine subjective aim. The internal relatedness of an emerging creature to creatures in its causal past and the immanence of the future in the present underscore the social character of existence and concern of the individual occasion for the many constituting the universe as a whole.

The other two principles of justice, equality appropriate to form and order/peace/harmony, are regulative rather than constitutive. Equality is grounded in human rationality, and order/peace/harmony are grounded in human community. They impose limits on the actions of the individual. People abuse their freedom, freedom and equality are not perfectly compatible, and the community can oppress as well as support human freedom. Consequently, the three principles of justice cannot be perfectly harmonized.

Equality is a mathematical ideal grounded in the notions of oddness, evenness, and congruence. It is never fully manifest under the conditions of existence, for no two creatures are *exactly* equal. In reality, the principle must be applied to creatures who are roughly equal, or who are equal for purposes of specific rules and regulations of justice. At a minimum, the principle requires that laws be applied equally to all the persons in the categories designated in the applicable law. The qualification "appropriate to form" is affixed to the principle of equality to acknowledge the legitimacy of the qualification to the principle of equality.

In spite of this general legitimacy, the precise limits which form imposes on equality in human life are subject to debate and review. No one denies that age legitimately limits equality. Young children are not expected to obey laws applying to adults. At the same time, there is ambiguity about the age at which children should be considered adults.

This biological limitation on equality is even more ambiguous in relation to human sexuality. Some sexual differences must be taken into account in formulating the rules and regulations of justice, but the extent to which they should inform the rules and regulations of justice is ambiguous. The limits which sexuality imposes on equality have undergone substantial change from one epoch to another and vary substantially between societies in the same historical epoch.

Social function also limits the principle of equality. Presidents, prime ministers, and chancellors are afforded some privileges by law which are not available to all people. The legitimacy of wage and salary differences among various types of employees rests in part on the implicit or explicit acknowledgement of the legitimacy of different rewards for various social functions. (The legitimacy also rests on consumer preferences, for the demand for various labor skills varies with the demand for the goods and services those skills can produce.)

Political conflict often emerges between those advocating a narrower and those advocating a broader understanding of human equality. The relative importance of human freedom and the limits the state may legitimately impose on people are other facets of this conflict.

The third principle of justice is order/peace/harmony. Rooted in God's harmonization of the forms of definiteness in Its primordial nature and in the derivative human experience of the lure for harmony and intensity of feeling, this principle recognizes the legitimacy of the quest for order, peace, and harmony in the life of a living community and in the relations between various living communities.

The tension between the rights of the individual and the rights of the community is reflected in the interplay between the three principles of justice. The freedom of individuals is both enhanced and repressed by the claims of equality and of the rights of the community. The proper balance between individual freedom and equality and between individual freedom and the claims of the community is not static. Changes both in the general climate of opinion and in technological developments affect the balance.

In one's constructive work, one is guided by one's assessment of the relative importance of the three principles in a given context, by one's view of the limits imposed on the harmony of life with life under the conditions of existence, and by one's prudential judgments about the likely consequences of particular public policies and particular forms of economic and political organization for human life.

The next section examines the bases for the frequently experienced disharmony of life with life. The concluding section draws on the delineation of the spheres of the human social order, the principles of justice, and the bases for disharmony in human life to develop a normatively desirable form of the arrangements between economic and political institutions.

IV
The Sources of Disharmony in Human Life

One of the persistent issues in religious social ethics is the basis for the disharmony in human life. In process thinking, evil is interpreted in aesthetic categories. Experiences which are evil evoke intense disharmony. Experiences which are good evoke heightened harmony and intensity of feelings. The embodiment of fitting principles of justice enhances harmony; their absence evokes disharmony.

The Bases of Evil in Human Life

The bases of evil in human life in order of the increasing level of intentionality evoking the evil are finitude, sloth and lethargy, ignorance, and inordinate self-interest.

The basic source of evil is finitude. Things perpetually perish. From the human point of view events embodying peak experiences pass away. The present fades into the past; objectification entails loss. Because some of the vivid experiences of the present evoke intense disharmony, some of this loss may be for the better. Unless succeeding creatures can encompass intensely disharmonious events as minor contrasts in a higher synthesis, the way of anesthesia is the way of peace. In spite of this positive evaluation of loss, the fact remains that the highest aspects of human achievement are lost.

Finitude also entails exclusion. If one decides to actualize some potentiality, other potentiality is not actualized. Coupled with the other factors contributing to disharmony in human life, the limits finitude imposes on human life may exacerbate the disharmonious aspects of experience.

The second source of evil is sloth and lethargy. Humans find the drag of the causal past to be greater than the lure for creative innovation in the present. Human acts of omission enhance evil patterns of social organization and creaturely practice. Sometimes humans simply do not have the willful energy to do that which needs to be done to reduce evil and to promote the good.

Ignorance is the third source of evil in human life. At a lower level, ignorance of the probable consequences of certain activities and/or of the understanding of certain laws may evoke substantial disharmony. Ignorance of certain laws, natural or human, is illustrative of this level of ignorance. Inadequate medical knowledge may lead to a prescribed course of treatment which is ineffectual or injurious. Inadequate economic knowledge may lead to public policies which evoke economic depressions and widespread human suffering.

At a higher level, ignorance of decisions contemporaries are making may evoke disharmony. The internal freedom of contemporary occasions prevents any one of them knowing unequivocally what its contemporaries are doing. A shared past and the ordering capacity of the divine subjective aim assure that contemporary occasions will not make utterly incompatible decisions, but these factors do not assure that contemporaries will make maximally compatible decisions.

Because human capacity to respond in a novel manner to the events of the causal past is greater than the capacity of other creatures on this planet to do so, humans are less certain than are members of sub-human species that the consequences of their actions will be the foreseen ones. Consequently, the prudential judgments one makes based on one's assessment of the probable consequences of particular public policy proposals and of particular courses of action are always more or less problematic. If unanticipated responses to one's actions occur, the actions may prove to be harmful.

Inordinate self-interest is the final source of evil in human life. All too frequently, human beings pursue their own self-interest excessively, placing their own interests and the interests of their family above the concerns for the well-being of the whole.

The boundary between legitimate self-interest and excessive self-interest is obscure. Some self-interest is necessary for a creature to actualize itself. Even if one acknowledges that authentic self-interest requires an interest for well-being of the whole, some self-interest is obligatory. Because of the necessity to become *some* thing rather than *no* thing, self-interest is inherent in the nature of things. One has the right to be just towards one's self.

The heightened human capacity to entertain contrasts, and contrasts of contrasts, and to exercise negative judgments—the peak of consciousness—both exacerbates human self-interest and also promotes altruism. Most humans are concerned both with their own being and well-being and also with the being and well-being of the whole. In fact, the two are intrinsically interrelated, for a wholesome sustaining environment is essential for personal well-being.

In advancing public policy proposals and in positing a desirable form of political economy, one must take account of the pervasiveness and the persistence of self-interest and of the intermingling of egoism and altruism in human actions.

Implications of the Bases of Evil for Economic and Political Life

People differ in their assessments of the degree of harmony of life with life possible under the conditions of existence, the plasticity of human nature, and the effect of the rearrangement of social institutions on the transformation of human nature.[10]

It makes a great deal of difference for social policy and for one's view of desirable forms of social organization whether one locates the sources of disharmony within the human being, in social institutions, or in some combination of the two. If one thinks that the locus of disharmony is essentially within the human being, one will be relatively disinterested in the transformation of social institutions. If one locates the sources of disharmony in factors external to the individual, one will be very interested in social transformation as *the* means to enhance the harmony of life with life possible under the conditions of existence.

If one locates the sources of disharmony as both internal and external, the situation is more complex. Both personal and social transformation may be seen as important ways to enhance the harmony of life with life.

One's views on these matters usually inform one's prudential judgments. If one is persuaded that both inordinate self-interest and also concern for the community as a whole are perenniel aspects of the human condition, one will be concerned with promoting social institutions that enhance the good of the community, protect the individual from the power of the community, promote the good of the individual, and protect the community from the power of individuals.

In the author's view, the loci of disharmony are both internal and external to the organism, and egoism and altruism are intermingled in human conduct. He bases these notions on personal experience and on the widespread experiences of humankind as embodied in the literature produced by the race. The constructive views advanced in the following section of this essay are informed by these notions and by the principles of justice enumerated here.

V
Capitalism and Democratic Polity: A Fitting Mode of Economic and Political Organization

Introduction

In the conclusion of this essay, the issues addressed in the foregoing sections are considered conjointly to develop a normative view of the fitting form of economic and political organization most likely to facilitate the following policy objectives:

1. Promote the embodiment of the principles of justice in the rules and regulations of justice.
2. Blunt and deflect widespread and persistent human propensities to promote their self-interests inordinately in economic and political activities.
3. Encourage and support widespread and persistent human propensities to promote the good of the community.
4. Protect the individual from the inordinate demands of the community.
5. Protect the community from the inordinate demands of the individual.
6. Foster growth and efficiency in the economic sphere.

The combination of a capitalist economic system and a democratic polity is best able to promote the six policy objectives just cited. This combination promotes individual self-initiative and self-determination, reduces gross inequalities, and facilitates the harmony of life with life in a living community. By separating economic and political power, by promoting checks and balances within and between institutions in the political and economic spheres, and by legitimating political intervention in the economic sphere for the sake of social justice, this arrangement blunts human self-interest and directs it into constructive channels. It also facilitates a concern with the whole by promoting democratic decision-making. The diffusion of power and the sustenance of multiple centers of initiative protect individuals and minorities from the powers of the community. At the same time, the community can limit through legal means the activities of individuals and corporations who violate the common good.[11]

The dynamic and emergent character of human life and the persistence of values and behavior patterns developed in other historical epochs underscore the need for flexible and innovative patterns of economic and political life. However, the direction of economic life should not be placed directly in the hands of politicians now or in the foreseeable future. The foreseeable future means at least several generations—beyond our present ability to discern the possibility. If human nature is substantially transformed, such full direction may eventually be warranted; but the author is skeptical about the likelihood of the radical transformation of human nature due to the structure of the human organism, the nature of the socialization process, and the necessity for some creaturely self-interest. At the same time, limited transformation has occurred, as the extension of freedom in some parts of the planet in the past three or four millenia shows. Moral progress is possible, and conditions for fostering moral progress should be encouraged.[12]

Because the well-being of the community is intimately related to its economic productivity, one must consider the impact both of the structural relations between economic and political entities and also of specific public policy proposals upon growth and efficiency in economic enterprises. This area is treated very lightly by most religious social ethicists, who are frequently more concerned with the common good of the community and the promotion of greater equality than with the growth and efficiency of economic enterprises. This omission is most unfortunate, for the unanticipated negative consequences of policies which diminish the growth and efficiency of economic enterprises endanger the quest for community as well as for the reduction of gross inequality.[13]

Democracy: A Fitting Form of Political Organization

The rule of the one, the some, or the many has characterized human political organizations. Monarchy, aristocracy, and democracy, the good forms of the rule of the one, the some, and the many, have been contrasted with despotism, oligarchy, and anarchy, the bad forms of the rule of the one, the some, and the many. It is beyond the scope of this essay to sort out the nuances between these types, but these broad formulations can serve to highlight the options available to humankind.

Democracy is most compatible with the constitutive principle of justice, i.e., freedom informed by excellence, for in a democracy many participate in the governing process. In large scale societies, representative democracy is required, for there are simply too many people for all to participate equally. Finitude is not the only limiting factor, for the necessity of a centered decision-making process demands that selected political leaders act on behalf of the group in any period of crisis.

Human capacity for justice is one of the bases for democracy, for human freedom and human concern for the well-being of the whole make democracy possible. Human capacity for injustice is the other basis for democracy. As noted earlier, humans not infrequently pursue their own self-interest inordinately. Human capacity for injustice makes democracy necessary, for democracy curbs the inordinate self-interest of political leaders by providing for their periodic election. The system of checks and balances within and between the executive, legislative, and judicial branches of government further blunts inordinate self-interest.

Universal suffrage furthers the principle of equality appropriate to form, for it minimizes the likelihood of inordinate inequality of income or political power in a society. The separation of economic and political power further curbs inordinate concentration of power in the hands of people in the political sphere or in the economic sphere and promotes multiple centers of initiative.

Democratic or Social Market Capitalism

Social market capitalism and democratic capitalism are terms used to describe the forms of economic and political organization that have emerged in several western democracies. The formal patterns considered here do not fit the details of any particular society, but they are embodied more or less fully in several countries in western Europe, the United States and Canada, and in some Pacific Basin countries.[14]

In democratic capitalism (the term used here to describe this arrangement of economy and polity), private ownership of the modes of production is combined with a democratic form of political organization. In such societies the government has the right to intervene in the economic sphere to promote the good of the community, to tax and to regulate economic enterprises, to engage in fiscal and monetary practices designed to promote stability and growth in the economic sphere, and to undertake various income redistribution schemes. At the same time, institutions in the economic sphere are not subsumed by the government.

As an economic system, capitalism possesses the following characteristics:

1. Private ownership of the means of production;
2. Free access to the market as a consumer, a producer, an investor, or a worker;
3. Pursuit of profit as a prime mover for economic activity; and
4. The use of a competitive pricing system to shape the allocation of land, capital, and labor, and to inform economic choices.

To function effectively, a capitalist economic system needs the support of a government and a legal order which (a) sustains voluntary and peaceful exchange through the enforcement of contracts and the maintenance of a viable monetary system, and (b) in most instances (some "natural" monopolies being the exception) prevents monopoly practices which disrupt normal supply-demand pricing mechanisms.

The government can intervene directly in the economic sphere in several ways. It counters monopolistic tendencies with appropriate antitrust actions, undertakes some types of research and development in the national interest, sponsors some forms of basic research, provides for some consumer protection, promotes programs to protect the environment from damage from industrial waste and emissions, maintains land use regulations and restrictions, protects humans from physically injurious products (particularly in health care), and requires reasonable safety standards in the work place.

The state has the responsibility for macroeconomic management through appropriate fiscal and monetary policy. These policies should promote the tendencies toward efficiency and growth fostered by a capitalist enterprise system. Finally, the government should engage in some income redistribution schemes to extend greater liberty to some and minimize inequality. All three principles of justice sustain the idea of some income redistribution. Gross inequality limits the freedom of some and threatens domestic tranquility.

The extent of income redistribution and the means that should be employed to undertake it are matters of considerable political debate. Issues centering around economic growth and efficiency and the appropriate level of inequality of income shape these debates. Because government economic policy should work with rather than against market forces, direct grants to persons needing economic assistance are generally preferable to elaborate government sponsored welfare schemes. Unfortunately, the inability or unwillingness of some of these potential grantees to support their children makes this principle moot in many instances.

One must assess the probable impact of proposed income redistribution schemes on growth and efficiency of the economy and on liberty, for proposals designed to attain greater equality may endager the liberty of some and evoke inefficiency and economic stagnation or decline. If such policies were enacted, less liberty and less equality for most people would be the probable long-run consequences.[15]

In formulating economic policy, one must take into account both the reality of finitude, sloth and lethargy, ignorance, and inordinate self-interest and also human concern for the whole. In addition, one must consider the need to reward individuals who work beyond the norm to promote growth and efficiency and/or make excellent decisions in allocating their resources, and to punish those who are indolent and/or make poor decisons in allocating their resources.

A capitalist enterprise economic system encourages risk-taking and the exercise of human freedom. Because capitalism places the risks for economic decisions on entrepreneurs, people with a very substantial interest in the success of an enterprise are responsible for making decisions and formulating policies.

Income redistribution schemes should seek to reduce gross inequality, but an egalitarian society is both impossible and undesirable.[16] At the foundational level, age grading, sexual differences, and the necessity for different social functions preclude a radically egalitarian society. Even if possible, such a society would be undesirable, for egalitarianism surpresses human freedom inordinately for the sake of equality and the community. Novel and innovative notions and actions do not mesh perfectly with equality and community. Public policy should seek to promote a minimal level of income in accord with the economic resources of a given community, but substantial differences in wealth and income do not necessarily denigrate the well-being of the community. In fact, they may enhance its well-being by promoting growth and efficiency in the economic sphere.

The separation of economic and political institutions promotes multiple centers of initiative in a society. This contribution is very important, for politicians all too frequently pursue their own self-interests inordinately. Politicians are deterred from usurping power and privilege by a democratic polity, the separation of economic and political power, the multiplication of factions, and a balance of power between the legislative, judicial, and executive branches of government. This arrangement—encouraged by tax policies designed to promote them—encourages the proliferation of voluntary associations so characteristic of some western societies and so vital to a vigorous public-serving private sector.[17]

In any economic system, production and consumption are two sides of the same coin. Consumer preference is central in a competitive enterprise system, for the pricing mechanisms based on supply and demand shape both consumption and production of goods and services.

Because of its reflection of consumer preferences, resource allocation based on supply-demand pricing mechanisms accentuates human freedom, the constitutive principle of justice. In spite of the merits of rooting consumption patterns on human choices, human freedom frequently is not informed by excellence. Finitude, sloth and lethargy, ignorance, and inordinate self-interest blunt or obscure the pursuit of excellence. The result is widespread market hedonism, in which people pursuing personal instant gratification degrade themselves and induce public vulgarity.[18]

Moralists have had much to say about conspicuous consumption and misallocation of human resources, but the solution to this condition is elusive. Every society must maintain a minimal level of public morality. Because bigots and fanatics are perennially tempted to try to use the state to foist their own views of proper morality upon others, public standards should not be unduly rigorous. Whenever possible, humans should be persuaded rather than coerced into higher levels of morality.

One of the most effective ways a democratic capitalist society can promote higher standards of morality is by its encouragement of voluntary associations through tax incentives and legal support. Associations in the private sector can contribute substantially to the promotion of higher standards of morality than those legally prescribed and to the development of the higher sensibilities of humankind evoked by the lure for the true and the beautiful. Religious institutions are significant participants in the private cultivation of public morality and in the promotion of the quality of life.[19]

Democratic socialists are persuaded that public ownership of the means of production will further the cause of social justice by enhancing equality and community and by promoting authentic instead of inauthentic freedom. These claims should be viewed with the utmost skepticism. Socialist policies would undercut the constitutive principle of freedom and would place far too much power in the hands of politicians and their families. The promoters of socialist schemes often place too much confidence in the perfectability of human nature, mistrust other people's exercise of human freedom, do not pay sufficient attention to economic growth and efficiency, and are too confident about the transformative capacity of socialist practices.

Democratic capitalist societies do sometimes experience too much inequality, fragmentation of community, and market hedonism. These undesirable traits are not unique to societies with capitalist enterprise systems; in fact, most of those societies with alternative forms of economy and polity suffer from the same maladies, frequently to a greater degree than do democratic capitalist countries.[20]

The government does have a role in countervailing these evils through some income redistribution schemes, appropriate consumer protectionism, protection of the environment, and the cultivation of a climate of opinion promoting community and the higher values of a civilized society—truth, science, art, adventure, and peace.

Nonetheless, perfection is not attainable, some inequality is desirable, and the government's role in these matters should be limited. As noted earlier, voluntary associations should play a major role in enhancing the quality of life in societies with a democratic polity and a capitalist enterprise economic system.

VI
Summary and Conclusions

The formulations developed in this essay are consonant with the propositions of process metaphysics, but these propositions are intermingled here with more specialized propositions pertaining to human beings and to human social institutions. The primacy of self-determination informed by excellence, the constitutive principle of justice, and the inevitable intertwining of harmonious and disharmonious components of experience have guided the constructive views developed here. Human capacity to manifest concern for the whole and human capacity to manifest inordinate self-interest suggest that power be diffused through the separation of the spheres of the human social order, the multiplication of factions, and a system of checks and balances in social organizations within and between the spheres of the human social order.

Utopians and idealists with visionary plans for the reconstruction of the social order grossly underestimate the persistence of inordinate human pursuit of self-interest. Cynics promoting *realpolitik* grossly underestimate human pursuit of justice and human concern for the common good. Neither the harmonies nor the furies prevail in human affairs.

The structure of economic and political institutions promoted here will not produce the perfect harmony of life with life, but democratic capitalism does make a more significant contribution to the enhanced harmonization of life with life consonant with the extension of human freedom than do other forms of economic and political organization now extant or likely to emerge in the foreseeable future.

Of course, no society embodies these forms perfectly; and the evolution of human life, coupled with new technological development, precludes idolization of any particular forms. In the economic sphere, more democratic forms of decision-making and work relations may well emerge.[21] It is conceivable that at some future time much less concern will have to be paid to economic growth and efficiency in the formulation of public policy and in the management of economic enterprises than is now the case. It is also conceivable economic abundance may modify human self-interest so markedly that a democratic socialist political economy would be desirable in some distant historical epoch.

In any event, this future is beyond the capacity of us in this generation to foresee. Although growth and efficiency should never unqualifiedly dominate public policy considerations, they will continue to be very important factors in public policy proposals for a long time to come. The quest for the novel and the innovative—so appealing to some followers of process thought—must be balanced by an awareness of the constraints which existing structures and practices impose on human beings. Some of these constraints may be surmounted in the future; others are intractable.

Process religious social ethicists promoting democratic capitalism assess the tractable and intractable facets of human existence differently than those promoting democratic socialism. Those affirming that freedom is the constitutive principle of justice and acknowledging the persistence of inordinate self-interest among humankind will be sympathetic to democratic capitalism. Those accentuating the principles of equality and community and envisaging the transformation of human nature in the direction of widespread and relatively unqualified altruism will be sympathetic to democratic socialism. In the author's judgment, the former assessment is more consonant with the facts embodied in the widespread experience of humankind than is the latter.

Notes and References

1. The major works of Whitehead which are directly pertinent to religious social ethics include the following: *Science and the Modern World* (Macmillan, 1925); *Religion in the Making* (Macmillan, 1926); *Process and Reality* (Macmillan, 1929); *Adventures of Ideas* (Macmillan, 1933); *Modes of Thought* (Macmillan, 1938).

2. Douglas Sturm is illustrative of persons informed by process thought who promote democratic socialism. The following essays illustrate his use of process thought: "Process

Thought and Political Theory: Implications of a Principle of Internal Relations," in John B. Cobb, Jr. and W. Widick Schroeder, editors, *Process Philosophy and Social Thought* (Chicago: Center for the Scientific Study of Religion, 1981), pp. 81-102; and "Toward a New Social Covenant: From Community to Commonwealth," in Bruce Grelle and David A. Krueger, editors, *Christianity and Capitalism: Perspectives on Religion, Liberalism and the Economy* (Chicago: Center for the Scientific Study of Religion, 1986), pp. 91-108.

Although he does not employ process thought, J. Philip Wogaman promotes a view of political economy close to Sturm's in his *Economics and Ethics: A Christian Inquiry* (Philadelphia: Fortress Press, 1986).

A more balanced view placing somewhat more emphasis on the principles of equality and community and relatively less emphasis on the principles of freedom and on growth and efficiency than is done here is advanced in Prentiss L. Pemberton and Daniel Rush Finn, *Toward a Christian Economic Ethic: Stewardship and Social Power* (Minneapolis: Winston Press, 1985).

Franklin I. Gamwell is less extreme than Sturm, but he also advocates substantially enhanced political participation in the economic sphere. The following illustrate his orientation: "Happiness and the Public World: Beyond Political Liberalism," in Cobb and Schroeder, ibid., pp. 38-54; *Beyond Preference: Liberal Theories of Independent Associations* (Chicago: University of Chicago Press, 1984); and "Freedom and the Economic Order: A Foreward to Religious Evaluation," in Grelle and Krueger, op. cit., pp. 49-65.

Although they are not informed by process modes of thought, Robert Benne and Michael Novak both support democratic capitalism. Benne's views are most fully developed in *The Ethic of Democratic Capitalism: A Moral Reassessment* (Philadelphia: Fortress Press, 1981), and Novak's view are elaborated in *The Spirit of Democratic Capitalism* (New York: Simon and Schuster, 1982).

It is beyond the scope of this essay to explore the relation of process thought to Marxism. In the main, Whitehead himself preferred social evolution to social revolution. The dialectic of negation is not a methodological tool for Whitehead, and the dialectic stops after a creature has become and is objectified in the Divine Life. Charles Hartshorne does address Marx in his *Insights and Oversights of the Great Thinkers: An Evaluation of Western Philosophy* (Albany, N.Y.: State University of New York Press, 1983). In that context he affirms the primacy of freedom and is critical of state controlled economies.

For a discussion of these relations, see Howard L. Parsons, "History as Viewed by Marx and Whitehead," *The Christian Scholar* 50 (1967), pp. 273-289. For a critique of process thought, see George V. Pixley, "Justice, and Class Struggle: A Challenge for Process Philosophy," *Process Studies* 413 (Fall, 1974), pp. 159-175.

In more recent times, process theologians have responded to liberation theologians, many of whom use Marxist modes of social analysis, in a variety of ways. Illustratively, see Delwin Brown, *To Set at Liberty: Christian Faith and Human Freedom* (Maryknoll: Orbis Books, 1981); John B. Cobb, Jr., *Process Theology as Political Theology* (Philadelphia: Westminster Press, 1982); and Schubert Ogden, *Faith and Freedom: Toward a Theology of Liberation* (Nashville: Abingdon, 1979). None of these texts deals directly with detailed issues of political economy, but none of them explicitly affirms democratic capitalism. They stress community and equality more forcefully than this essay does.

Because so much of liberation theology is indebted to Marxist modes of social analysis, this literature is not directly pertinent to the focus of this essay.

3. This understanding of human freedom is the "freedom informed by excellence" developed later in this essay.

4. Bernard M. Loomer highlights the contrasting views of power in his essay, "Two Conceptions of Power," *Process Studies* 6 (1976), pp. 5-32. The distinction between linear and reciprocal power is elaborated in the subsection "The Political Sphere" later in this section.

5. Max Weber is the classical figure who most saliently described the routinization and bureaucratization of modern society through the use of technical reason. (Technical reason seeks the most efficient means to attain a given end. It is truncated reason, for in itself it knows nothing directly of its grounding in the forms of definiteness. Ontic reason, which is aware of its participation in the forms of definiteness, must supplement technical reason.)

6. The central focus of this essay is the proper relation between economic and political institutions. Following a discussion of the bases for disharmony in human life under the conditions of existence and the development of the principles of justice which ought to guide human moral decisions, this topic will be discussed more fully than the delineation in this section permits.

7. In human life, both biological and social necessity combine with human rational shaping capacities to produce numerous forms of economic and political organization. In addition, relations between economic and political institutions vary substantially from epoch to epoch and between various socieites in the same historical epoch. It is beyond the scope of this essay to deal with these historical matters in any detail.

8. The potential for the emergence of small inclusivistic friendship groups exists in institutions in all the spheres of the social order. These groups frequently develop and "humanize" relations in these spheres. However, in most instances the settings limit the extent and shape of these groups. As noted earlier, most of this discussion is focued on post-traditional large heterogeneous societies. Pre-literate and many traditional societies do not differentiate the spheres of the social order as sharply as modern and post-modern societies do.

9. Franklin I. Gamwell makes a similar point in his "Happiness and the Public World: Beyond Political Liberalism," op. cit. Gamwell is more confident about the ability of humans to formulate transcendent principles than is the author. Gamwell's strong confidence in reason relates him to the rational strand of process thought associated particularly with Charles Hartshorne and Schubert Ogden.

The author retains some residual skepticism about the adequacy of Gamwell's formulations for two reasons. The first has to do with the ambiguity of linguistic symbols. Words have to be used to evoke experience. The "maximization of the harmony of the whole" requires the experience of harmony and the experiential correlation between the word "harmony" and the experience of harmony.

The second has to do with the relations of the forms to each other. The forms are a multiplicity, related to each other by their envisagement by God. Unlike Plato's use of the dialectic in *The Republic* to lead one to a vision of the Good, the dynamic power at the apex of the hierarchy of the forms, Whitehead insists that the forms are a multiplicity, not a class. If they be such, one's faith in rationalism is based on a transrational intuition that there is a relational essence in the nature of things which reason can hope to penetrate.

As a consequence, the author uses the term "quasi-transcendental" rather than "transcendental" to underscore both his hope that humans have been able to formulate some authentic transcendental principles and also his residual skepticism about the ability of humans to formulate *a priori* universal principles.

10. In classical Christian social ethics, the debates turned on contrasting views of the doctrine of sanctification and on the nature of human nature. Some felt human self-interest could be constrained, but even the saints continued to be sinners. Others held that the redeemed were indeed sanctified and were called to lead good and godly lives, informed by standards of perfection which were difficult but not impossible to attain. Still others took a middle position between these extremes. They urged Christians to strive toward full sanctification in their present lives, but they knew the goal could not be fully attained, at least for most if not all.

11. No Protestant theologian in the twentieth century has written more perceptively on

these matters than Reinhold Niebuhr. See especially *The Nature and Destiny of Man* (New York: Charles Scribner's Sons, 1949), vol. II, chapter 9, passim; and *The Children of Light and the Children of Darkness* (New York: Charles Scribner's Sons, 1944).

Because Niebuhr also notes the ambiguity of human motivation and formulates comparable principles of justice, the views on political economy developed here are similar to Niebuhr's. For the same reason they are similar to those of Robert Benne in his *The Ethic of Democratic Capitalism: A Moral Reassessment*, ibid., who is deeply in Niebuhr's debt for his constructive formulations.

These convergences occur in spite of the differences in the basic presuppositions informing this essay and the two authors just cited.

12. Because forms are a necessary part of any moral decision, progress is possible in morality. Better rules and regulations of justice and better forms of social organization can enhance moral decisions. For an illustrative contrasting view envisaging moral decisions involving a free transcendental decision beyond forms, see Paul Tillich, *Systematic Theology*, vol. III (Chicago: University of Chicago Press, 1963), pp. 333-339. Tillich entertains a more radical view of human freedom than does the author. In *Love, Power and Justice* (New York: Oxford, 1953) Tillich develops views regarding the relation of love, power, and justice in interpersonal, intergroup, and Divine relations similar to those developed here. However, he does not distinguish economic and political groups analytically and entertains a linear view of power.

13. For a perceptive discussion of the tension between efficiency and equality, see Arthur Okin, *Equality and Efficiency: The Big Tradeoff* (Washington: The Brookings Institution, 1975).

For an illumining analysis of Western economic growth, see Nathan Rosenberg and L.E. Birdzell, Jr., *How the West Grew Rich: The Economic Transformation of the Industrial World* (New York: Basic Books, 1986).

14. Although facets of the text are somewhat dated, *Capitalism Today*, edited by Daniel Bell and Irving Kristol (New York: Basic Books, 1970), addresses the ideological roots and the multi-faceted meaning of the term "capitalism" and explores the problems and promises of contemporary forms of capitalistic enterprise economies. For extended discussions of democratic capitalism, see Robert Benne, *The Ethic of Democratic Capitalism: A Moral Reassessment*, op. cit., and Michael Novak, *The Spirit of Democratic Capitalism*, op. cit.

For a defense of capitalism, see Irving Kristol, *Two Cheers for Capitalism* (New York: Basic Books, 1978).

15. See Arthur Okun, *Equality and Efficiency: The Big Tradeoff*, ibid. For some broad discussions of capitalism and equality, see *Capitalism and Socialism: A Theological Inquiry*, Michael Novak, editor (Washington, D.C.: American Enterprise Institute for Public Policy Research, 1979). The essays by Irving Kristol and Peter Berger in that volume are especially evocative.

For a suggestive critique of politically defined efforts to limit growth, see Edward Walter, *The Immorality of Limiting Growth* (Albany: The State University of New York Press, 1981).

It should be noted that economic growth includes both goods and services. Conservation of natural resources is not necessarily incompatible with economic growth. Technological innovation, shifting consumer preferences (which ought to be promoted primarily through the pricing mechanisms and not through rationing), and increased production and consumption of services may lead to economic growth and reduced consumption of non-replenishable natural resources at the same time.

16. Religious social ethicists sometimes appeal to the notion of creaturely equality before God to legitimate egalitarian ideals.

This notion is a curious one and cannot be justified by any appeal to the common experience of humankind. On the contrary, it would seem that God is supremely responsive to the contributions creatures of the world make to the Divine Life. If that is so, creatures could scarcely be equal before God. It would be a travesty for God to treat the contribution of a society of electrons to Its life equally with the contribution of the sequence of high grade occasions constituting the ultimate percipient occasions of the human soul. The contribution of human occasions to the Divine Life is unequal. Some humans experience richer and more complex feelings than others and hence make unequal contributions to the Divine Life. Even in the life of one individual the contributions of some of the occasions constituting the individual are greater than the contributions of others.

The author finds the views of orthodox Judaism on equality and inequality in human life more suggestive than those Christian formulations utilizing the idea of equality before God to inform religious social ethics.

17. In 1831 Alexis de Tocqueville in his remarkable *Democracy in America* commented astutely on the proliferation of voluntary associations in America. For contemporary reflections on this phenomenon, see James Luther Adams, *Voluntary Associations: Socio-Cultural Analyses and Theological Interpretation*, edited by J. Ronald Engel (Chicago: Exploration Press, 1986).

18. For a thoughtful analysis of this phenomenon, see Daniel Bell, *The Cultural Contradictions of Capitalism* (New York: Basic Books, 1976). For a perceptive discussion of some of the issues involved in promoting wholesome public life in America, see Richard John Neuhaus, *The Naked Public Square* (Grand Rapids: Eerdmans, 1984). Plato observed long ago that mediocrity and anarchy were twin dangers to which democracy was especially susceptible.

19. It is beyond the scope of this chapter to address directly the nature and character of religious institutions and their role in a democratic capitalist society. See Chapters 7, 8, 9 and 15.

20. Reliable comparative empirical data on the concentration of wealth in various historical epochs and in various societies in the current historical epoch are difficult to find. Marxists and non-Marxists are prone to use different sources of data and to interpret the same data in different ways.

For a reading that suggests increasingly rigid social stratification in the United States, see G. William Domhoff, *The Powers That Be: Processes of Rising Class Domination in America* (New York: Vintage Books, 1978). In a similar vein is the volume by Jonathan H. Turner and Charles E. Staines, *Inequality: Privilege and Poverty in America* (New York: Goodyear Publishing Co., 1976).

Others view the situation differently. See, for example, Warren G. Nutter and Henry A. Einhorn, *Enterprise Monopoly in the United States* (New York: Columbia University Press, 1969), and George Stigler, *The Economist as Preacher* (Chicago: University of Chicago Press, 1982).

For a critical assessment of third world development, see P.T. Bauer, *Reality and Rhetoric: Studies in the Economics of Development* (Cambridge: Harvard University Press, 1984).

Because of subsidies and privileges of social function, it is very difficult to compare the inequality in the Soviet Union with Western societies. Although the text is old, a major study by Abram Bergson in 1944 found the pattern of inequality between the highest-paid and lowest-paid workers in the Soviet Union were very similar to those in the United States. *The Structure of Soviet Wages* (Cambridge: Harvard University Press, 1944).

Because the "facts" are only one component in the interpretive contrasts between persons supporting democratic capitalism and those supporting democratic socialism, the debates would probably continue even if there were no evidence of gross income and wealth inequality or significant monopolistic practices. (Of course, socialists would normatively place more value on equality than would capitalists.)

For a trenchant critique of socialism, see Frank H. Knight, "Socialism: The Nature of the Problem," in his *Freedom and Reform* (New York: Harper and Bros., 1947).

Because of the primacy afforded the principle of freedom and the ubiquity of inordinate self-interest, the viewpoint developed here has some affinity to modes of thought informed by nineteenth century liberalism. See, for example, Milton Friedman, *Capitalism and Freedom* (Chicago: University of Chicago Press, 1962).

21. For one suggestive vision, see Louis O. Kelso and Patricia Hetter Kelso, *Democracy and Economic Power: Extending the ESOP Revolution* (Cambridge: Ballainger Publishing Co., 1986).

Introduction to Chapters 7 and 8

These two chapters rehearse the basic notions elaborated in Chapter 6. In spite of some repetitions, they are included in this volume because they address directly religious social ethicists who are very critical of democratic capitalism. They are somewhat polemical in character, for they promote an alternative vision as forcefully as they can. These essays illustrate how the general notions developed in the preceding chapter relate to contemporary discussions in religious social ethics. The chapters also have numerous bibliographical citations which illumine the sources stimulating my work. In contrast to the metaphysical portions of my work, the views elaborated in this part require consideration of novel, contingent data related to human beings and their behavior.

Compared to many religious social ethicists, I have found the work of the "Chicago School" of economics very helpful and very suggesting in pursuing these contingent matters. I have paid special attention to the work of Frank H. Knight, Milton Friedman, Harry Johnson, George Stigler, and Theodore W. Schultz. Even though their views of human freedom are truncated from my point of view, the liberal view of freedom as doing what one wants to do insofar as others are not injured by one's actions (dealt with in economics under the rubric of "the neighborhood effect") is very important. Similarly, their emphases on human self-initiation, consumer preference as central to the shaping of economic decisions, separation of economic and political institutions, and the centrality of the pricing mechanisms to facilitate the allocation of economic goods and services are, I think, of critical importance in shaping economy policy. Their skepticism about the efficacy of the government in economic matters and their concerns about growth and efficiency in the economic sphere are also worthy of careful attention.

Chapter 7, "American Democratic Capitalism: A Sympathetic Appraisal," was written for a festschrift for Gibson Winter, with whom I shared many seminars during the 1960s and 1970s. Influenced by the work of Martin Heidegger, Winter is very critical of the shape and substance of American society. His work helped stimulate my own reflections on political economy. My own views, contrasting sharply with his constructive views, were first put forth in this essay. (One is as much in the debt of a person with whom one disagrees as with a person with whom one agrees, for one's own understanding is enhanced and enriched with it is contrasted with alternatives.)

Chapter 8, "The Socialist/Communitarian Vision: New Dream or Old Nightmare?" is a revised version of a presentation made at a 1984 conference titled "Religion and the Economic Order: Historical Relations and the Normative Task" held at the Divinity School of the University of Chicago. The essay is a response to Douglas Sturm's paper entitled "Toward a New Social Covenant: From Commodity to Commonwealth." Drawing on the views elaborated most fully in Chapter 6, this essay makes a critical assessment of Sturm's promotion of democratic socialism and defends democratic capitalism as a better form of political economy.

The disagreements between Sturm and me constitute a family quarrel, for we both affirm the universality of the principle of relativity, taking shape here as a doctrine of internal relations. Nonetheless, we disagree about the implications of this doctrine for religious social ethics, and we give different priorities to the three principles of justice. Sturm emphasizes more forcefully the principle of equality and the saliency of community entailed in the principle of order/peace/harmony. I consider these notions to be regulative principles of justice and emphasize more forcefully the principle of freedom informed by excellence. Because of the ultimacy of creativity, I hold that freedom is the constitute principle of justice and give it priority. Sturm is also more optimistic about human ability to overcome propensities toward inordinate self-interest than I am. He also pays less attention to growth and efficiency in the economic sphere than I do.

This issue illustrates the way in which persons who share some common metaphysical principles disagree in their appropriation in human life and in social ethics. As discussed most extensively in Chapter 3, one cannot derive a process social ethic directly from process metaphysical propositions.

CHAPTER 7

American Democratic Capitalism: A Sympathetic Appraisal

INTRODUCTION

Economic and political institutions have been organized and related in a variety of ways in human societies. In the United States in the latter part of the twentieth century, capitalist organization characterized by private ownership of the modes of production and the use of pricing mechanisms to allocate resources in the economic sphere and a federated form of democracy in the political sphere have been combined in a relatively unique manner. Some observers have termed the form of economic organization embodied in this society "social market capitalism," and others have termed it "democratic capitalism."[1]

Democratic capitalism, the term used here to refer to the historical relations between democracy and market capitalism embodied in contemporary American society, has been subject to many criticisms by religious social ethicists. Many have been especially critical of market capitalism, and they often have promoted democratic socialism as a morally more defensible combination of economic and political institutions.[2]

Some critics, discerning the dominance of technical rationalism both in market capitalism and also in socialism, have advanced a more general critique of the dominant cultural values of Western civilization. Gibson Winter develops such a critique in *Being Free* and in *Liberating Creation*.[3]

While acknowledging the many imperfections and injustices of American democratic capitalism, granting the need for a more encompassing interpretation of the world than technical rationalism permits, and affirming the limitations of the understanding of freedom as doing what one wants to do, this essay interprets American democratic capitalism in an ambivalently positive manner. A capitalist economic system in association with a democratic polity constitutes a fitting combination of economic and political institutions to promote liberty, equality and community among humankind.

This essay is divided into four parts. The first section delineates the bases for the spheres of the human social order and sketches the relations between them. The second part elaborates principles of justice which provide criteria to evaluate American democratic capitalism and considers the implications of finitude, ignorance, sloth, lethargy, and inordinate self-interest for social policy and for forms of human social organization. The third part discusses the implication for American democratic capitalism of the principles of justice and the sources of disharmony among humans. The fourth part considers the results of the inquiry for the life of religious institutions in the United States. The basic categories shaping the analysis are informed by modes of thought associated with process philosophy.[4]

THE SPHERES OF THE HUMAN SOCIAL ORDER

Humans are embodied in a network of social relations in the familial, social, ethnic, economic, political, cultural and religious spheres of the human social order. They possess substantial capacities to surpass their pasts in their presents, to respond with novelty to circumstances, and to shape new and novel artifacts and ideas.

Because of these capacities human societies are more diverse and subject to more rapid change and innovation than sub-human societies on this planet. Consequently, human societies have embodied various forms of economic organization and various forms of political organization. In some societies institutions in the several spheres of the social order are sharply differentiated; in others they are more diffuse and intertwined.[5]

Generally, societies with a small number of members and/or with a traditional value orientation are less differentiated than societies with a large number of members and/or with a post-traditional value orientation. Post-traditional societies sustain technical rationalism, foster the individuation of members, and develop a complex legal order to define relations between members and sub-groups of the society.[6]

Families are rooted in biological necessity and in the needs of humans for inclusive, wholistic, and sustained relations. As is the case in all spheres of the human social order, the free play of imagination and the human capacity for choice combine with historical destiny to produce a variety of forms of family organization.

Social and ethnic groups are rooted in both biological and also socio-historical dimensions of life. Racial and ethnic groups are defined by real or imagined common biological and/or commonly shared historical experiences related to, but separable from, the larger community.

Economic institutions are grounded in biological necessity—the human need to attain adequate food, clothing and shelter—and human rational shaping capacity. Humans employ "technical" reason to calculate cost effective ways to attain specific ends.[7]

Although economic enterprises are grounded in biological necessity, the human imagination devises a wide variety of ways to satisfy basic human needs for food, fiber, and shelter. Human imagination results in an almost endless elaboration of material goods far exceeding those needed for human survival.

Humans aspire first to live and then to live well. Being and well-being are both goals of economic activity. Economic activity is accentuated by inordinate self-interest, for humans often seek economic power to attain their own goals.

The formal aspect of experience is dominant in the planning and the calculation associated with economic activity. The dynamic aspects are set, as it were, in a formal framework which is partly technical, partly monetary, and partly legal. The state enacts the laws embodied in the legal order which defines property rights, the "rules of the economic game," and the relations between economic activities and institutions and other human activities and human social institutions.

Political institutions are grounded in social necessity—the need for humans to coordinate their activities and to attain as much harmony of life with life as is possible under the conditions of existence—and human rational shaping capacity. The state includes humans in a specified geographical territory who are subject to its suasive and coercive authority.

Because social necessity is superior to biological necessity in the hierarchy of life, the state, a political institution, in principle has the right to intervene in economic affairs. The nature and shape of its intervention is much debated, and the evaluative part of this essay seeks to assess the fitting shape of its intervention.

As the dynamic dimension of human life is the leading component in institutions in the political sphere, power—both linear and reciprocal—is dominant in this sphere. Power is used to promulgate the laws which guide relations between humans and legitimate social institutions in the other spheres of the social order.

The free play of human imagination gives rise to the cultural sphere, the sphere of ideas and values. These ideas and values constitute the loci of meaning which provide people with the visions that ultimately determine the nature and character of social institutions in the other spheres of the social order.

Human responses to their awareness of the Divine Presence create institutions in the religious sphere. Love is the leading component in this sphere, and human awareness of the Supreme Love evokes the formation of religious institutions.[8]

This essay is focused primarily on relations between political and economic institutions in contemporary America and secondarily on relations between religious, political, and economic institutions. Before substantive issues dealing with these matters can be considered, it is necessary to discuss the principles of justice which provide criteria to evaluate American democratic capitalism and to note some salient factors limiting the harmony of life with life that is possible under the conditions of existence.

PRINCIPLES OF JUSTICE AND THE NATURE OF HUMAN NATURE

The becoming of a creature incorporates dynamic, formal, and unifying factors. Humans experience an emerging synthesis of forms and feelings shaped by their own self-determinations.

From this matrix of experience, three principles of justice may be abstracted. The first is self-determination informed by excellence. The second is equality appropriate to form. The third is order, peace or harmony.

Self-determination informed by excellence is at the very base of things, grounded in the ultimacy of the category of creativity. In affirming liberty or self-determination as a principle of justice, one is suggesting that the right of humans to deliberate and to come to their own decisions about actions informing their lives is fundamental.

The principle of equality appropriate to form is rooted in the notions of "oddness and evenness" and in the principle of congruence. Absolute equality is a mathematical ideal and is not literally embodied in the world. The phrase "appropriate to form" qualifies equality, for all creatures are manifestly not equal. In human life, legal equality and a measure of "equality of opportunity" may be drawn from this principle, but egalitarianism cannot be deduced from it.

The principle of order, peace or harmony is rooted in the experience of aesthetic satisfaction. The experience arises from the fitting synthesis of the formal and dynamic aspects of our emerging selves. In social relations this principle promotes a harmonization of the first two principles of justice in the name of the community, for liberty and equality are not perfectly compatable under the conditions of existence. Aesthetic satisfaction is the aim of existence, and aesthetic order is more fundamental than rational or moral order.

If the principle of liberty is accentuated unduly, equality for some is restricted inordinately. If the principle of equality is accentuated unduly, liberty for some is restricted inordinately. Given this situation, measures to extend equality must be assessed partly by their impact on liberty, and measures to extend liberty must be assessed partly by their impact on equality. Because liberty, grounded in the very nature of things, is the constitutive principle of justice, and equality, grounded on a rational mathematical ideal, is the regulative principle of justice, the question of the impact of policy proposals on humans begins—but does not end—with the question of its impact on liberty.

Human beings are inextricably related to others, for existence is characterized by community–in–individuation.[9] Both the individual and the community must be considered in a discussion of the relation of economic and political institutions. The attainment of a fitting emphasis on the individual creature and on the community is a vexing problem for social theory and for public policy.

Two other factors related to human nature must be considered before discussing the implications of the principles of justice for forms of human social organization and for public policy issues. The first is the capacity of humans to seek love and justice through reciprocal power. Humans are concerned with others, and they do seek to extend love and justice to others. The second is the limitation on the degree of the harmony of life with life possible under the conditions of existence. Finitude, ignorance, sloth, lethargy and inordinate self-interest combine to limit human efforts to maximize the harmony of life with life. Humans pursue their self-interests inordinately.

These dual tendencies combine to sustain and to thwart efforts to increase justice and harmony among humankind. People are concerned with the good of the whole and with both legitimate and also dubious efforts to enhance the self.[10]

As a result of these factors, the utilization of natural equilbria of power, intentional balance-of-power strategies, the multiplication of factions, the promotion of voluntary associations, the separation of economic and political power, a reasonable pluralism of values in the public realm, some state coordinating and interventionist activities, religious tolerance, religious pluralism and religious voluntarism will contribute to efforts to attain a reasonable measure of justice in the ongoing life of a living community. One should seek forms of social organization which promote these objectives. The following section considers the implications of these issues for American democratic capitalism.

IMPLICATIONS FOR AMERICAN DEMOCRATIC CAPITALISM

The principles of self-determination informed by excellence and equality appropriate to form sustain the idea of self-government by the members of a given living community. Democracy, in which leaders are selected to govern for a specified time and are subject to reselection or replacement by the adult members of the living community through fair and equitable election procedures, is most compatable with the principles of self-determination and equality appropriate to form.

In the American context, these procedures are set forth by a written constitution. Political and economic power are separated.[11] In addition, there is a diffusion of political power between federal and state governments. The checks and balances embodied in the American political system are designed to prevent the concentration of inordinate power in the hands of the powerful one or the powerful few.[12]

Capitalism as an economic system possesses the following characteristics:

(1) Private ownership of the means of production;

(2) Free access to the market as a consumer, a producer, an investor, or a worker;

(3) Pursuit of profit as a prime mover for economic activity; and

(4) The use of a competitive pricing system to shape the allocation of land, capital, and labor and to inform economic choices.

In order to function, the system needs the support of the legal order which (a) sustains voluntary and peaceful exchange through the enforcement of contracts and the maintenance of a viable monetary system and (b) tries in most instances (some "natural" monopolies being the exception) to prevent monopoly practices which disrupt normal supply-demand pricing mechanisms.[13]

As the coordinating and organizing center of the society, the government needs to carry on a variety of tasks which cannot be undertaken by its component parts. It must protect its citizens from physical attack by others. It needs to encourage the vitality of the "natural" groupings and to adjudicate conflicts between them. It should use all means of persuasion and negotiation to mitigate conflict between groups; and, when all other means fail, it should use its superior power to restrain social conflicts.

In addition to these activities, the state should initiate activities to ensure the ongoing health of the society. The conduct of foreign policy, the maintenance of a military organization for national defense, and the preservation of domestic tranquility are clear responsibilities of the government.

In the economic sphere, the government should intervene directly in several ways. It should counter monopolistic tendencies with appropriate antitrust efforts, undertake some kinds of research and development, provide for some consumer protection, promote programs to protect the environment from negative effects of production processes, maintain land use regulations and restrictions, protect humans from physically injurious products (particularly in the medical field), and require reasonable safety standards in the work place.

In addition, the government should pursue fitting fiscal and monetary policy to promote the orderly development of the economy. This macroeconomic program should seek to sustain reasonably stable prices.[14] The government should seek to follow policies that will promote the tendencies toward efficiency and growth already fostered by a capitalist economy.[15]

Finally, the government should intervene in the economic sphere to redistribute income to provide greater liberty and greater equality to all. Both principles of justice discussed earlier converge on this notion. Due both to differences in native ability and to social circumstances, not all persons have equal opportunity in the economic sphere.

The government clearly has a mandate to effect some modification of these conditions. In so doing, it must take account of finitude, differences in ability, and the intermingling of universal concerns and inordinate self-interest among humans. Consequently, in this area one must consider the impact of proposed public policies on efficiency and growth, for shorter term proposals designed to attain greater equality may sacrifice liberty, efficiency and growth. In such instances, the long term consequences may well mean less equality and less liberty for most of the people in the nation.

Given the reality of finitude, ignorance, sloth, lethargy and inordinate self-interest, public policy must take both incentives and human responsibility into account. Some economic incentives for individuals to work beyond the norm to promote growth and efficiency must be provided; some negative consequences for those who are indolent and/or make poor choices in pursuing their objectives must be built into policies seeking to redress inordinate inequality.

In the American experience, the greatest economic inequality lies between people in the upper five to fifteen percent income levels and in the lower five to fifteen percent income levels.[16] Intentional income redistribution schemes should affect primarily these groups. For the great middle group, market mechanisms should be permitted to allocate rewards for contributions made.

The supply-demand pricing mechanisms of a competitive economy are remarkably efficient in coordinating the allocation of resources and the production, distribution and consumption of goods and services. They obviate the need for a large governmental bureaucracy to attempt to allocate resources and to bring producers and consumers together.[17] The pricing mechanisms are grounded in the decisions of consumers and producers, thus accentuating the principle of self-determination. Government policies should work *with* these market forces rather than against them whenever possible.

Government policy should encourage the multiple centers of power—both economic and political—needed to sustain a rough natural equilibrium of power. Decentralization—wherever feasible—is desirable. The smallest unit able to carry on a specified function should be encouraged to do it.[18] The reductions of scale to a more human size and the promotion of multiple centers of initiative are both fostered by this principle of decentralization.

In human life one positive factor and one negative factor contribute to the desirability of substantial autonomy for economic enterprises. First, human self-determination is enhanced by multiple centers of initiative in a society. A large number of economic enterprises functioning without inordinate interference by the state enhances the range of human choices. Second, the persistence of inordinate self-interest among humans is blunted by the separation of economic and political institutions and by the multiplication of factions.

The principle of order, peace and harmony is also promoted by the separation of economic and political power, for the state does not have to take the blame for all economic woes. The responsibility for difficult economic decisions often lies with economic decision-makers rather than with political leaders. If responsibility is diffuse and the government is primarily a mediator rather than a protagonist on one side of economic conflicts, it can play a more constructive and fairer role in the resolution of these problems.[19]

Because economic efficiency frequently involves the closing of outmoded facilities and the loss of jobs, people and communities are hurt when business enterprises close and jobs are lost. Both private business and the government need to sustain people who are affected by these processes, but in many instances the closings must take place.

The alternative is government subsidy of inefficient enterprises. In the longer run, such practices both restrict the liberty of individuals in a society and also increase inequality. With appropriate macroeconomic policies, the government can promote growth in other sectors of the economy to produce additional jobs.

Although economic growth and efficiency often contribute to equality, this principle is not as directly enhanced by the separation of political and economic institutions as is the principle of liberty. In the efforts to realize the principle of equality, the state may intervene in the economic sphere through income redistribution measures and through programs to increase equality of opportunity. The impact on growth and efficiency of alternative ways to enhance equality of opportunity must be considered.

The separation of political and economic institutions, coupled with tax policies permitting deductions for charitable, religious, and educational contributions, promotes liberty in another way. It supports the proliferation of the numerous voluntary associations so characteristic of American life. While no simple casual relation can be established between the vigor of voluntary associations and the separation from each other of economics and political institutions, the multiple sources of funds available to voluntary associations certainly contribute to their number and vigor in the United States. Democratic institutions are enhanced by capitalism.[20]

In democratic capitalism, the state seeks to foster the self-determination of its citizens. From the societal perspective, freedom consists in doing what one wants to do. The state *qua* state maintains a minimal level of public morality. As noted earlier, it deters antisocial behavior, such as assault on persons, enforcement of voluntarily accepted contracts, robbery, graft, etc. However, the state does not contribute greatly to the understanding of self-determination informed by excellence. Indeed, its support of religious tolerance, freedom, and pluralism makes it difficult for the state *qua* state to do so.[21] The family, religious institutions, and, to a lesser extent, educational institutions should seek to nurture richer and deeper understandings of freedom than those which the state *qua* state can—or should—sustain.

Although the notion of a Divine Reality that is at least in some senses *sui generis* is mediated through the religion of America, the public sector does not embody a sustained or coherent theistic interpretation of experience.

The exploration of the multi-dimensional understanding of freedom, the cultivation of religious insight and meaning, the enhancement of belonging, and the broader shaping of human beings are left to institutions other than the state or economic institutions in American society. The concluding section addresses the implications of this situation for religious bodies.

RELIGIOUS INSTITUTIONS IN THE AMERICAN EXPERIENCE

The marked separation of the spheres of human social order and the privatization of religious institutions are modern phenomena manifest in post-traditional societies.[22]

Some interpreters lament this situation, but at the same time they affirm the merit of religious freedom, religious pluralism, and religious tolerance. One cannot have it both ways. If one rejects formal privatization, the consequence is the diminution or elimination of the religious freedom, religious pluralism and religious tolerance now sustained by the separation of church and state.

It is far better to affirm privatization than to suffer the consequences of the public support of a particular religious body. The human propensity toward idolatry is blunted when neither political nor religious leaders can fully anoint the other.

At the same time, religious institutions are called to become centers of meaning and belonging. They point to dimensions of experience and to realities which are not explicitly affirmed in economic and political life.

Two tasks confront members of religious institutions in this situation. First, they must sustain a context of belonging and meaning which they and their fellow participants can affirm with integrity. Second, they must define some way in which their social ethical concerns may be manifest in the public sphere.

In the first instance, representatives of most religious institutions will want to challenge aspects of the understanding of freedom informing the public realm. They will want to offer a theistic interpretation of reality to qualify and/or to augment the interpretations of the Divine Reality which are unevenly embodied in the public sphere.

In the second instance, they can either (a) seek to inform the magistrates of their tasks and responsibilities from a point of view unavailable to them from other sources, (b) affirm some version of natural law which will permit them to emphasize principles of justice common to all, or (c) affirm some distinctive principles inherent in their tradition and certain principles common to all. They may seek to provide a direction for society or directives to the society.

Persons in faith communities pressing for a coalescence of the community of faith and the community of politics will be more inclined to issue directives than to suggest a direction for the society. Persons in those faith communities maintaining more internal diversity in faith and works and resisting the identity of the community of faith and the community of politics will be more concerned with seeking to promote a direction for society. Religious leaders will encourage their members to pursue the quest for social justice through voluntary associations, political parties, and economic enterprises in the other spheres of the social order. They will acknowledge the legitimacy of some differences of viewpoint on public policy issues among their members.

One informed by the constructive formulations developed here will seek to enunciate principles which are common to all people in their public policy activities. He or she will promote a direction for the society, but will resist efforts to identify the community of faith and the community of politics.

In the American context, one will be a reformer rather than a revolutionary. One's efforts to extend social justice and to enhance the harmony of life with life that is possible under the conditions of human existence will be marked by innovation in the context of conservation, for evolutionary social change is preferable to cataclysmic social change. Democratic institutions provide the best framework through which such social transformations can be worked out.

Notes and References

1. The term "social market capitalism" was coined by the West German Social Democratic Party. At a 1959 conference at Bad Godesberg the party espoused economic competition and a market system which combined competition and planning in a fitting manner. The Social Democratic Party proposed an economic policy designed to limit great concentration of economic power and to separate economic and political power. Philip Wogaman uses the term "social market capitalism" to characterize the mixed economies of most of the English speaking world and western Europe in his *The Great Economic Debate: An Ethical Analysis* (Philadelphia: The Westminster Press, 1977).

   In his *The Ethic of Democratic Capitalism: A Moral Reassessment* (Philadelphia: Fortress Press, 1981), which deals primarily with the American economic system, Robert Benne uses Michael Novak's term "democratic capitalism" to denote the relation of economic and political institutions in the United States. That term has been appropriated here to indicate a form of democracy and market capitalism shaped by the American experience.

   Formally, there are only three ways in which institutions in the economic and political spheres can be related. They may be separated, they may be identified, or they may "overlap." The substance of a particular society will affect the nuances of the relations, and, in some instances, these nuances will be very important. Nonetheless, only a limited number of arrangements is possible.

   Protagonists of various forms of economic organization establish different priorities for liberty, equality, and community. They also have different views of liberty. Socialists usually entertain a more optimistic view of human nature than do capitalists.

   Laissez-faire capitalists emphasize liberty understood as doing what one wants to do. They seek to maintain a sharp separation between economic and political institutions. Equality is of secondary importance and the community is of tertiary importance. They also emphasize pursuit of self-interest as a dominant characteristic of humankind. Equality and community emerge from mutual self-interest.

   Democratic capitalists maintain more balance between liberty, equality, and community. They affirm a limited impingement of the government on economic institutions. Liberty is still the leading component, but it is balanced more evenly with equality and community. Often they are more ambivalent about human self-interest and human self-transcending capacities.

   Democratic socialists emphasize equality and set it in relation to liberty and community. They affirm the legitimacy of government ownership of the modes of production and distribution, but they may maintain some sphere for private property. In extreme cases, the relation posited between the individual and the community is similar to the Marxist vision. The emphasis on the community undoubtedly contributes to the appeal of democratic socialism to many religious social ethicists.

   Marxists emphasize community and accentuate state ownership of the modes of production. Equality is a strong secondary component and liberty is redefined so individual fulfillment is set in the context of community fulfillment. Marxist insistence on "right doctrine" is related to their insistence on the primacy of community. Although they would disagree with the substance of "right doctrine," Thomas Aquinas, John Calvin, and Menno Simons would all understand the need to suppress the deviant individual for the sake of the community.

   Both democratic socialists and Marxists entertain more optimistic views of the nature of human nature than do laissez-faire and many democratic capitalists.

   Democratic socialists and many Marxists advance contrasting views of social change. Democratic socialists advocate the transition to socialism through democratic and evolutionary means, but many Marxists, informed by the dialectic of negation, envisage more cataclysmic transformations.

2. The recent publication of Franklin Sherman's translation of Paul Tillich's *The Socialist Decision* (New York: Harper & Row, 1977) has evoked fresh discussion of the socialist alternative to democratic capitalism among religious social ethicists. Richard Shaull and Robert McAfee Brown are among the staunch critics of market capitalism. Dorothee Sölle and Jürgen Moltmann also criticize this mode of economic organization.

   Among Latin American "liberation" theologians, the mood is almost pervasive. Dom Helder Camara, Gustavo Gutierrez, Jose Miguez Bonino, and Juan Luis Segundo are representative. Their social analyses display a more pronounced Marxian character than do the analyses of many North American and western European theologians who espouse a socialist form of economic organization.

After a careful and balanced assessment of alternative forms of economic organization in *The Great Economic Debate*, (*op. cit.*) Philip Wogaman opts for socialism as a more adequate embodiment of a Christian morality.

For a classic critique of socialism, see the essay by Frank H. Knight, "Socialism: The Nature of the Problem" in his *Freedom and Reform* (New York: Harper & Bros., 1947).

For a volume encompassing contrasting views on the modern corporation from a variety of theological perspectives, see Oliver Williams and John Houck, editors, *The Judeo-Christian Vision and the Modern Corporation* (Notre Dame: University of Notre Dame Press, 1982).

3. Gibson Winter, *Being Free* (New York: Macmillan, 1970) and *Liberating Creation* (New York: Seabury, 1982). As the body of the text indicates, the point of view developed here is also concerned with a more inclusive understanding of reason than mere technical rationalism and a more encompassing understanding of freedom than the ability to do what one wants to do. However, the views developed here give more credence to technical reason and are more sympathetic to the existentialist view of freedom as doing what one wants to do. In addition, the extreme centrality of values rooted in the economic sphere in American life which Winter suggests seems too stringent. The dominant values shaping American life are more diffuse and pluralistic than this interpretation suggests.

Winter's constructive appropriation of Heidegger leads to an interpretation of experience grounded on a Being-being form of the classic essence-existence contrast. The notions of hiddenness and disclosure central to his work are reminiscient of the hiddenness and revelation of God in the classical Christian tradition. The implicit one-way God-world relations inherent in this view cannot be reconciled with a process view of God-world relations. The framework leads to a sharper critique of technology and a more intense vision of the possibility of a more harmonious human community than my appropriation of process philosophy permits. The nature of God-world relations, the nature of space and time, the nature of symbolic reference, the nature of immortality, and the relation of past, present, and future in a Heideggerian perspective all pose major problems for process thinkers. At the same time, the multidimensional character of human experience and the aim at aesthetic satisfaction provide the bases for some convergences between the two points of view.

Because the present essay is primarily a constructive one, these issues can only be noted here. Space limitations preclude an extended discussion of the problems embodied in a Heideggerian perspective from a process point of view. The basic contrast involves the Whiteheadian rejection of the essence-existence or Being-being contrast so central to Heidegger and to Winter. In addition, the principle of relativity is applied in a more through-going manner in a Whiteheadian perspective. The process view of the nature of an emerging subject-object further accentuates the contrast about the nature of the self between Whiteheadian and Heideggerian points of view.

My own thinking on the matters addressed in this essay were greatly stimulated by my association with Winter during the time he was at the Divinity School of the University of Chicago. We explored the issues addressed in this essay in numerous joint seminars. While we share a fundamental uneasiness about the non-theistic interpretations of experience embodied in the contemporary human sciences, we have developed contrasting constructive interpretations of the contemporary American experience. My ambiguously positive interpretation of that experience contrasts with his negative or ambiguously negative interpretation of it.

Winter's persistent criticisms of the American social order are a stimulus to us all, and those of us who do not share his primal vision are in his debt for the vigor with which he challenges us to pursue these issues in religious social ethics.

4. Process philosophy is associated with the seminal work of Alfred North Whitehead and Charles Hartshorne. Space limitations preclude an extended discussion of this movement here. For an example of the way in which process philosophy is informing social thought, see John B. Cobb, Jr. and W. Widick Schroeder, eds., *Process Philosophy and Social Thought* (Chicago: Center for the Scientific Study of Religion, 1981). Because of the contingent nature of human defining characteristics, the authors in this volume do not attain a consensus on fitting forms of human social organization.

For a related process assessment of capitalism see the chapter "Marxism and Metaphysics" in Charles Hartshorne, *Insights and Oversights of Great Thinkers: An Evaluation of Western Philosophy* (Albany: State University of New York Press, 1983). For a contrasting process interpretation, see John B. Cobb, Jr., *Process Philosophy as Political Theology* (Philadelphia: The Westminster Press, 1982).

The formulations developed in this essay may be characterized as standing in the "right wing" of process social theory. Liberty is accentuated more forcefully than equality or community, and formal elements in morality are also emphasized to a greater degree. In addition, the persistence of inordinate self-interest is more forcefully affirmed. In this "family quarrel," all proponents affirm the need to incorporate liberty, equality and community in their social analyses, deny the doctrine of "original sin" in its classical form, want to protect the ecosphere, and want to blunt the hellish prospect of nuclear warfare.

5. Space limitations preclude an extended development of the bases for the spheres of the social order and the structure of human nature. These topics are addressed more fully in several other chapters in this volume. See especially Part I, Chapters 4 and 5 in Part II, and Chapter 9 in Part III.
6. See Robert Bellah, "Religious Evolution" in *Beyond Belief* (New York: Harper and Row, 1970). His own constructive assessments, differing sharply from those developed here, appear in "Discerning Old and New Imperatives in Theological Education," *Theological Education*, Vol. XIX, No. 1 (Autumn, 1982), pp. 7-29. In that essay, he suggests "Since democratic capitalism seems an evermore self-contradictory idea, it may well be that only a form of democratic socialism will be compatible with a Christian life." (p. 26.)
7. Technical reason must be supplemented by ontic reason. In its more inclusive meaning, reason refers to human participation in forms of definiteness embodied in the primordial facet of the Divine Nature. Humans are able to contrast a variety of forms and to exercise negative judgments. These capacities give rise to consciousness and to human cognitive creativity.

   Neo-classical economics confines itself almost exclusively to human choices informed by technical rationalism. It is very "flat," unable either to illumine the depths and heights of human experience or to provide a set of ideas broad enough to encompass the richness of all human experience.

   Some economists, such as Gary Becker and George Stigler, have suggested using an economic model of humans maximizing their self-interests in all the spheres of the social order to interpret human behavior. Their approach represents an over-extension of an economic model.

   Marginal utility analyses dominant in mainstream economics emphasize gradual rather than dialectical change. The Marxian dialectic of negation does not fit the neo-classical economic model, and vice versa.
8. For fuller discussions of the spheres of the social order, see the references cited in note 5.
9. In process thought, the principle of relativity is the metaphysical basis for the social character of reality. The special intimacy with one's own causal past and the centeredness of the emerging subject contribute to the individuating and self-determining aspects of the human being. The necessary relation to other creatures contributes to the participation of the human being in and with others.

   Thus, the community and the individual must both be considered in a discussion of the relation of institutions in the economic and political spheres of the social order. Socialism and communism too readily subsume the individual to the community and are too egalitarian.
10. The ambiguity of human nature suggested here and the principles of justice developed here are similar to the views of Reinhold Niebuhr. Consequently, it is not surprising that the constructive views developed later are similar to his.

    This convergence occurs in spite of very substantial differences in basic interpretative frameworks. Niebuhr entertains a substance doctrine of the self, appeals to Newtonian conceptions of space and time, and envisages a "one-way" understanding of God-world relations

(God is imminent in and transcends the world, but the world is not imminent in and does not transcend God.)

The views are also very similar to those developed by Robert Benne in *The Ethic of Democratic Capitalism: A Moral Reassessment, op. cit.*, for Benne's constructive work is strongly influenced by Reinhold Niebuhr's anthropology. The principles of liberty and equality and the doctrine of human sinfulness also inform his constructive work. Benne's volume is a rich resource for empirical material pertaining to the issues considered here.

11. Radical critiques of American life center around charges that advertising, the pervasiveness of technical rationalism, monopoly capitalism, and/or the dominance of economic elites in the political sphere make a sham of the notion of democracy and/or the separation of institutions in the political and economic spheres. For various efforts to refute these points of view, see *Capitalism Today*, edited by Daniel Bell and Irving Kristol (New York: Mentor, 1971) and Benne, *op. cit.*

In the author's judgment, the allegations made by critics of American democratic capitalism contain some truth, but they overestimate the influence of advertising, understate the continued competition in the economic sphere, overstate the influence of conservative elitists in shaping public policy, and underestimate the psychic health of the citizenry.

The pervasiveness of technical rationalism is a major problem, and it needs to be supplemented, but not eliminated. The ambiguity of *techne* is acknowledged, but technology is interpreted in an ambivalently positive fashion.

For a sympathetically critical assessment of contemporary capitalism, see Irving Kristol, *Two Cheers for Capitalism* (New York: Basic Books, 1978). For a thoughtful critique of theories of dependent capitalism in third world development, see W. Arthur Lewis, *The Evolution of the International Economic Order* (Princeton, N. J.: Princeton University Press, 1978.)

12. James Madison, whose key role in the formulation and promulgation of the U.S. Constitution is well known, was a very astute lay theologian. He was much impressed by the doctrine of original sin and promoted political structures to blunt inordinate human self-interest.

The multiplication of factions and separation of powers were both designed to minimize the likelihood of inordinate concentration of political power. Many of Madison's essays in *The Federalist Papers* expound these views.

13. Space limitations preclude an adequate consideration of the complex problems of monopoly—both corporate and union. In earlier days many religious bodies rightly supported labor organizations to correct power imbalances between management and labor and to promote worker safety and health.

In the modern epoch, labor power in some industries—such as auto, steel, trucking and telecommunications—has become excessive, for workers in these industries are often paid substantially more than their counterparts in other industries due to monopoly practices by labor unions. The contemporary difficulties in many heavy industries are related to inordinate union power in them.

14. As the experiences of the past few years indicate, this goal is much easier to state than to actualize. Most mainstream economists acknowledge this difficulty, and they have no persuasive policy proposals designed to produce full employment and minimal inflation at the same time.

15. Efficiency and growth are critical to the extension of self-determination and equality. While efficiency and growth may be less important in some subsequent historical epoch, they are very important in the present epoch. Due to space limitations, this entire matter cannot be explored in detail here. For extended discussions, see Arthur Okun, *Equality and Efficiency: The Big Tradeoff* (Washington, D.C.: The Brookings Institute, 1975), and Edward Walter, *The Immorality of Limiting Growth* (Albany: State University of New York Press, 1981.)

16. See Paul Samuelson, *Economics, Eleventh Edition* (New York: McGraw-Hill Book Company, 1980), pp. 78-84. Transfer payments and age and family status differences must be taken into account in considering the needs of persons below the "poverty level."

17. Some economists sympathetic to socialism have advocated greater use of price mechanisms to allocate resources. See, for example, Oskar Lange, *Problems of the Political Economy of Socialism* (New Delhi: People's Publishing House, 1965).

18. This principle has been termed the principle of subsidiarity in Roman Catholic social teachings. It has been reaffirmed in many Catholic social pronouncements. See, for example,

Pope John XXIII, *Mater et Magistra.*

19. In Britain, for example, the government as the employer is often involved in a most difficult way in labor disputes.
20. Milton Friedman emphasizes the intimate relation between democracy and capitalism in *Capitalism and Freedom* (Chicago: University of Chicago Press, 1962). Ludwig Von Mises in *The Free and Prosperous Commonwealth* (Princeton: Van Nostrand, 1962.) and Friedrich Hayek, *The Road to Serfdom* (Chicago: University of Chicago Press, 1944), develop similar arguments.

    The presence of countries in western Europe that have been able to combine democracy and socialism raises some questions about these analyses. However, the time span has been quite short, and private centers of initiative do remain. In America, government income redistribution schemes redress gross inequality without eliminating private modes of production and private property.

    On the longer run, civil liberties are more apt to be sustained under arrangements separating economic and political institutions. Only a saintly government bureaucracy would give support to its staunch critics, and there are no such saintly bureaucracies. As Frank H. Knight observed, the persistence of the family in socialist societies poses another problem. Government officials are sorely tempted to give preferential treatment to their children.

    Individuals and government leaders are often tempted to equate their vision of the good with the common good. In light of this widespread propensity, one must be wary of self-appointed proponents of the common good.

    The "best" proponents of the common good—given the problems of finitude, ignorance, sloth, lethargy, and the persistence of inordinate self-interest among humans—are those who seek to defend civil liberties, to foster checks and balances, and to defend the separation of social institutions in the several spheres of the social order. In this framework, specific problems—of which the problem of the health of the ecosphere is perhaps the most urgent—can be most appropriately addressed. The capacity of the multiple factions to come to some judgments related to the "common good" attests to the ability of persons to surpass their self-interests in part.
21. The public faith of America—a complex mosaic including technical rationalism, a humanistic view of the sacredness of the human personality, and the religion of America—does contribute to the moral education of Americans. Space limitations preclude a discussion of this issue and the related discussion of "civil religion" here.

    Two of the major weaknesses of the understanding of human nature embodied in mainline economic theory and in the nineteenth century English liberal tradition that informs many social philosophies defending capitalism are their flatness and their inordinately individualistic bias. It is small wonder that many persons turn to Christianity, Marxism and other more inclusive social philosophies to answer human questions about meaning and belonging.

    Excessive individualism and excessive hedonism are major problems in the contemporary world. While democratic capitalism is not solely responsible for these problems (certainly hedonism is also manifest in socialist and Marxist countries), the overarching ethos in contemporary America does contribute to them.

    Religious institutions can seek both to cultivate a countervailing ethos and also to promote fitting public policy proposals to minimize some of the hedonistic excesses. In many instances it is difficult to go very far without unduly limiting human freedom. When the exercise of one's freedom limits the freedom of others, action can be taken. (Greater punishment for persons involved in alcohol related auto accidents is an example of an area where remedial action can be taken by the state.)
22. In some ways, the current American situation is analogous to the situation in the Roman Empire prior to the establishment of Christianity as the state church. However, the general cultural milieu is so different that the comparison is only a vaguely suggestive one. For a discussion of the evolution of religious institutions, see Robert Bellah, "Religious Evolution" in *Beyond Belief, op. cit.*

CHAPTER 8

The Socialist/Communitarian Vision: New Dream or Old Nightmare?

Many religious social ethicists related to major non-fundamentalist religious communities have not been very charitable in their assessments of American democratic capitalism. In fact, democratic socialism or communitarianism has been advanced by a goodly number of religious social ethicists.[1] Douglas Sturm and Cornel West, for instance, are representative of this line of critical thinking (in Grelle and Krueger 1986). These critiques have their cultural roots in the European experience and have been embodied in various facets of the American religious heritage. They began in Germany in the early decades of the nineteenth century among "left-wing Hegelians" who rejected the complex ontology of G. W. F. Hegel and sought alternative interpretations of the nature of things.[2]

Albrecht Ritschl (1822-89), in his Christological monism, initiated a line of liberal Protestant thinking that emphasized the life of Jesus as an exemplar of full human life. Walter Rauschenbusch (1861-1918), following graduate work in Germany, became the greatest figure of the American Social Gospel movement and helped interject socialist thinking into American religious social ethics.[3] F. D. Maurice (1805-72), and the English Fabians emerging in the latter part of the nineteenth century, also gave impetus to socialist thinking among American social ethicists (see

Hopkins 1940). The socialism and/or communitarianism evoked from these modes of thinking was gradualistic. Protagonists envisaged economic transformation through peaceful democratic processes.

Although not a major factor in these late nineteenth and early twentieth century developments, Marxist categories of analysis became more fashionable among religious social ethicists in the days of the Great Depression and have again emerged in the latter part of the twentieth century.[4] Latin American liberation theologians use Marxist categories of social analysis and interpretation very frequently in their constructive work (see, e.g., Gutierrez 1973; Gutierrez and Shaull 1977; Segundo 1976). This movement is complemented by various "theologies of hope" emerging out of the German experience following World War II. Some of these protagonists envisage more gradualistic moves to democratic socialism; others promote a revolutionary move. In the latter case, the dialectic of negation becomes a sociocultural as well as a theological methodological tool.[5]

All of these strands have interplayed with both indigenous American values and American appropriation of the Enlightenment notions of liberty, equality, and community to produce Liberation Theology. Most proponents of this style of theological thinking are critical of capitalism for its alleged promotion of inordinate individualism, materialism, elitism, hedonism, racism, sexism, classism, nationalism, militarism, colonialism, and exploitation of non-industrialized countries, or some combination of these evils.

It is beyond the scope of this essay to deal with all the facets of this complex social and intellectual movement. This essay focuses more narrowly on one key notion in most socialist/communitarian schemes, the promotion of public ownership of the means of production, and the factors that need to be considered in a moral appraisal of such a proposal. Douglas Sturm's article "Toward a New Social Covenant" (in Grelle and Krueger 1986) serves as a representative point of departure for understanding the issues at stake in this discussion.

Both Sturm and I, in our constructive work, are deeply indebted to the philosophy of Alfred North Whitehead and the movement of thought following his lead that came to be known as process philosophy, and its correlates, process theology and process social ethics.[6] In spite of this common legacy, however, we come to different conclusions about the most fitting relations between institutions in the economic and political spheres of the American social order.[7]

Sturm envisages the emergence of a new social covenant in this nation, resulting in a shift from humans being treated as commodities in the present situation to humans being treated as willing, self-determining persons in the new commonwealth.[8] In this shift to social democracy, the modes of production will become public property, and participatory democracy will expand greatly in both the economic and political spheres. Effecting this shift will enrich and deepen human life and enhance the harmony of life with life. Conflict and strife will be reduced, and in the new commonwealth, the common good will once again take precedence over individual good. The transformed relations between economic and political institutions will contribute to greater social justice, for community and equality—key components in Sturm's understanding of justice—will be enhanced by this projected transformation of economic and political institutions. Sturm's views may be taken as representative of many persons promoting democratic socialism.

In contrast to Sturm's views, I hold that in the current historical epoch and in the foreseeable future (certainly for the next two or three generations and probably much, much longer), economic and political institutions should be separated. A society combining an enterprise economic system based on private ownership of the modes of production (including widely diffused private ownership through personal shareholders and private pension plans) with appropriate government intervention in the economic sphere is more likely to attain both social justice and economic growth and efficiency than is a society coalescing economic and political power in the state. At the same time, I believe the democratic polity should intervene in the economic order in fitting ways to promote some common community interests, to limit some economic practices (monopoly, for example), to promote economic stability and growth through appropriate macro-economic policy (both fiscal and monetary) and to effect some income redistribution through taxation and welfare policies. I am generally wary of the counsel offered by many self-proclaimed proponents of the common good, for often their own self-interests and theories of social, economic, and political organization shape their policy proposals inordinately. Of course, properly defined self-interest, including due recognition of the neighborhood effect, does contribute to public policy deliberations in an ambiguously positive manner.

In sum, I affirm the creative possibilities and normative desirability of the emerging relations between economic and political institutions in the United States currently termed democratic or social market capitalism.[9]

The body of the essay seeks to establish the bases for this positive affirmation.

In this essay, the persistence of inordinate self-interest, the primacy of liberty as the constitutive principle of justice, and the values of pluralism and the multiplication-of-factions will be emphasized more forcefully than they are in Sturm's essay. These emphases lead me to a contrasting view of the common good, a more sympathetic reading of past American social, economic, and political history, and an alternative understanding of desirable future relations between economic and political institutions in the United States.

1

God, desiring not only that the human race might be able by their similarity of nature to associate with one another, but also that they might be bound together in harmony and peace by the ties of relationship, was pleased to derive all persons from one individual (Augustine 1950, XIV, 1).

And hence we enjoy some gratification when our good friends die; for though their death leaves us in sorrow, we have the consolatory assurance that they are beyond the ills by which in this life even the best of man are broken down or corrupted, or are in danger of both results (Augustine 1950, XIV, 8).

Sturm, in his discussion of the common good, cites Augustine to illumine the vision of a perfect harmony of life with life, in which all creatures are lured by the Divine will to coordinate and to harmonize their activities for the good of all. Augustine's description of human life after the fall, by contrast, calls attention to the persistence of disharmonious and discordant experiences among humankind. Taken conjointly, the two Augustinian epigrams attest to the pervasive and persistent interplay of both harmonious and discordant dimensions of experience in our personal and corporate life. Two critical issues emerge from reflection about these aspects of human experience: questions about the bases of these experiences, and the possibility of reducing or eliminating discord in the future through appropriate human action.

Karl Marx traced the alienation he discerned in the world to the objectification and thingification of the products of human labor. His salvific proposal centered on the elimination of private property to overcome the estrangement humans now experience. Non-Marxist socialists such as

Sturm are not that sanguine, but most of them affirm that some or most of the discord can be eliminated through the reorganization of the economic order and the public ownership of the means of production.[10]

In my view, the bases of disharmony in human life are finitude, ignorance, sloth, lethargy, and inordinate self-interest. *Finitude* demands exclusion, and from the human point of view, entails loss. The vivid immediacy of the present fades into the past and is only partially appropriated by the successors of the subject experiencing the present. Because of finitude, the evocation of harmony and intensity of feeling is shaped by the sustaining environment. In some instances, discordant experiences are necessary to evoke higher harmonies; in other instances, discordant experiences may evoke anesthesia.[11] *Ignorance* limits an experiencing subject's capacity to avoid all actions whose consequences may be deleterious, for emerging subjects do not know in detail what their contemporaries will decide to do. Consequently, some actualizations will evoke more discord than an emerging subject has any reason to suspect. *Sloth* and *lethargy* are too widespread among humankind to be ignored. Indeed, an efficient economic system must minimize these human tendencies through both suasion and coercion. Finally, human beings all too frequently conduct their lives with *inordinate self-interest.* The concern for others and for the broader human community is always present in human life, but self-interest qualifies and modifies the concern. Some self-interest, of course, is necessary for an emerging subject to become, but this metaphysical necessity all too often leads to excessive self-interest.

For all these reasons, I cannot envisage any form of human social organization that will eliminate the foundational experience of discord that fosters various theories of estrangement or alienation. Any scheme of social reorganization that proposes such an outcome is rightly viewed as utopian. The naive optimism frequently associated with such schemes all too often yields bitter fruits; for efforts to actualize such schemes frequently allow dictators or oligarchies to seize power and to claim the spoils of the reorganization for their own benefit.[12]

The plasticity of human nature and the possibility of alleviating persistent shortages of food, fiber and shelter prevent me from rejecting social democracy unequivocally and forever, though it does not seem very probable in the current historical epoch. However, as noted earlier, I see nothing emerging that would suggest a dramatic decline of inordinate self-interest among humankind in the foreseeable future or occasion the establishment of a socialist/communitarian society able to sustain both liberty and economic efficiency and growth.

The system of checks and balances embodied in the American system of government represents a fortuitous blending of Calvinistic and Enlightenment values. James Madison, who wrote many of *The Federalist Papers* elaborating the theory informing the structure of the proposed Constitution, was a very astute lay theologian. He took the doctrine of original sin very seriously and sought to develop a structure of government that would blunt inordinate self-interest through a system of checks and balances and through the multiplication-of-factions. Like Augustine, the U.S. Constitution envisaged both the harmony of the whole and the discord embodied within the whole.[13]

The inevitability of some discord in human life and the persistence of inordinate self-interest are two main reasons I resist democratic socialism and prefer democratic capitalism. I am very wary of the increased concentration of power in the hands of politicians that would occur if the means of production were owned by the state. The state, through its monopoly on the legitimate use of force, its capacity to make laws, and its administration of the judicial system, already has great power to coerce humans, to suppress individual liberty and self-initiation, and to bestow political favors. To give politicians—even those allegedly chosen through participatory democracy—vastly greater power over economic institutions would be to concentrate power inordinately.

2

A Great Society has nothing to do with and is in fact irreconcilable with "solidarity" in the true sense of unitedness in the pursuit of known common goals (Friedrich A. Hayek 1976, 111).

Democracy is not founded merely on the right of the private interest of the individual. This is only one side of the shield. It is founded equally on the function of the individual as a member of the community. It founds the common good on the common will, in forming which it bids every grown-up intelligent person to take a part (L. T. Hobhouse 1964, 115).

Our claim for freedom is rooted in our relationship with our contemporary environment. Nature does provide a field for independent activities (Alfred North Whitehead 1961, 251).

The epigrams of Hayek and Hobhouse that Sturm cited in the second section of his essay have been supplemented here by one drawn from the writings of Alfred North Whitehead. Taken conjointly, they pose the central issues of this section: the nature of liberty and its relation to equality and to community, and the implications of these principles and the persistence of inordinate self-interest for forms of economic and political organization.

In promoting the vision of social democracy as a normative form of economic-political organization, Sturm appeals to a doctrine of internal relations to legitimate the communitarianism he thinks democratic socialism will promote more effectively than democratic capitalism. This doctrine of internal relations is integral to process thinking. An explication of it and other foundational notions will illumine part of the basis for my view of normative relations between economic and political institutions. It will also illumine the role of continent empirical data in the elaboration of human social theory.[14]

Metaphysical propositions (if they be such) apply to all actual entities in all cosmic epochs. A metaphysical system seeks to coordinate and to integrate metaphysical propositions into a coherent whole. If a proposition is a metaphysical one, it will not discriminate one entity from another, for it will apply to all. The only way to develop metaphysical propositions is through the use of negative judgments. One must imagine the absence of that which is in fact always present. More specialized propositions apply to some but not to all actual entities. Consequently, a method of difference must be used to develop propositions applicable to a particular subject matter. These propositions must not violate the more general metaphysical propositions, but they necessarily will be more specific in characterizing particular subject matters.

As noted earlier, Sturm and I are both deeply influenced by process modes of thought. However, we order the primal notions of process philosophy somewhat differently, and we differ about contingent matters pertaining to human beings in the current historical epoch. Both factors contribute to the differences in our contrasting interpretations of the American past and our contrasting visions of the American future.

The doctrine of internal relations, which is a corollary of Whitehead's principle of relativity, is a very important notion for Sturm.[15] It permits him to reject the individualism which characterized much seventeenth-century social philosophy and which was salient in nineteenth-century English liberalism. The relations of the human organizing center with its body, with nature, and with other humans are fundamental in human experience. This doctrine of internal relations leads Sturm to affirm both participatory democracy and communitarianism. The primacy of the notion of community and a rather strong egalitarian bias are implicit in this affirmation. The merit of human self-determination is acknowledged, but human freedom is limited very substantially by the appeal to equality and community.

In my view, Sturm underplays the importance of the category of creativity, another primal notion in Whitehead's metaphysics. Creativity is the category of categories, the ultimate notion which can be characterized only by its manifestation in the creatures of the world. It stands behind the forms and is inexplicable by the forms. The sole appeal is to intuition. The freedom of the creatures of the world to respond with novelty to the influence of the causal past is an exemplification of the category of creativity. A given creature's capacity for novelty of response to its data cannot be determined *a priori;* this capacity must be assessed through comparative empirical observations of various types of creatures. Nature appears to be organized hierarchically, and on this planet, humans are the creatures possessing the greatest capacity for novelty of response to circumstances. Human purposiveness and self-determination are too pervasive and too salient to be dismissed as epiphenomenal.

Both community and freedom are important, but in my understanding, freedom is constitutive of human life, and community is regulative. Freedom of self-determination informed by excellence is the constitutive principle of justice, and the idea of order implicit in the notion of community is one of the regulative principles of justice.

The other regulative principle of justice, rather more implicit than explicit in Sturm's formulations, is the principle of equality. Equality is an idealized mathematical notion, and no two actual entities are exactly equal. In fact, equality as a regulative principle of justice is a vague notion, for equality can be applied only to creatures who are roughly equals. The way in which "form" ought to qualify equality is subject to disagreement. No one would argue, for example, that the same rules and regulations of justice should apply to children as to adults. Yet the nature of the qualifications, and the age at which a child becomes an adult, are subject to debate. In human life, the qualifications which form ought to give to equality are even more problematic when sex is the form qualifying equality. Social function is another form qualifying equality; but again, people differ substantially in their judgements about the extent to which one's social function should qualify equality.

In addition to these problems about the limits that forms should place on equality, there is a tension between freedom, equality, and order. Freedom evokes inequality, and the community limits human freedom for the sake of order and equality. Consequently, no perfect harmonization of the principles of justice is possible under the conditions of existence. A rough approximation or a tolerable balance is the most to be expected, and this balance will shift with changing circumstances.[16]

Because I hold that freedom is the constitutive principle of justice, I am wary about the overextension of equality and order, the regulative principles of justice. Sturm's views contain the danger that even in a relatively "ideal" situation that controlled inordinate self-interest, the pressure for equality and community in his socialist/communitarian society would make life very difficult for a non-conformist minority. There would be strong pressures for the state to suppress deviancy excessively. In fact, freedom would be redefined so that the person who was truly free would be the one who conformed to the expectations of the dominant group which claimed to speak for the community.[17] Given the widespread propensity toward inordinate self-interest, persons in charge of socialist political-economic systems could impose, and in many historical cases actually have imposed, excessive limitations on the self-initiative of persons in minority groups.

Democratic capitalism, which sustains multiple centers of initiative and power, fosters the development of voluntary associations, offers economic inducements without government sanction or approval, and promotes checks and balances within and between economic and political groups, can sustain the quest for liberty and equality while minimizing the dangers inherent in an omni-component government.

This view does not necessarily entail a laissez-faire economic policy. The state in principle has the right to intervene in the economic order for the sake of justice; because social necessity, the basis for the political sphere of human life, is superior to biological necessity, the basis for the economic order. Some income redistribution, unemployment compensation to sustain victims of technological change and/or the business cycle, appropriate measures to protect the environment and redress the neighborhood effect, and appropriate regulations of business illustrate some of the ways in which the polity may seek to attain economic justice for its citizens. In engaging in these activities, however, public policy should seek to sustain the private sector rather than impede it. Further, various forms of welfare should be designed to enhance the self-determination of recipients rather than to evoke continued dependence.[18]

3

> *This interrelation of agents, which makes the freedom of all members of a society depend upon the intentions of each, is the ground of morality . . . If we call the harmonious interrelation of agents their "community," we may say that a morally right action is an action which intends community . . . If the world is one action, any particular action determines the future, within its own limits, for all agents. Every individual agent is therefore responsible to all other agents for his actions (John MacMurray 1961, 118-19).*

> *As a nation we have become increasingly concerned, especially since 1929, about effecting fair and equitable balance between the conflicting goals of efficiency in production and the preservation of human values. The invisible hand of the market place did not provide compensation for men injured on the job, wages as a matter of right for men out of work, pensions for retired workers, or freedom from unjustified discharges. Much of the strength of this country, I believe, has derived from a strong drive for efficiency in completion, moderated, however, by an inherent compassion in the ultimation of one factor of production—labor. Here is the really revolutionary idea of the past century (George W. Taylor, "The Role of Labor Unions," in Samuelson 1973, 67).*

> *The conception [of socialism] actually lies in the realm of prophecy as well as in that of vague ideals or wishes well designated as "cloud-cuckoo land." . . . it is easy to imagine and to believe (as shown by the fact that intelligent people regularly do so imagine and believe) that the (supposed) evils in the world or any particular society (a) are economic in basis (b) more specifically are consequences of the form of economic organization and (c) can without serious difficulty be corrected by replacing the economic organization with a system of control by politicians (Frank H. Knight 1947, 133).*

One's retrieval of past American history is shaped by the interplay between one's basic presuppositions and the "facts." Sturm's reading of American political and economic history is an ambiguously negative one; he envisages the emergence of a new social covenant that will facilitate a shift from commodity to commonwealth. In my view, though, Sturm overstates the negative aspects of the American experience, and offers a highly dubious prescription for the future direction of American life.

My own reading at this history is an ambiguously positive one. Democratic capitalism as it has evolved in the context of the American experience has promoted the legitimate concern of the citizens of the republic to protect the humanity of persons in the work force, to reduce inordinate inequality in incomes, and to promote economic growth and efficiency. Obviously, much remains to be done to facilitate more human relations in the workplace, but much has been done. Because formal factors guided by technical rationalism must always be considered in any reasonably efficient economic system, an economic enterprise will always thwart communitarian dreams to a greater or lesser degree.

The epigram from Taylor is a balanced assessment of the fitting transformation of labor in the American experience, and the epigram from Knight is a trenchant statement of the problem inherent in socialism/communitarianism.

There has been a general drift toward the increased freedom of the individual over the past three thousand years or so. Slavery was presupposed in the ancient world, and it was not until the time of the Industrial Revolution in the eighteenth century that technological innovations made possible the freeing of more than a small segment of humankind from the necessity to spend almost all of their time in pursuit of food, fiber and shelter.[19] The Industrial Revolution, the popular appropriation of democratic and Enlightenment values, and the increasing differentiation of the spheres of the social order all contributed to the extension of some aspects of human freedom in some parts of the planet. The United States shared in and contributed to this development. The heightened individuation that began in the West in the latter part of the Middle Ages was marked by the increasing differentiation of the spheres of the social order. Institutions in the social, economic, political, and religious spheres became more autonomous, and increasingly the individual came to offer his or her labor for wages in the marketplace.[20]

As noted in Section 2, the Enlightenment and left-wing Calvinist values both contributed to the shape of the Constitution and the development of the American experiment. The next two centuries saw both the extension of voting rights to larger segments of the population and increased involvement of the government in economic matters.[21] During most of the nineteenth century, the dual values of growth and efficiency shaped American attitudes toward economic enterprises. By the latter part of the century, the inequities of laissez-faire capitalism led Congress to enact various measures to limit those inequities. The Interstate

Commerce Act (1887) and the Sherman Anti-Trust Act (1890) gave government the authority to limit monopoly practices.

In the twentieth century, equality became a more salient value.[22] Consequently, the limitations on corporate power in the latter part of the nineteenth century were followed in the twentieth century by various schemes to promote income redistribution. Fiscal policy became an increasingly popular way to seek to effect income redistribution.[23]

The capitalist system and its sustaining ethos harnessed human self-interest and motivated people to work diligently and efficiently. People affirmed the values of technical rationalism, a mind-set that sought to develop the most efficient means to attain a given end. As a result, very impressive economic growth took place in the past two centuries. Indeed, schemes of income redistribution developed in the twentieth century have themselves been greatly facilitated by economic growth. Food, shelter, and clothing—the primary creaturely necessities—have become available in very substantial quantities.

During the Great Depression in the 1930s, government involvement in the economic sphere increased dramatically. Faced with monumental economic problems, the government sought to foster economic recovery and to aid those left destitute. (In fact, much fiscal and monetary policy was contradictory.) Keynesian economic theory began to arrive in the mid to late 1930s, and it provided a legitimation for more active government intervention through monetary and fiscal policy to moderate fluctuations in the business cycle. The Depression also saw the extension of labor's rights and the beginning of a vast expansion of the welfare system that promoted the growth of a new bureaucratic establishment to oversee and administer welfare funds.[24] Overall, therefore, George Taylor's assessment quoted at the beginning of this section is a balanced one. Substantial progress was made in the United States in the past century to promote a more humane treatment of labor.

This broad interpretation needs to be supplemented by a consideration of two interrelated issues implicit in Sturm's discussion of socialism/communitarianism/participatory democracy. The first centers on the problem of growth and efficiency in the economic sphere; the second centers on the problem of the nature of the changes in the management of production which would actually occur in a socialist economy.

The quest for efficiency, the primacy of consumer preference in determining consumption, and the reliance on pricing mechanisms to guide the production and distribution of goods and services combine to produce "creative destruction," the term coined by Joseph Schumpeter to describe the dynamic capitalist enterprise system, a system that fosters technological innovation and rapid social change and evokes some human insecurity. With technological changes and shifts in consumer preferences, whole industries can be displaced, and new industries can emerge at a rapid pace. Workers caught in these transformations through no fault of their own are subject to both psychological and economical insecurity.

The problems associated with creative destruction would, I think, persist in a socialist economic system. They would likely be compounded by the preferential treatment politicians would extend to their families and friends to protect them from the impact of these changes. These actions would reduce growth and reduce efficiency.[25]

The second issue centers on the reliance on consumer preferences to guide the production of goods and services. Pricing mechanisms are a very effective and efficient way to guide the production and distribution of goods and services. The price of goods or services is set by the marketplace at the price at which supply and demand are in equilibrium. Price declines will clear the market of surplus goods and services through decreased production and increased demand, and price increases will induce the availability of under-supplied goods and services through increased production and reduced demand. The alternatives to the use of pricing mechanisms to guide production and consumption of goods and services would be rationing by coupon and/or some form of allocation of goods by governmental fiat. (Sturm does not propose to substitute those mechanisms for consumer preference and the pricing mechanism.)

A socialist/communitarian democratic society utilizing pricing mechanisms and consumer preferences to determine the availability and distribution of goods and services and seeking to attain some growth and some efficiency would probably confront the same economic problems as a democratic capitalist society. Indeed, the problems would most likely be exacerbated, because the government would be so much more deeply involved in economic activity.

Unless pricing mechanisms are permitted to continue to determine patterns of production and consumption, a scenario of decline becomes very possible. Without the discipline of a free market, great inefficiencies can arise throughout the economic system, greatly reducing human choices in the allocation of economic resources, and expanding government bureaucracy to deal with the new problems. The government may embrace complex long-range planning operations and make many errors in projections. Allocating goods and services by coupon rather than by price would allow black markets to evolve. Dispensing goods on a per capita basis would allow complex barter and swapping arrangements among consumers to emerge.[26] The risk and uncertainty inherent in the marketplace would not be eliminated, but political solutions would become much more tempting. Managers would probably be more timid and less willing to innovate, for socialist governments are less likely to reward managers for economic success than they are to punish managers who encounter difficulties. Faced with the possibility of censure if they go wrong, most plant managers and workers would no doubt be tempted to play it safe and try to maintain the status quo.

The most likely political consequences of an increasingly inefficient and stagnant economic system would be increasing unrest among members of the society. Because the government would be directly responsible for both managing the economy and producing goods and services, key government officials would be the targets of public unrest. Under these circumstances, the maintenance of democracy would become increasingly difficult. Politicians would seek to suppress unrest by appealing to the principle of order, and some entrepreneurs would seek to establish political hegemony so they could run the economy more efficiently and more profitably than the politicians.[27] Consequently, in this scenario a socialist/communitarian democratic society would run the risk of either totalitarian socialism or totalitarian fascism.

Sturm advances the ideal of participatory democracy in both the economic and political spheres of the American social order. His relatively egalitarian emphasis and his strong desire for community lead him to this ideal. Though participatory democracy conveys a multiplicity of meanings, ranging from *equal* participation to *selective* participation in all affairs of government, Sturm wants to apply equal participation very broadly in both the economic and political spheres. In fact, his proposal for interpenetration of the two spheres blurs very greatly the distinction between decisions in economic and political institutions.

In light of the above considerations, I argue that the principles of liberty and equality, along with the persistence of finitude, ignorance, sloth, lethargy, and inordinate self-interest among humankind, make democracy the most desirable form of political organization. These factors, though, do not legitimate participatory democracy. In the political sphere, a republican form of democracy is preferable to a participatory form because complex and interrelated decisions cannot be made by the mass electorate. Specialized knowledge and a backlog of concrete political experience are required, for a series of specific *ad hoc* decisions do not constitute a coherent public policy.

As noted earlier, the extension of voting rights to more groups in the United States over the past two centuries has promoted the principle of equality, for many voters have expected the government to countervail inordinate disparities in income and other inequities through various income redistribution plans and legal redress. This pattern has also facilitated increased government intervention in the economic sphere, for voters increasingly have expected the government to promote economic growth. These governmental activities have contributed to the emergence of democratic capitalism. Evaluated by the principles of liberty, equality and order, these developments deserve a generally sympathetic interpretation.[28] However, the process should not be extrapolated to condone the state appropriation of the modes of production in the name of communitarianism or the stifling of individual liberty in the name of equality and/or community. Nor should it suggest the desirability of promoting participatory democracy in lieu of representative democracy.

The appropriate degree of worker participation in management decisions is very difficult to discern. Growth and efficiency are important economic objectives, and no one knows precisely what impact alternative styles of decision making will have on an enterprise. The adversarial labor-management relations so widespread in contemporary America leave much to be desired, and experimentation with alternative forms has much to commend it. Worker rights certainly need to be protected, and legal restraints on arbitrary management decisions are entirely appropriate. However, the proposals Sturm offers for participatory democracy in the economic sphere ignore the need for specialized and professional guidance in economic enterprises. The government would have inordinate power if it could *mandate* such a decision making process.

These critical observations about proposals for democratic socialism/communitarianism should not blind one to the negative aspects of democratic capitalism. Capitalism does indeed appeal to self-interest very strongly as it presses with great vigor the quest for growth and efficiency, and it does lead to significant inequalities in income distribution. It has undoubtedly contributed to a materialistic bent in American life. Market hedonism has become a powerful force, with pursuit of material goods and instant gratification of wants an integral part of the American experience (see Bell 1976). However, market hedonism can be minimized if consumers will choose to allocate their resources through investment and support of alternative goods and services.

Unless one is prepared to empower the state with authority to direct human moral activity in substantial detail, one must rely in the current circumstances on suasion and fortitude. Families and various voluntary associations (including religious communities) may be able to cultivate persons to resist some of the debasing aspects of contemporary of life, but people should not be coerced to conform to inordinately high or arbitrary moral standards. The extent to which the state should coerce minimally acceptable societal standards of social behavior is subject to constant redefinition, but some such minimal standards are essential for the sustenance of human communities.[29]

In any reasonable efficient economic enterprise, human beings must be remunerated on the basis of their marketable competencies. Such a system cannot avoid the displacement of workers due to technological change and/or changes in consumer preferences. Nevertheless, humans are more than mere cogs in an economic engine, and they demand to be treated as such. They seek inclusive, holistic relations in which they are seen in their richness and complexity. Technical rationalism—the value informing role segmentation and the quest for efficiency and growth—is a truncated view of reason which needs to be supplemented by a broader view of reason grounded in the lure for beauty, truth, and goodness.

The communitarian appeal is rooted in these longings for holistic and inclusive relations, but these longings cannot be fulfilled in any reasonably efficient economic enterprise. The longings have the greatest hope of some fulfillment in the family, in small friendship groups, and in some types of voluntary associations, including some religious groups.

4

As long as a religion rests only upon those sentiments which are the consolation of all affliction, it may attract the affections of all mankind. But if it be mixed up with the bitter passions of the world, it may be constrained to defend allies whom it interests, and not the principle of love, have given to it; or to repel as antagonists men who are still attached to it, however opposed they may be to the powers with which it is allied. The church cannot share the temporal power of the state without being the object of a portion of that animosity which the latter excites . . . The American clergy were the first to perceive this truth and to act in conformity with it. They saw they must renounce their religious influence if they were to strive for political power, and they choose to give up the support of the state rather than to share its vicissitudes (Alexis de Tocqueville 1954, 321-23).

In his essay, Sturm neither discusses religious communities directly nor indicates what role they should play in facilitating the transition "from commodity to commonwealth." One can only speculate about the reasons for this omission. Perhaps he thinks the new "commonwealth" will so embody the substance of religion that religious communities will no longer be necessary. Whatever his reasons, it seems to me that any discussion of political and economic life must consider the role of religious communities, if only because they have appeared in all historical epochs.

Religious communities emerge from human response to an awareness of Divine immanence in human life. A religious community's constitutive act is worship. Religious communities provide some of the contexts in which humans may become aware of the Divine Reality, and the communities are the bearers of feelings and meanings embodied in religious traditions. They are both institutions and fellowships. As social fellowships they may counteract the hedonistic pressures of the broader culture by contributing to wholesome character formation of their members.

The separation of church and state, and the concomitant values of religious freedom, religious tolerance, and religious pluralism, are deeply embodied in the American experience. While no absolute separation was intended, substantial religious freedom exists. Communities of faith and communities of politics have rarely coalesced in the United States. Most religious communities have members of more than one political party and members who differ substantially on political and economic issues. In the American context, one does not usually expect to find one's religious association requiring a specific political association.

The inevitable contrast between the vision of the potential harmony of life with life and the actual intertwining of harmonious and discordant dimensions in the life of an actual living community legitimates a separation between religious and political communities.

These contrasts, a consequence of finitude and ignorance, are not, however, the only reason for resisting the coalescence of political and religious communities. The persistence of inordinate self-interest in human motivation is a second reason. Deification of government is one of the crudest forms of idolatry, and the temptation is increased in societies without independent voluntary associations, including religious communities. Conversely, a given faith community may be sorely tempted to equate *its* truth with *the* truth, and seek to impose its teachings on all members of the civil community. The existence of a plurality of religious communities and the separation of religious communities and the civil community can blunt the temptation to absolutism in either the religious or the civil sphere.

In political communities, power—both linear and reciprocal—is the leading component, and political life embodies both coercive and suasive elements. While justice and love are important in the political sphere, they are secondary and tertiary components; but without the form of justice and the lure of love, political power is naked. Such a realpolitik can not endure.

In religious communities, suasive love is the leading component, a love only partially actualizable in the world. Consequently, religious communities should not identify directly with any political community. They should seek to provide a direction for society, but they should be very wary about providing specific directives to a society. Religious communities furthermore should explore the bases for the principles of justice and consider their implications for forms of social organization and for the rules and regulations of justice. In addition, they should encourage their members to participate in other voluntary associations directly promoting particular public policies. In this way, they may promote the quest for justice and the enhancement of the harmony of life with life in a living community without becoming directly involved in the ambiguity of almost all economic and political activity.

Political and economic groups are important in human life, but they are not sufficient for human fulfillment. Humans need more inclusive holistic relations in the family, in small primary groups, and in some types of voluntary associations, including religious communities, for a rich and full life. Ultimate fulfillment is found in the Divine Life, and it is to this reality one must turn for a more encompassing fulfillment than is possible in the world. The sense of peace such fulfillment evokes is more a gift than achievement. Grace is more salient than works. This awareness of the reception and the transmutation in the Divine Life of the contributions of the creatures of the world can help us understand both the lure for the embodiment of love and justice in the world and also the inevitability of some evil and injustice in the world.

5

The art of progress is to preserve order amid change, and to preserve change amid order (Alfred North Whitehead 1978, 339).

In the light of both the positive and negative factors discussed in this essay, I conclude that the relative autonomy of economic, political and religious institutions in the United States should be supported. When these institutions are separated, this large, complex, heterogeneous, post-modern society can best realize the principles of freedom informed by ideals of excellence and equality appropriate to form in the life of the living community. In this historical epoch and in the foreseeable future, socialist/communitarian proposals to reorder these fundamental relations should be approached with the utmost skepticism. Their reordering would place additional burdens on government, reduce the centers of power and independent initiative that promote checks and balances in all spheres of the social order, and thus entail a reduction of human freedom, initiative, and self-determination in American social, economic, political, cultural, and religious life. Innovation in the context of the conservation of the basic structure of relations among economic, political, and religious institutions is the most appropriate way to pursue the quest for justice in the context of the American experience.

Notes and References

1. The following are some religious social ethicists who affirm some form of socialism as normatively desirable, or sharply criticize capitalism, or both: Hugo Assmann (1975); John Bennett (1975); Robert McAffee Brown (1981); Dom Helder Camara (1971); Gustavo Gutierrez (1973) Gustavo Gutierrez and Richard Shaull (1977); Jose Miguez Bonino (1975, 1983); Juan Segundo (1976, 1984); Paul Tillich (1977); and Philip Wogaman (1977). In *Liberating Creation* (1981) Gibson Winter offers a cultural critique of both socialism and capitalism. Following Heidegger, Winter is very critical of the technical rationalism which he sees at the base of both capitalism and socialism. Following his lead, many of the contributors to *Liberation and Ethics: Essays in Religious Social Ethics in Honor of Gibson Winter* (ed. Charles Amjad Ali and W. Alvin Pitcher, 1984) explore variations of the same theme.

2. Karl Marx is, of course, the best known figure in this movement. It is beyond the scope of this essay to trace these developments in detail. The following thinkers explore various facets of this complex development: G.D.H. Cole (1953); Louis Dupre (1983); Sidney Hook (1936); Bertell Ollman (1976); Robert C. Tucker (1972).

3. See especially, Walter Rauschenbusch (1912, 1917). The early writings of Reinhold Neibuhr (1932) also reflected this line of thinking.

4. For a detailed history of socialist thought in America, see Donald Drew Egbert and Stow Persons (1952).

5. See, for example, the following representative texts: Ernst Bloch (1970); Jürgen Moltmann (1974); and Dorothee Sölle (1977, 1983).

6. See John B. Cobb, Jr., and W. Widick Schroeder, eds. (1981) for a collection of essays dealing with issues in religious social ethics from a process perspective. In that volume, Sturm also promotes communitarianism in his essay "Process Thought and Political Theory: Implications of a Principle of Internal Relations: (81-102), and Max Stackhouse offers a perceptive critique in his "The Perils of Process: A Response to Sturm" (103-12). Whitehead's own social theory is developed in various places. *Science and the Modern World* (1925), *Religion in the Making* (1926), *Adventures of Ideas* (1961), and *Modes of Thought* (1938) are the most important resources for this aspect of his thinking.

7. The present paper is focused on the American experience. It does not address the complex problems of appropriate forms of social organization in countries with different historical destinies. It may be observed in passing, however, that socialist/communitarian visions in many different countries have consistently been thwarted.

8. Douglas Sturm uses the typologies "orthodox capitalism" and "heterodox capitalism" to contrast forms of economic organization in the United States and "protective democracy" and "participatory democracy" to contrast forms of political organization in the United States. The unique configuration of relations between economic and political institutions that has emerged in American democratic capitalism is distorted by these typological devices.

9. The term "democratic capitalism" was made popular by Michael Novak (1982) and Robert Benne (1981).

10. Socialists differ on the kinds and amounts of property persons may own for their own use and consumption in an ideal society. These family quarrels are not directly germane to the issues being considered in this essay.

11. It is beyond the scope of this essay to explore this issue further. For an extended discussion, see Chapter 1 of this volume.

12. For a perceptive analysis of these problems in the contemporary epoch, see Peter Berger (1974). For a perceptive critique of patterns of foreign aid, see P.T. Bauer (1984).

13. It is beyond the scope of this essay to trace in detail the complex socio-cultural movement leading to the breakdown of the medieval social order and the emergence of new forms of economic and political organization. For detailed and contrasting discussion of these matters, the following texts are illustrative: Joyce Oldham Appleby (1978); Albert O. Hirschman (1977); Leo Strauss (1953); R. H. Tawney (1920, 1926); Ernst Troeltsch (1931); Jacob Viner (1972); Michael Walzer (1968); Max Weber (1958).

14. For extended bibliographical references, see John B. Cobb, Jr., and W. Widick Schroeder, editors (1981).

15. In its most general form, Whitehead's principle of relativity states that every being is a potential for every becoming. It is the basis for understanding existence as inextricably social. Life involves both individuation and relationships.

16. While this religious social ethic seeks guidance from principles, it is ultimately a contextual ethic; for changing circumstances require changing responses to enhance the harmony of life with life under the conditions of existence.

17. Aquinas, Calvin, Lenin and Mao all sought uniformity of beliefs within a society.

18. For an interesting discussion of public policy proposals informed by this point of view, see Milton Friedman (1962). For studies exploring the impact of current forms of welfare on their recipients see George F. Gilder (1978, 1981). It is beyond the scope of this essay to deal with specific issues of public policy, for it is concerned with generic issues informing one's vision about normative forms of economic and political organization.

19. The pursuit of self-interest and the conditioning effects of one's sustaining environment are always a part of the human condition. One need not adopt a Marxist perspective to affirm the importance of these factors in human life.

The quest for laws that determine human life and the use of the dialectic of negation to interpret social change distort social analysis. The capacity of humans to surpass the past in the emerging present precludes the development of "laws" of human social change. One can indeed discern tendencies and configurations, but human freedom thwarts all efforts to write a deterministic history.

Marxist categorization of humans into the groupings "oppressor" and "oppressed" based on their location in the social structure of a given society is fallacious, for human beings surpass the nexus of relations in which they are embedded. Classes are abstractions. Their reification is an example of what Whitehead called "the fallacy of misplaced concreteness."

The Marxist bipolar categorization of human beings based on their position in the social structure is reminiscent of Augustine's bipolar categorization of human beings as "saved" and "damned" at the end of history based on Divine determination. For Marx, the bipolarity can be overcome *within* history, but only for those humans who are still extant at the time the public ownership of the modes of production occurs. Prior to that time, the "elect" will be those who are on the right side of the dialectic of the historical process. The tortuous issues of human freedom and inexorable historical process that Marx and his followers addressed are analogous to the concern of Augustine and his followers about human freedom and Divine predestination.

For a similar reason, humans are more than a factor in the production processes. They are that, but as human beings they are more than that. These issues are addressed briefly at the close of this section and in Section 4.

Socialists such as Sturm do not employ a full-blown Marxist analysis, but they selectively appropriate facets of the Marxist tradition. Their frequent reference to "oppressors" and the "oppressed," their widespread disdain of capitalist achievements, their frequent uncritical acceptance of the theory of dependent capitalism, their almost dogmatic view of the omnipresence of capitalist monopolies and excessive profits, their acceptance of Marxist critiques of advertising, and their conviction of the great benefits to accrue to humankind following the public ownership of many or most modes of production, all illustrate the complex influence Marxist modes of thought have had on advocates of democratic socialism.

Notions drawn from this tradition also appear frequently in the social analysis of advocates of one or another form of liberation theology.

20. For a suggestive discussion on this process see Robert Bellah (1970, 20-45).

21. In the present context, the author is interested in very broad tendencies and movements. More specialized monographs have amply documented these broad trends.

22. Insofar as economists were preachers, they emphasized growth and efficiency in the late eighteenth and in much of the nineteenth century. In the latter part of the nineteenth century and in much of the twentieth century they emphasized equality. Freedom is more closely related to growth and efficiency; equality is more closely related to community. For a perceptive discussion of these patterns, see George Stigler (1982, 3-37).

23. For a discussion of the tensions inherent between efficiency and equality, see Arthur M. Okun (1975). How successful these schemes have been is an empirical question about which there has been some debate.

24. It is beyond the scope of this essay to address specific public policy proposals, but freedom as the constitutive principle of justice provides a basis for judging public policy issues. Government income redistribution policies should seek to enhance the self-determination of the recipients. Therefore, government grants to the poor should be in the form of direct grants whenever possible. Further, the schemes should seek to avoid continued dependence.

25. The notion that politicians would suddenly be transformed into utterly altruistic beings devote to the pursuit of the common good in a socialistic/communitarian society is belied by human experience generally and by experience in many countries where the modes of production have been owned by the state.

26. Socialist economies in Communist countries have increasingly come to rely on free market pricing mechanisms to allocate resources. Such arrangements are compatible with government ownership of the modes of production. However, as noted in the body of the text, if they are used, the "creative destruction" and displacement of workers that occur in capitalist economies will also plague socialist economies. The negative impact of growth and efficiency is most likely to be much greater, for government "subsidies" to sustain declining industries will probably be easier to obtain. [The collapse of the Soviet Union a few years after this essay was written illustrates the issues cited here.]

27. In a socialist economy, some accounting mechanisms analogous to "profits" in a capitalist economy must be used to assess relative costs and returns on investment and the efficiency of particular enterprises.

28. Friedrich A. Hayek presents an extremely staunch opposition to government intervention in the economic sphere, holding that such economic reform is "the road to serfdom." Sidney and Beatrice Webb, on the other hand, strongly support communitarianism, holding that without the economic democracy coming from collectively equal ownership of the means of production, political democracy is nothing. Sturm comes close to this latter view.

29. For a suggestive exploration of some of the issues involved in this problem, see Richard John Neuhaus (1984). It is beyond the scope of this essay to consider the public faith of America and the relation of the religions of America to the religion of America.

Bibliography

Amjad-Ali, Charles and W. Alvin Pitcher (eds.). 1984, *Liberation and Ethics: Essays in Religious Social Ethics in Honor of Gibson Winter.* Chicago: Center for the Scientific Study of Religion.

Appleby, Joyce. 1978. *Economic Thought and Ideology in Seventeenth Century England.* Princeton: Princeton University Press.

____. 1984. *Capitalism and a New Social Order: The Republican Vision of the 1790's.* New York: New York University Press.

Assmann, Hugo. 1975. *Theology for a Nomad Church.* Maryknoll, N.Y.: Orbis Books.

Augustine. 1950. *The City of God,* trans., Marcus Dods. New York: Modern Library.

Bauer, P.T. 1984. *Reality and Rhetoric: Studies in the Economics of Development.* Cambridge: Harvard University Press.

Bell, Daniel. 1976. *The Cultural Contradictions of Capitalism.* New York: Basic Books.

Bellah, Robert. 1970. *Beyond Belief.* New York: Harper & Row.

Benne, Robert. 1981. *The Ethic of Democratic Capitalism: A Moral Reassessment.* Philadelphia: Fortress Press.

Bennett, John. 1975. *The Radical Imperative—From Theology to Social Ethics.* Philadelphia: Westminster Press.

Berger, Peter. 1974. *Pyramids of Sacrifice: Political Ethics and Social Change.* New York: Basic Books.

Bloch, Ernst. 1970. *A Philosophy of the Future.* New York: Herder & Herder.

Bonino, Jose Miguez. 1975, *Doing Theology in a Revolutionary Situation.* Philadelphia: Fortress Press.

____. 1983. *Toward a Christian Ethics.* Philadelphia: Fortress Press.

Brown, Robert McAffee. 1981. *Making Peace in the Global Village.* Philadelphia: Westminster Press.

Camara, Dom Helder. 1971. *Revolution Through Peace.* New York: Harper & Row.

Cobb, John B., Jr. and W. Widick Schroeder (eds.) 1981. *Process Philosophy and Social Thought.* Chicago: Center for the Scientific Study of Religion.

Cole, G.D.H. 1953. *History of Socialist Thought,* vol. 1, *The Forerunners, 1789-1850.*New York: St. Martin's Press.

Dupre, Louis. 1983. *Marx's Critique of Modern Culture,* New Haven: Yale University Press.

Egbert, Donald Drew and Stow Persons. 1952. *Socialism and American Life,* 2 vols. Princeton: Princeton University Press.

Friedman, Milton. 1962. *Capitalism and Freedom.* Chicago: University of Chicago Press.

Gilder, George F. 1978. *Visible Man.* New York: Basic Books.

____. 1981. *Wealth and Poverty.* New York: Basic Books.

Grelle, Bruce, and David A. Krueger, eds. 1986. *Christianity and Capitalism: Perspectives on Religion, Liberalism and the Economy.* Chicago: Center for the Scientific Study of Religion.

Gutierrez, Gustavo. 1973. *A Theology of Liberation: History, Politics and Salvation.* Maryknoll, N.Y.: Orbis Books.

Gutierrez, Gustavo and Richard Shaull. 1977. *Liberation and Change.* Atlanta: John Knox Press.

Hayek, Friedrich A. 1961. *The Road to Serfdom.* Chicago: University of Chicago Press. (First published in 1944).

____. 1976. *Law, Legislation and Liberty.* Vol. 2: *The Mirage of Social Justice.* Chicago: University of Chicago Press.

Hirschman, Albert O. 1977. *The Passions and the Interests: Political Arguments for Capitalism before its Triumph.* Princeton: Princeton University Press.

Hobhouse, L.T. 1964. *Liberalism.* London: Oxford University Press. (First published in 1911.)

Hook, Sidney. 1936. *From Hegel to Marx: Studies in the Intellectual Development of Karl Marx.* New York: Reynal & Hitchcock.

Hopkins, Charles H. 1940. *The Rise of the Social Gospel in American Protestantism, 1865-1915.* New Haven: Yale University Press.

Knight, Frank H. 1947. *Freedom and Reform.* New York: Harper & Brothers.

____. 1976. *The Ethics of Competition and Other Essays.* Chicago: University of Chicago Press. (First published in 1935.)

MacMurray, John. 1961. *Persons in Relation.* London: Faber & Faber.

Moltmann, Jürgen. 1974. *The Crucified God.* New York: Harper & Row.

Neuhaus, Richard John. 1984. *The Naked Public Square.* Grand Rapids, Michigan: Erdmans.

Niebuhr, Reinhold. 1932. *Moral Man and Immoral Society.* New York: Charles Scribner's Sons.

Novak, Michael. 1982. *The Spirit of Democratic Capitalism.* New York: American Enterprise Institute, Simon & Schuster.

Okun, Arthur. 1975. *Equality and Efficiency: The Big Tradeoff.* Washington, D.C.: The Brookings Institution.

Ollman, Bertell. 1976. *Alienation: Marx's Conception of Man in Capitalist Society,* 2nd ed. Cambridge: Cambridge University Press.

Rauschenbusch, Walter. 1912. *Christianizing the Social Order.* New York: Macmillan.

___. 1917. *A Theology of the Social Gospel.* New York: Macmillan.

Samuelson, Paul. 1973. *Readings in Economics.* New York: McGraw-Hill Co. [selection by George W. Taylor.]

Segundo, Juan. 1976. *Liberation of Theology.* Maryknoll, N.Y.: Orbis Books.

____. 1984. *Faith and Ideologies.* Maryknoll, N.Y.: Orbis Books.

Scumpeter, Joseph A. 1950. *Capitalism, Socialism, and Democracy.* (Third edition), New York: Harper & Row.

Sölle, Dorothee. 1977. *Revolutionary Patience.* Maryknoll, N.Y.: Orbis Books.

____. 1983. *The Arms Race Kills Even Without War.* Philadelphia: Fortress Press.

Stackhouse, Max. 1981. "The Perils of Process: A Response to Sturm." In *Process Philosophy and Social Thought,* ed. John B. Cobb, Jr., and W. Widick Schroeder, 103-12. Chicago: Center for the Scientific Study of Religion.

Stigler, George. 1982. *The Economist as Preacher*. Chicago: University of Chicago Press.

Strauss, Leo. 1953. *Natural Rights and History*. Chicago: University of Chicago Press.

Sturm, Douglas. 1981. "Process Thought and Political Theory: Implications of a Principle of Internal Relations." In *Process Philosophy and Social Thought*, ed. John B. Cobb, Jr. and W. Widick Schroeder. Chicago: Center for the Scientific Study of Religion.

____. 1986. "Toward a New Social Covenant: From Commodity to Commonwealth." In *Christianity and Capitalism: Perspectives on Religion, Liberalism and the Economy*, ed. Bruce Grelle and David A. Krueger, 91-108. Chicago: Center of the Scientific Study of Religion.

Tawney, R.H. 1920. *The Acquisitive Society*. New York: Harcourt, Brace and Howe.

____. 1926. *Religion and the Rise of Capitalism*. New York: Harcourt, Brace & Co.

Tillich, Paul. 1977. *The Socialist Decision*. New York: Harper & Row. (First published in 1933.)

Tocqueville, Alexis de. 1954. *Democracy in America*. New York: Vintage Books. (First published in 1835-40.)

Troeltsch, Ernst. 1931. *The Social Teaching of the Christian Churches*, 2 vols. London: George Allen and Unwin.

Tucker, Robert C. 1972. *Philosophy and Myth in Karl Marx*. Cambridge: Cambridge University Press.

Viner, Jacob. 1972. *The Role of Providence in the Social Order: An Essay in Intellectual History*. Princeton: Princeton University Press.

Walzer, Michael. 1968. *The Revolution of the Saints: A Study in the Origin of Radical Politics*. New York: Atheneum.

Weber, Max. 1958. *The Protestant Ethic and the Spirit of Capitalism*. New York: Charles Scribner's Sons.

West, Cornel. 1986. "Neo-Aristotelianism, Liberalism and Socialism: A Christian Perspective." In *Christianity and Capitalism: Perspectives on Religion, Liberalism and the Economy*, ed. Bruce Grelle and David A. Krueger, 79-90. Chicago: Center for the Scientific Study of Religion.

Whitehead, Alfred North. 1925. *Science and the Modern World*. New York: Macmillan.

____. 1926. *Religion in the Making*. New York: Macmillan.

____. 1938. *Modes of Thought*. New York: Macmillan.

____. 1961. *Adventures of Ideas*. New York: The Free Press.

____. 1978. *Process and Reality*. New York: The Free Press.

Winter Gibson. 1981. *Liberating Creation*. New York:: Seabury Press.

Wogaman, J. Philip. 1977. *The Great Economic Debate: An Ethical Analysis*. Philadelphia, Westminster Press.

PART THREE

On Religious Institutions: Constructive and Analytical Studies

Introduction to Part Three

The essays in Part Three address issues centered on the Christian churches and on methodological issues in the sociology of religion. My research in the sociology of religion has focused on the church, for I have wanted my empirical studies to be useful to leaders and laity in the Christian tradition. Due to the intertwining of fact and value noted earlier, both analytic and constructive elements appear in all these essays. However, the amount of space devoted to each element varies, depending upon the emphases of a given essay. Those essays in Section A address more attention to constructive issues; those in Section B address more attention to analytic issues.

In this part, the voluntary church is highlighted as the dominant form of religious organization in the United States in the latter part of the twentieth century. It is compared with the intentional fellowship. People belong to the voluntary church because they *will* to belong. The voluntary church has loosely defined and lax criteria for membership, and it tolerates substantial variations in belief and practice. In contrast, the intentional fellowship has rigorous membership requirements, and it expects its members to adhere to a strictly defined set of beliefs and practices.

Ernest Troeltsch, in his classic study *The Social Teaching of the Christian Churches,* distinguished between church type and sect type religious organizations. The church was the established inclusive body, emphasizing the membership of all who had been baptized, accepting some differences in levels of individual commitment, and maintaining lay/clergy distinctions. The sect was a "believer's church," emphasizing the intentional commitment of its adherents, pressing for a high level of commitment for all participants, and minimizing lay/clergy distinctions. Because of the separation of church and state in the American experience, neither type applies in the United States without interpretation. The intentional fellowship and the voluntary church are products of the interplay in the United States between those within the Christian movement who expect intense involvement by all participants and those who tolerate differential involvement among participants. In this historical context, the intentional fellowship is analogous to the European sect, and the voluntary church is analogous to the European church, with one major exception. The American voluntary church is not supported by the government. In this sense, all American churches are "believers' churches."

In the 1980s and 1990s scholars have given increased attention to the congregation as the central entity within the Christian church. In a seminal recent article, Stephen Warner has promoted this thesis. I have advanced this view in my work for over two decades. Shaped by the general cultural values of religious liberty, religious pluralism, and religious tolerance, and of the legitimacy of the separation of church and state, the European church, dominated by religious professionals, has been transformed.

In the voluntary church of the American experience, lay people expect to have a significant role in shaping the program and policies of the local congregation. They have a regard for the direction of the professional, but they reserve the right to make up their own minds on many issues. In this sense, the voluntary church may be seen as a hybrid between the European church and the European sect.

Chapters 9, 10, and 11 in Section A of this part incorporate substantial constructive considerations. In these chapters I am concerned not only with analyzing what the churches are doing, but what they ought to do. Because I do not ground my warrants on particular phenomena within the Christian movement, I hold that the guidelines developed here should apply to *all* religious institutions, not merely those fostered within the Christian movement. The particularity emerges from my own embodiment within that movement and my primary audiences. The universal claims one makes *must* be drawn from some particular experience; on the physical side, one necessarily is enmeshed in a particular history.

Since the essays in Part Three were written, large numbers of immigrants from the Middle East and Asia have altered the religious complexion of this country. As was the case with earlier migrations, these newcomers cannot bring their economic and political institutions with them, but they can bring their religious ones. The substantial presence of Muslim, Hindu, Buddhist, and other religious bodies has modified the traditional Protestant-Catholic-Jewish tripartite structure of religious identity in this country. At the same time, the religion of America is qualifying and partially transforming the religious institutions which these new immigrants bring, just as Protestant, Catholic, and Jewish religious bodies were and are continuing to be transformed in the context of the American experience. For example, a Buddhist temple in a Chicago suburb has weekly services attended by a large "congregation," for whom social relations with persons from similar historical backgrounds intertwine with religious observances. One can scarcely imagine a Buddhist "congregation" of this shape in the historical settings in which Buddhism is predominant.

Adherents of Buddhism, Hinduism, and some other predominantly Asian religions, which—at least in principle affirm syncretism or pluralism—may more readily appropriate the values of religious plurality, religious liberty, and religious tolerance than the adherents of Islam. As was the case with many historic forms of Christianity, many historic forms of Islam do not promote religious tolerance, religious pluralism, and religious liberty. Thus, the transformation of the Islamic religion in the American experience may be more difficult. On the constructive side, their religious belief systems must be transformed in such a way that these key values, rooted historically more forcefully in the Enlightenment than in either historic Islam, Judaism, or Christianity, can be supported with integrity. (The world-wide resurgence of "fundamentalism" is related both to the absence of the embodiment of Enlightenment values in many societies and to their rejection by some people in all societies, and also to the propensity of humans to pursue their own self-interests inordinately. Consequently, some adherents of those religions which in principle may affirm pluralism and/or syncretism may manifest much intolerance. Followers of eastern as well as of western religious movements display such attitudes and engage in such behavior.)

SECTION A

Constructive Studies

Introduction to Chapter 9

This chapter was originally written in the mid-1970s for discussion in a colloquium on religious foundations for the human future conducted under the auspices of the Center for the Scientific Study of Religion. The process perspective informing all of these essays is very salient in this chapter, for it employs basic notions discussed in Part One to order the discussion and to ground the constructive formulations. At a time when many clergy and laity both called for the churches to issue directives to American society and also entertained negative or ambiguously negative assessments of American society, I sought to maintain distinctions between communities of faith and communities of politics, to advance an ambiguously positive assessment of American society, and to develop principles to permit religious institutions to offer a direction in which human societies in general and American society in particular ought to move. I also sought to develop the grounds for the various functions of religious institutions and the relations between them. The essay retrieves historical data to interpret the impact of the American experience on religious institutions in this setting.

In the two decades since this essay was writen, public perception of the political activity of highly visible religious leaders has shifted. In the 1970s most press coverage centered on the views of highly visible religious leaders promoting causes popular with those in the left-wing of the Democratic party. In the 1990s, it centers on highly visible religious leaders promoting causes popular with those in the right-wing of the Republican party.

CHAPTER 9

Religious Institutions and Human Society: A Normative Inquiry into the Appropriate Contribution of Religious Institutions to Human Life and to the Divine Life

Introduction

This essay is more normative than descriptive, for it delineates the appropriate contributions religious institutions *ought* to make to human life and to the Divine Life. It does incorporate a descriptive dimension in one section. In that section the broad structure of the contemporary American social order is characterized and correlated with normative forms of social organization outlined in a preceding section.

The term "religious institution" is used in the title for a specific reason. Religious institutions, whose constitutive acts center on worship of the Divine Reality, are ubiquitous in human history. They are a genus of which the Christian Church is a species. The Christian Church bears a tradition through which most people in the West in general and the United States in particular have been led to develop interpretations of the Divine presence in human life. Most of the illustrative material cited here will be drawn from Christian thinkers, but analogous patterns are discernable in other religious traditions.

Christianity is a species of the genus "religion." No categorically unique qualities are ascribed to the Christian Church or to its founder, Jesus of Nazareth; nonetheless their contributions to a network of feeling and meaning evoking sensitivity and theological reflection are gratefully acknowledged.[1] In its origins Christianity does differ substantially from the other great world religions. The other great world religions emerged with full-blown metaphysical interpretations of God and Its relations to the world; Christianity has always been a religion seeking an adequate mode of interpretation. Its founder's teachings were direct and intuitive sayings and observations. His utterances were concrete and usually commonplace. His person is a salient factor in the emergence of the Christian movement, and He has evoked people in that movement to reflect on God-world relations.

The term "human society" is used to indicate the presence of an entity — or more properly, a complex clustering of entities in patterned relations to one another through a multiplicity of social institutions with a variety of defining characteristics — characterized by the presence of religious institutions and of institutions in the other spheres of the social order. Taken conjointly, the social institutions in the several spheres of the social order, in conjunction with the human beings from which the spheres are abstracted and with the defining characteristics embodied in the past and present of human beings, constitute human society.

Theologians in the Christian tradition have held various views of appropriate relations between the church and institutions in the other spheres of the social order.[2] Some have held that a sharp contrast ought to exist between the church and the world. Significant segments of the early church and various withdrawing sects, such as the Mennonites, saw such contrasts and urged their adherents to have as little to do with nonbelievers as possible.

Others accepted a sharp contrast between life among Christians in the church and life among Christians and others in the world, but they saw a paradoxical relation between the church and other social institutions. Hence, as in the case of Martin Luther, they counseled for participation by Christians in both spheres, but they saw different leading principles manifest in the two spheres. In Luther's view, for instance, love (understood as outgoing concern for others, kindness, sweetness, and charity) was the leading principle in relations among Christians in the church, but power (understood primarily as the use of force, physical or psychic, to establish the superiority of one will, individual or collective, over another) was the leading principle among people in the state. The strange work of God's love was manifest through the state.

Still others sought to effect a coalescence or a movement toward an identification of the church and the world. Thomas Münzer in the Reformation and some protagonists of contemporary "liberation" theologies illustrate interpretations in which the sword was or is to be used to bring forth an increased harmony of life with life under the conditions of existence. Others, including many twentieth century "liberal" Protestants, have urged the extension of the suasive power of love to the public spheres to enhance the harmony of life with life under the conditions of existence.

In both of these instances, some vision of the harmony of life with life rooted in a Christian experience provides the basis for efforts to effect a radical transformation of the world. Current protagonists of a radical transformation of the social order are more apt to locate the crux of the problems increasing disharmony of life with life in the economic or cultural spheres than earlier proponents did, but they all share a common vision of a sharp contrast between the existing rather miserable state of disharmony of life with life and a potential future state of an enhanced harmony of life with life. They relate such a possibility to changes in the religious, cultural, political, economic, social, and/or familial spheres of life.[3]

Although not as frequently manifest in the Christian tradition, a more conservative reading of the possibilities of human life may lead proponents to seek to restore some past state of the social order or to defend the *status quo* as that situation most likely to maximize the harmony of life with life possible under the conditions of existence.[4]

Classically, social conservatives related the doctrine of the Fall to a vision of the perfect harmony of life with life under the conditions of an earlier state of affairs. Affirming the persistence of sin among humans, they rejected a perfectionist vision and sought to conserve existing institutions as the best possible under the conditions of existence. Sometimes they supported the existing political forms as the best possible ones, granted the persistent inordinate self-centeredness of humans; sometimes they supported existing economic forms. In other instances a more inclusive model was defended, incorporating social institutions in most or all the spheres of the social order.

All of these views have one thing in common; they involve a rather sharp contrast between a vision of perfection and the current condition of humankind. In spite of this common element, they differ markedly in their assessments of its implications for present and future human life. The Lutheran vision is the most conservative, and the "radical transformation" vision is the most innovative. The Anabaptist vision develops the most clarity about church-world and Christian-non-believer distinctions, and the "radical transformation" vision develops the least clarity.

One other broad view remains for consideration. Proponents of this view discern an overlap or a point of contact between the vision of the harmony embodied in the beatific vision of the Good and the degree of harmony of life with life possible under the conditions of existence. Protagonists vary in their assessment of the contribution of the forms embodied in human experience to the harmony of life with life.

The possibility of a necessary contribution of *a priori* static forms to human life represents one polar view. The possibility of an emergent and dynamic context providing the basis for the emergence of forms represents the other polar view. In this instance, all forms are constantly being outgrown and outrun by the emerging present.[5]

Whether anyone is guided unequivocally by a view of *a priori* static forms or an emerging dynamic context is a moot question. Historically, Catholicism has had the most formalistic bias (natural law, causistry, natural theology, etc.), Calvinism a moderate formalistic bias (natural law, ambivalently positive relations between love, justice, and forms of social organization, emphasis on third function of the law, i.e., a positive contribution of the law to human life, and a rejection of natural theology), and so-called "contextualists" the most dynamic bias (no natural law, strong emphasis on God's freedom, no natural theology, principles emerging from context, strong emphasis on novelty of contexts). The strongly formalistic versions of this "overlap" or contiguous view of love-justice relations have close relations with the more conservative or "contrast" interpretations discussed earlier; the strongly dynamic versions have close relations with the more innovative "contrast" interpretations.

The view elaborated in this essay has more in common with this "overlap" perspective than with any of the others. Because it holds that forms are necessarily included in every experience, it has some affinities with the more formalistic versions of this "overlap" interpretation. Because it holds that the emerging present subject surpasses the past and appropriates novel forms as well as forms embodied in creatures lying in its causal past (implying the ultimacy of a category of creativity), it has some affinities with the more dynamic versions of the "overlap" theory. In sum, the view developed here is intermediate with a moderate dynamic bias. It is more Catholic than classical Protestantism, and more Protestant than classical Catholicism.

Because of the relations envisaged between the formal, dynamic, and unifying components of experience, some will see the normative connections suggested here between the church and social institutions in the other spheres of the social order as standing between a "two kingdom" view and a transformative view. In relation to church-state connections, the view advanced here is more Lutheran than classical Calvinism, and more Calvinistic than classical Lutheranism.

The "Isness-Oughtness" Contrasts in Human Life

Humankind has been haunted by the lure of perfection. The vision of the perfect harmony of life with life is manifest in many cultural contexts.

Augustine envisaged a perfect harmony of life with life in a literal Garden of Eden. Adam and Eve had been so created that their wills were perfectly united with the Divine will. This perfect harmony led to a harmony of their reason with the Divine reason and the perfect harmony of the components of their bodies. A similar harmony of sub-human and supra-human creatures in relation to the whole prevailed.

In his formulation of a hierarchy of nature, angels, creatures with minds and wills but without bodies, were intermediate between humans and God. An angel turned away from God before humans did, so there was some prior propensity toward disharmony — evil being a privation or lack of being — in the cosmos. Nonetheless, though the action was foreknown by God, Adam and Eve through inevitability but not necessity turned away from the Divine will and centered their lives upon themselves. This disruption led to the cleavage between Divine reason and human reason and subsequently disrupted the harmony between the body, the mind, and the will. Consequently, because of the sin of Adam and Eve, death entered the human situation and disrupted the harmony of creation.

In the present context, the point warranting emphasis is the Augustinian vision of a perfectly created and harmonious world disrupted by human and trans-human agents. The Fall is contrasted with the vision of a pre-existing harmony and a future restoration of that harmony for some but not all creatures.

The Stoics' notion of a pre-existing Golden Age from which humankind had fallen, Plato's envisagement of the Good, and Aristotle's notion of a Supreme Being reflexively thinking thoughts about Itself all illustrate the persistence of a vision of perfection among humankind.

In the present epoch, Karl Marx's view of the enhanced harmony of life with life to be attained by an appropriate reorganization of the social order, Jean Jacques Rousseau's vision of the harmony of nature, and Sigmund Freud's entertainment of the possibility of understanding the forces and factors shaping human behavior in order to live in conformity with them may all be interpreted as responses to a pervasive intuition of perfection.[6]

Contemporary Protestant theologians have frequently rejected the cosmological side of Augustine's interpretation of the "isness-oughtness" contrast embodied in human experience, but they have usually affirmed the inner spiritual and existential dimension of that analysis. The wretchedness or estrangement of humans is contrasted with their reunion with the Divine reality effected by Divine initiative. They often differ in their views on sanctification, leading them to contrasting views on the extent to which the harmony of life with life may be attained under the conditions of existence. The broad shape of these alternatives has been discussed in the introduction, and it is not necessary to elaborate them further in the present context. It is important to note, however, that alternative assessments lead to differing diagnoses of and remedies for the disharmony and the injustice discerned in the social order.

At a more everyday level of less fully interpreted experience, people are constantly contrasting a projected or experienced "better" state of affairs with an existing "worse" state. These widespread experiences of humans suggest the pervasiveness of an experience of harmony and intensity of feeling in emerging creatures.

These experiences of perfection do not float into the world from nowhere; they must find their locus in a subject-object whose qualities are objectified in human experiences.

God's primordial envisagement of all potentiality constitutes such a locus for the human experience of perfect harmony. Its subjective aim orders and harmonizes all of the forms and lures creatures to aesthetic satisfaction and enhancement of feeling. The forms constituting the primordial facet of Its nature are not internally related to each other; they are related through their common participation in Its subjective aim. In this sense, the forms do not constitute a class but are a multiplicity.

Because of this relationship an unequivocally convincing and self-evident rational proof for the existence of God cannot be developed. A religious intuition that there is a relational essence to the universe sustains and supports the rationalistic faith that the relational essence can be illumined by reason. A metaphysical system may enhance human religious feelings, but it cannot — on its own — create them.

This view of God's subjective aim seeking satisfaction through the evocation of creatures in a world is closely related to the Platonic understanding of the Good, but the lack of internal relations of all the forms means that philosophy cannot lead one to a vision of the Good as directly as it does for Plato in Books V-VII of *The Republic.*

This view of the relation of the forms to each other through their common envisagement by God also provides a coherent explanation for the becoming of some creatures without eliciting the becoming of all creatures. If the forms were internally related to each other, the actualization of one form would elicit the actualization of all forms. Potentiality and actuality would coincide; the result would be a static universe in which all that could become would have become. There would be no contrast between that which is and that which might be but is not; hence, there would be no consciousness.

The "isness-oughtness" contrast, the reality of which is expressed in common history of humankind and to which illustrative references have been made earlier in this essay, is rooted in the perfection of God's harmonization of the forms in Its subjective aim and the limitations necessarily imposed by the finitude of actuality. As they become, creatures cannot actualize everything; some selectivity, some exclusion, and some limitations are unavoidable.

The "oughtness" of the perfect harmony of God's subjective aim is experienced with varying intensity by the creatures of the world. In certain of the occasions which in serial order constitute the life history of a human being, the intensity of this perfection is unusually strong; in other occasions, it may be markedly diminished. The rather exceptional experiences of great intensity are what are termed "mystical" or "ecstatic" experiences. In such occasions the subject-object structure of the experience, which is *always* embodied in the structure of the world, is not overcome, but the human subject-object is in an especially intense way experiencing the objectification of a facet of the Divine Nature in his or her experience.[7] This experience is interpreted frequently as the "oughtness" of perfect harmony.

The limitations of existence impose themselves upon creatures as an "isness," a givenness which necessarily precludes the actualization of the perfect harmony embodied the primordial aspect of God. When conscious creatures, such as human beings, compare the "oughtness" of the intense experience of God's subjective aim with the "isness" imposed by the limitations of existence and, through the exercise of negative judgment imagine the possibility of the actualization of that which is necessarily only potentiality, they experience an "isness-oughtness" contrast.

The confusion of potentiality and actuality has led some people to seek an inordinate harmony of life with life under the conditions of existence. Because of the intensity of their convictions, many have considered them to be religious fanatics and have been concerned about the dangers to social, economic, and political stability embodied in their views. From the constructive view informing this essay, there is substantial wisdom in such popular assessments of proponents of radically transformative visions.

The inexorable and inviolable foundation for the contrast, as has been noted, is the limitation which actuality imposes on potentiality. Other factors also contribute to the "isness-oughtness" contrast. These factors are discussed in the following section.

The Factors Contributing to the "Isness-Oughtness" Contrast

As noted above, the "isness-oughtness" contrast in human experience is rooted in the difference between the harmonization of all potentiality in one facet of the Divine Life and the necessary limitations on the infinity of potentiality imposed by the actualization of some but not all potentiality in the finite becoming of a particular creature in the world. There is no such thing as a single mode of perfection in the cosmos. Each actualization must be assessed in relation to the context in which it emerges. The actualization will be more or less appropriate to its context, but "best" is always a relative term and *the* "best" is possible only from the Divine perspective. Other creatures have to settle for a relative "better" or "worse."

In addition to this foundational limitation on the degree of harmony possible under the conditions of existence, other secondary factors may intensify the "isness-oughtness" contrast embodied in human experience. Finitude imposes other limitations on the degree of harmony of life with life possible in a particular context in a particular cosmic epoch.

The capacity of organisms to respond novelly to their past is intimately related to the limitations of finitude. Their freedom may lead them to seek, consciously or unconsciously, the actualization of new and novel forms of potentiality in the present. These actualizations may prove to be evil if they are born out of season; on the other hand, without the actualization of novel forms, the complex development of societies and the emergence of organisms with enhanced capacities for intensity of feeling could not have taken place in the evolution of the cosmos.

Often two potentially meritorious actualizations are mutually exclusive. For example, it is not possible for a human being to actualize all of his or her potentialities. Granted some relative differences due to ability and temperament, no one person can actualize numerous professional competencies. If one chooses to become a physician, it will be almost impossible for that person to become a distinguished musician. Who can say which is "better" and which is "worse?"

In addition, decisions now lying in the causal past of emerging creatures may limit the degree of harmony possible in a given locus. For example, a network of decisions made by preceding generations of Americans has contributed to the emergence of a society in which the influence of technical rationalism and high technology is very substantial. Granted the need to modify technical rationalism and to restrain the multiple impact of high technology, it is impossible to effect many qualifications on the shorter run without very substantial disharmony.

In addition to finitude in its primal and secondary manifestations, ignorance and sloth and lethargy contribute to human experiences of the "isness-oughtness" contrast. Emerging creatures do not possess fully adequate knowledge of creatures lying in their causal past, and contemporary creatures actualize themselves in causal independence of their contemporaries. Both factors contribute to the inability of emerging creatures to actualize themselves in such a fashion as to maximize the degree of harmony possible in a given context.

Inadequate knowledge of the creatures in one's causal past may cause one to do things which are at cross purposes with what other contemporaries are deciding to become, thereby attenuating the richness of future creatures. For example, a lack of awareness of certain traumas in the life of another, such as intense fear of automobile accidents because of experience of a terrifying crash, may lead a person to drive more aggressively than his or her companion would desire.

Even if one had a fully adequate knowledge of the causal past, one could not know for certain what an emerging creature was going to become, for contemporary physical events happen in causal independence of one another. Two emerging creatures may share much of a common past and may appropriate and respond to that past similarly. These responses may enhance the harmony and intensity of feeling of future creatures, but there is no way to be certain of such compatible responses. Indeed, the independence of contemporary creatures from the causal influence of each other provides some "elbow room" in the universe. Without such independence, novel creatures could not emerge.[8]

Sloth and lethargy also contribute to disharmony by fostering inordinate creaturely self-interest. The point of view elaborated here, as noted earlier, does not appeal to a doctrine of original sin in either its classical or contemporary forms. Nonetheless, the persistence of the doctrine suggests it is pointing toward a recurrent and pervasive aspect of human experience, i.e., inordinate human self-interest. Self-interest is grounded in the necessity to actualize something, for there must be "selves" who are aiming their becoming at their "interests." The vision of the larger whole to which the parts are contributing may qualify and modify self-interest, but the vision cannot eliminate self-interest. Indeed, any whole which does sensitively sustain its parts is pernicious. A whole ought to foster some diversity in its parts.

Finitude, ignorance, sloth, lethargy and inordinate self-interest in their interrelatedness and inter-penetration create the "isness-oughtness" contrast embodied in human experience. This contrast cannot be eliminated, but there are principles of justice which can give some guidance to the shape of structures which may enhance the possibilities of increased harmony of life with life and to the appropriate relations between human social institutions in the familial, ethnic, social, economic, political, cultural, and religious spheres. Subsequent sections address these issues.

Form, Dynamics, and Unification in Human Life

Human experience begins with an emerging creature's appropriation of creatures lying in its causal past. From the human point of view, the past is never fully objectified in an emerging creature; the objectification involves some loss. Nonetheless, every creature in the causal past contributes *something* to the structure and the feelings of a novel emerging subject-object. Eternal objects, those forms of definiteness embodied in the primordial facet of God's nature and representing potentiality capable of being actualized again and again in the creatures of the world, provide the basis for the objectification of creatures in the past in emerging creatures. Some of the eternal objects contribute forms and feelings to an emerging creature; all of them contribute feelings, including the negative feeling of elimination from the definiteness of a particular creature.

The importance of necessary relations of the causal past to the emerging present inherent in this view should be underscored. Cause and effect are intertwined in human experience. In the appropriation of the creatures of the world, the body functions as a giant amplifier, feeding data into the organizing center of the human being. The organizing center is an ultimate percipient occasion, sometimes conscious and the locus for all our data about ourselves and the world. Humans do not merely impose their categories of understanding on the world; the patterns embodied in the order of nature are appropriated by humans in the initial phase of their experience. Facts and values are interrelated, for the "facts" contribute their share of feeling, meaning, and form to an emerging creature.

This initial physical phase in the emergence of a creature is "succeeded" by a mental phase, in which novel eternal objects embodied in the Divine Life are appropriated directly by the emerging creature. The verb "succeeded" is placed in quotation marks to indicate that the emerging subject-object being discussed is literally out of physical time, for such time itself is measured by the sequence of occasions which become. The "movement" of eternal objects constitutes the passage of time. The emerging entity can only be separated analytically into earlier and later phases. In fact, it is an inextricably interrelated entity unified by its own subjective aim.

In this supplemental phase, contrasts between the initial data appropriated in the physical phase of the becoming of a new creation and the eternal objects appropriated in the mental phase develop. The emerging creature aiming at aesthetic satisfaction and intensity of feeling synthesizes and contrasts its physical and conceptual feelings. The more complex the organism, the more salient the conceptual phase, and the richer the contrasts emerging in the later phases of the creature's becoming. The peak of consciousness is the negative judgment, when a creature contrasts what is with what might be but is not. In this sense, God is the supremely conscious creature, for It contrasts all that might be with all that is. God is becoming more conscious in the evolution of the cosmos; for, as more and more creatures become, It has more actual subject-objects to contrast with what might be but is not.

The emerging creature unifies its physical and conceptual data and their concomitant feelings as it seeks its satisfaction. Its initial subjective aim, through which it is able to unify its feelings and objects, is derived from God's overarching subjective aim. God's subjective aim, as noted earlier, involves Its unification of the forms of definiteness in the primordial facet of Its nature. God is a suasive force in the universe; for the Divine is an evoker, luring forth creatures seeking aesthetic satisfaction and intensity of feeling.

Three components-in-relation are all pervasive in experience. The first component is a formal component, involving both creatures who have become and, hence, are objects for all subsequent creatures, and also forms of definiteness embodied in the primordial facet of God's nature.

The second component is a dynamic component, involving the process of the appropriation of objects, the emerging synthesis of those objects and related feelings into an evolving subject, and the process of the objectification of that subject into the Divine Life. The rhythm by which the many in the cosmos first become an integrated unity and then become one more of the many is perennial. The ultimate category is the category of creativity. All creatures, including the Divine creature, are subject to the emergent process.[10] In affirming the ultimacy of this category one can appeal only to intuition, for the category is more inclusive than any other one. Creativity is manifest in all creation, and appeal to nothing more general than it can be made to illumine it.

The third component is the unification of the formal and dynamic components in concrete, actual entities. Emerging creatures aiming at their satisfaction synthesize and harmonize the feelings and objects constituting their data into an emerging unity. This unification is dependent upon God's subjective aim.[11]

Form, dynamics, and unification are three-in-relation. No one component of experience can be understood except as it is set in the context of the other two. There are differences in the priority of the components in various dimensions of experience. These differences permit a characterization of the leading dimension in various facets of life and the development of normative views about principles of justice and forms of social organization. They also permit a formulation of the appropriate relations between religious institutions and institutions in the other spheres of the social order. Such relations guide the assessment developed here of the contribution religious institutions ought to make a human life in the present and in the future.

The Priority of Justice, Power, and Love in the Dimensions of Human Experience

As form, dynamics, and unification are three-in-relation, these components are present in every sphere of human life. In spite of these necessary interrelations, a leading component, a secondary component, and a tertiary component are discernable in the various spheres of human life. The saliency of a particular component in one or more of the spheres of human life permits an assessment of the potential contributions of social institutions in the several spheres of the social order to human life. It also permits an interpretation of the appropriate relations of social institutions to each other.

There are six possible sequences of relations between these three components: dynamics, unification, and form; form, unification, and dynamics; form, dynamics, and unification; dynamics, form, and unification; unification, dynamics, and form; and unification, form and dynamics.

Before relating these components to human life, these symbols referring to basic metaphysical processes need to be correlated with more familiar ones. The form component of human life embodies the notion of justice, for it entails the rational side of things. The dynamic component embodies the notion of power, for it entails both causal influence and self-determination. The unification component embodies the notion of love, for it entails the harmonization of formal and dynamic components into a unity and the sensitive responses of creatures one to another.

The first sequence of priority, power, love, and justice, refers to the basic process of the emergence of the novel creature *per se*. Any emerging creature under the necessity to actualize itself (power) is able to do so through the derivation of its subjective aim from God's subjective aim (love). As it emerges, it synthesizes forms (justice) and feelings derived from the causal past and from God's primordial nature into a whole.

The second sequence of priority, justice, love, and power, refers to the relations between human beings in face-to-face relations. The form of the person can be most fully respected in such relations; for, at least potentially, one can be more fully accepted and understood in such small group contexts than in any other context. Love, involving sympathetic and empathic responses to the needs of others, is second in emphasis. Self-determination is third in emphasis; for, at least in principle, one's own aims are intimately related to the aims of the other.

The third and fourth sequences, "justice, power, and love" and "power, justice, and love," relate to human groups of social institutions in their abstraction from the concrete network of social relations in which human beings are enmeshed. These abstractions refer to intergroup relations in the racial, ethnic, status, economic, cultural, and political spheres of the social order.

The justice, power, and love sequence is predominant in all of these spheres except the political, for the values shaping these relations are defined by cultural forms. These cultural defining characteristics are themselves the product of the response of the shaping capacities of human beings to factors inherent in the conditions of human existence. These forms shape the way people are lured or coerced to participate in the social institutions in these spheres.

The state may enact and enforce laws which reinforce or run counter to the forms predominant in one or more of these spheres. As this law-making and law-enforcing function of the state suggests, the sequence of priority in the state is power, justice, and love. Power considerations are predominant; the state acts to shape and to enforce laws helping to define the character of the social institutions in the other spheres of the social order. If a state is to endure, its citizens must participate in some commonly shared values and give at least tacit approval to the political elders of the state. Leaders seeking to impose their wills upon a citizenry without regard for justice or for the expectations of the citizens may be able to do so for a time, but eventually such leadership will modify its views or be deposed. The "better" the state, the greater its reliance on reciprocal suasive power and the less its reliance on linear power.

The state seeks to develop forms and patterns to facilitate both domestic and international order and harmony. Within a state, understood as a geographical territory with some common shared values in which an organizing center has a monopoly on the legitimate use of force and on the shaping of domestic and foreign policy, a consensus formation process is often successful, for the members of a state share enough common values to accept or to acquiesce to the policy decisions developed by the leaders in the organizing center of the state. If members do not share enough common values to permit the consensus formation process to evolve, internal strife and civil wars will develop.

The nurture of order and harmony in the domestic side of a state's life is often difficult, but such nurture is even more difficult in international affairs. There is little consensus about justice and a minimal participation in common values among the peoples of the several national states on this planet, so the dimension of power looms even larger in international affairs than in national affairs.

This reality limits the capacity of any nation state to shape policy which will enhance the harmony of th whole. Political leaders must always consider the expectations of their own citizens in the formulation of foreign policy; the predominance of self-interest among all peoples suggests only those policies fostering the common good of all humankind which also clearly enhance the welfare of the peoples of particular nations have any chance of adoption. Any view of the human future fostering the adoption of policy which ignores the pervasiveness of self-interest among the nations of the world will not only create internal discord but also will increase rather than diminish the fragile order currently extant among the nations of the world.

The sequences "love, power, and justice" and "love, justice, and power" refer to God-world relations. From the Divine point of view, the sequence of priorities is love, power, and justice. God manifests Its love by sensitively responding to the becoming of the creatures of the world and by then seeking to evoke the becoming of new creatures who will maximize the harmony and intensity of feeling of which they are capable. God does so by providing them with seasonally relevant forms of definiteness from which the creatures may appropriate those which they "decide" to incorporate in their emerging selves. These creatures are then objectified in the Divine Life, and the sequence is repeated for emerging creatures. In Its totality God functions in the universe as a locus of potentiality, a lure for feeling, a mediator of experience, and an ultimate receptor of all that has become.

From the human point of view, the sequence of priorities is love, justice, and power. Love refers to the development of the emerging creature's subjective aim evoked by God's subjective aim. Justice refers to the emerging creature's appropriation of creatures lying in its causal past and of forms of definiteness embodied in the primordial facet of God's nature. Power refers to the dynamic process of self-development and to the actualization of the creature who then becomes a "power" which all subsequent creatures must take into account.[12]

Religious institutions are grounded in human religious experience and in interpretations of that experience. The priority of love in the love, justice, power sequence provides the basis for the development of criteria to guide the relations between religious institutions and institutions and groups in the other spheres of the social order.

The Divine Reality functions by persuasion in the cosmos, and institutions lured forth by that reality should do likewise. Religious institutions should not use physical force or threat of physical force either to attract participants or to relate to people. Except in the most extraordinary circumstances, they should not be involved directly in the conflict of political group with political group in the political sphere. The necessary inclusion of form in human experience implies that reason contributes positively to human experience of the Divine Presence, but the saliency of love means that religious experience is more fundamental and elemental than any analysis of it or of the supreme subject-object of religious devotion. Faith is prior reason in human religious experience, but reason may enhance faith.

Because justice and love are more salient than power in interpersonal relations and because social institutions involve abstractions from the concrete net of relations to which humans are bound, the fullest dimensions of human life are realizable only in interpersonal relations. Some forms of social organization are more consonant with human nature than others. When a given society can sustain them, these forms should be supported; but it is a mistake to criticize inordinately forms of familial, ethnic, status, economic, political, cultural and religious organizations on the grounds that they thwart the fulfillment of human life. Those forms of social organization which offer the possibilities of more adequately enhancing human life should be fostered, but the most any form of social organization can ever do is to provide a more favorable environment for the cultivation of richer, fuller, and more harmonious life.

Because human actualization involves some loss of the past, even the most congenial forms of social organization and the most satisfying interpersonal relations cannot provide an ultimate fulfillment. Religious institutions should seek to evoke human intuitions of an ultimate fulfillment beyond the temporal. In the Christian tradition, this non-temporal locus of fulfillment has been characterized by the symbol "the Kingdom of God." These symbols bear witness to the everlasting objectification of the creatures of the world in the Divine Life. The creatures are objectified in the consequent facet of God's nature and then flow back into the world — the Kingdom of God is with us now and forever more.

Temporal fulfillment of human life surpasses social institutions and historical groups and is embodied in individual human beings in their concrete relations with other creatures — human and non-human; eternal fulfillment of human life surpasses the perpetual perishing of the temporal and is embodied in the everlasting full and complete objectification of the creatures of the world in the Divine Life.

The contrast between the priority of power in political life and the priority of love in the religious life is the foundational reason for the similarity between this view and the classical Lutheran "Two Kingdom" interpretation of church-world relations. The necessary embodiment of form in *all* experience, the universality of general principles of justice, and the ambivalently positive contribution of desirable forms of social organization to human life are the foundational reasons for the similarity between this view and classical Calvinism and Catholicism.

The question of the appropriate contribution of religious institutions to human life is inextricably related to an understanding of the principles of justice and desirable forms of human social organization in the several spheres of the social order. The subsequent section of this essay addresses these issues.

Human Principles of Justice and Desirable Forms of Social Organization

Human Principles of Justice

The process of creaturely actualization involves the unification of data derived from a given creature's causal past and from the primordial facet of God's nature. The "power" component involves both the givenness of data and the dynamic decision by which an emerging creature becomes what it is to be. Power in human social systems involves the actualization and implementation of decisions made by various participants in the system. It is necessarily reciprocal, but the intensity and the reciprocity varies.

"Justice" involves the forms which give shape to creaturely actualization. Justice in human social systems relates to the principles of justice, to the rules and regulations of justice informed by the principles and shaped by the decisions of people in the organizing center of a state, and to the application of the rules and regulations of justice in a particular situation by seasonally relevant participants in that situation.

"Love" refers to the unification of power and justice in a particular context. In human societies, the unification of power and justice takes place in a twofold manner. First, people have to make decisions to embody the principles of justice through particular rules and regulations of justice in a specified context. Second, people have to apply the rules and regulations of justice in a particular situation. The power component, as noted earlier, is the leading component at each level, so the encounter of wills with wills, both individual and collective and also domestic and international, is characteristic of political life.

The form, dynamics, unification triad inherent in the actualization of all creatures provides the basis for the formulation of the principles of justice. The rational component of form provides the basis for equality appropriate to form as a principle of justice. The rational component initially gives rise to the recognition of odd and even. The recognition of even and the intuition of the idea of congruence entail the idea of equality. Differences among creatures require some limitations on the principle of equality, for the principle can apply only to equals. Thus the qualifying phrase "appropriate to form" must be added to the notion of equality.[13]

The dynamic component of power provides the basis for self-determination informed by excellence as a principle of justice. The dynamic bias inherent in the cosmos in general and human beings in particular limits the fit of forms to facts. As befits high grade organism, the shaping capacity of human beings is substantial. The lure for harmony and intensity of feeling, both within and between creatures, qualifies self-determination; for it is informed by the excellence of harmony and intensity of feeling. Thus the qualifying phrase "informed by excellence" must be added to the notion of self-determination.

Some humans have greater shaping capacities than others, so self-determination modifies and qualifies equality among humans. Some social differentiation is necessary and desirable, but protagonists disagree on the degree of differentiation that ought to be sustained within and between nations.

The problems inherent in efforts to harmonize the principles of equality appropriate to form and self-determination informed by excellence lead to a consideration of order, peace, or harmony, the third principle of justice. Both equality and self-determination must be manifest, but they cannot be harmonized perfectly. A tolerable balance is obtained in a healthy society, but the precise integration cannot be determined *a priori*. It depends on contextual factors and the give and take that is part of the life of a living community.

Protagonists of either excessive equality or excessive self-determination are apt to ignore the principle of order, but its saliency in human life should not be underestimated. In its political organization, humankind is also imperiled by the danger of tyranny on the one hand and anarchy on the other hand. The excessive disorder of anarchy encourages the excessive order of tyranny, and vice versa.

Equality appropriate to form, self-determination informed by excellence, and order are thus universal principles of justice. These principles taken in conjunction with the sequence of priorities of form, dynamics and unification discussed earlier and with the characteristics of human beings, can inform the development of forms of social organization most likely to permit — but not to guarantee — the maximization of the harmony of life with life under the conditions of human existence. The next portion of this section elaborates these forms.

Normative Forms of Social Organization

The capacity of human beings to surpass their pasts and to shape their emerging presents is substantial, compared to other organisms on this planet. This freedom is limited by destiny, for the human past and the conditions of nature combine to place limits on what is possible in the present. Human capacity to shape the defining characteristics giving form to human social institutions in the spheres of the social order is more substantial than human capacity to shape the defining characteristics of nature, but even these capacities are not unlimited. The multiplicity of forms of familial, racial, ethnic, social, economic, political, cultural, and religious institutions underscores the interplay of human decisions and historical destiny. Even though these forms are the product of human intentionality, such intentionality becomes a causal factor limiting the freedom of expression of future creatures.

As a consequence of the interplay of freedom and historical destiny, the forms elaborated here are not seasonally relevant in many human societies now or in the foreseeable future. In spite of this limitation, the vision of normative forms of human social organization in the several spheres of the social order can serve as a lure for people to seek such forms in societies where they are not institutionalized and for people to sustain and to enhance them in societies where they are institutionalized.

The family is grounded in biological and social necessity. It is the elemental and fundamental unit of the social order. The diadic nature of human procreation, the needs for intimacy, and the prolonged maturation process for humans all encouraged the emergence of the monogamous family. Human self-determination plays a role in the initiation of the family unit, but this freedom occurs in the context of structures which qualify it. The monogamous family is most apt to harmonize self-determination informed by excellence and equality appropriate to form, and it is the most desirable form of family organization.

The problems centered around the notions "equality appropriate to form" and "order" in the family are manifold. As the visibility of women's liberationists indicates, there is no full consensus on the forms which give the proper equality in family life. Age differences qualify the relations within the family unit, but neither age or sex differences provide definitive directives about intra-family relations.

It is doubtful if the plasticity of human nature is sufficiently great to permit humans to redefine radically traditional sexual roles. Certainly, the predominant role of women in the procreation process is not changeable now or in the foreseeable future. This basic elemental biological and psychic reality limits the extent of familial "equality."

In spite of this limitation, human ability to surpass natural forms permits some modifications of traditional patterns. Radical revisions must be challenged, based on the forms to which human organizing centers are intimately related, but gross inequalities must also be challenged.

Self-determination informed by excellence centers on the promise-giving and promise-receiving embodied in the public aspects of the marriage ceremony. Persons exchanging promises are under substantial obligation to honor such promises.

In spite of such intentionality, marriages do cease when partners no longer feel married. Divorce, though scarcely a desirable action, is sometimes necessary. People who will to dissolve their marriages should be forgiven, but the guilt involved should not be trivialized.[14]

Awareness of the relations between potentiality and actuality raise major problems with abortion. However the issue is rationalized, there is no question that in most instances an evolving fetus would become a human being. It is life, and it bears the potential of a more complex form of life. It is beyond the scope of this essay to explore this issue in detail, but the understanding expressed here occasions serious reservations about the sanction of abortion on demand.[15]

Other primary groups besides the family frequently emerge in human life. They incorporate relatively inclusive relations, and they permit a fuller recognition of the person than do institutions in which technical rationalism is predominant. Often the net of interrelations in social institutions in these latter spheres elicit primary friendship groups.[16] A reasonable number of such groups to supplement primary groups shaped by familial relations is desirable. Due to finitude, a person may participate in only a small number of primary group relations.

Human creating, shaping capacities especially related to self-determination informed by excellence combine with biological and social necessity to produce social groups including racial, ethnic, and status groupings in human societies. Social identity based on real or imagined racial differences, regional or nationality characteristics, and/or style of life is very widespread in human societies. A "good" society will harmonize these groups into a contrasting whole in which the parts enhance the complexity and richness of the whole. Such a synthesis requires a harmonious blending of freedom informed by excellence and equality appropriate to form. It is not possible to stipulate the precise range of pluralism that is desirable except in a given context. There are limits to the diversity any society can sustain, but those limits are shaped by the historical destiny of a given people.

Equality appropriate to form in the social sphere suggests the desirability of varied racial, ethnic, and status groups in a particular society blended into a harmonious whole. In a "good" society, overarching commonly shared values encourage mutual respect and tolerance among the several racial, ethnic, and status groups, groups sharing a measure of equality in economic, political and cultural life.

Human rational shaping capacities, particularly those associated with technical reason, and biological necessity combine to foster the emergence of economic institutions. The biological bases for the production of goods and services are primary human needs for food, fiber, and shelter. These basic needs are elaborated through the free play of imagination into endless varieties of means to produce products to satisfy these primal needs and an array of other needs related to human life. Some of the other "needs" are incidental and become the basis for critical assessments of inordinate production and consumption.

Every economic system seeks to harmonize people's demands for goods and services (the shape of self-determination informed by excellence in the economic sphere) with available resources and the provision for responsible growth and efficiency (the shape of equality appropriate to form in the economic sphere). Some pricing mechanism based on supply and demand is necessary, but there is no "best" form of economic organization.

The propensity of humans to abuse their power suggests that government ownership of all the means of production is undesirable and that unbridled private ownership is undesirable. In the first instance, too much power would be concentrated in the hands of the government bureaucracy, and political opposition would be impaired. In the second instance, too much power would be concentrated in the hands of owners, or, as is more likely in contemporary America, in the hands of a managerial elite. In neither instance would service to the common good be maximally enhanced.

Social necessity is more human than biological necessity, so the state, grounded in the human rational shaping capacities and social necessity, has the right to intervene in economic affairs; but the shape of the intervention cannot be decided except in a given context. Government incomes redistribution policies can modify markedly an enterprise economy without radically changing it.

As just observed, human rational shaping capacities and social necessity combine to produce political groups and have fostered the emergence of complex entities termed nation-states. The government, which is the organizing center of the state, is the co-ordinating, integrating, and directing center of a society. It cannot attain a perfect harmony between the principles of self-determination informed by excellence and equality appropriate to form, but it must seek to sustain a tolerable harmony between the two principles as they are embodied in the complex interplay of individuals and groups in the life of the living community.[17]

Democracy is the form of political organization most able to order the other two partially contradictory principles of justice. The principle of self-determination (albeit not always informed by excellence) is inherent in the democratic process. The principle of equality appropriate to form is enhanced by the participation of large numbers of citizens in political processes, but this participation may sometimes foster moves toward politics that are too egalitarian. A federated form of democracy is better able to balance self-determination and equality than forms offering the electorate a more direct role in policy formation. The electorate should have a voice in giving direction to public policy, but the specifics should be left to smaller and more coherent bodies.[18]

Granted human propensities toward inordinate self-interest, the balance of power and multiplication of faction doctrines informing the American democratic structures have much to commend them.

The free play of human imagination (rooted in the substantial capacity of humans to contrast what is with what might be but is not) and human shaping capacities combine to produce cultural objects, of which education, science, and art (including music, literature, and visual arts) are salient. For the same reasons as were cited for the social sphere, cultural diversity and pluralism are desirable, but there are limits to the degree of pluralism a particular society can sustain without disintegration. Generally, the greater the differentiation within and between the spheres of the social order, the greater the degree of pluralism, for the very presence of the differentiations suggests that mutual pluralism and tolerance are foundational values in such a society.

Human awareness of the Divine Presence in the world and human rational shaping capacity combine to produce religious institutions. The insistent particularity of human existence ties humans inextricably to special lived histories, including particular religious traditions. On the conceptual side, one may envisage the possibility of an emerging world theology which will co-ordinate and harmonize the theologies developed thus far in human history. On the physical side one must note the enmeshing of people in particular matrices of religious feeling and meaning.

This particularism and the multiplicity of alternative interpretations of the Divine Reality practically present and theoretically possible among humankind suggest the desirability of religious liberty and religious pluralism set in the context of some overarching unity.

Worship, education, and the cultivation of sociability constitute the primary internal facets of religious institutional life. The articulation of principles of justice and of desirable forms of social organization constitute its primary functions in relation to institutions in the other spheres of the social order.

In sum, monogamy, racial, ethnic, status, cultural, and religious pluralism and tolerance, economic organizations permitting a rational allocation of resources based on a supply - demand mechanism, and democracy are the forms of social organization most apt to maximize the actualization of the three principles of justice. The following section discusses the public faith of America and the religions of America to permit an assessment of the relation between the public faith of America, the religions of America, and authentic religion.

America's Public Faith and the Religions of America

Introduction

Religious institutions, such as temples, churches, monasteries, shrines, and synagogues have been part and parcel of the fabric of social life in all human societies. The modern occidental historical epoch is distinguished from all others by the sharper separation of the religious sphere from the other spheres of the social order. It is also distinguished by the widespread questioning by the people in many social strata of interpretations of life affirming the reality of the Divine presence in the world.

This section is focused on foundational notions or grounding assumptions Americans hold about the bases for the values associated with America's public faith and the several religions of America. Many of the observations will appear to be "self-evident" — once they have been brought to consciousness. The reason for this self-evident character is rooted in the nature of human experience. We habitually think by a method of difference. Sometimes we see a giraffe, and sometimes we don't. Our awareness of the presence of the giraffe is heightened by our recall of those experiences in which we did not see a giraffe.

To discover a component of experience that is always present, one must employ a negative judgement, imaginatively considering the absence of the omnipresent component. This is the method used in this section to examine those foundational notions shared by most Americans. These notions are characterized under the rubric of "America's public faith." They are generally presupposed in discussions of religious beliefs and values. In a very significant sense then, the religious communities are not ultimately foundational, for the notions informing particular religious traditions are shaped and directed by ideas somewhat more general and pervasive — ideas presupposed but rarely discussed explicitly.

The public faith of America, as the term is being used here, is composed of three diverse value components. The first complex component is the "Religion of America," a common religion shared by most Americans. This common Religion of America is to be contrasted with the religions of America, the multiplicity of faith communities commonly understood as "religious" groups. The second component of the public faith of America is "technical rationalism," the idea that human reason should be used to calculate the most efficient means to attain a given end. The third component is "secular humanism," the notion that emerging human beings are worthy of concern, dignity, and respect. Certain moral notions, such as the values sustaining the forms of social organization in the familial, social, economic, political, and cultural spheres, shade into the Religion of America.

The religions of America are embodied in the familiar tripartite structures of faith communities in America — Protestant, Catholic, and Jewish. Within Protestantism and Judaism, there are a number of sub-communities. People may move from one such sub-community to another without undercutting their basic identities as Protestant or Jews. Within Protestantism, a White Protestant - Black Protestant division is also part of sub-community differences.[19]

The Emergence of the Voluntary Religious Institution in the American Experience

A sequence of events that was one of the most significant in the history of Christianity transpired in the United States in the latter part of the eighteenth and the early part of the nineteenth centuries; the federal government, and subsequently all the state governments, affirmed the principle of religious liberty by disestablishment of all religious institutions. Some voluntary sectarian Christian groups — among whom the Mennonites and some left-wing Calvinist groups are salient examples — and Jewish faith communities had existed in Europe, but an officially established state church had long been the practice in Europe. Now, in the Age of Reason, the Bill of Rights of the new republic affirmed the principle of church-state separation at the national level.

In human affairs, critical actions of leaders in an epoch-forming period shape the feelings, customs, habits, social institutions, and cultural values of succeeding generations, for their decisions become causal components contributing to the decisions of others both in their own time and in later historical periods. In this sub-section, salient aspects of America's past are retrieved to enhance the understanding of contemporary church-state relations and to illumine the factors shaping the emergence of the voluntary religious institution to a position of preeminence in the United States.

American churches and synagogues are rooted primarily in Europe, for the vast waves of European immigrants brought their own religious institutions with them. Unable to transplant their social, economic, or political institutions in the new world directly, they were able to implant their religious institutions with fewer modifications. Some American Indian and some Oriental religious institutions have resisted assimilation, but the overwhelming majority of religious institutions in America are related to some facet of the Christian movement. The most influential minority religion in America is Judaism, which has some shared history with Christianity and with the European tradition. Black religious groups, rooted both in the American and in the African heritages, are, in some senses, a minority group within the Christian movement in America.

The early post-feudal period during which the first white settlers migrated from Europe to the new world was scarcely conducive to the idea of religious liberty. With the notable exceptions of Rhode Island and Pennsylvania, the early colonists established their versions of established churches in the colonies they settled. These early settlers may have had doctrinal disputes with the established churches of Europe, but they did not repudiate the idea of establishment *per se.*

Social and cultural realities, however, made the maintenance of the established church difficult in the American colonies. Immigrants to a given colony came from different parts of Europe with different established state churches. This religious diversity made the establishment of one state church difficult and contributed to the trend toward disestablishment.

This sociological reality was augmented by ideological trends, for both non-Christian thought forms, particularly French Deism and various forms of naturalism and romanticism, and also various Christian views of the Believers' Church rooted in the left wing of both the Lutheran and Calvinist versions of the Reformation, led more and more people in the colonies to question the wisdom of an established church.

The framers of the Constitution were very aware of the potentially divisive effect of religious sects upon the body politic, and they were determined to mitigate such possible conflicts by minimizing the involvement of the government in religious matters. The First Amendment to the Constitution, prohibiting Congress from enacting any law establishing a state church, reflected this concern.

The Supreme Court held that the amendment applied only to the federal government and not to the state governments, but its suasive power was considerable. By 1833 the last of the states had disestablished the church, and the separation of church and state in America was substantially completed.

The importance of this historical development for the style and shape of the religions of America can scarcely be overemphasized, for it minimized the hostility toward religious institutions manifested so frequently in Europe. It also reinforced the emerging norms of religious liberty, religious tolerance, and religious pluralism. It provided the framework for the mass evangelism of the frontier era and made the voluntarily gathered congregation the normative form of religious organization in the United States.

This vision of the intentional gathered church as normative had been fostered by various groups related to the left wing of the Protestant Reformation. Neither sixteenth century Lutherans nor Calvinists had supported this view of the church; they had sought to substitute an established Protestant church for an established Catholic one in the areas where they were predominant.

The sociocultural homogeneity of the small European principalities of the late feudal period and the elitism of both state and church made this transition from an established Catholic church to an established Protestant church possible in parts of Europe, and groups emphasizing the Believers' Church were subject to various forms of persecution in most of Europe.

The First Amendment to the Constitution contributed to the development of a radically different situation in the United States, for the left-wing vision of the church as an intentional gathered fellowship of believers was sanctioned politically in the United States. Religious voluntarism, religious pluralism, and religious tolerance, inevitable correlates of the doctrine of the separation of church and state, were evolving into a central place in the emerging public religion of America. The denomination, representing an amalgamation of the more inclusive, less evangelical, less intentional, and less demanding church with the more exclusive, more evangelical, more intentional, and more demanding intentional fellowship, was destined to emerge as the predominant form of religious organization in the United States.

Jews, long subject to various forms of persecution in Europe and already having a voluntary religious association, readily affirmed the separation of church and state and the related notions of religious voluntarism, religious tolerance, and religious pluralism. At the time of the founding of the nation, the few Roman Catholics in the United States — forty thousand out of a population of about four million — did likewise.

By the time of the Civil War, something of a consensus on this issue had been attained in America, but the consensus was challenged between 1865 and 1915 by the large number of Roman Catholic and Lutheran migrants coming from European lands where these faith groups were established churches.

These migrants altered markedly the religious composition of America. By this time the separation of church and state had become a core integrative value in American society, a central part of the Religion of America. Consequently, if the national consensus were to be sustained, separation of church and state, religious liberty, religious tolerance and religious pluralism had to be accepted by these more recent migrants. Since these notions were alien to many of the migrants, especially Roman Catholics from eastern and southern Europe, considerable disharmony and conflict about church relations developed in the United States during this period. The continued debates about state aid to church related schools and some issues of public morality and public policy show that these issues are not completely resolved, but a broad consensus has now been attained on the basic idea of state neutrality in these affairs.[20]

The separation of church and state precluded the use of government monies for the support of religious institutions and their salaried professionals. The implications for the religions of America are far-reaching.

Religious professionals in America have had to be more sensitive to the needs and interests of their members than have their European counter-parts. A simple explanation for the much higher religious institutional involvement of American lay people than European lay people is impossible, but the long-established voluntarism of American churches and synagogues is certainly a most significant factor. In order to sustain their institutions, American clergy have had to develop much more innovative and often more imaginative programs than their European colleagues.

Voluntarism, coupled with the pragmatism and the lack of intellectualism in the nineteenth century American ethos, contributed to the activistic and programmatic emphases of American religious institutions, looked upon with such disdain by many European church people. The fund-raising aspects of the church socials of American Protestantism, the bingo nights of American Catholicism, and the sisterhood activities of American Judaism all reflect this pragmatism and activism.

The lack of any significant feeling of anti-clericalism in the United States is also related to religious voluntarism, pluralism, and tolerance, for no ecclesiastical group was able to impose either its teachings on any significant segement of the learned community or its socioeconomic views on any large segments of the country. The dependence of the clergy on voluntary lay contributions had ameliorated potential lay-clergy conflicts, for the lay people could readily withhold their talents and their money. Suasion was the only means by which church people could seek members or pursue matters of public policy.

In relating to their lay people, religious leaders in America have had to pay much more attention to the consensus formation process, for in the final analysis — regardless of polity or of doctrine — a person in America is a member of a church or synagogue because he wills or she to be a member. If a given person finds a particular church or particular denomination unsatisfactory for any reason, he or she can probably find some religious institution which will welcome him or her to membership without undue difficulty. One can also become inactive in one's given faith community or one can withdraw from any and all religious institutions at will. Consequently, most local clergy focus on adjustive and integrative issues, seeking to attract and to keep members in their fellowships.

In this situation it is easier to be a priest than a prophet, for comfort is less disruptive to the life of a church or synagogue than challenge. The relative balance one envisages between priestly and prophetic functions depends ultimately upon one's understanding of the nature of religion, the principles of justice informing one's view of the social order, the forms of social organization considered to be normatively desirable, and one's assessment of the current situation. The point deserving emphasis in the present context is the necessity for an adjustive, integrative style of leadership in the voluntary church.

The only alternatives are either an established church, funded by tax monies, or a multiplicity of highly intentional communities sustaining values in substantial opposition to the predominant culture but on which the members concur. In such an instance, clergy are "prophetic" externally but "priestly" internally. The first alternative is unacceptable to those who think religious liberty is one of the hallmarks of high civilization, and the second, coherent with the basic values of the Religion of America, will result in small groups relatively isolated from the center of American life.

As a result of religious voluntarism, people tend to join churches and synagogues whose constituents reflect their own ethnic and social situation. This self-selection process contributes to the status and/or ethnic exclusiveness of many churches and synagogues. Insofar as exclusiveness obscures people's visions of the inclusiveness of humankind, it is evil. At the same time, insofar as exclusiveness enhances the novelty of the parts of a whole and gives rise to contrasts contributing positively to the whole, it is good.

Technical Rationalism and Secular Humanism

Before turning to a discussion of the major substance of the Religion of America, the other two components that are part of the public faith of America, technical rationalism and non-theistic or "secular" humanism, should be noted.

Technical rationalism seeks the most efficient means to attain a given end; secular humanism affirms individual dignity and the value of the human personality. Both motifs of the public faith of America had their genesis in elements of the Judeo-Christian tradition. Technical rationalism is a product of the transformation of the inner worldly asceticism and the truncation of redeemed ontic reason of Calvinism; secular humanism is a truncation of the value of the human personality as a child of God, a salient value in portions of the Judeo-Christian heritage.

The two motifs cannot be perfectly harmonized with each other, and some conflict between them is inevitable. Technical rationalism tends to atomize people and to foster competition, but secular humanism tends to unify them and to foster cooperation. In spite of this conflict, the two motifs are interrelated, for a person appropriating technical rationalism is apt to challenge traditionalist views of life. Such traditionalist views restrict the potentiality of some groups, such as women, beyond the limits placed by nature. Thus, an uneasy alliance exists between proponents of technical rationalism and secular humanism. They both reject theistic interpretations of life and seek to minimize the limits which history and nature place upon human life.

These facets of America's public faith also have their impact on the religions of America. Technical rationalism has given impetus to the proliferation of ecclesiastical bureaucracies and the concerns with "efficiency" within the churches and synagogues. Non-theistic humanist notions, such as are embodied in the Human Potential Movement, have encouraged the development of multiplicity of small group emphases within churches and synagogues.

In the public realm, secular humanism, technical rationalism, and the public Religion of America interplay, partly reinforcing one another and partly conflicting with one another. No strong coherence exists, and the same person may emphasize different motifs at different times and in different contexts. Indeed, the co-existence of piety and secularity in the context of the American experience, a phenomenon of great interest, is dependent upon the capacities of people to appropriate these differing motifs without sensing undue disharmony and incoherence between them.

Technical rationalism has fostered the transformation of America from a folk society to a large-scale technological society, for technical reason knows nothing of history and of social honor. It only asks "What are the most efficient means to attain a given end?" In this way technical reason supports the pragmatism and activism which are deeply embodied in the American experience. The transition from a folk society to a large-scale technological society has altered the shape of the religions of America, for it has contributed to the separation of the religious sphere from the other spheres of the social order and to the segmentation of human social interaction.

Over the past two centuries the scale of social organization in the United States has increased tremendously. At the time of the first census in 1970, the population was slightly less than four million. Farm and rural residents comprised 95 percent of the population, and the two hundred thousand urban dwellers lived in what would now be considered small towns.

At the present time over two thirds of the nation's population of over two hundred million live in urban centers. They live in a society shaped by big business, big labor, and big government. Without the mind set encouraged by technical rationalism, the large bureaucracy — corporate or governmental — would not have emerged. This emergence was coterminous with the industrialization and urbanization of America. Technical rationalism was the foundational value fostering the vast extension of urbanization, bureaucratization, and industrialization that characterized the transformation of America from a folk society to a large-scale technological society.

Prior to this transformation, people knew each other in many different contexts. Church-goers on Sunday saw the people with whom they dealt every day in social, economic, and political activities. The gradual disestablishment of state churches and the influx of different immigrant groups increased the number of religious institutions. This increase reduced the likelihood that people worshipping together on Sunday would interact in other social contexts during the week, but these non-urban people still encountered each other in many different circumstances.

The vast extensions of the urbanization, industrialization, and bureaucratization in the late nineteenth and twentieth centuries have greatly segmented human social interaction. Today the likelihood that a person attending a given church or synagogue would encounter a fellow member in other social contexts during the week is much less than in earlier periods. This is especially true in the urban centers where the majority of Americans live. This segmentation of social interaction reinforces the privatization of the religious sphere, i.e., the separation of churches and synagogues from direct participation in public life and from direct contributions to public policy issues.

The church-state separation discussed earlier gave impetus to the privatization of the religious sphere, for no doctrine associated with a particular religious group could hold sway in the public spheres. Religious beliefs became private matters not directly pertinent to the public realm. Thus technical rationalism and the separation of church and state factor in the Religion of America reinforced the privatization of the religions of America. This privatization of the religions of America, in turn, has contributed to the emergence of a technological society par excellence in the United States, for it largely freed the market place from the restraints of religious convictions. The demise of Sunday business closings in the past two or three decades is evidence in the continued erosion of the impact of particular religious values in the economic sphere.

The small group emphases associated with secular humanism have also contributed to this privatization, for the introspection and focus on group processes not infrequently leads participants to excessive preoccupation with themselves and their small groups.

The Emergence and Substance of the Religion of America

Most Americans share America's public religion and also identify with one of the major faith groups. The separation of the church and state and the correlates of religious liberty, religious tolerance, and religious pluralism discussed in the preceding subsection are one aspect of the Religion of America. In this subsection the emergence and the development of the central core in the Religion of America, a common faith in which members rooted in different religions of America may participate, are elaborated.

In order for the members of a society to sustain themselves over an extended period of time, most of them must share some common integrative values. Coupled with the privatization of particular religious beliefs fostered by the emergence of the idea of separation in church and state and the notion of technical reason, a Religion of America emerged in the seventeenth, eighteenth and nineteenth centuries. This Religion of America does not monopolize the faith of the public realm, for as already suggested, it shares this domain with non-theistic or "secular" humanism and technical rationalism. America's public faith, somewhat inchoate and amorphous, is a blending of motifs drawn from these three sources.

The broad contours of America's public religion have been shaped by the epoch-making events in American history — the settlement of the country, the Revolutionary War and the unification of the colonies, the Westward expansion and the doctrine of manifest destiny, the Civil War and the assassination of Abraham Lincoln, the mass European immigration between the Civil War and the First World War, and, in the first half of the twentieth century, the emerging consciousness of a national vocation to extend democracy to all people. This analysis is concentrated on major national holidays and major cultural heroes, for these events and figures elucidate the major components of the Religion of America.

The analogue between the early colonists and the people of Israel is striking. Old Testament imagery was frequent in public references in seventeenth and eighteenth century America. The early settlers saw themselves carving new colonies out of the wilderness of the Atlantic seaboard. Many of them believed they were a chosen people, freed from the bondages of Europe and starting afresh in the land which had known no feudal period.[21]

An unduly romantic reading of this historical epoch is clearly unwarranted for, as previously noted, most religious leaders intended to establish their version of a state church in the American colonies. In addition more people probably were drawn to the New World by economic motives than by religious vision.

In spite of these cautionary observations, the novelty and freshness of the New World were facts of major importance in shaping colonial America and in the interpretative retrieval of that period made by later generations of Americans.

George Washington, seen as the one who led his people to liberty from the oppressor, is the Moses of the Religion of America. As the "father" of his country, he helped unify the colonies into a new nation. In these formative years, liberty, equality, and brotherhood in a democracy under God, a notion reflecting the Deistic influences drawn from eighteenth century European thought, particularly French, began to emerge as another central motif in the evolving Religion of America.

The notion of manifest destiny, giving divine sanction to America's westward movement, emerged as an interpretive motif in the Religion of America between the time of the Revolutionary War and the Civil War. Manifest destiny gave an overarching theological rationale for activities and practices shaped in large part by self interest and desires for economic betterment, and it contributed to the popularity of the doctrine of progress, also a part of the public religion.

During the fusion of Deistic and Christian motifs in the period between the Revolutionary War and the Civil War, the idea of a transcendent creative and judging God, shorn of Christocentric emphases, emerged into a central position in America's public region. This concept was personified in the public theological interpretation of life offered by Abraham Lincoln.

Just as George Washington may plausibly be interpreted analogically as the Moses of America's public religion, Abraham Lincoln may plausibly be interpreted as the Jesus of Nazareth of that religion. In his December, 1862, message to Congress, in his Gettysburg Address, and in his second Inaugural Address, Lincoln powerfully reinforced the idea of a transcendent, creative, and judging God in the public sphere.

Lincoln's sacrificial death sanctified what he had said and done. His life and death gave impetus to the emergence of the value complex "liberty, equality, and brotherhood in a democracy under God" to a central position in the American moral order and in the Religion of America.

The great symbolic importance Americans attach to the birthdays of Washington and Lincoln and to Independence Day and Thanksgiving Day give credence to this symbolic interpretation of Washington and Lincoln and of the emergence of America's public religion.

The vast immigration of persons from southern and eastern Europe in the period between the Civil War and World War I engendered considerable disharmony in the United States. It produced the melting pot vision of American society, for no society in history sought to assimilate so many diverse groups in so short a time.

As Americans sought to interpret and to adjust to this increasing internal diversity, the Statue of Liberty began to attain symbolic significance. America was to be the recipient of the poor and oppressed from other parts of the world and to be a model of democracy for all the world.

During the first half of this century, America's sense of national vocation came to fruition. Earlier America had sought to become a new nation, free from foreign entanglements. During this period, people began to suggest that America was called to extend democracy to all people. In World War I, Woodrow Wilson proclaimed that America sought to make the world "safe for democracy;" in World War II, Franklin Roosevelt sought to extend the "four freedoms" to all people. It is too early to be certain, but the Vietnam War may mark the end of this expansionist era; new imagery may now be developing to interpret the end of this era.

Shifting and unstable "prophetic minorities" are also components of the Religion of America. In recent times Martin Luther King, Jr., William Fulbright, Eugene McCarthy, and their followers illustrate the prophetic utterances and unstable character of these minorities.

Presidents serve as high priests of the Religion of America and the Constitution serves as its Bible. Presidents are especially apt to evoke ideas embodied in the Religion of America in their inaugural addresses, in addresses and proclamations related to Memorial Day, Independence Day, and Thanksgiving Day, and in periods of national crisis.[22] The death of major national heroes also evokes aspects of the Religion of America. This public religion — vague, diffuse, and only fitfully self-consciously held — is shared by almost all Americans and serves to unify diverse and conflicting values.

The dark underside of human experience symbolized in the Christian tradition by the doctrine of original sin accentuates the element of inordinate self interest and conflict in human life. It is a subdued motif in the Religion of America, but it is not absent.

For instance, one finds such a motif clearly manifest in the writings of Nathaniel Hawthorne. It is embodied in the political life of the American experience through the multiplication of factions and balance of power doctrines incorporated in the Constitution and articulated most forcefully by James Madison in *The Federalist Papers*. It also is entwined with the life and death of Abraham Lincoln.

This interplay between America's public faith and the religions of America constitutes the context in which Americans respond to the Divine Presence in their lives. In the final portion of this essay, a normative interpretation of this situation is undertaken.

Religious Institutions and the Human Future: A Normative Interpretation

Human beings are inextricably intermeshed in a complex network of societies and hierarchies of societies. The insistent particularity of existence and the historicity of human experience interject a note of caution about discussing the "human future," for there is no such thing as a "human in general." Each of us is what he or she is because of the context in which he or she is set, including his or her relations to his or her own past and to his or her more immediate net of societies. Americans approach the future in a different way than Chinese, Russians, or Indians. There is no way to discuss the human future in the economic and political spheres except in the context of particular lived histories of the several peoples of the world.

Because of the privatization of the religions of America and the separation of church and state discussed in the preceding section, it is extremely difficult for Americans in particular religious traditions to address directly matters of public policy and to receive a hearing unless they are able to appeal to values and notions embodied in America's public faith. Because of its relations to the principles of justice and to normative forms of social organization, the assessment of the public faith of America advanced here is ambivalently positive. This view runs the risk of making idols out of the nation and of underplaying a prophetic critique of facets of American society. Nonetheless, if one is prepared to affirm constructively the desirability of the separation of church and state and the related values of religious liberty, religious tolerance, and religious pluralism, one cannot be unambivalently negative about the relation of religious institutions to American society. Those periods in history when the Christian church had more direct influence and power than it does in contemporary America do not suggest that church people possessed peculiar political and economic acumen.

Similarly, if one believes that monogamy is the most desirable form of family life, that racial, ethnic, and social pluralisms are desirable, that a modified free enterprise system is a viable form of economic organization, that democracy is the best possible form of political organization, and that cultural pluralism is desirable, one cannot make an unqualifiedly negative assessment either of American society or of American religious life.

The nature of the Divine Reality and the sequence of priority of the form, dynamics, unification triad discussed earlier permits a delineation of appropriate functions and activities of religious institutions.

The priority of unification in the form, dynamics, unification triad in God-world relations accentuates the suasive role of religious institutions and indicates that worship, which is human response to the awareness of the Divine Presence in the world, is the constitutive function of religious institutions. In worship humans are led to an increased awareness of the Divine Presence. God is always immanent in human experience, but human awareness of Its presence varies from person to person and from time to time.

Human awareness of God is enhanced in three interrelated ways, as the unification, form, dynamics triad would suggest. The first — and in some ways the foremost — is through aesthetic sensitivity. Beauty in art, beauty in music, beauty in thought, and beauty in expression all can serve to heighten the human sense of the Divine.

The second way in which human awareness of the Divine is enhanced is through reason. The quest for truth is not all-important, but it is very significant in human experience. Because of its contribution to human apprehension of the Divine, rational discourse as well as aesthetic attainment is important in worship.

The third way in which human awareness of the Divine is increased is through the doing of good. Issues involving justice and the common good are interwoven in worship services. Aesthetic sensitivity, rational understanding, and the good act reinforce and evoke each other. Beauty, truth, and goodness in their interrelation ought to be embodied in worship services.

Other activities of religious institutions flow from these relational qualities. The educational aspects of the life of religious institutions focus on the quest for truth, but beauty, involving feelings and sensitivites, and morality, involving an appreciative respect for people, are also important in the educational process.

The whole pastoral side of ministry — professional and lay alike — is rooted in the sharing and caring concerns of people seeking to do the good. The enrichment of life through the fostering of close interpersonal relations and through group activities is an important aspect of the life of religious institutions.

Sharing and caring are not only an internal aspect of the life of religious institutions. They are bound to a concern for others beyond the immediate fellowship. Love of others and interest in the common good ought to lead participants in religious institutions to seek justice in the social order and in relations between groups and between nations.

It is at this point substantial problems emerge, for there is a multiplicity of views about the proper relation between religious institutions and the public sphere. Further, justice is much more difficult to attain in intergroup relations, due to differences in the sequence of priorities in the form, dynamics, unification triad discussed earlier. According to the view developed here, religious institutions should seek to accentuate the principles of justice and to affirm normative forms of social organization, but religious institutions qua religious institutions should be wary about issuing directives to a society.

Too close an identity with some of the protagonists in most complex social, economic, and political issues compromises the religious institutions' unique position among social institutions. Obviously, no such stricture should be made with reference to individual participants in religious institutions, but they are likely to be found entertaining conflicting views on complex policy issues. Informed by a sense of cause, a sense of proportion, and a sense of responsibility, members of religious institutions may hope to make some contributions to the quest for justice, but they cannot expect undue success.

Strife and conflict are a perennial aspect of the human situation, and they are especially salient in the political realm. Without some sense of a peace surpassing this realm and suggested by the idea of a Kingdom of God beyond the temporal world, people cannot sustain their spirits in the face of persistent strife and turmoil. The religious institution which loses its balance and proportion by confusing its constitutive and derivative components and/or by becoming too preoccupied with issues of morality and justice is in danger of losing its life for the wrong reasons. Conversely, the religious institution ignoring issues of morality and justice is perverse.

Notes and References

1. It is obvious from these observations that the assumptions shaping this essay differentiate the author from the vast majority of Christian theologians, who emphasize more forcefully the categorical uniqueness of Jesus of Nazareth, and, frequently, of the Christian church. Similarly, they accentuate the discontinuity of Divine-human relations and entertain a "one-way" immanent-transcendent God-world relation. God is immanent in the world, but the world is not immanent — at least not in accord with the structural principals they develop — in God. The emphases on the Christian movement as a sub-conscious matrix of feeling and meaning and a self-conscious affirmation of that matrix as a locus for feeling the Divine Presence and for interpreting God-world relations are the bases on which the author affirms his allegiance to Christianity.

2. Although the epistemological assumptions in this essay differ from those of the theologians of "typical" groups cited here, there is a common factor relating all these perspectives. In spite of differing assessments about the means by which humans become aware of the Divine Presence and in spite of different interpretations of the implications of this awareness for God-world relations, common experiences of a beatific vision more fundamental and elemental than the abstractions made from it underlie all these assessments and interpretations.

3. In *Being Free*, (New York: Macmillan, 1970) Gibson Winter centers his critique of contemporary American society on the cultural sphere. In *A Theology of Liberation* (Mary Knoll, N.Y.: Orbis Books, 1973), Gustave Gutierrez centers his critique on the economic sphere. These differences are a matter of degree rather than of kind, for both analysts note the interrelatedness of the spheres of the social order. Both are critical of high technology and capitalist forms of economic organization.

Jürgen Moltmann's *Theology of Hope* (New York: Harper and Row, 1967), J. Deotis Roberts' *A Black Political Theology* (Philadelphia: The Westminster Press, 1974), and Letty M. Russell's *Human Liberation in a Feminist Perspective — A Theology* (Philadelphia: The Westminster Press, 1974) illustrate this general perspective.

In contrast to most classical theologians, these interpreters relate Christian "liberation" quite directly to the social, economic, and political spheres of life.

4. Richard Baxter represents such a perspective in his *A Holy Commonwealth.* Some of James Madison's essays in *The Federalist Papers* may be read in this way. Persuaded that human beings are inordinately motivated by self-interest, Madison elaborates balance-of-power and multiplication-of-factions doctrines to evolve structures to blunt and deter the efforts of humans to attain inordinate power. Once such structures have evolved, they ought to be supported and sustained.

Those seeking to defend a capitalist enterprise economic system on theological grounds (see, for example, William Lawrence, "The Relation of Wealth to Morals," *The World's Work,* Vol. 1, No. 3, January, 1901, pp. 286-292) reflect a similar conservative perspective.

5. T. S. Eliot's *The Idea of a Christian Society* (New York: Harcourt, Brace, and Company, 1940) illustrates a Christian social theory with a formalistic bias that seeks to life up the medieval period as a model of a "good" social order. Thus he moves toward the perspective of those accentuating the past as "good." H. Richard Niebuhr's *The Responsible Self* (New York: Harper and Row, 1963) illustrates a Christian social theory with a dynamic bias that seeks to transform the present social order. These figures do not attack the existing order as sharply as the more radical visionaries; hence they are more centralist in their interpretations of the created order.

6. Of course, it is not being suggested that these thinkers would concur with the assessment being made here or that they shared either a common interpretation of the world or the view informing this essay. From the constructive viewpoint elaborated here, it is held that they were attracted by the lure for truth and for harmony embodied in the Divine Nature.

7. We reject the notion of Tillich and others that God is beyond the subject-object structure of experience. Because of the priority of the mental pole in Its experience, God is a unique subject-object, but It is not beyond this structure. God is, rather, the supreme exemplification of the subject-object structure of existence. As the supreme subject who never "closes up," God is able to receive into Itself all the subject-objects of the world who have become. For this reason, Tillich wrongly concluded that God was beyond the subject-object structure of the world.

The subject-object structure of the world involves a two-fold character. First, all objects, i.e., creatures who have become, are data for emerging subjects. Second, every creature is both a subject and an object. As it is becoming it is an emerging subject aiming at its own satisfaction. After it has become, it is an object which is objectified everlastingly in the Divine Life and is a datum for all emerging subjects which "succeed" it.

8. It should be noted that the lure for harmony is in partial contradiction to the lure for intensity of feeling. Harmonies involving minimal contrasts, and, hence, minimal intensities of feeling, may be less "good" than the temporary increases in disharmony needed to attain richer and more complex harmonies, and, hence, greater intensities of feeling. For example, the disharmonies engendered in America by the resurgence of the civil rights movement in the 1960s were a necessary prerequisite for the attainment of higher harmonies with richer and more complex contrasts among the component parts. Such an emergence is not guaranteed, but without some risks more complex societies and hierarchies of societies needed to sustain the mix of breadth and depth required for rich and complex harmonies could not have evolved.

9. This affirmation of philosophical realism separates this perspective from Hume's understanding of cause-effect relations. Humans do have some sense of antecedent causes contributing to present experiences. The appropriations of forms from subject-objects in the causal past necessarily relate human reason to forms and patterns embodied in the external world. The Kantian bifurcation between pure reason and practical reason and its attendant fact-value disjunction does not accord with our foundational experiences. H. Richard Niebuhr's distinctions between internal and external history and between speculative and practical reason are based on this Kantian understanding of perception. This view is pervasive in contemporary Protestant theology.

10. Because of this view of the ultimacy of the dynamic dimension in experience, the perspective elaborated here has a Protestant bias. Nonetheless, the necessary presence of formal components in every experience implies a rejection of the notion of the radical freedom of God and the transcendence of forms in the height of human freedom fashionable in contemporary neo-orthodox forms of Protestantism. In this sense, this view has a Catholic bias. This is the basic reason for the possibility of progress in morality; each "moral act" incorporates forms. Some of these forms enhance morality. The evolution of better forms provides the basis for some "progress" in morality.

11. From this point of view, the frequent appearance of trinitarian modes of thought in the Christian tradition is based on factors rooted in the nature of things. The symbol "God the Father" is rooted in the dynamic dimensions of experience, the symbol "God the Son" is rooted in the formal dimensions of experience, and the symbol "God the Holy Spirit" is rooted in the unifying dimensions of experience. Protestantism has tended to emphasize the

Father and to set the Son and Holy Spirit in relation to the Father. Catholicism has tended to emphasize the Son and to set the Holy Spirit and the Father in relation to the Son. The perspective developed here emphasizes the Holy Spirit and sets the Son and the Father in relation to the Holy Spirit.

12. This sequence of priority is the basic reason for the qualification of the classical Protestant idea of justification by grace through faith. God's grace is manifest in Its overarching subjective aim, but the saliency of structures in the emergence of an entity permits the use of reason to illumine facets of the Divine Nature. Indeed, God-world relations are not intuitively self-evident. They require rational interpretation.

13. In human life, differences in age, sex, ability, and social functions are salient limits on equality. A continued discussion about the forms legitimately limiting equality occurs in the life of a living community. The current struggle in the United States about the Equal Rights Amendment to the Constitution illustrates the ambiguity inherent in the notion "appropriate to form." Interestingly, opposition to the amendment is greatest in the South, the region of the country most influenced by the Anglican tradition. Conservative seventeenth century English divines, persuaded that the medieval social theory having a formalistic bias was true, implanted notions related to that tradition in the South.

14. In American society, social forces contribute to an inordinately high divorce rate. The contract theory of marriage, minimizing the organic side of marriage, reflects the widespread popular understanding of freedom as the ability to do what one wants to do.

The predominance of technical rationalism and an inordinate emphasis on achievement, upward social mobility, and geographical mobility accentuate the pressures on marriages, particularly among white collar people. The inordinate emphasis among such groups on the conjugal family accentuates the problem, for humans need the sympathetic support of relatives in the extended family.

A theological critique of facets of American life based on its negative impact on the family is certainly legitimate. At the same time, religious institutions should do all they can to sustain and to support wholesome family life in the midst of these environmental pressures.

15. Complex problems focused on the need for substantial reductions in the birth rate cannot be explored here. Limitations on conception are a much more acceptable means of birth control than abortion.

16. In societies in which the spheres of the social order are markedly differentiated from each other, such as in contemporary American society, substantial disharmony may be induced in primary group relations by the network of secondary relations fostered by membership in a bureaucracy in one or the other spheres of the social order. For example, a manager who is asked to evaluate the productivity and the competence of a colleague may feel substantial pressures in evaluating a colleague who is also a friend.

17. The use of the term "organizing center" to refer to the political leadership empowered to act in the name of the state is based on an analogy between the individual and the state. The state itself is an abstraction from the nexus of individuals who participate in it. It is not a living organism in the sense a person is. Therefore, there are limits to this analogy; the state is not an organism, and the individuals who participate in it surpass the state in their individuality. The state cannot claim the individual as a part in the same sense that the individual person can claim its constituent parts. Even in the person, some of its societies function in relative independence from the organizing center. At the same time, in both instances all of the constituent parts are qualified by their participation in that particular whole.

18. Democracy is obviously not seasonally relevant in many human societies. Religious institutions should seek to foster governmental concern with the common good rather than the good of the rulers, whether the government in a given society is predominantly a rule of one, of some, or of many.

19. As noted in the Introduction to Part Three, in the two decades since this essay was written in 1976, the flow of immigrants from Asia and the Middle East has substantially raised the number of people in the United States related to Hinduism, Buddhism, Shintoism, and Islamism. As observed there, unless these more recent migrants (as well as other Americans) affirm the key values of religious freedom, religious pluralism, and religious tolerance embodied in the Religion of America, religious strife in America may well increase.

20. In a recent study, lay people in three Roman Catholic parishes in a cross section of suburban Chicago overwhelmingly supported the proposition that the government should be neutral toward religious institutions. (Schroeder, W. Widick, *et. al., Suburban Religion* [Chicago: Center for the Scientific Study of Religion, 1974] p. 20.)

21. This imagery was particularly prevalent in New England. These Puritan motifs were not salient in the South, where, as observed in an earlier note, conservative Anglican influence was very pervasive in the seventeenth century. It is interesting to speculate on the relation of the English civil war between the Royalists and the Puritans in that century and the American civil war in the nineteenth century. Certainly, the medieval legacy Anglicans left to the South contrasted sharply with the Puritan influence in the North and exacerbated the contrasts between the two regions of the country.

22. The intense agony of the Watergate experience for Americans is deeply rooted in the character of the American presidency as shaped by the American experience. Not only is the president a political leader — the president also is the high priest of the public Religion of America. The emotions, the wounds, and the divisiveness engendered by the Watergate events are grounded in the failure of President Nixon to perform satisfactorily either as high priest or as political leader. The dishonesty, the deceitfulness, and the failure to observe the constitutional processes all stain the public Religion of America. The positive aspect of the experience is also rooted in the Religion of America — the Constitution was preserved and the wisdom of the multiplication of factions doctrine and of the principle of the separation and balance of powers was illustrated.

The ambivalences of technical reason in the context of the American experience were also manifest in the Watergate phenomenon. The expediency, the willingness to use highly dubious means to attain a desired end, the calculation, the hair-splitting, the circumvention embodied in the legal order, the efforts to avoid the spirit of the law — all of these factors were present. The unique character of the individuals involved points to the episodic aspects of the Watergate phenomenon. The use of calculating reason and inordinate concern with self-interest point to the systemic aspects of the phenomenon.

Clergy and lay people did not speak with a clear voice on the Watergate problem — a reflection of the complexity of the issues, the diverse understandings they have about the relation of the church to the public sphere, the privatization of the religious sphere, and the predominance of adjustive and integrative activity in church and synagogue life.

Introduction to Chapter 10

Members of religious institutions have always struggled with questions about both the appropriate role of their religious institutions and also of lay and professional participants in the quest for social justice in the world. World Council of Churches support for some paramilitary groups, United Church of Christ support for the "Wilmington Ten," and liberation theological support for the coalescence of communities of faith and communities of politics are dramatic examples of the efforts of some Christians to involve Christian churches quite directly in the political sphere of the human social order.

Several major denominations in the United States have promulgated numerous public policy statements offering specific counsel on complex issues. Many such pronouncements fail to recognize the complexities of most social issues, and they do not develop coherent and persuasive arguments for the viewpoint they espouse. Frequently, they also fail to address the legitimacy of reasonable dissent from their views.[1]

As the views elaborated in Chapter 9 show, my own constructive efforts have led me to question such direct involvement of religious institutions *qua* religious institutions in the body politic. In relation to theologians within the Christian movement, I have come to appreciate, in more general forms than they would have affirmed, both the "Two Kingdoms" doctrine of Martin Luther and also the transforming views of many people in the Calvinist tradition. I share Luther's views of the distinction which ought to be maintained between the priority of love in the church and power the state, but I also share the beliefs of many Calvinists who believe that religious institutions should provide a direction for the transformation of human life. These dual convictions are manifest in both the preceding chapter and also in this chapter.

This chapter is organized into three sections. The first section discusses several alternative perspectives on social change to illumine the interplay between metatheory and interpretations of social change. The second section, drawing on the basic notions developed in Part One, outlines my understanding of the bases for social change.

The third section elaborates the views developed in the last portion of Chapter 9. It suggests a way in which religious institutions could both honor the legitimacy of contrasting prudential views on the best means to sustain the quest for social justice and also support those seeking to promote specific projects and programs. To shape the argument, it retrieves notions developed in both Part One and Part Two and in Chapter 9.

Notes and References

1. For an examination of one such effort, see my *Flawed Process and Sectarian Substance: Analytical and Critical Perspectives on the United Church of Christ General Synod Pronouncement "Christian Faith: Economic Life and Justice."* (Chicago, IL: Exploration Press, 1990.)

CHAPTER 10

Religious Institutions and Social Change

Alternative Perspectives on Social Change

The phenomenon of social change is of self-conscious interest to all humans who reflect on the contrast between what has been, what is, and what might be. Change is ubiquitous, but the past is reproduced with less novel innovation in some subhuman entities than in others, in people in some human societies than in other human societies, and in some people in the same society than in other people in that society. Compared to other entities of which we have any direct knowledge, humans possess the greatest plasticity and the most enhanced capacities for surpassing the past in the present.

Humankind has some sense of where it has been and of where it is going, but it is never certain of either. The experiences of permanence and change, the influence of the causal past in the emerging present, the intuition of a perfect harmony, the lure of the future embodied in the present, and the attainment of some satisfaction in the present have been interpreted in diverse ways.

Some theologians have maintained that God knows where humans have been and where they are going, but humans do not. They affirm God's providence, and they develop doctrines of predestination. Augustine and Calvin have put the doctrine of predestination in classic form.

The doctrine emerges whenever thinkers press the doctrines of God's unqualified omnipotence, omnipresence, and omniscience to a logical and coherent conclusion. Divine flat "imposes" laws on the world. God's will accounts for the laws and patterns due to finitude, ignorance, and sin. Humans discern these patterns darkly and also experience disharmony.

The idea of the "orderliness" of things, implicit in doctrines of predestination, became a motive force in the emergence of the natural sciences in the early modern period. Isaac Newton, for example, held that the Deity imposed laws on nature. Though shorn of Christocentric emphases, eighteenth-century Deists held that the laws of nature were a consequence of Divine ordering. Deprived of its theological underpinning, the notion of the lawfulness of nature has persisted in truncated forms in the natural and human sciences of the nineteenth and twentieth centuries.

The Greek atomists, of whom Democritus is representative, were the only Greek philosophers who sought underlying laws which they held determined human behavior. The Sophists' focus on human self-determination emphasized the significance of individual agents in social change. Aristotle's understanding of freedom and reason in the human sphere led him to distinguish between the degree of precision to be expected in the practical disciplines compared to the theoretical disciplines. Plato's view of the spontaneity of the Divine *eros* and the concomitant spontaneity of creatures in the world led him to suggest that nature could provide only a likely tale.

Because western philosophy did not have an autonomous existence from about the time of Augustine until about the time of Erasmus, European philosophic speculations about the relation of the past to the present and to the future in human affairs did not emerge again until the modern period. Gottfried Wilhelm von Leibnitz and Baruch Spinoza both elaborated views in which Divine ordering was an integral part of their philosophic viewpoint. By separating theoretical from practical reason, Immanuel Kant attempted to affirm both the legitimacy of the quest for causal laws in the sciences and also the freedom of the individual to shape his or her own decisions.

Karl Marx represents a nineteenth-century effort to discover a necessary development of human history. Marx interpreted change driven by a dialectic of negation in relation to an underlying substructure.

In many respects a tantalizing relation exists between Augustine's determinism and Marx's determinism. Augustine goes "up" to the

Divine, as it were, to establish his theory of predestination, and Marx goes "down" to underlying forces and structures to establish his theory of the dialectical evolution of human history. Both theorists struggle with the question of human freedom and the contribution of human agents to the "inevitable" processes they discern.

Sigmund Freud represents an early twentieth-century effort to focus on the causal past to understand the present and the future. Though he concentrated his attention on the causal past of the individual and cast his analysis in the framework of an interplay between the id, the ego, and the superego, Freud shared Marx's rejection of the *sui generis* character of religious phenomena. He also sought to discern universal causal factors shaping human behavior.

The impact of the modes of thought of people such as Marx and Freud on the contemporary human sciences in America is very pervasive indeed. It is reflected in the views of those who think that the predictive capacity of social scientific theories is the criterion of their validity and who reject the notion of a Divine Reality who is in some sense *sui generis.*

Talcott Parsons, a distinguished contemporary sociologist, affirms this objective as he formulates this proposition framed in the style of thought of Newtonian mechanics:

> It may be taken for granted that all scientific theory is concerned with the analysis of elements of uniformity in empirical processes. This is what is ordinarily meant by the "dynamic" interest of theory. The essential question is how far the state of theory is developed to the point of permitting deductive transitions from one aspect or state of a system to another, so that it is possible to say that if the facts in A sector are W and X, those in B sector must be Y and Z. In some parts of physics and chemistry it is possible to extend the empirical coverage of such a deductive system quite widely. But in the sciences of action dynamic knowledge of this character is highly fragmentary, though by no means absent.
>
> (*The Social System,* Glencoe, Ill.: Free Press, p. 20.)

Though Parsons acknowledges that no definitive theory to predict the changes in a macroscopic social system exists, he hopes sociological theory will develop the point that such prediction is possible.

This quest for precise laws of social change in the contemporary human sciences is balanced by another view rooted in the neo-Kantian tradition. This perspective seeks to discern tendencies and configurations in human societies, but it rejects the quest for precise laws.

Max Weber is the most distinguished exemplar of this approach. According to Weber, humans are meaning-seeking, meaning-positing animals who make decisions and who interact with other decision-making humans. Because of the primacy of human "will" in social relations, Weber did not think one could develop laws in the human sciences as precise as those developed in the natural sciences. Weber's own emphases on "charismatic" leadership and the significance of general cultural conditions in shaping human action reflect his views of the basic motive forces contributing to social change.

In the modern period, C. Wright Mills continues this tradition, emphasizing the importance of the actions of humans in effecting social change. Mills was more willing to politicize his social theories than Weber, for Weber attempted to differentiate sharply between statements of fact informing social scientific analysis and statements of value informing human moral decisions.

Many contemporary Protestant theologians have elaborated views which are more akin to the perspectives of Max Weber and C. Wright Mills than of Talcott Parsons, for they emphasize the importance of the human will in decision-making, leading them to more dynamic emergent views of social change.

Reinhold Niebuhr, for example, has held that the freedom of the human spirit, manifest in its capacity for indefinite self-transcendence, enables humans to contribute to the shaping of history. Though humans are limited by the causal past, they are not determined by it. The ambiguity of human historical achievement reflects the ambiguity inherent in all human cultural achievements; for humans, who in the height of their creative freedom stand between the abyss of nothingness, on the one hand, and the infinity of potentiality, on the other hand, inevitably but not necessarily sin. Their inordinate self-interest results in the persistence of some disharmony and conflict in human affairs.

In a manner reminiscent of Immanuel Kant's distinction between practical and theoretical reason, H. Richard Niebuhr sought to resolve the freedom-determination contrast by distinguishing between internal history and external history. He held that internal history is holistic, simultaneous, and self-determining, and that external history is atomistic, temporally sequential, and causal. By developing this distinction, he contrasted "confessional" studies with "scientific" ones, and compromised the issue of freedom and determination in human affairs. His "double vision" views place him in the company of Augustine and John Calvin, for Richard Niebuhr held that there was only one history from God's point of view. Human "double vision" is a result of finitude, ignorance, and sin.

In the past two or three decades, neo-Marxist modes of thought have become more widespread among selected human scientists and theologians. The influence of the Frankfurt school associated especially with Jürgen Habermas can be seen in the promotion of critical theory. Analysts informed by this theory assess the vested interests of a proponent of a viewpoint based on his or her social location, and they appeal to the dialectic of negation to develop a conflict model of social change. Humans are categorized in groups, unusually bipolar groups based on some specified social location, gender, or race. Conflict between these groups is the key to understanding social change.

The influence of the deconstructionist movement associated especially with Foucault can be seen in the work of analysts who seek to discern the underlying factors which they claim give rise to ideas and values. Social location and/or gender and race also loom large in their interpretations.

The enumeration of distinguished philosophers, scientists, and theologians who have struggled with freedom-determination and change-permanency problems could be expanded greatly. The point of this discussion is neither to enumerate exhaustively the major thinkers, past and present, who have struggled with this question, nor to illumine adequately the theoretical schemata they developed. Rather, it has been undertaken to demonstrate that these issues, which are fundamental to the question of social change, have been perennial ones in the history of civilized humankind. No one who develops a theory of social change can avoid dealing with them. In the following section of this presentation, I shall sketch my constructive views of a framework from which I interpret the phenomenon of social change.

An Outline of a Framework for Interpreting Social Change

Social change is inherent in the nature of things. Every creature in the cosmos appropriates both components in its causal past and also forms of definiteness embodied in the primordial facet of the Divine Nature. It unifies these components in a unique synthesis, placing its stamp of individuality, however feeble, upon them. The completed creature, who has been an emerging subject, now becomes a superject who is objectified everlastingly in the consequent facet of the Divine Nature. It becomes a datum for other creatures that are in its causal future. These emerging creatures appropriate aspects of the completed creature as they become what they are to be. They, in turn, become data for other creatures.

In this view, creativity is the category of categories, the most general category one can envisage. Because creativity is the ultimate category inexplicable by appeal to a notion more universal than it, one must appeal to intuition to elicit recognition of the category. Creativity cannot be characterized, for any characterization would incorporate dimensions less general than it. It must be intuited. This view of the ultimacy of creativity is a Protestant one, in the sense that a dynamic or power dimension is viewed as dominant over form in the nature of things. The pure conservative, political or scientific, is fighting the universe and cannot win. In a similar vein, the pure rationalist does not appreciate the trans-rational bases for rationality.

Creativity is inextricably related to the once-for-all envisagement of all potentiality in the primordial facet of God's nature and to the actualization of creatures in the world. Consequently, the emerging togetherness of the disjunctive "many" of the universe into a conjunctive "one" is a generic notion whose recognition may also be intuited; it cannot be demonstrated by appealing to more fundamental or elemental notions.

Social change in human societies is set in the context of social change in a wider network of societies. Without a relatively stable congenial wider sustaining environment, human society would be impossible.

The most inclusive society of entities in the present cosmic epoch is the electro-magnetic society. Electro-magnetic occasions themselves presuppose the ubiquity of selected geometrical forms and the actualization of specific families of straight lines. Inorganic and organic societies, more or less living, are more specialized societies that have developed within the context of the more general electro-magnetic society. Humans organisms are composed of myriads of highly specialized and coordinated societies culminating in a regnant center. Humans are at the apex of those creatures discernible on this planet.

In this view, laws are immanental, developing with the societies that come into existence. As the societies that sustain them pass away, the laws associated with those societies also pass away. When Plato observed in the *Timaeus* that all nature could give was a likely tale, he was advancing an immanental view of the law, qualified by the notion of Divine persuasion.

The precision of the laws that can be developed in a particular science and the goals for which a particular science develops its laws depend upon the nature of the subject matter of the science. As the subject-object of investigation for the human sciences is humankind, one must consider the nature of human nature in elaborating a theory and style of social scientific research on social change.

Humans possess a regnant center. This organizing center partly depends on the complex of societies that constitute the body, partly interacts with the body, and is partly independent of the body. This regnant center responds novelly to the data presented to it, and it elaborates a complex conceptual symbolism that helps distinguish humans from the rest of the primates.

The emergence of humankind is the product of eons of history. In this evolutionary process, the Divine Lure for harmony and intensity of feeling has evoked some creatures whose capacities for novelty of response to circumstances and for integration of physical and conceptual data are richer and more complex than others. On this planet humans are at the apex of this evolutionary process, and they constitute the highest grade organisms of which we have any direct knowledge at present.

Compulsion and suasion interplay in the process of social change transpiring in human societies. This interplay may be illumined by examining the process by which an actual occasion begins, becomes, and is objectified in the consequent facet of the Divine Life, and in other occasions in the world.

Every creature is dipolar. With the exception of God, a creature begins to become by appropriating data from its settled past. This "physical" conformal stage of a creature's emergence is "succeeded" by a "conceptual" phase. In this phase the emerging entity appropriates forms of definiteness embodied in the primordial facet of the Divine Nature. This process of creaturely becoming is *sui generis*; neither God nor any other creature knows in detail what the emerging creature will decide to become. The creature's subjective aim, elicited by the Divine Lure for harmony and intensity of feeling, permits the creature to decide what data to include and what data to exclude in its process of becoming. This view of the *sui generis* nature of creaturely formation is incompatible with either classical or contemporary forms of predestinarianism or unqualified causal determinism.

The richness and complexity of the emerging entity are dependent on the character of conceptual phase of the creature. If it is prolonged, an array of novel forms of definiteness permit the emerging creature to respond more novelistically and more intensely to its initial data.

Human organizing centers are rich and complex. They possess a greater degree of internal freedom than do the organizing centers of any other creatures on this planet.

Due to the richness of the supplemental phase of their becoming, humans are not bound by their causal pasts. This fact belies the efforts of some human scientists to develop precise "laws" of human behavior and to predict the precise rate and shape of social change.

At the same time, the causal past does condition the present, for people are lured to reproduce values and feeling tones they mutually share. Consequently, human scientists may legitimately seek to discern tendencies and configurations in human societies, but they cannot expect to attain the degree of precision in projecting the behavior of creatures of the past to creatures of the future which some natural scientists develop with respect to their subject matters.

Because societal defining forms are immanent in the creatures constituting human societies, comparative studies must be undertaken with caution; for comparable structures may not incorporate the same meanings, feeling tones, and values in different historical epochs, and/or in different human societies.

Humans are lured to reproduce patterns and to participate in commonly shared meanings, but they are not bound to do so. Some structural components, especially those rooted in human physical and biological characteristics, are universal in human life; but they are inextricably intertwined with more particularistic feelings and beliefs rooted in the human organizing center. These dual aspects of human nature give rise to the conflicts between some sociologists and some historians about the relative significance of generalizing and individualizing components in human life.

This process perspective on social change has considerable affinity with the theory of the distinguished German social theorist, Max Weber. According to Weber, human beings are meaning-seeking, meaning-positing creatures. Their abilities to make decisions led Weber to reject the notion that precise laws could be developed for the human sciences. He sought to discern tendencies and configurations. At the same time, Weber's fact-value disjunction and his unqualified view of power as the ability to attain one's own will in conflict with other wills, do not cohere with a process understanding. This process view is not reconcilable with Talcott Parson's interpretive theory, for Parsons considers social systems independently of the creatures who constitute them, has a bias toward system equilibrium, seeks inviolate laws, and interprets human behavior on the basis of a gratification-deprivation balance.

This perspective cannot be reconciled with the neo-Marxist view of those associated with the Frankfurt school or with those associated with the deconstructionist movement, including those theologians identified with various forms of liberation theology who use those modes of analysis and interpretation. The dialectic stops when a creature becomes, creatures cannot be identified with contributing causal factors related to one's body or to one's social location, gender, or race (albeit they are *influenced* by these factors), the emerging creature is more than the sum of its parts, and the emerging creature shares some forms with all creatures.

Social change may be gradual or cataclysmic. In some instances the dialectic of negation may help one discern some aspects of social change; such social change will likely entail much bloodshed. The interplay of conflicting interest groups, a view promoted by John Stuart Mill to interpret social change, is widespread, but it may involve many groups and may involve suasion more saliently than coercion. In any case, the dialectic of negation is not at the base of things.

Because social location, gender, and race may be associated with a cluster of values and feelings, these factors are frequently very significant in shaping the feelings and values of an emerging creature. One need not be a Marxist to affirm this fact. According to the view being advanced here, this influence is understood as an example of the principle of relativity that is integral to process thought. As noted in other contexts, the principle states that every being is a potential for every becoming. The forms and feelings associated with the appropriation of data from a creature's causal past *do* contribute to the concreteness of the emerging creature; they *do not* determine it. The absolutizing of these influences is the flaw in the Marxist-oriented view.

The integration of the parts comprising the whole creature cannot be adequately understood by merely examining the parts, for the gestalt view conforms to our experience. One cannot eliminate a shade of pink from a sunset with altering the whole of the experience; one cannot characterize adequately a human experience by dissecting it into its component parts.

Finally, the solipsism inherent in deconstructionist views does not fit the facts. Humans do share some aspects of experience with other humans and with subhuman entities. As we begin to become, we do appropriate forms and feelings from creatures in our causal past. The objectification of these forms and feelings insures a linkage with other creatures. Without some common components, symbolic reference would be impossible. There is a kernel of truth in the radically existentialist viewpoint, for no two creatures participate in exactly the same world. Further, excepting the Divine Entity, they never appropriate the past without some loss. Nonetheless, they do share some common components of experience. The more shared experience, the more common components.

Although Weber overemphasizes conflict in human life, compulsion and violence are inevitable aspects of human life. Elements of coercion in human affairs include the limits some entities in the causal past impose on emerging creatures, the causal independence of contemporary creatures (at least on the physical side) which limits the coordination of contemporary events, and the *sui generis* decisions of some emerging creatures who manifest inordinate self-interest. These factors limit the degree of harmony and intensity of feeling possible in the emerging present.

Suasive factors are also present in human life. Elements of suasion in human affairs include the Divine suasion toward harmony and intensity of feeling in the present, the "order of nature" embodied in the creatures in the causal past of an emerging creature, and sensitive empathetic acting of human beings toward each other. Values, humane or otherwise, are "trapped universals" helping shape the form of a human social order and human behavior. Hence, one should be sensitive to ideas initially developed by creative elites. Better ideas enhance life.

Thus, human history reflects the interplay of coercion and persuasion. The element of strife, coercion, and conflict, noted by such diverse thinkers as the Sophists, Niccolo Machiavelli, Thomas Hobbes, John Stuart Mill, and Max Weber, are very evident in human life, but this element is intermingled with cooperative and harmonizing tendencies. This interplay between force and persuasion has been noted by such diverse thinkers as Plato, Aristotle, most classical Christian theologians, G.W.F. Hegel, Paul Tillich, Pope John XXIII, Reinhold Niebuhr, and Alfred North Whitehead.

Social change is both ubiquitous and ambiguous. Sometimes it enhances human life; sometimes it degrades human life. This ambiguity raises the normative question of the fitting relation of religious institutions to the processes of social change and social transformation. The concluding portion of this essay elaborates a constructive perspective on the fitting role of religious institutions in the shaping of social change. This assessment must be undertaken in the context of a discussion of the principles of justice and of the fitting relation of religious institutions to social institutions in the other spheres of the human social order. The principles of justice and the vision of fitting forms of human social organization developed in the preceding chapters shape this discussion.

Religious Institutions and the Shaping of Social Change

Introduction

This section is constructive, not analytical. No effort is made to empathize with the protagonists who hold alternative interpretations of the nature of various religious institutions and their role in the promotion of social change. The argument is undertaken without a direct reference to those holding contrasting views. Because the conclusions reached are at variance with some of the current practices of many religious institutions and with the interpretation of those practices by other theologians and social ethicists, these formulations represent one more contribution to the conflict over the proper relation between the religious institutions and institutions in other spheres of the human social order. Because every possible view of relations between institutions in the religious sphere and institutions in the other spheres of the human social order is extant in contemporary America, one cannot develop a constructive understanding without engendering some conflict. Because the natural theology at the base of this perspective is anathema to many contemporary theologians, the approach employed here will also evoke conflicts about theological method.

In the view affirmed here, God is immanent in all creatures whether they are aware of it or not. God's presence or human sensitivity to Its presence need not be channeled through religious institutions. Nonetheless, they may bear special witness to the Divine Reality and heighten human consciousness about the divine. Because of religious institutions' special focus, clergy should strive to maintain functional differences between religious institutions and social institutions in the other spheres of the human social order.

Religious institutions and their professional leaders should not be too intimately involved in the claims and counterclaims of conflicts rooted primarily among protagonists related to social institutions in the other spheres of the human social order. The primary responsibility of religious institutions in promoting social change is the cultivation of an ethos that may promote the emergence of more harmony and justice in human society. In America, leaders of religious institutions should seek to provide a direction for American society and for America's relations with other nation states, but they should be extremely wary about issuing directives for the society.

The next portion of this section delineates the bases for religious institutions and their functions. The final portion retrieves the earlier discussions on love, power, and justice, and forms of human social organization to suggest the direction religious institutions should take.

The Bases for Religious Institutions and Their Primary Functions

Religious institutions are grounded in the religious experience of humankind. They have arisen out of the interplay between ritual and emotion in the dawn of the human race, for very early in human history people sought to express their intuitions of the supreme fusion of the fact and value dimensions of experience in the Divine Life. In the religious experience of humankind, ritual and feelings are more elemental than beliefs and rationally developed theologies, but the latter two aspects are a necessary part of the religious expression of civilized humankind.

Though religious institutions bear witness to God's entire nature, they are especially related to human experiences focused on the primordial face of Its nature. As noted earlier, the primordial facet of the Divine Nature is Its one-for-all envisagement of all potentiality. The primordial facet is perfect in the sense that it perfectly harmonizes and orders all the forms of definiteness.

This facet of the Divine Life serves as a Locus of potentiality and as a Lure for feeling. Taken in their unity, the primordial facet and the consequent facet, which is God's reception into Itself everlastingly of the creatures of the world, permit God to serve as a Mediator of experience from one creature to another, and as the Ultimate Receptor of all that has become.

The experience of perfect harmony is part of human experience. It gives rise to the "isness-oughtness" contrast, a contrast which is perennial in human life. It is grounded in the contrast between the limitlessness of potentiality, which can be universal and inclusive, and the finitude of actuality, which must be particularistic and exclusive. The contrast is exacerbated by ignorance, sloth, lethargy, and inordinate self-interest.

Persons who confuse potentiality with actuality advance all sorts of utopian schemes to effect the perfect harmony of life with life under the conditions of existence. Their recurrences and their failures point to the persistence of the "isness-oughtness" contrast in human experience.

The immanence of God in the world is the basis for the quest of religious institutions for a fitting harmony of life with life in the human social order. The transcendence of God, the perfection of the primordial facet of Its nature, the limits which existence places on perfectibility, and the multiplicity of perfections possible in the world are the bases for the distinction between religious institutions and the social order.

Religious institutions have no monopoly on the embodiment of human intuitions of the beautiful, the true, and the good, but it is their special business to accentuate them and to bear witness to their presence in the life of humankind. This distinction permits a functional differentiation between religious institutions and institutions in the other spheres of the social order.

Worship, grounded in the transrational human awareness of the Divine Presence, is the constitutive base for religious institutions. Education, grounded in the presence of forms for human life and and in the quest for truth, and the fostering of close interpersonal relations, grounded in the desire for harmony and intensity of feeling in human life, should be central derivate activities of religious institutions. They should seek to cultivate an ethos in which greater harmony of life with life is possible.

Except under the most extraordinary circumstances, involvement of religious institutions in politics should be indirect and three-fold. First, they should foster a vision of forms of social organization that are normatively desirable in human society and articulate the principles of justice that can guide humans in the quest for harmony in human life. Second, they should foster programs that directly serve people in need. Third, they should help motivate and guide people to seek justice directly in the human community.

In the quest for justice the primary but not exclusive locus of lay involvement should be in social institutions in the political sphere, for the government is primarily concerned with the promulgation and the application of the rules and regulations of justice. Through a multiplicity of public and private associations, members of religious institutions may cooperate with others who are seeking greater justice in the social order.

There is no reason in principle why religious professionals should not participate directly in the claims and counterclaims of the political process through involvement in groups in the other spheres of the social order. However, in fact, because of their religious leadership roles, they should be most circumspect in their involvements. In the main, it would be more desirable for them to aid and abet laypersons in their involvement in groups in the other spheres of the social order than for them to participate directly in groups related primarily to these spheres.

As noted in the preceding section, social change in human societies is a baffling admixture of compulsion and suasion. The way of religious institutions is the way of suasion, for they bear special witness to the persuasive aspects of the Divine Nature. Consequently they should almost always avoid coercion in their internal lives and in their relations to social institutions and groups in the other spheres of the social order.

No such stricture can be applied to individual Christians. Even though the persuasion of reciprocal power is always preferable to coercion, they may have to resort to compulsion in their involvements in groups in other spheres of the social order to facilitate the quest for justice and peace.

Principles of Justice and Normative Forms of Human Social Organization

One of the most important suasive tasks of religious institutions in their relations to the public sphere is the enunciation of principles of justice and the elaboration of normative forms of human social organization. In these ways they can contribute to the cultivation of an ethos which may permit more adequate embodiment of the principles of justice in the rules and regulations of justice and more adequate realization of desirable forms of human social organization.

Because forms of definiteness are a necessary aspect of all entities, including the Divine, love and justice are interrelated. The quest for justice entails the quest for a greater harmony of life with life, and principles and rules and regulations of justice make an ambivalently positive contribution toward the attainment of such harmony. As old forms may be inadequate to changing circumstances, some rules and regulations of justice may be inadequate; but *some* forms are necessary in every context. Calculating justice seeks to apply the rules and regulations of justice to a particular context; transforming justice seeks to surpass old forms for the sake of more fitting forms.

Because calculating justice focuses on the rational or formal side of things, the quest for justice includes the quest for principles of justice. There are three principles of justice: self-determination informed by excellence, equality appropriate to form, and order, peace/harmony. They are grounded in the universal experiences of dynamics, form, and their unification in the actualization of human experience. These elements are three-in-relation, so they mutually qualify and presuppose each other. The dynamic nature of life and the ultimacy of the category of creativity give rise to self-determination informed by excellence, the first principle of justice, for self-actualization is partly *sui generis.* The many senses of human freedom are grounded in this fundamental dimension of human experience. The qualification "informed by excellence" modifies self-determination and urges forth the more excellent way of love, the enhancement of harmony and intensity of feeling. Because of the ultimacy of creativity at the base of things, self-determination informed by excellence is the constitutive principle of justice.

The other two principles of justice—equality appropriate to form and order, peace, and harmony—are regulative principles of justice. They help shape self-determination in a particular context.

The presence of geometric forms occasioning the notions of oddness, evenness, and congruence gives rise to the notion of equality appropriate to form, the second principle of justice. The equal application of the rules and regulations of justice to all who fall under their domain is one of the implications of this principle. Equality also suggests the idea of equality in the several spheres of the social order, but social equality is equivocal. It is qualified by the ascribed and achieved statuses of human beings and by self-determination informed by excellence and order, the other two principles of justice. An egalitarian human society is impossible and undesirable. At the same time, the principle of equality appropriate to form suggests that members of a human society should seek a minimally adequate level of housing, clothing, food, medical care, and education for its members.

The unification of the formal and dynamic aspects of human experience gives rise to order, peace/harmony, the third principle of justice. In human life, the first two principles of justice—self-determination informed by excellence, and equality appropriate to form—must be harmonized in a tolerable manner. There is no single mode of perfection in the cosmos and human decisions are frequently shaped by sloth, lethargy, ignorance, and inordinate self-interest. Therefore, because some disorder is inevitable, the principle of order underscores the necessity of the state, the organizing center of a human community, to attain some harmony between the first two principles of justice to enhance the harmony of life with life.

As political leaders translate the principles of justice into the rules and regulations of justice applicable to a given living community, some tolerable order between liberty and equality will emerge in the give and take of its life. After the rules and regulations of justice have been promulgated, some persons will have to apply them particular situations.

The principles of justice are less ambivalent than their incorporation in rules and regulations of justice, which, in turn, are less ambivalent than the application of the rules and regulations of justice in a given context. Due to this differential ambivalence, religious institutions are on firmer ground in enunciating the principles of justice than in supporting particular combatants in struggles centered in the political sphere of human society.

The principles of justice may be set in relation to the biological, social, cognitive, moral, aesthetic, and religious characteristics of humankind to suggest forms of social organization most appropriate for creatures possessing these defining characteristics. This topic has been considered at length in Part One and in Part Two of this volume, so the matter will be developed in summary form here.

The family is rooted in social and biological necessity. Due to humankind's dominantly bisexual nature, its need for intimacy, and the prolonged period of childhood, the monogamous family can best harmonize the principles of equality appropriate to form and self-determination informed by excellence.

Racial, status, and ethnic groups are grounded in biological characteristics and socio-historical traditions. Racial, status, and ethnic diversity in a society is desirable. ("Society" is understood here to mean a nation-state in which common laws exist in a specified geographical area in which the members are related to the same organizing center. The organizing center has a monopoly of the legitimate use of force within the geographical limits of the society.) A society in which a rich diversity can be harmonized in a common unity is a better society than one which cannot tolerate much racial, status, or ethnic diversity. There are limits to the degree of diversity which can be harmonized within a given state, but the limits cannot be determined without knowledge of the particular context in which the diverse social and ethnic groups are set.

Humankind's biological needs combine with its rational and creative capacities to produce an economic sphere. No unequivocally normative form of economic organization can be derived from a joint consideration of the principles of justice and the characteristics of human kind, but legitimate differences in human tastes and preferences required that every complex economic system must include adequate pricing mechanisms to reflect consumer desires and to permit reasonably efficient allocation of resources. Although no unequivocal support for a modified enterprise economic system can be developed on the basis of the principles of justice and the characteristics of humankind, it is a highly viable form of economic organization in most contexts in the present historical epoch. Very dramatic changes in "human nature," most unlikely in the foreseeable future, would have to occur for a socialist form of political economy to enhance greatly the quality of human life. For reasons detailed in Part Two, my prudential judgment about the likely consequences of socialist and capitalist political economies leads me to support democratic capitalism.

Humankind's social needs combine with their rational and creative capacities to produce a political system. Democracy is the form of political organization most able to balance equality appropriate to form and self-determination informed by excellence. Because humankind's social necessities surpass its economic necessities, the state in principle has the right to intervene in the economic sphere. The nature of the intervention ought to be determined by political judgments and economic judgments about the impact of alternative government policies on the economic system.

Culture is a product of the interplay of human rational capacity with "unessential" factors in existence. In this context, "unessential" means not bound by biological or social necessity. Cultural diversity in a society is also desirable. Again, there are limits to the degree of cultural diversity which a given society can harmonize in a reasonably adequate manner, but they can only be discerned contextually.

Humankind's religious experiences are rich and multi-faceted. The principles of self-determination informed by excellence and equality appropriate to form are most adequately harmonized by fostering religious liberty, tolerance, and some pluralism in belief and practice. As noted earlier, religious institutions are rooted in human awareness of the Divine Presence. Consequently, worship is constitutive of religious institutions and is at the center of their existence. Education, involving the exploration of theological alternatives and the cultivation of an ethos receptive to the more adequate embodiment of principles of justice and normative forms of social organization, is a key activity. The provision of a context in which people can engage in wholesome interpersonal relations is the third central focus in the life of the religious institutions.

Religious Institutions and the Quest for Justice in American Society

Spokespersons for American religious institutions do not speak with one voice on many complex public policy issues. In groups with a connectional and hierarchical form of institutional organization, of which the Roman Catholic Church is the most outstanding exemplar, religious professionals speak for the church on moral and public policy issues. Involving some collegial clergy relations but organized with hierarchical lines of authority, the Roman Catholic Church offers official teachings and pronouncements on both personal and public policy issues. In many connectional Protestant bodies, lay people participate directly with clergy in the development of church teachings on these matters. In religious institutions that support local autonomy, congregations may formulate their own views. They may be guided by the teachings and the pronouncements of broader bodies, such as regional, national, or international bodies with which they are association; but they retain the right to accept, modify, ignore, or reject such teachings and pronouncements.

Many factors lead me to prefer congregational religious organizations: the ambiguity of linguistic symbols, the primacy of self-determination in the nature of things, the propensity of humans to equate *the* truth with their efforts to approach the truth, the saliency of beauty in experience, the legitimacy of variety in religious beliefs and practices, and the legitimacy of reasonable dissent on many personal moral matters and on many public policy issues. Congregational organizations are best able to legitimate reasonable dissent and to support a variety of beliefs and practices within a broader faith community. At the same time, they may become very idiosyncratic, inordinately self-serving, and narrow in focus.

In the quest for justice, religious institutions should seek to provide a direction for American society, but they should be very wary about providing directives for the society. The principles of justice and the desirable forms of human social organization suggested earlier offer guidelines for religious institutions. They should seek to contribute to an ethos in which such principles and such forms of social organization can be embodied in the life of the living community. They should focus on interpretation and persuasion.

In the past three or four decades the members of the ecclesiastical bureaucracies of some American denominations concerned with denominational programs and public policy formulation have been so preoccupied with direct "relevance" that they have neglected the culture-shaping, culture-forming role of religious institutions. Political ecclesiastical activists, often informed by ideas dominant in the left wing of the Democratic political party, have dominated much of the political activity of the National Council of Churches, and of several denominations of Anglo-American origin, such as the American Baptists, the United Methodists, the Presbyterians, and the United Church of Christ. As advocates of particular public policy proposals, they have frequently failed to focus sufficient time and resources on efforts to cultivate an ethos which would facilitate the incorporation of higher ideals of justice and better forms of social organization in American society. Frequently they have appealed to the regulative principles of justice. Relatedly, they have paid less attention to the constitutive principle of self-determination informed by excellence and have given minimal attention to the impact of their proposals on growth and efficiency in the economic sphere.

In the past decade or two, other Protestant groups have promoted public policy positions contrasting with those of the denominations just cited. The "Christian Coalition," described by some as the "religious right," has frequently been at loggerheads with other people described by some as the "religious left." Issues on which the two groups differ range from abortion and homosexuality to forms of affirmative action.

People in both groups speak with vigor on complex social, political and economic issues. Whether either group should issue such directives to the American people is moot.

This critique of the way in which some religious professionals have sought to involve their religious institutions in the political sphere does not mean that religious institutions should ignore public life and the quest for justice. It is fitting and proper for religious institutions to call attention to the principles of justice that ought to inform human life, and to promote values fostering desirable forms of human social organization. As citizens, religious professionals and lay people should be informed and motivated by theological understanding in their quest for justice. Though they should be more circumspect than has frequently been the case, spokespersons for religious institutions may well support some specific rules and regulations of justice, for the dividing line between principles, on the one hand, and rules and regulations, on the other hand, is fuzzy.

It is easier to call attention to a problem than it is to suggest specific public policy to redress the situation. The issue of inflation is illustrative. Inflation impacts different people unequally and endangers domestic tranquility. Both regulative principles of justice, equality appropriate to form, and order/peace/harmony, indicate the danger of "high" inflation rates. It is entirely appropriate for religious bodies and their spokespersons to call attention to the problem and to support initiatives to curb inflation. However, spokespersons for religious institutions and religious bodies have no business prescribing in detail the mix and shape of monetary and fiscal policy initiatives which the politicians should develop to redress the problem. These discussions should be developed by participants in nonreligious, voluntary associations, political parties, and economic entities.

It follows from this line of reasoning that religious benevolence funds should be used primarily for "spiritual" things. The use of general ecclesiastical funds to promote community organizations, to provide bail money for members of political groups, and to promote highly specific economic and political causes requires the most considered reflection.

Because no view of fitting religious institution-public sphere relations is shared by all religious professionals or laypeople in any American denomination, noncoercive ways of funding projects related directly to these and comparative initiatives in the public spheres should be encouraged. If the principles of pluralism and voluntarism in the religious sphere are to be actualized, individual clergy and laypersons ought to have a definitive voice in the allocation of resources for benevolences used primarily for purposes related to such initiatives. One fitting way of denominational funding of programs involving direct involvement of religious groups in the other spheres of human society is through special benevolence offerings designated for these specific programs and through the cultivation of special interest groups of members of religious institutions wanting to pursue specific activities in the other spheres. Those laypersons who feel such programs and activities are a necessary expression of their religious convictions could thus support those programs without involving entire religious institutions, and those persons who could not in conscience support the proposed programs could refrain from contributing to them.

This designated giving approach to public policy and social action initiatives would probably reduce the funds available for some mission projects. However, religious leaders could use these contributions with the clear knowledge that donors intended for their benevolence money to be used to develop the designated initiative. As a by-product, this approach would force protagonists of particular projects to clarify the presuppositions guiding them and would focus attention on basic issues in religious institution-world relations. The "religious right" has sometimes been clearer on this special giving emphasis than has the "religious left."

A Concluding Note

The indirect shaping of social change to promote social justice is an important aspect of the work of clergypersons, but it is not all-important. Even though the beautiful, the true, and the good are three-in-relation, at some times and in some contexts one may be a bit oblivious as to their interrelation. Without being tempered by the beautiful and restrained by the true, the moralist becomes ugly and malicious. Those puritans, old and new, who are inordinately preoccupied about the future, miss all they actually possess—the specious present.

Introduction to Chapter 11

Most of my professional life has been spent on the faculty of a "liberal" theological seminary. Few words are more ambiguous and chameleon than "liberal." Both in reference to views on political economy and on religious phenomena, the term has multiple meanings. In the nineteenth century, John Stuart Mill's *On Liberty* represented a major statement on the freedom of individual expression and governmental limits in the social, economic, cultural, and religious spheres. Liberals promoted policies designed to limit the role of government in the society, and conservatives sought to defend traditional substantial government involvement in affairs in the other spheres of the social order. In the twentieth century, the meanings have been reversed.

In the religious sphere, the term "liberal" carries several meanings. It can indicate the views of those who do not entertain literalistic views of a sacred scripture, in contrast to "fundamentalists" who do hold to the inerrancy of one or more sacred texts. It can indicate those who support public policy proposals generally associated with the left wing of the Democratic party in the United States and in comparable political groups in other countries. It can indicate those who are associated with a particular theological movement in nineteenth and twentieth century Protestantism. It can mean those who promote a contextual rather than a principled religious social ethic. It can mean those who are prepared to embrace selectively contemporary culture and many of its artistic and scientific accomplishments. It sometimes is used positively to commend the views of a person or a group; it is sometimes used pejoratively to criticize the views of a person or a group.

This essay was originally published in a festschrift entitled *Theology and the Human Spirit: Essays in Honor of Perry D. LeFevre,* a colleague who had contributed much to the life of the liberal theological institution with which I have been associated. I seek to identify the core values giving shape to a liberal Christian theological seminary. In this epoch politically correct views are as much a part of the life of this institution as they are a part of the life of many American colleges and universities. Free and open inquiry and discussion, which are at the heart of the intellectual life both of American colleges and universities and also of liberal theological seminaries, are being challenged by proponents of political correctness, a new form of authoritarianism.

This essay distinguishes between core liberal values and doctrines identified with specialized forms of liberalism. It argues that the loss of the core values of liberalism will transform the liberal Christian theological seminary into an indoctrination center. Both in the secular university and in the liberal theological seminary, persons affirming core liberal values have sometimes supported the actions of those who reject such values.

This essay argues that these persons must sometimes have to fight to resist such anti-liberal actions. Because the core values of liberalism include the legitimacy of freedom of expression, tolerance of other views, and the merits of pluralism, liberals sometimes find it difficult to fight actions and ideas that undermine these core beliefs. If they do not do so, they risk the loss of those institutions that embody those core values to those who do not cherish free inquiry and open debate.

While individual participants in a liberal institution have the right to entertain anti-liberal core values, the institution *qua* institution must guarantee the right of free and open discussion. If it does not, it loses its basic character.

CHAPTER 11

The Idea of a Liberal Christian Theological Seminary

Introduction

The editors of this volume have invited present and some former faculty members of the Chicago Theological Seminary to contribute essays to this Festschrift honoring Perry LeFevre, Professor of Constructive Theology, on the occasion of his retirement. He has served on its faculty with great distinction for thirty-one years. He was also academic dean of the seminary for the first twenty years of its reconstitution as a separate school following the dissolution of the Federated Theological Faculty of the University of Chicago in 1961. In this role, he made major contributions to the theory guiding the organization of the seminary's curriculum and to its embodiment in a program of study.

The chapter titles of this volume reveal the broad range of issues faculty members have addressed and the diversity of interpretive frameworks they have employed. LeFevre embraced this variety with enthusiasm, for he sought faculty people who were both able scholars and who held contrasting theological interpretations. In pursuing these objectives, he was informed by a cluster of foundational liberal values which will be addressed in this essay. Some aspects of this discussion are idiosyncratic to this particular institution, but many of the issues considered here emerge in most liberal Protestant theological seminaries in the United States in this historical epoch.[1]

This essay examines the liberal heritage enmeshed in the history of this Christian theological seminary. In this context it explores both specialized secondary forms of liberalism and the foundational liberal values which are intertwined with them. In addition, it addresses the implications of foundational liberal values for the life of a liberal Christian theological seminary. If such a seminary is to survive with integrity, most students, faculty, administrative officers, members of its Board of Trustees and members of its broader constituencies must share a basic commitment to these foundational liberal values.

The Liberal Heritage

As noted in the introduction, Perry LeFevre, both as an administrator and as a professor, is strongly committed to the foundational liberal ideas. He incorporates these inclusive ideas within a more specialized form of liberalism associated with one facet of the history of this institution. It is necessary to retrieve selected aspects of this history in order to understand better the current situation.

The Social Gospel movement, though informed in part by the specialized theological liberalism of nineteenth century German Protestant thought (particularly the anti-metaphysical thought of Albrecht Ritschl), was an indigenous American movement in theology. It emerged in the latter part of the nineteenth century and flowered in the early decades of the twentieth century. Its influence was widespread in several American denominations, including the Congregational churches associated with the Chicago Theological Seminary and the Baptist churches associated with the Divinity School of the University of Chicago. During the first three or four decades of the twentieth century both of these institutions attracted numerous faculty who were leaders in that movement and many students who were broadly sympathetic to it. They were very concerned with social justice issues, and many envisioned the progressive embodiment of a love ethic in the social order. Skeptical about the validity of ontological and metaphysical analyses, the proponents of this movement sought to utilize the emerging human sciences, especially sociology and psychology, to further the "Christianizing" of the social order. They entertained a relatively optimistic view of human nature and focused their theological interpretations on the life and teachings of Jesus of Nazareth. In their selective abstraction from the Biblical records, they developed a social ethic of love modeled after Jesus' life and teachings. They promoted a love ethic as a basis both for personal conduct and for the progressive transformation of the social order. They hoped that persuasion, harmony and equality would reduce or eliminate coercion, conflict, and injustice in the social order.

By the time Perry LeFevre arrived at the seminary as a student in 1943, the Social Gospel was under serious attack and its direct influence in liberal American theological institutions was in decline. The radical neo-orthodoxy of Karl Barth which developed in Europe after the first world war and the more moderate neo-orthodoxy of Reinhold Niebuhr which evolved in the United States during the 1930s, coupled with the Great Depression and World War II, led many to challenge the theological assumptions informing this specialized form of theological liberalism. People assailed it, claiming it was excessively confident about the goodness of human nature, was unduly optimistic about social progress, and was theologically shallow.

In the Chicago context, people associated with the Social Gospel form of theological liberalism began to explore alternative philosophical and theological moorings for their interpretations of the Christian movement. In the 1930s Henry Nelson Wieman in the Divinity School and Charles Hartshorne in the philosophy department of the University of Chicago led the quest for the development of new forms of theological liberalism. In the 1930s and 1940s members of the "Chicago School" utilized the resources of the pragmatism of John Dewey and William James, the emergent evolution of Henri Bergson, the interaction social psychology of George Herbert Mead, the value theory of Ralph Barton Perry and, above all, the philosophy of Alfred North Whitehead in their work. In the late 1930s and early 1940s Bernard Meland, Bernard Loomer and Daniel Day Williams joined Wieman and Hartshorne in the development of neo-liberal thought, elaborating richer and more complex interpretations of the Christian movement than those associated with the Social Gospel.

By the time Perry LeFevre matriculated at CTS, this neo-liberal movement of thought was a major factor in the Chicago complex.[2] The scholars just noted were central to the early development of what subsequently has been called process theology. As one would expect in the development of any rich theological movement,"family quarrels" and contrasting emphases developed among the initiators of this theological and philosophical movement. Three strands of process theology, expressing contrasting views of the status of human reason and its relation to experience, have developed. Further, these cited people differed in the attention they gave to Christian beliefs, doctrines and practices in their constructive work. Because these contrasting emphases and understandings illumine the context stimulating LeFevre's early work, it is fitting to sketch the contrasts between these initiators of process theology and to locate LeFevre's work within this group.

Wieman and Hartshorne, both in Whitehead's debt, accentuated different facets of his thought and held contrasting views about the status of reason and its ability to illumine the nature of things. Whitehead himself emphasized both rational and empirical factors in the development of speculative philosophy. Coherence and logic were the rational criteria; applicability and adequacy were the empirical criteria. Because adequacy entailed the applicability of the schematism to all occasions, it is necessary. This necessity tied the rational and empirical sides of the schematism together.

Whitehead's faith in rationalism was grounded on a transrational intuition that there was a relational matrix inherent in the nature of things which reason could penetrate. Limitations of insight and of language precluded the development of a fully adequate metaphysics, but progress was possible. Because the ultimate of ultimates for Whitehead was a creativity beyond forms, the ultimacy of that creativity could be shown only by an appeal to intuition. Further, eternal objects (comparable to the Platonic forms) constituted a multiplicity, but they were not a class. One could not, therefore, be led to a vision of the Good, the transformal form at the base of things, by the proper use of the dialectic, as Plato maintained in *The Republic*. Consequently, reason played an important but not an unqualified role in illumining the nature of things. In his philosophical writings, Whitehead maintained a careful balance between the rational and empirical facets of his work.

While Whitehead held that the Divine Reality served as the principle of order, the locus of potentiality, and the mediator of experience from one creature to another and was the ultimate receptor of all that had become, he refused to advance proofs for the existence of God. Instead, he simply explored the implications of his metaphysics for the Divine Reality, which was the supreme exemplification of metaphysical propositions.

Wieman rejected some facets of Whitehead's philosophy as too speculative and focused on the empirical side of things. Hartshorne strongly emphasized the more rational side of Whitehead's philosophy and was less restrained about the limits of reason than was he.

Consequently, three strands of process thinking have emerged in the past several decades. Perry LeFevre, Bernard Loomer and Bernard Meland have minimized the speculative side of Whitehead and are more closely identified with Wieman. Others, such as John Cobb, Daniel Day Williams, David Ray Griffin, Marjorie Suchocki, William Christian and Lewis Ford, are seeking to maintain the balance between the rational and empirical sides of Whitehead's philosophy and are more closely identified with Whitehead himself. Still others, such as Schubert Ogden, David Tracy and Franklin I. Gamwell, have accentuated the rational side of Whitehead's philosophy and are more closely identified with Hartshorne. LeFevre, Meland, Cobb, Williams, Griffin, Suchocki, Ogden and Tracy have focused more explicitly on the Christian movement in their work, but all are interested in the relation of their work to other fields.

The Two Meanings of Liberalism

In the preceding section, the Social Gospel and neo-liberalism, two specialized forms of theological liberalism, were noted. Both of these specialized forms contain generic liberal ideas more inclusive than those embodied in these particular species. At its foundational level Christian liberalism is a mode of thought requiring a methodological commitment to free and open inquiry and debate into the beliefs and practices embodied in the Christian movement. It does not entail a commitment to a particular set of beliefs and practices.

The seventeenth and eighteenth century movement of European thought known as the Enlightenment and nineteenth century English liberalism contributed greatly to these ideas. The Enlightenment also played a major role in legitimating human rights, religious liberty, religious pluralism, and religious freedom, ideas which are also part of the fundamental liberal values informing the institutional basis of this liberal Christian theological seminary. In these days when in some theological circles Europhobia is widespread and the ideas of the Enlightenment and/or nineteenth century English liberalism are widely criticized for the shallowness of their rationalism and their excessively individualistic view of human nature, the contributions of these movements of thought to the core matrix of ideas sustaining a liberal Christian theological seminary need to be reaffirmed.

While sharing these core values with a substantial majority of persons associated with modern Western universities, Christian liberalism has a more focused subject matter — the beliefs, feelings, and practices associated with the Christian movement.

Writing fifty years ago, the late Daniel Day Williams, a CTS alumnus, for many years a member of the seminary faculty, and a leading proponent of one form of process theology, expressed his understanding of the foundational meaning of Christian liberalism in this way:

> Christian theology is an inquiry for the correct expression of those truths which are discovered within the Christian movement and which can be expressed in Christian symbols. It arises within the Christian movement and is organically related to it as its frame of reference. Thus it is to the Christian movement as a whole, in all its breadth and depth and ramifications, that theology belongs; but no presuppositions about the absolute or supernatural character of any portion of the beliefs or objects of the movement need be accepted as the starting-point. The theologian may legitimately inquire as to the truth of any proposition which appears within the Christian fold, and the nature and significance of Christianity itself may be a legitimate object of theological inquiry.[3]

Williams goes on to suggest some propositions with which a Christian might agree, such as "The Christian movement offers a significant body of experience and idea related to the objects of religion; it is therefore worthy of exploration" or "Somewhere within the Christian movement there are significant clues to truth." Acknowledging that such beliefs are not the beliefs of all Christians, Williams notes that they constitute the "... most general judgments of importance and relevance which theology, like any inquiry, must make about its subject matter."[4]

He then elaborates a view which is primary for the liberal Christian view:

> The plain fact is that there is no one set of propositions about any of the objects of Christian concern or about the method of Christian thinking which all Christian churches are agreed upon. In the creedal churches, apart from Rome, interpretation of the creeds is left to the

> individual. Further, the basis on which the creed is believed and recited is not prescribed by the creed itself. Christians do arrive at their beliefs by different routes, and their beliefs differ. How then can any one starting-point and any one theological method be prescribed for Christian thought?...No Christian or church can prescribe any dogma which is not open to Christian inquiry and revision in the light of the truth which the Christian movement has always professed to seek.[5]

While Daniel Day Williams and Perry LeFevre have both used notions drawn from facets of pragmatism and process theology to interpret key Christian doctrines and practices, neither insists these modes of thought — or any other specialized mode of thought — should be imposed upon one who is seeking to discern the truth of Christian doctrine and practice.

In this spirit, the Chicago Theological Seminary has been open to students of all denominations and of no denomination and has freely called scholars to its faculty who do not share the more specialized forms of theological liberalism of people such as Williams and LeFevre. The institution requires no confessional or creedal commitment from its faculty or its students. Neither an orthodoxy nor an orthopraxis is a criterion for admission to its student body or appointment to its faculty. Members of the community are free to explore the Christian movement and other religious and secular movements without any *a priori* restrictions or limitations, other than seriousness of intent and responsible intellectual work. Attesting to the depth of the seminary's commitment to these principles, only a minority of the students and of the faculty as the seminary is presently constituted is affiliated with the United Church of Christ, its primary supporting denomination.

Tensions are greatest when persons in the seminary community insist their way of doing theology is *the* way theology must be done and/or affirm that their understanding of social ethics and the public policy implications of their views should become institutional policy. The community can sustain some people in its midst who entertain such monolithic views; but if one such view were to become dominant, the liberal idea informing the institution would be in serious trouble.

This liberal theological institution is grounded on three primary values — tolerance for alternative interpretations of the beliefs and practices of the Christian movement, the legitimacy of theological pluralism in its midst, and the right of participants in the community to pursue freely their own modes of theological inquiry.[6] These fundamental values do not require one to commit oneself either to the particular species of theological liberalism dominant in this school in the first part of this century, forms rooted in the Kantian *Critiques* and/or the thought of the nineteenth century neo-Kantian revisionists and their Social Gospel successors, or to the so-called process theology associated with Alfred North Whitehead and his school. They do require one to commit oneself to sustain an institutional ethos which supports its members as they pursue multiple modes of inquiry informed by any of a variety of metatheories.

While these core values give shape to the understanding of the seminary as an institution, its participants must appropriate a more specialized understanding of the Christian movement into their own work. Their engagements with the Christian heritage and with contemporary theology, ethics, and culture are the matrix out of which such personal convictions emerge. Their encounters with the forms through which ministry is practiced focus their professional understandings. Students have access to the faculties of the seminary, other theological institutions in the area, and the University of Chicago. As seminary students struggle to develop constructive theological viewpoints which they can maintain with spiritual, intellectual and emotional integrity, they can utilize these immense resources. Because of the liberal interest in both Christian and non-Christian modes of thought and also in the universality of the faith entailed in the *Logos* doctrine, liberal Christian seminaries are enriched by close proximity to major universities. The Chicago Theological Seminary is extremely fortunate in this regard, for it is adjacent to the University of Chicago, one of the great research universities of our epoch.

Because the seminary is not a creedal, confessing and/or committed community espousing particular Christian beliefs, rituals or practices, it is at most an amorphous or formless church. Members of the seminary community may participate in churches and those in the Believers Church tradition may choose to form churches emerging from the relations they develop in the seminary. However no member of the seminary community is required to participate in a particular community of faith.

The Implications of Foundational Liberal Values for the Life of a Liberal Christian Seminary

Thus far this essay has explored the relation between the primary liberal values shaping the self-understanding of this institution and the secondary liberal values affirmed by some of its participants. It has done so in order to illumine the "orthodoxy" shaping its life. It is also necessary to address Christian practice, exploring the orthopraxis (right conduct) expected of participants in the seminary community and of the seminary's role in promoting a particular understanding of Christian orthopraxis.

Both in the past and in the present many in the seminary community have been deeply concerned about questions of social justice. Presently, various forms of liberation theology are very fashionable in some parts of the Christian movement and also in this seminary. Its proponents strongly emphasize an orthopraxis, accentuate equality as *the* principle of justice, affirm a "preferential option" for some oppressed group or groups, and provide little space for alternative prudential judgments as to the best means to attain a given end.

Just as there has not been a consensus within the Christian movement as a whole about the interpretation of the beliefs and symbols embodied within it, so there has not been a consensus concerning proper action. Participants in the Christian movement disagree about the relation of the Christian community to the civil community; about the nature of justice, power, and love, individually and in their interrelationships; about the implications of Christian beliefs for the rules and regulations of justice within and without the Christian movement; and about the truth of a teleological or a deontological ethic. Further, they disagree about the nature of the historical situation in which they find themselves; about the possibilities of describing normative forms of social organization in the familial, social, economic, political and/or religious spheres and, if they hold it is possible to suggest normative forms, about their structure; about the desirability of particular public policy proposals; and about fitting theories and methods to use in social and psycho/spiritual analyses.

Just as a liberal Christian theological seminary must seek to provide a supportive framework for the exploration of Christian beliefs, it must also seek to provide a supportive framework for the exploration of Christian practices. Insofar as practice is more concrete, more personal and more encompassing than theory, a liberal Christian seminary must impose relatively more limits on interpersonal conduct within the institution than upon the exploration of the theory informing various practices. The principles of respect for the human person and the limitation of practices directly harmful to others — principles endemic to the primary values of liberalism discussed earlier — shape the rules and regulations of justice in interpersonal relations within the seminary community.

In practice, further limits are imposed on the members of liberal Christian theological seminaries. For example, some scriptures and some Christian social ethical teachings condemn homosexual activity, promote patriarchal forms of family organization, and tolerate or legitimate slavery. Many contemporary Christians find at least some of these biblical passages and attendant social teachings very offensive. Others want to affirm at least some of them, teachings which historically have been widespread within the Christian movement.

Some feminists, some homosexuals, and others sympathetic with the rights they affirm are so outraged by some Christian social teachings on homosexual and male-female relations that they contribute to a climate of opinion leading almost all participants to reject soundly certain Christian social teachings. Those members of the Christian movement affirming some historic beliefs and practices relating to homosexuality and patriarchal forms of family organization may find it difficult — if not impossible — to pursue free and open inquiry on these matters in "liberal" seminaries in this historical epoch.

All are offended by historic social teachings on slavery; those few in the Christian movement in our day defending slavery or caste-structured societies would find it even more difficult to pursue their inquiries in the midst of a liberal seminary. Thus the climate of opinion sets informal limits on free and open inquiry and debate, even in a liberal Christian theological seminary.

Contemporary Threats to a Liberal Christian Theological Seminary

The Loci of Pressures for an Institutional Orthopraxis — Biblical fundamentalism (because of its requirements about biblical orthodoxy), Roman Catholicism (because of its ecclesiastical definition of proper Christian doctrine), some specialized forms of Christian liberalism and some African-American religious beliefs (because of their lack of distinction between communities of faith and communities of politics), some forms of confessional Protestantism (because of their demands for commitment to particular interpretations of Christian doctrine), and some forms of liberation theology (because of the centrality of the dialectic of negation and critical theory in their interpretations of proper Christian practice) constitute major challenges to the theory and practice of a liberal Christian theological seminary.

Because of their attraction to persons associated with groups historically related to liberal Christian theological institutions, some specialized forms of Christian liberalism itself, some forms of African-American religious beliefs and some forms of liberation theology pose the most serious intellectual and institutional challenge to liberal Christian theological seminaries in the United States in the current epoch. Only a small number of biblical fundamentalists and confessional Protestants are attracted to liberal Christian seminaries. The sympathetic understanding of Roman Catholic participants of the nature of non-Catholic liberal theological institutions minimizes threats from this group. Hence, people seeking to promote an institutional orthopraxis are drawn largely from those adherents of the first three types which do not make some principled distinction between their community of faith and their community of politics.

People associated with the Social Gospel movement, as observed earlier, sought to Christianize the social order. People in this tradition have frequently sought to have their communities of faith endorse particular public policy proposals and to support particular political programs. Many African-Americans have historically expected their clergy and their churches to "promote the race." African-American clergy have not infrequently run for public office, seeing no contradiction between an ordained clergy status and that of a public officeholder.

Because some people in these two groups may understand the distinction between a seminary and a church and may affirm foundational liberal values for the former institution, they may be willing to tolerate institutional neutrality on most public policy issues. Others, seeing no distinction in principle between a church and/or a denomination and a liberal Christian theological seminary and using the analogical method to legitimate their claims, seek to persuade a seminary to adopt church and/or denominational statements on public policy issues. Still others try to persuade a seminary to adopt their views, seeking to convert it into a confessing congregation.

In the current period, the most consistent and coherent challenges to the idea of a liberal Christian theological seminary come from proponents of some forms of liberation theology. This particular theological movement emerged in Germany after World War II and became a major movement in the 1960s and 1970s. Emphasizing the coalescence of theory and practice in an orthopraxis and incorporating a properly defined orientation on ecological, sexual, social, economic and/or political matters, people in this theological movement frequently desire persons and institutions to take what its proponents envisage to be politically correct stances on public policy issues.

As is the case with all rich theological movements, liberation theology is complex and multi-dimensional. Some species, informed by the Social Gospel movement, may not pose on principle a threat to the idea of a liberal theological school. Other species, informed by the dialectic of negation as a proper mode of social analysis and critical theory as a basis for the coalescence of *theoria* and *praxis* in an orthopraxis (the generic notions cited earlier and associated with the so-called "Frankfurt School" of sociology), constitute a direct threat to that idea. Rooted directly in the thought of Karl Marx and indirectly in the thought of G. W. F. Hegel and expressed most fully today in the thought of Jürgen Habermas, these notions are in direct conflict with the presuppositions of the foundational liberal values which have shaped the life of liberal Christian theological seminaries in the twentieth century. Consequently if one sought with intellectual and emotional integrity to embody the dialectic of negation and critical theory in one's work, one would have to challenge both the primary notions of religious pluralism, religious tolerance and religious liberty informing the intellectual life of liberal seminaries and also the contrast between theoria and praxis legitimating the distinction between a theological seminary as seminary and a particular community of faith and politics.

Liberation theologians employing the dialectic of negation in social analyses discern inherent conflicts between people who on the basis of selected ascribed characteristics are situated in one of two mutually exclusive social groups. They term one polar group the "oppressor" and the other the "oppressed." Liberation theologians differ in the categories they use to place people in particular social groups. However they always use primary categories grounded on one or more ascribed characteristic, such as sex, race, or age, or on social location. If social location is the basis for categorization they employ ethnicity, nationality, social status, social class, political affiliation, and/or religious affiliation in their analyses. Analysts characterize one group — the one they perceive to have the greatest linear power — as the oppressor and the other group — the one they perceive to have the least linear power — as the oppressed. They interpret history as a dynamic struggle between these interest groups leading to a reconfiguration of the social order and some realignment of power relations. The more utopian liberation theologians envisage a future time of greatly enhanced harmony of life with life, once the dialectical process of social struggle has rendered the polar types obsolete in a transformed social order.

Liberation theologians affirming critical theory hold that all social analyses except their own are ideologies designed to mask the self-interest of their designated dominant group. They use critical theory to unmask ideology and to promote proper political action. They insist that the end of analysis in human affairs is action, where *theoria* and *praxis* coalesce. They think proper analysis will lead to an orthodoxy of orthopraxis. In theological contexts, they replace God talk with God walk. They hold that if one does not take a stand for a proposed public policy view or a prescribed course of political action, he or she is taking a stand against it.

When proponents couple critical theory with the dialectic of negation, they undercut a "middle" ground; for they insist one is either for or against them in the struggles for human liberation. They argue that no person or institution can be neutral in these struggles. Unless proponents of species of liberation theology informed by the dialectic of negation and critical theory are willing to make an exception in the case of liberal theological schools, they are bound to seek to politicize these institutions.

Because this exception would violate the intellectual and emotional integrity of one holding such views, others will have to view such concessions as tactical. They must assume that proponents of critical theory and the dialectic of negation want to establish their values as the core beliefs of the institution to which they are related. Persons holding to the primal values of a liberal Christian theological school have no option but to resist them. In this way, the fact that some people believe that the dialectic of negation is correct (even though it may not be inherent in the nature of things) impacts the life of a liberal Christian theological seminary.

It is difficult to know how many American proponents of liberation theologies have appropriated the dialectic of negation and critical theory, for many motifs in American liberation theologies incorporate ideas promoted by the Social Gospel movement. Unless one knows what species of liberation theology a given proponent is advancing, one cannot know whether liberal or neo-Marxist values are primal for that proponent. If the dialectic of negation and critical theory are primary values, the defender of a liberal Christian theological seminary, as noted in the preceding paragraph, must resist efforts to embody those values at the core of the seminary and must affirm the integrity of those liberal values sustaining the institution.

This seminary has consistently resisted efforts from some of its constituencies to take official positions on public policy issues. In so doing, it has been guided — at least implicitly — by core liberal values. These efforts have been made infrequently, for most members have rejected the idea of an institutional orthopraxis, in spite of their strong interests in human rights and issues of social justice.

In fact, the only issue that has found its way to an official body of the seminary since the Vietnam War was a proposal to declare the seminary a nuclear free zone. That proposal, developed in the late 1980s, was voted down by the seminary's Academic Council. There is no way to know whether the proposal would have been adopted by the Board of Trustees had it reached that body. The fact that some faculty, staff, and students developed and promoted such a declaration reveals the uneven embodiment of fundamental liberal ideas among the seminary's primary constituencies.[7]

In the discussion of this proposal, no one explicitly appealed to critical theory or the dialectic of negation to legitimate their position. Some appealed to denominational statements on nuclear war. Others argued that the seminary should be in the vanguard of social transformation and lead the way toward a nuclear free world. By voting down this proposal, the Academic Council reaffirmed the primary liberal values of the institution.

If the seminary as such is not a church, then the use of the analogical method to legitimate seminary endorsement of church or/and denominational public policy statements is inappropriate. If the seminary is to provide a context in which persons may freely explore a variety of interpretations of Christian ethics and public policy proposals and is to resist the temptation to become a community of politics, then it should be most restrained in adopting public policy positions.[8]

Many of its members may be in the vanguard of social transformation, for the value commitments required to sustain a liberal Christian theological school do not apply to the diverse more specialized beliefs which members of a seminary community hold. If they want to form Believers Churches whose adherents covenant to promote particular public policy proposals, they should be encouraged to do so. If they want to participate in one or more of the numerous voluntary associations in American life promoting particular public policy viewpoints, they should be encouraged to do so. The only restriction a liberal Christian theological seminary should impose is a limiting one. Members of a seminary community should make it clear that they do not speak for the seminary as such with respect either to particular public policy issues or to the specialized religious social ethic influencing their judgments on these issues.[9]

The Future

Perry LeFevre is deeply committed to the primary liberal values which have sustained this seminary during the almost half-century he has been associated with it. His commitment to fundamental liberal values is reflected in the care with which he seeks to explore contrasting interpretations of the Christian movement.

Wary of what he considers to be the excess speculation of Whitehead and Hartshorne, he has focused more sharply on the empirical side of experience. Persuaded that there is an immanental good more basic than any created good, he has sought to identify and to nurture those structures and processes in human life which evoke creative personal and social transformations to counter the evil and the banal in the world.

In light of his embodiment of the fundamental values informing the life of this liberal Christian theological seminary, it is fitting to conclude this essay with some reflections about its future. Both the fragility of the liberal idea and the relative paucity of financial resources provided by individuals and churches committed to the liberal idea raise questions about its survival beyond the first two decades of the twenty-first century.

The liberal idea is challenged by various forms of religious fundamentalism. Some, such as Islamic fundamentalism, pose no real threat to liberal Christian theological seminaries. Others, such as the so-called religious right in the United States and other forms of Christian orthodoxy, pose a minor threat; but it seems most unlikely that adherents to the modes of thought represented in that movement will impact directly on most liberal Christian seminaries.

As observed earlier, due to its widespread popularity among people in some groups historically related to liberalism, liberation theologies using the dialectic of negation and critical theory potentially pose the most serious threat to the idea of a liberal Christian theological seminary. Taken conjointly, the dialectic of negation and critical theory limit the freedom of inquiry and debate which is at the heart of a liberal seminary.

Unless people are willing to maintain a distinction between *theoria* and *praxis*, they will seek to transform the liberal Christian theological seminary into a political community committed to an orthopraxis. The embodiment of either an orthodoxy or an orthopraxis as primary institutional values would transform this liberal seminary into an indoctrination center. It would cease to be a liberal Christian theological seminary.

This liberal Christian theological seminary is a fragile entity; it needs the support of a broad company within and without an immediate seminary community to survive and to serve in the twenty-first century. It needs a student body and a faculty who, by substantial majorities, both share the fundamental liberal idea of free and open inquiry and debate about the meaning and practice of the Christian movement and also seek to develop interpretations of the Christian movement which they can maintain with intellectual and emotional integrity. It also needs the financial support of those persons within the Christian movement who share these primary liberal values and who are persuaded this particular liberal Christian theological seminary is worthy of their support.

To warrant such support, this seminary must sustain people who develop modes of thought reflecting the profundity of meaning and practice embodied within the Christian movement. Its graduates must demonstrate leadership capacities within the Christian movement and must contribute positively to the life of the broader society in which religious institutions are set.

Perry LeFevre has given full measure to foster an ethos evoking these qualities among its faculty and its graduates. It has been a privilege to be his colleague for more than thirty years. Through devotion and perspicuity he has contributed much to the self-definition of this institution and to the understanding of the meaning of a liberal Christian theological seminary. It is my hope that those who are associated with this seminary may continue the quest for scholarly and professional excellence, theological integrity, and seasonal relevance so deeply embodied in the life, thought, and work of Perry LeFevre.

Notes and References

1. The Chicago Theological Seminary was founded by Congregationalists in 1855. Because that denomination and its successor, the United Church of Christ, both have a congregational form of polity, its governance is different than seminaries related to denominations with Presbyterian or Episcopal polities. Its Board of Trustees is self-selected and self-perpetuating.

2. In this essay, that portion of a larger whole which impinges most directly on the development of LeFevre's thought is highlighted. Both within and without the Federated Theological Faculty, critics and those indifferent to process modes of thought were plentiful.

3. Daniel Day Williams," Theology and Truth" *The Journal of Religion* (October, 1942), Vol. XXII, No. 4, pp. 382-97, reprinted in Daniel Day Williams, *Essays in Process Theology*, edited by Perry LeFevre, (Chicago: Exploration Press, 1985) p. 30.

4. *Ibid*, pp. 33-34.

5. *Ibid*. pp. 34-35.

6. As noted earlier in the text, shorn of their Christian particularity, the fundamental values of religious tolerance, religious pluralism, and religious liberty are also embodied in the Enlightenment and in nineteenth century English liberalism. Historically a complex interplay of Baptist, Quaker, Enlightenment, English liberal, later Congregationalist and Social Gospel ideas has contributed to the core notions which have shaped the life of this seminary for most of the twentieth century.

As noted in the body of the text, LeFevre's commitment to fundamental liberal values is reflected in the care with which he seeks to explore contrasting interpretations of the Christian movement. In his required courses in constructive theology, he sought to introduce his students to a broad and representative range of thinkers. Students were expected to develop their own constructive positions at the conclusion of their work in these courses.

7. The author was visited by a student who sought his participation in some meetings designed to develop the nuclear free proposal. The author told the student that he detested nuclear weapons, thought they were a curse on humankind, and believed their widespread use would be catastrophic for humankind. He also observed that in his judgment the mutually assured destruction strategy being pursued by the U.S. and its allies was the one most likely to prevent a nuclear holocaust. He then observed that others may disagree with his prudential judgment in this matter. In any event, he stated he was opposed on principle to any statement on the issue, pro or con, by the seminary *qua* seminary, for it should not become a community of politics.

If the seminary is to be conceived as a church, it should be understood as a catholic institution, possessing a "formless form" so protean it can encompass multiple forms of beliefs and practices within it.

8. The author says "most restrained" because he can envisage a most extraordinary situation which might require an institutional statement. Even in such a situation, members of the seminary community should seek other avenues to advance their views if at all feasible.

9. People associating with diverse interest groups and interacting with each other enrich the intellectual life of a liberal Christian theological school. Reflecting the fashionableness of the ascribed bases for social location today, the organizational bases for most of the special interest groups at this liberal seminary are gender and race. Whether this interest group configuration is adequate to evoke rich and complex intellectual interchange is moot.

Of the five special interest groups active at the Chicago Theological Seminary in the 1990-91 academic year, four were constituted primarily by gender issues and racial issues. These include a woman's concerns group, a men's concerns group, a gay and lesbian concerns group, and an African-American concerns group. The only special interest group organized on a different basis was a student chapter of the Fellowship of Reconciliation, a body with a pacifist orientation.

In addition to the FOR, the only other inclusive student groups were a Worship Committee and a Community Life Committee which are organized by the seminary to coordinate some inclusive events, largely for social activities or for spiritual formation.

Because special interest group and multiplication of factions ideas are deeply rooted in the American liberal tradition (e.g., *The Federalist Papers*), special interest group principles of organization are commonplace in this institution. The dialectic of negation and critical theory extant in some theological circles have played a role in creating a climate of opinion encouraging gender and race defined interest groups, but special interest group principles seem to be dominant informing notions among this seminary's participants.

Introduction to Chapter 12

Survey research methods have been widely used to study religious phenomena during the past fifty years. During the 1960s and 1970s, led by the work of Andrew Greeley of the National Opinion Research Center and Charles Y. Glock of the University of California at Berkeley, several major studies utilizing survey research methods and data analysis techniques were undertaken in the United States. I myself was involved in two substantial studies using survey research during that time. In this context, I focused my attention to the issues addressed here.

This essay addresses foundational problems that are inherent in the collection, analysis, and interpretation of interview and questionnaire data used in the social scientific study of human religious experience. These foundational data include the ambiguity of linguistic symbols, the relation of the causal past to the emerging present, the relation of a whole to its constituent parts, the role of creative minorities in human societies, and the use of a method of difference in data analysis and interpretation. These problematic issues are interpreted from the perspective of process philosophy, the constructive point of view informing all the essays in this volume. An appeal is made to common sense to act as a restraint on specialists who circumscribe too narrowly their grounds for model building and/or over-analyze inherently vague linguistic data. The essay challenges interpretations of survey research data denying the authenticity of religious experience or ignoring a consideration of the question by appealing implicitly or explicitly to a fact-value disjunction in human experience.

CHAPTER 12

Measuring the Muse: Reflections on the Use of Survey Methods in the Study of Religious Phenomena

Social scientists frequently utilize survey research questionnaire and interview data to analyze various facets of human religious experience. These studies have been undertaken in numerous countries, but more have been conducted in the United States than elsewhere. The pervasiveness of technical rationalism and the relatively greater availability of financial resources in the United States have contributed to the predominance of American studies.

The most fashionable style of analysis of interview and questionnaire data is causal analysis. Scholars employing this style seek to establish that knowledge of one set or cluster of variables, termed the independent variables, will enable them to predict the configuration of another set of variables, termed the dependent variables. Advocates of this style of analysis are apt to criticize workers using survey research data to establish correlates, tendencies, and configurations for their lack of rigor and/or methodological naivete. Sometimes these critiques may be legitimate; but they usually reflect a critic's foundational presuppositions about the problematic issues inherent in the collection, analysis, and interpretation of questionnaire and interview data.

This chapter discusses five persistent and interrelated problems inherent in use of survey research methods: the ambiguity of linguistic symbols, the relations of the causal past to the emerging present, the relation of a whole to its constituent parts, the role of creative minorities in human societies, and the method of difference in data analysis and interpretation.

These problems are perennial. This discussion is focused on survey research studies of religious phenomena using interview or questionnaire data; but the issues addressed are common to all studies using survey research methods and/or interview and questionnaire data.

From some points of view, a scholar sensitive to these persistent problems could qualify his or her research design, his or her methods of data collection and analysis, and his or her style of interpretation to take them into account and terminate his or her work at that point. If one is persuaded that a rational interpretation of this problematic is necessary, one is led to seek a logical and coherent interpretation of this problematic which does justice to the facts. For one having a faith in rationalism, a deeper understanding of the nature of things is thus attained.

Process philosophy pushes one in this direction, for it holds that all "facts" are interconnected and that there is a relational essence to the universe which reason seeks to penetrate.[1] These notions are affirmed here; so this chapter seeks to resolve the problematic in survey research studies of religion by using categories of interpretation drawn from process philosophy.

The Problematic in Survey Research Studies of Religious Phenomena

Introduction

The foundational problems considered in this section emerge from reflection on human experience done in conjunction with the reading of the major survey research studies of religious phenomena undertaken in the past two to three decades. The problems are discussed and then interpreted in categories derived from process modes of thought. To provide a measure of concreteness to the discussion, illustrative references to *Christian Beliefs and Anti-Semitism* by Charles Y. Glock and Rodney Stark are made in the Notes and References section. The Glock and Stark work is used because it is very well known and is a lucid example of the predominant style of survey research analysis.

The Ambiguity of Linguistic Symbols

The primary data in survey research are the words humans use to communicate feelings and meanings. Data are gathered from a sample population through the use of questionnaires and/or interviews.[2] Sometimes social scientists used forced option responses in their questionnaires and interview schedules. If they do, they place responses in preconceived categories derived by empirical examination, logical reflection, or both. Sometimes they use open-ended questioned and categorize the responses later. Sometimes they devise even more unstructured interviews.

Because of the high cost of data collection, the need for a large number of cases for statistical analysis, and the need for discrete categories for most statistical tests, forced option responses have been used most frequently in survey research studies of religious phenomena.[3] The formalistic bias resulting from the cumulative effect of forced option responses often encourages analysts employing them to overemphasize the static dimensions of experience and to accentuate the autonomy of the parts of a whole.[4] These issues will be discussed subsequently, but the implications of forced-option responses for form-dynamics and part-whole relations should be noted here.

The degree of precision possible in survey research studies utilizing interview and questionnaire data is limited by an inherently vague relation between linguistic symbols and human experience. Survey data may be used to illumine major tendencies and configurations; but they cannot adequately illumine the subtle tendencies, the shifts in mood, and the complex dynamic relations between feeling, thinking, and acting to which reflection on our own inner experience attests.[5] Relatively unstructured depth interviews in which subjects illumine the way in which they integrate the various components of their experiences into a whole are better able to illumine the complexity of human experience; but such data are not amenable to precise formulizations and catagorizations.[6]

Doubts about the validity and reliability of interview and of questionnaire data are inevitable, for linguistic symbols are intrinsically vague. Linguistic scholars remind us that the predominant meanings of words shift over a period of time.

The vagueness of linguistic symbols is rooted in the fact that no two creatures share exactly the same experience or inhabit precisely the same world. In order for linguistic symbols to communicate, the initiator of the symbol and the recipient of the symbol must share a common experience. The initiator of the symbol hopes to elicit an experience into the consciousness of the recipient comparable to an experience the symbol elicits in the initiator's consciousness.

Linguistic symbols evoke not only clear and distinct ideas and experiences in the recipient's consciousness but also a penumbra of feelings and meanings. These ancillary feelings and meanings may bring forth vivid memories of significant events in the lives of some of those appropriating the symbols but not in others. For example, people perceive "physical" objects, such as the green forest and the blue sky, with the aid of geometric forms and sense data. Symbols referring to such shared experiences are relatively lucid for these linguistic symbols refer to human experiences of phenomena whose defining characteristics are quite "objective" and persistent.

Nonetheless, even when the linguistic symbols refer to physical objects, they may elicit markedly different ancillary feelings among people. When one auditor hears the term "green forest," he or she may recall the experience of an evergreen forest in the Rocky Mountains; another may recall the experience of a deciduous forest in Arkansas. In the first instance, the auditor may associate the memory with a mountain picnic; in the second, the auditor may associate the memory with a case of poison ivy. Thus, the same symbol may evoke feelings of well-being or disharmony in different auditors, depending on the associations evoked by the symbol.

All linguistic symbols involve both interpretative and descriptive elements, but the relative significance of the elements varies from symbol to symbol. The term "green forest" refers to the qualification of geometric forms by a sense datum, greenness, in the experience of a human subject. The phrase "God is love" ascribes the quality "love" to the Supreme Subject-Object. In the first instance, the descriptive element is dominant; in the second the interpretative element is dominant.[7]

Linguistic symbols also change their meanings in the course of events, for new events modify the experiences to which the symbols refer. The dynamic side of life cannot be captured by linguistic forms, and their shifting meanings are manifestations of this truth.

The vagueness of linguistic symbols limits inherently the validity and reliability of interview and questionnaire data. Broadly speaking, the validity of such data is limited by the extent of congruence of shared experiences between the interviewee and interviewer, and the reliability is limited by the shifting meaning of symbols in the course of events.

A pattern of increasing precision of linguistic symbols based on the movement from the most private aspects of experiences to the most public is evident in human life. Symbols referring to inner feelings and foundational religious experiences are less precise than symbols referring to cognitive propositions. Such symbols, in turn, are less precise than symbols referring to human actions and activities.

This pattern of increasing precision as one moves from private to public dimensions of experience permits an assessment of the degree of clarity to be expected in questionnaire and interview data dealing with religious phenomena. Overt public activities, such as attendance and membership patterns and ritual activities, are easier to assess than religious beliefs. Symbols referring to religious beliefs in turn are clearer than symbols referring to attitudes, inner feelings, and foundational religious experiences.

Experience itself is more fundamental than any of the abstractions made from it, for it consists in the way an emerging subject synthesizes the physical and conceptual sides of its experience into a unity. Consequently, symbols referring to religious experience are always abstractions from an experience more fundamental and elemental than the symbols. It is credulous to assume linguistic symbols referring to the Divine Reality evoke the same understanding in all people, for differences in intensity of feeling and in interpretative frameworks modify the meanings and feelings evoked by theistic symbols.

The abstract character of linguistic symbols should never be forgotten. Forms are found in facts, and they are abstractions from facts. Survey research methodology encourages the reification of symbols, for the initially vague linguistic symbols are codified into discrete categories. These categories are then manipulated with the aid of mathematical symbols.

Some codifications and quantitative assessments of the intensity and frequency of human feeling, thinking, and acting are certainly appropriate, for authentic differences do exist between human beings. At the same time, these efforts to quantify *human* feelings, meanings, and actions are limited by the intermingling of qualitative and quantitative factors in human experience and by human capacities to modify some intensities of feeling volitionally and quite rapidly.

This understanding of the interplay of qualitative and quantitative patterns in human experience provides some guidance in evaluating measurements of *human* feelings, meanings, and actions.[8] Interview and questionnaire data are readily susceptible to nominal and ordinal measurement, for categorization by class and crude measures of intensity of feeling are fitting for the subject matter. Interval and ratio measurement are much more questionable, for *human* feelings and meanings are relatively more dynamic and qualitative than are the feelings and meanings of lower forms of life.

Even so, the analyst interpreting the significance of findings based on nominal and ordinal measurements should be mindful of the vagueness of the linguistic symbols on which the categorizations and measurements are based, the relation of forms to facts just considered, and the whole-part problem to be discussed subsequently. He or she may then minimize the temptation to think a study based on survey research methods conveys great clarity and precision.

The Relation of the Causal Past to the Emerging Present

The findings of all the major survey research studies of religious phenomena reveal some correlations between patterns of feelings, meanings, and actions; but they rarely show extremely high correlations. People will disagree in their interpretations of the implications of such findings for past-present-future relations. Two contrasting polar views and a mediating centralist view are possible.

Some social radicals disavow interest in empirical studies and suggest they are trivial, irrelevant, and/or dehumanizing. They hold such studies distract people from the urgent task of building a more viable future by focusing their attention too strongly on the causal past and by objectifying the subjective. They reject causal studies and affirm the freedom of humans to build their futures.[9]

Social or biological determinists are understandably interested in causal studies, for they hold an adequate understanding of the human causal past would enable one to predict the shape of the emerging present and the anticipatable future.[10]

Social radicals are unlikely to conduct survey research studies of religious phenomena, but social or biological determinists may well develop such studies. As noted earlier, even among those who are not full blown environmental determinists, the causal mode is very fashionable in survey research.[11] Those committed to causal models envisage further refinements of research instruments and more sophisticated elaboration of causal models and social theory to increase the predictive capacity of their studies.[12]

It is probably not possible to dissuade one dogmatically committed to a position of causal determinism by calling attention to the relatively modest correlations between most variables in survey research studies of religious phenomena; but less doctrinaire persons may interpret such findings differently. Such centralists may think the findings reflect a blending of the influences of the causal past and the self-initiated decisions humans make in the emerging present.[13] Persons holding this voluntaristic view of human beings might well utilize survey research to discern tendencies and configurations in human affairs and to accentuate salient correlates of religious feelings and meanings; but they would discount the efforts of some scholars to discern or to anticipate a very high degree of precision and predictability in such studies.[14]

Process views cohere with this centralist interpretation of the relation of the past to the emerging present and the anticipated future. People are conditioned by events lying in their causal pasts, but they are not determined by them. Life would be chaotic without some coherence and patterning related to the causal past, but it would by tyrannical without some novelty in the emerging present. Purposiveness, intentionality, and a quest for being and well-being shape the whole tone of human life. If personal responsibilities for human actions are denied, the whole character of the life of civilized humankind would be altered.

Though the voluntaristic strand of social scientific theory is in closer harmony to process modes of thought than the causal strand, it deals inadequately with the problems of perception and causation. A general theory of perception and causation is needed, and process philosophy offers such a theory. According to process views of perception and causation, creatures lying in the causal past of an emerging creature are objectified in that creature. This objectification is an illustration of the principle of relativity, integral to process thought. In its most general form, the principle states that every being, i.e., every creature that has become, is a potential for every becoming, i.e., for every creature in the process of actualizing itself.

Every creature in the cosmos that has become contributes something to every creature that is becoming. Often the contribution is trivial, but it is actual. The scientist focusing his or her studies on the contribution of the causal past to the present is dealing primarily with efficient and material causes. Such studies are important, because all creatures, including humans, are conditioned by their causal pasts.

This focus on material and efficient causes needs to be balanced by an emphasis on formal and final causes because an emerging creature, aiming at aesthetic satisfaction and intensity of feeling, synthesizes forms of definiteness derived from the causal past and from one facet of the Divine Nature into a novel unity. The aim for harmony and intensity of feeling, elicited by the Divine, accentuates the importance of final cause in the actualization of creatures. As creatures synthesize the entities objectified in them in a novel unity, they are more than the sum of their parts.

All creatures are dipolar. The physical phase of experience is derived from creatures in the settled past of an emerging subject-object, and the conceptual phase is derived from forms of definiteness embodied in the Divine. The two sides are unified by the creature's subjective aim, also derived from the Divine.

The relative importance of the causal past in the self-determination of creatures depends on the significance of the physical and conceptual poles in the becoming of various creatures. The physical pole is accentuated in low grade organisms; so they reproduce the past in the present with little change. The creatures constituting the subject matter of the physical sciences are dominated by their causal pasts. Since they reproduce their pasts in their presents with little novelty, objective species of forms of definiteness, i.e., the mathematical forms, are especially salient. Therefore, mathematical laws describing their behavior are predominant, and prediction of future behavior on the basis of past behavior is central in the physical sciences.

Nature appears to be ordered hierarchically, so far as we can observe; and the conceptual pole is accentuated in some of the creatures constituting more complex organisms. Life is a bid for freedom from the bonds of the causal past. Living creatures are concerned primarily with the vivid immediacy of their presents. Subjective species of forms of definiteness and feeling tones related to vivid aesthetic experiences become more important in such creatures.

Humans are constituted by a complex hierarchy of societies, culminating in a regnant center of a very high grade. Their experiences are unified in the soul, a formless form so protean it can encompass all the experiences constituting it.

As is the case with all creatures, human experience is also dipolar. The conceptual or supplemental phase is greatly enhanced in the soul; so the higher phases of experience, involving consciousness and correlated intellectual, aesthetic, moral and religious experiences are very significant in human life.

The interplay between feeling, thinking and acting in human life is complex, interrelated, and reciprocal; so it is arbitrary to apply clear causal priority to any one component.[15] Feeling is, however, most fundamental and elemental. For this reason the basic interpretation of becoming emphasizes the aesthetic experience.

The contribution of the causal past to the emergent present focuses human interests on the past, the present, and the future. The persistence of forms, feelings and structures limits the possibilities that may be actualized in the present and in the foreseeable future; but human capacities to surpass the past in the present and to transform the present in the future open up novel actualizations. Social scientific findings may condition judgments about what is possible and desirable in a given context, but they do not determine them.

Since final and efficient causation are necessarily related to each other, it is arbitrary unqualifiedly to separate methodological discussions about the study of religious phenomena from substantive ones about the nature of religious phenomena. Religious phenomena are the result of rather exceptional conscious intellectual, moral, and aesthetic experiences. Social scientific analyses can explore some of the consequences of this foundational experience, but they cannot adequately illumine it.

The interrelation of efficient and final cause involves a rejection of the "fact-value" dichotomy fashionable among some social scientists. The necessary relation of creatures to each other and their participation in common forms calls for a normative interpretation of these experiences.

The social scientist interested in the everyday doing of sociological studies of religion cannot distinguish categorically the analytical from the evaluative dimensions of an investigation. In the case of the study of religious phenomena, the social scientist either ignoring the presence of a Divine Reality evoking human religious experience or interpreting religious experience on non-*sui generis* grounds is seriously distorting his subject matter. There are no Olympian heights from which a disinterested observer may "study" religious phenomena. For the interrelation of truth, beauty, and goodness may lure forth authentic religious experience in the investigator as well as in the investigated—unless the conceptual framework he or she affirms so distorts his or her religious experiences he or she is led to suppress or disavow them.

The Relation of a Whole to its Constituent Parts

Survey research methodology atomizes constituent wholes at two levels. At the societal level, the sampling procedure results in the selection of particular individuals from whom data are to be obtained by using questionnaires or interviews. They are isolated from the net of social relations in which they are enmeshed, and they are approached as individual cases. At the individual level, discrete linguistic stimuli embodied in the schedules are employed to evoke discrete linguistic responses from the subject.

The codification and categorization of the responses, as noted earlier, encourages the isolation of discrete parts of a whole. These component parts are often then combined to construct a new whole, consisting of indices derived from data obtained discretely.[16] No analyst can examine all the component parts of a whole, for there are simply too many. He or she focuses on some he or she has reason to believe are important, and he or she ignores others. He or she then seeks to assess the contribution of the component parts to the human beings from whom he or she initially abstracted the parts. This morphological approach is useful, for it may illumine salient forms affecting the phenomenon under consideration. Morphology cannot, however, deal adequately with the whole for a whole is more than the sum of its parts.

It is necessary to elaborate the discussion begun in the preceding subsection to illumine the view of the whole-part relations leading to the judgment just advanced, for the description of the process of the emergence of a creature sketched there led to the conclusion that a whole is more than the sum of its parts.

The significance of this fact in scientific work depends upon the complexity of the subject matter. The unity of simple creatures is not so seriously distorted as the unity of complex creatures when the scientist focuses primarily on the mathematical forms in which the creature participates.[17]

As noted earlier, an emerging creature unifies data from its causal past and forms of definiteness embodied in God into a novel synthesis. Conscious human experience is the result of a complex contrast of data drawn from the physical side of one's experience with forms of definiteness derived in a supplemental phase of the conceptual side of one's experience. The whole *is* the experience; and the removal of any constituent part removes *that* experience, with its shades of feeling and meaning unified in a particular way.

In morphological analysis, the scientist dissects the unified creature into some of its component parts. The unity of the creature is destroyed in this analysis and abstraction. Wordsworth aptly described the nature of morphological investigations when he observed, "We murder to dissect."

The relative importance of the analysis of the component parts contributing to a whole depends upon the significance of the conceptual pole in the experience of the creatures constituting the subject matter of a particular science. In the natural sciences, geometrical and temporal extensions, abstractions rooted in the physical side of experiences, are correlated with the observed patterns of behavior of subhuman organisms. In the physical sciences, geometric extension is still most salient. It is very important in the biological sciences, but organismic purposes and aims assume greater significance. In the human sciences, such factors assume dominant proportions.

Components of feeling and meaning become dominant in studies of human beings. The abstraction and the analysis of crucial components of human experience through interviews and questionnaires are useful because these components contribute to human decisions. But the unity of a human experience is distorted by this analytic focus.

The codification of verbal propositions inverts the relations between forms and facts in human experience, for forms are always found in concrete entities, not *vice versa.* If the forms are overtly or covertly reified, the balance between formal and dynamic elements in human experience is distorted. As a consequence of this reification, an interpreter may place too much emphasis on the causal past and on the component parts contributing to a whole.

Comparative studies in the social sciences are suggestive, but they are limited by the whole-part relations discussed here. Two people may synthesize comparable components in different ways, or the same person may synthesize the same component differently at different times.

A historical epoch may be interpreted analogically as a unique whole constituted by a synthesis of its component parts. Social institutions are given shape by the dominant values of the human beings comprising them. The universality of social institutions, rooted in the nature of human nature, and the limits nature imposes on forms of social organization encourage comparative study; but the synthesis of the components into a novel unity limits it.

One needs to exercise an artistic intuitive judgment to attain a proper balance in assessing the importance of the universal and the particular in a given context.[18] In this way an analyst may grasp the way in which the component parts of a whole fit together or grasp the way in which the present and the future may emerge from the past. Such intuitive judgments, rooted in the participation of many creatures in the same forms and in each other guided by the Divine Subject-Object, are non-statistical. For this reason, historians and sensitive observers employing non-statistical means may have a surer vision of the emerging human future than statistically oriented social scientists.[19]

The Role of Creative Minorities in Human Societies

Survey research has egalitarian and ahistorical biases, for most studies focus on the "average" in human societies. Purposive interviewing of creative minorities may minimize some of the problems of the bias toward the average characteristic of most survey research studies; but survey research methods must be supplemented by other means of data gathering, data analysis, and data interpretation to assess adequately the actual and potential impact of creative minorities in a society or in the encounter between societies.[20]

Interpretations of social change based on the actions of individual agents as makers and shapers of history are more useful in dealing with creative minorities than are the interpretations of social change based on a reflection of the average. This latter view is at least implicit in most survey research studies. Historians have more frequently interpreted history as a consequence of the novel and idiosyncratic activities of human beings. If a social scientist is too closely tied to data derived from his survey research studies, he or she may be insensitive to emergent factors having profound implications for the phenomena being studied.

The impact of creative minorities on human life illustrates the differential capacities of human individuals and human groups to respond novelly to situations. Sub-ordinate super-ordinate relations in human life and the tendency toward some type of hierarchical ordering of every human society are inherent in these differential capacities.

The impact upon human societies of the emergent novelty initiated by creative minorities is unknown in its details. Survey research methods cannot deal adequately with creative minorities, for interview and questionnaire instruments neither anticipate fully nor assess adequately the impact of novel feelings, thoughts, and actions upon human life. Since initiating events may affect an entire historical epoch and shape many values, comparative assessments may be difficult or impossible.

Analysts may be tempted to ignore such pervasive influences, for they are extremely difficult to evaluate. The innovative and novel feelings, thoughts, and actions of creative minorities accentuate the emergent and unanticipatable side of human life. Formal analysis, such as are represented by Max Weber's traditional, legal, and charismatic types of authority, illumine aspects of the functions of culture-bearing, culture-creating elites; but they do not permit social scientists to discern *a priori* the impact of charismatic leaders in a society.

The role of creative minorities in history is an especially dramatic illustration of the dominance of dynamics over form in the nature of things. The examination of forms and patterns rooted in the past to interpret the present and to anticipate the future is valuable, for forms and patterns tend to persist. The value of causal analysis is limited by the capacities of creatures to surpass the past in the present.[21]

Survey research data dealing with the "average" contribute to an understanding of facets of the dominant sustaining ethos, but they do not enable us to grasp the emerging future. One may minimize the ahistorical and egalitarian biases of survey research by purposive sampling, longitudinal interviews, and recall questions; but one cannot eliminate them.[22]

The Method of Difference in Data Analysis and Interpretation, Model Building, and Broader Generalities

The method of difference is at the base of all causal analysis of interview and questionnaire data. The effects of some factors, usually termed independent variables, on other factors, usually termed dependent variables, are assessed by manipulating data statistically.

The use of the method of difference results in the systematic exclusion of universal components in a given environment and of other specific components not considered in the particular study. In factor analysis, for example, axes are rotated to discern the components most strongly associated with the differences between two or more variables. In the rotation, components not contributing "independently" to the variations observed between two or more variables are eliminated from further consideration. The analyst simply assumes that the individual "stripped" of the eliminated components and of the contribution of the ignored universal components would possess the same character. Such an assumption is moot.

In survey research analysis, the pervasive significance of general components in the wider environment not considered in the investigation is systematically ignored. The impact of these general factors on the phenomenon being studied cannot be evaluated by the method of difference, for the general factors are always present in the environment. These more general factors may be present in a particular sub-culture, in an entire culture, in all human societies in a given historical epoch, in all human societies in some or all historical epochs, or in some or all societies extending beyond human societies.

The universality of certain factors in an ethos is illustrated by the pervasiveness of religious institutions in American society. Without their presence, the whole tone and character of American life would be different. Detailed studies seeking to compare and to contrast the impact of various religious beliefs on the American people must presuppose the ethos to which religious institutions contribute. Nothing can legitimately be held "constant," for the sustaining environment being held constant would be different in the absence of the components isolated for study.[23]

Metaphysical propositions, i.e., propositions applying to all creatures in all cosmic epochs, are clearly excluded from consideration in these analysis. Consequently, among other things, a consideration of a Divine Reality who is, at least in some sense, *sui generis* and present in all experience, is systematically excluded from consideration; for God exemplifies supremely the metaphysical categories.

Those seeking to develop generic notions cannot rely on the detailed results of a single investigation in a single field. This development requires the coordination of fundamental notions applicable in all fields of scientific endeavor and the elaboration of propositions applicable to all subject matters. Such generic notions, in turn, may provide guidance to workers seeking to develop specific notions applicable to a particular subject matter.

The dominant modes of survey research data analysis of religious phenomena preclude this voyage toward larger generalities, for their methods of analysis and model building are closely tied to data gathered by questionnaires and interviews. Neither the relatively modest causal analysis undertaken by Lenski (1961), the more complex method of elaboration used by Glock and Stark (1966), nor the most complex path analysis used by NORC (1971) gives one sufficient scope to develop generic notions.

One must exercise negative judgments to evolve generic notions, for one must imagine the absence of components which are in fact always present in experience. The development of metaphysical propositions has a rational and empirical side. The rational side includes coherence and logicality; the empirical side includes applicability and adequacy. A proposition is applicable if it applies to some subjects, and it is adequate if it applies to all subjects. Adequacy, then, ties the rational and empirical sides of metaphysical speculation together.

A Concluding Note

This chapter has considered persistent problems confronting scholars using survey research methods to study religious phenomena. Most workers have acknowledged many of the problems noted here, but few have sought to explore the foundational issues contributing to the persistence of the problems. Persons need a broader interpretative framework to appropriate the myriad monographs utilizing questionnaire and interview data and/or using survey research techniques. Some of the implications of one such broader perspective for the interpretation of survey research data have been discussed here.

Process philosophers have struggled with the problematic of survey research: the relation between linguistic symbols and human experience, the relations of the causal past and the emerging present, the relation of the parts to a whole, the nature of creative minorities, and the method of difference. As they addressed these issues in a broader context, they have considered related problems, including the relation of formal and dynamic elements in human experience, the relation of efficient and final cause, the bases for authentic religious experience, the bases for forms of human social organization, and the interpretation of perception, including memory.

In their quest for a logical and coherent interpretation of these problems that fit the facts, process philosophers have had to appeal to a Divine Reality who is *sui generis* in a qualified sense. From the perspective of process philosophy and dipolar theism, a consideration of the Divine nature is necessary for an adequate interpretation of religious experience, the subject matter of social scientific studies of religious phenomena. Studies not incorporating such a consideration are truncated and partially misleading.

The common sense of humankind may serve to restrain specialists using survey research methods to study religion, for most humans have affirmed the reality of religious experience. As they interpreted their actions, they also have appealed to purposiveness and intentionality. Any interpretation of human experience explaining away or ignoring these widespread intuitions of humankind is itself suspect.

Notes and References

1. Process philosophy is rooted in the Platonic tradition, but it inverts Plato's general point of view by emphasizing "becoming" rather than "being." It was initially elaborated by Alfred North Whitehead (1925, 1926, 1927, 1929, 1933, and 1938). Charles Hartshorne (1941, 1948, 1962, 1967, and 1970) is one of the foremost contemporary exponents of this mode of thought. Basic assumptions of this informing perspective on reality include the ultimacy of the category of creativity, the universality of the principle of relativity, the notion that reasons for things are to be found in actual entities, and a faith in rationalism. Platonic styles of thought are not currently fashionable in the social sciences. Consequently, some of the formulations developed in the body of this essay will be unappealing to most readers whose intellectual roots are in one of the social sciences. The predominant social scientific styles of interpretations of religious phenomena are phenomenological, reductionistic, or residualistic. For an elaboration of these issues see Schroeder (1970) and Winter (1966).

2. Deliberate deception, the most obvious manifestation of the ambiguity of linguistic symbols, is so self-evident that it is not discussed in the body of the paper. Human capacity for deliberate deception is rooted in the ability of people to surpass and to transform their pasts in their presents.

3. For example, Glock and Stark (1966) used forced option responses to gather their data. The researchers devised the alternative responses to the included items, and the respondents chose the statement with which they most fully agreed. For instance, in one item designed to contribute to an Orthodoxy Index, respondents were asked to indicate their views toward rather simplistic and crude interpretations of Biblical materials. The items included: the existence of a personal God, the divinity of Jesus Christ, the authenticity of Biblical miracles, and the existence of the Devil. Most people do not have clear and lucid views on these matters; but the alternative responses provided by the questionnaire helped people formulate—at least for the moment—their views quite sharply. As a result, lay people were reported to have sharp and rather formally defined views on Christian "orthodoxy."

4. Glock and Stark (1966), for example, root their method of elaboration in the responses people make to discrete, forced option responses. The causal sequence they sought to develop assumed the priority of beliefs in relation to the more dynamic facets of feeling and action in human experience. Such an assumption coheres with the formalistic bias introduced by the use of forced option responses. The method of causal analysis they employed accentuated this formalistic bias.

5. The resistance of clinically oriented psychologists and psychiatrists to inordinate statistical analysis and their suggestive use of case studies reflect some awareness of the complex, dynamic, and wholistic relation between symbolism and human experience. Chein's (1972) support of the "clinical" method in psychology represents one effort to legitimate an alternative style of research.

6. If Glock and Stark (1966) had used such case studies, they might have sensed more clearly the way in which prejudiced people employ the beliefs with which they are most familiar to legitimate their prejudices. In other words, if Glock and Stark had talked in depth to prejudiced people, they might have more forcefully emphasized ethocentricity, personality types, and salient reference groups in their interpretations of the grounds for anti-Semitism. These observations in no sense deny the importance of their findings about the widespread prevalence of anti-Semitism among members of Christian churches in the United States. The pervasiveness of such beliefs ought to be of concern to all Christians; and efforts to counteract them, including the reformation of Christian beliefs, ought to be undertaken. These observations do lead one to question, however, the clarity of the causal relations between Christian beliefs and anti-Semitism which Glock and Stark propose.

7. Not all interpretative schemata have the same power to illumine human experiences of the Divine Presence, but an analyst must choose some schematism to order and to interpret his or her data. His or her choice will be shaped by his or her own foundational assumptions about the nature of religious experience. Most of the survey research studies of religious phenomena have not addressed this issue directly, suggesting that the authors were maintaining some sort of dichotomy between scientific and religious belief systems. From the constructive understanding of human experience being developed here, the bifurcation is arbitrary. Tentative and provisional distinctions based on one's primary focus of attention, external or internal, are legitimate; but ultimately science and religion must find their appropriate places within one coherent mode of thought.

8. Sub-human dimensions of experience, such as tactile, auditory or visual perception, are more amenable to interval or ratio measurement.

9. Richard Shaull (1971), for example, reflects such a mood.

10. As noted previously Glock and Stark (1966) are attracted to a causal model. The method of elaboration they employ seeks to establish the way in which one set of variables produces another set. In this instance, they seek to show how "orthodox" Christian beliefs not qualified by "libertarianism" produce anti-Sematic attitudes.

11. Gerhard Lenski (1961) expresses ambivalent views on the issue of causal determinism. He rejects any monocausal theory of social determination and wants to assess the influence of the religious factor, as he defines it, on human feelings, beliefs, and actions. In this way he opts for a multi-causal model. At the same time, he acknowledges responsibility for any deficiencies in the study in the closing paragraph of the preface. Unless one is willing to distinguish between scientific and confessional studies, as is done in the Kantian tradition, this dual approach is contradictory. Lenski does not address the philosophic problem relating theoretic to practical reason in this volume; so it is not possible to discern how he would resolve this issue.

12. Talcott Parsons (1951) and B. F. Skinner (1971) both advance such views.

13. In this vein, persons acknowledging both the contribution of the past to the present and also the capacity of high-grade organisms such as human beings to surpass the past in the present would interpret the Glock and Stark (1966) findings differently than the authors do. From this point of view the presence of positive correlations between "orthodox" Christian and anti-Sematic attitudes (qualified by "libertarianism") reflects the contribution the past makes to the present, the persistence of aspects of "orthodox" Christian teachings.

The fact the correlations are nowhere near 1.00 and are qualified by "libertarianism" reflects the capacity of human beings to surpass and to transform their pasts in their emerging presents.

14. Max Weber is perhaps the most distinguished sociologist of religion holding this viewpoint. It is revealing that his studies were historically and typologically oriented. He sought to discern tendencies and configurations in human affairs but did not seek to establish sharp causal patterns. Clark (1965), Schroeder and Obenhaus (1964), Schroeder, Obenhaus, Jones, and Sweetser (1974), and Underwood (1957) illustrate this approach to the use of interview and questionnaire data in the study of religious phenomena. See Schroeder (1970) for an extended discussion of Max Weber's ordering of the sciences. Schroeder, Obenhaus, Jones, and Sweetser are self-consciously aware of these problematics in their study.

15. In the elaboration of their causal model, Glock and Stark (1966) accentuate a sequential process in human experience. Beliefs lead to feelings, which in turn lead to action. They acknowledge some feedback but suggest the predominant sequence is beliefs to feelings to action. According to the view of human perception advanced here, the relation between feelings, beliefs, and action is much more dynamic than the Glock-Stark model presupposes. There is constant interplay between emotions, reasons, and decisions; so a relatively clearcut causal sequence is spurious. In contrast to Glock and Stark, however, the view advanced here is that human experience begins with a flood of feelings, i.e., with aesthetic appropriation from the causal past. Intellectual feelings emerge in the later phases of experience. They flicker and are less forceful than emotional feelings. (This view is closer to contextual, interactionalist and Gestalt theories than to the Glock-Stark view.) The data Glock and Stark present could readily be reordered to cohere with this interrelational and dynamic view, for their correlations are all far below 1.00. It would have been just as easy to have begun one's elaboration of a causal chain, if one wanted to elaborate a causal chain at all, with acts of anti-Semitic behavior and to elaborate their relations to feelings and beliefs or to have begun with anti-Semitic feelings and to elaborate their relations to anti-Semitic beliefs and actions. There is a "lure toward coherence" between feelings, beliefs, and actions, so a prejudiced person will get his or her beliefs where he or she can find them. If one of his or her predominant reference groups is a Christian group, he or she can selectively abstract from the complex mosaic that constitutes Christian "beliefs" to support his or her anti-Semitic feelings and actions. This line of reasoning would lead one to emphasize the focus of prejudice in the individual and in salient reference groups rather than in "Christian" beliefs. The basic interpretation of human experience differs; but this view has some relation to the efforts of T.W. Adorno and his colleagues to relate prejudice to the authoritarian personality, to the efforts of Milton Rokeach to relate prejudice to the closed mind, and to the efforts of Gordon Allport to compare persons who have extrinsic religious orientations with persons who have intrinsic religious orientations.

16. Glock and Stark's (1966) method illustrates this process. The initial sample was drawn from church membership rolls, and a questionnaire was mailed to each individual in the sample. Each individual filled out the questionnaire in private and returned it to the center sponsoring the study. No consideration of the respondent's net of social relations was made. Each individual was a discrete case, isolated from the other respondents. The forced option response questions were coded, and the data were analyzed in a manner consonant with a model developed by the authors. In this analysis discrete items were combined to make indices taken as representative of certain factors, such as religious orthodoxy, libertarianism, hostility to Jews, and the like. By proceeding in this way, the authors developed a model they felt was adequate to explain the relation between Christian beliefs and

anti-Semitism. The legitimate critiques leveled at the study by those who claim they ignored reference group theory and studies on authoritarian personalities illustrate the hazards of building an explanatory model in this manner. Both salient groups to which the individual relates and the characteristics of the whole person from whom bits of data have been obtained are lost in this style of data collection and analysis.

17. For this reason, the argument that individual uniqueness sets limits to all the sciences is both true and also not directly to the point so far as comparisons between the human and non-human sciences are concerned. The difference in the degree of uniqueness and the novelty of the response of a rock and a human to their sustaining environments is so great as to *almost* be a difference in kind.

18. For example, the egalitarianism espoused by the Levellers in seventeenth century England represents a persistent and recurrent phenomenon in human affairs; but the peculiar shape of this movement in that historical epoch in England requires consideration of the unique character of that epoch. Similarly, the universality of religious experiences encourages the comparative study of the religious institutions. At the same time, the manner in which they are woven into the social fabric of a given society in a given historical epoch limits the usefulness of a comparative study.

19. It is beyond the scope of this paper to explore this issue at length. For a suggestive discussion of statistical and non-statistical grounds for a probability judgment, see Whitehead (1929): 303-316.

20. Among classical sociologists of religion, Max Weber was most sensitive to this issue. His concern with the charismatic leader and his discussions of the routinization of charisma reflect this sensitivity. Similarly, *The Protestant Ethic and the Spirit of Capitalism* (1930) focuses attention on a unique phenomenon giving rise to unique historical consequences. He cites individual people in that work and notes the novel and innovative contributions they made to the breakdown of the medieval synthesis and to the development of people willing to exchange their labor for money in the open market. Glock and Stark (1966) make some historical references in the introduction of their work, but it then unfolds without further historical references. They neither elaborate the Jewish understanding of the Jews as chosen people as a continuing source of prejudices nor refer to contemporary Jewish theologians struggling with the ethnocentric implications of such a view. There is no discussion of the state of Israel and of the implications of Arab-Israeli conflict on American foreign policy or on the American economy. These dynamic situations shaped in part by the decisions of creative minorities probably will have more to do with the shape of prejudice toward American Jews by other Americans than anything related to Christian beliefs; yet they are ignored in a volume whose concluding chapter addresses ways to ameliorate prejudice toward Jews in American society. Two other examples drawn from survey research literature of causally oriented survey research studies may be noted. Lenski (1961) projected the continued strength of the Roman Catholic Church in the United States at a time its adherents were beginning to drift away in substantial numbers. He was also concerned about the possibility of religious compartmentalization in the United States at a time major reforms in the Catholic Church were under way. Similarly, by focusing on survey research data in a causally oriented study, Andrew Greeley and Peter Rossi (1966) foresaw the continued health of the Catholic parochial school system in the U.S. at the time a marked contradiction of the system was beginning.

21. Laws are immanental from the perspective of process thought, but they are lured forth by God's evocation seeking harmony and intensity of feeling. Laws come into existence as the creatures in a given ethos share common forms and defining characteristics and they pass out of existence as the ethos changes. According to this view, the relatively greater capacity of humans to surpass their pasts results in more rapid changes in the "laws" shap-

ing human societies than in the laws shaping sub-human societies. Social scientific laws change more rapidly than physical laws because humans are able to modify their environment more rapidly than are other creatures on this planet, but all laws change over a longer period. The immanental "laws" shaping the character of Chinese or American society shift more rapidly than the "immanental" laws shaping the behavior of electrons. Nonetheless, the presence of the geometric forms permitting measurement is "arbitrary" in the sense that these forms need not be present in all cosmic epochs. Plato put it poetically in the *Timaeus* when he suggested that all nature could give was a "likely tale."

22. When "average" opinions are equated with normative opinions, political leadership may be too prone to follow public opinion and too cautious about helping to create it. For a polemical attack on public opinion polls see Lindsay Rogers (1949).

23. This issue is obviously related to the "whole-part" problem discussed earlier. Because Glock and Stark (1966) employ the method of difference, they are unable to assess the positive role Christianity in America has played in fostering feelings, beliefs, actions, and social institutions which ameliorate tendencies toward inordinate prejudice. Definitive assessments are impossible, but the impossibility of precise evaluation is no excuse to ignore factors of obvious cultural significance. Greeley and Rossi (1966) also illustrate the problems of evaluation encountered when analysts employ the method of difference. The whole character of the Roman Catholic Church in America has been deeply influenced by the evolution of the parochial school system. The survey research methods they used cannot assess this impact. The comparisons they made between Catholics attending parochial schools and Catholics attending public schools presuppose the presence of a Church profoundly affected by the existence of a large parochial school system. If most parochial schools closed or had not been extant, their findings would probably be different, for the Catholic Church in America would be a different institution.

Bibliography

Chein, Isidor
1972 *The Science of Behavior and the Image of Man.* New York, N.Y.: Basic Books.
Clark, Henry
1965 *The Church and Residential Desegregation.* New Haven, Conn.: College and University Press, 1965.
Glock, Charles Y. and Rodney Stark
1966 *Christian Beliefs and Anti-Semitism.* New York, N.Y.: Harper and Row.
Greeley, Andrew M. and Peter H. Rossi
1966 *The Education of Catholic Americans.* Chicago, Ill.: Aldine.
Hartshorne, Charles
1941 *Man's Vision of God.* New York, N.Y.: Harper and Company.
1948 *The Divine Relativity.* New Haven, Conn.: Yale University Press.
1962 *The Logic of Perfection.* LaSalle, Ill.: Open Court Press.
1967 *A Natural Theology for Our Time.* LaSalle, Ill.: Open Court Press.
Lenski, Gerhard
1961 *The Religious Factor.* Garden City, N.Y.: Doubleday.
National Opinion Research Center
1971 *American Priests.* Chicago, Ill.: National Opinion Research Center.
Parsons, Talcott

1951 *The Social System.* Glencoe, Ill.: Free Press.
Rogers, Lindsay
1949 *The Pollsters.* New York, N.Y.: Knopf.
Schroeder, W. Widick
1970 *Cognitive Structures and Religious Research.* East Lansing, Mich.: Michigan State University Press.
Schroeder, W. Widick and Victor Obenhaus
1964 *Religion in American Culture.* New York N.Y.: Free Press.
Schroeder, W. Widick *et al.*
1974 *Suburban Religion: Churches and Synogogues in the American Experience.* Chicago, Ill.: Center for the Scientific Study of Religion.
Shaull, Richard
1971 "The Church and the Making of a Counter Culture." *The Chicago Theological Seminary Register* 61 (May):15-27.
Skinner, B.F.
1971 *Beyond Freedom and Dignity.* New York, N.Y.: Knopf.
Underwood, Kenneth
1957 *Protestant and Catholic.* Boston, Mass.: Beacon Press.
Weber, Max
1930 *The Protestant Ethic and the Spirit of Capitalism.* London, Eng.: George Allen and Unwin, Ltd.
Whitehead, Alfred N.
1925 *Science and the Modern World.* New York, N.Y.: Macmillan.
1926 *Religion in the Making.* New York, N.Y.: Macmillan.
1927 *Symbolism: Its Meaning and Effect.* New York, N.Y.: Macmillan.
1929 *Process and Reality.* New York, N.Y.: Macmillan.
1933 *Adventures of Ideas.* New York, N.Y.: Macmillan.
1938 *Modes of Thought.* New York, N.Y.: Macmillan.
Winter, Gibson
1966 *Elements for a Social Ethic.* New York, N.Y.: Macmillan.

Section B

Analytical Studies

Introduction to Section B of Part Three

The four essays in this section focus on analytic rather than on constructive work, but constructive elements are present in each of them. They were written in the 1970s and the early 1980s. Retrieving and augmenting some of the historical motifs developed in Chapter 9, Chapters 13 and 14 explore the factors contributing to the emergence of the voluntary church as the dominant form of religious organization in the United States today and consider efforts to invigorate religious bodies. Chapter 15 considers the quest for denominational identity and the limits of pluralism in the United Church of Christ. Chapter 16 takes a retrospective look at sociological religious research in the United States and considers its prospects. It examines the emergence of three professional organizations devoted to the scientific study of religious phenomena and suggests the possibility of new metatheories more sympathetic to *sui generis* interpretations of religious experience.

As note in the general introduction to Part Three, the American religious experiment has continued since the time that Chapters 13 and 14 were written, for the influx of immigrants in the past two decades from the Far East, and to a lesser extent, from the Middle East, has altered the American religious landscape. Muslim, Buddhist, Shintoist, Hindu, and various ethnic Christian groups have become more numerous. These groups have already taken on some aspects of the "voluntary church."

The extent to which these various faith communities will be incorporated into the religion of America in the coming decades is a matter of much interest. The shape of this accommodation will impact the religious identity of persons in all the faith communities in America. Unless most Americans share common central values transcending those of any particular faith community, the country runs the danger of balkanization. If past patterns are repeated, these newer faith communities will be transformed as were the churches of European origin in earlier times. Because the basic views of most of these newer immigrants are not informed by the Judeo-Christian tradition, the transformations, assuming they occur, will be of a different character than the earlier ones. If these newcomers and their descendants affirm religious liberty, religious pluralism and religious tolerance, the American religious experiment will enter a new epoch. If they reject these notions, conflict and acrimony in the religious sphere will become more widespread.

Chapter 15 addresses problems of identity and diversity in the United Churches of Christ. This denomination was created in 1957 through a merger of the Congregational-Christian Churches and the Evangelical and Reformed Church. The two denominations differed substantially in polity, social status, lived history, and beliefs. These differences have exacerbated the identity issues which any church merger raises.

Chapter 16 considers the development of religious research in the United States. It takes a retrospective look at the emergence of four different professional societies having an interest in the scientific study of religious phenomena and ponders the future direction of religious research in the United States.

Introduction to Chapters 13 and 14

All religious institutions in the United States have been transformed by the American social context. The American religious experiment, which in one sense was a question of sovereignty, led to the separation of religious institutions from the state. This separation, as noted in Chapter 9 as well as in Chapters 13 and 14, required the transformation of views supporting the idea of a state church, the norm in Europe from which the vast majority of migrants came during the colonial period. In the early modern period, the state was expected to support the established church in both Protestant and Catholic regions. Toleration came very slowly over several centuries. Indeed, to this day some church bodies occupy a privileged place in most European countries.

Chapter 13 was written as a contribution to a conference which the Chicago Theological Seminary was sponsoring as a part of the nation's bicentennial celebration. It was originally published in the collection of essays developed for that conference under the title *The American Religious Experiment: Piety and Practicality,* edited by Clyde Manschrcek and Barbara Brown Zikmund. The essay highlights the historical factors leading to the emergence of the voluntary church. It also addresses the question of church renewal, for many Protestant religious professionals seek to transform the voluntary church into an intentional fellowship. The essay advances an ambivalently positive interpretation of the voluntary church.

Chapter 14 was also developed for a conference at the Chicago Theological Seminary and was included in the collection of essays emerging from that conference under the title *Sources of Vitality in American Church Life,* edited by Robert L. Moore. It recapitulates the material in Chapters 9 and 10 in order to delineate the framework that promotes and legitimates the wide variety of religious expression found in the United States. The American experiment encourages the proliferation of religious bodies and facilitates the emergence of new ones. Not all of them promote either individual or social well-being. The concluding section of the essay raises some formal questions to help one evaluate the relative merit of a given form of religious expression.

CHAPTER 13

The Emergence of the Voluntary Church

The separation of church and state is the most important single socio-cultural factor affecting the shape and style of American religious institutions. This separation has made the principle of religious voluntarism preeminent and has fostered the emergence of the related values of religious pluralism and religious tolerance.

The notions of church-state separation, religious liberty, religious pluralism and religious tolerance have become central core values shared by most Americans. They hold these foundational convictions more fundamentally than they hold most particular religious beliefs. Consequently, the beliefs of those faith communities holding alternative views of church-state relations have been qualified and transformed by the American religious experiment. The predominance of these widely held convictional values in contemporary America has made the voluntary church the predominant form of religious organization in America.

This historic development is traced through selective historical retrieval in the first half of this essay. In the second half the contemporary situation is assessed, and alternative views of "church renewal" are discussed.

THE EUROPEAN AND AMERICAN ANTECEDENTS OF THE VOLUNTARY CHURCH

Human beings differ in the intensity of their involvements in faith communities. Some people are extraordinarily sensitive to the Divine Presence in the world, and they frequently respond to their awareness of the Divine Presence by very substantial involvement in a faith community. Others are moderately and still others marginally involved.

Shifting climates of opinion in the various epochs of Christian history have affected the proportions of the population with high, moderate and low involvement in faith communities in different historical periods, but every epoch has had some people in each group.

In Europe varying religious sensitivities and institutional involvements contributed to the development of "church" and "sect" type faith communities, so astutely analyzed by Ernst Troeltsch some two generations ago. According to Troeltsch, church type faith communities are more inclusive in membership, less demanding of members, less biblically focused, and less egalitarian than sect type faith communities. Sects seek the total involvement and total commitment of their members, and they often accentuate the New Testament model of the church. They minimize the clergy-laity contrast, and they often have egalitarian emphases. They usually contrast more sharply the disparity between the church and the world.

In America, a hybrid institution which is neither a church nor a sect in the European sense has evolved. It is a "voluntary" church, distinguished by the fact that members belong because they **will** to belong. The denomination has become the predominant form of "connectional" institution, relating various "gathered" fellowships.

These summary observations require clarification and elaboration. A selective historical retrieval will facilitate this process.

THE EUROPEAN ANTECEDENTS

Neither Luther nor Calvin envisaged religious liberty in the contemporary American sense. Both sought to substitute their version of an established state church for the Catholic version.

In the sixteenth century, the princes of the small principalities of what is now Germany determined whether a given area would become Protestant or remain Catholic. Their decisions were often shaped as much by political and economic factors as by religious issues.

In the theocracy of Calvin's Geneva the religious liberty of the nonconformist was severely circumscribed. The state stood ready to coerce those persons whom the church determined were violating church teaching or practice.

The people associated with the movements subsequently called the "Left Wing of the Reformation" are the precursors of the contemporary voluntary church. They emphasized the primacy of the intentional fellowship, a faith community composed of those whose experiences had led them to form churches in which discipline under God, the authority of Scripture, right belief and right conduct were central.

In the German speaking portion of the Reformation Anabaptists such as the Mennonites were representative of the intentional fellowship; in the English speaking world, various Baptist bodies related to the Calvinistic tradition were representative. These groups had markedly different views of church-world relations. Mennonites sought to withdraw from worldly entanglements, and most Baptists sought to influence public policy. In spite of these differences, they both believed the gathered fellowship was the proper type of faith community.

THE AMERICAN ANTECEDENTS

The religious organization of the American colonies was shaped by the expectations of the early English settlers. Seventeenth century English Puritan-Anglican struggles spilled over into the colonies, for Puritans predominated in New England and Anglicans predominated in the South.

As was the case with sixteenth century Lutherans and Calvinists, neither Puritans nor Anglicans sought to disestablish the church. They disagreed on the type of church to be established, but they affirmed the general principle of establishment **per se.** The notions of religious liberty and a pluralism of fellowships were affirmed in principle only in Rhode Island and Pennsylvania.

As time passed, the colonies became more and more heterogeneous religiously, for settlers coming from various parts of Europe with different established churches became more numerous in all of the colonies. This social reality which encouraged disestablishment was accentuated by cultural and political developments in the eighteenth century.

Deistic modes of thought emerging in the Enlightenment fostered the ideas of religious pluralism, voluntarism, and tolerance, complementing the Quaker and Baptist views. The sectarian wars that had plagued Europe made an impact on American leadership, and most American political leaders were very anxious to avoid the religious wars that had devasted parts of Europe.

Thus, the embryonic secularity of Deism, the piety of some Christian bodies, and the practicality of American political leadership contributed to the emergence of the doctrine of the separation of church and state. The Congress of the new republic affirmed this doctrine by adopting the First Amendment of the Constitution, guaranteeing religious liberty. The Supreme Court subsequently ruled that the First Amendment applied only to the Federal Government, but its suasive power was considerable. In 1833, Massachusetts, the last state to have an established church, disestablished it. The American religious experiment, informed by piety and practicality, was fully launched.

FROM WASHINGTON TO LINCOLN: A PROTESTANT PLURALISM

In the early days of the Republic the nation was nominally Protestant in overwhelming proportions. In 1790 there were only 40,000 Catholics and at most a few thousand Jews in a population of almost 4,000,000.

Fewer than five percent of that population belonged to a church, so the field was ripe for intensive evangelism. The revivalistic activities in the latter half of the eighteenth century and the first half of the nineteenth century were set in the context of this dual situation — a very low proportion of the population associated with the churches and an evolving disestablishment. If the churches of America were to survive, they had to have more members. America's religious leaders — often with more evangelical zeal than theological perspicacity — set about this recruitment task with vigor and enthusiasm.

Under the dual influences of evangelism and church-state separation the pluralism of Protestantism caused by the migration of people affiliated with different Protestant bodies in Europe was augmented by the proliferation of indigenous groups in the nineteenth century. The extraordinarily large number of denominations in America is an outgrowth of these factors.

The seventeenth century pattern of Puritan migration to the New England colonies and of Anglican migration to the Southern colonies was noted earlier. The impact of those migrations was still observable in the nineteenth century. The unique character of Southern religion in America is a result of the blending of earlier Anglican influences with the biblicism and revivalism of the eighteenth and nineteenth centuries. The medieval social theory so predominant among seventeenth century Anglican divines who migrated from England to Virginia and some of the other Southern colonies contributed greatly to the quasi-feudal character of the Old South. The aristocracy, the style of chivalry, the elevated status of women, and the interpretation of slavery as a white man's burden were rooted in this conservative Anglican tradition. Formal involvement in the Anglican Church was very low in the latter part of the eighteenth century, and the South was ripe for the evangelism and the biblically informed revivalism that became firmly entrenched in this region. Despite this overlay, the early Anglican "layer" contributed substantially to the emergence of a distinctive style of Christianity in this region.

The Puritan influence was widespread in the North and the West in the first half of the nineteenth century and exacerbated regional conflicts. It is possible to trace some of the roots of the Civil War to the contrasting beliefs of the seventeenth century Puritan and Anglican immigrants — contrasts which had produced a Civil War in seventeenth century England.

During this epoch, the idea of religious disestablishment was firmly embodied in the American experiment. The public school was evolving to a central position in American education and the "Sunday School," a typically American enterprise integrally related to the voluntary church, was taking form.

The overwhelming Protestant character of the country was modified somewhat during this time. The number of Catholic immigrants increased, particularly in the latter part of the period, for the potato famine in Ireland and the European political unrest in 1848 encouraged more Catholics to immigrate.

FROM LINCOLN TO WILSON: URBANIZATION, INDUSTRIALIZATION, AND THE EMERGENCE OF A MULTI-FAITH PLURALISM

In the post-Civil War epoch the United States was transformed from a predominantly rural, agrarian and overwhelmingly Protestant country to an urban, industrial, and less predominantly Protestant country. The tremendous mass migrations in this period, particularly from 1885-1915, altered markedly the ethnic and religious composition of the nation. Between 1880 and 1920 almost 25,000,000 immigrants settled in this nation, and the proportion of Catholics in the population increased dramatically.

Catholics coming from Southern and Eastern Europe knew almost nothing of religious liberty, religious pluralism, religious tolerance and church-state separation. They developed an extensive parochial school system and numerous Catholic welfare institutions during this time, for they sought to develop religious institutions similar to the ones they had known in their homelands.

The Jewish population of America increased substantially during this time, for they participated in the migrations from both Northern and Eastern Europe. They still remained a small proportion of the American population (less than three percent), but their actual number increased markedly.

The earlier consensus attained on church-state separation was shaken but not shattered during this epoch. Subject to various forms of persecution at the hands of both Catholics and Protestants in Europe, the Jewish immigrants enthusiastically affirmed the principle of church-state separation. Catholic affirmation was more restrained and less enthusiastic, for many Catholic immigrants came from areas of Europe in which Catholicism was the predominant religion and in which the church enjoyed special privileges and support from the state. These contrasting interpretations of church-state relations created difficulties, compounded by the fact that many of these immigrants came from parts of Europe with monarchical or aristocratic govenments and knew little or nothing about a democratic form of government. Crowding into the burgeoning industrial cities of the North, they often became urban villagers, seeking to claim some turf as their own. In this context, the Statue of Liberty took on major symbolic significance, and the "melting-pot" theory of culturalization became popular.

During this period the black church in America became a visible social institution. There were a few black churches among free blacks in the antebellum period, but the end of slavery saw the tremendous expansion of black churches in the South. The shape and style of the black church was affected not only by the commingling of Anglican and evangelical influences in the South but also by the character of the black experience in America. The black church emerged as an inclusive social institution, dealing not only with religious matters but also with social, economic, and political issues.

THE PREEMINENCE OF THE VOLUNTARY CHURCH IN TWENTIETH CENTURY AMERICA

Within the framework of religious voluntarism, three major faith communities have evolved: Protestant, Catholic, Jewish. Because of different early histories and the persistence of segregation, American Protestantism divided into predominantly white denominations and predominantly black denominations. Thus, the cultural and social realities of the American experience have differentiated white Protestantism from black Protestantism, giving rise to four major faith communities.

The contemporary voluntary church differs markedly in one respect from the intentional fellowships of the Reformation epoch discussed previously. The voluntary church does not demand that its members affirm the strong emphases on right discipline under God, the authority of Scripture, right belief and right conduct, emphases characteristic of the "Believers' Church" of the Reformation era. It accepts almost anyone who chooses to belong. Intentional fellowships do exist, but they incorporate fewer people than do the voluntary churches.

Because the separation of church and state precludes the use of tax money for the support of faith communities, American clergy in the voluntary church have had to develop more innovative and often more imaginative programs than their European counterparts. The fund-raising aspects of bake sales, auctions, and many faith community sponsored programs reflect the practicality and activism of the voluntary church.

The paucity of significant anti-clericalism in the United States is also related to the voluntary church, for no faith community has been able to impose directly its teachings in the public realm. Most members in the voluntary church prefer priestly activities to prophetic ones. At the cultural level, the separation of church and state has limited the power of the church to address public issues. At the personal level, members of the voluntary church do not want undue internal conflict; they prefer adjustive, integrative styles of leadership to challenging and disintegrative ones. Leaders may engage in prophetic activity from time to time, provided they engage predominantly in priestly activities.

Local professionals are under substantial pressure to conform to lay expectations, for lay people in every tradition are free to dissociate themselves from their faith community if they will to do so. In some traditions they may dismiss leaders if the contrast in clergy-lay expectations become inordinate. In all traditions, lay people make things difficult for clergy with whom they have substantial disagreement.

THE MAJOR FAITH COMMUNITIES IN CONTEMPORARY AMERICA: WHITE PROTESTANT, BLACK PROTESTANT, CATHOLIC AND JEWISH

Four major faith communities have evolved in the context of the American religious experiment: white Protestant, black Protestant, Catholic, and Jewish. Protestantism is the majority religion, and Judaism is a small minority. Church membership data are not very reliable, but the best estimates indicate a relatively steady increase in the proportion of the American people affiliated with a faith community from the time of the founding of the country until the late 1950s, at which time between 65 and 70 percent of American adults were affiliated with a religious institution. Since then a modest decline in the proportion of adults belonging to churches has taken place.

About 65 to 70 percent of Americans belonging to religious institutions belong to Protestant churches, about 25 to 30 percent belong to Catholic churches, and about two or three percent belong to Jewish synagogues. Of the 70 to 75 million Protestant church members, some 10 to 12 million are black.

The principles of organization and authority differ within and between these faith communities. The impact of the American religious experiment on these principles needs to be considered.

VOLUNTARISM, PRINCIPLES OF ORGANIZATION, AND AUTHORITY IN THE MAJOR FAITH COMMUNITIES

As noted earlier, the principle of church-state separation and the concomitant principles of religious liberty, religious tolerance, and religious pluralism undergird the American religious experiment. These principles are more foundational for the vast majority of Americans today than are the principles of any particular religious tradition. As a consequence, the understanding of faith communities as "gathered fellowships" has become the normative understanding among most Americans. As noted earlier, relatively few highly intentional religious fellowships exist in contemporary America; most Protestant faith communities and the Catholic Church have been transformed or are being transformed into predominantly voluntary churches.

There is one major historical difference between most Protestant faith communities and Catholicism. Most Protestant bodies have had two or three centuries to accommodate themselves to the American religious experiment. By contrast the Catholic Church has had only three generations, for the flood of Catholic immigrants between 1885 and 1915 knew nothing of the emergence of the American religious experiment and of the foundational values embodied in it.

This historical difference is compounded by ecclesiastical and doctrinal contrasts, for the predominant principle of organization has differed in the faith communities. In American Protestantism as a whole, the **congregational** principle of the primacy of the local congregation has predominated. Episcopal and Presbyterian principles of organization are extant, but they are substantially qualified and modified by the congregational principle. As noted earlier, the congregational principle is reinforced by the principle of voluntarism embodied in general American cultural values. Both lay people and clergy can move from one of the more than 250 Protestant denominations to another without renouncing their Protestant faith identity, providing substantial internal diversity and opportunities for lay and clergy self-selection.

In Protestantism, the question of authority centers on the authority of Scripture. Some persons and groups think it is the unequivocal locus for matters of faith and order; others think it is not. Among the former group, conflict emerges about alternative interpretations of Scripture and differing implications to be drawn from it. Among the latter, internal differences emerge, for no consensus about the locus of authority or the shape of faith and order exists.

In Catholicism, a **cultic** principle of organization has been predominant. A specially designated, hierarchically organized body of priests has set policy, prescribed doctrines, and administered rites for the laity. The multiplicity of Catholic religious orders and the distinction between secular and religious priests have provided some internal diversity within Catholicism, but Catholic emphases on "true" doctrine and a hierarchial system of authority culminating in the authority of the Pope have substantially limited the extent of internal diversity. A Catholic cannot move from one subcommunity to another and retain his or her basic Catholic faith identity in the same way a Protestant can.

The inner turmoil currently manifest in American Catholicism, which is substantially greater than in Protestantism or Judaism, is a result of the recent widespead affirmation of the voluntaristic principle by Catholic clergy and laity. The increased emphasis on the laity since Vatican II coheres with the principle of voluntarism. The development of various structures to facilitate lay involvement in the decision making processes within the American Catholic Church in the past decade or two is also in tune with the principles informing the American religious experiment. In Catholicism, the question of authority centers on the authority of the tradition. Laity-laity, clergy-clergy, and laity-clergy conflicts about the degree of voluntarism compatible with Catholicism and about the locus of authority within the church are commonplace.

In Judaism, a **communal** principle of organization is predominant, for the Jewish religious community is inextricably intertwined with the history of the Jewish people. Jews may move from one of the three sub-communities to another without renouncing their basic Jewishness. In addition to the religious subgroups numerous "secular" Jewish agencies exist. Since many American Jews have great difficulty affirming the "religious" side of their historic community, these "secular" agencies also serve as a way for Jews to retain Jewish social identity in the context of their detachment from synagogues. The communal principle of organization coheres with a congregational principle, so the voluntarism of the American religious experiment was readily compatible with the Jewish experience. In Judaism the question of authority centers around the question of the authority of the Jewish community. The debate is multi-faceted, since the relation of the "religious" community to the "historic" community and the authority of the historic community are intertwined issues.

Previously it was noted that the earlier "Believers' Church" emphasized discipline under God, the authority of Scripture, right belief, and right conduct. The members of the voluntary church in contemporary America do not uniformly affirm these emphases, and the implications of this situation warrant special consideration.

THE VOLUNTARY CHURCH AND LEVELS OF INTENTIONALITY

In the voluntary church, which all evidence indicates is the preeminent form of the church in contemporary America, members belong because they **will** to belong. Strict membership criteria are rare, and any person who wants to belong to a church will have no difficulty in finding one which will be happy to have him or her. Only among some "Believers' Churches" do strict covenants and membership criteria exist, and these communities are distinguished by their paucity.

In most of the Protestant churches of the major denominations, such as the American Baptist Churches in the USA, Episcopal Church, the Lutheran Church in America, the United Church of Christ, the United Methodist Church, and the United Presbyterian Church, and in Catholicism, people with widely varying levels of intentionality and commitment coexist in the same congregations. A few members (usually less than ten percent) are highly involved and deeply committed to their church; many (usually about one-half to two-thirds) have a significant measure of commitment; some (usually about one-quarter) are marginally involved, and a few (usually about ten percent) are merely on the membership roll. Since the level of one's commitment and the **substance** of one's commitment may differ, the members in a given congregation whose levels of commitment are high may differ in the substance of their commitments. In more evangelical groups, such as churches in the Southern Baptist Convention and the Lutheran Church-Missouri Synod, the level of intentionality is higher than in the previously cited denominations, but these denominations also have substantial proportions of marginal and dormant members. In Judaism the same general patterns prevail, except that the proportions of marginal and dormant members are higher than in Catholicism or Protestantism. People are free to "shop" for an appropriate religious institution in Protestantism and Judaism. Catholics are encouraged to attend the church in their geographical parish, but in recent decades more of them are seeking a church that fits their religious and social style. Most people will to belong to religious institutions with people of similar social status and ethnicity, so particular congregations tend to have members in about the same social status and tend to be ethnically homogeneous.

The voluntary church places primacy on the local congregation. Those denominations with episcopal or presbyterian polities are connectional, and are not as directly subject to the will of local congregations as are denominations with a congregational polity, but in America they must also pay considerable attention to the expectations and interests of local congregations. Local lay people expect to be consulted in major decisions; and they expect to have some voice in the decision making process, regardless of the form of church government prevailing in their denomination. They are willing to listen to their leader's views on faith and morals, but they reserve the right to make up their own minds.

The widely varying levels of participation, theological understanding and spiritual maturity among the members of the voluntary church in America place very special demands upon religious leaders. Their responses depend upon their theories of religious leadership and their theological interpretations of this situation.

Interpretations of the situation and strategies for "church renewal" abound. It is fitting to conclude this essay with a brief discussion of alternative strategies for "church renewal."

THE VOLUNTARY CHURCH AND STRATEGIES FOR "CHURCH RENEWAL"

The core values informing the lives of most Americans emerge from a variety of sources. The religions of America discussed here are one source of meaning. The public faith of America, including the religion of America (a complex faith incorporating belief in separation of church and state, religious liberty, religious pluralism and religious tolerance and other motifs not discussed here), technical rationalism and secular humanism, are another source of meaning. Taken together they constitute a blending of piety and practicality shared unevenly and in a less than fully coherent way by most Americans.

Participants in the voluntary church affirm many aspects of the public faith of America, resulting in complex and subtle transformations of their historic faith communities. One's evaluation of this situation and one's suggested responses to it will be guided by one's views on the following issues: the nature of "authentic" religion; the relation between "authentic" religion, other religions, and human culture; the relation between love, justice, and forms of social organization; and the extent of the harmony of life with life possible under the conditions of existence. These issues cannot be elaborated adequately here, but some observations about the way in which theological understanding informs some of the diverse strategies for "church renewal" can be made.

Persons preferring the intentional fellowship inevitably criticize the voluntary church and offer various strategies to intensify the depth of commitment of church members. They often lament the loss of discipline characteristic of earlier intentional fellowships and seek to restore it. Since only a fraction of the members of the typical voluntary church respond to such "renewal" efforts by professional leadership, some self-conscious "elites" emerge who have different visions of the nature of the church than most of the participants. Such contrasting views not infrequently lead to internal struggles within congregations, for not all members share either the style or substance of the understandings being advocated by the "renewalists."

Some persons seeking the restoration of intentional communities are informed by kerygmatic styles of theology. Consequently, they focus attention on the Bible and/or facets of the tradition (often the early church). They seek to cultivate groups engaged in Bible study in the context of reflection on current experience. Others are informed by apologetic styles of theology. They also cultivate small groups, but they are more apt to be informed by humanistic psychology and other contemporary modes of thought. Persons seeking the restoration of the intentional fellowship entertain differing views of the church's involvement in politics. Some seek direct involvement in the political sphere, but others accentuate the need for substantial distance or withdrawal from politics.

Persons whose views on the nature of the church permit them to accept the reality of the voluntary church with more equanimity than more sectarian protagonists offer more moderate and balanced suggestions for "church renewal." Because "institutional maintainence" is not such a negative word for them, they are likely to be more supportive of activities sustaining existing enterprises. Since only the most insensitive do not see the need for innovation and for opportunities to cultivate deeper theological understanding and spiritual maturation, such persons support some innovative and "renewing" efforts. Those are set, however, in the context of a more sympathetic interpretation of the current situation.

The vision of the religious professional as a "pastoral director," "a facilitator," and/or an "enabler" is compatible with this latter view. Accepting members with markedly different degrees of commitment and spiritual maturation, protagonists of this perspective are able to foster and to support the multiple programs of worship, education and social activities typical of the voluntary church.

Professionals willing to commit themselves to a process of consensus formation in a faith community, seeking to sustain a spiritual and moral community bearing witness to the Divine Presence in human life and desiring a limited pluralism in style and substance can serve the voluntary church with integrity. They know full well their efforts will be fragmentary, imperfect, and ambivalent, but they believe the positive aspects of the voluntary church justify these efforts. Informed by a sense of cause, a sense of proportion, and a sense of responsibility, such professional leadership may legitimately hope to enhance human life and to contribute to the Divine Life.

NOTES:

Much of the material summarized in this essay is elaborated and documented in detail in W. Widick Schroeder, Victor Obenhaus, Larry A. Jones, and Thomas Sweetser, *Suburban Religion: Churches and Synagogues in the American Experience* (Chicago, 1974). In the last chapter of the volume, the author of this essay offers a sympathetic constructive interpretation of the voluntary church. Thomas P. Sweetser's *The Catholic Parish: Shifting Membership in a Changing Church* (Chicago, 1974) focuses on the Catholic data reported in the preceeding citation.

Sydney E. Ahlstrom's *A Religious History of the American People* (New Haven, 1972) is an encyclopedic treatment of American religious history. Martin E. Marty's *Righteous Empire: The Protestant Experience in America* (New York, 1970) emphasizes the Puritan influence in America. Sydney Mead's *The Lively Experiment: The Shaping of Christianity in America* (New York, 1963) focuses of religious liberty and the physical fact of the "frontier" in interpreting Christianity in America.

Winthrop Hudson's *American Protestantism* (Chicago, 1961), John Tracy Ellis' *American Catholicism* (Chicago, 1956) and Nathan Glazer's *American Judaism* (Chicago, 1972) are useful surveys of the histories of these three faith communities in America. E. Franklin Frazier's *The Negro Church in America* (New York, 1963) and Joseph Washington's *Black Religion: The Negro and Christianity in the United States* (Boston, 1964) are helpful analyses of the black church in America.

Useful sociological studies of contemporary American religion include: Will Herberg, *Protestant, Catholic, Jew* (New York, 1955); Gerhard Lenski, *The Religious Factor* (New York,

1961); Rodney Stark and Charles Y. Glock, *American Piety: The Nature of Religious Commitment* (Berkeley, 1968); and Martin E. Marty, Stuart E. Rosenberg and Andrew M. Greeley, *What Do We Believe? The Stance of Religion in America* (New York, 1968).

Franklin H. Littell's *From State Church to Pluralism* (Garden City, 1962) combines historical analysis with an appeal for church renewal of the kerygmatic intentional community type. Philip and Phoebe Anderson elaborate their views of church renewal of an apologetic intentional community type in *The House Church* (Nashville, 1975).

The following volumes deal with "church renewal" from the perspective of the voluntary church: H. Richard Niebuhr, *The Purpose of the Church and Its Ministry* (New York, 1956); James Gustafson, *Treasure in Earthen Vessels* (New York, 1961); James Dittes, *The Church in the Way* (New York, 1967); and James Nelson, *Moral Nexus* (Philadelphia, 1971).

CHAPTER 14

The Variety of American Religious Expression: A Framework for Interpretation

INTRODUCTION

The kaleidoscopic composition of the religious sphere of the American social order has been and continues to be a source of surprise to the European observer. Accustomed to the twin phenomena of overwhelmingly preponderant formally established churches and widespread self-conscious secular movements, Europeans are struck by the variety and the relative vitality of American religious institutions and by the paucity of militant secularist groups. Piety and secularity co-exist in the American experience in a novel manner.

According to *The Yearbook of American Churches*, which contains the most reliable statistical material on American religious bodies, the number of religious bodies has ranged between 250 and 300 in recent years. The variety of American religious expression is not quite as dramatic as these data would suggest, for between eighty and eighty-five percent of the members of religious bodies belong to the eighteen largest groups. Nonetheless, compared to other nations in which Christianity has been the predominant historical religion, the variety of American religious expression is remarkable.

In the examination of any religious group one must consider four factors: the nature of the Divine Reality and Its Presence in human life; the effect of the causal past on the emerging present; the predominant values and forms of social organization extant in a particular society; and the impact of highly visible and articulate religious leaders on a particular group. Human awareness of the Divine Presence in human experience is the foundational and elemental basis for the emergence of religious bodies.[1] Again and again in the course of human history, people reaffirm this experiential basis for the development of religious groups.

Human responses to this living flame produce the perennial reassertion of religious vitality. Without this experiential grounding, religious expression would flounder and die.

The universality of this experience occasions a dimension of religious unity transcending the religious particularity involved in the embodiment of this experience in specific religious bodies. However, this human experience of the Divine Presence is necessarily enmeshed in a specific heritage and a particular mode of interpretation.

Due to this synthesis of universal and particular factors in human religious expression, the impact of the causal past needs to be considered to understand the context giving form to a particular religious institution. The lived histories of particular peoples in a particular society inevitably affect the shape of religious expression and the character of religious association. Selective historical retrieval is essential to understand the variety of human religious expression. The examination of the predominant values in a given society is closely related to the consideration of the influence of the causal past, for the values incorporated in a particular human society affect the nature of religious bodies, the relations between various religious bodies, and the relations between various religious bodies and social institutions in the other spheres of the social order.

Finally highly visible and highly articulate religious leaders affect the character and emphases of particular religious movements. Religious virtuosos, who seem able to express the grandeur of their religous visions to their adherents, often have marked influence on their followers. In some instances, these charismatic leaders (to use a term elaborated by Rudolph Sohm and generalized and popularized by Max Weber) demand very substantial allegiance from their followers. They embody the unique particularity of a given religious movement and become causal components which must be considered in the historical retrieval necessary in the analysis of a particular religious movement.

In this chapter the Divine Presence, the impact of the American causal past on contemporary forms of religious organization, and the predominant values in contemporary American society which affect the shape of all religious bodies are considered in some detail. These factors provide the context out of which particular religious movements emerge.

A discussion of the influence of particular religious leaders is not developed here. This discussion would lead to detailed analyses of particular religious emphases, bodies and movements. In this chapter, the context out of which particular emphases bodies and movements emerge is the focus of attention. Since all forms of religious expression are effected by the Divine Presence and the socio-cultural context in which they are set, a consideration of these factors is a necessary component in the analysis of any particular form of American religous expression.

Human religious expression differs in quality and in richness. Some criteria are necessary to evaluate and to assess this dimension of human experience. Although this chapter is primarily analytical, some guidelines to help assess the quality of various forms of religious expression will be suggested in the conclusion of this essay.

THE DIVINE PRESENCE AND RELIGIOUS EXPRESSION

Religious experience is ultimately grounded in human awareness of the

Divine Presence. Although It requires a world for Its completion, this Divine Reality is partially *sui generis*. Consequently, phenomenological, residualistic, or reductionistic interpretations of religious experience are inadequate.

Human awareness of the Divine Presence may occur in any context, for the Divine subjective aim, some of the forms of definiteness embodied in the primordial facet of Its nature, and some components of the creatures of the causal past embodied in the consequent facet of Its nature are immanent in an emerging human occasion.

Human religious experience is evoked by a trans-rational intuition of an ultimate harmony of harmonies which is at the base of things. Moral, cognitive or aesthetic experiences may lead to or enhance religious experience.

Humans may be more or less aware of the Divine Presence, leading to different levels of human religious awareness. The emerging character of the Divine Life Itself may lead to increasingly complex varieties of religious experience.

Although humans may be intuitively aware of the Divine Presence, the nature of the Divine Life and the shape of God-world relations are not self-evident. Humans seeking to interpret their religious experiences employ a variety of modes of thought. Consequently, even though the Divine Presence is ubiquitous in human life, humans interpret their experience of that Presence in markedly different ways. They also synthesize their religious experiences with markedly different lived histories of feeling and meaning.

In this manner humans combine the unity and authenticity of religious experience evoked by the ubiquity of the Divine Presence with diverse interpretations, varying intensity of involvement, and differing historical antecedents to produce a complex array of human religious expression.

THE CAUSAL PAST AND THE VARIETIES OF AMERICAN RELIGIOUS EXPRESSION

Introduction — Individuals, human societies, and human social institutions do not emerge *de novo*. They are the product of a complex past; the actions of individual agents, the persuasion of the Divine Agency, and the coercive and persuasive factors embodied in the causal past condition the shape of contemporary religious expression.

The contemporary American religious situation has been affected by the peculiar character of the American experience. Selective historical retrieval is undertaken here to illumine the bases for the predominant forms of contemporary religious expression.

The Established Church and the Colonial Epoch — Viewed broadly, the established state church pattern predominant in Europe until the past century or so was transplanted from England to the New World by the early colonists. The Pilgrims disagreed with the form of the established church in England, but they did not reject the idea of establishment *per se*. Guided by the fervor of their own religious convictions, they sought to establish a theocracy in the New World encompassing all the dimensions of life.

About the same time, Royalists began to colonize the South, seeking to establish the Church of England in their territories. The idea of religious liberty *per se* was advanced only in Rhode Island and Pennsylvania. Even in these colonies, the lot of those informed by non-Christian thought forms was not easy.

Those colonists active in establishing state churches in the New World were probably motivated by more intense religious convictions than were many in England. Persons with more moderate convictions were probably more likely to remain in their homeland. Relatively satisfied with existing forms of religious expression, they were less likely to attempt radical revisions of existing religious institutions.

The New England colonists frequently appealed to the vision of a New Israel in the wilderness, and they commonly used Old Testament imagery in their interpretations of their experience. They sought to establish a new and true theocracy in the New World. The Southern colonists appealed to a vision of a feudal social pattern and an idealized social order of the high Middle Ages.

The early immigrants were overwhelmingly Protestant, and the vast majority came from northern and western Europe. During the seventeenth and eigtheenth centuries, the colonies became more heterogeneous religiously, for disparate groups coming from various parts of Europe settled in the same colonies. Religious interest waned, and the established churches had many nominal or dormant members.

In 1790 some 40,000 of the nearly 4 million residents of the emerging new republic were Catholic, and a tiny segment (certainly less than 2,000) were Jewish. Furthermore, according to the best estimates available not more than five to ten percent of the population actually belonged to a religious body.

The Doctrine of the Separation of Church and State — The notions of religious liberty, religious pluralism and religious tolerance began to emerge during the latter part of the colonial epoch. Both political prudence and religious conviction contributed to this emergence Some religious people, particularly those associated with churches in the left-wing of the Calvinist movement, preferred broader religious liberty in principle. Many politicians, desiring to spare the fragile evolving republic from the religious wars that had plagued Europe, supported religious liberty on pragmatic grounds.

The First Amendment to the Constitution, which guaranteed religious liberty, gave powerful impetus to the development of these notions. Although the Supreme Court ruled that the Amendment applied only to the Federal Government, its suasive power was considerable. By 1833 the last state with an established church disestablished it, and the American religious experiment was fully launched.

The values of religious liberty, religious tolerance and religious pluralism are necessary correlates of the doctrine of the separation of church and state. These values began to emerge into central components of a religion of America during the nineteenth and twentieth centuries.

These notions are of extreme significance in the American experience, for they sustain the legitimacy of a multiplicity of religious bodies. In the context of the American experience, it became legitimate for one to express one's private faith as one sees fit, so long as the private faith does not challenge some of the basic tenets of the religion of America — separation of church and state, religious liberty, religious pluralism and religious tolerance.

The New Immigrants and the Protestant Monopoly — After the Civil War, immigration patterns began to shift. Many people from southern and eastern Europe began to immigrate to America. Due to the religious composition of these areas of Europe, a vast increase in the Catholic population of the country and a significant increase in the Jewish population took place between 1865 and 1915.

The emancipation of the slaves led to the emergence of the visible black church. Shaped primarily by the Southern experience, and very secondarily by the African experience, the black church had its roots in the Protestant tradition. In a sociological sense, blacks also became "immigrants" during the late nineteenth and early twentieth centuries, for they were beginning to achieve a new status in American life and were beginning to migrate from the rural South to urban centers, both North and South.

Consequently, the basic faith structure in the American experience began to be modified. The predominantly Protestant nation became more religiously diverse, and four major faith groupings emerged — white Protestant, black Protestant, Catholic and Jewish. Other religious bodies are grudgingly tolerated, but they are somewhat suspect.

The vast immigration occurring between 1865 and 1915 contributed to the emergence of many ethnic churches in America. Unable to bring their economic or political institutions with them, the new immigrants were able to transplant their religious institutions in the New World. Although these churches have been qualified and transformed by the American experience, they still bear the marks of their origins. Their adherents have synthesized various religious and cultural traditions to produce unique religious institutions.

The Melting Pot and the New Ethnicity — This vast influx of immigrants produced great contrasts in the emerging industrializing and urbanizing nation. The "melting pot" theory of acculturation evolved in the first third of the twentieth century. According to this popular view, America was to receive and to incorporate into its national life diverse groups and nationalities to fulfill its own life.

This "melting pot" theory began to be transformed after World War II. Ethnic consciousness — always present but somewhat subdued in the earlier epoch — re-emerged, transmuted but not eliminated by the

American experience. Grandchildren sought to rediscover that which the children of immigrants had sought to forget.

Black ethnicity came to the fore in the fifties and sixties, and it contributed to the increasing self-awareness of other ethnic groups. Since churches were an integral part of ethnic identity, these institutions were affected by renewed ethnic consciousness.

To help understand the dynamics of this renewed ethnic consciousness, a distinction should be made between two types of relations people maintain with religious bodies. The first type is *associational*, involving formal membership and participation. The second type is *communal*, involving a broad identity with persons in a particular religio-cultural tradition. In this instance, one may identify vaguely with a particular religio-cultural tradition, but one may be only remotely related to formal religious institutions rooted in that tradition. In this fashion, religious institutions contribute to broad feelings of religio-ethnic identity, but they have minimal direct impact on many of the persons broadly identifying with a particular religious body. The dramatic decline in Catholic church attendance in the past two decades illustrates this phenomenon.

The following section utilizes the selective historical retrieval developed here and data drawn from a number of historical and sociological studies to state formally the predominant values in the American context and to consider their impact on the multifarious forms of American religious expression.

THE PUBLIC FAITH OF AMERICA AND THE VARIETIES OF AMERICAN RELIGIOUS EXPRESSION

Church-State Separation and the Forms of American Religious Expression — To understand the basic notions sustaining the variety of American religious expression, one must discern those aspects of America's public faith fostering the continual emergence of new forms of religious expression. Selected aspects of the religion of America, including the doctrine of church-state separation, religious pluralism, religious tolerance and religious liberty, were noted in the preceding section.

Taken conjointly, these values have contributed to the emergence of the voluntary religious institution as the predominant form of religious organization in the United States. People are free to associate or to disassociate from religious institutions at will. As a result of this situation, religious bodies compete for members in the "marketplace."

Most religious institutions have relaxed criteria for membership. Voluntary religious institutions impose minimal requirements for membership and tolerate wide variations in belief and practice among their members. They stand in sharp contrast to intentional fellowships requiring rigid tests of membership and high levels of discipline.

Religious Virtuosos and the Intentional Fellowship — The "minimal" criteria for membership in religious institutions characteristic of the voluntary church are never satisfying to all. Religious virtuosos, experiencing an intense awareness of the Divine Presence, emerge again and again, calling any who will listen to more intense religious commitment and involvement. This emphasis on heightened intentionality has existed in many times and in many places; it is the basis for Ernst Troeltsch's classic church-sect dichotomy. Although Troeltsch's typology cannot be applied to the American scene without substantial reformulations, it does point to this perennial issue of differential religious interest, involvement and commitment.

In the context of the American experience, the quest for more intense religious commitments and involvements has taken two main forms. In some instances, proponents of heightened intentionality have sought primarily to "renew" existing congregations or denominations.

These emphases may lead to internal disruptions and the establishment of new groups, but they emerge out of and in reaction to existing religious institutions.

In other instances religious virtuosos have launched "new" religious movements, attracting followers wherever they can find them. In most instances a new movement is related to Christianity or Judaism, the predominant religious groups in American culture. In some instances, the new movements draw on another tradition (usually related to the Orient) or transmute drastically the predominant expressions of Christianity or Judaism.

Since the religion of America embraces religious tolerance, pluralism, and voluntarism, it supports these endeavors at a foundational level. The vigor and variety of such movements are limited by the ability of religious leaders to formulate their beliefs and to attract followers. If adherents deviate too markedly from the predominant Judeo-Christian forms of religious expression, they encounter some social pressures, but the state stands ready to protect the adherents of a particular faith community from inordinate societal pressures for conformity.

There are limits to the tolerance and liberty a religious group may enjoy. Legal battles centering on pacificism, public aid to church schools, medical practices, and sexual patterns illustrate the limits imposed on the variety of religious expression by members of the broader American society.

Forms of Religious Expression — As noted in the preceding section, four predominant forms of religious expression have evolved in the context of the American experience: white Protestant, black Protestant, Catholic, and Jewish. According to the religion of America, it is fitting for Americans to express their religious experience in one of these forms. Within Protestantism and Judaism, a variety of sub-forms exist. Consequently, a person may move from one Protestant group to another or from one Jewish group to another and retain one's basic identity as a "Protestant" or a "Jew." Catholics have no such internal diversity, but the multiplicity of Catholic orders provide some bases for internal diversity within Catholicism.

Secular Humanism and Technical Rationalism — Other facets of the religion of America need not be delineated here, for the notions of separation of church and state, religious liberty, religious tolerance, and religious pluralism illumine those aspects of a commonly shared religion of America fostering the variety of American religious expression. Secular humanism and technical rationalism, the other two components of America's public faith, do need to be considered, for they also affect the shape and tone of American religious expression.[2]

Secular humanism presupposes the essential worth and dignity of the human person. Although secular humanism has its roots in the Christian tradition, it has shed the theocentric focus of Christianity. Human worth and dignity, derivative in Christianity, have become primary in secular humanism. It has a more optimistic view of human nature than most Christian interpretations, and it advances a rather positive view about the possibility of human progress.

Secular humanism is deeply embedded in predominant modes of thought in the public schools and in some forms of humanistic psychology.

Technical reason is calculating reason. It is reason divested from any ontic grounding. Technical reason seeks to discover the most efficient means to attain a given end. It is "secular" reason.

Technical rationalism is very pervasive in the American experience. Technical rationalism has fostered the vast extensions of bureaucracies, the use of means-ends analyses, the development of the applied sciences, and the relatively sharp separation of the spheres of the social order. These phenomena are all characteristic of post-traditional societies and are exemplified very forcefully in the American experience.

People blend the religions of America, the religion of America, secular humanism, and technical rationalism in complex and diverse ways. This blending accounts for the co-existence of piety and secularity in the American experience for two centuries or more. America is both very pious and very secular.

From the point of view of theism, secular humanism and technical reason are not adequate to sustain the human spirit. One would anticipate periodic protests against and rejection of secular humanism, technical rationalism, or both. One would also anticipate the re-emergence of various forms of theistic interpretations of human existence. Both phenomena have developed again and again in the context of the American experience.

NOVEL CONTEMPORARY FORMS OF RELIGIOUS EXPRESSION

Introduction — During the nineteen sixties and the nineteen seventies a complex array of religious and quasi-religious movements challenging aspects of both the public faith and also the religions of America has emerged. The re-kindling of interest in Eastern "religions" (if non-theistic interpretations of life can be termed religion), the Civil Rights Movement (which tapped the ideas of liberty, equality, and fraternity in a democracy under God deeply rooted in the religion of America), the re-assertion of ethnic consciousness, the emergence of highly intentional fellowships of many varieties, the development of social action oriented interest groups, the charismatic movement, the emerging social action concerns of churches related to the National Association of Evangelicals, the development of youth oriented religious cults shaped and directed by religious virtuosos (and some charlatans), and the cultivation of persons and groups seeking to "renew" voluntary religious institutions through various group processes and/or the application of organizational development theory and practice have burst onto the scene in the past two decades.

Historical Factors Unique to this Epoch — Introduction —

In addition to the general cultural factors informing the religious ferment of the sixties and seventies two specific historical phenomena must be considered in any analysis of the components contributing to contemporary forms of American religious expression.

The Viet Nam War — The first phenomenon was the Viet Nam War. It spawned a wide variety of protest movements, some of which were religiously based. Protest leaders were able to recruit substantial numbers of followers, for many people were strongly opposed to the War. Although the motives of the followers were often not as pristine as those of the religious leaders, they were attracted to their views on this particular issue.

The Age Structure of the American Population — The second factor was the changing age structure of the American population. This factor requires some explication, for its significance is not as self-evident as the Viet Nam War.

Many interpreters, informed by a wide range of theoretical viewpoints, have noted that during adolescence and early adulthood many people manifest especially intense religious interests and are questing for personal identity. Frequently, youth reject — at one level — significant aspects of their own past history. Questing for meanings they can affirm with integrity, they often reject some of the values and loci of meaning they have known in their childhood. They subject symbols of meaning and belonging — parental associations and values, religious traditions and associations, and commonly held cultural values to challenge and to re-evaluation.

Youth think and feel with vivid intensity, and they are especially concerned with issues of both meaning and belonging. Consequently, they are likely candidates for intentional fellowships of one form or another. Some youth find intentional fellowships very attractive, for they provide powerful loci of meaning and sustain intimate and inclusive human social relations.

The attraction of Eastern religions among the youth of America is twofold. First, they have an aura of novelty and mystery; they permit one to stand against one's own heritage without rejecting all "religion." Second, the meditations and spiritual exercises advanced by many proponents of Eastern religions offer a form of justification by works. Although the understanding of reason informing Eastern religions is not strictly comparable to technical rationalism, there are some interesting parallels; for the guru, spiritual advisor, and religious virtuoso promise to teach their adherents a method they can use to attain spiritual illumination. In this way, one aspect of the public faith of America is compatible with a major component in many Eastern religions.

Even though only a small proportion of American youth has been attracted to intentional religious fellowships in the past two decades, the "pool" from which potential devotees to various forms of intentional fellowships may be drawn has increased dramatically since 1960.

A resume of the changes in the 20-34 age group between 1950 and 2000 will illumine the effect of this factor on the formation of intentional fellowships. These data are summarized in Table One.

Table One. The 20-34 Age Group in the U.S. Population, 1950-2000 and the Percentage Change by Census Period, 1950-2000

	Year					
	1950	1960	1970	1980	1990	2000
Population in thousands	35,716	34,042	42,449	57,065	59,016	52,631
Percent change from previous census	....	-4.7	+24.7	+34.4	+3.4	-10.8

Source: *Statistical Abstract of the United States*, 1973, p. 6 and *Population Estimates and Projections*, Series P-25, no. 541 (Feb., 1975) Table 2, pp. 8-12, U.S. Department of Commerce, Bureau of the Census.

As the data in Table One reveal, the age structure of the population was not conducive to an increase in highly visible intentional fellowships and new varieties of religious expression between 1950 and 1960. The age structure is very favorable for such movements during the 1960-1980 period, and it will be moderately unfavorable during the later part of this century.

The 35-64 age group will increase very substantially between 1980 and 2000. This age mix is more conducive to the voluntary church than to the intentional fellowship. It augers well for the relative vitality of this form of religious organization during this period.

No single factor can explain the variety of American religious expression. Epochal shifts make comparative studies between different historical periods suspect, but the shifting age structure of the American population does affect the shape and tone of American religious expression.

From Public Confrontations to Private Meditation — The esoteric character of some intentional religious movements, human attraction for the novel and/or the esoteric, the implicit or explicit preference for the intentional fellowship by some religious professionals (including many associated with theological faculties), and the news-worthiness of the novel and unique all contribute to interest in these groups. (The very selection of the title of this volume illustrates the way in which some religious professionals are attracted to the intentional fellowship or highly visible sources of vitality.)

Many of these movements are numerically insignificant. Most of them are evanescent. Some will attain stable institutional form and will persist. Those which do survive will possess leadership able to adapt to the institutionalization and routinization characteristic of all religious bodies.

The shift from more politically active to more withdrawn and meditative religious groups has been one of the fascinating phenomena of the nineteen seventies. The visible presence of religious professionals, mass assemblies, public demonstrations and confrontations, commonplace in the nineteen sixties, are almost absent in the late seventies.

Several factors have contributed to this shift in emphasis. In the public realm, the end of the Viet Nam War, which galvanized and focused much religiously motivated social action, undermined the most visible unifying social issue. In addition, the successful enactment of much civil rights legislation has led to new and more complex problems making it difficult to focus on dramatic issues.

A decline in church membership and reductions in benevolences have also affected religious activity, for the funding of social action projects has been reduced sharply in most denominations in the past decade.

The aging of the population has also affected the shape of religious activity. The quest for personal identity and integrity requires more than public activity; it also requires intellectual reflection, meditation, and privacy. In contrast to the activist mood of a decade ago, the inner introspective side of the quest for theological and spiritual maturation has come to the fore.

RELIGIOUS LEADERSHIP AND THE VARIETY OF AMERICAN RELIGIOUS EXPRESSION

The final factor contributing to the variety of American religious expression is the activity and interpretation of particular people who provide religious leadership, lay or professional. As noted earlier, this factor is formally recognized in this essay, but it is not elaborated. To do so would lead beyond a framework for interpretation and toward a consideration of a particular form of religious expression in the context of the American experience.

A CONCLUDING NOTE

The varieties of American religious expression receiving most attention are highly visible and highly intentional fellowships. Some may be sources of vitality, but others are detrimental to the enhancement of human life. Some criteria for evaluation not inherent in the manifestation of particular forms of religous organization are needed.

This chapter has focused on analytic and/or descriptive rather than on evaluative dimensions. However, some evaluation is necessary for two reasons. First, the fact and value dimensions of experience are interrelated. Second, many intentional fellowships may be sources of religious vitality, but their overall contribution to human life may be more negative than positive. The following questions may be raised about any religious group:

1) Does it maintain some balance between individuation and participation? Is the individual being suppressed and consumed by the group or, conversely, does the individual have some opportunity to attain some distance from the group?

2) Are members of the group seeking rational interpretation of its dynamic dimensions? Is such reflection encouraged, or is it put down as "head-tripping?"

3) Do the members of the group have some sense of concern for the larger whole of which they are a part? Do issues of social justice and of the principles of justice emerge?

4) Do the members of the group balance the intentional dimension of their lives with the destiny dimension, i.e., the way in which the causal past qualifies and conditions the present and the future?

5) Do the members have some appreciation of institutions as well as of fellowships?

One final observation. Inordinate concern with "vitality" may overplay this aspect of human experience. A fitting balance between conservation and innovation and between the dynamic and formal dimensions of experience is desirable.

Most clergy serving Protestant churches affiliated with the National Council of Churches relate to voluntary churches. Their congregations are not as visible or as controversial as are intentional fellowships and may not be as "vital" as some of the groups discussed here. Nonetheless, in their efforts to deal with humans at various levels of religious intentionality, these clergy in quiet and undramatic ways may be contributing as much or more to the vitality of religious institutions and to the well-being of humankind as the highly visible leaders of intentional fellowships and highly promoted causes.

Without the contributions of persons serving voluntary churches to the maintenance of the church as an institution, the Christian movement would lose its focus and its tradition in a generation.

Notes and References

1. This understanding differentiates the interpretation of American religious experience developed here from most contemporary social scientific analyses. These analyses are usually rooted in Marxist, Freudian, Durkheimian, Weberian or Husserlian frameworks of interpretation. They are either reductionist, residualistic or strictly phenomenological.

2. For a more extended discussion of the religions of America and America's public faith, see W. Widick Schroeder, Victor Obenhaus, Larry A. Jones and Thomas Sweetser, *Suburban Religion* (Chicago: Center for the Scientific Study of Religion, 1974) pp. 17-31. This volume also contains substantial bibliographic references.

Space limitations have precluded extensive citations in this chapter or explicit references to alternative modes of interpretation. In addition to the citations in *Suburban Religion,* the author found the following volumes especially useful in considering the topic of this chapter:

Robert Bellah, *The Broken Covenant,* (New York: Seabury, 1975).

Robert Benne and Philip Hefner, *Defining America,* (Philadelphia: Fortress Press, 1974).

Charles Y. Glock and Robert N. Bellah, eds. *The New Religious Consciousness* (Berkeley: University of California Press, 1976).

Sidney Mead, *The Old Religion in the Brave New World,* (Berkeley: University of California Press, 1977).

Robert Wuthnow, *The Consciousness Reformation,* (Berkeley: University of California Press, 1976).

Irving I. Zaretsky and Mark P. Leone, eds., *Religious Movements in Contemporary America,* (Princeton, N.J.: Princeton University Press, 1974).

Introduction to Chapter 15

Chapter 15 is the final essay focusing on the life of religious institutions. I am affiliated with the United Church of Christ, and the seminary on whose faculty I served is a closely related seminary of this denomination. I was affiliated with the Congregational-Christian Churches, one of the merger partners discussed in this essay before the United Church of Christ was formed in 1957. Consequently, I have been a participant observer of its emerging life since the new denomination was formed.

As the constructive portions of this essay and other essays in this volume suggest, I am more sympathetic with beliefs and practices associated with the Congregational-Christian Churches wing of the merged bodies. Ecclesiastical bureaucrats responsible for promoting the well-being of the denomination generally have tried to minimize the persistent contrasts in styles and emphases between churches rooted in the two traditions, but differences in beliefs and practices between former Evangelical and Reformed congregations and former Congregational-Christian congregations persist. Some denominational leaders have recently proposed a new initiative to promote a renewed biblical emphasis. This effort will likely highlight the differences extant between persons committed to kerygmatic approaches and to apologetic approaches to the interpretation of the Christian movement. Whether the effort, if it is in fact undertaken, will contribute positively to the quest for denominational unity is moot. As the constructive portion of this chapter reveals, I would prefer to emphasize other notions to provide denominational identity, Legitimate theological pluralism and congregational autonomy do not seem to be among the beliefs current denominational leadership want to accentuate.

This chapter originally appeared in *The United Church of Christ: Studies in Identity and Polity,* edited by Dorothy C. Bass and Kenneth B. Smith.

CHAPTER 15

The United Church of Christ: The Quest for Denominational Identity and the Limits of Pluralism

Introduction

The theme of this essay was suggested by four events the author recently experienced. These events will serve to illustrate the problem of unity and diversity in the United Church of Christ in this historical epoch. They will be recounted anecdotally to introduce the analysis and interpretation of some issues in the contemporary life of the United Church of Christ. In this analysis, selective historical retrieval is utilized to illumine the contemporary situaton. In the concluding sections, some constructive observations emphasizing the normative and practical desirability of congregational polity to help define denominational identity and to shape the limits of pluralism, the merits of theological diversity, and the desirability of maintaining distinctions between the community of faith and the community of politics are advanced.

The first event was a meeting of a Ministerial Advisory Board of the Chicago Theological Seminary. The immediate topic was a statement signed by a group of United Church seminary or divinity school professors calling for the development of a statement of faith for the denomination. Almost half of the signatories taught at one of the three seminaries having had close historic ties with the Evangelical and Reformed denomination, the denomination uniting with the Congregational-Christian Churches in 1957 to form the United Church of Christ.

The setting served to highlight the problem of denominational identity and the limits of pluralism, for this proposal was undoubtedly a response to a widely felt need for a formulation that would contribute to denominational identity. How to develop a statement that both would do justice to the plurality of theological outlooks currently extant in the UCC and also would promote a central identity—unless the acknowledgement of openness, the primacy of congregational polity, the legitimacy of diverse modes of interpretation of the Christian movement, and the manifestation of an irenic spirit were at the center of the statement—was no small task! It was possible that the very effort to develop a statement of faith could be a process fostering denominational identity, but it was also possible that such an effort would accentuate the differences already extant within the denomination.

In the course of the discussion at this meeting, a distinguished and learned denominational leader whose roots in the Evangelical and Reformed tradition are very deep made some observations about Chicago Theological Seminary graduates and about other denominational matters. He noted that in ordination examinations CTS graduates did pretty well on questions dealing with God and Jesus, but they did not do very well on questions involving liturgical practices and the sacraments. He went on to criticize the emphasis often placed on the involvement of seminary faculty in the American Academy of Religion (the learned society in the field of religious studies dominated by faculty members in departments of religious studies in colleges and universitites and in university based divinity schools). He further criticized most denominational public policy pronouncements for their too frequent convergence with proposals offered by Americans for Democratic Action, the political action body dominated by people in the left wing of the Democratic party. He finally criticized the laxity of an ordaining body for ordaining persons whose theological views were quite unorthodox.

Others in the group responded to his comments by defending the practices he criticized. As it happened, all but one of these respondents had their roots in the Congregational-Christian denomination.

The second event was a conversation with a member of a local United Church of Christ formed by the organic merger of two local congregations. One of these congregations had been a Congregational-Christian church prior to the union, and the other had been an Evangelical and Reformed Church.

The person observed that "The E & R's have taken over. Many of the Congregationists have died or transferred their membership to another church, and the people we have been attracting are a different kind of people."

When asked what he meant by " . . . different kind of people," he responded, "Well, there are a lot of people with German names, and there are more working people. We don't have as many professional people as the old Congregational Church did."

The third event was a conversation with a person who had attended a former Evangelical and Reformed Church in Pennsylvania prior to her husband's corporate transfer to the Chicago area. She was asked what church she was attending here. She replied, "Oh, the ____________ Lutheran Church."

When asked if she had gone to a United Church of Christ here, she said, "Yes, our family attended the ____________ Congregational Church (a United Church of Christ affiliated church which had voted to retain its original name), but we didn't feel at home there. Their order of service was different than ours, and we didn't feel comfortable with the people. The Lutheran Church is more like the one we left."

The final experience was a conversation with a person whose small UCC church with roots in the Congregational tradition had merged with a nearby larger UCC church whose roots were in the Evangelical and Reformed tradition.

When asked whether he was going to join the church with which his congregation had voted to merge, he replied, "I don't think so. Their service is so much more formal than ours, and the minister is too authoritarian for me. We're going to look around for a church more like our old one."

1. Historical Antecedents[1]

These incidents reveal that after twenty-eight years practices, feelings, and meanings embodied in the different causal pasts of the uniting denominations persist. The contrasts have been attenuated during this time, but the persistence of many local congregations embodying values sustained by one or the other of the uniting bodies and the persistence of theological seminaries which continue to reflect the diversity of the two groups sustain some of the historical contrasts. The recitation of these anecdotes should not be construed to imply that the union has not had numerous positive consequences, but the observations do point to persistent problems. Various survey research data point in the same direction.[2]

The issues revealed by these anecdotes are important; for to establish its identity and to evoke the loyalty of its adherents, a social institution must evolve a set of core meanings and practices which its adherents affirm. The foundational meanings a given group shares are often embodied in written form, but they partly transcend formal codification.

The written forms themselves represent an effort to interpret the practices in which human beings engage. In fact, many of the most fundamental notions people hold are so foundational they are not often articulated and are not easily formulated; these notions are often embodied in specialized practices which, in turn, serve to evoke a penumbra of feeling and meaning.

The difficulty in articulating our most fundamental notions is grounded in the nature of our experience. We habitually think by contrasting the presence of something with its absence. Our foundational notions are *always* present, so the needed contrast to evoke our awareness can be evoked only by a negative judgment, imagining the absence of that which is present. These foundational notions can range from the unspoken notions that unite the members of a social group to metaphysical notions which apply to all actual entities.

This essay does not address the quest for metaphysical propositions. It addresses the relatively easier task of examining some of the contrasting and unifying meanings and practices embodied in the United Church of Christ. In this instance, the meanings and practices are more visible, and the contrasts leading to understanding are more readily evoked.

Members of a religious institution share some common fundamental meanings and loyalties, and they engage in some common practices. At the same time, they differ in some meanings and loyalties, and they differ in some practices. Some of the beliefs, loyalties and practices they share come from other salient loci—familial, ethnic, status, economic, political, and cultural. Sometimes the contribution of the various spheres of the social order to a person's matrix of practice, feeling and meaning is fairly clear-cut; more often the matrix of practice, feeling and meaning contributing to a person's life experience is vague and diffuse. It is a mistake to confuse clarity in thought with priority in influence.

The United Church of Christ is a so called "main-line" Protestant denomination in the United States. Its leaders participate in a variety of inter-denominational activities, and the large majority of its churches are "voluntary churches" in contrast to "intentional fellowships." In a "voluntary church" criteria for membership are relatively lax. In an "intentional fellowship" criteria for membership are rigorous.[3]

In the voluntary church members usually join because they "will" to belong. These churches tolerate considerable latitude in belief and practice, and church discipline in the congregation is minimal. Individual members often differ substantially in their commitment to the formal beliefs and practices of their congregation and in their degree of involvement in their church.

These patterns are common to many Protestant denominations in the United States, and they are the distinguishing marks of what it means to be a main-line denomination. Illustratively, the United Church of Christ, the Presbyterian Church (U.S.A.), the United Methodist Church, the Protestant Episcopal Church, the American Baptist Churches, the Lutheran Church in America, and the Disciples of Christ are main-line denominations.

However, mainline Protestant denominations in the United States differ among themselves, based on their polities and on their particular lived histories. Congregational, presbyterian and episcopal polities produce different patterns of association and different types of formal authority. Connectional and hierarchical relations loom largest in churches with episcopal polities, are intermediate in churches with presbyterian polities, and are least significant in churches with congregational polities. Becaues the United Church of Christ has a congregational polity, local churches may differ substantially in faith and order and in life and work.

Two factors contribute to the uniqueness of the United Church of Christ among denominations in the United States. First, although they were both "Anglo-American" in origin, the Congregational-Christian denomination had its primary roots among English speaking people in England and in the New World. Although indigenous to America, the origins of what was later to become the Evangelical and Reformed Church denomination are found among eighteenth-century German speaking immigrants. It was influenced much more by continental European churches and clergy in its formative period than was the Congregational-Christian denomination. Liturgical and theological emphases appropriated from the complex interplay of Lutheranism, Zwinglianism , and Dutch Calvinism in eighteenth-century America contributed to the markedly different historical roots of this denomination. Wesleyan influences affected this body in the nineteenth century.

Second, the two merging denominations had different polities. The Congregational-Christian denomination had a congregational polity, emphasizing the autonomy of the local congregation in matters of faith and order as well as life and work. This polity accentuated decision-making by local congregations and minimized the authority of denominational agencies and instrumentalities and denominational leaders. The Evangelical and Reformed denomination had a presbyterian polity, emphasizing the connectional character of the church and giving more formal authority to denominational agencies and instrumentalities and to denominational leadership.

The United Church of Christ retained the congregational polity of the Congregational-Christian churches, but the relative importance of associations, conferences, denominational leadership and national agencies and instrumentalities has generally been enhanced in the new denomination.

(Congregational-Christian churches were adament on the polity issue. Without the acceptance of congregational polity by the Evangelical and Reformed Church, the 1957 union would not have been approved by the Congregational-Christian churches.)

Because of their closer ties to the dominant English settlers in the seventeenth and eighteenth centuries and to the intellectual elites of American culture in the nineteenth and twentieth centuries, Congregational clergy both influenced and were more forcefully influenced by intellectual currents in the broader culture than Evangelical and Reformed clergy. Harvard and Yale provided indigenous theological education for Congregational clergy in the colonial epoch.

The 1931 union of the Congregational and Christian churches was a merger of indigenous American bodies; but the Congregational body was the much larger partner, and its style dominated the merged body. Both groups had a congregational polity.

Because the German Reformed Church and the Evangelical Church emerged among German speaking immigrants in the eighteenth century, these groups had to rely more heavily on continental European educated clergy immigrants for their leadership in their formative days. By the middle of the nineteenth century many clergy were educated in the United States; but aided by substantial immigration from Germany after the Civil War, German ethnic identity persisted during the nineteenth and on into the twentieth century. Indeed, the 1934 merger of the Evangelical and German Reformed denominations to form the Evangelical and Reformed Church was facilitated by their common ethnic heritage. Earlier perceived differences had been reduced by the acculturation process in America.

The 1957 merger of these two bodies to form the United Church of Christ would not have been predicted by most sociologists, for the social, economic and cultural differences between the two merging bodies were very substantial. Salient socio-cultural and religious contrasts between the Congregational-Christian and the Evangelical and Reformed denominations at the time of the union warrant enumeration, for they help illumine the tensions prompting much of the current discussions about pluralism in the United Church of Christ and accentuate the urgency of the quest for identity. (To be sure, subsequent developments in the new denomination also contributed to these tensions. Some of these factors will be considered later in this essay.)

(1) *Ethnic and racial character:* The German roots of the Evangelical and Reformed denomination gave this denomination a distinctive ethnic flavor. German was widely used in many churches well into the twentieth century, and the denomination had many more first and second generation immigrants than did the Congregational-Christian churches. A Germanic paternalism was common in pastor-congregation relations. The English and

American roots of the Congregational-Christian Churches placed the denomination in the center of predominately white Anglo-Saxon Protestant bodies. Although each uniting group had small proportions of blacks, both were predominately white denominations.

(2). *Socio-economic status:* The membership of the Congregational-Christian denomination ranked higher in various indices of socio-economic status than did the membership of the Evangelical and Reformed denomination. The Congregational-Christian denomination had a higher proportion of college graduates, and its members had a higher median income.

(3.) *Size and geographical distribution:* The Congregational-Christian denomination was almost twice the size of the Evangelical and Reformed denomination at the time of the union. The Congregational-Christian membership was about 1,400,000; the Evangelical and Reformed membership was about 735,000.

The Congregational-Christian membership was concentrated in New England and the Upper Midwest, with substantial membership in the rest of the Midwest, the Mountain states and the West Coast. Evangelical and Reformed membership was concentrated in Pennsylvania, the Upper Midwest, and the area around St. Louis, with smaller groups in the South, the rest of the Midwest and the Far West.

(4.) *Theological emphases:* Reflecting their complex relation to Lutheran, Zwinglian, and Dutch Reformed theological movements in Europe, the liturgical and confessional emphasis of the Evangelical and Reformed denomination sustained liturgical patterns emphasizing the sacraments and a fusion of Lutheran and Reformed patterns of worship.
The Heidelberg Catechism loomed large it its life, and the denomination was not so deeply affected by the liberalism which Congregationalism both helped shape and also shared in the nineteenth and twentieth centuries. At the same time, the Heidelberg Catechism was given an experiential, pious and conciliating interpretation by the early leaders of the "German Reformed Church."

The Congregational-Christian churches also traced their roots to the Reformed tradition, but the Lutheran liturgical and sacramental influences impinging on the German Reformed Church were not a part of the tradition.

At the time of the union, this Reformed influence had been greatly modified by liberalism and the Social Gospel, to which Congregationalists contributed so much. The liturgical and sacramental emphases were more diffuse and less central to the life of many Congregational-Christian churches.

Both denominations demanded an educated clergy, and in recent times both college and seminary degrees were normally a requisite for ordination. However, the substance of the expected education and the institutions providing it varied substantially from denomination to denomination.

Congregational-Christian clergy were educated in a broader range of theological schools than were Evangelical and Reformed clergy. Most of the latter were educated at one of the three Evangelical and Reformed seminaries, Eden, Lancaster, and Mission House. Congregational clergy were more likely to be exposed to so called secular education, for they were more likely to attend university related theological schools.

Several factors contributed to the greater theological and liturgical commonality of the Evangelical and Reformed clergy: a common ethnic heritage and common educational experiences; a relatively small movement of clergy of other denominations into the denomination compared to the Congregational-Christian denomination; and a connectional polity, which brought them into closer relation with their colleagues and which limited the diversity in belief and practice between congregations.

Both denominations had statements of faith, but the relatively less formalistic and diffuse statement of the Congregational-Christian churches, coupled with its congregational polity and the factors just cited, contributed to greater variety in belief and practice in the Congregational-Christian denomination than in the Evangelical and Reformed denomination.

(5.) *Polity:* No issue was more important to the Congregational-Christian participants in the union discussions than the polity issue. The principle of congregational autonomy was very important to members of the Congregational-Christian denomination. The interplay between local congregations and associations of Congregational churches has a long and complex history that need not be rehearsed here. By the time of the merger the congregational polity had contributed to the variety of beliefs and practices found in the Congregational-Christian churches, for local congregations had wide latitude in formulating particular beliefs and in fostering particular patterns of worship. Similarly, lay persons and clergy knew that in their public statements regional and national bodies were speaking for themselves and not necessarily for a particular church. This recognition blunted conflict and sustained diversity in beliefs, patterns of worship, modes of education, and relations with the world, for people recognized the legitimacy of alternative beliefs and practices—so long as the principle of local autonomy was sustained.

As a consequence of this polity, a rather loose relation existed between local Congregational-Christian churches and denominational agencies, instrumentalities, and theological schools. Most of them were responsible for raising at least part of their funds through their own efforts, and they enjoyed considerable independence in thought and action.

The Evangelical and Reformed denomination was a connectional church of a presbyterian type. Its synods played a major role in shaping the life of the church, and its general synod provided substantial direction to the life of the denomination. Its agencies and instrumentalities were creations of the church and were more closely related to the denomination as a whole than was the case for Congregational-Christian counterparts.

Because of their connectional associations, local congregations—particularly local pastors—felt more closely bound by the pronouncements of the broader collective associations than did their Congregational-Christian counterparts.

(6.) *Social action concerns:* The Congregational churches were deeply involved in the Social Gospel movement in liberal American Protestantism in the latter part of the nineteenth century and the first part of the twentieth century. This movement had waned before the union of the Congregational-Christian and Evangelical and Reformed denominations in 1957, but many Congregationalists continued to express strong interests in social justice issues and in various programs which they felt would further the cause of social justice.

The Evangelical and Reformed denomination was touched by these concerns (indeed, the most distinguished spokesperson on social issues in mainline American Protestant Christianity in the period prior to the union was Reinhold Neibuhr, a member of this denomination), but the relative isolation of the denomination from the Social Gospel movement and its synodical structure resulted in limited involvement in social action concerns compared to the Congregational-Christian denomination.

In sum, the two uniting denominations had substantially different lived experiences and memories. Relatively speaking, compared to the Evangelical and Reformed denomination at the time of the union, the Congregational-Christian denomination was closer to the center of the white Anglo-Saxon Protestant establishment, had a membership of higher socio-economic status, was more diverse in its theological and ethical outlook, was less concerned with liturgical and sacramental issues, was less closely related to the Reformed tradition in its current life and work, and was more concerned with social action and social witness.

Its congregational polity contrasted with the presbyterian polity of the Evangelical and Reformed denomination. This form of polity promotes a collegial style of leadership, for denominational leaders must rely primarily on persuasion in promoting their views.

The Contemporary Situation

Introduction—Most Americans have internalized core values derived from facets of the public faith of America to define relations between various faith communities. The separation of church and state and the concomitant values of religious liberty, religious tolerance, and religious pluralism are deeply internalized by the vast majority of the American people. These Enlightenment notions help define relations between and within religious bodies, for they deflate any magisterial propensities of a particular religious body and promote an irenic spirit.

Conflicts and tensions in the broader society have exacerbated internal tensions within the UCC, for UCC people have entertained contrasting views on a variety of public policy issues and on the appropriate relation between the church and the public sphere.

The congregational polity of the United Church of Christ contributes both to its unity and to its diversity. Because of the autonomy of the local congregation, a given church has substantial latitude in defining its core beliefs, its style of worship, its level of discipline, its educational program, its pattern of administration and governance, its expression of social witness, and its evangelical emphasis. In this way local congregations both affirm their distinctiveness and also contribute to diversity in the denomination. Congregational polity and the appreciation of theological diversity thus provide unifying values for the denomination.

Status and ethnic homogeneity in local congregations—Most local congregations are relatively homogeneous by ethnicity and by social status. This reality is partly a function of the territorial base of most congregations and partly a function of the self-selection process by which persons decide to affiliate with a particular church.[4]

In American communities the most important single factor contributing to neighborhood homogeneity is the cost of housing. Because of the likelihood that housing stock of comparable value will be located in the same geographical area, persons of comparable economic class tend to live in a given neighborhood. Because social status and economic class have a very high positive correlation in the United States, people living in a given neighborhood are likely to share common value orientations and common life styles.

In addition, people of the same ethnic background tend to cluster in particular neighborhoods, especially in the larger cities. Blacks, Germans, Swedes, Hispanics, Poles, etc. are frequently dominant in a given geographical area.

In addition to neighborhood homogeneity, human intentionality also contributes to relatively homogeneous local congregations by race, ethnicity and social status. In the context of the American experience many Protestants shop for a church. They decide to join a given congregation for a wide variety of reasons—the appearance of the sanctuary; the perceived quality of the worship service, including the music, sermon and liturgy; the educational program; the quality of group life; their assessment of the lifestyle of the members; their interest in a given denomination; their assessment of the substance and style of the clergy person; their evaluation of the formal and informal beliefs of a given congregation; their relations with current members; their concurrence with the social outreach and social justice emphasis of the church. All of these factors and others contribute to a potential member's decision to become a member of a particular local congregation.

These ecological and purposive factors contribute to the relative social and ethnic homogeneity of a particular congregation, but they also contribute to the heterogeneity of the United Church of Christ as a whole by race, ethnicity, theological beliefs, worship patterns, liturgical practices, and educational, evangelical, social witness emphases, and, to a lesser extent, by social status. (Because of the selective involvement of various social status groups in religious institutions in America and the higher social status of the Congregational-Christian wing of the denomination, the denomination is underrepresented in lower status persons compared to the population as a whole.)

The quest for denominational identity—As a result of this complex interplay of historical antecedents and contemporary racial, ethnic, socioeconomic, theological and liturgical factors affecting both faith and order and also life and work, the United Church of Christ is a denomination seeking an identity.

The call for "statements of faith" is one manifestation of the quest for denominational identity.

Although the issue of beliefs is central, two related issues are salient in the contemporary quest for denominational identity: polity and the relation between the community of faith and the community of politics.

Members of the ecclesiastical bureaucracy experience this diversity most forcefully, for they have to deal with clergypersons and laypersons related to the diversity of local congregations comprising the United Church of Christ. The elbow room provided by congregational polity amongst a varied constituency permits substantial variety in faith and order and in life and work between local congregations.

Pressures mount when those various constituencies want their views of proper beliefs and practices to be adopted by the denomination as a whole. Granted the amorphous meaning of "the denomination as a whole" in a denomination with a congregational polity, many persons do look to representatives of associations, conferences, and national bodies to speak, in some sense, for the denomination. The president of the church and the General Synod become focal points for these debates and concerns. One suspects these issues are more important for persons whose roots are in the Evangelical and Reformed wing of the denomination, for these matters are more important in denominations with a connectional polity than in denominations with a congregational polity.

The polity issue continues to be a subject of debate and discussion. The involvement of representatives of associations, conferences and national bodies in the life of local congregations and other church bodies illustrates the fuzziness of the relations between various bodies in the denomination. In part, the emerging patterns represent a more or less conscious response to a denomination composed of churches with memories of both congregational and presbyterian polities.

For example, in the recent inauguration of a president of the Chicago Theological Seminary, the minister of the Chicago Metropolitan Association of the Illinois Conference of the United Church of Christ installed the president. Because the seminary is an autonomous body with a self-perpetuating Board of Trustees, the authority behind this installation was unclear. Historically, it would have been more fitting for a representative of the Evangelical and Reformed Church to install a president of one of their seminaries than for a representative of the Congregational-Christian churches to install a president of the Chicago Theological Seminary, an institution closely related to but organically separated from the Congregational-Christian churches.

The ecumenical movement is most likely to evoke a major debate about polity in the coming years. Denominational leaders have been actively exploring merger possibilities with the Disciples of Christ and are in continued dialogue with other bodies involved in the Consultation on Church Union discussions. In fact, COCU delegates have recently recommended that the United Church of Christ join the other COCU discussants to create a new inclusive denomination of more than twenty million members. Diverse views on the merits of these mergers exist in the denomination, but the mechanisms by which individuals and and local congregations may express their views on those matters have been fragile and/or non-existent. To date, contributions by local congregations to these discussions have been minimal. Denominational representatives have been the visible discussants. And, the authority they possess to engage in such discussions is much fuzzier than it would be in denominations with presbyterian or episcopal polities.

The final salient issue contributing to contemporary discussions about unity and diversity in the United Church of Christ is the relation between communities of faith and communities of politics. The articulate leadership in associations, conferences and national bodies has often been in the vanguard of the promotion of specific public policy issues. The recent endorsement of the first draft of the American Catholic Bishops' pastoral letter on the American economy by the president of the denomination is a case in point.[5] While few would quarrel with the efforts to alleviate poverty, the particular policy proposals advanced in the pastoral letter to reduce poverty and the interpretations made of the more affluent are certainly subject to question on many grounds.

The sanctuary movement, in which some local congregations have voted to shelter illegal refugees from the conflicts in Central America, represents the coalescence of the community of faith and the community of politics on one public policy issue. It illustrates the tensions embodied in the social action concerns of the denomination and raises forcefully the question of the appropriate relation between the community of faith and the community of politics.

This historical retrieval has suggested some of the roots of the multiple diversities present within the United Church of Christ and has suggested the reasons for the persistence of the diversity. In the midst of this dynamic, emergent situation, the United Church of Christ is seeking to establish an identity and to explore the limits of diversity.

In human affairs even socio-historical retrieval at a relatively low level of abstraction reflects an implicit constructive interpretation. However, a relative distinction can be made between analytical and constructive work. In the final portion of this essay, constructive observations are dominant, for an assessment of the issues examined in this section is undertaken.

A Constructive Assessment

In defense of theological diversity[6]—Many in the Congregational-Christian wing of this denomination dealt with the question of unity and diversity in the nineteenth and twentieth centuries both interpretatively and organizationally.

On the interpretive side, a primal conviction usually underlay the varieties of theological formulations they developed. No formulation could adequately characterize the depth of the human experience of Divine immanence in the world. Complimentariness and not exclusivity of theological interpretation was a dominant motif in this latter day Congregational heritage.

Congregationalists felt that the autonomy of the local congregation was closely related to this primal idea. No presbytery, no bishop, no so-called doctor of the church was to tell a local congregation what it *must* believe to become a part of the fellowship of Congregational churches. The Divine Spirit working through individuals gathered together in local congregations was central. Scripture and tradition—including non-Christian religious traditions and so-called secular culture—were taken seriously by the most, but they were not the ultimate focus of authority.

At its best, the liberal spirit embodied in this view is irenic. One is willing to live amid substantial diversity of theological interpretations, respecting other views and expecting one's own views also to be respected. At its core, the liberal spirit affirms that the method of open inquiry and free discussion of alternative theological interpretations of human experience is more important than any particular content, important as particular content may be.

This inclusivistic and irenic viewpoint is not congenial to all. Indeed, some, informed by alternative viewpoints, will have to resist this view if they are going to affirm their own positions with integrity.

Some members of the Biblical Witness Fellowship, a contemporary UCC group calling for the exclusiveness of the Bible as the focus of authority and affirming the primacy of the Reformed tradition, clearly understand this dilemma. If people are persuaded that the Biblical forms are *the* forms God in the height of Its freedom has decided to employ to convey Its revelation to humankind, apologetic theology must be rejected. In their eyes, those who employ it are highly suspect, if not downright unfaithful.

In this dilemma one can discern one of the limits of diversity. How does one reconcile the view that one may use biblical forms to illumine God's relations with humans with the view that one *must* use biblical forms to do so?

If one is seeking to draw a circle which includes another, and that person is drawing a circle which excludes you, it is very difficult to effect a reconciliation. At this point liberals must fight, for they must insist on the legitimacy of alternative interpretations within *their* community of faith. One could expand the list of illustrations dealing with the issue of inclusivity and exclusivity, but the central problem has been illumined by the question of the authority of scripture.

Unless one at the foundational level affirms the legitimacy of a variety of ways to abstract from the matrix of meaning and feeling embodied in the Christian movement and retains at least a residual skepticism about the adequacy of his/her own formulations, theological diversity and the liberal intent are in jeopardy. The alternative is an insistence on the unequivocal legitimacy of a particular theological method and/or interpretation of religious experience and the Christian movement.

Religious experience is more foundational and fundamental than any abstractions derived from it. Particular liturgical practices and particular linguistic symbols can never exhaust the meaning of religious experience. Efforts to state formally our foundational religious experience are necessary, but they are laden with ambiguity. Cognitive formulations are needed to interpret and to deepen our religious experience, but these forms can never exhaust the experience.

Ritual and emotion are prior to beliefs and rational theologies. Rational theologies emerge with the attempts of our ancestors and ourselves to interpret and to bring coherence to the religious practices and beliefs in which we find ourselves immersed.

Religious institutions seek to bear witness to the Divine persuasive presence amongst humankind. The primacy of the Divine Spirit and the centrality of human religious experience are basic to this interpretation. Religious institutions are evoked and sustained by human awareness of the Divine Presence in one's own experience. By employing the analogical method, one can empathize with comparable experiences in other human beings.

Freedom is at the very base of things, for every new emergent event stamps its own authenticity on the data it appropriates in the process of becoming. This basic freedom and the persuasive facets of the Divine Nature have implications for the style of religious institutions. Persuasion and not coercion ought to be the way of religious institutions. Religious liberty is a prized value and should be guarded preciously.

The diversity of religious institutions on this planet and the internal diversity within the Christian movement are a result of the interplay between the physical and conceptual sides of our experience. Abstract thought seeks generalizations and seeks to probe the universals embodied in particular experience. Religion seeks to synthesize the more abstract side of human experience with the concreteness of particular religious traditions which are the bearers of more specialized feelings and meanings with which conceptual feelings are intertwined.

In defense of congregational polity—The primacy of liberty and persuasiveness in religious matters and the multiplicity of religious traditions are fittingly synthesized in religious institutions with a congregational polity. A given gathered community has substantial latitude to shape its own patterns of both faith and order and also life and work. Persons in these institutions may learn from other religious communities, but they are not bound by their beliefs and practices. Mutual respect and complimentariness do not preclude diversity and some conflict. Indeed, from this point of view, one must resist those who insist so forcefully on the rightness of their own views that they want to deny others admission to the fellowship.

Many who prize congregational autonomy would not affiliate with a religious institution having any other form of polity, for they believe that the voluntary associational principle is the most fitting form of religious association. They hold that this principle respects the primacy of persuasion and liberty in religious matters and sustains most fittingly a collegial style of religious leadership. They also believe congregational polity legitimates diversity of belief and practice in different gathered communities who voluntarily will to relate to other congregationally based faith communities.

Ecumenical efforts to effect an organic unity of the various religious institutions embodied in the Christian movement are highly suspect. One may certainly support many types of functional co-operation between Christian bodies and between Christian bodies and other religious and secular groups, but one should oppose an organic unity of the various faith communities related to the Christian movement unless they are prepared to affirm a congregational polity. There is no evidence to suggest that either many of the denominations involved in COCU discussions or the Roman Catholic Church would consent to this form of polity.

A common sharing of the awareness of the Divine immanence is an adequate basis for the unifying facet of religious expression. Diversity in visible ways is a fitting check on imperialistic tendencies and on the inordinate press for uniformity in belief and practice, with resultant inordinate limitations on religious liberty.

The voluntary association of local congregations provides both for a broader relationality and also for legitimate diversity in belief and practice. At this inter-congregational level, some contrasts between the beliefs and practices of local congregations who associate with each other is fitting and proper. These relations can serve to remind the local constituent bodies of the universality of the experience of the Divine presence and the diversity of particular modes of expression and interpretation of that experience. They can also serve to inform the related congregations of issues they may need to consider in their own lives.

Local congregations, informed by an irenic spirit and represented by learned clergy persons, can sustain, support and interpret the theological diversity of various churches in a complementary fashion.

In defense of a separation between communities of faith and communities of politics—The relation between communities of faith and communities of politics has been a perennial issue in the Christian movement. Among some people in the denomination implicit political orthodoxy and an explicit theological pluralism seem to provide a basis for denominational identity.

The emergence of various forms of liberation theology in the 1960s and 1970s exacerbates the question of the relation between the community of faith and the community of politics, for in many of these forms of theology a particular theological formulation is wedded with a mode of social analysis and social interpretation which *insists* on the coalescence of the community of faith with a particular community of politics.

One must challenge their views of the relation of theological understanding and moral action. In most instances it is very difficult to derive prudential moral judgments directly from theological understanding. Most of the time persons participating in the same community of faith may legitimately disagree on many particular public policy issues.

Most people long for as much harmony of life with life as is possible under the conditions of existence. Almost all members of Christian religious groups seek to attain as much earthly peace as is possible under the conditions of existence, but they may not concur on the most effective means to attain it.

For example, some may hold a unilateral nuclear freeze and/or unilateral disarmament by the United States would enhance the prospects of peace. Others may think that such actions would have the opposite effect.

Because none of us possesses omniscience, each of us must must make a prudential judgment with regard to such an issue. If members of a given community of faith seek to incorporate such a political proposal in their community of faith, they may force some people to leave that particular community of faith because they cannot support its politics.

Due to the selective way persons affiliate with congregations in the United Church of Christ, some particular congregations may be able to attain a greater coalescence between the community of faith and the community of politics than others can. Such a consensus should be respected so long as these congregations, respecting the principle of congregational autonomy, can understand with some charity why all congregations do not follow their lead.

In most congregations, people entertain contrasting prudential judgments on many social justice issues. Certainly, members of these congregations should look to their church to offer a *direction* on public policy matters, but they may legitimately be wary of efforts by some to offer *directives* on public policy matters.

Persons within a given congregation should be encouraged to participate in other specialized voluntary associations to express their religious convictions on public policy issues. Special interest groups *within* a congregation and *between* congregations may well pursue particular public policy issues, so long as they make it clear they are speaking *to* and not *for* their congregations. Designated giving for particular projects and programs can serve to permit persons seeing particular projects and programs as an outgrowth of their religious convictions to support them. It can also symbolize the legitimacy of the distinction between the community of faith and the community of politics and permit persons to withold their funds from projects they cannot in conscience support.

The Centrality of Congregational Polity

Congregational polity is the linchpin for the sustenance of theological diversity within the denomination, for the maintainence of appropriate distinctions between the community of faith and the community of politics, and for the promotion of a collegial style of leadership. The general drift of the ecumenical movement, the support of biblical theology as *the* way to do theology in some parts of the denomination, and the increasing fashionableness of various forms of liberation theology, all of which in different ways press for theological exclusivity, make it unlikely that a consensus on the basis for denominational identity will emerge in the forseeable future.

So long as the principle of congregational polity is affirmed, the press for theological exclusivity can be blunted. If denominational spokespersons press for the abandonment of congregational polity in response to the proposals of the Consultation on Church Unity, very substantial conflict will emerge. Some of us will refuse to affiliate with a denomination with a presbyterian or episcopal polity; others will do so with great reluctance.

In the meantime, in the complex interplay between the casual past and the emerging future which is shaping the identity of the United Church of

Christ, one may hope that many will continue to foster the merits of congregational polity, the legitimacy of theological diversity within the denomination as a whole, and the desirability of maintaining some distinctions between communities of faith and communities of politics within many of the congregations comprising the United Church of Christ.

Notes and References

1. See the following for detailed discussions and documentation of the factors summarized here: Sydney E. Ahlstrom, *A Religious History of the American People*, New Haven: Yale University Press, 1972; Kenneth Cauthen, *The Impact of American Religious Liberalism*, New York: Harper and Row, 1962; Edwin S. Gaustad, *Historical Atlas of Religion in America*, New York: Harper & Row, 1966; Louis H. Gunnemann, *The Shaping of the United Church of Christ: An Essay in the History of the American Christianity*, New York: United Church Press, 1977; Winthrop S. Hudson, *American Protestantism*, Chicago: University of Chicago Press, 1961; Charles H. Hopkins, *The Rise of the Social Gospel in American Protestantism, 1865-1915*, New Haven: Yale University Press, 1940; Douglas Horton, *The United Church of Christ: Its Origins, Organization and Role in the World Today*, New York: Nelson, 1962; William R. Hutchison, ed., *American Protestant Thought: The Liberal Era*, New York: Harper and Row, 1968; Alan Bowe Peabody, *A Study of the Controversy in Congregationalism over Merger with the Evangelical and Reformed Church*, Ann Arbor: University Microfilms, 1966; Carl E. Schneider, *The German Church on the American Frontier*, St. Louis: Eden Publishing House, 1939; William Warren Sweet, ed., *Religion on the American Frontier*, Vol. 3, *The Congregationalists*, Chicago: University of Chicago Press, 1939; Barbara Brown Zikmund, ed., *Hidden Histories in the United Church of Christ*, New York: United Church Press, 1984; Lowell H. Zuck, *European Roots of the United Church of Christ*, New York: United Church Press, 1976.

2. Because of the expenses involved in obtaining survey data and the flowering of this style of research after the union, quality data are rare. The following studies provide some suggestive data: Yoshio Fukuyama, *The Ministry in Transition: A Case Study in Theological Education*, University Park: Pennsylvania State University Press, 1972; George Gallop, Jr., *Religion in America, 1984*, Princeton: Princeton Religion Research Center, 1984; Victor Obenhaus, *And See the People: A Study of the United Church of Christ*, Chicago: Chicago Theological Seminary, 1968; W. Widick Schroeder and Victor Obenhaus, *Religion in American Culture: Unity and Diversity in a Midwestern County*, New York: Free Press, 1964; Rodney Stark and Charles Y. Glock, *American Piety: The Nature of Religious Commitment*, Berkeley: University of California Press, 1968.

3. For an elaboration of the issues discussed here, see, for example, the following: James Gustafson, "The Voluntary Church: A Moral Appraisal," in D.B. Robertson, ed., *Voluntary Associations: A Case Study of Groups in Free Societies*, Richmond: John Knox Press, 1966; W. Widick Schroeder, *et. al.*, *Suburban Religion: Churches and Synagogues in the American Experience*, Chicago: Center for the Scientific Study of Religion, 1974; W. Widick Schroeder, "The Emergence of the Voluntary Church" in Clyde L. Manschreck and Barbara Brown Zikmund, ed., *The American Religious Experiment: Piety and Practicality*, Chicago: Exploration Press, 1978, appearing in this volume as Chapter 13.

4. See Schroeder, *et. al.*, *Subui ɔan Religion: Churches and Synagogues in the American Experience, op. cit*; and Walter E. Ziegenhals, *Urban Churches in Transition*, New York: Pilgrim Press, 1978.

5. "Post Hails Bishops' Letter on U.S. Economy," in *Keeping You Posted*, New York: Office of Communication of the United Church of Christ, Vol. 20. No. 2 (Feb. 1985).

6. In this discussion, a setting in the context of the Christian movement is presupposed. The relation of communities of faith rooted in the Christian movement to communities of faith rooted in other religious traditions is not explored directly in this essay, for it is addressed primarily to persons affiliated with a United Church of Christ congregation.

Introduction to Chapter 16

This essay examines the professionalization of religious research in the United States and related topics. Because professional societies illumine value orientations and practices among workers in a given field, the nature of the American Catholic Sociological Society, the Society of Christian Ethics, the Religious Research Association, and the Society for the Scientific Study of Religion are briefly considered. The differential appropriation of religious research in various ecclesiastical bodies, the problem of funding religious research in the American situation, and the shift in emphases from a pragmatic problem-solving approach focused on institutional survival to more theoretical approaches to the understanding of religious phenomena are discussed. The bifurcation between persons interested in religious research educated under theological faculties and those trained under human science faculties is noted.

At the time Chapter 16 was written, there was much ferment in the human sciences. Many were challenging the social systems theory associated with Talcott Parsons, and people were searching for alternative metatheory. It was my hope that neo-Platonic, neo-Hegelian, and neo-Aristoletian frameworks of interpretation might attract some people doing work in the sociology of religion. Such a hope has not been realized. In addition to reductionistic and phenomentological interpretations popular at that time, neo-Marxist modes of thought associated with the Frankfurt School and deconstructionist modes of thought associated with Foucault and his followers have become more fashionable during the past two decades.

In spite of their current popularity, I am still hopeful that some may appropriate other modes of interpretation in their work. Human imagination is conditioned but not bound by social location, race, gender, ethnicity, or the influence of the causal past. Using their imagination, being guided by the rational criteria of logicality and coherence and by the empirical criteria of applicability and adequacy, and willing to pursue the quest for truth informed by intellectual and emotional integrity, scholars can help shape the development of alternative interpretive frameworks.

Scholars need not explain religious experience on the basis of some factors held to be more basic and elemental. They may interpret it by appealing to the immanence in human experience of a Divine Reality that is, in at least some ways, *suit generis.*

As noted earlier, people cannot evade the question of the ultimate grounds for religious experience by appeal to a fact-value disjunction. This neo-Kantian distinction stands or falls on the adequacy of its view of sense perception. If sense *re*ception is more fundamental in human experience than sense *per*ception, then the fact-value disjunction is spurious. If an emerging subject begins to become by appropriating forms and a flood of feelings embodied in its causal past, fact and value are interrelated.

I hold this interrelationship does exist. We begin to become by valuing that which we appropriate in the initial phase of our becoming. The free play of imagination, which permits one to transcend the past in part, emerges in the later phases of our becoming. The partial truth in gender, race, ethnic, or social location theories of value is based on the concrete particularity of entities in an emerging subject's causal past and on their emotional and intellectual influence on the emerging subject.

The error in such theories is the equation of this partial truth with the whole truth. It is one thing to say that one's values and sensibilities are effected by one's causal past. It is quite another thing either to suggest that there are no propositions in which all creatures participate or to suggest that human beings lack the capacity to surpass partially the past in the present, to discern general principles of justice, or to develop desirable forms of human social organization. It does not follow that an "explanation" of the relations between past and present valuations necessarily undercuts the moral validity of such valuations. Some values persist because they enhance the harmony of life with life and fittingly embody principles of justice and forms of human social organization.

CHAPTER 16

The Development of Religious Research in the United States: Retrospect and Prospect

Scholarly interest in religious phenomena and lay involvement with religious institutions in the United States increased for the decade or so following the Second World War. Lay participation in religious institutions increased until the late 1950s, with a bimodal peak of 49 percent of American adults attending religious services reached in 1955 and 1958. The figure declined to 42 percent in 1969 (Gallup, 1969).

During this postwar period, two professional organizations composed of persons interested in the social scientific study of religion, the Society for the Scientific Study of Religion (SSSR) and the Religious Research Association (RRA) were incorporated. Each of them founded journals devoted to the "scientific" study of religious phenomena.

Though the American Catholic Sociological Society (ACSS) was founded prior to World War II, its focus was shifted in the early 1960s. Prior to that time, it dealt with many sociological topics, but its members decided to center its interest primarily in the sociology of religion. Its journal was renamed *Sociological Analysis* and is now devoted to papers in the sociology of religion.

The emergence of three journals devoted to the social scientific study of religion in the post-World War II era attests to increased scholarly interest in the social scientific study of religion. The need for more publication outlets is related both to increased scholarly interest and to the "publish or perish" syndrome so prevalent in American academia.

All three professional groups are avowedly interfaith, but their origins differ significantly. The SSSR originated with a group of scholars along the Eastern seaboard in the late 1940s and became a national society in the 1950s. It is the largest and most prestigious of the three professional societies. More scholars who are not confessionally related to one of the major faith categories are attracted to it. Its *Journal for the Scientific Study of Religion* is larger, more inclusive of academic disciplines, and more prestigious than either *Sociological Analysis* or the *Review of Religious Research.*

The ACSS, the oldest of the three societies devoted to the social scientific study of religion, was founded by Catholic sociologists prior to World War II. It is still composed primarily of Roman Catholic sociologists, but in keeping with the ecumenical mood of recent years the Society has encouraged broader participation, especially by Protestants, and in 1971 became the Association for the Sociology of Religion. It is also the most focused of the three professional groups, for the other two are avowedly *interdisciplinary.*

Persons conducting religious research under the auspices of Protestant denominational and interdenominational bureaucracies were the initiators of the Religious Research Fellowship from which the RRA emerged in the early 1950s. It is now interfaith and interdisciplinary, but functionaries in various Protestant ecclesiastical bureaucracies continue to dominate its policy-making body. It is the smallest and possibly the least prestigious of the three societies.

The RRA avowedly is more exclusively focused on empirical religious research, but in practice the programs at its meetings and the papers in its journal tend to parallel the interests of the ACSS and the SSSR.

Although it is not directly focused on religious research, a fourth professional society which may significantly affect the shape and direction of religious research has emerged in the past decade. The Society of Christian Ethics, composed primarily of professors of social ethics, may provide a context for social research which has implications for public policy.

This discussion of the development of religious research in the U.S.A. has been initiated with a characterization of the professional societies, for this is a very useful way to illumine value orientations and practices among professionals in a given field. The emergence of professional societies in the modern world is one facet of the development of voluntary associations, which has played a significant role in shaping contemporary American life (Robertson, 1966; see Whitehead, 1933). This, in turn, is related to the increasing rationalization of the social order and the concomitant elaboration of bureaucracies in the several spheres of the social order (Weber, 1930, 1946).

The existence of three professional societies and emergence of a fourth in the same general field is unusual, but it reflects the social and intellectual distance between academicians in dominantly secular institutions, Roman Catholic sociologists, and Protestant religious researchers. Though the professional societies were related historically to different constituencies, their journals have been dominated by academicians whose primary training and professional interests are in sociology, anthropology, or psychology. Historians and political scientists are conspicuously absent. A few social ethicists have published papers in these journals, but the dominant authors are "behavioral scientists." As a result, an unfortunate bifurcation has taken place, for precious little interchange between social ethicists and social scientists has occurred either in these societies or in their official journals.

The Ecclesiastical Institutionalization of Religious Research in the United States

The institutionalization of religious research in the United States is part of a historical movement during which technical rationalism has emerged to a position of preeminence in some portions of the Western world. The development of religious research is inextricably intertwined with the emergence of science, the increased differentiation of the spheres of the social order from each other, the elaboration of large bureaucracies in the economic, political, cultural, and religious spheres, and the popularization of thought forms interpreting religious phenomena in non-*sui generis* ways. Since technical rationalism is more pervasive in America than anywhere else in the world, it is understandable that empirical religious research is more widespread in America than in any other country (Ellul, 1964; Hughes, 1958; Kornhauser, 1959; Moore, 1963; Rieff, 1966; Stein, 1960; Williams, 1970).

Religious research in America began earliest in those denominations most closely related to the main currents of non-theological thinking. The Congregational-Christian wing of the United Church of Christ and the Presbyterian Church in the U.S.A. were early supporters of rational (non-ontic) pragmatic (empirical) religious research. Both denominations were providing some support for the religious research in the 1920s and 1930s. As more religious professionals turned to empirically based research to help them understand their situation and to provide guidance for policy and program development, the interest in selected aspects of religious research spread to other religious groups.

Relatively, religious research under Jewish auspices has been extensive. This sponsorship is related to the very considerable secularization of Jewish culture in America and to the preoccupation of many Jews with problems of prejudice and acculturation. The $500,000, for example, which social scientists at the University of California at Berkeley received from Jewish sources to study prejudice in the 1960s is a much larger research grant than has come from Protestant sources in recent times.

Roman Catholicism and the more conservative Protestant groups were slower to embrace religious research. In the case of Catholicism, both isolation from the mainstream of American intellectual life and proper concern about the presuppositions informing religious research contributed to the slowness of its institutionalization. Since World War II, however, more evaluative research has been done under Catholic ecclesiastical auspices. The relative objectivity of criteria for church membership and the relatively rational organization of the Roman Catholic ecclesiastical bureaucracy have contributed to the clarity of Roman Catholic research on these topics. The $425,000 recently granted by Catholic sources to NORC for a study of Catholic priests is also a much larger grant than any Protestant group has given to foster religious research in recent years.

Because of Catholic scholars continued concern with the question of the Truth of its belief system, reflected publicly in most prominent form in the papal critiques of situational ethics and Freudian psychology and in the imprimatur required on many works by Catholic religious professionals, they have been more reserved in their use of contemporary social theory and fashionable styles of social research. Their intellectual hesitancy has been reinforced by ecclesiastical inertia and traditionalism, for parish priests and members of the Catholic hierarchy have scarcely been in the vanguard of those who have sought to appropriate the findings of religious research.[1]

The relatively "conservative" Protestant denominations, such as the Southern Baptist Convention, and inter-denominational agencies, such as the National Association of Evangelicals, have had relatively more objective criteria for membership and theological norms than more "liberal" Protestant groups. As a result, they have made increased use of demographic and attitudinal data in the past decade (Zuck and Getz, 1968; Barkman et al., 1969). Evangelicals may have been slow to appropriate some of the values of technical rationalism, but once they accepted them they have been very willing to use them to evaluate church growth and program effectiveness (Read et al., 1969).

Most religious research conducted under Protestant ecclesiastical auspices has been shaped by the pragmatic, activistic, and relatively anti-intellectual ethos which has pervaded much of the institutional expression of religious experience in the United States (Mead, 1963). Relatively few religious researchers employed by Protestant ecclesiastical bodies have been self-consciously concerned about the relation between theological and social scientific views of human beings. Few have considered the implications of alternative perspectives on the nature of human nature for the shape and style of religious research.[2]

The Focus of Ecclesiastically Sponsored Religious Research

Members of the ecclesiastical bureaucracies in the several denominations and religious professionals serving local religious institutions have been interested in religious research primarily for the assistance it may give in ecclesiastical policy formulation, program evaluation, cultivation of parish life, and understanding the contemporary situation. Most of the people doing research under ecclesiastical auspices have undertaken studies related to the first three issues and have drawn on other studies which interpret the contemporary situation.

These studies are generally done by research and planning staff members for some group within a denomination and are rarely published for the benefit of the larger scholarly and ecclesiastical community. For example, during the four years from 1965 to 1969, only three papers were submitted to the *Review of Religious Research* by staff members of ecclesiastical bureaucracies who had conducted research under such auspices.[3]

Contract research grants made by ecclesiastical groups to academic research centers are hazardous, for social scientists are guided by criteria which differ in part from those of religious professionals. They are also often interested primarily in securing funds to sustain facilities and staff already in existence.

The combination may result in the development of inordinately expensive research designs producing findings and analyses of limited usefulness to the agency contracting the research. Since most graduate students employed in such research projects are heading for academic posts, funds expended may not even contribute to the education of people who will later use their skills under ecclesiastical auspices. Administrators responsible for expending ecclesiastical monies would be well advised to be wary of contract research unless the closest kind of continued consultation and collaboration is maintained between the sponsoring agency and the group doing the research.

Though religious research has been undertaken by some religious bodies in the U.S.A. for more than fifty years, no denomination devotes much of its budget to research and evaluation. In most Protestant denominations, a research "staff" is minimal or nonexistent. The evaluation of work undertaken by mission boards is rare indeed. In most circumstances, budgets for evaluative research are also minimal or nonexistent. The diffuseness of the goals of mission projects makes evaluative research in the religious sphere difficult. The lack of funding makes it almost impossible.

In the past decade or so, religious professionals strongly concerned about social justice and critical of the past activities of religious institutions in the public sphere have moved into policy positions in several Protestant denominations. This "new breed" of church leader, critical of ecclesiastically sponsored program maintenance and church extension research focused on demographic and attitudinal phenomena, has been more interested in sponsoring policy studies and fostering action research focused specifically on political problems.[4]

The Funding of Empirical Religious Research

Negative lay reactions to the leadership style of the "new breed" of highly visible members of the ecclesiastical bureaucracy have been developing in the past several years. The extent to which lay resentment of the activity of American religious institutions in the public sphere has contributed to the relative decline in church participation and in benevolence giving in the past several years is problematic, for the rapid inflation and economic slow-down of recent years and the changing age composition of the American population have also affected giving to religious institutions. The voluntary nature of religious institutions precludes the use of coercive measures, such as taxation, to fund the work of the institution, so declines in benevolence giving necessarily mean program reductions. Benevolence giving declines more sharply than total giving, for local staff and building needs are less deferrable.

As a result, every major Protestant, Catholic, and Jewish ecclesiastical bureaucracy is under increasing financial strain. It is almost axiomatic that novel and experimental programs are among the first to be cut when funds are short. New programming and staff additions in such a marginal area as religious research are most unlikely in such a climate. Maintenance of the *status quo* for the funding of religious research under ecclesiastical auspices is the most one may expect in the next several years; reduction in such funding is quite likely.[5]

The prospects for substantial support of religious research by government agencies are almost nil. The American tradition of separation of church and state makes it very difficult to fund research in this sphere through overt government grants. Some funding through various federal agencies has occurred, but the grants constitute a small segment of total research grants, receive minimal publicity, and are politically sensitive.

The prospects for university funding of religious research are not much better. Because of the general reduction of funds for research in the social sciences by the federal government in the late 1960s, university departments are under increased pressure to secure funds to sustain the staffs they accumulated when research monies were easier to come by. It seems unlikely that many departmental or divisional chairpersons will allocate monies for empirical studies of religious phenomena in the present climate, for the prospects of external funding of such studies are slim.

Since individual scholars may and do develop individual studies with minimal funding, the flow of papers and monographs under educational auspices will continue, but it is unlikely that many large-scale studies will be made in the foreseeable future.

The diminished prospect of economic support of religious research, which has never been heavily supported since the Institute for Social and Religious Research spent some of the Rockefeller millions in the 1920s and 1930s for religious research, leads to this rather glum prognosis for the future development of certain types of empirical research, but there is a positive dimension to this situation.

The shortage of funds for expensive empirical research, especially for interview and questionnaire studies, may encourage more persons interested in religious research to reflect more intensively on the theoretical issues confronting the field and to initiate research which does not require large staffs and costly data processing. Archival research, historically grounded research, evaluative research, and participant observation research, all of which have yielded important results in the past half-century, still offer rich opportunities for significant and relatively inexpensive empirical religious research. The need to explore alternative interpretations of the meanings discerned by religious research is urgent.[6]

Advances in computer technology make certain types of statistical analysis more feasible and less costly than in earlier decades but this development is ambiguous. On the one hand, since the past conditions the present, analysis of causal components conditioning present phenomena are useful. On the other hand, since the present transcends the past, creativity is dominant over form in the nature of things, linguistic symbols are equivocal, and a whole is more than the sum of its parts, the feasibility of certain statistical manipulations may lead to an inordinate interest in quasi-quantified analysis.

These observations lead to some reflections on theoretical frameworks which have guided religious research in America and judgments about the future development of the theory informing empirical studies of religious phenomena.

Some Reflections on Theory and Religious Research

The American Ethos and the Emergence of Religious Research

As noted previously, religious research in the United States was stimulated by the processes of urbanization, industrialization, and bureaucrazation which began with the Renaissance and Reformation, for each contributed to the development of technical rationalism. The Industrial Revolution gave them impetus. The U.S.A. was uniquely situated to appropriate the Industrial Revolution with its concomitant technical rationalism. Since religious research was unlikely to develop without the widespread acceptance of technical rationalism, the same root value orientation which contributed to the emergence of industrialization, urbanization, and bureaucrazation also fostered the development of religious research.

By 1900 the rural church in the United States, along with many other rural social institutions, was in trouble, for urbanization was adversely affecting rural life. The decline in the proportion of population in rural areas, which had been under way since before the time of the first Census in 1790, was soon to give way to an absolute decline in the rural segment of the population.

This social problem, more than any other single factor, gave religious research its early impetus. Concern with the use of research to help resolve a practical problem has been one of the motivating factors in religious research under ecclesiastical auspices from that day to the present. Members of the ecclesiastical bureaucracies are wary of funding research which does not have programmatic implications.

The emergence of religious research was coterminous with the establishment of departments of sociology in American colleges and universities. It was natural for persons interested in religious research to turn to sociology to develop research methods and inform theory to shape their research interests.

It was soon apparent that urban churches were also affected by shifting population movements and by the dynamics of urban life. Thus the same pragmatic concerns with institutional survival which gave rise to study of the rural church also sustained interest in studying the urban church in its environment. Two pioneers in this effort were H. Paul Douglass, who studied both phenomena, and Samuel C. Kincheloe, who studied primarily the urban church and its environment. Both were concerned with the impact of the social environment on religious institutions and *vice versa*.[7]

The American ethos was pragmatic, activistic, and anti-intellectual. The early style of religious research reflected this ethos. The research was oriented toward problem-solving and, though not anti-intellectual, was anti-metaphysical and anti-theological. This strand has persisted in religious research under ecclesiastical auspices and is still prevalent among some research workers employed by denominational and inter-denominational agencies.

A Shift in Perspectives: Theological Revival, Social Theory, and Religious Research

The theological revival, which began in America in the 1930s and has continued to the present time, has affected markedly the interests and theoretical perspectives of most persons interested in religious research who were trained in the 1950s and 1960s in theological centers. The shift in emphasis is especially evident among graduates of the divinity schools of Yale University and the University of Chicago. It has led many of them to have a primary interest in policy questions and to use research to help them formulate policy. The studies of Waldo Beach (1969), Thomas Campbell and Yoshio Fukuyama (1970), Henry Clark (1965), Paul Harrison (1959), Victor Obenhaus (1957, 1963, 1968), Robert Terry (1970), Kenneth Underwood (1957, 1969), Oliver Whitley (1959, 1964, 1969), Gibson Winter (1961, 1963, 1966, 1969), the author of this paper (1970), and Schroeder and Obenhaus (1964) are illustrative of the dual interests of people who have been associated with these institutions during the past two decades.

At the same time as persons interested in religious research within Protestant theological faculties were increasingly concerned about the theological rationale for their work and were struggling with the problem of the relation between theology and the social sciences, persons interested in religious research under social science faculties were also increasingly interested in theoretical issues. Members of theological faculties turned to distinguished theologians for guidance in shaping theoretical perspectives; members of social science faculties turned to distinguished European social theorists of the preceding generation for guidance in shaping theoretical perspectives. Protestant social theorists turned to such figures as Karl Barth, Paul Tillich, Emil Brunner, and the Niebuhr brothers; and social scientists turned to such figures as Emile Durkheim, Sigmund Freud, Max Weber, Vilfredo Pareto, Karl Marx, and George Simmel.

The result has been a rather sharp bifurcation of points of view among persons interested in religious research between those educated under Protestant theological faculties and those educated under American social science faculties. A generational contrast also exists, for the increased interest in theory began about 1940. Thus, religious researchers trained in the 1920s and 1930s under either sociological or theological auspices were educated in an ethos which was activistic and pragmatic. Those educated later under theological faculties often sought to relate religious research to both theology and social science theory; but those educated later under social science faculties usually sought to relate religious research only to more general social science theory. In the former case, research workers almost always either distinguished scientific studies from confessional ones or interpreted religious phenomena on *sui generis* grounds. In the latter case, research workers almost always interpreted religious phenomena from some non-ontological, phenomenological perspective or from a reductionist perspective. Thus, deep and irresolvable contrasts in interpretation of religious phenomena are developing among those interested in the empirical study of religious phenomena.

Religious researchers informed by *sui generis* perspectives are apt to be more sensitive to the root philosophical and theological issues involved in their analysis. They *necessarily* must have pondered a broader range of options as they shape their interpretations of empirical religious research than is *necessarily* the case for those informed by non-ontological phenomenological or reductionist perspectives.[8]

At the moment, most religious research published in the United States is informed by non-*sui generis* perspectives, for it is being done by social scientists who, either implicitly or explicitly, do not undertake *sui generis* interpretations of religious phenomena. Persons interested in religious research who can affirm the *sui generis* character of religious experience need to develop these interests and to publish material informed by this perspective to broaden the understanding of religion and society.

Not only do studies informed by alternative interpretations of religious phenomena need to be developed. Religious researchers also need to free themselves from unduly constrictive social scientific methodologies. Efforts to seek inordinate precision in social scientific studies in general and in social scientific studies of religious phenomena in particular are highly suspect. Microscopic studies of particular phenomena need to be augmented by macroscopic ones in order to attain a more synoptic vision of the interplay of people as it is shaped through religious institutions and the other spheres of the social order.

These observations presuppose that forms are found in facts, feeling and meaning are inextricably intertwined, dynamics is dominant over form, a whole is more than the sum of its parts, and an adequate explanation of a phenomenon must include a consideration of the functioning of the Divine in the universe. It seems unlikely at the present time that many will pursue studies informed by these modes of thought. Very few workers educated under social scientific faculties are prepared to affirm these presuppositions. Some educated under theological faculties are willing to affirm some or all of them, but such are few in number. Financial support for empirical studies of religious phenomena under the auspices of theological seminaries and departments of religion is meager.

The unfashionable nature of *sui generis* perspectives on all religious phenomena among social scientists makes many suspect *a priori* all studies shaped by *sui generis* interpretations. The unfashionableness of presuppositions leading to holistic and dynamic studies of humans make many social scientists critical and wary of such "non-scientific" and interpretative studies.

One factor may qualify this judgment. The pervasive unrest among graduate students in the social sciences today is fascinating, for they are intuitively seeking alternative methodologies and interpretations of reality to those which dominate these fields today.[9] It is plausible to interpret this ferment as a religious quest, in which the protagonists are seeking Truth among truths. The emerging generation of scholars may be more sympathetic to *sui generis* interpretations of religious phenomena and more concerned about the interplay of fact, value, and decisions in policy formulation than their predecessors. It is too early to be clear about consequences of this movement, but it could lead younger scholars to return to an explicit consideration of the nature of the true, the good, and the beautiful in the context of religious research in particular and all research in general.

The Future

Several lines will probably characterize the future development of religious research in the United States. Functionaries in the ecclesiastical bureaucracies will continue to carry on program maintenance types of research, but it is difficult to see any expansion in this type of research, considering the financial pressures which most denominations are likely to confront in the 1970s. Some younger functionaries, trained in certain theological centers, are likely to open up new lines of thinking, but budgetary limitations are likely to restrict sharply new and innovative efforts.

Interest in religious studies in state-supported institutions is likely to continue. The current national crisis is a profoundly moral one, and administrators in the educational system are likely to foster the development of departments concerned with religion, morality, and social ethics.

Because of the peculiar church-state problems of America, it is likely that many theological issues will emerge in such disciplines as the psychology and sociology of religion. Unfortunately, they probably will do so in truncated and relatively undisciplined ways, for the separation of these disciplines from the classical philosophic and theological tradition of the West is quite sharp.

Finally, parallel development of religious research under theological auspices and social scientific auspices is likely to continue in the United States. The extent of interplay between the two groups will depend on the possibilities of the context for interchange in the several professional societies and the extent to which some social scientists are freed from unduly constrictive methodologies and truncated interpretations of religious phenomena.

Notes and References

1. Paul H. Furfey, Joseph H. Fichter, and Andrew M. Greeley are among the more distinguished Catholic social scientists who have studied Catholic religious institutions in the post-World War period. Little work was done by Catholic social scientists prior to the Second World War. Both Fichter and Greeley have been more concerned with the development of empirical studies than with the issue of the shape of social scientific theory *vis-a-vis* theologically rooted social theory.

2. Though I cannot provide definitive data, I am willing to advance a judgment about the value orientations of many religious researchers employed by Protestant ecclesiastical bureaucracies in the U.S. on the basis of my experience in the life of the RRA since its inception, observational participation in the educational processes of a large theological education complex over a period of twenty years, and my knowledge of the types of publications produced by members of the Protestant ecclesiastical bureaucracy. I think many Protestant religious researchers employed by ecclesiastical bureaucracies have been attracted to such positions because they were disinterested in other forms of religious leadership, had serious problems with theological interpretations dominant in their particular tradition, and/or were not attracted to theological and philosophical reflection.

3. This statement is based on the author's observations, since he served as Editor of the *Review of Religious Research* during this period. David O. Moberg, the current editor, reports that the situation has improved only slightly since 1969.

4. For a somewhat exaggerated assessment of the implications of this situation, see Hadden (1969). For a qualitative description of the phenomenon, see Cox (1967). The sociological parallel is the work of C. Wright Mills and members of the so-called "New Left" in sociology. Insofar as this movement attempts to get humans back into sociological theory, their critique of some styles of sociological research is valuable. The structural-functional approach to human society, as best exemplified in the work of Talcott Parsons, dissects people into too many roles. Protagonists of this approach rarely discuss the action of any individual humans in their studies.

5. This quotation, drawn from the observations of the Conference minister of the Illinois Conference of the United Church of Christ in the February, 1970, issue of a monthly letter titled *Concerns,* illumines the processes at work:

> In view of our continuing decline in support, the Budget Committee is recommending to the Board of Directors that there be a drastic reduction in present budget expenditures to help compensate for the expected deficit of 1970. Though this will greatly reduce our services and program, there is no other way to be financially responsible given the fiscal facts of the last three years.

The United Church of Christ is also under increased financial pressure at the national level. Total giving at the national and conference level in 1969 was up .56 percent, counting a non-repeatable item. Since the rate of inflation in 1969 was over 6 percent, real income was down.

Most major denominations are encountering comparable financial pressures at the national level. In 1970, national leaders of the United Presbyterian Church reported that their buying power had been reduced 33 percent in the past three years, based on a 15 percent decline in income and an 18 percent inflationary factor.

6. Winter (1966) represents a major beginning in this exploration, and Ricoeur (1970) undertakes a masterful explication from a phenenological perspective of the issue of meaning noted here.

7. Douglass' early work was on the rural community; *The Little Town* was published in 1919. The movement of his interests from the empirical study of churches in non-metropolitan areas in the pre-World War I period to the empirical study of city churches in the 1920s and 1930s and to the study of faith and order in the late 1930s and the 1940s parallels the dominant mood in Protestantism. For a perceptive analysis of Douglass' work, see the first H. Paul Douglass Lectures (Brunner, 1959).

Kincheloe began his pioneering studies of city churches in the late 1920s. *The American City and Its Church* (1938) is the best example of his interests.

8. In the United States, sociology faculties have generally divorced themselves from historical, philosophical, and theological faculties. The number of sociologists in the United States who interpret reality ontologically is minute. For example, in a recent work on sociological theory, Wallace (1969) dismissed all "super-natural" social theory from consideration. Though ontologists would resist the term "supernatural" to characterize their ontological interpretation of the nature of things, Wallace included no readings of or references to their work. Whitehead was cited in one footnote, but there was no serious consideration of social theory in the classical sense in the readings in this book.

9. This mood is not confined only to graduate students. Some work by respected scholars in the field reflecting this unrest is emerging. For example, Berger (1969), Friedrich (1970), and Gouldner (1970) all express dissatisfaction with the dominant shape of contemporary sociological theory. None reflect the neo-Platonic understanding implicit in this paragraph, but they do illumine the current dissatisfaction about contemporary styles of sociological theory.

Bibliography

Barkman, Paul F., *et al.*
1969 *Christian Collegians and Foreign Missions.* Monrovia, California: Missions Advanced Research and Communications Center.
Beach, Waldo
1969 *Christian Community and American Society.* Philadelphia: The Westminster Press.
Berger, Peter
1969 *A Rumor of Angels.* Garden City: Doubleday.
Brunner, Edmund de S.
1959 "Harlan Paul Douglass: Pioneer researcher in the sociology of religion." *Review of Religious Research 1* (Summer and Fall): 3-16, 63-75.
Campbell, Thomas, and Yoshio Fukuyama
1970 *The Fragmented Layman.* Philadelphia and Boston: Pilgrim Press.
Clark, Henry
1965 *The Church and Residential Desegregation.* New Haven: College and University Press.
Cox, Harvey G.
1967 "The 'New Breed' in American church: Sources of social activism in American religion." *Daedalus* 96 (Winter): 135-150.
Douglass, Harlan Paul
1919 *The Little Town.* New York: Macmillan.
Ellul, Jacques
1964 *The Technological Society.* New York: Knopf.
Friedrich, Robert
1970 *A Sociology of Sociology.* New York: The Free Press.
Gallup, George
1969 "Churchgoing slides in U.S." *Chicago Sun Times* (December 28, 1969): 5.
Gouldner, Alvin
1970 *The Coming Crisis of Western Sociology.* New York: Basic Books.
Hadden, Jeffrey K.
1969 *The Gathering Storm in the Churches.* Garden City: Doubleday.
Harrison, Paul
1959 *Authority and Power in the Free Church Tradition.* Princeton: Princeton University Press.
Hughes, Henry Stuart
1958 *Consciousness and Society.* New York: Knopf.
Kincheloe, Samuel
1938 *The American City and Its Church.* New York: Friendship Press.
Kornhauser, William
1959 *The Politics of Mass Society.* Glencoe, Illinois: The Free Press.
Mead, Sidney
1963 *The Lively Experiment: The Shaping of Christianity in America.* New York: Harper and Row.
Moore, Wilbert E.
1963 *Social Change.* Englewood Cliffs, New Jersey: Prentice-Hall, Inc.
Obenhaus, Victor
1957 *The Responsible Christian.* Chicago: University of Chicago Press.
1963 *The Church and Faith in Mid-America.* Philadelphia: The Westminster Press.

1968 *And See the People*. Chicago: Chicago Theological Seminary.
Read, William R., Victor M. Monterroso and Harmon A. Johnson
1969 *Latin American Church Growth*. Grand Rapids: Erdmans Pub. Co.
Ricoeur, Paul
1970 *Freud and Philosophy: An Essay on Interpretation*. New Haven: Yale University Press.
Rieff, Philip
1966 *The Triumph of the Therapeutic*. New York: Harper and Row.
Robertson, D.B., ed.
1966 *Voluntary Associations*. Richmond: John Knox Press.
Schroeder, W. Widick
1970 *Cognitive Structures and Religious Research*. East Lansing: Michigan State University Press.
Schroeder, W. Widick, and Victor Obenhaus
1964 *Religion in American Culture*. New York: The Free Press.
Stein, Maurice
1960 *The Eclipse of Community*. Princeton: Princeton University Press.
Terry, Robert
1970 *For Whites Only*. Grand Rapids: Erdmans Pub. Co.
Underwood, Kenneth
1957 *Protestant and Catholic*. Boston: Beacon Press.
1969 *The Church, the University and Social Policy*. Middletown, Connecticut: Wesleyan University Press.
Wallace, Walter, ed.
1969 *Sociological Theory*. Chicago: Aldine Pub. Co.
Weber, Max
1930 *The Protestant Ethic and the Spirit of Capitalism*. London: George Allan and Unwin, Ltd.
1946 "Science as a Vocation" and "Bureaucracy" in *From Max Weber: Essays in Sociology*. New York: Oxford University Press.
Whitehead, A. N.
1933 "Aspects of Freedom" in *Adventures of Ideas*. New York: Macmillan.
Whitley, Oliver
1959 *Trumpet Call of Reformation*. St. Louis, Missouri: Bethany Press.
1964 *Religious Behavior: Where Sociology and Religion Meet*. Englewood Cliffs, New Jersey: Prentice-Hall, Inc.
1969 *The Church: Mirror or Window? Images of the Church in American Society*. St. Louis, Missouri: Bethany Press.
Williams, Robin, Jr.
1970 *American Society: A Sociological Interpretation*. New York: Knopf.
Winter, Gibson
1961 *The Suburban Captivity of the Churches*. Garden City: Doubleday.
1963 *The New Creation as Metropolis*. New York: Macmillan.
1966 *Elements for a Social Ethic*. New York: Macmillan.
1969 *Religious Identity*. New York: Macmillan.
Zuck, Roy B., and Gene A. Getz
1968 *Christian Youth: An In-Depth Study*. Chicago: Moody Press.

PART FOUR

Alternative Primal Interpretations: Analyses and Critiques

Introduction to Part Four

In order to set dipolar theism, as the process view of God has often been called, in perspective, this view of the Divine Reality needs to be contrasted with alternative views. The three chapters in Part Four deal analytically and critically with the thought of three twentieth century interpreters. Two are theologians in the Protestant facet of the Christian movement; the other is an interpreter of scientific work. Paul Tillich and Jürgen Moltmann, the two theologians, are influential theologians whose work has been widely read in theological circles. Ralph W. Burhoe, less well known, has pioneered in the movement to relate religion and science. His thinking represents an alternative way to see the relation between the two fields. In each discussion the subject's viewpoint is criticized from my constructive viewpoint. In this way, the basic assumptions informing the subject's work and the basic assumptions informing my work are made clearer.

Greek Interpretations of the Divine

Introduction — Not surprisingly, several of the alternative interpretations were developed in ancient Greece, for Greek thought is the fountainhead of western thought. (Augmented by Hebraic views, classical theism emerged in the early Christian era. God was conceived as eminently real, at whose fiat the world was created and sustained. It possessed aseity. It was an unmoved mover, unaffected by the world.) Four interpretations of the Divine Reality were salient in classical Greek thought. Democritus advanced a reductionist interpretation, the Sophists undertook an existentialist skeptical interpretation, and Plato and Aristotle formulated theistic interpretations.

Subsequent thinkers have linked these interpretations with contrasting methodological and epistemological assumptions. However, these primal interpretations have emerged time and again in the history of human thought, for the foundational notions in relation to which contingent notions are set were explored early in the development of human reflection. (Those scientists who think science should not be interested in historical retrieval are insensitive to the necessity to consider more inclusive propositions in which to set their more specialized propositions.) All these interpretations address the meaning of freedom, power, law, nature, knowledge, and God, but they understand these terms and the relations between them differently.

Broadly speaking, reductionistic interpretations initiated by Democritus or skeptical, agnostic and/or strongly relativistic interpretations initiated by the Sophists are dominant in the universities and among the literati in this post-modern epoch, and the theistic interpretations initiated by Plato or Aristotle are subordinate. For this reason, theistic interpretations of experience are highly suspect in learned circles in this period.

The Existential Phenomological Interpretation of the Sophists — The Sophists entertained a skeptical existentialist interpretation of human experience. One begins one's interpretation with one's experience and one's perspective. As Protagoras observed, humans are the measure of things. In this context the meaning of measure is not that of a yardstick, but, rather, that of a master or a maker.

Thus, people make the laws. In the first book of Plato's *Republic,* the younger Sophist defines justice as the interest of the stronger, i.e., the interest of the one who has the most power to pursue his/her own interests. Consequently, the interest of the weaker is to do what is in the interest of the stronger. The weaker is free to pursue his or her own interests in areas where the strong have no interest. In this existentialist interpretation, power is seen from the perspective of the agent.

Sophists give indirect meaning to nature, knowledge, and God. The agent determines from his/her perspective whatever "is." The framework of the perspective of the observer defines nature, for everyone sees nature from a different perspective.

Similarly, human agents create or make knowledge, which depends upon the orientation of the knower and upon what the knower does. If protagonists of this interpretation differentiate knowledge from God, they characterize God as that which a person creates. Just as persons make knowledge, so they make God. (In the modern epoch, Max Weber and his successors focused their attention on the religious virtuoso, a charismatic leader who evoked adherents to follow the leader's views about human relations to an alleged Divine Reality. As noted earlier, Max Weber, grounded in the neo-Kantian tradition, maintained a fact-value disjunction which permitted him sympathetically to contrast his "scientific" analysis with "confessional" studies. Rodney Stark, a contemporary sociologist utilizing this perspective, is less restrained. He holds very firmly to the charismatic interpretation.)

Proponents of this interpretation of the nature of reality hold that the debate is the appropriate way to discuss knowledge. All protagonists have a right to a hearing, and each person advances a point of view that remains an alternative. An option which is rejected now may later be preferable.

For existentialists, freedom is self-determination. One is free if one has the power to do what one pleases, what one is inclined to do. To the extent one can do what one wants to do, one is free. To the extent one cannot do what one wants to do, one is bound. One's power is assessed by what one can do. One makes one's self, one makes others, and one makes one's external world. There is no "world behind the world" to which appeal should be made to understand truly. Proponents of this existentialist phenomenological interpretation appeal neither to the forms which Plato affirmed nor to atoms in motion which Democritus affirmed to understand their experiences.

The Contextual or Situational Phenomological Interpretation of Aristotle — A second phenomenological approach focuses on the circumstances which influence the knower or agent. One begins one's analysis with these circumstances, and then one differentiates various components found in these circumstances. One doesn't begin with the independent individual and his/her own mind; rather, one begins with the individual in society, affected by cultural and political forms. Experiences are conditioned by these circumstances.

Aristotle, who utilized this situational interpretation, held that law was the fundamental notion. Laws are statements of the relational context in which power operates. This relational context includes both natural and political laws. If one wants to undertake the task of explaining what a person does in the state, which is never natural in the sense that nature is natural because human choices are involved in the formulation of the state, one examines the way in which a person's actions are influenced by institutional arrangements and by the habits a person acquires. In this interpretation, laws and virtues are the basic notions guiding the analysis.

Aristotle held that humans are to be conceived as a part of the circumstances which make them what they are. It is impossible to rip humans out of their context. They exist in a physical, biological, moral, and political context which affects them and their habits. Because of the reflexive relations which exist between people in a familial, economic, and political context, politics and ethics are two facets of a single science.

Because different circumstances applied to different entities, Aristotle made basic distinctions between the theoretical, the practical and the aesthetic disciplines. The theoretical sciences include the natural sciences, mathematics, logic and metaphysics. The practical or social sciences examine the interplay between the choices humans make and their social situation. The aesthetic disciplines include those whose subject matters were made by humans, such as art, drama, music, and rhetoric. They serve a carthartic function, effecting human feelings.

Theoretical or speculative reason applies to the first sphere; practical reason applies to the second. God is discerned through the use of speculative reason. God "exists" and thinks thoughts about itself. It is the prime mover and is the locus of human contemplation. (Aristotle rejected the reality of Platonic forms and the essence/existence contrast involved in that ontological interpretation.) Humans participate reflexively in the eternal law which is embodied in God. This participation gives rise to natural law and permits reason to inform the will of its fitting action.

Aristotle's work is very important for Christian theology and Christian ethics, for Thomas Aquinas, who is still the dominant informing spirit in the Roman Catholic tradition, was greatly influenced by his thought. Aristotle provides the basic framework which Thomas supplements with his views on supernatural revelation, transcending the understanding which human reason can develop but compatible with it. (From the perspective of the process thought informing the constructive portions of this volume, the view of the Divine Reality elaborated by Aristotle and by Aquinas is most unfortunate, for it precludes the possibility of reciprocity of influence between God and the world. From the Aristotelian and Thomistic point of view, God influences the world, but the world does not influence God.)

In this contextual approach, freedom is the freedom of self-realization. Freedom constitutes a social problem, and one's task is to follow the consequences of one's choices in one's social institutional context. Practical reason, discerning the ends to which various human actions should be directed, informs the will of the fitting choices which it should realize.

The Elemental Ontological Interpretation of Democritus — In contrast to these two classical Greek phenomenological interpretations of the nature of freedom, focusing on freedom understood as self-determination and as self-realization, two other interpretations evolved in that seminal setting. These "ontological" interpretations began with something which is more fundamental that "mere appearance" and which constitutes the basis of knowledge. The understanding these interpretations give to the notions of power and law depends upon or is related to the structure of something more basic than that which existentialists or contextualists hold is fundamental in human experience.

Democritus discerned something more fundamental that mere sense experience—atoms in motion. Thus he held that nature, as he understood it, was the fundamental notion, and he set power, law and knowledge in relation to it. Atoms were the fundamental indivisible entities back of or underlying experience.

A proponent of this elemental or atomistic interpretation, as it may be called, assumes that the agent may determine knowledge of himself or herself by examining the operation of the entities that make him or her what he or she is. (Contemporary reductionistic and deterministic social theorists find their intellectual roots in the line of interpretation that began with Democritus and the Greek atomists. In the modern world, some people holding an elemental interpretation, such as Sigmund Freud, discern the determining entities within one. For others, such as Karl Marx and present day deconstructionists, the determining entities are external. For others, such as Talcott Parsons, they are both internal and external.)

Democritus and those in this tradition discern two kinds of power, two kinds of knowledge, two views of God, and two meanings of law. The first kind of power is the power which a body in motion manifests. The second kind of power is the power which a physical body exerts on other physical bodies. The former kind of power is dependent on the later kind.

The first kind of knowledge is sense experience. It is never true and cannot be trusted. Democritus observed that empirical knowledge was a kind of bastard knowledge. The second kind of knowledge, which can be trusted, is the knowledge or understanding of bodies in motion.

The inferior understanding of God is that which is fashionable or conventional in a particular context. The true understanding of God is knowledge of the underlying factors that give rise to the idea of God. (Freud and his successors, for example, sought to "explain" the God who has been affirmed by a person or a group by appealing to the psychological notions of "father figure," projection, and transference. Durkheim and his successors explained God on the basis of the human experience of society, which was both immanent in them and transcendent of them.)

The first kind of laws are those which humans create in states. These laws are arbitrary or conventional. The second kind of laws are those based on knowledge of the motion of the underlying atoms; they "explain" the arbitrary and conventional laws.

Scientists seek to construct a series of more and more adequate formulations about what goes on among the elemental components underlying human experience. Ethics falls into an area of non-science, for human behavior is guided by the pleasure-pain principle. The good is what pleases, and the evil is what causes pain. From this point of view, it may be possible to develop a science which would determine what causes certain things to evoke pleasure in human beings and what causes certain things to evoke pain in human beings. This science would be indirectly related to ethics, but it would be prior to ethics and more fundamental than ethics.

For the elemental interpretation, freedom consists in acting in accord with a standard, i.e., action in accord with one's own nature. One seeks to discern one's nature by discovering the forces and factors which cause one to be what one is and to live in accord with them. Some versions of psychiatry, strongly influenced by this approach, assume that self-knowledge, i.e., knowledge of one's own nature, will release one from internal obstacles and will give one the freedom to "be oneself." Some versions of Marxism assume that an understanding and readjustment of social institutional configurations will liberate humans and make them free.

The Transcendent Rationalistic Ontological Interpretation of Plato — The second basic ontological interpretation emerging in Greek thought is a transcendent species in which knowledge is the central notion in relation to which power, law and nature are set. Plato, who employed this mode of interpretation, held that the most intelligible is most true. The basic reality is the "idea," which is truer than any imitation and is the source of any becoming and of any opinion. For him, the universe operates according to the laws of reason. Nature refers to becoming, and the creatures that become participate in the ideas. (In the early modern period Spinoza held that God had two infinite attributes, thought and extension. The order of things is the same as or corresponds to the order of the connection of thought.)

Plato, as did Democritus, set up secondary relations between power and law, so he ascribed two meanings to each term. The basic law of being the law of reason. The secondary kind of law is that which can be set up in the ordinary state. Only the wise person has true power, that is to say, has knowledge. A person who uses power without reason is exercising an inferior kind of power. Plato characterized the power of the Sophists as an inferior kind of power.

Thus, nature, power, and law are assimilated to knowledge. In the ideal world, knowledge is identical with law and power. Kings are philosophers, and philosophers are kings. The Good unifies the forms (ideas), so ethics inevitably involves a consideration of knowledge and the Good. One is saved by wisdom or knowledge of the Good, a "formless form" which unifies the forms and to which one can be led by properly using the dialectic.

Freedom is located entirely in the individual. Although Socrates apologized for using the term, he spoke of the self superiority of the wise person, that is, of the person who controls emotion by reason. Freedom consists in acting in accord with reason. A foolish person acting according to his or her emotions is not free. Even though such a person initiates his or her own actions, that person is bound, for emotions refer to that which one suffers or endures. Therefore, Plato devoted a great deal of attention to education, for it was the institutional form by which one could attain freedom, which is the approximation to a standard, reason, and is the freedom of self-perfection.

The Transcendent Theo-dynamic Ontological Interpretation of Early Classical Christianity and the Modern Period

Numerous thinkers within the Christian movement have had a close relation with Plato's views, but most have differed with him on the bases for human experience of the Divine. For them, unaided human reason cannot lead one to the vision of the Good; God in the height of Its dynamic creative freedom must reveal Itself to humankind. The specific locus of this Divine self revelation is Jesus the Christ, who is illumined as such to the human spirit when it is grasped by the Divine Spirit in a moment of ecstasy. This theo-dynamic transcendent ontological interpretation, as it may be termed, begins with Divine power and views the world as a created whole, dependent on the God Who transcends and creates both forms and the world. Augustine was the classical figure who most fully articulated this viewpoint.

Ontic will or spiritual power becomes the basic term in relation to which knowledge, nature, power, and law are set. (Protagonists of this interpretation differ on the relation of ordinary human experiences to the experience of the Divine Spirit in a moment of ecstasy. Augustine and Paul Tillich, for example, hold that in the Fall [Adam and Eve turning their own wills from their locus in God's will to themselves, disrupting the harmony of creation in Augustine's literalistic interpretation of the Fall; the movement from essence to existence in Tillich's symbolic interpretation of the Fall] human relationships with the Divine are sharply distorted but not completely lost from the human point of view. For Augustine, human craving for the Divine remains; for Tillich, humans can raise but cannot answer the question of the meaning of existence.

For some, of whom the contemporary Protestant theologian Karl Barth is an outstanding exemplar, the Fall is more radical. Neither the craving after happiness nor human questioning shaped by the distortion of proper God-human relations remains after the Fall. God is utterly transcendent. All human longing for and all human awareness of the Divine Reality depends on Its self revelation through Jesus Christ in the height of Its freedom. True knowledge, then, depends on God's initiative, and is contrasted with the inferior knowledge of the fallen and unredeemed human. The redeemed person is the free person. For Barth the biblical forms are the forms through which God's revelation in Jesus Christ is carried. Others frequently absolutize these forms.

These epistemological differences persist when persons utilizing a theo-dynamic ontological interpretation address the issues of nature, power, and law. Those holding that the Fall resulted in the distortion but not the complete loss of any human understanding of the Divine will discern a distortion of authentic interpretations by the unredeemed person; those holding that the Fall resulted in a complete loss of any human relation with the Divine will discern a radical contrast between authentic and false understandings of nature, power and law. In the subsequent paragraphs dealing with this topic, these contrasts will be ignored.

Proponents of this theo-dynamic species of the transcendent ontological interpretation discern two views of nature. The false view sees nature as self sufficient and autonomous; the true view sees nature as a Divine creation, dependent on God's sustaining and guiding creative power. (Interestingly, Augustine and many of his followers promoted the notion of divine omnipotence. The doctrine of predestination entailed in this view leads to a form of causal determination, which gives it some analogs to the views of Democritus and other proponents of an elemental interpretation. The tantalizing relation between Marx and Augustine noted earlier is related to this analogy.).

God's will, which manifests perfect love, is the basic law of being. Secondary or inferior laws may be set up in the ordinary state. Such laws are necessary due to sin, finitude and/or ignorance. Only the blessed person has true power, which is contrasted with the inferior power of the unredeemed. Only the redeemed person has true knowledge and true power. (In the Christian movement, the issue of the capacity of the redeemed person to actualize his or her power invariably emerges in the consideration of true wisdom and true power. Does the redeemed person who has wisdom have the power to actualize the law of love? There are three possibilities. The redeemed person may actualize his or her power completely, partially, or not at all. It is beyond the scope of this introduction to trace the ramifications of these alternatives within the Christian movement. Alternatives have been considered earlier in this volume, especially in Chapter 9.) In summary, proponents of this view locate freedom primarily in God and derivatively in human beings. Freedom consists in acting accord to a standard, God's will.[1]

An Interpretation of the Relation of Process Thought to These Classical Interpretations

The relation of the perspective informing the constructive portions of this volume to Greek thought and to the dominate views in the Christian movement is complex. The ontological principle, which, as noted frequently, is basic to process thought, states that the reasons for things are to be found in actual entities, both in entities in the world and in God. This phenomenological interpretation relates this view to the Sophists and to Aristotle.

The principle of relativity, a second notion basic to process thought, states that every being, i.e., every entity that has become, is a potential for every becoming. This intrinsic relationality of entities leads to a view which affirms the impact of the causal past on the present and the need to explore the social institutional consequences of one's decisions for future entities in the world. Thus, Sophistic existentialism is blended with Aristotelian situationalism.

As was the case with Aristotle, God exists. However, in contrast to Aristotle, God is not a changeless Supreme Being. Instead, God is an actual entity who is changing as the world evolves. God differs from all other actual entities in two salient ways. First, the primordial facet of God's nature envisages all potentiality and is prior to the consequent facet of God's nature. (Whether the eternal objects which God envisages are a continuum which are atomized when the creatures of the world appropriate them and whether, under the aegis of creativity, new eternal objects are created are not considered here.) Second, through Its consequent facet, God receives fully into Its life all the creatures of the world which have become. It is this never ending and full reception of the emerging creatures of the world in the Divine Life which produces Its growth.

The primordial facet of the Divine Life is analogous to the Platonic Good, but it does not have the high stature Plato assigns to the Good, for It is deficient in actuality. It needs a world for Its completion. In his conception of the Divine actuality, Whitehead, the founder of the mode of thought informing the constructive portions of this volume, thus blended Aristotelian and Platonic modes of thought. (The unfashionableness of both these modes of thought in most intellectual circles in the current epoch helps account for the relatively modest influences of process of thought in the human sciences at the present time.)

The ultimacy of the category of creativity in process thought entails the dominance of dynamics over form in the nature of things. An emerging creature appropriates forms of definiteness from creatures embodied in its causal past in the physical phase of its becoming and from God in the conceptual phase of its becoming, but the creature itself, guided by but not determined by the Divine subjective aim, shapes its own synthesis of the data and feeling tones it receives from the creatures in its causal past and from God. After it has become, it is a datum for all the creatures that succeed it. As superject, it then contributes to the emergence of other emerging entities.

As noted in earlier chapters, this dynamic bias results in a contexualist consequentialist social ethic. One seeks to respond in a given context in such a manner that one's actions will enhance the harmony and intensity of feeling of the creatures in its causal future. In so doing, one seeks to assess the probable consequences of alternative decisions. In such an assessment, one may be informed by formal guidelines, but one's actions need not be unequivocally shaped by such guidelines. In other words, forms are very useful but are not definitive in a given situation. This concern for tracing the social institutional consequences of one's actions relates process thought to Aristotelian social ethics, but it is not as formal as is Aristotle's social ethic. In the context of the Christian movement, this social ethic is less formalistic than Catholic social ethics, but more formalistic than much Protestant social ethics. It is also more sympathetic to the universality of some principles than is a biblically centered Protestant social ethic. (For detailed discussion of these issues, see Parts One and Two of this volume.)

Freedom is self determination informed by excellence. In this formulation, the self determination of the Sophistic view is qualified by the experience of the lure for harmony and intensity of feeling embodied in the Divine Nature. As just noted, the fitting action to enhance harmony and intensity of feeling is shaped by one's assessment of the future consequences of one's actions. In this way, this understanding involves a qualification of the classic Sophistic view and a convergence with facets of Aristotle's thought.

The aesthetic language of harmony and disharmony is Platonic. Although process thought is not reductionistic, its understanding of causal efficacy does mean that the creatures lying in the causal past of an emerging entity do condition its feelings and form. In this way Democritus' emphases are incorporated in process modes of thought.

Laws are viewed as imminent, coming into existence and passing out of existence as the creatures embodying them change. This atomistic view of nature has some resemblance to the views of Democritus, but the mental pole is emphasized and the "atoms" do not persist. They become and then perish. They never really "are." Power is relational, not linear.

This process view contrasts with substance views of the nature of reality advanced by both Aristotle and Democritus. It is in accord with Plato's view of the becoming of occasions, but for Plato the "really real" were the changeless forms in the realm of being. According to the ontological principle, for process thought the "really real" are the actual entities of the world. (Overall, the debt of process thought to Plato is very great indeed. As noted earlier, this inversion of Plato's thought and the application of the principle of relativity to the Divine Life constitute major shifts from Plato. Nonetheless, much of his thought is very compatible with process interpretations. Whitehead himself is very explicit about his intellectual debt to Plato.)

None of the three thinkers examined in Part Four entertains the two-way God world relation characteristic of dipolar theism. Both Moltmann and Tillich affirm a Divine Reality of the one-way variety, and both emphasize the priority of the dynamic facet of the Divine nature. Both insist on the necessity of a Divine initiative to reveal Its nature to humans, and both emphasize the categorical differences between God and the creatures of the world. They are more closely related to the views developed in early classical Christianity.

Burhoe has a more deterministic view of the emergence of humankind, and he draws on the French anthropological tradition in his interpretations. His views are more closely related to the Greek atomists who advanced elemental interpretations of law, nature, freedom, power, knowledge and God.

Notes

1. People in the Roman Catholic tradition have drawn upon Aristotelian ideas to develop their notion of the Divine Being, for St. Thomas and his successors were greatly influenced by his thought. They affirmed the validity of natural theology, for they held unaided human reason could illumine facets of the Divine Nature. God was the unmoved mover, the first cause Who thought thoughts about Itself. Human reason participated in this eternal law, the embodiment of which was called natural law. People promulgated human laws, informed by natural law. God, in the height of Its freedom, supplemented natural law with Divine law. While Divine revelation supplemented the understanding of God developed by human reason, revelation did not contradict human reason. Forms are more strongly emphasized than in classical Protestantism.

The Church is the bearer of God's revelation to humankind through Jesus Christ, and the Church is the promulgator and defender of the Truth. The church plays the role which the Bible plays in classical Protestantism. (As noted earlier, the constructive view developed here also affirms the existence of God, but the nature of the Divine Subject-object differs from the conceptions of Aristotle and St. Thomas. In addition, this view does not give either the church or the Christian scriptures the authority which many in the Christian movement claim for the one, the other or both.)

Introduction to Chapter 17

This chapter is a revised version of an essay prepared for a conference sponsored by the Meadville/Lombard Theological School, a Unitarian-Universalist theological institution, in connection with a seminar series celebrating its 125th anniversary. Not surprisingly, both Paul Tillich and Alfred North Whitehead have attracted substantial interest among Unitarian-Universalists. Tillich's apologetic approach to Christian theology, utilizing facets of contemporary existentialist philosophy to interpret the Christian movement, and his very broad scope are of interest to many Unitarians. In many of his writings his Christological views were not richly elaborated, even thought they are at the center of his systematic theology. This obliqueness is congenial with the views of many in that denomination.

Similarly, Whitehead's low Christology is attractive to numerous Unitarians. His philosophical theism, rooted in universal propositions not categorically tied to any extant historical religion, appeals to the universalism of many Unitarians.

The analysis is focused on the fundamental notions Tillich elaborated in his *Systematic Theology,* his *magnum opus.* It does not address his intellectual development or trace his subsequent work. His last work in the history of religions offers hints of a possible shift in his views toward other great world religions, but that work is too fragmentary to discern what systematic shifts he might have made. If he had made a shift, it would have most likely centered on his view of Jesus as the Christ.

Both Tillich and Whitehead rank among the great intellects of the human race, so a comparative study of these two figures should be of general interest. As the body of this chapter reveals, my constructive sympathies are with Whitehead rather than with Tillich; but I have long been a great admirer of Tillich's systematic power and of the architectonic character of his theological system. I have found his analyses very suggestive; and, as this chapter shows, I find many points of contact between my constructive views and those of Tillich.

CHAPTER 17

The Neo-Orthodox Philosophical Theology of Paul Tillich

Paul Tillich in Theological Context

The use of the term "neo-orthodox" in the title of this chapter to refer to the theology of Paul Tillich presupposes some criteria on the basis of which theological perspectives can be ordered and assessed. Tillich has been praised by some theologians and assailed by others for his theological liberalism, but such praises and critiques are usually made from points of view rooted in Protestant Christianity.

In the main, Tillich's debt to the tradition of Paul, Augustine, and the sixteenth century reformers, especially Luther, is great indeed. In fact, at all critical points Tillich's theology coheres with the central tenet of the Protestant reformation, i.e. humans are justified by grace through faith. He insists on the universalism-particularism of the Christian faith, affirms the centrality for Christians of Jesus as the Christ, and grounds the religious institution he calls the Christian church on the Spiritual Presence it bears and elicits through its confessional witness to Jesus as the Christ. Because he affirms the ontological polarities are distorted but not abrogated under the conditions of existence and understands religion to be a function of the freedom of the spirit interplaying with the freedom-destiny polarity, his thought is perhaps best understood as closer to Augustine than to the sixteenth century reformers. Certainly *sola scriptura* is not a methodological presupposition for him. This interpretation coheres with Augustine's view that even fallen humans crave the happiness due to the relation to God they have lost; hence, not all awareness of the Divine is "lost" in the fall.

With the exception of some tantalizing and puzzling observations in Part V of his *Systematic Theology* about the essentialization of finite beings, Tillich adheres to classical views about the unconditional and unconditioned nature of the Divine, Who is independent of and unaffected by creatures in the world. His Protestant emphasis is apparent in his view of the dominance of a "trans-dynamic" dimension in the Divine and in the priority of dynamic over static dimensions in human experience.

If one holds these emphasis are consonant with the major thrust of the Protestant reformers of the sixteenth century, it is entirely appropriate, as is done here, to characterize Tillich as a neo-orthodox theologian. Those who deny Tillich status as a neo-orthodox Protestant theologian place greater emphasis on the form through which the Christian message is mediated and deny that humans can even raise questions about the "really real" aside from God's grace.

One of Tillich's major opponents, for example, is Karl Barth, whom Tillich thinks is arbitrary when he seeks to confine the theological explication of the Christian message to biblical forms. Though Tillich insists on the finality and concreteness of the Christian revelation in Jesus as the Christ, he acknowledges the multiplicity of symbolic linguistic forms through which the Christian message may be communicated. Such forms are cultural creations and are a consequence of the creating capacity of the human.

Both Barth and Tillich are attacked by biblical fundamentalists and Protestant scholastics for their refusal to make absolute the form through which the Christian message is delivered. While Barth obviously bears tantalizingly close relation to fundamentalism, Tillich is a major enemy of this branch of Christianity.

Tillich's appeal to people in liberal Protestantism is undoubtedly related to his willingness to use philosophical language, particularly the language of some forms of twentieth century existentialism, in the explication of his theological system. Tillich's understanding of the universality of the *logos* structure of reality permits him to suggest a method of correlation for theological analysis.

Philosophy, whose task it is to elaborate the universal structures humans experience in their encounters with reality, is able to raise questions about ultimate reality, but it is unable to give answers to questions of human ultimate concern because of the irrationality of the movement from essence to existence and the distortion of the ontological polarities under the conditions of existence. Theology, whose task it is to elaborate the meaning of the human experience of the New Being in Jesus as the Christ, is able to give answers to the questions which philosophy raises. The "method of correlation" relates philosophic questions to theological answers.

Each major part of Tillich's *Systematic Theology* is therefore organized in two major sections. The first section, based on philosophic analysis, raises questions about the nature of ultimate reality. The second section, based on theological analysis, gives answers to the questions about the nature of ultimate reality raised in the first section.

Tillich rejects the formalism embodied in Roman Catholic theology, but his use of philosophy in theological apologetics relates him loosely to Roman Catholicism. Just as he can be seen as a "bridge" figure between biblically centered Protestant theology and Protestant liberalism, so he can also be seen as a "bridge" figure between Protestant and Catholic philosophical theology. His rejection of natural theology, "super-naturalism," his critique of the dominance of form in Aquinas, his insistence that God is beyond the subject-object structure of human experience, and his rejection of the claims of the "heteronomous" authority of the Roman Catholic Church place him at odds with Roman Catholicism, but his interest in philosophic analysis does permit some communication with traditional Roman Catholic thinkers. Broadly viewed, Tillich is more in debt to the Platonic heritage than to the Aristotelian heritage informing the dominant modes of Roman Catholic thought. At the same time, his epistemological views separate him from both Plato and Aristotle.

In addition, Tillich is ambiguously related to phenomenological perspectives on reality and negatively related to reductionistic views of reality.

His insistence on the legitimacy of empirical studies using the canons of evidence and criteria of evaluation appropriate for particular subject matters within the realm of ordinary knowledge leads him to evaluate historical and scientific studies positively, so long as they do not preclude the possibility of increased illumination by "extraordinary" knowledge, i.e., the human experience of Spiritual Presence in a moment of ecstasy.

It is this qualification which leads him to a negative evaluation of reductionistic interpretations of reality.

Tillich's both/and approach to the "scientific" study of religious phenomena is analogous to the "external-internal" history contrast of H. Richard Niebuhr, to the "fact-value" dichotomy of Max Weber, and to the "theoretical reason-practical reason" bifurcation of Immanual Kant. His insistence that values must be grounded in ontology separates him from ethical humanism.

Because he denies that reason can penetrate to the ultimate nature of things, insists on the finality of Christian revelation, and is very Christocentric, Tillich is out of tune with a theological liberalism affirming the intrinsic reasonableness of things, questioning the finality of Christian revelation, entertaining a relatively low Christology and envisaging a different God-world relation. As he affirms the authenticity of a *sui generis* Supreme Reality, Tillich maintains a point of contact with such theistic thinkers, even though they may disagree with his understanding of the Divine Nature and of the means by which humans become aware of It.

The relation of Tillich's thought to the form of theological liberalism informing this critique is tantalizing. As will become clear in the following sections of this chapter, the basic ontological structure and the ontological elements, central to the way in which Tillich posits his philosophical questions and considers life and the spirit, are translatable into the categories of process thought.

Tillich and process informed thinkers discern similar dimensions in experience, but they diverge in their interpretation of these dimensions and their implications for the life of civilized humankind and for the Divine Life. From the point of view of process thinkers, Tillich is better at raising questions than he is at giving answers.

Even this assessment is tentative, for Tillich assumes the movement from essence to existence is irrational, affirms the Divine Reality is beyond the subject-object structure of existence, entertains a substance view of the nature of the self, deals inadequately with problems of perception, fails to apply the principle of relativity to Divine-world relations, and over-emphasizes the dynamic side of things.

The following section delineates the basic notions shaping Tillich's analyses, the third section considers his understanding of the Divine, and the final section criticizes Tillich's view from a perspective of process theology and dipolar theism.

The Fundamental Informing Notions in the Neo-Orthodox Philosophical Theology of Paul Tillich

Spiritual Presence

The religious experience of Spiritual Presence is absolutely central to Tillich's theological system. Regardless of the amount of intellectual analysis one makes of Tillich's thought, one will be unable to fathom its central core unless one has had an experience analogous to Tillich's description of being grasped by Spiritual Presence, the state of ecstasy. Though the interpretation of this experience of Divine Presence is necessarily related to one's constructive viewpoint, one who has not had a "religious experience" cannot empathize with the Tillichian schematism.

Tillich's description of Spiritual Presence and his interpretive framework are both illumined in this discussion of the manifestation of the Divine Spirit in the human spirit:

> . . . spirit as a dimension of life unites the power of being with the meaning of being. Spirit can be defined as the actualization of power and meaning in unity. Within the limits of our experience this happens only in man — in man as a whole and in all the dimensions of life which are present in him. Man, in experiencing himself as man, is conscious of being determined in his nature by spirit as a dimension of his life. This immediate experience makes it possible to speak symbolically of God as Spirit and of the divine Spirit. These terms, like all other statements about God, are symbols. In them, empirical material is appropriated and transcended. Without this experience of spirit as the unity of power and meaning in himself, man would not have been able to express the revelatory experience of "God present" in the term "Spirit" or "Spiritual Presence." This shows again that no doctrine of the divine Spirit is possible without an understanding of spirit as a dimension of life.
>
> The question of the relation between Spirit and spirit is usually answered by the metaphorical statement that the divine Spirit dwells and works in the human spirit. In this context, the word "in" implies all the problems of the relation of the divine to the human, of the unconditional to the conditioned, and of the creative ground to creaturely existence. If the divine Spirit breaks into the human spirit, this does not mean that it rests there, but that it drives the human spirit out of itself. The "in" of the divine Spirit is an "out" for the human spirit. The spirit, a dimension of finite life, is driven into a successful self-transcendence; it is grasped by something ultimate and unconditional. It is still the human spirit; it remains what it is, but at the same time, it goes out of itself under the impact of the divine Spirit. "Ecstasy" is the classical term for this state of being grasped by the Spiritual Presence. It describes the human situation under the Spiritual Presence exactly.
>
> . . . The Spiritual Presence creates an ecstasy in both . . . [revelatory and saving experiences] . . . which drives the spirit of man beyond itself without destroying its essential, i.e., rational, structure. Ecstasy does not destroy the centeredness of the

> integrated self. Should it do so, demonic possession would replace the creative presence of the Spirit.
>
> Although the ecstatic character of the experience of Spiritual Presence does not destroy the rational structure of the human spirit, it does something the human spirit could not do by itself. When it grasps man, it creates unambiguous life. Man in his self-transcendence can reach for it, but man cannot grasp it, unless he is first grasped by it. Man remains in himself. By the very nature of his self-transcendence, man is driven to ask the question of unambiguous life, but the answer must come to him through the creative power of the Spiritual Presence. "Natural theology" describes man's self-transcendence and the questions implied in his consciousness of its ambiguity. But "natural theology" does not answer the question.
>
> This illustrates the truth that the human spirit is unable to compel the divine Spirit to enter the human spirit. The attempt to do so belongs directly to the ambiguities of religion and indirectly to the ambiguities of culture and morality. If religious devotion, moral obedience, or scientific honesty could compel the divine Spirit to "descend" to us, the Spirit which "descended" would be the human spirit in a religious disguise. It would be, and often is, simply man's spirit ascending, the natural form of man's self-transcendence. The finite cannot force the infinite; man cannot compel God. The human spirit as a dimension of life is ambiguous, as all life is, whereas the divine Spirit creates unambiguous life.[1]

This passage has been quoted at length because it also illumines clearly Tillich's understanding of the way in which humans become aware of Spiritual Presence. God, symbolically speaking, takes the initiative to reveal Itself to humans. God grasps humans who become aware of Its revelatory and saving power in this experience of Spiritual Presence.

For Christians, the regeneration, justification, and sanctification present in the objective side of Spiritual Presence is manifest through the New Being in Jesus as the Christ, who is the power of salvation.[2] The term "justification by grace through faith" points to the unanticipatable and unmanipulatable nature of this experience.

Tillich insists that the principle of justification by grace through faith is the first and basic expression of the Protestant principle. It affirms ". . . that, in relation to God, God alone can act and that no human claim, especially no religious claim, no intellectual or moral or devotional 'work', can reunite us with him."[3] This insistence leads to the judgment expressed earlier that Tillich is a "neo-orthodox" theologian.

Tillich's view of God-human relations revealed in this quotation means he appeals to a dynamic principle to establish a relation between a human and that which is conceived to be the "really real." This "world behind the world" relates Tillich to theistic thinkers, even though God is beyond the subject-object structure of existence. God "is," but God does not exist.

The Essence-Existence Contrast

For Tillich, humans are essentially related to but existentially estranged from the Divine Reality. This formulation is exceptionally important for Tillich. It is no exaggeration to say that the entire schematism stands or falls on the adequacy of Tillich's view of the relation of essence to existence. In the final part of this chapter, Tillich's essence-existence contrast and his view of the movement from essence to existence to essentialization will be challenged. In the present context, it is important to explicate it as clearly as possible.

Tillich interprets existence to mean "standing out of non-being."[4] He opens up the question of essence and existence dialectically, indicating that all things stand out of non-being. He notes that non-being can be understood in two ways, as absolute non-being and as relative non-being. By asserting that everything that exists stands out of absolute non-being, one says they are in both being and non-being. To exist is to be something finite, a mixture of being and non-being. To exist is to stand out of one's own non-being.

One can stand out of one's own non-being only if everything participates in being, whether or not it exists. Things participate in potential being before they can come into actual being. Mere potentiality is relative non-being. It is, metaphorically speaking, the power of being which has not realized its power. Something exists when it leaves the state of mere potentiality and becomes actual. It then stands out of mere potentiality, i.e., relative non-being.

Something which exists is never out of mere potentiality, for it never manifests its power of being completely in its state of existence, i.e., it never fully exhausts its potentiality.

The distinction between actuality and the potentiality of relative non-being gives rise to a split in reality between potentiality and actuality. Tillich observes:

> Within the whole of being as it is encountered, there are structures which have no existence, and things which have existence on the basis of structures. Treehood does not exist, although it has being, namely, potential being. But the tree in my back yard does exist. It stands out of the mere potentiality of treehood. But it stands out and exists only because it participates in the power of being which is treehood, that power which makes every tree a tree and nothing else.
>
> This split in the whole of reality, expressed in the term "existence," is one of the earliest discoveries of human thought. Long before Plato, the prephilosophical and the philosophical mind experienced two levels of reality. We can call them "essential" and the "existential" levels. The Orphics, the Pythagoreans, Anaximander, Heraclitus, and Parmenides were driven to their philosophy by the awareness that

> the world they encountered lacked ultimate reality. But only in Plato does the contrast between the existential and the essential being become an ontological and ethical problem. Existence for Plato is the realm of mere opinion, error and evil. It lacks true reality. True being is essential being and is present in the realm of eternal ideas, i.e., in essence. In order to reach essential being, man must rise above existence. He must return to the essential realm from which he fell into existence. In this way, man's existence, his standing out of potentiality, is judged as a fall from what he essentially is. The potential is the essential, and to exist, i.e., stand out of potentiality, is the loss of true essentiality. It is not a complete loss, for man still stands in his potential or essential being. He remembers it, and through his remembrance, he participates in the true and the good. He stands in and out of the essential realm. In this sense "standing out" has a meaning precisely opposite that of the usual English usage. It means falling away from what man essentially is.[5]

Tillich uses the phrase "transition from essence to existence" to characterize the myth of "the Fall." The symbol "the Fall" is a symbol for the human situation universally. Finite freedom makes possible the transition from essence to existence.

Creation and the Fall coincide for Tillich ". . . in so far as there is no point in time and space in which created goodness was actualized and had existence."[6] Though creation is good in its essential character, it falls into universal estrangement through freedom and destiny when it is actualized.

Tillich insists that the transition from essence to existence is not a structural necessity. It has the character of a leap, so essence cannot be derived from existence. This understanding is critical for Tillich's doctrine of justification by grace through faith; for if essence were derivable from existence, rational reflection on existence could lead one to an understanding of essence. The paradox of Christianity, the appearance of the New Being under the conditions of existence, yet judging and conquering them, is a paradox only if this essence-existence contrast is tenable. This paradox is that which is against human self-understanding and expectations, both empirical and rational.

Tillich emphasizes the irrationality of the transition from essence to existence in this passage:

> . . . the transition from essence to existence, from the potential to the actual, from dreaming innocence to existential guilt and tragedy, is irrational. In spite of its universality, this transition is not rational; in the last analysis it is irrational. We encounter the irrationality of this transition from essence to existence in everything, and its presence is irrational, not paradoxical. It is an undeniable fact which must be accepted, although it contradicts the essential structure of everything created.[7]

The Ontological Concepts

Tillich organizes his theological system by using ontological concepts, i.e., concepts which are more universal than any concept designating a realm of beings but less universal than being. He distinguishes four levels of ontological concepts: 1) the basic ontological structure which is the implicit condition of the ontological question; 2) the elements which constitute the ontological structure; 3) the characteristics of being which are the conditions of existence; and 4) the categories of being and knowing.[8]

The first level of ontological concepts is a self-world structure of being which gives rise to the subject-object structure of being. This subject-object structure of being is presupposed when the ontological question is asked, for the ontological question, i.e., the question of being, requires an asking subject and an object about which the question is asked. The relation between subject and object is one of polarity, not that of identity from which neither subject nor object can be derived. Tillich does not think the basic ontological structure can be derived. This quotation illumines Tillich's way of using philosophy to raise questions and pointing to theology to give answers:

> The question, "What precedes the duality of self and world, of subject and object?" is a question in which reason looks into its own abyss — an abyss in which distinction and derivation disappear. Only revelation can answer this question.[9]

The ontological elements constituting the basic structure of being are the second level of ontological concepts. Because they share the basic polar character of the basic structure, they are principles and not the highest generic concepts. Due to their polar character, one pole of an ontological element "is meaningful only in so far as it refers by implication to the opposite pole."[10]

The three outstanding polarities — Tillich does not indicate any others — constituting the basic ontological structure are individuality and participation, dynamics and form, and freedom and destiny.[11] Individuality, dynamics, and freedom express the "self-relatedness of being, its power of being something for itself."[12] Participation, form, and destiny express ". . . the belongingness of being, its character of being a part of a universe of being."[13]

The third level of ontological concepts deals with the duality of essential and existential being, their relation to each other, and their relation to being itself. Because finite freedom, freedom in unity with finitude, is the turning point from being to existence, ". . . it is the analysis of finitude in its polarity with infinity as well as in its relation to freedom and destiny, to being and non-being, to essence and existence, which is the task of ontology in third level."[14]

The fourth level deals with the basic forms of thought and being, traditionally called categories. The categories ". . . participate in the nature of finitude and can be called structures of finite being and thinking."[15] Tillich holds four main categories — time, space, causality and substance — must be analyzed from a theological point of view.

For Tillich, time "flows." His own view emerges in the context of other views of time. From the negative side, there is ". . . movement of time from a past that is more toward a future that is not yet through a present which is nothing more than the moving boundary line between past and future."[16] From the positive side, there is a ". . . creative character of the temporal process, to its directness and irreversibility, to the new produced within it."[17] Tillich holds that ontology can only state a balance between the positive and negative character of time; it cannot discern its meaning.

To be is to have space, which is implied in the present. "Time creates the present through its union with space."[18] Like the other categories, space is ambiguous. On the one hand, space is necessary for life; on the other hand, space will eventually be lost.

Causality also has positive and negative aspects, expressing both being and non-being. "If something is causally explained, its reality is affirmed, and the power of its resistance against nonbeing is understood."[19] On the other hand, the notion of ". . . the cause of a thing or event presupposes that it does not possess its own power of coming into being."[20]

Similarly, substance, which points to something relatively static and self-contained underlying the flux of appearances, also has positive and negative elements. Substance gives accidents their ontological power, but without accidents there is no substance.

The Dimensions and Ambiguities of Life

Tillich envisions several realms or dimensions of life, but he recognizes the fuzziness of the gradations. His own preference for the dynamic side of things leads him to resist inordinately sharp formalizations. Acknowledging the gradations, Tillichs posits the inorganic, organic, psychological, the spiritual, and the historical dimensions of life. In humans the dimensions of Spirit are dominant, but all the other realms are also present. Spirit is a unity of power and meaning. It implies a totally centered self, i.e., one that is free. Psychological self-awareness is presupposed by the presence of the spirit. The dimension of the spirit gives rise to the historical dimension. "This last and all-embracing dimension of life comes to its full actualization only in man, in whom as bearer of the Spirit the conditions for it are present."[21] This dimension gives rise to the quest for the kingdom of God within history and at the end of history.

Tillich uses the ontological polarities to organize his treatment of the self-actualization of life and its ambiguities. The individuality-participation polarity orders his discussion of the self-integration of life, the dynamics-form polarity orders his discussion of the self-creativity of life, and the freedom-destiny polarity orders his discussion of the self-transcendence of life.

He discusses self-integration and disintegration (health and disease), self-creativity and destruction (life and death), and self-transcendence and profanization (the greatness of life and its ambiguities) outside the dimension of spirit. In addition, he discusses self-integration, self-creativity and self-transcendence in relation to the dimension of the spirit. In the dimension of the spirit, self-integration gives rise to morality, self-creativity gives rise to culture, and self-transcendence gives rise to religion. All are ambiguous and elicit the quest for the unambiguous.

Finally, Tillich discusses life and history, considering the structure of historical processes and the logic of historical knowledge, the movement of history within this structural frame, the ambiguities of historical existence, and the quest for the meaning of historical movement. The "Kingdom of God" is posited as the answer to the question of the meaning of history. Tillich relates the "Kingdom of God" symbol to an "inner-historical" meaning, referring to "Spiritual Presence," and to a trans-historical meaning, referring to "Eternal Life."

Tillich's Interpretation of the Divine Reality

The use of the notions informing Tillich's schematism can be illustrated by considering his discussion of the Divine. Because Tillich's conception of the Divine contrasts sharply with process views, this topical treatment enhances the critique of Tillich in the following section.

Though he does reject some views of predestination, Tillich's view of God's unconditional character constitutes a clear and lucid formulation of the classical view of God-world relations, a view overwhelmingly dominant in the Christian tradition. Three passages in which Tillich discusses the aseity of God illuminate Tillich's view of the unqualifiedly unconditional character of the Divine.

In the context of discussion of casualty, Tillich observes: "The anxiety in which causality is experienced is that of not being in, of, and by one's self, of not having the 'aseity' which theology traditionally attributes to God."[22]

In the context of a discussion of God as being, Tillich writes:

> A theology which does not dare to identify God and the power of being as the first step toward a doctrine of God relapses into monarchic monotheism, for if God is not being-itself, he is subordinate to it, just as Zeus is subordinate to fate in Greek religion. The structure of being-itself is his fate, as it is the fate of all other beings. But God is his own fate; he is "by himself"; he possesses "aseity." This can be said of him only if he is the power of being, if he is being-itself.[23]

In the context of a discussion of the way in which the ontological elements are symbolically applicable to the Divine Life, Tillich makes this sharp formulation about the unconditioned nature of God. It is quoted at length, for it is very important in the critique in the final section of this essay:

> If we consider the polarity of freedom and destiny in its symbolic value, we find that there hardly is a word said about God in the Bible which does not point directly or indirectly to his freedom. In freedom he creates, in freedom he deals with the world and man, in freedom he saves and fulfills. His freedom is freedom from anything prior to him or alongside him. Chaos cannot prevent him from speaking the word which makes light out of darkness; the evil deeds of men cannot prevent him from carrying through his plans; the good deeds of men cannot force him to reward them; the structure of being cannot prevent him from revealing himself; etc. Classical theology has spoken in more abstract terms of the aseity of God, of his being *a se*, self-derived. There is no ground prior to him which could condition his freedom; neither chaos nor non-being has power to limit or resist him. But aseity also means that there is nothing given in God which is not at the same time affirmed by his freedom. If taken nonsymbolically, this naturally leads to an unanswerable question, whether the structure of freedom, because it constitutes his freedom, is not itself something given in relation to which God has no freedom. The answer can only be that freedom, like the other ontological concepts, must be understood symbolically and in terms of the existential correlation of man and God. If taken in this way, freedom means that that which is man's ultimate concern is in no way dependent on man or on any finite being or on any finite concern. Only that which is unconditional can be the expression of unconditional concern. A conditioned God is no God.
>
> Can the term "destiny" be applied symbolically to the divine life? The gods of polytheism have a destiny — or, more correctly, a fate — because they are not ulti-

mate. But can one say that he who is unconditional and absolute has a destiny in the same manner in which he has freedom? Is it possible to attribute destiny to being-itself? It is possible, provided the connotation of a destiny-determining power above God is avoided and provided one adds that God is his own destiny and that in God freedom and destiny are one. It may be argued that this truth is more adequately expressed if destiny is replaced by necessity, not mechanical necessity, but structural necessity, of course, or if God is spoken of as being his own law. Such phrases are important as interpretations, but they lack two elements of meaning which are present in the word "destiny." They lack the mystery of that which precedes any structure and law, being-itself; and they lack the relation to history which is included in the term "destiny." If we say that God is his own destiny, we point both to the infinite mystery of being and to the participation of God in becoming and in history.[24]

This view of the Divine puts God beyond the basic ontological structures, the ontological elements, finitude, the categories, and essential and existential being. These notions can be used symbolically to characterize the Divine Life because It is the ground of the structure of being. Tillich puts the issue in the following terms:

> Since God is the ground of being, he is the ground of the structure of being. He is not subject to this structure; the structure is grounded in him. He *is* this structure, and it is impossible to speak about him except in terms of this structure. God must be approached cognitively through the structural elements of being-itself. These elements make him a living God, a God who can be man's concrete concern. They enable us to use symbols which we are certain point to the ground of reality.[25]

Tillich's discussion of the Divine is organized about the ontological levels considered in his treatment of being and the question of God. In his theological answer, he explores the implications of the notion that God is being-itself beyond the subject-object cleavage embodied in the self-world relation, beyond the ontological polarities, infinite, the ground of the categories, and beyond essential and existential being.

As noted earlier, Tillich insists that God is not *a* being, for then he would be subject to the categories of finitude, especially space and substance. Tillich puts the matter thusly:

> Whenever infinite or unconditional power and meaning are attributed to the highest being, it has ceased to be *a* being and has become being-itself . . . . the concept of being as being, or being-itself, points to the power inherent in everything, the power of resisting nonbeing. Therefore, instead of saying that God is first of all being-itself, it is possible to say that he is the power of being, in everything and above everything . . .[26]

It follows that God is also beyond the essence-existence contrast. Tillich observes:

> As being-itself God is beyond the contrast of essential and existential being. We have spoken of the transition of being into existence, which involves the possibility that being will contradict and lose itself. This transition is excluded from being-itself (except in terms of the christological paradox[27]), for being-itself does not participate in nonbeing. . . . Logically, being-itself is "before," "prior to," the split which characterizes finite being.[28]

Tillich is unequivocal in his rejection of the notion that God is universal essence. He states:

> If God is understood as universal essence, as the form of all forms, he is identified with the unity and totality of finite potentialities; but he has ceased to be the power of the ground in all of them, and therefore he has ceased to transcend them. He has poured all his creative power into a system of forms, and he is bound to these forms.[29]

Similarly, Tillich rejects attempts to speak of the existence of God, for ". . . an existence of God which is not united with its essence is a contradiction in terms."[30] Tillich comments: "It makes God a being whose existence does not fulfill his essential potentialities; being and not-yet-being are 'mixed' in him, as they are in everything finite. God ceases to be God, the ground of being and meaning."[31]

Tillich refers to the creative and abysmal nature of the Divine to discuss what others have termed the immanence and transcendence of God. As is necessarily the case, he translates other ways of putting God-world relations into his own terms. This passage illumines this central notion in Tillich's understanding of the Divine:

> As the power of being, God transcends every being and also the totality of beings — the world. Being-itself is beyond finitude and infinity; otherwise it would be conditioned by some thing other than itself, and the real power of being would lie beyond both it and that which conditioned it. Being-itself infinitely transcends every finite being. There is no proportion or gradation between the finite and infinite. There is an absolute break, an infinite "jump." On the other hand, everything finite participates in being-itself and in its infinity. Otherwise it would not have the power of being. It would be swallowed by nonbeing, or it never would have emerged out of nonbeing. This double relation of all beings to being-itself gives being-itself a double characteristic. In calling it creative, we point to the fact that everything participates in the infinite power of being. In calling it abysmal, we point to the fact that everything participates in the power of being in a finite way, that all beings are infinitely transcended by their creative ground.[32]

According to Tillich, humans use causality and substance, which are the two categories of relation, to interpret the relation of being-itself to finite beings. As is true of all statements about God except for the statement, "God is being-itself," causality and substance are used symbolically when they refer to God. In this case, the difference between substance and causality disappears. In this way, Tillich seeks both to affirm the ultimacy of divine creation and of creaturely freedom. He expresses the notion in this passage:

> . . . if God is the cause of the entire series of causes and effects, he is the substance underlying the whole process of becoming. But this "underlying" does not have the character of a substance which underlies its accidents and which is completely expressed by them. It is an underlying in which substance and accidents preserve their freedom. In other words, it is substance not as a category but as a symbol. And, if taken symbolically, there is no difference between *prima causa* and *ultima substantia*.[33]

After this discussion of God as Being, Tillich examines God as living, creating, and relating. In the section on "God as Living," Tillich deals with God in Himself, symbolically characterizing the being of God. He uses the ontological elements to give symbolic expression to the nature of the Divine Life itself.

Tillich uses the symbolic power of the categories — space, time, cause, and substance — to discuss the relation of God to the creatures. Because the Divine Life is given expression by the ontological elements — individualization-participation, dynamics-form, and freedom-destiny — these polarities are also used in Tillich's discussion of relation of the creator to the created. The section on "God as Related" can be looked upon as a continuation of the section on "God as Creating," since creation is Tillich's basic description of God-world relations.

In the section on "God as Creating," Tillich explores the implications of the creativity of the Divine Life, using the three modes of time — past, present, future — to symbolize it. Tillich speaks of originating creation, sustaining creation, and directing creation as he discusses the doctrine of creation.

In the section on "God as Related," Tillich explores creator-creature relations. He rejects the notion God can be related to creatures in the proper sense of the word; the word "holiness" symbolizes the unapproachable character of God. He also discusses divine power and the creature, divine love and the creature, and the symbols "Lord" and

"Father." The *logos* structure of being is included in Tillich's consideration of "The Meaning of Omniscience" in the treatment of divine power and the creature and in his consideration of "The Divine Love and the Divine Justice" in the treatment of divine love and the creature. The symbol "Lord" basically expresses human relations to God Who is holy power; the symbol "Father," basically holy love.

Since there is no distinction between potentiality and actuality in God, the word "life," the process in which potential being becomes actual being, as used to characterize God is used symbolically. None the less, since every true symbol participates in the reality it symbolizes, it is possible to speak of God as living. Tillich observes:

> If we call God the "living God," we deny that he is a pure identity of being as being; and we also deny that there is a definite separation of being from being in him. We assert that he is the eternal process in which separation is posited and is overcome by reunion. In this sense, God lives. Few things about God are more emphasized in the Bible, especially in the Old Testament, than the truth that God is a living God. Most of the so-called anthropomorphisms of the biblical picture of God are expressions of his character as living. His actions, his passion, his remembrances and anticipations, his suffering and joy, his personal relations and his plans — all these make him a living God and distinguish him from the pure absolute, from being-itself.[34]

As noted earlier, Tillich employs the ontological elements to give symbolic expression to the nature of the Divine Life. This passage, quoted at length because it will be cited in the critical portion of this chapter, is a powerful statement of Tillich's conception of the Divine Life:

> The polar character of the ontological elements is rooted in the divine life, but the divine life is not subject to this polarity. Within the divine life, every ontological element includes its polar element completely, without tension and without the threat of dissolution, for God is being-itself. However, there is a difference between the first and the second elements in each polarity with regard to their power of symbolizing the divine life. The elements of individualization, dynamics, and freedom represent the self or subject side of the basic ontological structure within the polarity to which they belong. The elements of participation, form, and destiny represent the world or object side of the basic ontological structure within the polarity to which they belong. Both sides are rooted in the divine life. But the first side determines the existential relationship between God and man, which is the source of all symbolization. Man is a self who has a world. As a self he is an individual person who participates universally, he is a dynamic self-transcending agent within a special and a general form, and he is freedom which has a special destiny and which participates in a general destiny. Therefore, man symbolizes that which is his ultimate concern in terms taken from his own being. From the subjective side of the polarities he takes — or more exactly, receives — the material with which he symbolizes the divine life. He sees the divine life as personal, dynamic, and free. He cannot see it in any other way, for God

is man's ultimate concern, and therefore he stands in analogy to that which man himself is. But the religious mind — theologically speaking, man in the correlation of revelation — always realizes implicitly, if not explicitly, that the other side of the polarities also is completely present in the side he uses as symbolic material. God is called a person, but he is a person not in finite separation but in an absolute and unconditional participation in everything. God is called dynamic, but he is dynamic not in tension with form but in an absolute and unconditional unity with form, so that his self-transcendence never is in tension with his self-preservation, so that he always remains God. God is called "free," but he is free not in arbitrariness but in an absolute and unconditional identity with his destiny, so that he himself is his destiny, so that the essential structures of being are not strange to his freedom but are the actuality of his freedom. In this way, although the symbols used for the divine life are taken from the concrete situation of man's relationship to God, they imply God's ultimacy, the ultimacy in which the polarities of being disappear in the ground of being, in being-itself.[35]

Tillich builds up the meaning of spirit through the examination of the ontological elements and their unity. In this passage, also quoted at length because it will be cited in the following critical section, Tillich illumines his understand of spirit:

The meaning of spirit is built up through the meaning of the ontological elements and their union. In terms of both sides of the three polarities one can say that spirit is the unity of power and meaning. On the side of power it includes centered personality, self-transcending vitality, and freedom of self-determination. On the side of meaning it includes universal participation, forms and structures of reality, and limiting and directing destiny. Life fulfilled as spirit embraces passion as much as truth, libido as much as surrender, will to power as much as justice. If one of these sides is adsorbed by its correlate, either abstract law or chaotic movement remains. Spirit does not stand in contrast to body. Life as spirit transcends the duality of body and mind. It also transcends the triplicity of body, soul, and mind, in which soul is actual life-power and mind and body are its functions. Life as spirit is the life of the soul, which includes mind and body, but not as realities alongside the soul. Spirit is not a "part," nor is it a special function. It is the all-embracing function in which all elements of the structure of being participate. Life as spirit can be found by man only in man, for only in him is the structure of being completely realized.

The statement that God is Spirit means that life as spirit is the inclusive symbol for the divine life. It contains all the ontological elements. God is not nearer to one "part" of being or to a special function of being than he is to another. As Spirit he is as near to the creative darkness of the unconscious as he is to the critical light of cognitive reason. Spirit is the power through which meaning lives, and it is the meaning which gives direction to power. God as Spirit is the ultimate unity of both power and meaning.[36]

Tillich goes on to discuss the trinitarian principles:

God is spirit, and any trinitarian statement must be derived from this basic assertion.

God's life is life as spirit, and the trinitarian principles are moments within the process of the divine life. Human intuition of the divine always has distinguished between the abyss of the divine (the element of power) and the fulness of its content (the element of meaning), between the divine depth and the divine *logos.* The first principle is the basis of Godhead, that which makes God God. It is the root of his majesty, the unapproachable intensity of his being, the inexhaustible ground of being in which everything has its origin. It is the power of being infinitely resisting nonbeing, giving the power of being to everything that is. . . .

The classical term *logos* is most adequate for the second principle, that of meaning and structure. It unites meaningful structure with creativity. . . . The *logos* opens the divine ground, its infinity and its darkness, and it makes its fulness distiguishable, definite, finite. The *logos* has been called the mirror of the divine depth, the principle of God's self-objectification. In the *logos* God speaks his "word," both in himself and beyond himself. . . .[37]

Tillich concludes his discussion of God as living with an analysis of God and the infinite. This notion is also a major interest in the subsequent critique of Tillich, so it is quoted here in its entirety:

The divine life is infinite, but in such a way that the finite is posited in it in a manner which transcends potentiality and actuality. Therefore, it is not precise to identify God with the infinite. This can be done on some levels of analysis. If man and his world are described as finite, God is infinite in contrast to them. But the analysis must go beyond this level in both directions. Man is aware of his finitude because he has the power of transcending it and of looking at it. Without this awareness he could not call himself mortal. On the other hand, that which is infinite would not be infinite if it were limited by the finite. God is infinite because he has the finite (and with it that element of nonbeing which belongs to finitude) within himself united with his infinity. One of the functions of the symbol "divine life" is to point to this situation.[38]

Tillich indicates that the doctrine of creation is the answer to the question implied in human finitude and in finitude generally. This answer comes to humans; it does not emerge out of the question. As noted earlier, Tillich subsumes both preservation of the world and providence under the notion of divine creativity.

In the treatment of God's originating activity, Tillich considers the following:

(1) Creation and Nonbeing
(2) Creation, Essence, and Existence
(3) Creation and the Categories
(4) The Creature.

Some of the notions discussed here have been noted earlier, but some key ideas need to be highlighted.

For Tillich, the doctrine of creation out of nothing means that the tragic character of existence is not rooted in the Divine and that there is an element of nonbeing in creatureliness.

Tillich seeks the answer to the question of the relation between creation and time from the creative character of the Divine Life. He never fully explicates his view of space, but this statement about the nature of time is illumining and contrasts with the view posited in the critique:

> If the finite is posited within the process of the divine life, the forms of finitude (the categories) also are present in it. The divine life includes temporality, but it is not subject to it. The divine eternity includes time and transcends it. The time of the divine life is determined not by the negative element of creaturely time but the present, not by the "no longer" and the "not yet" of our time. Our time, the time which is determined by nonbeing, is the time of existence. It presupposes the separation of existence from essence and the existential disruption of the moments of time which are essentially united within the divine life.
>
> Time, then, has a double character with respect to creation. It belongs to the creative process of the divine life as well as to the point of creation which coincides with the fall. Time participates in the destiny of everything created to be rooted in the divine ground beyond essence and existence and to be separated from the divine ground through creaturely freedom and creaturely destiny. Therefore, if one speaks of time before creation, this can only mean the divine time which is not "before" in any sense of temporal existence. And if one speaks of creation *in* time, this can only mean the transformation of the time which belongs to the divine life into the time which belongs to creaturely existence. It is more adequate to speak of creation *with* time, for time is the form of finitude in the creative ground of the divine life as well as in creaturely existence.[39]

In this discussion, Tillich holds humans are the *telos* of creation:

> In maintaining that the fulfillment of creation is the actualization of finite freedom, we affirm implicitly that man is the *telos* of creation. Of no other being that is known can it be said that finite freedom is actualized within it. In other beings there are preformations of freedom, such as Gestalt and spontaneity, but the power of transcending the chain of stimulus and response by deliberation and decision is absent. No other being has a complete self and a complete world; no other being is aware of finitude on the basis of an awareness of potential infinity. If another being were found which, in spite of biological differences, had these qualities, it would be human. And if among men a being were found of a like biological nature, but without the previously mentioned qualities, it would not be called "man." But both cases are imaginary, since biological structure and ontological character cannot be separated.[40]

Tillich contrasts God's originating and sustaining creativity by comparing power, the creative ground which is the dominant factor in the former, and form, the structure of reality dominant in the latter.

Tillich prefers the concept "*telos* of creativity" to the concept "the purpose of creation." The latter term is too ambiguous, for creation has no purpose beyond itself. The concept "*telos* of creativity" means ". . . the inner aim of fulfilling in actuality what is beyond potentiality and actuality in the divine life."[41]

God is always directing everything towards its fulfillment, but It ". . . always creates through the freedom of man and through the spontaneity and structural wholeness of all creatures."[42] Providence ". . . uses all factors, both those given by freedom and those given by destiny, in creatively directing everything towards its fulfillment. Providence is a *quality* of every constellation of conditions, a quality which 'drives' or 'lures' toward fulfillment."[43]

In his discussion of providence, Tillich appeals to the unity of the poles of individualization and participation in the creative ground of the Divine Life to refute the doctrine humankind is separated into the saved or the condemned. In this context, he explicates his view of the way in which God participates in the disharmonies of existence. Because it contrasts sharply with the process view guiding the critique of Tillich, it is quoted here:

> The principle of participation drives us one step further. God himself is said to participate in the negativities of creaturely existence. This idea is supported by mystical as well as by christological thought. Nevertheless, the idea must be stated with reservations. Genuine patripassianism (the doctrine that God the Father has suffered in Christ) rightly was rejected by the early church. God as being-itself transcends nonbeing absolutely. On the other hand, God as creative life includes the finite and, with it, nonbeing, although nonbeing is eternally conquered and the finite is eternally reunited within the infinity of the divine life. Therefore, it is meaningful to speak of a participation of the divine life in the negativities of creaturely life.This is the ultimate answer to the question of theodicy. The certainty of God's directing creativity is based on the certainty of God as the ground of being and meaning. The confidence of every creature, its courage to be, is rooted in faith in God as its creative ground.[44]

Tillich organizes his discussion of "God as Related" into three major sections, the divine holiness and the creature, the divine power and the creature, and the divine love and the creature. In addition, he has a concluding section, noted earlier, dealing with the symbol "God as Lord and Father."

Tillich passionately denies the possibility of having a relation with God in the proper sense of the word. Proponents of dipolar theism explicitly affirm this view, so these crucial paragraphs must be cited:

> "Relation" is a basic ontological category. It is valid of the correlation of the ontological elements as well as of the interrelations of everything finite. The distinctly theological question is: "Can God be related and, if so, in what sense?" God as being-itself is the ground of every relation; in his life all relations are present beyond the distinctions between potentiality and actuality. But they are not the relations of God with something else. They are the inner relations of the divine life. The internal relations are, of course, not conditioned by the actualization of finite freedom. But the question is whether there are external relations between God and the creature. The doctrine of creation affirms that God is the creative ground of everything in every moment. In this sense there is no creaturely independence from which an external relation between God and the creature could be derived. If God is said to be in relation, this statement is as symbolic as the statement that God is a living God. And every special relation participates in this symbolic character. Every relation in which God becomes an object to a subject, in knowledge or in action, must be affirmed and ended at the same time. It must be affirmed because man is a centered self to whom every relation involves an object. It must be denied because God can never become an object for man's knowledge or action. Therefore, mystical theology, inside and outside Christian theology, speaks of God's recognizing and loving himself through man. This means that if God becomes an object, nevertheless he remains a subject.
>
> The unapproachable character of God, or the impossibility of having a relation with him in the proper sense of the word, is expressed in the word "holiness." God is essentially holy, and every relation with him involves the consciousness that it is paradoxical to be related to that which is holy. God cannot become an object of knowledge or a partner in action. If we speak, as we must, of the ego-thou relation between God and man, the thou embraces the ego and consequently the entire relation. If it were otherwise, if the ego-thou relation with God was proper rather than symbolic, the ego could withdraw from the relation. But there is no place to which man can withdraw from the divine thou, because it includes the ego and is nearer to the ego than the ego to itself. Ultimately, it is an insult to the divine holiness to talk about God as we do of objects whose existence or nonexistence can be discussed. It is an insult to the divine holiness to treat God as a partner with whom one collaborates or as a superior power whom one influences by rites and prayers. The holiness of God makes it impossible to draw him into the context of the ego-world and the subject-object correlation. He himself is the ground and meaning of this correlation, not an element within it. The holiness of God requires that in relation to him we leave behind the totality of finite relations and enter into a relation which, in the categorical sense of the word, is not a relation at all. We can bring all our relations into the sphere of the holy; we can consecrate the finite, including its internal and external relations, through the experience of the holy; but to do so we must first transcend all these relations. Theology, which by its nature is always in the danger of drawing God into the cognitive relation of the subject-object structure of being, should strongly point to the holiness of God and his unapproachable character in judgment of itself.[45]

Tillich defines ". . . divine omnipotence as the power of being which resists nonbeing in all its expressions and which is manifest in the creative process in all its forms."[46] The symbol of omnipotence should be correlated with the faith which gives the courage to conquer the anxiety of finitude.

Tillich then explores the meaning of omnipotence with respect to time, which is eternity, space, which is omnipresence, and the subject-object structure of existence, which is omniscience. These three symbols focus on the relation of God to the created.

Tillich affirms that eternity includes temporality. He appeals to ". . . the only analogy to eternity found in human experience, that is, the unity of the remembered past and anticipated future in an experienced present."[47] Because the present predominates in temporal experience, an eternal present is the first symbol of eternity. This eternal present is neither simultaneity nor the negation of an independent past or future. Tillich comes tantalizingly close to a process view of the relative openness of the future in this passage, though he does assume time "flows."

> The eternal present is moving from past to future but without ceasing to be present. The future is genuine only if it is open, if the new can happen and if it can be anticipated. This is the motive which led Bergson to insist upon the absolute openness of the future to the point of making God dependent on the unforeseen that might happen. But in teaching the absolute openness of the future, Bergson devaluated the present by denying the possibility of its anticipation. A God who is not able to anticipate every possible future is dependent on an absolute accident and cannot be the foundation of an ultimate courage. This God would himself be subject to the anxiety of the unknown. He would not be being-itself. Therefore, a relative although not an absolute openness to the future is the characteristic of eternity. The new is beyond potentiality and actuality in the divine life and becomes actual as new in time and history. Without the element of openness, history would be without creativity. It would cease to be history. On the other hand, without that which limits openness, history would be without direction. It would cease to be history.[48]

In contrast to a process view of the past, Tillich holds that the past is not complete for God, ". . . because through it he creates the future; and, in creating the future, he re-creates the past. . . . The past becomes something different through everything new which happens. . . . From the point of view of eternity, both past and future are open. The creativity which leads to the future also transforms the past. If eternity is conceived in terms of creativity, the eternal includes past and future without absorbing their special character as modes of time."[49]

Tillich also holds God's relation to space must be interpreted in qualitative terms. "God creates extension in the ground of his life, in which everything spatial is rooted. But God is not subject to it; he transcends it and participates in it. God's omnipresence is his creative participation in the spatial existence of his creatures."[50]

Because God is beyond the subject-object structure of the world, Tillich rejects the idea that omniscience is ". . . the faculty of a highest being who is supposed to know all objects, past, present, and future, and, beyond this, everything that might have happened if what has happened had not happened."[51] Instead, omniscience symbolically ". . . expresses the spiritual character of the divine omniscience expresses the spiritual character of the divine omnipotence and omnipresence."[52] ". . . God is not present in an all-permeating manner but . . . he is present spiritually."[53]

In the last major section of his discussion of "God as Related," Tillich considers divine love and the creature. He distinguishes four types of love, *agapé, libido, eros,* and *philia.* Tillich discusses the four types in this passage:

> If we say that God *is* love, we apply the experience of separation and reunion to the divine life. As in the case of life and spirit, one speaks symbolically of God as love. He *is* love; this means that the divine life has the character of love but beyond the distinction between potentiality and actuality. This means therefore that it is mystery for finite understanding. The New Testament uses the term *agapé* for divine love. But it uses the same term also for man's love to man and man's love to God. There must be something in common in the three love relations. In order to discover it, one must compare the *agapé* type of love with the other types. One can say in abbreviated form: Love as *libido* is the movement of the needy toward that which fulfills the need. Love as *philia* is the movement of the equal toward union with the equal. Love as *erõs* is the movement of that which is lower in power and meaning to that which is higher. It is obvious that in all three the element of desire is present. This does not contradict the created goodness of being, since separation and the longing for reunion belong to the essential nature of creaturely life. But there is a form of love which transcends these, namely, the desire for the fulfillment of the longing of the other being, the longing for *his* ultimate fulfillment. All love, except *agapé,* is dependent on contingent characteristics which change and are partial. It is dependent on repulsion and attraction, on passion and sympathy. *Agapé* is independent of these states. It affirms the other unconditionally, that is, apart from higher or lower, pleasant or unpleasant qualities. *Agapé* unites the lover and the beloved because of the image of fulfillment which God has of both. Therefore, *agapé* is universal; no one with whom a concrete relation is technically possible ("the neighbor") is excluded; nor is anyone preferred. *Agapé* accept the other in spite of resistance. It suffers and forgives. It seeks the personal fulfillment of the other.[54]

Since process views of love presuppose reciprocity of relations between creatures, including human-God relations, Tillich's rejection of this view in the following passage will help illumine the contrast between his view of God-human relations and process views:

> God works toward the fulfillment of every creature and toward the bringing-together into the unity of his life all who are separated and disrupted. Since *agapé* is usually (though not always and not necessarily) connected with the other types of love, it is natural that Christian symbolism has used these types in order to make the divine love concrete. In so far as devotional language speaks of the longing of God for his creature and in so far as mystical language speaks of the need that God has for man, the *libido* element is introduced into the notion of the divine love, but in poetic-religious symbolism, for God is not in need of anything. When biblical and devotional language suggest that the disciples are the "friends of God" (or Christ), the *philia* element is introduced into the notion of the divine love, although in a metaphorical symbolic way, for there is no equality between God and man. If God is described in religious and theological language as driving toward the *eschaton,* i.e., the ultimate fulfillment in which he is "all in all," it can be compared with the *erós* type of love, the striving for the *summum bonum;* but it can only be compared, not equated, with *erós,* for God in his eternity transcends the fulfillment and nonfulfilment of reality. The three types of love contribute to the symbolization of the divine love, but the basic and only adequate symbol is *agapé.*[55]

In addition to the discussion of the meaning of divine love in this section, Tillich also considers the relation of divine love to divine justice and divine love as grace and predestination.

Justice is grounded in the form side of reality, for it is the " . . . side of love which affirms the independent right of object and subject within the love relation."[56] "Divine love includes the justice which acknowledges and preserves the freedom and the unique character of the beloved."[57] In seeking reunion, justice resists and condemns that which is against love. A creature who violates the structure of justice violates love itself, and that creature is consequently judged and condemned. As noted earlier in the discussion of creation and the fall, this violation occurs universally, so "God's wrath" is experienced by all humans.

This formulation leads to Tillich's final statement about the love of God in relation to the unjust creature. The symbol of justification ". . . points to the unconditional validity of the structure of justice but at the same time to the divine act in which love conquers the immanent consequences of the violation of justice."[58] In relation to the sinner, divine love is grace.

In this context, Tillich makes the same observation discussed earlier, i.e., grace is no way dependent on human works. He states:

> The term "grace" (*gratia, charis*) qualifies all relations between God and man in such a way that they are freely inaugurated by God and in no way dependent on anything the creature does or desires. One may distinguish two basic forms of grace — the grace which characterizes God's threefold creativity, and the grace which characterizes God's saving activity. The first form of grace is simple and direct; it provides participation in being to everything that is, and it gives unique participation to every individual being. The second form of grace is paradoxical; it gives fulfillment to that which is separated from the source of fulfillment, and it accepts that which is unacceptable. It is possible to distinguish a third form of grace, one which mediates between the two preceding ones and unites elements of both, namely, God's providential grace. On the one hand, it belongs to creative grace and, on the other hand, to saving grace, since the purpose of God's directing or providential creativity is fulfillment of the creature in spite of resistance. The classical term for this kind of grace is *gratia praeveniens* ("prevenient grace"). It prepares for the acceptance of saving grace through the processes of nature and history."[59]

The question of predestination, the problem of the relation of divine love to ultimate human destiny is raised by the fact that some are not prepared to accept saving grace. The symbolic meaning of predestination which Tillich affirms points ". . . to the existential experience that, in relation to God, God's act always precedes and further, that, in order to be certain of one's fulfillment, one can and must look at God's activity alone."[60]

This elaboration of Tillich's view of divine love and the creature concludes the explication of Tillich's theological viewpoint. It began and ended on the "neo-orthodox" note. Though it is fairly extended, these formulations are necessary to provide the basis for the critique of Tillich's thought from my perspective.

A Process Critique

The Basic Notions Shaping this Critique

Four fundamental ideas shape the perspective informing this critique of Tillich's neo-orthodox philosophical theology. They are a principle of rationality, a principle of concrete explanation, a principle of relativity, and the category of creativity.

A faith in rationalism is fundamental to this viewpoint. There is a relational structure to the universe, and it is the task of metaphysics to try to penetrate that structure. This premise cannot be "proved," for it arises from an intuition inherent in the nature of things. It is an ideal seeking satisfaction and not the end product of a line of reasoning. This faith shades off into religious experience and is sustained by the belief that the intellectual endeavor embodies hope and offers the prospect of some success. Reason seeks to penetrate to the nature of things and to develop propositions applying to all entities.

The principle of concrete explanation (often called the ontological principle, a term coined by Whitehead) holds that the reasons for things are to be found in concrete entities in the world. Explanations are sought among actual occasions, so the search for an explanation is necessarily the search for an actual entity. This principle implies that the ultimate appeal in philosophic analysis is to one's experience — one's experience of oneself and one's relation to other entities in the world.

The principle of relativity, stated in its most general terms, is that every being is a potential for every becoming. This principle means that every actual entity which has become contributes, however feebly, to every entity that is becoming. The creatures of the world are inextricably part one of another. The notion of reciprocal God-world relations is a direct consequence of this principle.

The category of creativity is the category of categories. It implies the notions of "one," "many," "identity," and "diversity." It is the principle by which the many, which is the universe disjunctively, become the one, which is the universe conjunctively. Novelty emerges in this unification, producing a concrete togetherness. The notions of "production of novelty" and "concrete togetherness" cannot be explained in terms either of more general notions or in terms of the many participating in the emergence of the one. One must appeal exclusively to intuition.

A Critique of the Fundamental Notions in Tillich

Introduction. In this section the Tillichian system is critiqued from my constructive perspective rooted in my appropriation of process philosophy. The basic contrasts with Tillich center on the nature of the Divine Reality, the nature of actual entities, and the status of reason. Before turning to the detailed critique, the basic differences in the views of God and of reason should be highlighted.

In accord with the principle of concrete explanation, I hold that God is an actual entity. This existentialist phenomenological interpretation contrasts with Tillich's dynamic ontological interpretation of experience.

God is not beyond the subject object-structure of existence, as Tillich holds. Rather, God is the Supreme Subject-Object.

God does differ from other subjects-objects in one respect: Its conceptual pole is prior to Its physical pole. For this reason, It is able to contrast all that is with all that might be but is not. God never "closes up," but It supremely manifests the processes entailed in the becoming of an actual entity. God is forever being enriched and is forever growing with the creative advance of the world as emerging new actual entities become and are objectified everlastingly in Its life.

Creativity, the principle of rationality, and human "works." Because Tillich makes an essence-existence contrast, conceives of the movement from essence to existence as a fall out of potentiality into actuality, and believes that the move is irrational, he rejects the notion that reason can penetrate to the "really real." Rather, God, Who is beyond the subject object structure of the world must reveal Itself to the human spirit in a moment of ecstasy. For him, ontological structures which are essentially united are existentially distorted.

As will be explicated in this section, I think Tillich's essence-existence contrast is spurious. I have more faith in the ability of reason to penetrate to the nature of things than Tillich does. (As noted in the Introduction to Part Four, the existentialist phenomenological view of God as an actual entity advanced here relates my view to the phenomenological views of Aristotle and Thomistic thinkers in the Roman Catholic tradition indebted to Aristotle, for they also affirm that God exists. In contrast to St. Thomas Aquinas, I hold that God is conditioned by the world and is not unequivocally omnipotent and omniscient. Although I do not make the distinction between speculative and practical reason in the way Aristotelian and Thomistic thinkers do, I do share their higher regard for reason than do Tillich and most other Protestant thinkers.)

The category of creativity is suggestive of the abysmal dimension of "power" in the Divine in Tillich. All creatures, including the Divine, are in its grip, for the creative advance into novelty is inherent in the nature of things. Of course, creativity, God, and the world must be discussed conjointly, for they are all necessary to the description of the becoming of an emerging creature.

Tillich would hold that the ultimacy of creativity in process thought is a God above God and is more fundamental that the actual entity which process thinkers term "God." In response, I would say that God, creativity and the world are intrinsically interrelated. God is both a product of creativity and a precondition for creativity.

The ultimacy of creativity does give this interpretation of things of dynamic transrational bias. In this sense this view bears a close relation to Tillich's view that power is the primal dimension in the power, form, unification triad of trinitarian thinking.

The principle of rationality is in direct conflict with Tillich's view that the movement from essence to existence is irrational. As will be noted in detail subsequently, I reject the way Tillich puts the essence-existence contrast. In the present context, the important point is that the alleged irrationality of the essence-existence movement permits Tillich to argue that one cannot understand one's essence through an analysis of existence. The disruption of the structures of a human's essential nature can be restored only on the basis of Divine initiative.

On the contrary, I hold that, at least in principle, an adequate analysis of experience can illumine not only what humans are but what they are meant to be. God is not the chief exception to metaphysical propositions; It is their supreme exemplification. Therefore, philosophy cannot only raise questions about the nature of things; it can also give answers. The "method of correlation" Tillich employs, in which philosophy raises questions and theology gives answers, is spurious; it involves artificial and unreal distinctions grounded in Reformation theology. Philosophy seeks to develop propositions applicable to all creatures; theology seeks to develop propositions applicable to the Supreme Creature.

Humans are not justified by grace through faith alone, for works — intellectual, aesthetic, and moral — may help humans experience and interpret the Divine Presence and contribute to the Divine Life. To be sure, God contributes to the emergence of every creature, whether the creature is aware of it or not. God's grace, evoking a faith in rationalism, does precede human works. However, human awareness of the Divine Presence and of God's "acceptance" of one is not a one-way street. Intellectual analysis of religious experience *may* contribute to that experience. At the same time, moral and aesthetic intuition *may* illumine the nature of Divine Presence.

Intellectual acumen is no guarantee of religious wisdom, for religious experience is more fundamental than the intellectual analysis of it. In this sense, the concreteness of Tillich's description of Spiritual Presence is valid, though the interpretation he offers is inadequate. None the less, the proper interpretation may enhance and elicit religious experience.

The creatures of the world are justified by God's subjective aim which lures creatures to become and by their everlasting reception into consequent facet of God's nature, which is the objectification of the creatures of the world in the Divine Life. In this way, that which they have become live forever and flow back into the world.

The ultimacy of the subject-object structure of existence and relationality. The principle of concrete explanation presupposes that the subject-object structure of reality is fundamental. However, the subject-object structure of reality is different from that which Tillich presupposes. Every emerging creature is a subject as it appropriates the data from the world (as the principle of relativity states) for its becoming, and every creature is an object — a datum for other emerging creatures — after it has become. Thus, every creature is a subject-object. Tillich's distinction between subjects and objects presupposes a substance doctrine of the self, in which a substantial self undergoes accidents, and does not envision the subject-object relation inherent in the "becoming-being" character of actual entities.

In contrast to other creatures, God's conceptual experience, i.e., Its envisionagement of all potentiality, is prior to Its physical experience, i.e., the objectification of the creatures of the world in God. The former side of the Divine is termed the primordial facet of Its nature; the latter, the consequent facet of Its nature. Nevertheless, God exists and is not beyond the subject-object structure of reality. It is the Supreme subject-object.

The universality of the principle of relativity and the subject-object nature of all entities, including God, lead to a rejection of the idea of an unconditional and unconditioned God. A God Who cannot respond tenderly and sensitively to the creatures of the world is no God. God needs the world just as the world needs God; each contributes to the life of the other. God is not unconditioned; It is supremely conditioned. Relations between God and the world are reciprocal.

Every creature contributes to the life of every other creature, but every creature except God is selective in its appropriation of the world as it begins to become; some things are lost. On the contrary, God is able to appropriate completely and everlastingly all the world has to offer to It. This observation is a direct consequence of the implication of the principle of relativity and the priority of the mental pole in the Divine Life.

The essence-existence contrast. The principle of rationality, the principle of relativity, and the principle of concrete explanation considered conjointly lead to the rejection of the way Tillich puts the essence-existence contrast. His concern with the contrast between potentiality and actuality is certainly legitimate, but his doctrine of essence and his view of the irrationality of the movement from essence to existence must be questioned.

The sheer givenness of things limits the extent to which existence may be rationalized. The theorist must have some material on the basis of which to theorize. This affirmation is the way in which one informed by process thought may interpret the Tillichian view about the irrationality of the movement from essence to existence. This "givenness " cannot be fully rationalized; it is contingent and, however extensively it is rationalized, it must finally be accepted as "given." In fact, one may compulsively become too rationalistic, for ultimately a creature does what it does because it "decides" to do so.

On the basis of experience, one is aware that something might have been which is not and that other things which are not may become. This experience gives rise to the ideas of potentiality and of a potentiality-actuality contrast.

Because everything must be located somewhere, potentiality must also have a locus. That locus is the primordial facet of God's nature, Who has once-for-all envisaged all potentiality. All forms of definiteness are embodied in Its nature, but some forms of definiteness are also embodied in other creatures.

This differentiation gives rise to a distinction between general potentiality, the bundle of possibilities embodied in the primordial facet of God's nature, some of which are mutually exclusive, and real potentiality, the potentiality of seasonally relevant forms for a given creature in a given cosmic epoch. The "essences" which are pertinent for particular creatures are the complex "bundle" of forms of definiteness unified into a pattern sustaining a particular type of creature and embodied in those creatures.

God and the settled past conjointly produce the analog of that which Tillich calls "essences." Tillich's contrast between essential and existential being is in fact a contrast of forms of definitions embodied in the primordial facet of God's nature and the forms embodied in creatures in the settled past with the appropriation of those patterns in an emerging creature with comparable defining characteristics. God and creatures combine to create "essences." The Tillichian contrast between essential and existential being is spurious. God is not beyond essence and existence; in God's actuality, God is a unity of the envisagement of all potentiality and of the embodiment of all of the creatures that have become.

The "isness-oughtness" contrast. Actual entities are the "really real." Existence is concrete; essences are abstract, mere potential. There is no "Fall" from essence to existence, as Tillich suggests. The "really real" are actual entities, not essences which are prior to existence.

The fundamental human experience of an "isness-oughtness" contrast, arising from the contrast between the human experience of the lure for harmony and intensity of feeling embodied in God's nature and the Divine ordering of forms of definiteness, on the one hand, and the limitations of existence, on the other hand, has led humans to develop doctrines of the Fall. Humans contrast their vision of the primordial facet of God's nature with the disharmonies which physical realization evokes and posit a fall from a perfectly harmonious state.

In fact, finitude, ignorance, sloth, lethargy and inordinate creaturely self-interest account for the experience of alienation and disharmony which is a part of human experience. There is no fall from potentiality to actuality.

Potentiality is boundless, without limit, infinite; actuality is bound, limited, and finite. By contrasting infinite being and finite being, Tillich has muddled the distinction between potentiality and actuality. He has further muddled it by affirming God is beyond potentiality and actuality.

The ontological elements and the categories. From the point of view of one informed by process philosophy, the richness of the Tillichian schematism is due to the fact Tillich organizes his theological system around notions inherent in the nature of things. The basic subject-object structure of experience, the contrast between potentiality and actuality, the reality of the Divine, the dominance of a transdynamic element in the nature of things, the pervasiveness of individuality and participation, of dynamics and form, and of freedom and destiny, the hierarchical ordering of nature, and the reality of space, time and cause combine to make the Tillichian schematism very suggestive, especially when dealing with human life.

The ontological elements are, as Tillich suggests, basic and universal. The individual-participation polarity is rooted in the subject-object character of an actual entity and the principle of relativity, the dynamics-form polarity is rooted in the dynamic appropriation of forms of definiteness in the becoming of an actual entity, and the freedom-destiny polarity is grounded in the freedom of an actual entity to surpass but be limited by the causal past in its emerging present.

Tillich holds that these ontological polarities are perfectly balanced and unified in the Divine Life. I affirm the dynamic character of the Divine Life, but I envision a different rhythm than the process of separation and reunion with Itself which Tillich proposes. In my view, the creative advance of the world entails the initial creative phase of God's primordial envisagement of the forms of definiteness, the physical realization of actual entities in the world, and the objectification of these entities everlastingly in the Divine Life. In this sense, there is separation and reunion in the Divine Life. However, the separation and reunion is not merely within God Itself; the separation and reunion are between God and the creatures of the world.

Tillich affirms that God includes time and space but transcends these categories. His formulation of space and time are Newtonian. As noted earlier, time "flows" and is the measure of motion, which significantly, is not one of the categories around which Tillich organizes his treatment of the Divine. Space is that which creatures occupy. It has extension and an existence "independent" of the creatures which "occupy" it.

Tillich contrasts *chronos,* time which flows, with *kairos,* the existential moment of the present. These notions of external and internal time parallel my views of "macro" and "micro" time, except that "macro" time does not flow. "Macro" time is the time produced by the succession of events which become. The experience of time is the experience of the forms of definiteness as they "move" from one entity to another. Time is measured by the ingression of eternal objects in a sequence of occasions.

"Micro" time or duration is the "thickness" of time embodied in a creature who is becoming. As a creature becomes, it is "out of time," that is, it is emerging in causal independence of its contemporaries. Metaphorically, one can speak of the thickness of time to illumine this internal process of becoming.

God, Who includes the creatures who have become in the consequent facet of Its nature, thus includes time in the "macro" sense, but "micro" time is internal to each emerging creature. Since the creature's satisfaction includes the initial aim to become, God participates indirectly in this "time." Because of a creature's everlasting objectification without loss in the Divine Life, God *may* share fully the "micro" time of an emerging creature. I leave the issue open.

Because he affirms the extension of space, Tillich presupposes a continuity of becoming. In fact, there is a becoming of continuity but not a continuity of becoming. Some creatures "spatialize" the world through participation in geometric forms as they become. These forms define geometric relations between these creatures and contribute to their forms of definiteness, but only some creatures are self-conscious of these relations. Societies which appear to be "substances" share many common defining characteristics. Not all creatures have a geometric seat; such entities cannot spatialize the world. For such entities rest and motion cannot be defined.

The Divine Life participates in all geometric forms conceptually and in those geometric forms actualized physically. Its conception of space is the richest conceivable type, for God contrasts all possible forms with all actualized forms. No other creature is able to do this. God is not "beyond" space, as Tillich puts it; rather, all space is immanent in God's experience.

Tillich and I also differ in our understanding of causation. Actual entities lying in the causal past of an emerging occasion affect that occasion. In this sense, they are causes. Some entities merely reproduce that past in the present with almost no change. For these entities, the laws of nature hold sway. At the same time, such low grade organisms, under the aegis of creativity, put, however feebly, their stamps of individuality on themselves. Other entities have greater capacities to respond novelly to circumstances, for the conceptual phase of their becoming is prolonged. Such entities manifest greater freedom from the influence of the causal past. Because God serves as the locus of potentiality, the mediator of forms of definiteness and of feelings from one entity to another, and the lure for feeling, It is also a cause.

Tillich makes a categorical contrast between Divine causality and other types. On the contrary, I hold the principle of relativity applies to all entities, including God. God is a cause, but God is also caused. Aspects of God's life are contingent, just as are aspects of the lives of all other creatures. I reject the notion of Divine aseity in favor of the notion of a God Who is supremely receptive and inclusive.

The question of substances and accidents, or the one and the many in process terms, is a very difficult one. Tillich rightly notes that process philosophers cannot avoid the problem of substance " . . . because questions about that which *has* functions or about that which *is* in process cannot be silenced. The replacement of static notions by dynamic ones does not remove the question of that which makes change possible by not (relatively) changing itself."[61]

The issue is one of emphasis, for personal identity is as much a fact as personal diversity. In my view, some "formless form," an elusive notion because it cannot be characterized independently of the entities which comprise it, is needed. This "formless form" is the soul.

The multidimensional unity of life. My process view of the hierarchy of nature, elaborated in Part One, is very similar to Tillich's, but it more forcefully accentuates the manner in which lower grade organisms and lower grade societies are incorporated in more complex organisms. Tillich emphasizes the creatures' efforts to increase their power of being as they grow in complexity and differentiation; I emphasize the creatures' efforts to increase sensitivity of feeling and aesthetic satisfaction.

Both Tillich and I affirm the enhanced capacity of higher grade organisms to respond novelly to causal influences. Humans possess the greatest degree of freedom from the bonds of the causal past of any organisms of which we have any direct knowledge. Tillich uses the term "self-transcendence" to identify human freedom. I prefer the term "self-surpassment," for I hold the organizing center of the human being is constituted by a sequence of ultimate percipient occasions which surpass each other in serial order.

For Tillich, humans fragmentarily and anticipatorily participate in unambiguous life in a moment of ecstasy. For me, humans experience an intense aesthetic awareness both of God's subjective aim which orders and harmonizes the forms of definiteness and also of the peace which emerges from a glimpse of the everlasting objectification of the creatures of the world in the Divine Life. For Tillich, the experience is unequivocally a result of Divine grace, not human works. For me, the experience is more a function of Divine grace than human works, but not unequivocally so.

These differing understandings of what I think is a universal albeit exceptional human experience illumine the way in which contrasting world views lead to different interpretations of this foundational experience. [Many Asian thinkers offer other interpretations of these universal experiences. It is beyond the scope of this chapter to explore this issue. Because of its rejection of the substance doctrine of the self, process thought has some similarities with many Asian modes of thought.]

Jesus of Nazareth and the church. For Tillich, Jesus is the Christ according to the claim of the Christian Church, whose followers have portrayed Jesus of Nazareth as one who, as a medium, is transparent to the ground of being and who, under the conditions of existence, is unambiguously related to the ground of being. This revelation of God is final, for it cannot be superseded. It is paradoxial, i.e., contrary to human experience.

On the contrary, for me the appearance of the Divine under the conditions of existence is not paradoxical, i.e., it is not contrary to interpreted experience. God is necessarily immanent in the world, and reason has the capacity to illumine that presence.

Jesus of Nazareth is a lure for feeling and meaning in the world and may well be the locus from which religious experience and interpretation emerge; but he is not "the Christ" in the Tillichian. With two exceptions, my Christological view is similar to the view prevalent in the specialized forms of Protestant liberalism manifest in the latter part of the nineteenth century and the early part of the twentieth century. In the earlier forms of liberalism, metaphysics was disavowed and the possibility of the early embodiment of a love ethic in the social order was popular. As the discussions in the first three parts of this volume reveal in detail, I employ a specialized metaphysics in my interpretation of the Christian movement; and I do not foresee the embodiment of a love ethic in the social order in the foreseeable future. In fact, I do not think public policy proposals should be based on such an assumption. At the same time, I do think that some progress in morality and in the development of better forms of social organization is possible, but certainly not inevitable.

In contrast to Tillich, there is no "final" revelation, for the Divine Life surpasses Itself as the creative advance of the cosmos continues. Because of the principle of rationality and the principle of concrete explanation, any experience may elicit religious experience and foster the emergence of thought leading to the formulation of metaphysical propositions.

As noted earlier, these principles apply supremely to the Divine Reality, so theological interpretation may develop out of any experience. Since this evaluation involves both experiential and interpretative components, it is not based exclusively on the experience of Spiritual Presence. Though unequivocally grounded in religious experience, the experience of the lure toward harmony and intensity of feeling grounded in the base of things, a reasonably adequate *sui generis* interpretation of such experience may serve to enhance it. Conversely, non *sui generis* interpretations of religious experience may diminish it.

In a similar vein, the religious institution, identified by worship, education, and the context in which close interpersonal relations may emerge, is a genus of which the Christian church is a species. There is no reason for any religious institution to affirm its distinctively universalistic and particularistic character. In fact, it will emerge out of some concrete context, but there is no reason on the conceptual side to affirm its unequivocal uniqueness as a vehicle of Spiritual Presence. This view of religious institutions has been discussed at length in Chapter 9.

A Critique of Tillich's Doctrine of God

Both Tillichian and process views of God have been cited frequently in the earlier portions of this critique because they are intertwined with their fundamental informing notions. In this section, the contrasts are considered in a more focused manner.

As noted earlier, Tillich holds "God is being-itself" is the only literal statement which can be made about God. All other statements, rooted in ontology, are symbolic because God transcends ontological structures. Nevertheless, theology can use the ontological structure of being as the material for symbols which point to the Divine Life.

In principle, one informed by process philosophy may allow for more literal statements about the Divine. Because God is their Supreme exemplification, metaphysical propositions apply literally to the Divine. Two qualifications should be noted. First, the inadequacy and elliptical character of linguistic symbols require one to make an "imaginative" leap if they are going to communicate adequately the underlying experience to which they point. Second, the tentativeness of metaphysical propositions suggests at least a modicum of restraint on those who think they have developed propositions which are applicable to every conceivable creature, i.e., metaphysical propositions. A fully adequate theology awaits a fully adequate metaphysics. Because the latter can be approached only asymptotically, a fully adequate theology is impossible. It is an ideal seeking satisfaction, but it will never be fully achieved.

In process thought, God is dipolar, as are all other creatures. However, as observed earlier, God's conceptual pole, Its once-for-all envisagement of all potentiality, is prior to God physical pole, its everlasting objectification of the creatures of the world. The former side of God's nature is called the primordial facet; the latter side, the consequent facet.

The primordial facet of God is free, complete, infinite, eternal, actually deficient, and unconscious. The consequent facet is determined, incomplete, finite, "everlasting," fully actual, and conscious, for it ". . . is the weaving of God's physical feelings on His primordial concepts."[62] God is a unity comprising these two poles.

God's subjective aim is perfect, for it is derived from the absolute completeness of the primordial facet of God's nature. It affects the consequent facet, for there is no loss or obstruction in the consequent facet.

The term "everlasting" means ". . . the property of combining creative advance with the retention of mutual immediacy. . . ."[63]

By relating these facets of the Divine nature to Tillich's view of God, one may discern, on the terms of dipolar theism, how Tillich formulated his doctrine. First, Tillich did not differentiate the category of creativity from God. Thus, Tillich is led to emphasize power and unconditionality in his characterization of the Divine. Second, Tillich used some of the characteristics of the primordial facet of God's nature to define the Divine. Freedom, completeness, infinity, and eternality are the notions he uses, rejecting the idea that in this way God is actually deficient. Tillich's discussion of consciousness and the concomitant problem of perception is minimal, but it is difficult to fathom how that which is beyond the subject-object cleavage is "conscious."

Having defined God as unconditional, Tillich has no direct consideration of the consequent facet of God's nature. The attributes of determination, incompleteness, and finitude are incompatible with Tillich's conception of God. Because God is beyond potentiality and actuality for Tillich, he can use neither the terms "actually deficient" and "fully actual" nor "unconscious" and "conscious" in referring to the Divine. The Tillichian analog to "everlasting" is essentialization. As is observed subsequently, Tillich is hard put to explain, on his terms, how or what the world process contributes to the Divine Life.

Though the bases are different, Tillich's doctrine of providence is not far removed from the view of dipolar theists. Because God's subjective aim is luring forth creatures who are becoming, God is creatively urging creatures toward their fulfillment, as Tillich suggests. As noted subsequently, however, the understanding of "fulfillment" is marked differently in Tillich and in my version of dipolar theism.

It is not possible to reconcile my views and Tillich's views on the meaning of omnipotence. In one sense, both Tillich and I agree that God is always present in creatures and can cope with whatever the creatures decide to do. Tillich casts his understanding in the framework of a power of being resisting nonbeing, but I cast my understanding in the framework of becoming and everlastingness. God is omnipotent in the sense the divine can make the best of whatever becomes.

Tillich rejects the idea that eternity is timelessness, because God embraces temporality though It is "eternal." I hold this view is mistaken, for the primordial facet of the Divine nature is eternal, i.e., changeless. The consequent facet is "everlasting," appropriating forever the vivid immediacy of the creatures who have become. This appropriation is the analog of simultaneity in classical Christian thought.

Tillich errs in suggesting the past changes. The past does not become something different through everything new which happens, but the creatures who appropriate it, both Divine and temporal, do.

Tillich's understanding of God's omnipresence as Its creative participation in the spatial existence of Its creatures is close to my view, though his discussion of the nature of space is truncated. The notion of omnipresence as meaning the ubiquity of God is compatible with my view, for every creature derives its subjective aim from the Divine.

Tillich's view of God's omniscience is less adequate than his view of omnipresence. His suggestion that omniscience means God is present spiritually is very similar to his view of omnipresence. I prefer a revision of the classical view Tillich calls an absurdity. The omniscience of God consists of Its "knowledge" of all potentiality and his retention everlastingly of all actuality. God does not foreknow the future because it has not happened and does not "know" the becoming of creatures in their present; but God does "know" perfectly all that has become, i.e., the past.

God's judgment on the world is the tender reception of the world into Itself, losing nothing which can be saved and using destructive evil in the temporal world by relating it to the completed whole.

The conception of the creative act and the relation of God to it is different in process thought than in Tillich. This quotation from Alfred N. Whitehead puts the matter lucidly and poetically:

> Another image which is also required to understand his [God's] consequent nature, is that of his infinite patience. The universe includes a threefold creative act composed of (i) the one infinite conceptual realization, (ii) the multiple solidarity of free physical realization in the temporal world, (iii) the ultimate unity of the multiplicity of actual fact with the primordial conceptual fact. If we conceive the first term and the last term in their unity over against the intermediate multiple freedom of physical realizations in the temporal world, we conceive of the patience of God, tenderly saving the turmoil of the intermediate world by the completion of his own nature. The sheer force of things lies in the intermediate physical process: this is the energy of physical production. God's role is not the combat of productive force with productive force, of destructive force with destructive force; it lies in the operation of the over-powering rationality of his conceptual harmonization. He does not create the world, he saves it; or, more accurately, he is the poet of the world, with tender patience leading it by his vision of truth, beauty, and goodness.[64]

Tillich's view of the unconditional character of *agapé* was delineated earlier. In contrast to that view, I hold that *agapé* should be redefined as supremely conditioned love. After the creatures of the world which have become are received everlastingly in the Divine Life, the perfected actuality flows back into the temporal world, for each temporal entity incorporates it as an immediate fact of pertinent experience. In commenting on this reality, Whitehead adds a fourth creative phase to the three cited above:

> For the kingdom of heaven is with us today. The action of the fourth phase is the love of God for the world. It is the particular providence for particular occasions. What is done in the world is transformed into a reality in heaven, and the reality in heaven passes back into the world. By reason of this reciprocal relation, the love in the world passes into the love in heaven, and floods back again into the world. In this sense, God is the great companion — the fellow-sufferer who understands.[54]

This formulation is analogous to Tillich's exposition of the state of the creature in what he calls essentialization or in Eternal Life, but it is much more lucid and coherent. Tillich holds it is not possible to deal with the issue except in religious poetic-symbolism. Tillich observes:

> In this view the world process means something for God. He is not a separate self-sufficient entity who, driven by a whim, creates what he wants and saves whom he wants. Rather, the eternal act of creation is driven by a love which finds fulfillment only through the other one who has the freedom to reject and to accept love. God, so to speak, drives toward the actualization and essentialization of everything that has being. For the eternal dimension of what happens in the universe is the Divine Life itself. It is the content of the divine blessedness.[66]

This formulation is an empty one, a necessary consequence of the assumptions on which his theological system is based. From my point of view, this statement is incomprehensible, for it is inconceivable that a God Who is infinite and unconditional can be a God for Whom the world process means something. Unconditional love is not love at all; it is tyranny, masked in pious garb. Supreme love is supremely conditioned love, Divine love responding fully and adequately to all temporal creatures.

Both process philosophy and Tillich's neo-orthodoxy philosophical theology have a trinitarian (pre-trinitarian in Tillich's terms) structure. In my view, forms embodied in the primordial facet of God's nature and other creatures in the world are appropriated by an emerging creature who, informed by its own subjective aim, gives a stamp of individuality, however feeble it may be, to the data it appropriates in the process of becoming. One Supreme entity and many other entities unify formal elements in a dynamic process of becoming. These components are intrinsically interrelated, so their separation for analytic purposes is heuristic and provisional.

Coupled with the relatively easy translation of Tillich's ontological elements into process categories, noted previously, Tillich's analyses of human life are very suggestive.

Tillich overmphasizes the contextual aspect in morality, for he holds that moral decisions are made at the apex of human freedom beyond forms. For this reason, there can be no progress in morality.

On the contrary, forms are a necessary part of the becoming of an actual entity. The embodiment of better forms in the human social order and their internalization in human beings can lead to progress in morality.[67]

Interestingly, Tillich only discusses three of the six possible relations between love (unification in my view, reunion in Tillich's view), power (reciprocal in my view, linear in Tillich's view), and justice (intrinsic, legal and transformative in my view, intrinsic, tributive, and creative in Tillich's view). Tillich rightly notes that the sequence "justice, love and power" is the pattern for interpersonal relations and the sequence "power, justice and love" is the pattern for interaction in the political sphere. However, he does not suggest a pattern for the economic sphere. In my view, the pattern of interaction in that sphere (and also in the social and ethnic spheres) is justice, power and love.

Power is less linear and more reciprocal in all the spheres of the human social order than Tillich suggests. In addition, he should have further elaborated the sequence in the sphere of the holy. The sequence he delineates, love, power and justice, is fitting from the human point of view. However, Tillich does not look at the sequence from the Divine point of view, for he does not allow for God-world reciprocity. In my view, the proper sequence from the Divine point of view is love, justice and power. In this view, God receives the creatures of the world into Its life (love) by embodying the forms and feelings of their becoming (justice) and then lures forth new creatures through the overarching rationality of Its subjective aim (power).

These sequences are discussed in detail in Part One, Part Two, and Chapter 9 of Part Three.

Divine love lifts up forms of definiteness seasonally relevant for a given creature in its context, but divine love does not force "justice" on the creature. If the creature defies some of the appropriate forms, it must pay the consequences; for neither God nor the creatures of the temporal world can eliminate the forms embodied in other creatures and in primordial facet of God's nature. In Its judgment, God will make the best of what the creatures decide to become, but God and the world will be enhanced if the creatures make decisions which increase the harmony and intensity of feeling among them.

This summary statement by Whitehead illumines the dipolar nature of the Divine and underscores the reasons for the contrasts and conflicts with Tillich:

> It is as true to say that God is permanent and the World fluent, as that the World is permanent and God is fluent.
>
> It is as true to say that God is one and the World many, as that the World is one and God many.
>
> It is as true to say that, in comparison with the World, God is actual eminently, as that, in comparison with God, the World is actual eminently.
>
> It is as true to say that the World is immanent in God, as that God is immanent in the World.
>
> It is as true to say that God transcends the World, as that the World transcends God.
>
> It is as true to say that God creatures the World, as that the World creates God.
>
> God and the World are the contrasted opposites in terms of which Creativity achieves its supreme task of transforming disjoined multiplicity, with its diversities in opposition, into concrescent unity, with its diversities in contrast. In each actuality these are two concrescent poles of realization — "enjoyment" and "appetition," that is, the "physical" and the "conceptual."[68]

This discussion of God's judgment in relation to divine love concludes my critique of Tillich's neo-orthodox philosophical theology. Though my differences with Tillich are fundamental, I am greatly in his debt. It is an aesthetic delight to analyze such a clear and lucid systematic work. To my mind, anyone who reads him with care cannot but be stimulated and challenged to reflect on the issues he addresses with such acumen.

Notes

1. Paul Tillich, *Systematic Theology*, Vol. III, Chicago: University of Chicago Press, 1963, pp. 111-113.

2. Paul Tillich, *Systematic Theology*, Vol. II, Chicago: University of Chicago Press, 1957, pp. 165-180.

3. Paul Tillich, *Systematic Theology*, Vol. III, *op. cit.*, p. 224.

4. Paul Tillich, *Systematic Theology*, Vol. II, *op. cit.*, p. 21. The explication in this and the following two paragraphs is drawn from pages 20 and 21 of Volume II of *Systematic Theology*.

5. *Ibid.*, pp. 21-22. It is interesting to observe that Plato held reason and the proper use of the dialectic could lead the wise human to the good, the fountainhead of essence. Tillich rejects this way of "saving knowledge."

6. *Ibid.*, p. 44.

7. *Ibid.*, p. 91.

8. Paul Tillich, *Systematic Theology,* Vol. I, Chicago: University of Chicago Press, 1951, p. 104.
9. *Ibid.,* p. 174.
10. *Ibid.,* p. 165.
11. Tillich uses the term "universality" rather than "participation" in his enumeration of the polarities on p. 165 of *Systematic Theology,* Vol. I. However, in the subsequent elaboration of polarities (*Systematic Theology,* Vol. I, pp. 174-178) and in most other contexts he uses the term "participation."
12. Paul Tillich, *Systematic Theology, Vol. I, op. cit.,* p. 165.
13. *Ibid.,* p. 165.
14. *Ibid.,* p. 165.
15. *Ibid.,* p. 165.
16. *Ibid.,* p. 193.
17. *Ibid.,* p. 193.
18. *Ibid.,* p. 194.
19. *Ibid.,* p. 195.
20. *Ibid.,* p. 196.
21. Paul Tillich, *Systematic Theology,* Vol. III, p. 25. The formulations in this and the following three paragraphs are a compact statement of the bases for the notions developed by Tillich in pages 11-110 and 297-423 of Volume III of his *Systematic Theology.*
22. Paul Tillich, *Systematic Theology* Vol. I, p. 196.
23. *Ibid.,* p. 236.
24. *Ibid.,* p. 248.
25. *Ibid.,* p. 238.
26. *Ibid.,* p. 236.
27. As noted earlier, those who affirm Jesus as the Christ acknowledge the paradoxical (contrary to popular opinion) unambiguous manifestation of being-itself in existence.
28. Paul Tillich, *Systematic Theology,* Vol. I, *op. cit.,* p. 236.
29. *Ibid.,* p. 236.
30. *Ibid.,* p. 236.
31. *Ibid.,* p. 236.
32. *Ibid.,* p. 237.
33. *Ibid.,* p. 238.
34. *Ibid.,* p. 242.
35. *Ibid.,* p. 243-244.
36. *Ibid.,* p. 249-250.
37. *Ibid.,* p. 250-251.
38. *Ibid.,* p. 251-252.
39. *Ibid.,* p. 257.
40. *Ibid.,* p. 258.
41. *Ibid.,* p. 264.
42. *Ibid.,* p. 266.
43. *Ibid.,* p. 267.
44. *Ibid.,* p. 270.
45. *Ibid.,* p. 271-272.
46. *Ibid.,* p. 273.
47. *Ibid.,* p. 275.
48. *Ibid.,* p. 275-276.
49. *Ibid.,* p. 276.

50. *Ibid.*, p. 277.
51. *Ibid.*, p. 278.
52. *Ibid.*, p. 278.
53. *Ibid.*, p. 279.
54. *Ibid.*, p. 280.
55. *Ibid.*, p. 281.
56. *Ibid.*, p. 282.
57. *Ibid.*, p. 283.
58. *Ibid.*, p. 284-285.
59. *Ibid.*, p. 285.
60. *Ibid.*, p. 286.
61. *Ibid.*, p. 197.
62. Alfred N. Whitehead, *Process and Reality*, New York: Macmillan, 1929, p. 524.
63. *Ibid.*, p. 524-525.
64. *Ibid.*, p. 525.
65. *Ibid.*, p. 532.
66. Paul Tillich, *Systematic Theology*, Vol. III, *op. cit.*, p. 422.
67. For an elaboration of the principles of justice and forms of social organization normatively desirable for human beings from the point of view of this version of process philosophy, see Part I. Tillich and I differ in our prudential judgments on political economy. I opt for democratic capitalism rather than for democratic socialism. Part II discusses this issue in detail.
68. Alfred N. Whitehead, *Process and Reality*, *op. cit.*, p. 528.

Introduction to Chapter 18

In the 1960s and 1970s various strands of a theological perspective termed "Liberation Theology" emerged within both Protestant and Catholic facets of the Christian movement. Although it is a complex movement, its various protagonists seek to "liberate" humans from what they consider to be oppressive sexual, racial, social, economic, political, and/or cultural conditions by promoting a very substantial transformation of the spheres of the social order. Many proponents hold egalitarian and socialistic values, at least in principle. Neo-Marxist modes of social analysis are fashionable among its leaders. The work of Jürgen Habermas and the French deconstructionists directly or indirectly has impacted the work of many liberation theologians. In addition to its influence in North America and some parts of Europe, the movement has been influential in Latin America, Africa, and Asia.

This chapter considers a major work of Jürgen Moltmann, an early German proponent of one form of liberation theology. Moltmann uses both the dialectic of negation and the analogical method in his constructive work. He elaborates his views of the implications of God's revelation in Jesus Christ for the human being and for the human social order. His version of liberation theology relates him to Protestant neo-orthodoxy, for he rejects the idea of a natural theology in which unredeemed human reason may lead to an adequate interpretation of the Divine Reality. His promotion of democratic socialism reflects a view of political economy which is widespread among liberation theologians. (The essays in Part Two of this volume have addressed these matters in detail.)

This chapter undertakes an internal analysis of Moltmann's views as developed in a major writing and offers a critique of them drawing on the foundational notions outlines in Part One of this volume.

CHAPTER 18

Liberation Theology: A Critique from a Process Perspective

Introduction

The inclusive terms "Liberation Theology" and "Process Perspective" used in the title of this chapter mask a difficult problem of symbolic reference, for each phrase points toward rich, complex and multifarious contemporary movements of thought. There is no single mode of "Liberation Theology," and there is no single mode of "Process Theology." In spite of this internal pluralism, the phrases do point toward families of thinkers who share common traditions and relate to common precursors.

Paul, Luther, Hegel, Marx, and Barth are frequent loci of reference for Protestant "Liberation Theologians," most of whom have emerged in the German speaking world. Plato, Whitehead, and Hartshorne are frequent loci of reference for "Process Theologians," most of whom have emerged from the English speaking world, particularly the United States.

These differing historical roots are important, for the shape and tone of varying interpretations of the Christian movement are deeply affected by the ethoses to which humans are related. At this level, most German Protestant theologians are steeped in the feeling and thinking of Martin Luther and of Teutonic culture. In contrast, most American theologians have experienced a more diffuse and less focused religious and cultural matrix. Protestant-Catholic, Lutheran-Calvinist, Lutheran-Anabaptist, Christian-"Secular," and Christian-Marxist conflicts and contrasts are more forcefully embodied in the life experiences of German theologians than of American theologians. Because of different forms of church-state relations and different understandings of religious liberty in the United States and in Germany, Germans are forced to make more explicit and self conscious decisions to disaffiliate with the Christian movement than are Americans.

As I have sought to understand some of the reasons for the theological emphases of German Protestant theologians and for the relatively greater difficulty of Germany to attain a degree of political sanity and stability compared to England or the United States, I have often pondered these contrasts. Although I do not intend to dwell on this issue here, I do want to call attention to it, for one's historical context conditions one's sensibilities, feelings, loyalties and attention to particular intellectual issues.

These socio-cultural contrasts between protagonists of various forms of liberation theology and various forms of process theology are compounded by cognitive ones, for salient contrasts in foundational presuppositions differentiate liberation and process theologians.

Process and liberation theologians differ in their understandings of reason and revelation, Jesus of Nazareth, eschatology, and psychological and political liberation. Related contrasts emerge on such topics are God-world relations, form-dynamic relations, the nature of the church, normative forms of social organization, the nature of perfection, the relation of the church to the other spheres of the social order, the function of principles of justice, the relation of joy and sorrow in human experience, and the nature of "liberation."

The complexity is compounded by the fact that significant "family" quarrels exist between various "liberation" theologians and various "process" theologians. In order to provide a sharp focus for this chapter and to keep it at a manageable length, I will center my exposition of liberation theology on one distinguished representative of that broad perspective, Jürgen Moltmann. I am going to concentrate my attention on selected topics in one of his major works, *The Crucified God*.

I will base my critique on my own constructive appropriation of the process tradition. My version of process theology is somewhat more formalistic and socially conservative than some other versions, but I will not involve myself in this family quarrel here. Whatever the defects of this approach, it has the merit of putting salient problems sharply. I hope this posing of the issues will be evocative and will highlight the contrasts between Moltmann's version of liberation theology and my version of process theology.

Although the issues are intrinsically interrelated, I shall discuss the topics of reason and revelation, Christology, eschatology, psychological liberation and political liberation sequentially. This sequential discussion is made necessary by the serially related succession of events which constitute the thread of experience constituting our conscious organizing centers.

REASON AND REVELATION

Moltmann's View:

For Moltmann, the basic principle of knowledge is the dialectical principle of negation. Quoting Schelling's words with approbation, Moltmann affirms: " 'Every being can be revealed only in its opposite. Love only in hatred, unity only in conflict'."[1]

This principle is foundational for Moltmann's theological method. He observes:

> Applied to Christian theology, this means that God is only revealed as 'God' in his opposite: godlessness and abandonment by God. In concrete terms, God is revealed in the cross of Christ who was abandoned by God. His grace is revealed in sinners. His righteousness is revealed in the unrighteous and in those without rights, and his gracious election in the damned. The epistemological principle of the theology of the cross can only be this dialectic principle: the deity of God is revealed in the paradox of the cross. This makes it easier to understand what Jesus did: it was not the devout, but the sinners, and not the righteous but the unrighteous who recognized him, because in them he revealed the divine righteousness of grace, and the kingdom. He revealed his identity amongst those who had lost their identity, amongst the lepers, sick, rejected and despised, and was recognized as the Son of Man amongst those who had been deprived of their humanity. And this makes it easier to understand Paul's theology of the cross in his doctrine of justification: in his revelation in the cross God justifies the godless, and always justifies them alone (E. Käsemann). One must become godless oneself and abandon every kind of self-deification or likeness to God, in order to recognize the God who reveals himself in the crucified Christ. One must abandon every self-justification if one is to recognize the revelation of the righteousness of God amongst the unrighteous, to whom basically one belongs oneself.[2]

In this critical methodological passage, Moltmann affirms the bedrock importance of the Protestant principle of justification by grace through faith. It is God and God alone who takes the initiative to reveal Itself to humankind in the crucified Christ.

Once this dialectic of negation is experientially grasped, the method of analogy, i.e., like is known by like, can be used to bring humans into correspondence with God. Moltmann expresses his understanding of the proper relation between the dialectic of negation and the method of analogy in this quotation:

> The dialectical principle of 'revelation in the opposite' does not replace the analogical principle of 'like is known only by like', but alone makes it possible. In so far as God is revealed in his opposite, he can be known by the godless and those who are abandoned by God, and it is this knowledge which brings them into correspondence with God and, as I John 3.2 says, enables them even to have the hope of being like God. But the basis and starting point of analogy is this dialectic. Without revelation in the opposite, the contradictions cannot be brought into correspondence. If the principle of analogy alone is followed, the result would be a *theologia gloriae*, applicable to heaven alone. It is the dialectical knowledge of God in his opposite which first brings heaven down to the earth of those who are abandoned by God, and opens heaven to the godless.[3]

In these passages, Moltmann posits the radical discontinuity between humans and God and attacks human efforts to create a natural theology. All attempts to discern the Divine nature from categories drawn from human experiences other than the experiences of godlessness and the sense of abandonment by God are manifestations of self-deification. To be sure, one may use "redeemed" reason to illumine human understanding of the divine, but one may use the method of analogy only after one has experienced revelation in the opposite.

A Process Critique:

From my point of view, the dialectic of negation, though not foundational to the illumination of the Divine Reality, is pointing to a phenomenon embodied in some human experiences. It is grounded in the capacity of human consciousness to entertain negative judgments, i.e., to imagine conceptually the presence of that which is in fact absent or to imagine conceptually the absence of that which is in fact present. Even though the Divine Reality is necessarily immanent in every occasion, human beings, by the exercise of negative judgments, may imagine Its absence. Such human affirmation of God's absence may have complex and reciprocal relations with human feelings, leading humans to express agony, despair and feeling of abandonment by the Divine.

My faith in rationalism prompts me to affirm that there is a relational essence to the universe and that it is the task of speculative reason to seek to elaborate that essence. The violation of that relational essence, as is implied by the dialectic of negation affirmed by Moltmann, is irrational and incoherent.

Having so stated, I also want to affirm the transrational basis of my faith in rationalism. There are no self-evident first principles on the basis of which one may construct a matrix of metaphysical propositions nor is there an adequate language in which to frame them.

The transrational nature of this intuition of the rational character of the universe shades off into religious experience and is sustained by it. This intuition is rooted, I believe, in the envisagement of the eternal objects by God's subjective aim. My awareness of aesthetic satisfaction, order, peace, harmony, and the lure for intensity of feeling is rooted in this intuition. Though transrational, the intuition is not irrational and is not paradoxically related to other experiences.

In my view the transrational character of this intuition is the foundational reason for the persistence of the Protestant doctrine of justification by grace through faith. However, and in contrast to the view Moltmann advances, growth in theory about the nature of Divine-world relations can enhance human religious experience. Justification by grace through faith and justification by human works reciprocally enhance and reinforce one another. Greater conceptual understanding of the nature of the Divine may enrich and deepen human religious experience. Though I would want to qualify Moltmann's bald-faced notion of "self-deification," I would plead guilty to the charge that I seek justification by works as well as by grace. There is a basic continuity between human efforts to understand various subject-objects, including the Supreme Subject-Object.

At the same time, there is one categorical difference between God and all other creatures: the conceptual pole of God's experience is prior to Its physical experience, whereas in all other creatures, the physical pole is prior to the conceptual pole. From my interpretive framework, this difıerence has also lent some plausibility to the dialectic of negation in the treatment of Divine-human relations.

From my perspective, the dialectic stops when a creature has become. The creatures of the future surpass but do not negate the creatures that have become. They selectively appropriate them and integrate them into a new, novel emerging unity. Contrasts are essential to experience and to understanding, but they involve selective appropriations and not negation.

The experience of loss—common to all creatures except the Divine creature—, the presence of contrasts and conflict in human experience, and the human capacity to entertain negative judgments lend some plausibility to the dialectic of negation; but it is, I think, a misreading of the human situation to posit it as foundational for the elaboration of Divine-human relations and for the illumination of the Divine nature.

ON CHRISTOLOGY

Moltmann's View:

As Moltmann indicated in a passage previously quoted, the dialectic of negation, which is of absolutely central methodological importance for him, provides the basis for his Christology and a Trinitarian theology. The life and teachings of Jesus are of minimal consequence for him, and the cross of Jesus becomes the focus for his Christology.

He succinctly summarizes his approach in the following passage:

> The place of the doctrine of the Trinity is not the 'thinking of thought', but the cross of Jesus. 'Concepts without perception are empty' (Kant). The perception of the trinitarian concept of God is the cross of Jesus. 'Perceptions without concepts are blind' (Kant). The theological concept for the perception of the crucified Christ is the doctrine of the Trinity. The material principle of the doctrine of the Trinity is the cross of Christ. The formal principle of knowledge of the cross is the doctrine of the Trinity.[4]

After an effort to relate his views to Paul, Moltmann summarizes his synthesis of the material principle of the cross of Christ and a doctrine of the Trinity. He observes:

> But if one begins by leaving on one side any concept of God which is already presupposed and taken from metaphysics, one must speak of the one whom Jesus called 'Father' and in respect of whom he understood himself as 'the Son . In that case one will understand the deadly aspect of the event between the Father who forsakes and the Son who is forsaken, and conversely the living aspect of the event between the Father who loves and the Son who loves. The Son suffers in his love being forsaken by the Father as he dies. The Father suffers in his love the grief of the death of the Son. In that case, whatever proceeds from the event between the Father and the Son must be understood as the spirit of the surrender of the Father and the Son, as the spirit which creates love for forsaken men, as the spirit which brings the dead alive. It is the unconditioned and therefore boundless love which proceeds from the grief of the Father and the dying of the Son and reaches forsaken men in order to create in them the possibility and the force of new life.[5]

He continues this discussion by emphasizing its "event-character," and the implications for a doctrine of salvation:

> Faith understands the historical event between the Father who forsakes and the Son who is forsaken on the cross in eschatological terms as an event between the Father who loves and the Son who is loved in the present spirit of the love that creates life.
>
> If the cross of Jesus is understood as a divine event, i.e. as an event between Jesus and his God and Father, it is necessary to speak in trinitarian terms of the Son and the Father and the Spirit. In that case the doctrine of the Trinity is no longer an exorbitant and impractical speculation about God, but is nothing other than a shorter version of the passion narrative of Christ in its significance for the eschatological freedom of faith and the life of oppressed nature. It protects faith from both monotheism and atheism because it keeps believers at the cross. The content of the doctrine of the Trinity is the real cross of Christ himself. The form of the crucified Christ is the Trinity. In that case, what is salvation? Only if all disaster, forsakenness by God, absolute death, the infinite curse of damnation and sinking into nothingness is in God himself, is community with this God eternal salvation, infinite joy, indestructible election and divine life. The 'bifurcation' in God must contain the whole uproar of history within itself. Men must be able to recognize rejection, the curse and final nothingness in it. The cross stands between the Father and the Son in all the harshness of its forsakenness. If one describes the life of God within the Trinity as the 'history of God' (Hegel), this history of God contains within itself the whole abyss of godforsakenness, absolute death and the non-God. *'Nemo contra Deum nisi Deus ipse.'* Because this death took place in the history between Father and Son on the cross on Golgotha, there proceeds from it the spirit of life, love and election to salvation. The concrete 'history of God' in the death of Jesus on the cross on Golgotha therefore contains within itself all the depths and abysses of human history and therefore can be understood as the history of history. All human history, however much it may be determined by guilt and death, is taken up into this 'history of God', i.e. into the Trinity, and integrated into the future of the 'history of God'. There is no suffering which in this history of God is not God's suffering; no death which has not been God's death in the history on Golgotha. Therefore there is no life, no fortune and no joy which have not been integrated by his history into eternal life, the eternal joy of God. To think of 'God in history' always leads to theism and to atheism. To think of 'history in God' leads beyond that, into new creation and *theopoiesis*. To 'think of history in God' however, first means to understand humanity in the suffering and dying of Christ, and that means all humanity, with its dilemmas and its despairs.[6]

Moltmann concludes his discussion of the Trinitarian theology of the cross by interpreting the implications of his doctrine of the Trinity for the phrase "God is love." He states:

> the doctrine of the Trinity can be understood as an interpretation of the ground, the event and the experience of that love in which the one who has been condemned to love finds new possibility for life because he has found in it the grace of the impossibility of the death of rejection. It is not the interpretation of love as an ideal, a heavenly power or as a commandment, but of love as an event in a loveless, legalistic world: the event of an unconditioned and boundless love which comes to meet man, which takes hold of those who are unloved and forsaken, unrighteous or outside the law, and gives them a new identity, liberates them from the norms of social identifications and from the guardians of social norms and idolatrous images. What Jesus commanded in the Sermon on the Mount as love of one's enemy has taken place on the cross through Jesus' dying and the grief of the Father in the power of the spirit, for the godless and the loveless. Just as the unconditional love of Jesus for the rejected made the Pharisees his enemies and brought him to the cross, so unconditional love also means enmity and persecution in a

world in which the life of man is made dependent on particular social norms, conditions and achievements. A love which takes precedence and robs these conditions of their force is folly and scandal in this world. But if the believer experiences his freedom and the new possibility of his life in the fact that the love of God reaches him, the loveless and the unloved, in the cross of Christ, what must be the thoughts of a theology which corresponds to this love? In that case it is a love which creates its own conditions, since it cannot accept the conditions of lovelessness and the law. Further, it cannot command love and counterlove. As its purpose is freedom, it is directed towards freedom. So it cannot prohibit slavery and enmity, but must suffer this contradiction, and can only take upon itself grief at this contradiction and the grief of protest against it, and manifest this grief in protest. That is what happened on the cross of Christ. God is unconditional love, because he takes on himself grief at the contradiction in men and does not angrily suppress this contradiction. God allows himself to be forced out. God suffers, God allows himself to be crucified and is crucified, and in this consummates his unconditional love that is so full of hope. But that means that in the cross he becomes himself the condition of this love. The loving Father has a parallel in the loving Son and in the Spirit creates similar patterns of love in man in revolt. The fact of this love can be contradicted. It can be crucified, but in crucifixion it finds its fulfilment and becomes love of the enemy. Thus its suffering proves to be stronger than hate. Its might is powerful in weakness and gains power over its enemies in grief, because it gives life even to its enemies and opens up the future to change. If in the freedom given through experience of it the believer understands the crucifixion as an event of the love of the Son and the grief of the Father, that is, as an event between God and God, as an event within the Trinity, he perceives the liberating word of love which creates new life. By the death of the Son he is taken up into the grief of the Father and experiences a liberation which is a new element in this de-divinized and legalistic world, which is itself even a new element over against the original creation of the word. He is in fact taken up into the inner life of God, if in the cross of Christ he experiences the love of God for the godless, the enemies, in so far as the history of Christ is the inner life of God himself. In that case, if he lives in this love, he lives in God and God in him. If he lives in this freedom, he lives in God and God in him. If one conceives of the Trinity as an event of love in the suffering and the death of Jesus—and that is something which faith must do—then the Trinity is no self-contained group in heaven, but an eschatological process open for men on earth, which stems from the cross of Christ. By the secular cross on Golgotha, understood as open vulnerability and as the love of God for loveless and unloved, dehumanized men, God's being and God's life is open to true man. There is no 'outside the gate' with God (W. Borchert), if God himself is the one who died outside the gate on Golgotha for those who are outside.[7]

A Process Critique:

It is scarcely surprising that Moltmann cites Kant's famous observations about concepts and perceptions in his discussion of the cross of Jesus and the doctrine of the Trinity, for the concrete particularity of the cross of Jesus is the foundational beginning point for Moltmann's Christology. The concepts used to interpret the cross involve the dialectic of negation and an event understanding of the cross.

From my perspective, I wish Moltman had elaborated and clarified the relation between perceptions and conceptions. From a process viewpoint, one begins one's experience with the perception of other occasions. The initial phase of the becoming of a new creature involves sense reception in the mode of causal efficacy. In this appropriative phase of the becoming of a creature, forms of definiteness and feelings associated with them are objectified into the emerging creature. In this manner, perceptions necessarily include concepts. Further, the order embodied in the creatures of the world is appropriated by an emerging creature. Conscious creatures are able to contrast that potentiality which might be with that which is. In this process of contrasting contrasts and contrasting contrasts of contrasts, conscious creatures, exercising negative judgments, can compare what is with what might be but is not. In this way conceptions and perceptions may well differ. Nonetheless, conceptions are rooted in perceptions and refer to a real world embodying forms providing particular patterns of order.

The cross of Christ, the material principle of the doctrine of the Trinity to which Moltmann appeals, is thus objectified in the experience of the interpreter in the same fashion as any other complex cluster of events. Further, the doctrine of the Trinity, the formal principle of knowledge of the cross to which Moltmann appeals, embodies an explication of the Divine Nature which is congruent with understandings which in principle could be derived from any fully and adequately explicated experience. There may be a difference in degree and in focus of feeling between a Christian reflecting on the meaning of the cross and a Christian reflecting on the meaning of other events, but there is no difference in kind. By focusing inordinately on the cross, Moltmann distorts or ignores other salient aspects of the complex matrix of feeling and meaning embodied in the life of Jesus of Nazareth.

Moltmann indicates that he seeks to leave "...on one side any concept of God which is already presupposed and taken from metaphysics..."[8] In the quoted passage Moltmann does not explicitly indicate what he means by metaphysics, but he is seeking to reject the classical doctrine of the two natures. If metaphysics is understood to include epistemology, as I so understand it, Moltmann's affirmation about the way humans attain knowledge or awareness of the Divine through the dialectic of negation is a metaphysical proposition. It seems to me that his effort to leave "...on one side any concept of God which is already presupposed and taken from metaphysics..." is impossible. The critical theological question is "To what metaphysics does one appeal as one formulates one's conception of the Divine?" Moltmann finds Kant's view of the relation between perception and conception and Hegel's formulation of the dialectic of negation metaphysically more adequate than Whitehead's understanding of the relation between causal efficacy and presentational immediacy and his conception of Divine-world relations. This affirmation does not resolve the adequacy of one metaphysical proposition or another, but it does challenge Moltmann's assertion that he is not dealing with a concept of God rooted in a metaphysic.

Moltmann's discussion of the Trinity illumines the way in which the dialectic of negation relates Father, Son, and Spirit. In the quoted passages, Moltmann notes the reciprocal relation between the Father and the Son. In negation, the Father forsakes the Son and the Son is forsaken by the Father. This negation is the deadly aspect of the relation. In affirmation, the Father who loves the son suffers grief at the death of the Son, and the Son suffers in love being forsaken by the Father. From this event then proceeds the spirit which creates love for forsaken humans and brings the dead alive.

According to Moltmann in the quoted passage, the love which proceeds from the grief of the Father and the dying of the Son and reaches forsaken humans to create the possibility and force of new life is "...the unconditioned and therefore boundless love..."[9]

From my interpretive perspective Moltmann has confused the Son's sense of being forsaken by God with being forsaken by God. God is immanent in all creatures as they become, whether they are aware of God's immanence or not. At the same time, as creatures become, they transcend God. Their becoming is *sui generis*, shaped by but not determined by God and other creatures.

The human capacity to exercise negative judgments explicated earlier certainly can produce a sense of forsakenness, but this sense of forsakenness does not alter the structural necessity for relationships and for reciprocity.

The understanding of the love proceeding from the Father as unconditioned and unbounded must be challenged from my process perspective. Divine love is not unconditioned and unbounded. On the contrary, it is supremely conditioned and supremely bound. Such love is a result of God's response to and appropriation of the creatures of the world. The notion that God would or could forsake Jesus of Nazareth or any other creature of the world is grotesque. As noted earlier, Jesus—or any other creature with the richness of conceptual capacity to exercise negative judgments—may well have felt forsaken by God, but this feeling does not alter the structural necessity of relationship between God and other creatures. God does not and cannot forsake Its creatures, regardless of what they think God does.

I think Moltmann's attempt to see God suffering in the crucifixion is legitimate, but I must question his interpretation of it. For me, it poignantly reflects God's capacity to respond sensitively and empathetically to the creatures of the world. Jesus' agony and sense of forsakenness did grieve God, and, metaphorically speaking, God responded as sensitively as God could to the circumstances surrounding Jesus' crucifixion and death.

I am quite impressed with the persistence of trinitarian modes of thought, but I would not ground them in a high Christology and a theology of the cross. Rather, it seems to me that the notions of Father, Son, and Holy Spirit are rooted in three dimensions manifest in all experiences.

The first dimension is the dynamic creative growing together of a drop of experience; this dimension, grounded in the category of creativity, gives rise to various formulations of "God the Father" in Christian theology. The second dimension is the forms of definiteness manifest in all our experiences; this dimension, grounded in the reality of eternal objects, embodied in God's primordial nature and in creatures in the causal past of an emerging creature, gives rise to various formulations of "God the Son" in Christian theology. The third dimension is the lure for the unification of these dynamic and formal components in an emerging creature; this dimension, grounded in God's subjective aim, gives rise to various formulations of "God the Holy Spirit" in Christian theology. Because these dimensions are three-in-relation, the discussion of any one dimension involves the other two. Hence, the effort to formulate the relation of dynamics, form, and unification evokes trinitarian (small't') modes of thought.

In concluding this critique of Moltmann's "Trinitarian Theology of the Cross," I would like to direct attention to several of the passages in the last long quotation from Moltmann cited in the first part of this section. (pp. 247-249 in *The Crucified God.*)

Moltmann discerns the world apart from his doctrine of the Trinity as a loveless, legalistic world. He affirms that the love manifest in the event of the Cross is "...an unconditioned and boundless love which comes to meet man, which takes hold of those who are unloved and forsaken, unrighteous or outside the law, and gives them a new identity, liberates them from the norms of social identifications and from the guardians of social norms and idolatrous images."[10]

He proceeds by using the method of analogy, grounded in the prior dialectic of negation, to describe the situation of the Christian believer:

> Just as the unconditional love of Jesus for the rejected made the Pharisees his enemies and brought him to the cross, so unconditional love also means enmity and persecution in a world in which the life of man is made dependent on particular social norms, conditions and achievements.[11]

In the passage, Moltmann goes on to trace the implications of his understanding of the cross of Christ. This reality may enable believers to experience a liberating word of love which is a new element in a dehumanized and legalistic world and to live in the inner life of God Itself.

This assessment of the forms embodied in the natural and social world provides the basis for his critique of the social order and the framework for his understanding of political liberation, a topic to be discussed subsequently.

In my view, forms are necessarily embodied in all human experience. I strongly suspect that in spite of the "event" language Moltmann uses in describing the cross of Christ, a substance doctrine of the self is embedded in his formulations. It certainly seems apparent in these passages. Moltmann is suggesting that humans possess some "inner core," a center more elemental than the relations and patterns that are embodied in it. Otherwise, how can he refer to their liberation "...from the norms of social identifications and from the guardians of social norms and idolatrous images"?[12] Presumably, one could strip away these external layers and arrive at a love which can be liberating. I think the analogy of the peeling of an onion is more fitting. As one strips away the layers to get down to the irreducible core, one finds nothing left. Put more philosophically, "substance" and "accident" are inextricably interrelated. (It also follows that forms may contribute positively to the harmony of our lives together. This topic is addressed subsequently.)

Moltmann's focus on the cross leads to gross underestimation of the contribution Jesus of Nazareth has made to the enhancement of tenderness and sensitivity of feelings in human life. My own assessment of his life and teachings is closer to that of Whitehead: Jesus revealed in fact what Plato divined in theory, i.e., the primordial facet of the Divine agency in the world functions by persuasion. Although the liberal interpretations of the life and teachings of Jesus and of His persuasive role in human life have fallen into disfavor in the theological world in the last fifty years, I still think, granted the superficiality of much of American liberal Protestantism, there is much merit in many of its emphases.

I think the crucifixion of Jesus is best interpreted by lifting up two motifs. The first is the persuasive function of the Divine in the cosmos which was just noted. The second is the persistence of coercion in human affairs. The state, symbolized by the person of Pilate, had to be concerned with an earthly peace and rightly discerned that in the present state of human development and social organization the social teachings of Jesus were not applicable. Subject to many and diverse interpretations, these tales embodied in the synoptic gospels are, I think, more evocative than the Pauline corpus to which Moltmann is so deeply indebted.

ON ESCHATOLOGY

Moltmann's View:

Moltmann holds that eschatology has assumed a more significant place in contemporary theology than in many other theological epochs. He interprets the present emphasis as pointing toward a reading of the Bible as a

> ...testimony to the history of promise, and faith is seized as a living hope and as a contradiction to the present which establishes itself in inner apathy and external systems. ...Jesus is given a new title as *the anticipator of the future* of God, his righteousness and the freedom of man. This anticipation of the future, which can be recognized in his whole manifestation, in his person, his functions and his history of crucifixion and resurrection, has led to his being seen as the unconditional and universal *realization of the promise*. He has been named the unique *anticipation of the end* in the midst of history, or *God's lieutenant* in a godless world, as the *provisional representative* of the still absent God.[13]

Moltmann addresses the question "Does Christ make himself superfluous when the kingdom of God comes?"[14] through an historical retrieval of alternative responses to this question in the Christological tradition.

Moltmann's own answer to this question is "No." He summarizes his reason in the following passage.

> This is no historical-eschatological event in which the provisional is replaced by the final, but a process within the Trinity. The 'kingdom of God' passes from the incarnate Son to the Father. As a result Jesus becomes superfluous as 'Christ' and 'Kyrios'. His mediating functions between the Father and abandoned mankind come to an end. But he remains as 'Son', indeed his Sonship only becomes complete as he hands over the kingdom to the Father. For Paul, the title Son not only expresses a function of Jesus for men, but also denotes his whole being in relationship to the Father. The obedience of Jesus is accomplished in the subordination of the Son to the Father (v. 28). The word used for subordination does not mean making superfluous, but obedience. The relationship of Jesus to his God and Father is described by Paul as Sonship in the formulae which denote surrender. The title 'Son' does not therefore concern a Godhead separated from the manhood of Christ, but the whole person of the Christ who is delivered up, raised and given power to rule, in his relationship to the Father. The relationships in the Trinity between Father and Son are not fixed in static terms once and for all, but are a living history. This history of God or this history in God begins with the sending and delivering up of the Son, continues with his resurrection and the transference of the rule of God to him, and only ends when the Son hands over this rule to the Father. The delivering up on the cross is the central point of this history in God, not its conclusion. Only with the handing over of rule to the Father is the obedience of the Son, and thus his Sonship, consummated.
>
> In the light of this future it becomes clear that the rule of the crucified Christ, too, is not just that of a forerunner of the coming sole Lordship of Christ, but in its eschatological provisionality already itself represents the lordship of the Son. However, the rule of Christ involved not only representation for the coming rule of God but also the incarnation and the realization of this rule of God. The Christ does not just intervene for the future consummation, but this consummation already acquires its permanent form in his suffering love. The eternal God has by no means merely 'veiled' his majesty in the manhood of Jesus, in order to draw near to men in grace. Such a modalistic christology must ultimately end in un-Christian monotheism or pantheism. A merely functional christology must end in a non-Christian eschatology of being, obtained from somewhere else. Here the purpose for which Christ has come cannot be defined in terms of Christ, but must be defined in some other terms. Only when, as in Paul, eschatological-functional christology is taken up from beginning to end into a trinitarian christology, is it and does it remain Christian. But conversely, for trinitarian christology that means an alteration in the concept of God. The cross does not bring an end to the trinitarian history in God between the Father and the Son in the Spirit as eschatological history, but rather opens it up. The goal of the subordination of the Son to the Father and the significance of the transference of the kingdom to the Father is not simply the sole rule of God, but the consummation of the Fatherhood of the Father. If according to I Cor. 15.49 man will bear the image (*eikon*) of the heavenly, this will be accomplished in men being made like the image of the Son, so that, as Rom. 8.29 says, he may be the firstborn among many brothers. The goal of the consummation does not lie in the dissolution by Christ of his rule so that it is taken up into the rule of God, but in the consummation of the obedience of the Son and thus in the consummation of the brotherhood of believers. In respect of the world, the godless powers and death one can see the consummation of salvation in the transition from the rule of Christ to the sole rule of God. But in respect of the inner relationship of the Son to the Father, the consummation of the salvation of the world lies in the consummation of the history of God within the Trinity. In the first respect it is possible to speak of the provisional functions of God's Christ as representative and mediator becoming superfluous. In the second

respect, however, one must speak of the abiding significance of the Son who is delivered up and then raised. It follows from this that the crucified Christ does not disappear when the fulfillment comes, but rather becomes the ground for redeemed existence in God and the indwelling of God in all. In that event the crucified Christ in fact no longer has representative functions. But new existence is indebted to him for ever. The functional and soteriological representative-christology then becomes a doxological Son-christology. And as the end brings about this reversal, so too it is present in the confession of the Christian believer from the beginning. Historical christology, too, must do more than provide a functional representation of the significance and use of Christ for salvation, righteousness and identity; it must itself be an expression of the brotherhood of the believer with the Son and express that doxologically in thanksgiving and praise. Thus the necessity of representation 'for us' becomes the freedom of thankfulness 'from us'. Christ is more than necessary; he is free and sets free. He belongs both to the realm of necessity and the realm of freedom, because he is himself the transition.[15]

Moltmann concludes his discussion of the theology of the 'crucified God' with a corresponding anthropology. The following two quotations summarize his views. In the first he affirms that the cross represents the suffering which is the beginning of the trinitarian history of God.

Life in communion with Christ is full life in the trinitarian situation of God. Dead in Christ and raised to new life, as Paul says in Rom. 6.8, the believer really participates in the suffering of God in the world, because he partakes in the suffering of the love of God. Conversely, he takes part in the particular suffering of the word, because God has made it his suffering in the cross of his Son.[170] The human God who encounters man in the crucified Christ thus involves man in a realistic divinization (*theosis*). Therefore in communion with Christ it can truly be said that men live *in God* and *from God*, 'that they live, move and have their being in him' (Acts 17.28). Understood in pantheistic terms, that would be a dream which would have to ignore the negative element in the world. But a trintarian theology of the cross perceives God in the negative element and therefore the negative element in God, and in this dialectical way is panentheistic. For in the hidden mode of humiliation to the point of the cross, all being and all that annihilates has already been taken up in God and God begins to become 'all in all'. To recognize God in the cross of Christ, conversely, means to recognize the cross, inextricable suffering, death and hopeless rejection in God.[16]

He then turns to a discussion of the culmination of the trinitarian history of God at the end of history.

It is necessary to remember the martyrs, so as not to become abstract. Of them and of the dumb sacrifices it is true in a real, transferred sense, that God himself hung on the gallows, as E. Wiesel was able to say. If that is taken seriously, it must also be said that, like the cross of Christ, even Auschwitz is in God himself. Even Auschwitz is taken up into the grief of the Father, the surrender of the Son and the power of the Spirit. That never means that Auschwitz and other grisly places can be justified, for it is the cross that is the beginning of the trinitarian history of God. As Paul says in I Cor. 15, only with the resurrection of the dead, the murdered and the gassed, only with the healing of those in despair who bear lifelong wounds, only with the abolition of all rule and authority, only with the annihilation of death will the Son hand over the kingdom to the Father. Then God will turn his sorrow into eternal joy. This will be the sign of the completion of the trinitarian history of God and the end of world history, the overcoming of the history of man's sorrow and the fulfillment of his history of hope. God in Auschwitz and Auschwitz in the crucified God—that is the basis for a real hope which both embraces and overcomes the world, and the ground for a love which is stronger than death

> and can sustain death. It is the ground for living with the terror of history and the end of history, and nevertheless remaining in love and meeting what comes in openness for God's future. It is the ground for living and bearing guilt and sorrow for the future of man in God.[17]

A Process Critique:

The deep contrast between my process understanding of a doctrine of last things and that of Moltman may be illumined by considering the question "Does Christ make himself superfluous when the Kingdom of God comes?" which Moltmann uses as a way into his discussion of the topic "Trinity and Eschatology."

Having rejected the dialectic of negation and Moltmann's high Christology, I find Moltmann's question itself superfluous. Moltmann thinks it is meaningful to talk about "the end" and "fulfillment" as the culmination of history as

> ...the resurrection of the dead, the murdered and the gassed, only with the healing of those in despair who bear lifelong wounds, only with the abolition of all rule and authority, only with the annihilation of death will the Son hand over the kingdom to the Father. Then God will turn his sorrow into eternal joy. This will be the sign of the completion of the trinitarian history of God and the end of world history, the overcoming of the history of man's sorrow and the fulfillment of his history of hope.[18]

This passage is puzzling and cryptic. There is no doubt that Moltmann's vision of what God is doing to make life more human, coupled with the conviction that the notions "completion of the trinitarian history of God" and "the end of world history" are meaningful ones, may provide motivation for a cruciform existence. These ideas may encourage some to try to co-operate with God to break down forms and structures limiting the harmony of life with life and move toward the emerging kingdom.

At the same time, I must question the understanding of the nature of God-world relations and the understanding of the nature of perfection embodied in these views of fulfillment and the end of world history.

To speak of fulfillment and the end of world history as Moltmann does, one must presuppose a single mode of perfection in the cosmos. The world had a beginning, has a "middle" and will have an end. The end involves the turning of sorrow into "eternal joy," whatever that means. In some fashion, it must mean a "changeless harmony" in which the creatures of the world cleave to their Creator and redeemer. This single mode of perfection is that toward which the creation is moving and the crucified Christ is "...the basis for the new being and the new identity which goes beyond the self-identity that men always desire."[19]

In contrast to Moltmann, I hold that there is no single mode of perfection in the cosmos. "Perfection," involving the harmonization of the parts into a whole of intense aesthetic satisfaction, depends on a context for its realization. Moltmann's single mode of perfection represents an over-moralization of thought and an inherent limitation on the zest for novelty and intensity of feeling. The inexhaustable potentiality envisaged by God and the ultimacy of the category of creativity suggest that there will always be perfections beyond perfections, world without end.

From my perspective, Moltmann has identified the human experience of the perfection of potentiality rooted in God's harmonization and ordering of the forms of definiteness embodied in the primordial facet of Its nature with the perfection of historical existence. In other words, he has confused potentiality and actuality. Actuality always implies limitation and a finite "perfection." Finite perfections, fitting in relation to a context, may always be surpassed.

The "doctrine of last things" does point to the human experience of an "end," a "termination," a "cutting off." One who analogizes from this experience to the notion of an end of world history, which is, in my view, cosmic history and not merely human history, misreads the nature of the foundational experience giving rise to the intuitions of beginning, middle, and end.

Our experience emerges in drops or "buds." As a creature begins to become, it appropriates forms of definiteness and tones of feeling from creatures in its causal past and from the primordial facet of God's nature. This appropriation constitutes the "beginning" of the creature, a facet of the experiencing of the creature which can be separated only analytically from its "middle" or its "end." The "middle" of the becoming of a creature is constituted by an emerging integration of the data appropriated by a creature as it evolves toward its actualization. The "end" of the creature is its completion of this complex synthesis and the attainment of its measure of aesthetic satisfaction and intensity of feeling. The creature, which has been an emerging subject, now becomes an object for all the creatures which are to follow it.

In sum, the notion of a "beginning" is rooted in the human experience of an initial phase in the becoming of a creature, the notion of a "middle" is rooted in the human experience of the emerging integration of the components of the data and feelings in the becoming of a creature, and the notion of an "end" is rooted in the human experience of the completion or "closing up" of a creature.

The "doctrine of last things" does point to the intuition of the everlasting appropriation of the creatures of the world into the consequent facet of God's nature—a peace beyond the strife and turmoil of the temporal world. God's all-inclusive rationality permits God to receive the creatures of the world into Itself without loss and to synthesize conflicting and disharmonious components into the richest possible harmony. In this manner the creatures of the world are transformed and pass into the Kingdom of Heaven. Retained everlastingly in the Divine Life, these "completed" creatures pass back into the world as they are appropriated by new emerging entities. The Kingdom of Heaven is ever with us.

ON THE PSYCHOLOGICAL LIBERATION OF MAN

Moltmann's View:

In *The Crucified God,* Moltmann engages in an extended discussion of the psychoanalysis of Sigmund Freud and Freud's criticism of religion.[20] He appreciates Freud's assessment of the sickness of the natural person and Freud's critique of "human-made" religion, but he accentuates the redemptive character of the crucified God and develops the typical neo-orthodox contrast between the idolatry of human-made religions and the authenticity of the Christian faith.

He holds that the Christian faith provides the basis for a critique of Freudian understanding of maturity as a wise resignation to overcome infantile illusions. In contrast to the acceptance and apathy of wise resignation, Moltmann holds that hope for the future, rooted in God's revelation in the cross, is the basis for Christian maturity. He notes:

> Openness to the future is conditioned by openness to the past. Constant faithfulness to hope is reciprocally bound up with faithfulness to the earth. Christian faith understands itself as faithfulness to hope as it is mindful of the resurrection of Christ, and as faithfulness to the earth as it is mindful of the cross of Christ. Because it leads man into this history of God, it frees him for an acceptance of human life which is capable of suffering and capable of love.
>
> ...To free sick man from his psychological vicious circles it offers not only the critical rationality and ego-support which are often summoned up against the psychological strategies of evil, but also the new spontaneous liveliness which that critical rationality needs as the atmosphere in which it can develop freely.[21]

Moltmann concludes this facet of his discussion by noting the relation between the logic of understanding and the level of feeling and instinct and by offering a critique of technological society. He observes:

> As is well known, the logic of the instinct differs from the logic of the understanding and is not always influenced by it. Therefore the logic of the understanding needs a corresponding level of instinct and feeling on which it can develop freely. It needs a barrier against anxiety and the threat of death on the level of the feelings also, that is, a love of life which brings intelligence to the understanding and orients it. These are fundamental decisions of the interest which make possible rationality and lead to the human use of rationality. On the level of the feelings and instincts man 'thinks' in notions and symbols. As is already shown by language, rational thought is directed for its freedom towards notions and symbols which do not constrict and fixate it, but open up free space for it. Rightly understood, the Christian symbolism which represents the situation of man in the passion of God, which wakens his remembrance and keeps alive his hope, cannot be a superstitious, dogmatistic and pathological pattern formation. It does not liberate an apathetic rationality of domination, but sympathetic reason. 'We know in so far as we love,' said Augustine, and in so doing made love the enabling ground for knowledge. The Christian symbolism of the situation of man in the *pathos* of God leads to the loving and suffering knowledge of man. It can therefore only take up the iconoclasm that is critical of religion and the psychotherapeutic liberation of man from his vicious circles and develop its own prophetic criticism of idolatry in parallel to that.
>
> Any therapy is directed towards *health.* But health is a norm which changes with history and is conditioned by society. If in today's society health means 'the capability to

> work and the capability for enjoyment', as Freud could put it, and this concept of health even dominates psychotherapy, the Christian interpretation of the human situation must nevertheless also question the compulsive idolatry which the concepts of production and consumption introduce into this definition, and develop another form of humanity. Suffering in a superficial, activist, apathetic and therefore dehumanized society can be a sign of spiritual health.[22]

A Process Critique:

Given his doctrine of sin and the paradoxical nature of God's revelation in the cross, it is not surprising to find Moltmann attracted provisionally to Freud's pessimistic interpretation of human nature and to Freud's critique of religion as a human .construct. Moltmann contrasts his provisional pessimism with the hope offered humans through the crucified God. The hope that God is acting in history to redeem humankind frees humans to accept a human life capable both of suffering and of love. It provides a basis for criticizing and surpassing Freud's pessimistic assessments. Similarly, Moltmann's critique of human efforts to move toward the Divine permits him both to affirm Freud's analysis of the source of religion, and also to appeal to the Christian faith which contrasts with and judges human religion.

It is beyond the scope of this essay to undertake a process critique of Freud, but I do affirm the Moltmannian critique of Freud's pessimism and of his inordinate focus on the causal past. Freud's analyses reflect a Newtonian world view. The pleasure-pain principle and the rewards-punishment theory of motivation so salient in his analyses cohere with a mechanistic world view. Although the bases differ from Moltmann's, I also want to affirm the possibility of some greater enhancement of the harmony of life with life in the future through human effort and Divine Lure.

When Moltmann contrasts the "logic of understanding" with the "level of instinct and feeling," he is pointing to the complex interplay of feeling and thinking inherent in human experience. Unfortunately he does not elaborate and clarify his understanding of the relations between reason, instinct and feeling in this context.

In the last quoted passage, Moltmann delineates a sympathetic reason embodied in Christian symbolism, a reason emerging out of decisions of interest shaped by Christian experience and Christian symbolism. Because I hold that feeling is prior to thinking and that a transrational (not *irrational*) ground undergirds one's faith in rationalism, I have some sympathy with this view. However, I think Moltmann too closely identifies "redeemed" reason with the Christian faith.

I wish Moltmann had elaborated the structural relations he envisages between the "logic of understanding" and the "level of instinct and feeling on which it can freely develop." One could relate the "level of instinct" to causal efficacy, "feeling" to the aim at aesthetic satisfaction, and the "logic of understanding" to the appropriation of forms of definiteness and to the capacity to exercise negative judgments, contrasting what is with what might be but is not. Undoubtedly Moltmann does not have such process categories in mind; more likely, he entertains a Kantian understanding of the relation of theoretical to practical reason.

My critique of Freud's interpretation of religion is based on different grounds than Moltmann's. Religion is grounded in human responses to the Divine Presence in the world, and human awareness of that Presence has emerged in many contexts. Because more adequate categories of interpretation may enhance human religious experience, human "works" as well as God's grace may contribute to human religious experience. The transrational character of faith leads me to deny the unequivocally persuasive character of any natural theology or rational proofs for the existence of God, but the necessary embodiment of forms in all experiences and the contribution of reason to an understanding of the Divine nature and Divine-world relations lead me to appreciate human efforts to illumine the Divine nature. Because Freud rejects the notion of a Divine Agency, he is unable either to discern a locus of potentiality in the cosmos or to explain the lure for harmony and intensity of feeling embodied in our experience. He is also unable either to provide a rational explanation for the mediation of experience from one creature to another or to provide an ultimate receptor for all that has become.

Moltmann's critique of "...production and consumption..." "...in a superficial, activist, apathetic and therefore dehumanized society..." in the final two sentences of the last quotation in the preceding sub-section provides a transition to his discussion of "Ways Towards the Political Liberation of Mankind" in the final chapter of *The Crucified God*. There is some legitimacy in his critique, but it is too sweeping and too inclusive. Because the next section of this paper focuses on Moltmann's views on the political liberation of humankind, a critique of this dimension of Moltmann's "Liberation Theology" will be developed in that context.

ON THE POLITICAL LIBERATION OF HUMANKIND

Moltmann's View:

As the concluding quotation in the preceding section indicated, Moltmann posits a reciprocal but not a direct relation between psychological suffering and the suffering in society. In a limit situation, psychological suffering "...becomes the suffering of society and suffering in society, and is determined by that. The psychological hermeneutics of life in the situation of the crucified God... therefore remains incomplete, if it is not supplemented by a corresponding political hermeneutics."[23]

Moltmann then raises four questions about a political hermeneutic.

> What is meant by the contemporization of the crucified God in the political religions of society? In what dimensions must a human society develop in the free sphere of the history of this God? What are the economic, social and political consequences of the gospel of the Son of Man who was crucified as a 'rebel'? In the Reformation, the

theology of cross was expounded as a criticism of the church; how can it now be realized as a criticism of society? If in the political trial of Jesus, the Caesar was the external reason for his end on the cross, how can the risen Christ become the internal reason for the end of Caesar?[24]

He then goes on to affirm the necessity to attend to the concrete particularity of problems in the public spheres:

If we attempt to draw the consequences of the theology of the cross for politics, the matter cannot be exhausted in general and abstract definitions of the relationship between church and state or dogmatic faith and political action. Concrete attention must be paid to religious problems of politics and to laws, compulsions and the vicious circles which for economic and social reasons constrict, oppress or make impossible the life of man and living humanity. The freedom of faith is lived out in political freedom. The freedom of faith therefore urges men on towards liberating actions, because it makes them painfully aware of suffering in situations of exploitation, oppression, alienation and captivity. The situation of the crucified God makes it clear that human situations where there is no freedom are vicious circles which must be broken through because they can be broken through in him. Those who take the way from freedom of faith to liberating action automatically find themselves co-operating with other freedom movements in God's history. Political hermeneutics calls especially for dialogue with socialist, democratic, humanistic and anti-racist movements. Political hermeneutics reflects the new situation of God in the inhuman situtations of men, in order to break down the hierarchical relationships which deprive them of self-determination, and to help to develop their humanity. So there is need for critical solidarity with these movements; for solidarity with them in the struggle against the forms of inhumanity which threaten mankind; and for criticism and acceptance of criticism of the aims and methods of liberation. Political hermeneutics of faith is not a reduction of the theology of the cross to a political ideology, but an interpretation of it in political discipleship. Political hermeneutics sets out to recognize the social and economic influences on theological institutions and languages, in order to bring their liberating content into the political dimension and to make them relevant towards really freeing men from their misery in certain vicious circles. Political hermeneutics asks not only what sense it makes to talk of God, but also what is the function of such talk and what effect it has. Even here, none of the so-called substance of faith is lost; rather, faith gains substance in its political incarnations and overcomes its un-Christian abstraction, which keeps it far from the present situation of the crucified God. Christian theology must be politically clear whether it is disseminating faith or superstition.[25]

Moltmann discerns a dialectic relation of identity and difference between God and humankind and between the history of liberation and the Kingdom of God. God and humankind are bound together and distinguished from each other through the history of the crucified Christ. Cohering with his view of the paradox of the crucified God informed by the dialectic of negation, Moltmann insists that the human history of God's liberation must begin with the crucified God. In this manner, the specie becomes the genus, and this genus informs the species. Rejecting alternative understandings of church-world relations because they deal first in the abstract and only then in the concrete, Moltmann makes the following constructive affirmation:

To make a correct distinction between God and the world, the absolute and the relative, the last things and the things before the last is one thing. To look for what corresponds

> to God in the world, to the last things in the things before the last, to the great hope in the lesser hopes, is something else. But must we not go beyond that and from the start understand God *in* the world, the beyond *in* the this-worldly, the universal *in* the concrete and eschatology *in* the historical, in order to arrive at a political hermeneutics of the crucified Christ and a theology of real liberations.? That would lead beyond difference and parable in thought and language to a synecdochic understanding of the 'explosive', liberating presences of God in the extremities of inhuman misery. In that case we would have to understand the incarnations and anticipations of the presence of God in a history of 'transformations of God'. That would lead beyond difference and parable to a perception of God's identifications in history. The criterion of perception would be the identification of God with the crucified Christ. The horizon of perception would then be the kingdom of the perfected indwelling of God in the new creation, that is, the consummation of the trinitarian process of God in history. History is the 'sacrament' of Christian ethics, not just its material.[26]

Moltmann sees similarities and differences between the new political theology and political hermeneutics he propounds and the views of the early church. He presupposes "...the early church's criticism of the political theology of political religions...,"[27] but he is more radical because he seeks "...to reclaim from the biblical tradition the awareness of a trial between the eschatological message of Jesus and social and political reality."[28]

Moltmann elaborates the implications of this understanding for the new political theology in the following passage. It is rather lengthy, but it is so critical for an understanding of his views that it is quoted here in its entirety.

> Christian theology which wants to be aware of the present political restraints on and functions of its language, rites, institutions and practice will therefore do well to recall the political crucifixion and divine resurrection of the Christ who was executed as a 'rebel' and the consequence of discipleship. The memory of the passion and resurrection of Christ is at the same time both dangerous and liberating. It endangers a church which is adapted to the religious politics of its time and brings it into fellowship with the sufferers of its time. It frees the church from politico-religious church politics for a critical Christian political theology. The new political theology is not concerned with the dissolution of the church into left-wing or right-wing politics, but with the Christianization of its political situation and function in terms of the freedom of Christ.
>
> Christian theology has continually interpreted in soteriological terms the history of the Christ who was condemned in the name of the law, and in his exaltation by God brings to an end the law and the demands made on men by the law: man is not made righteous before God by works of the law, but by God's grace in faith. Faith brings liberation from the compulsion of works. But a theological interpretation of the political dimension of the crucifixion and resurrection of Jesus is absent. Because it has been assimilated to the state, the church has left this dimension unexplained. Now the death of Christ was the death of a political offender. According to the scale of social values of the time, crucifixion was dishonour and shame. If this crucified man has been raised from the dead and exalted to be the Christ of God, then what public opinion holds to be lowliest, what the state has determined to be disgraceful, is changed into what is supreme. In that case, the glory of God does not shine on the crowns of the mighty, but on the face of the crucified Christ. The authority of God is then no longer represented directly by those in high positions, the powerful and the rich, but by the outcast Son of Man, who died between two wretches. The rule and the kingdom of God are no longer reflected in

political rule and world kingdoms, but in the service of Christ, who humiliated himself to the point of death on the cross.

The consequence for Christian theology is that it must adopt a critical attitude towards political religions in society and in the churches. The political theology of the cross must liberate the state from the political service of idols and must liberate men from political alienation and loss of rights. It must seek to demythologize state and society. It must prepare for the revolution of all values which is involved in the exaltation of the crucified Christ, in the demolition of relationships of political domination. Now political representations and master-slave relationships continually arise when a people is capable of action in the medium of history. The citizen surrenders the right of self-determination to his representatives, so that they may act for him. This process of unburdening in political action is associated with the alienation of those who are relieved of their burdens. 'In representative insitutions there is always subjection to a visible image, and that is idolatry. Political idolatry and political alienation arise when the representatives go over the heads of those whom they are meant to represent, and when the people bows to its own rulers. Alienation between government and people is then shown in an all-embracing apathy of the people towards those 'up there'. Because the representatives are out of their control, the citizens lapse into a passivity which allows further misuse of power to go unhindered. The democratic movement has clearly seen the connection between political idolatry, with the consequent apathy of its subjects, and the deprivation of political rights. 'Democracy has no monuments. It mints no medals. It does not bear a man's head on its coins. Its true nature is iconoclasm.' If the nature of democracy is political iconoclasm, its reality lies in the demolition of master-slave relationships, in the limitation and control of the political exercise of power, and in activating the people from their apathy as subjects towards responsible participation in the processes of political decision.

If the Christ of God was executed in the name of the politico-religious authorities of his time, then for the believer the higher justification of these and similar authorities is removed. In that case political rule can only be justified 'from below'. Wherever Christianity extends, the idea of the state changes. Political rule is no longer accepted as God-given, but is understood as a task the fulfillment of which must be constantly justified. The theory of the state is no longer assertive thought, but justifying and critical thought. The early church rejected the cult of the emperor and replaced it with prayer for the emperor which represented a limitation of his power. The Middle Ages and the Reformation relativized political ordinances so that they became necessary ordinances in the world, which served the well-being of people but not their salvation. Puritanism abolished the feudal system and replaced it by the covenant or the constitution of the free citizen. A critical political theology today must take this course of desacralization, relativization and democratization. If the churches become 'institutions for the free criticism of society', they must necessarily overcome not only private idolatry but also political idolatry, and extend human freedom in the situation of the crucified God not only in the overcoming of systems of psychological apathy, but also in the overcoming of the mystique of political and religious systems of rule which make men apathetic.

Christianity did not arise as a national or a class religion. As a dominant religion of rulers it must deny its origin in the crucified Christ and lose identity. The crucified God is in fact a stateless and classless God. But that does not mean that he is an unpolitical God. He is the God of the poor, the oppressed and the humiliated. The rule of the Christ who was crucified for political reasons can only be extended through liberation from forms of rule which make men servile and apathetic and the political religions which give them stability. According to Paul, the perfection of his kingdom of freedom is to bring about the annihilation of all rule, authority and power. which are still unavoidable here, and at the same time to achieve the overcoming of equivalent apathy and alienation. Christians will seek to anticipate the future of Christ according to the measure of the possibilities available to them, by breaking down lordship and building up the political liveliness of each individual.[29]

Moltmann enumerates a number of vicious circles which prevent better mutual relations and do not allow humans to be human. They contribute to each other and mutually influence each other, but they are not reducible to one another. These dimensions, in order of increasing inclusiveness, include the economic, the political, the cultural, and the natural. There is also another more inclusive and deeper dimension grounded in the meaning of life. Liberating action seeks to free life from the vicious circles of death rooted in these interacting and interpenetrating dimensions.

In the economic dimension of life, the vicious circle of poverty, consisting of hunger, illness and early mortality, oppresses life. According to Moltmann, it is provoked by exploitation and class domination. Inequality exists within and between countries. Globally, the underdeveloped countries are increasingly economically disadvantaged and cannot obtain freedom. Liberation involves provision for food, fiber, housing, and medical attention. It also involves:

> ...a social justice which can give all members of society a satisfying and just share in the products they produce. In so far as the vicious circle of poverty is produced by exploitation and class domination, social justice can only be achieved by a redistribution of economic power. The privileges of capital over labour strengthen the vicious circle of poverty. The vicious circle of poverty can be broken only through economic co-determination and control of economic power by the producers. Social welfare for those who are economically weak and development aid for the so-called underdeveloped nations are necessary as transitional measures to keep men alive who would otherwise go to the wall. But they are only justified by a social policy which brings social justice to the poor, the exploited and the weak. If and in so far as socialism in this sense means the satisfaction of material need and social justice in a material democracy, *socialism is the symbol for the liberation of men from the vicious circle of poverty.*[30]

In the political dimension of life force is a vicious circle related to poverty. It is manifest both within particular societies and between nation-states. Liberation in this dimension is the manifestation of democracy. Political responsibility enhances human dignity. Moltmann observes:

> This includes participation in and control of the exercise of economic and political power. The vicious circle of force can only be broken by giving each individual political responsibility and an active part in the processes of decision. Otherwise the exercise of power is not freed from the privileges and hegemonies of particular classes and groups. Only through equal and just distribution of political burdens can the alienation of the people from political power and its political apathy be overcome. The *Universal Declaration of Human Rights* may be taken as a standard for democratic justice. In the formulations which have been hitherto held to be valid it derives from the civic revolutions of the eighteenth and nineteenth centuries, and to that degree needs to be supplemented. Democracy means the recognition of human rights as the basic rights of the citizen in a state. The aim of the democratic movement, for we must speak of a movement and not of a condition or an ideal, is the making possible and the realization of human dignity through liberation from political oppression and control. If and to the degree that the democratic movement means the abolition of privilege and the establishment of political human rights, *democracy is the symbol for the liberation of men from*

the vicious circle of force. This is true not only within a state but also between competing states, for the abolition of military deterrent systems and the construction of systems for political peace and control.[31]

In the cultural dimension of life, racial and cultural alienation constitutes a vicious circle. People are "... robbed of their identity and characteristics and have been degraded to the point of becoming manipulable factors in the system. ...The conquest of poverty and political oppression is often achieved only at the cost..." of racial, cultural and technocratic alienation.[32] In this instance humans become non-self-determining cogs in a technocracy.

Moltmann asserts that "...liberation from the vicious circle of alienation means identity in the recognition of others. By this we mean the 'human emancipation of man' (Marx), in which men gain self-respect and self-confidence in the recognition of others and fellowship with them."[33] He concludes:

> The human emancipation of men from self-alientation and alienating dealings with each other is only possible when different kinds of people encounter each other without anxiety, superiority or repressed feelings of guilt and regard their differences as fruitful, working together productively. If and in so far as emancipation means personalization in socialization and finding one's identity in the recognition of others, *emancipation is the symbol for liberation from the vicious circle of alienation.*[34]

Moltmann further suggests that "... the vicious circle of poverty, force and alienation are now bound up in a greater circle, *the vicious circle of the industrial pollution of nature.* Mindless faith in progress has irreparably destroyed the balance of nature by industrialization."[35] He calls for peace with nature, a liberation from the vicious circle of industrial pollution. He believes that humans must seek new models of co-operation with nature and calls for a relation of intercommunication with nature "...which pays respect to the circumstances."[36]

Finally, in the deepest dimension, Moltmann discerns a vicious circle of senselessness and godforsakenness, giving rise to apathy. This sense of apathy not infrequently occasions an unconscious death-wish. It is overcome by divine initiative.

> ...the presence of meaning is termed the presence and indwelling of God in a new creation. ...In a situation of godforsakenness and senselessness the knowledge of the hidden presence of God in the godforsaken Christ on the cross already gives 'courage to be', despite nothingness and all annihilating experiences."[37]

Because the five vicious circles are reciprocally interrelated, Moltmann holds that "...liberation must be sought in all these five dimensions simultaneously in every specific situation."[38] In his view, democracy without socialism—understood in the sense of involving economic co-determination and control of economic power by the workers and of bringing social justice to all the members of a society—or socialism without democracy is not liberating. In a similar vein, he argues for their necessary relation to identity in recognition, peace with nature, and the internal presence of meaning in everything.

This interrelatedness leads Moltmann to conclude "...that in any *theology of liberations* the universal must be understood *in* the particular and the eschatological *in* the historical.Otherwise it is impossible to think universally without becoming abstract."[39]

Moltmann then rehearses his identification of liberation in the economic dimension with social justice, in the political dimension with democratic human rights, in the cultural dimension with identity in recognition, in the natural dimension with peace with nature, and in the "religious" dimension with the courage to be in faith.[40] He has termed "...these identifications *symbols,* because they both show liberation in real terms in various spheres and at the same time invite further thought."[41] They are evocative in character, and the dialectical character of symbolic thought "...which makes fast in negatives and takes matters further in positives is iconoclastic of language. ...Thus the cause of liberation is not established, but is constantly in process and is only comprehended by participatory, dialectical thinking."[42]

Moltmann concludes this section by developing his view of the relation of symbols to sacraments and the presence of God in liberation efforts. He states:

> The symbol in thought is matched by the conception of reality as a *sacrament,* that is, as a reality qualified by God's word and made the bearer of his presence. These realities are not another kingdom separate from God, nor are they just similes and equivalents of his kingdom. They are synecdochically, to take up Luther's language, real presences of his coming omnipresence. In this sense a theology of liberation cannot get by without corresponding materializations of the presence of God, unless it means to remain idealistic. For it, the identifications of the presence of God with the matter involved in liberation from vicious circles are real symbols, real ciphers and material anticipations of the physical presence of God. They are incarnations which point beyond themselves. They stand in parallel to the traditional real presence of God in the sacraments, and do not replace this. If we allow the theological language of the real presence of God to run through these dimensions of misery, we reach the following sequence of identifications. In the vicious circle of poverty it can be said: 'God is not dead. He is bread.' God is present as bread in that he is the unconditional which draws near, in the present sense. In the vicious circle of force God's presence is experienced as liberation for human dignity and responsibility. In the vicious circle of alienation his presence is perceived in the experience of human identity and recognition. In the vicious circle of the destruction of nature God is present in joy in existence and in peace between man and nature. In the vicious circle or meaninglessness and godforsakenness, finally, he comes forward in the figure of the crucified Christ, who communicates courage to be.
>
> In accordance with theological tradition it is possible to see this real presence of God, pointing beyond itself, as the history of the Shekinah wandering through the dust, as the history of the spirit which comes upon all flesh. We understand it here in the process of the trinitarian history of God. Thus the real presences of God acquire the character of a '*praesentia explosiva*'. Brotherhood with Christ means the suffering and active participation in the history of this God. Its criterion is the history of the crucified and risen Christ. Its power is the sighing and liberating spirit of God. Its consummation lies in the kingdom of the triune God which sets all things free and fills them with meaning.[43]

A Process Critique:

Affirming the universality of the principle of relativity and the finality of the self-determining creature, I also see reciprocal but not direct relations between psychological and societal suffering. Moltmann does not elaborate the structural bases for the relations between the psychological and the societal nor does he elaborate the bases for the five dimensions of society. He does see the triune God participating in the liberation of humans in all these dimensions and, through the dialectic of negation, does indicate how humans can co-operate with what God is doing to make life more human.

From my point of view, the various societal dimensions are rooted in and are abstractions from the concrete network of relations in which people are embodied. The individual surpasses the societal and cannot expect to find a rich fulfillment outside of close interpersonal relations—relations which may emerge out of interaction in any of the spheres of the social order. By positing a single mode of perfection and by failing to distinguish between leading, secondary, and tertiary components in interpersonal and intergroup relations, Moltmann exaggerates the degree of the harmony of life with life possible in the various spheres of the social order and underplays the persistence of disharmony in some of the spheres.

Moltmann's use of the dialectic of negation leads him to underappreciate the extent of aesthetic satisfaction attained in the emerging present and to overestimate the enhancement of the harmony of life with life possible in-the future. By focusing inordinately on the suffering of the crucified God, Moltmann does not adequately indicate the dimension of joy and aesthetic satisfaction actualized in the present by the most "oppressed" creature. Because of his vision of a single mode of perfection at the end of history, Moltmann underestimates the positive contributions of past and present forms of social organization to the life of humankind.

In spite of these critical comments about Moltmann's assessment of the spheres of the social order, I also affirm the vision of more desirable forms of human social organization to enhance the quality of human life. In other contexts, I have elaborated principles of justice and forms of social organization which can enhance human life.[44] In the present context, I will summarize these notions and contrast them with those of Moltmann.

In my view, three constitutive principles of justice are embodied in human experience and serve to provide some formal criteria to evaluate human forms of social organization. These principles are rooted in the emerging unification of a drop of experience. The dynamic unification of formal components in a novel unity illustrates the principles of unification, form, and dynamics.

Unification gives rise to the notion of order or harmony as a principle of justice.

The recognition of oddness and evenness and the intuition of the notion of congruence gives rise to the idea of equality, the second principle of justice. The presence of different types of creatures and societies of creatures requires a qualification of equality by restricting the principle to creatures with comparable defining characteristics. Consequently "equality appropriate to form" becomes a second principle of justice, for the principle of equality should apply only to comparable creatures.

The experience of the process of becoming and the awareness of a capacity for decision-making give rise to self-determination, the third principle of justice. The lure to sustain the harmony of the whole leads to the qualification of self-determination by the quest for the more excellent way of the harmonization of the totality. Consequently, the third principle of justice becomes "self-determination informed by excellence."

Because of finitude, ignorance, sloth and lethargy and because of the metaphysical necessity for self-interest for a creaturely self-actualization, the principles of equality appropriate to form and self-determination informed by excellence are not perfectly harmonizable. Inordinate self-interest accentuates the disharmony. Consequently, one must appeal to the principle of order, embodying both suasion and coercion, to attain a reasonable harmony between these two necessary but partially competing principles of justice.

These principles, taken in conjunction with the leading components in the various spheres of the social order suggested later in this section, may serve to guide one's assessment of normatively desirable forms of social organization: an economic system fostering some risk-taking and responsible growth and relying on some type of supply-demand mechanisms to allocate resources, democracy, a pluralism of social, ethnic, and racial groups, a cultural pluralism, and religious pluralism and liberty.[44]

Although there is a "lure toward the coherence" of these forms, I am much more reserved about socialism as the normative form of economic organization than Moltmann; and I am opposed to Moltmann's view of the role of the church in the public spheres. Because Moltmann does not elaborate his view of liberating forms of family organization in this text, I am unable to compare our view on this matter. Although the bases differ, I concur with Moltmann's views about the desirability of democracy and fitting social, ethnic, and cultural pluralism.

Moltmann is too radical, but I share his concerns about the industrial pollution of nature. From my process perspective, the distinctions Moltmann makes between spirit and flesh are spurious, but I certainly do affirm the intimacy between and the mutual interdependence of humans and nature. When he says "Mindless faith in progress has irreparably destroyed the balance of nature by industrialization," Moltmann overstates his case. Further, when he cites Meadows and his colleagues to support his observation, "It is possible to calculate the 'limits of growth'," Moltmann is not sufficiently critical of their methods.[46]

In spite of these reservations I do think the Calvinistic view that humans should master nature needs to be balanced by the Lutheran view that nature should be received and appropriated. Nature does impose limits—albeit malleable ones—on humans which they violate at their peril.

Moltmann's assertion that the vicious circle of poverty "...is provoked by exploitation and class domination" is far too simple an explanation of an exceedingly complex phenomenon.[47] It is not at all clear that the poor would be richer if the rich were poorer; similarly, it is very doubtful whether the redistribution of economic power Moltmann calls for would reduce the vicious circle of poverty.

I think Moltmann does not adequately consider the perennial tension between the principles of equality and self-determination. If the principle of equality—even when it is properly qualified by the notion "appropriate to form"—is pushed too vigorously, some people will find that their capacities for self-determination are truncated. Conversely, if the principle of self-determination is pushed too vigorously, some people will attain inordinate wealth and power, attenuating the principle of equality. Moltmann's vision of God's action *in* history and God's action in moving toward the establishment of the Kingdom of God may lead him to think this persistent problem will be transformed in the future, but I am unwilling to make this leap of faith.

Because of his understanding of the transvaluation of values revealed to the believer in the crucified God, Moltmann underestimates the contribution of elites to the well-being of humankind. Without the theoretical and practical developments in science and technology since the time of the Renaissance, the possibility of more than a tiny fraction of humankind living above the poverty level would be nil. The hierarchical ordering of nature and the differentiations among humans lead me to suspect that at least a qualified hierarchical ordering is deeply embodied in the nature of things. Such patterns limit the extension of equality in human life.

Although I would not suggest that social market capitalism is necessarily the *best* possible form of economic organization, I do think it is a very viable form. I reject Moltmann's assertion that socialism and democracy must go hand-in-glove in the movement toward human liberation. Unless one is willing to put very substantial confidence in the beneficience of the state and the willingness of governmental functionaries to support diverse efforts at self-initiation, one must be wary about coalescence of the economic and political spheres. I am not persuaded that human self-determination would necessarily be enhanced by this movement.[48]

I also think Moltmann underestimates the current positive contributions of the magistrates to our lives together. The principle of order is one of the principles of justice, and governments do contribute to the order of human society. His understanding of a single mode of perfection and his vision of the coming of the kingdom lead him to an inordinate critique of the contribution of existing governments to human well-being.

Although better forms of economic and political organization may enhance human life, they cannot insure human fulfillment, for the form and needs of a person cannot be fully considered in these spheres of the social order. The reasons for this situation are to be found in sequence of priority of the principles of form, dynamics and unification in the several spheres of human life and in the necessary abstractions made from the concrete net of human relations in these spheres of the social order. In the familial sphere and in interpersonal relations in small groups, form is the leading component, unification is the secondary component, and dynamics is the tertiary component; and abstractions from the concrete interaction of people are minimal. Thus the form of the person and a sensitive loving response to the person are more fully realizable in these spheres than in the economic and political spheres.

In the economic and political spheres, abstractions are made from the concrete net of relations in which humans find themselves. In the economic sphere, the sequence of priority is form, dynamics, and unification. Technical rationalism—using calculating reason to discern the most efficient means to attain a given end—looms large in this sphere. Only in the most primitive form of economic organization can the individual be considered wholistically.

In the political sphere, the sequence of priority is dynamics, form, and unification. Governments live in a house of power, and political leaders must deal with this reality. Although suasive power of the Divine Lure is never absent, the coercive power of causal efficacy and the clash of conflicting purposes is frequently most painfully evident in inter- and intrastate relations.

In an earlier section, I criticized the dialectic of negation which is at the heart of Moltmann's theological method. The radical discontinuity in Divine-human relations Moltmann suggests is incompatible with my understanding of process theology. For me, religious institutions emerge in human history as a response to human intuitions of the Divine Presence. Moltmann's distinctions between human-made religions and the divinely initiated Christian faith are not compatible with my views, for I hold the Divine may illumine Itself in any context. There are differences in degrees of religiously significant events but there are no differences in kind. Therefore, to point to the categorical supremacy of one religious tradition or one religious institution is spurious; the Christian church is a species of the genus "religious institution."

The sequence of priority of the form, dynamics, unification triad in the religious sphere is twofold. From the Divine perspective, the sequence of priorities is unification, dynamics and form. God manifests Its love in sensitive response to creatures who have become and then evokes new creatures, lifting up fitting forms of definiteness for them.

From the human perspective, the sequence of priorities is unification, form, and dynamics. The emerging creature's subjective aim is evoked by God's subjective aim, its forms of definiteness are appropriated from the causal past and the primordial facet of God's nature, and its dynamic process of self-development gives rise to its actualization. The creature then becomes a superject, a power of being for all subsequent creatures.

Because unification, embodying love, peace, and harmony, is the leading component in God-world relations and because the primordial facet of God's nature functions by suasion in the cosmos, religious institutions should not use physical force to recruit members or to relate to human beings. Only in the most extraordinary of circumstances should religious institutions *qua* religious institutions be involved directly in the economic or political spheres. The contrast with Moltmann's view is obvious.

Moltmann insists in this section "...that in any *theology of liberations* the universal must be understood *in* the particular and the eschatological *in* the historical. Otherwise it is impossible to think concretely without becoming pragmatic and impossible to think universally without becoming abstract."[49]

He makes these observations without universalizing the principle of relativity or without reformulating the notions of end and of perfection. If he had done so, he would have suggested that the particular is universal in the sense that the particular that has become is a datum for all that is to become and that the end is always coming and yet the end that has become lives forevermore in the Divine Life. Less obsessed with the vision of a single mode of perfection, he might be somewhat more sanguine about and assess somewhat more positively the complex multiplicity of forms of social organization that have emerged in the history of humankind.

In the final paragraph of his text, Moltmann develops a moving classical trinitarian formulation of Father, Son and Holy Spirit and the consummation of brotherhood in the kingdom of the triune God. Because Moltmann has insisted throughout the text that God is unconditioned and that God does not have necessary relations with the world (hence the insistence upon the primacy of the dialectic of negation), I find these passages puzzling. Thus, I conclude this process critique of a liberation theology with three typical process questions: If the Divine nature and God-world relations are of the types Moltmann suggests, what does it mean to talk about the consummation of brotherhood in the kingdom of the triune God? How can God receive into Itself that which the world has to offer? What do suffering (and joy) mean if one of the parties is unconditioned and is not necessarily related to the other?

CONCLUSION

Moltmann's version of liberation theology and the process perspective informing the constructive views elaborated here contrast markedly. My process perspective places a greater emphasis on reason than does Moltmann's liberation theology. It affirms multiple loci of revelation and does not focus so sharply upon the crucifixion. It establishes another mode of explanation of the experience of negation and rejects Moltmann's understanding of the dialectic of negation. It affirms a qualified doctrine of justification by works, for it holds that advances in conceptual understanding can both deepen our understanding of the nature of Divine-world relations and also enhance human religious experience.

In contrast to Moltmann's high Christology, the view entertained here holds that there is no categorical difference between Jesus of Nazareth and other creatures. The necessary presence of forms in all experiences is affirmed, and a liberal understanding of the person of Jesus of Nazareth is sketched. An alternative basis for a trinitarian understanding of experience is suggested.

Moltmann's understanding of "the end" and of "fulfillment" are contrasted with a process view of God-world relations and the nature of perfection. The process view of the beginning, the middle, and the end of the becoming of a creature is seen as the basis of an understanding of "the end" and of "fulfillment," and the process doctrine of a multiplicity of perfections is contrasted with Moltmann's entertainment of a single mode of perfection.

Moltmann's understanding of the relation between reason, instinct and feeling in human experience is questioned, and reasons for a common disagreement with Freud's interpretation of the human situation are discussed.

Finally, Moltmann's views on the political liberation of humankind are considered. According to the process perspective advanced here, Moltmann underestimates the dimension of joy and aesthetic satisfaction actualized in the present and underestimates the positive contributions of past and present forms of social organization to the life of humankind. The differences are not dramatic, for Moltmann's critiques of human-nature relations and his critique of high technology are qualifiedly affirmed.

Moltmann's views of desirable forms of social organization are compared and contrasted with an alternative understanding. His view that poverty is provoked primarily by exploitation and class domination is challenged, and a more positive evaluation of the principle of order is advanced. The process perspective developed in this section is more formalistic than other versions of process social theory, and substantial family quarrels among process thinkers about these matters may be anticipated.

In spite of these internal differences among process thinkers, the contrast in basic presuppositions between Moltmann's liberation theology and most process thinkers' is very substantial. Persons thinking they discern a convergence on specific issues of public policy or on forms of social organization between process perspectives and Moltmann's version of liberation theology should be mindful of these basic contrasts in interpretation of the Christian movement.

Notes and References

1. Jürgen Moltmann, *The Crucified God: The Cross of Christ as the Foundation and Criticism of Christian Theology*, New York: Harper and Row, 1974, p. 27.
2. *Ibid.*, p. 27.
3. *Ibid.*, pp. 27-28. The widespread appropriation of the dialectic of negation in social analyses by liberation theologians inordinately accentuates contrasts between human groups. These analyses are analogous to classical Christian contrasts between the saved and the damned. Augustine and Marx both reflect this type of categorical thinking.
4. *Ibid.*, pp. 240-241.
5. *Ibid.*, p. 245.
6. *Ibid.*, pp. 246-247.
7. *Ibid.*, pp. 247-249.
8. *Ibid.*, p. 245.
9. *Ibid.*, p. 245.
10. *Ibid.*, p. 248.
11. *Ibid.*, p. 248.
12. *Ibid.*, p. 248.
13. *Ibid.*, p. 256.
14. *Ibid.*, p. 257. From my perspective, this question itself is wrongly put. This issue is discussed in the critique of Moltmann's eschatology in the following subsection.
15. *Ibid.*, pp. 264-266.
16. *Ibid.*, p. 277.
17. *Ibid.*, p. 278.
18. Ibid., p. 263.
20. *Ibid.*, p. 291. Interestingly, Moltmann's only references to other psychologically oriented interpreters are Norman O. Brown, H. Marcuse and Erich Fromm. In this context, he rightly insists on the different dimensions of the psychological and the societal.
21. *Ibid.*, pp. 313-314.
22. *Ibid.*, pp. 314-315.
23. *Ibid.*, p. 317.
24. *Ibid.*, p. 317.
25. *Ibid.*, pp. 317-318.
26. *Ibid.*, p. 321.
27. *Ibid.*, p. 326.
28. *Ibid.*, p. 326.
29. *Ibid.*, pp. 326-329.
30. *Ibid.*, p. 332.
31. *Ibid.*, pp. 332-333.
32. *Ibid.*, p. 331.
33. *Ibid.*, p. 333.
34. *Ibid.*, pp. 333-334.
35. *Ibid.*, p. 331.
36. *Ibid.*, p. 334.
37. *Ibid.*, p. 335.
38. *Ibid.*, p. 336.
39. *Ibid.*, p. 336.
40. The term "religious" placed in italics is my term and not Moltmann's. He uses the term "meaning of life" to denote this dimension. The relation of these dimensions to the old Lutheran "orders of creation" should be obvious.
41. Moltmann, *op. cit.*, p. 337.
42. *Ibid.*, p. 337.
43. *Ibid.*, pp. 337-338.
44. See, for example, Chapter 9 of this volume.

45. For an elaboration of these notions, in addition to the reference cited in note 44, see W. Widick Schroeder, *Cognitive Structures and Religious Research* (East Lansing, Michigan State University Press, 1970), pp. 180-191, and W. Widick Schroeder, *et all.*, *Suburban Religion* (Chicago: Center for the Scientific Study of Religion, 1974), pp. 191-210.
46. Moltmann, *op. cit.*, p. 331. For a wide range of assessments of Meadows' *The Limits to Growth* (New York: Universe Books, 1972) see Willem L. Oltman's *On Growth* (New York: G. P. Putman's Sons, New York 1974). For a critique see H. S. D. Cole *et al.*, *Models of Doom: A Critique of the Limits to Growth* (New York: Universe Books, 1973).
47. *Ibid.*, p. 330. For an excellent selection of essays interpreting this issue from various perspectives, see Kenneth E. Boulding and Tapan Mukerjee, editors, *Economic Imperialism* (Ann Arbor: University of Michigan Press, 1972). For a series of trenchant critique of many types of economic and political "reformers," see Frank H. Knight, *Freedom and Reform* (New York: Harper and Brothers, 1947).
48. For a suggestive discussion of these issues, see Milton Friedman, *Capitalism and Freedom* (Chicago: University of Chicago Press, 1962).
49. Moltmann, *op. cit.*, p. 336.

Introduction to Chapter 19

Ralph Wendell Burhoe has devoted his life to exploring the relations between science and religion and to facilitating discussions of this topic. In his own writing, in his work for the Institute on Religion in an Age of Science, and in his work as founding editor of *Zygon: Journal of Religion and Science,* he has made major contributions to the facilitation of discussions of the relation between religion and science. In recognition of his work, he was awarded the Templeton Prize.

This essay is a revised version of a presentation given in an advanced seminar of the Center for Advanced Study in Religion and Science in cooperation with the Chicago Cluster of Theological Schools which was devoted to a discussion of his views on the relation of religion and science. Because this essay draws so explicitly on the foundational notions elaborated in Part One, it is a fitting concluding chapter of this collection of essays, all of which have been concerned implicitly or explicitly with the relation of religion and science.

CHAPTER 19

"The Human Prospect and the 'Lord of History'": A Process Critique

Ralph Wendell Burhoe uses the discussion of Robert L. Heilbroner's *An Inquiry into the Human Prospect* in the September 1975 issue of *Zygon* to elaborate his own theory of the bases of religious phenomena and to project his own views of the contribution of religion to the future of humankind. He seeks "to show from a wider perspective of the scientific study of religion and a study of the religious implications of science that there is no need to fear that religion is necessarily incompatible with either the basic freedom or the basic rationality or truth of science."[1] He seeks to "provide evidence that religion has been what has made human freedom and the rise of science possible and . . . does indeed have . . . the capacity to generate in men a readiness or motivation to the kind of social altruism and concern for the long-range future that is not possessed by governments."[2] He aims to show that "the sciences depict a more-than-human reality that determines human destiny in very much the same manner as a traditional deity of religion."[3]

In his remarks on the contributions of the other papers to the *Zygon* issue on Heilbroner, Burhoe summarizes the intent of his essay:

> It is my intent to show that the "Lord of History" [a phrase used to denote the reality which determines human destiny] is nowhere shown to be more "meaningful and true" than by some of the recent revelations of the sciences.[4]
>
> Since I think we have some information from both genetic and cultural evolution on the role and capacity of reason to convince and convert, and since we have an obligation to our posterity now, I shall seek to set forth in this paper some scientific grounds for religious hope.[5]
>
> I shall seek to show new scientific grounds for understanding how the "Lord of History" produces saints and suffering servants.[6]
>
> I shall seek to adduce more evidence on how . . . religion and science can get together.[7]
>
> We shall need . . . to make clearer how . . . *processes* of the "evolutionary adaptive generalizations" may be said to be related to the gods of religion, on the one hand, and how, on the other hand, societal selection can run counter to the genetic selection . . . geneticists have shown cannot produce altruistic creatures in a genetically diverse population. I think . . . simple, linear projections of disastrous futures for living systems are often invalidated because the "projections" of such disastrous futures often may be a part of the very negative-feedback mechanisms that prevent the disasters.[8]

Burhoe concludes his agenda with the following comment:

> In general, I shall seek to address myself to the elaboration of a scientific picture of religion that will be convincing to the scientific and skeptical minds who have not yet been provided with much scientific evidence for its virtues and potential. I shall build on the very significant elements of the situation presented by the other contributors to this issue and seek to provide additional information to show how religion (and the sovereign and often obscure system of transcendent realities to which religion has for thousands of years sought to relate us) may be reformulated and revalidated in the light of the sciences as salvatory for the present human predicament.[9]

In this formulation of his intentions Burhoe uses such terms as "science," "scientific study of religion," and "scientific grounds" in a global manner. He does not discriminate various understandings of science or explore alternative philosophies of science. Because of this global usage, it is very difficult to discern why he has selected a particular social scientific interpretation of religion and has rejected others.

As subsequent sections will make clear, he has drawn primarily on the French sociological tradition of Auguste Comte, Émile Durkheim, and Claude Lévi-Strauss. The German tradition, of whom Max Weber may be taken as the exemplar par excellence, is ignored completely. Burhoe does not indicate the bases for his selective appropriation of social theorists, but the French positivistic school is more congenial to his general way of interpreting religious phenomena than the neo-Kantian heritage manifest in Germany.

Here I shall elaborate what I take to be the salient aspects of the discussion in each section of Burhoe's paper. I shall then raise critical questions and discuss problems I encounter with Burhoe's discussion.

Ancient Biological Roots of Religion

A Summary of the Section. Burhoe begins his discussion by exploring the ancient biological roots of religions. He finds these "roots in ancient, genotypically programmed patterns of the central nervous system, . . ."[10]

He appeals to recent scientific findings to provide a rational interpretation of religion. He notes three phylogenetic levels in the human brain: "(1) the very old reptilian level which generates our *instincts* including those involved in religion, (2) the limbic system of our old mammalian brain which is involved in generating deeply religious feelings and emotions, and (3) the human neocortex, which can associate diverse elements from several sensory modalities into *symbols,* and then associate symbols and establish symbols of symbols of symbols in systematic hierarchies."[11]

He then makes the following interpretation of this view of human instincts, feelings, and thinking:

> These functions of the brain provide new grounds for understanding the reality of religion, the usefulness and validity of deep religious feelings and emotions. They give a tangible basis for the power of religion to motivate morals as well as provide hope and courage. They give a clue on how the brain may mediate to us the rare spiritual mixtures of the combined products of all three of these genetically given levels of our brain, programmed from the outside by combinations of high cultural, genetic, and environmental information, to produce in conscious self-awareness the idealistic rapture and vision of deeper reality in the mystical experience of the love of God and beatific vision. That is, they allow us to account for religious experience. It also becomes clear how such projections may reflect validly not only man's needs but also a picture of the objective reality that is sacred for him and to which he must adapt.[12]

Burhoe indicates that social motivation and altruism beyond the nuclear family cannot be produced by genetically programmed patterns of human behavior. He finds the basis for social motivation and altruism in the emergence of a "culturetype" (". . . cooperative human societies are composed of *genetically diverse members of the same species* . . . who are genetically much more diverse than cousins, but nevertheless are programmed or *motivated to altruistic behavior* . . . by certain necessary additional *cultural* 'information' [in the technical sense, as in the 'information' in a genotype or computer])."[13]

Discussion. Burhoe's intent to root his explanation of religious phenomena in the elemental and fundamental structures of the brain becomes clear in this section. Drawing on data ordered by a particular type of evolutionary theory, he roots *instincts* in the oldest level of the brain, *feelings and emotions* in a more recently evolved level, and *symbols* in the most recently evolved level. The emergence of symbols is related to the emergence of culturetypes.

The formulation developed here is extremely compact and raises a number of questions for me. The most fundamental has to do with the relation between the brain and my awareness of a conscious center which receives diverse input from my body, including my brain. I have no doubt that my organizing center—an ultimate percipient occasion—is intimately related to my body and to my brain. However, my own experience—which must be the ultimate court of appeal in this matter—does not lead me to identify myself with my brain or my body. Sometimes I am preoccupied with my body and it influences me tremendously. Sometimes I am able to influence my body substantially. Sometimes I am preoccupied with an intellectual problem and am oblivious of my body. My wholistic experience cannot be explained adequately by appeal to genetic, cultural, or environmental phenomena.

Instincts, feelings and emotions, and symbols are clearly a part of my self-conscious experience. However, I wish Burhoe would elaborate and clarify the relation between the contribution of forms and feelings derived from the causal past (which I take to be the basis of *instinct*), novel forms of definiteness (which I take are included in *symbols*) not derived from the causal past, and their integration into an aesthetic whole which is my own experiencing.

It seems to me that the process of perception, reflection, and conception is much more complex than Burhoe's formulation suggests. He neither elaborates the means by which symbols are mediated from one creature to another (including the sequence of entities constituting the human organizing center) nor explains the basis for consciousness.

Finally, I am in substantial sympathy with the vision of the increasing complexification of creatures in the evolutionary process and in the increasing importance of symbols in the life of higher organisms. I am not persuaded that the locus of such symbolism can be centered in culture as definitively as Burhoe suggests. A transcendent locus of potentiality which has envisaged all potentiality is needed to provide a coherent interpretation of the contrast between potentiality and actuality which humans encounter in their becoming and in their experience of symbols.

If this be so, a notion of a Divine Reality, *sui generis* in at least some senses, is required. I do not think Burhoe's attempt to "explain" the "mystical experience of the love of God and beatific vision" by instinctual, emotional, and symbolic genetically given levels of the brain and "programmed from the outside by combinations of high cultural, genetic, and environmental information" is adequate. Some "outside" ordering of reasonably relevant forms of definiteness is necessary to interpret the emergence of a creature, but the locus of this ordering is beyond cultural, genetic, and environmental information. At the same time an emerging creature must take account of its context, so data rooted in the cultural, biological, and natural world of a creature are important.

One final observation. The terms "information" and "programming" convey a flatness and aesthetic insensitivity to me. My own experience of the vivid immediacy of my specious present involves a flood of feeling and thinking aiming at aesthetic satisfaction. It may be that Burhoe's use of these terms is not meant to deny this dimension of my inner experience, but the terms frequently are associated with a mechanistic, objectivistic, and reductionist interpretation of human experience.

Religion's Role in Cultural Evolution

A Summary of the Section. Because religion is a central contributor to the transmission of values in cultural evolution, Burhoe considers religion's role in cultural evolution. He draws substantially from the understanding of Anthony F. C. Wallace, an anthropologist deeply indebted to the theoretical work of the French sociological tradition (of whom Durkheim is representative), to interpret religion.[14] Burhoe's summary of Wallace's view is stated as follows: "Religious rituals and beliefs, then, are outgrowths of very ancient roots of genetically programmed modes for ritual communications directly tied to the genetically programmed mechanisms that mediate suitable feelings and responses to provide adaptive or viable behavior relative to fellow creatures and the larger environment."[15]

Though this part of the section is titled "What Is Religion?" the discussion actually seeks to "explain" the underlying forces and factors which give rise to patterns of ritual and belief which are "a process of maximizing the quantity of organization in the matrix of perceived human experience."[16]

In the second part of the subsection entitled "Religion as Cultural

Evolution's Agent for Transforming Apes into Men" Burhoe interprets religion as the agent of cultural evolution which socializes humans and fosters altruistic behavior. The sociocultural system becomes the unit of selection in cultural evolution.[17] Making an analogy drawn from the genotypes of biology and using a mechanistic model, Burhoe sees heritable information stored

> as a "culturetype" in a "culture pool," in such coded memory patterns as rituals and languages inscribed in the neurological patterns of brains. The feedback insemination of this information—from the successful behavioral responses it produces—to shape the next generation of new "culturetypes" . . . does not require a biological generation but may even be immediate in a verbal response. Also, because culturetypes may be stored in "artifacts," the "sexual recombination" potential may sleep for fifty biological generations and come to life in contemporary culture, as in the discovery of a nonliving artifact or book of a previous culture. . . . If a culture's evolved system of information patterns does not produce viable organisms or phenotypes, then, as a "higher court of judgment," nature (the total reality involved in the system) obliterates those phenotypes and hence that culturetype, just as she obliterates inadequate DNA information in biological evolution.[18]

Human capacity for rapid response to cultural codification and transmission of information has greatly accelerated the pace of evolution in the sociocultural sphere. Burhoe believes that the information transmitted in ritual and belief is essential to shape human adaptation to its environment and its fellow humans. He suggests that the evolving systems of socially transmitted rituals and beliefs, usually called religions, have contributed to "the emergence of the conscious feelings of the self as more than a body, as a larger being with sociocultural loyalties and cosmic connections, . . ."[19]

He suggests that "the present crisis in human cultural evolution will require and will produce the emergence of a reformation of traditional religions that will unite traditional, deeply felt, emotive, pietistic, religious feelings with fully scientific 'myths' or beliefs."[20]

Discussion. This section focuses on the factors in the causal past allegedly giving rise to religion and on the functions it allegedly plays in human life.

As noted, the first part of the section is titled "What Is Religion?" but it focuses on the structure of the brain permitting the emergence of patterns of ritual and belief and on the functions religion allegedly has in human life.

I myself do not think religion is defined adequately by characterizing these structures and functions. It is one thing to note the factors which are associated with the human organizing center and its relations to its fellow creatures and its environment. It is quite another to assume that this structure and these relations account adequately for the emergence and persistence of religion among humankind. Since Burhoe (and the anthropological tradition from which he draws in this section) rejects the idea of a *sui generis* or partly *sui generis* Divine Reality as the ground for religious experience, he must turn to the biological and cultural spheres to "explain" its origin.

The second part of this section focuses on the emergence of social cultural systems. The long quotation cited from this part illustrates the mechanistic and materialistic perspective informing Burhoe's constructive interpretation. I do not know what "such coded memory patterns as rituals and languages inscribed in the neurological patterns of brains" means. The idea that the experiences of the past are "inscribed in the neurological patterns of brains" relocates the locus of memory, but it does not provide an explanation for the way in which the vivid immediacy of past "presents" can be appropriated in an emerging present. Even if the sequence of events constituting the experiences of the past are "located" in various parts of the brain and reproduced serially by the creatures constituting those parts, the events must be mediated to the ultimate percipient occasion "remembering" its past. I do wish Burhoe would illumine this process. I suspect that the idea of enduring substances which retain these experiences is inherent in Burhoe's formulation. In any case, I think this discussion needs expansion and clarification. I think an adequate explanation of memory requires the elaboration of an interpretative framework appealing to the canalization of living experiences, the objectification and everlasting retention of these experiences in the Divine Life, and the mediation of these experiences to the emerging percipient occasion through the common participation of past and emerging creatures in the same forms of definiteness.

In the long citation just referred to, Burhoe identifies nature as the total reality involved in the system. Nature "obliterates" those culturetypes not producing viable organisms or phenotypes. I wish this notion of "the total reality involved in the system" was explicated more fully. (Burhoe's deification of nature implicit in this formulation becomes explicit later in the paper.) I also find the notion of "obliteration" harsh and ultimately unsatisfying. If this be all one can say about the creatures that have become, Burhoe is saying nature ultimately gives its beloved sleep—and nothing more.

The Evolution of Scientific Theology

A Summary of the Section. Burhoe posits four broad stages of religious evolution: primitive ritual, primitive beliefs or myths, theology, and scientific theology. Theology emerged out of primitive beliefs or myths some one to three thousand years ago, and scientific theology emerged in recent decades.[21] He holds that "Christian theology was a high step toward converting primitive or 'mythical' explanations of religious ritual into the sophisticated, rational, scholastic 'myths' of Greek philosophy."[22]

Burhoe traces the breakdown in classical Christianity precipitated by the emergence of science sometime after 1500. In this discussion he appeals to an analogy provided by some terms in contemporary computer analysis. It is quoted here in its entirety because it illumines Burhoe's basic vision of the relation of the biological, cognitive, and social dimensions of human experience:

> For understanding the relation between religion and other elements of culture and the relation of these to the more slowly changing information that shapes our biological nature, it may be helpful to use an analogy nicely provided by some terms common in contemporary computer technology, where "hardware" denotes the electronic and material machinery and "software" denotes the special linguistic or logical rules that program the machinery with information that makes it useful for human purposes. Before each new job, the software is fed into the machinery by information on punched cards or magnetic tape as the machine's program. The machine "reads" this program or incorporates it so that it becomes a part of itself. In analogy we may say that culturally formulated or evolved religious information became the basic motivational software of the hominid *Homo sapiens,* to program this "ape" to become the human nature we know. The hardware in religion is the fixed, genetically programmed motivational mechanisms of the lower brain centers to which religiously evolved ritual behaviors and beliefs tied the new, culturally transmitted information about self, society, duty, and hope. The special hardware to "read" programs from cultural software is the brain's neocortex. It is this new, cultural, socially transmitted level of information or software that provides the characteristic human patterns of feeling and logic in conscious choice making. In several thousands of years of evolution the hardware of the human gene pool has changed little. It is the software (or belief systems) that has evolved increasingly rapidly and has become for all practical purposes the program that motivates (so long as it remains cathected to the hardware) man's sociocultural behavior.[23]

In this discussion Burhoe affirms the importance of convincing beliefs for human behavior, notes the personal and social disorganization entailed by the decline in the "convinceability" of traditional Christian beliefs in the West, and then points to the coming of scientific theology. It is here he sees the possibility of the emergence of new, credible beliefs which will enhance social altruism.

He does not discuss in detail the way in which reason, feeling, and ecstasy are related, but he does indicate reason fails to elicit feeling when it "becomes confused by conflicting reasons."[24] He expresses a strong conviction that modern science offers a way to human salvation. The following quotation illumines the substance and force of Burhoe's conviction:

The new religious and theological language will be as high above that of five centuries ago as contemporary cosmology is above the Ptolemaic, as contemporary medicine, agriculture, communications, and transportation concepts are above those of the fifteenth century.

Modern science is the new revelation about human nature and the world that is universally credible and compelling for most men today, as already shown by the spread of scientific medicine and other scientific technologies to all cultures of the world. When it becomes successfully integrated with religious traditions, scientific understanding will tend to pull them more closely together, as it has pulled the world's varied medical beliefs and practices together into a more universal system. At the same time, the scientific theologies will find genuine virtues and validities in each of the great religious traditions and will adapt themselves to each local culture, as scientifically based medicine or agriculture has adapted to the local situation's particularities without losing its universality.[25]

His extraordinarily high view of the morality of the scientist is reflected in this observation: "One need not fear any domination by scientists, as one now may properly fear domination by one or another political dictator, for science is the element of human cultural evolution that has learned most deeply to understand that the evolution of valid knowledge is not be be entrusted to any individual human wish, prejudice, or person."[26]

One of the reasons for Burhoe's faith in science is "its insistence on getting a truth-value judgment from *the external reality system itself,* no matter how plausible or well confirmed a new hypothesis or statement might be within the rational scheme of the scientists making it."[27] Burhoe discerns a split between human-value culture which provides *meaning* and the scientific culture which provides *truth.*[28] Burhoe seeks to overcome this bifurcation by deifying nature. The following quotation illustrates this deification:

In Christian theology the symbol of the ultimate and true reality which created man, shaped and shapes his destiny, and provides meaning, purpose, hope, and direction for human life is the term "God." Central in religions generally are such symbols for the ultimate source and context of human life. In a world that has been converted to a very different world view from that of Plato and Aristotle, the effectiveness of this "God" symbol requires its credible translation into the new world view. In the new scientific world view, the "reality" which possesses very similar attributes is called "nature." In the sciences, "nature" has come to denote the total reality system, including the laws or ways in which it operates in time, the dynamic history of its sources as far as they can be traced in time and space, and hypothetical entities or

> constructs that may not be directly observable but on the basis of which what is observable logically follows. . . . The scientific picture tells us how the often inexplicable or seemingly irrational world of our commonsense experience is the natural and rational product of a long history or cosmic evolution of a system of hitherto hidden or unknown particles and forces, portrayed in different aspects by various sciences and yet all essentially integrated around a common, universal, everlasting, all-determining "ultimate reality system."[29]

He then completes the deification of nature: "To the extent that there could be shown to be an equivalence between what is denoted by the theological term 'God' and this scientific term 'nature,' to that extent we could say that scientists are engaged in the attempt to talk about God and hence are doing theology. But I would guess that in the last fifty years more than nine hundred out of a thousand people I have known in the sciences and in theology do not see any relation remotely approaching identity between 'nature' and 'God.' "[30]

Discussion. In the early portion of this exceedingly important discussion Burhoe delineates four stages of religious evolution: primitive ritual, primitive beliefs or myths, theology, and scientific theology.

It is striking to me that the dimension of feeling or emotion is not explicit in this categorization of religious evolution. If feeling and patterns of religious behavior are reciprocally and dynamically interrelated—as I think they are—then somewhat different stages of religious evolution are needed. I would see religious ritual and religious emotion as emerging very early in human religious evolution.

I am also uneasy about Burhoe's understanding of "primitive beliefs or myths." I think it might be useful to elaborate the bases for my uneasiness, for it will illumine facets of the contrasting "grounding intuitions" informing Burhoe's work and my critique of it.

I think that religious experience is grounded in the human intuition of a Divine lure for harmony and intensity of feeling. The Divine subjective aim evokes novelty and seeks to enhance the aesthetic satisfaction in the creatures of the world. The Divine subjective aim primordially envisaged all potentiality and orders it to provide fitting forms of definiteness for emerging creatures. These forms of definiteness are not a class; rather, they are a multiplicity, all of them having one thing in common—their envisagement by the Divine subjective aim. Because of the transrational (not irrational) character of this envisagement, there are no self-evident first principles which the philosophical theologian may employ to "prove" the existence of the Divine or to use as clear and self-evident basic premises to elaborate a metaphysic. Human faith in rationalism—that there is a relational matrix to the universe whose essence reason seeks to penetrate—is sustained by this transrational experience. Thus faith in rationalism shades off into religious experience and is sustained by religious experience.

It follows that "myth" is richer for me than for Burhoe, who uses the epithet "primitive" to describe myth. Myth points toward human experience of the transrational "power" of God's subjective aim at the base of potentiality. To be sure, "myth" has been, is now, and will be identified with particular "beliefs"; such "primitive" reification of myth must be resisted if its capacity for evocation of the Divine Presence in human life is to be sustained. Nonetheless, its evocative power is perennial and is not to be identified with the primitive.

Humans do seek cognitive explanations of what they feel and do, so the emergence of religious beliefs to interpret religious feeling and religious ritual is universal and perennial among humans. The term "primitive" may be used to refer to religious beliefs which are relatively uncoordinated and incoherent. Such beliefs may be contrasted with the more coherent and logical systems of thought evolved by theologians seeking to provide a rational interpretation of the religious emotions, rituals, and beliefs which they inherit.

In sum, I would also see an emergence of religious beliefs, but I would characterize them differently from the way Burhoe does. The emergent sequence is ritual, emotion, beliefs, and rational interpretation. The relation between these components is dynamic and reciprocal.

Burhoe's "theology" and "scientific theology" are both forms of rational interpretation. As subsequent discussion will make clear, I am dubious about the prospects for a "scientific" theology of the type Burhoe proposes. I do think an adequate theology must "fit the facts," but I am not as certain as Burhoe is that one can evolve a "science" independent of metaphysics. The relation between philosophic propositions and propositions applying to the subject matter of the various sciences is subtle and complex, and the "facts" which the various sciences consider are subject to a variety of fundamental interpretations.

Burhoe's discussion of the relation between the biological, cognitive, and social dimensions of human experience elaborates the perspective cited earlier. It is interesting that he begins his discussion with a reference to contemporary computer technology and draws an analogy to human experience. Since one begins one's reflection with human experience, I would have thought one employing an analogical method would want to have begun with that experience and see how far analogies in the other direction would be fitting, rather than vice versa.

I cite this passage and note Burhoe's use of the analogical method to illumine the mechanistic, deterministic, and materialistic base of his thinking. I strongly suspect that the "metaphysics" implicit in his view of science has its roots in a Newtonian world view. (This issue will be raised again later in my remarks on his conception of the nature of time and space.) For Burhoe, "mind" is dependent on "matter," located either in the body, in culture, in society, or in nature.

The internal and social disharmony occasioned in the personality and in society by the absence of convincing beliefs which Burhoe suggests is persuasive. Personal integrity or wholeness—insofar as it can be attained under the conditions of existence—does require a substantial measure of coherence among feeling, thinking, and acting. It seems to me that the lure evoking this desire is rooted in the ordering of the forms of definiteness in God's primordial nature. In this way the quests for the "truth" in science and in philosophy, for the beautiful in art, and for the good in ethics are evoked by foundational religious intuition and experience.

The path to the renewal of the meaning evoking power of religious symbolism does not lie, it seems to me, in the direction of an emerging scientific theology. Rather, it lies in the direction of reinterpretation of foundational religious intuition and experience evoking religious symbols such that persons can affirm with integrity the authenticity of a Divine Reality which is in some senses *sui generis.*

Burhoe's faith in modern science and human scientists is put forcefully and eloquently in this section. Without derogating either facets of the scientific method or the moral character of scientists, I would suggest this faith is excessive.

Burhoe deifies nature in a way comparable with the way Durkheim deified society. This quoted section provides some clues about his view of this ultimate reality system and about aspects of some implicit philosophic notions embodied in his thinking.

He observes that the term "nature" is used in the sciences "to denote the total reality system, including the laws or ways in which it operates in time, the dynamic history of its sources as far as they can be traced in time and space, and hypothetical entities or constructs that may not be directly observable but on the basis of which what is observable logically follows."

Note the phrases "in time" and "in time and space" included in this characterization of the total reality system. Is time something which flows and in which bits of mind and matter persist? Is space something which extends evenly in all directions? Is time measured by motion or is motion measured by time? Is there a becoming of continuity or a continuity of becoming? In other words, is a Newtonian or a

Platonic view of space and time being advanced? Alternatively, does Burhoe want to opt for P. W. Bridgman's operational definitions of space and time or an Einsteinian-Kantian view?

Note the phrase "integrated around a common, universal, everlasting, all-determining 'ultimate reality system.' " Does the "ultimate reality system" incorporate the differentiated and singular as well as the common? What is the understanding of the particular and what is its relation to the universal? What is the relation of the temporal and the eternal to the everlasting? Is any entity "all-determining?"

Note the phrase "hypothetical entities or constructs that may not be directly observable but on the basis of which what is observable logically follows." Are these entities merely hypothetical or constructs or are the forms to which they relate also embodied in creatures observed in nature? What is involved in the process of direct observation? What is the meaning of "logic" in this context?

I raise these questions to point to philosophic assumptions I think are implicit in this formulation of nature. I think these issues are perennial in human experience and cannot be resolved by appeal to work in one or several of the specialized sciences. One cannot avoid metaphysical questions by appealing to the authority of science.

In the specialized natural sciences one customarily thinks by a method of difference and the use of the experiment. The effects of various phenomena are assessed by comparing specified characteristics of other phenomena in the light of the presence or absence of the former phenomena on the observed phenomenon. The experimental method collapses when one is seeking to discern those factors and structures always present in human experience. In metaphysics one may use an experiential method, but one cannot use an experimental method. By employing a negative judgment, one may consider imaginatively the absence of that which is always present in experience. In such a manner one may envisage the factors and structures which are always present and evolve a set of metaphysical propositions.

Thus both the specialized sciences and metaphysics share a common concern with testing the results of one's propositions; both are concerned with the truth. From my point of view *the* truth is nothing else but the way in which the creatures of the world are objectified in the Divine Life. Our more limited truths are selective abstractions from this objective truth. Metaphysical propositions are more general and universal than the propositions applying to specific subject matters, but they must not be inconsistent with those more specialized propositions.

My final observation has to do with Burhoe's view of the morality of the scientist. While there are highly "moral" scientists, finitude, ignorance, sloth, lethargy, and inordinate self-interest are very pervasive among humankind. I do not believe scientists are immune from the jealousies, squabbles, self-seeking, or power conflicts so common among us. I myself would be and am concerned about domination by scientists.

I concur with Burhoe's observations about the checks and balances inherent in the scientific enterprise. Nonetheless, although scientists may prize rationality within their own spheres of endeavor, they often are dogmatically irrational outside their own spheres and not infrequently resist revisions in the basic modes of thought within their own sphere of specialization.

WHAT IS MAN'S FREEDOM?

A Summary of the Section. In this section Burhoe advances the notion that natural selection is a nonrandom or determined process. He sees the process of increasing complexification exhibited in the evolutionary process as a nonrandom or determined process working by means of random variations given by another layer of nature.

He struggles with the ancient problem of predestination and human freedom, translated into the framework of his "scientific theology." He puts his formulation of the question in this manner:

> In general, I would say that the new scientific pictures of man's creation by natural selection again allow for the restoration of the validity of a god concept as a reality which maintains perpetually a concern for what is going on in the cosmos, even a complete control of the process. This concept of "complete control" or "scientific determinism" is another stumbling block with which theologians themselves have been struggling since long before modern science began. How can one speak of "God" as designating that which controls everything and yet allows man freedom to make choices and be responsible for his choices?[31]

He subsequently puts the relation of humans to nature (God) in this manner: "With the scientific picture of an omnipotent and sovereign environment within which man is a small and completely dependent incident, we come into a problem of human motivation found by earlier theologies depicting a sovereign God's foreordination or predestination of man."[32]

He then formulates a proper view of freedom, freedom interpreted as understanding the forces and factors making one so that one can live in conformity to them: "We can properly say that freedom (whether as capacity to maintain life's present patterns or to search for potentially better patterns) has been and is determined by inputs from man's environment. Instead of requiring freedom from determinism, man's responsibility or duty to carry out goals or values turns out to be completely dependent upon it. Duty to some goal is determined by having been inscribed in the "heart" (central nervous system) of man by the larger environment."[33]

He then summarizes what he considers to be the current scientific picture:

> From the present scientific pictures of *Homo sapiens,* it could be said that man's freedom from the disordering elements of his environment is an ordered (determined) cybernetic or homeostatic system that provides that freedom; that this system itself has been determined by natural selection; and that nature's evolving systems insist upon or determine that he continue an open or free search for ever higher adaptive levels. Man's freedoms constrain him to compete in an everlasting program to maintain and extend the ever-expanding hierarchical levels of dynamic patterns of stratified stability (or of dynamic homeostasis) of the open-ended flow patterns of dissipative energy that we know as life. From this task or ordination, established and continued for billions of years by the specific parameters of cosmic processes on earth, man has no possibility of escaping. *Man has no freedom to do other than adapt to what this "nature" requires—except to cease to be.* As ancient theologians have said, to be a slave of the true God is man's greatest freedom. That is, to cherish and ever to seek better adaptations to the cosmically given or determined patterns of how to live and to evolve is the way unto life. But in this process man has far more of the first kind of freedom (the freedom to maintain life's dynamic patterns against myriads of disruptive interventions) than any other creature on earth. He has infinities of the second kind of freedom (the freedom to search and find better patterns of life).[34]

The way Burhoe seeks to translate theological symbols into scientific ones is illustrated in this passage: "When thus properly translated or interpreted, not only our traditional Western religious species but all the great religions can again become more effective in enculturating in the 'brain pool' of mankind an integrated and unifying perception of the self as larger than the 'natural' or commonsense self of the body, a new being that integrates not merely with the immediately ambient sociocultural system but ultimately with the species and with the ultimate reality system called 'nature,' the 'natural system,' or 'the way things are' in the sciences and called God or the Kingdom of God in Christian theology."[35]

The contrast between human genetic and cultural systems gives rise to the "isness-oughtness" contrast embodied in human experience. Man's social freedom "depends on the state of mutual adaptation of two essentially different units, both resident in his central nervous system but only one of which is resident in his genotype. . . . The mismatches between the programs of sociocultural systems and an individual's biological drives have caused the problem of evil and original sin to exercise mythmakers and theologians from the beginning, undoubtedly, of human culture."[36]

Burhoe concludes this section by locating fully human freedom in the recognition of the good or right in three separate systems:

> (1) his organism, (2) his society, and (3) the total ecosystem which is ultimately the creator and sustainer of his society as well as of his individual nature. If his attitude and behavior are correctly informed concerning what to do with respect to the two superior, transcendent realities which enable his organism to *be* or to have life, then he will have the first freedom or power for maintaining life and also the second freedom or power for participating in the creation of new and better life. . . . The new scientific pictures can revitalize this ancient religious wisdom by showing better than ever its essential validity or truth. Briefly, man's greatest freedom comes from his proper service to his society and God; man's freedom is a heritage or gift ordained or fully determined by the reality system that produced us.[37]

Discussion. Burhoe's view of the relation between his "Lord of History" (nature) and the classical Christian view of the Divine is intriguing. Instead of going "up" to seek a deterministic explanation of things, Burhoe goes "down" or "out." He views nature as having "complete" control of the process of emergent evolution. His sharpest formulation is in the quoted passage beginning "with the scientific picture of an omnipotent and sovereign environment within which man is a small and *completely dependent incident*" (italics added).

It seems to me that the broad view of the increasing complexification of creatures and hierarchies of creatures in the evolutionary process is very persuasive. Whether it need be interpreted in the deterministic manner Burhoe suggests is moot and is rooted in a world view not directly derived from "the scientific picture" (certainly not the scientific picture of humanistic psychology or *verstehen* sociology).

I do not think humans are a "completely dependent incident." It seems to me that all emerging creatures appropriate aspects of the creatures that have become and contribute something to all creatures in their causal future. This universalization of the principle of relativity means no creature is merely dependent. Every creature receives data from its environment (including an authentic and partially *sui generis* Divine Presence) and synthesizes it in private. Thus freedom and determination are characteristics of every creature. Life is a bid for freedom from the bonds of the causal past, and high-grade organisms are not bound by their "environment" as they decide what they are to be.

This capacity for some novelty of response extends to all creatures, though it is minimal in the case of inorganic entities. It follows that laws are immanental, coming into existence as creatures and societies of creatures appropriate and reproduce particular forms of definiteness and passing out as new societies emerge. This desire to share common defining characteristics is enhanced by the Divine lure for harmony and intensity of feeling.

The element of novelty inherent in life means that no one —including the Divine—foreordains what is to happen. The universality of the category of freedom and determination means that God (or nature) is limited by the freedom of creatures to "decide" what they are to be. It also means that the laws of nature are limited by the shifting, defining characteristics appropriated by creatures and societies of creatures.

I am in substantial sympathy with Burhoe's intent to relate humans to other humans and to lift up a concern for the whole, but I am not persuaded that the deification of nature is the way to do so.

I have great difficulty with Burhoe's interpretation of the "isness-oughtness" contrast in human experience. I affirm the experience of a contrast between a very substantial harmony in some of the sequence of events constituting my person and the disharmony experienced in other of the events constituting my person, but I think the contrast is rooted in something more fundamental than the contrast between individual biological drives and the programs of sociocultural systems. It is grounded in the contrast between one's experience of the perfection of God's subjective aim which orders and harmonizes the forms of definiteness and limits on this perfection caused by finitude, ignorance, sloth, lethargy, and inordinate self-interest.

I respond very positively to the quote concluding the summary of this section—provided the meaning of "total ecosystem" can be reformulated to include an authentic Divine Reality in part transcending the ecosystem, and the category of freedom and determination can be universalized to apply to all creatures, including the Divine creature.

MAN'S CAPACITY TO SACRIFICE HIS PRESENT FOR HIS FUTURE SELF

A Summary of the Section. In this section Burhoe affirms that humans gladly have, can, and must deny present satisfactions for the sake of future generations. Burhoe notes that the "natural history of all organisms shows that self-sacrifice for the larger whole of which it is a part is the order of the day."[38] He also sees the emergence of death and sex as the ways in which the "Lord of History" enhanced the evolutionary process.

In an oblique reference to the question of immortality Burhoe notes that human somatic death is genetically prescribed. He speaks disparagingly of "otherwise sound biologists, who are not really clear about this, perhaps because so great is their misconceived desire for the infinite continuation of the individual body that the truth of the essential goodness or virtue of somatic and genotypic death is not acceptable to them."[39] For Burhoe, the ecosystem of advancing forms of life provides the basis for altruism and self-sacrifice.

Discussion. The attainment of the proper balance between the realization of present satisfaction and the anticipation of future satisfactions is a salient moral problem. Similarly, the balance between proper individuation and concern for the community is a persistent problem. Burhoe affirms very strongly the propriety of concern for the future and for the community.

There is obviously much merit in this emphasis from many perspectives. I would make only two observations. First, there must be some satisfaction in the present, for, although the future is real in the present, it is not actual. Further, sometimes novelty and aesthetic satisfaction are enhanced if one is a bit oblivious of the future. Second, in order to actualize oneself, one must be separated from the community. Burhoe has given us little guidance to help us discern legitimate from tyrannical community interests and to sustain proper individuation from the whole.

I cannot resolve the problem of death as easily as Burhoe does. For me, the ultimate evil is loss—the vivid immediacy of the present is perpetually perishing. The attempt to resolve this problem by appealing to human contributions to the biological and cultural future is not satisfying, for, ultimately, these creatures also shall pass away. I think something more is needed than biological and cultural immortality to deal with this haunting problem.

Two other possibilities suggest themselves. One is the everlasting retention of the creatures that have become in the Divine Life. The other is the persistence of the "soul" after the demise of the organism with which, currently, it is associated intimately. I do not see how Burhoe's formulations permit him to envisage either of these possibilities.

The former possibility requires an interpretative schematism positing mutual interaction and reciprocity between creatures and God who is in some senses *sui generis* and in some senses dependent on the world and who can retain everlastingly and without loss all that the world has to offer. The latter possibility requires the notion of an intense mutual immanence between God and the soul and an interpretative framework allowing the possibility of further evolutionary states and a multiplicity of layers or levels of experience such that the existence of entities not so dependent on an organic and inorganic substructure may emerge and be sustained. Burhoe provides no house for such hope.

Natural Selection and Human Salvation

A Summary of the Section. Burhoe introduces his discussion by reaffirming his faith in "scientific theology." He believes modern physics is in process of replacing "metaphysics" (undefined in this section) and "supernatural," which Burhoe translates to mean a "scientific picture of human destiny as completely determined by forces entirely beyond man's control, quite superhuman."[40]

He reaffirms and elaborates his confidence in the future viability of religion, understood as the transmitter of human value-culture and "the sociocultural cumulated wisdom for salvation."[41] In the current epoch Burhoe locates religious propagation in the popular arts and in the humanism of the secular universities. He summarizes his understanding of nature, the true "Lord of History," in this section:

> If we understand the "nature" described by the sciences as the system of laws, according to which events in the history or evolution of the underlying reality system proceed in time, which, together with the given or "initial conditions" and the "hidden relations" or "preferred configurations" of the reality system, explain (as far as man can explain it) the varied history or evolution of the universe and the living systems (including human minds and societies) in it, then we do have a concept akin to the ultimate reality or God of the high religions. It possesses the aseity (absolute self-sufficiency), omnipotence, and other traditional attributes of God that make it natural to speak of a "Lord of History."[42]

The new religious virtuosos, those who genuinely understand the true Lord of History, are the bearers of scientific theology. They are to enculturate the information necessary to maintain life. Burhoe elaborates the elitist view of these religious virtuosos:

> For enculturation in human societies—with all their diverse levels of ages, education, and genetic endowments—it requires continuing reinforcement programs from the most elementary rituals through the most sophisticated scientific theology. It should be carefully noted that a scientific theology is no more and no less necessary for a population that would live in the "kingdom of heaven" (symbol for ultimate reality for life) than is the science of a medical technology for a population that would be healthy. Only a few persons in ten thousand need to be consciously aware of the full scientific details involved in certain medical inoculations; but without them health for millions would be impossible. The same is true for effective religion in the modern world.[43]

Discussion. The impossibility of substituting the theories of a special science for metaphysics was discussed earlier and will not be elaborated further here, but it is necessary to comment on Burhoe's view of the new religious virtuosos—the bearers of scientific theology.

Since there are alternative ways of abstracting from and interpreting the drops of human experience, it seems most unlikely that humankind will attain a consensus on foundational interpretations of religious experience in the foreseeable future. Burhoe has rejected those philosophic and theological traditions that think it is necessary to interpret religious experience as a response to a Divine reality which is in some sense *sui generis* and has chosen to deify nature.

In so doing he has rejected the Aristotelian and Platonic philosophic traditions and almost all forms of Christian theology. He may have rejected metaphysics formally, but he has grounded his views in propositions reminiscent of Democritus, Newton, and/or the Sophists. It is not possible to be definitive on this grounding, for Burhoe's own formulations are not explicitly related to historical thinkers. I am here referring to the primacy of nature and the epiphenomenal character of consciousness associated with the atomistic tradition, the notions of space, time, matter, and minds posited by Newton, and the operationalism (construction of concepts and theories) associated with the Sophists.

I would shudder at the thought of inculcating his view of scientific theology in the educational system, just as I would shudder at the thought of inculcating any other particular interpretation of human religious experience in the educational system. The reinforcement program he suggests I find equally distasteful. This proposal smacks of manipulation and violates the human quest for freedom and integrity.

I do not think nontheistic interpretations of religions can sustain the human spirit or elicit some measure of social altruism in the longer run.

In any event, people must continue to explore both ancient and contemporary interpretations of human religious experience and to affirm perspectives which they can affirm with intellectual and emotional integrity. Some may find the sort of scientific theology Burhoe elaborates in this essay to be logical, coherent, applicable, and adequate to the complexity of human religious experience, but others will find other perspectives more adequate. I would hope that educational and religious institutions will continue to seek to sustain at least a limited pluralism of styles of religious rituals, feelings, beliefs, and interpretations.

A Concluding Note

The issues Burhoe has raised in his essay are perennial. My own questions and critiques, rooted in the Platonic tradition and in the perspective of process philosophy, illustrate how a proponent of another tradition, familiar with at least the broad contours of modern science, reacts to the formulations Burhoe has advanced.

In a basic sense our disagreement centers on the status of metaphysics. I do not think it is possible to eliminate metaphysics, for every approach to human understanding embodies first principles and makes assumptions not resolvable by any simple appeal to the facts. In this sense I would say Burhoe employs an implicit metaphysics in his analysis.

I have tried to illumine some of its elements by raising critical questions about it and the interpretations of religion emerging from it.

It has not been possible in the context of the space available to elaborate an alternative interpretation, but the critique I have advanced is grounded in an alternative, foundational vision of the nature of things—one which refuses to deify nature and which affirms the reality of a Divine entity that is both immanent in and transcendent of the world. This Divine reality is qualifiedly *sui generis* and is the locus of potentiality, the lure for feeling, the mediator of experience from one creature to another, and the ultimate receptor of all that has become.

NOTES

1. Ralph Wendell Burhoe, "The Human Prospect and the 'Lord of History,'" *Zygon* 10 (1975): 301.
2. Ibid.
3. Ibid., p. 302.
4. Ibid.
5. Ibid., p. 303.
6. Ibid.
7. Ibid.
8. Ibid., p. 304.
9. Ibid.
10. Ibid.
11. Ibid., p. 306.
12. Ibid.
13. Ibid., p. 310.
14. A. F. C. Wallace, *Religion: An Anthropological View* (New York: Random House, 1966). Émile Durkheim's classic work is *The Elementary Forms of the Religious Life,* trans. Joseph Swain (London: G. Allen & Unwin, 1915). For an extended analysis and critique of Durkheim which elaborates some of the critical observations developed later in this paper, see "Émile Durkheim's Ordering of the Sciences: A Résumé and a Critique," in

my *Cognitive Structures and Religious Research* (East Lansing: Michigan State University Press, 1970).

15. Burhoe, p. 312.

16. Ibid., p. 313. The quote is a quotation drawn from Wallace.

17. Although Burhoe does not cite Talcott Parsons in this discussion, it seems to me he is drawing on notions which Parsons helped develop and popularize (see, e.g., Talcott Parsons, *The Social System* [Glencoe, Ill.: Free Press, 1951]). In Parsons's later work he became very interested in sociocultural evolution. Again, this line of thinking was initiated in the later part of the nineteenth century in both England and France. Durkheim, Morgan, and others elaborated ideas comparable with those Burhoe develops here.

18. Burhoe, pp. 313–14. This quotation illumines Burhoe's deification of nature and his use of a mechanistic model.

19. Ibid., p. 316.

20. Ibid., p. 317. Burhoe does not indicate what he means by "fully scientific" in this context. He does say: ". . . for those exposed to scientific beliefs, the scientific extension of previous myths and theologies would be as essential to aesthetic and motivational religion of the twenty-first century as were the informational patterns of the DNA necessary for the evolution of cells and organisms. It also seems to me that such an interpretation of religion in terms of modern natural philosophy or science is as necessary and as big a step in the advancement of religion as was the synthesis of Platonic and Aristotelian philosophy with religion in the preparation for Western civilization as successor to the classic Mediterranean civilization." The global quality of this characterization should be noted. From many points of view, modern natural philsophy or science is extremely complex and variegated and more closely related to alternative traditional philosophic schemata than Burhoe's characterization would suggest. Similarly, the synthesis of Plato and Christianity that Augustine undertook differs substantially from the synthesis of Aristotle and Christianity that Aquinas undertook. The alternative understandings of the relation of human forms of understanding to the order of nature exhibited by Einstein and Whitehead, two of the greatest philosophers of nature of the modern epoch, may suggest to some the extraordinarily subtle and complex relations between scientific formulations, philosophic perspectives, and religious understanding. P. W. Bridgman's operationalism illustrates an approach coherent with a Sophistic perspective. The question, "Which modern natural philosophy will be most widely appropriated in the twenty-first century to interpret religious experience?" seems to me to be the crucial one. As the critical portion of this essay suggests, I have grave doubts about the adequacy of the mechanistic-materialistic mode Burhoe uses in his paper to interpret religious experience and to sustain the human spirit.

21. Ibid., p. 319. The parallel between Burhoe's vision and that of Comte is striking (see Auguste Comte, *Positive Philosophy* [New York: Appleton, 1853]). Similarly, the outline Burhoe suggests is strikingly similar to that of Durkheim. (See, e.g., the last chapter of *Elementary Forms of the Religious Life.*) Wallace, whose work Burhoe cites with approval in several parts of his paper, is probably the figure linking Burhoe to this tradition.

22. Burhoe, p. 321. In his discussion in this section Burhoe notes the influence of Plato and Aristotle on Christian theology. Interestingly, he does not note the influence of the Greek atomists and Sophists. It seems to me that a synthesis of these two heritages is reflected in Burhoe's own constructive efforts. The materialism of the atomists is combined with the interactionalism, operationalism, and antimetaphysical outlook of the Sophists to produce a "scientific theology."

23. Ibid., pp. 321–22. The term "cathected" may relate Burhoe to the Freudian heritage, but he does not elaborate his usage of the term here.

24. Ibid., p. 326.

25. Ibid., p. 328.

26. Ibid.

27. Ibid.

28. Ibid., p. 329. In recent Western history this distinction is grounded in the bifur-

cation between theoretic reason and practical reason. Burhoe does not explore this tradition and its Kantian roots in this paper.

29. Ibid., p. 330. Note the implicit Newtonian view of time as that which flows and of space as that which extends evenly in all directions in the passage ". . . including the laws or ways in which it operates *in time*, the dynamic history of its sources as far as they can be traced *in time and space*, . . ." (italics added). In spite of his strong interest in evolution, Burhoe does not cite such evolutionary thinkers as Henri Bergson, S. Alexander, Whitehead, Charles Hartshorne, or Teilhard de Chardin. Significantly, none of these thinkers deified nature.

30. Ibid.

31. Ibid., p. 335.

32. Ibid., p. 336.

33. Ibid., p. 338.

34. Ibid., pp. 338–39.

35. Ibid., p. 342.

36. Ibid., p. 345.

37. Ibid., p. 346.

38. Ibid., p. 347.

39. Ibid., p. 347–48.

40. Ibid., p. 352.

41. Ibid., p. 357.

42. Ibid., p. 361.

43. Ibid., p. 367.